The Best of Two Lives

Best Wishes To Eileen

Doris Clifford

The Best of Two Lives

Al Ahsan fi Hayat Ithnain

———◆———

DORIS AYYOUB

Foreword by A. Mary Murphy

RESOURCE *Publications* · Eugene, Oregon

THE BEST OF TWO LIVES
Al Ahsan fi Hayat Ithnain

Resource Publications
An Imprint of Wipf and Stock Publishers
199 W. 8th Ave., Suite 3
Eugene, OR 97401

www.wipfandstock.com

PAPERBACK ISBN: 978-1-4982-9837-7
HARDCOVER ISBN: 978-1-4982-4888-4
EBOOK ISBN: 978-1-4982-9838-4

Manufactured in the U.S.A.   09/01/16

For Ibrahim Ayyoub, Family Storyteller

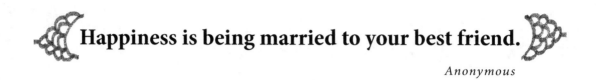 **Happiness is being married to your best friend.**

Anonymous

Ahsanshee!

Contents

Foreword

DORIS RIGNEY AYYOUB HAS lived her life in the Pacific Northwest—Idaho, Oregon, and Washington—so there is a strong local interest component to her story, but this is far more than a regional interest vehicle. The desire to speak against anti-Arab sentiment is perhaps the driving force behind the writing of this book. But, it simultaneously is a vital, experiential, piece of Americana. And, maybe, also of Jordania, if there is such a term. There are ways of doing described here that might just enable a bunch of urbanites, utterly detached from where their food is sourced, to survive if there's a prolonged power failure. The pioneering sensibility is strong and inspiring and humbling.

At a time when it was most unusual, the 1950s, Doris and Ibrahim Ayyoub were a so-called "mixed" couple. A respected advisor told them mixed marriages never work. At their wedding, people wanted to touch Ibrahim's hair, to see if Ay-rab hair was soft or coarse. When their first daughter was born, a rumour spread that Ay-rabs bury baby girls in the sand. In more recent years, Doris and Ibrahim became deeply troubled by widespread anti-Arab commentary and actions, and they decided to tell their story, of a Jordanian immigrant committing himself to an American girl and to America, to serve as an example of the positives that can result from the average immigrant life, regardless of origin or destination.

Their love story is shaped as a journey, woven from the threads of family, beginning with the cultural foundations of Jordan and the United States. Doris meticulously prepares those foundations and shows that the similarities far outweigh the differences. That's a large part of the point. Ayyoub or Rigney, the people are hardworking and socially committed. Jordanian or American, most people are working to secure and improve the lives of their children. Doris' family migrated from Oklahoma and Michigan, overcoming obstacle after obstacle, and Ibrahim likewise left the familiar to seek opportunity in Oregon.

Their story relates anecdote after anecdote, creating compelling characters and vividly showing ways of life that would be lost but for projects such as this. It makes traditional village life in Jordan familiar and engaging, showing that it is not fundamentally different, as many think. A mother painstakingly preparing and preserving food is the same no matter where she is. A mother teaching her child a lesson, whether by breathtakingly throwing him off the roof or immovably making her go without Christmas is the same no matter where she is.

Chapter by chapter, Doris draws on every detail she can muster, making a reader respond to her characters, whether it's with admiration or resentment, laughter or anger. She never shrinks from showing the negative attributes that she couldn't be blamed for wanting to hide, and that's what keeps this from being a purely family history. There's something here to help all of us see our own families more clearly and honestly and understand them more thoroughly and compassionately.

Doris and Ibrahim are so clearly the product of their parents, from Jo Rigney's dogged, cheerful determination to Toufiq Ayyoub's quiet, purposeful wisdom. We know it by the orange-crate cupboards, by the constant bread making, by the business dealings (astute and otherwise), the desire for education, the storytelling, the love. *The Best of Two Lives* seeks to establish the two backgrounds and then brings them together to suggest that the blend distills and strengthens. It creates two full worlds and makes them one.

Over a number of years, the data and the stories and the pictures that went into creating the story were collected and organized and culled, in a concerted effort to produce this genuine labor of love. I have watched and read as Doris and Ibrahim worked diligently toward their shared goal, which surely is a metaphor for their two lives. I have admired the tenacity. I have appreciated the ambition to examine their lives and not just to dash off a quick memoir with some amusing and interesting snippets and call it done. I have been impressed by the willingness to cut something that just doesn't contribute. That's what writing is.

As a specialist in writing life stories, I know the importance of the research stage, of the subsequent verification of facts, of the constant need to make choices, to step away and question why something gets in and something else stays out, and the commitment to craft, so that, in the end, the story lives and speaks to someone else. Doris and Ibrahim knew their story had something to say. I know it has something to say. I am delighted that Doris now has the opportunity to hold their book in her hands, just as Ibrahim wanted.

A. Mary Murphy PhD

Prologue

Ahsanshee Laila! The very best Laila!

Ibrahim and Baby Laila

Ahsanshee Tammy! The very best Tammy!

Ibrahim and Baby Tamam

THIS WAS THE SONG sung to our daughters by their Daddy when they were tiny. *Ahsanshee*, the very best! This Arabic term has significant meaning for our family, as do the names of our daughters. The literal Arabic translation of *Laila* is "the special night," but in Arabic poetry it implies the deepest description of "true love." So Ahsanshee Laila translates to "the best of true loves." And *Tamam* means "complete or perfect." She was the perfect completion to our family. *Ahsanshee!*

As I contemplate the intertwining of our lives, Ibrahim's and mine; I am struck with the realization that *Al ahsan fi hayat ithnain,* the best of two lives, is an apt description for this book. Ibrahim in Jordan, and Doris in America grew up in families vastly distant geographically, but not as culturally disparate as one might assume. The story of our separate backgrounds and how we eventually came together moves back and forth between Jordan and America.

Our children were blessed to inherit the best of both cultures. In fact, we have a family joke about the word "heredity." When our oldest daughter, Laila, could barely speak, her Daddy taught some clever answers to his questions and carried on the tradition to Tammy when she arrived. Ibrahim asked each of his baby daughters, "What is the cube root of 31?" She grinned triumphantly because this test was one Daddy had practiced for weeks. Brown eyes sparkling, she proudly answered in her loudest voice, "Pi." "That's right." Now here is the next question, "What makes you so smart?" Once again she was ready with a quick answer, "Heridetery!"

When I reflect on this playful conversation between Ibrahim and his daughters, it reminds me that our children are a combination of heredity and culture. He, the son of a wise Arab father and gentle mother in the small Jordanian village of Al Husn, traveled halfway around the world to meet me at college in America. I was the daughter of a strong-willed mother who grew up in a poverty-ridden German-English household to marry my introverted, conservative, and stubborn father of Irish-French-Cherokee descent.

The quiet Jordanian town, where Ibrahim's ancestors lived during the early 1900's, is very like the struggling, hard-scrabble American towns and homesteads during the same time period. This story will reveal our backgrounds and early lives, full of similar experiences. From then on, the tale evolves into the mix of these two people together, as we lived our Best of Two Lives.

Doris and Ibrahim

CHAPTER 1

The Lives of Our Elders

IBRAHIM'S FATHER, TOUFIQ SULEIMAN Ayyoub, was born in Al Husn, Jordan, in 1890.

He was ten years old when Ottoman Sultan Abdul Hamid began to construct the Hejaz railroad running from Damascus through the length of Jordan and on to the Holy City of Medina. Railroads built at this time were intended to strengthen Turkish authority, spanning six centuries, over Arab provinces. The route ran fairly close to Al Husn, and construction of the railroad was significant because it meant obligations on the men of the area, who were given the option either of cutting trees to fuel the steam engines or of being conscripted into the Turkish army. Many opted for the former, which ravaged Jordan's hardwood trees and turned extensive forests into desert wastelands.

Toufiq Ayyoub

Because the Ayyoubs, in general, bemoaned the deforestation, Toufiq chose to join the army where he served for several years. Living in the Ottoman Empire made it imperative to have at least some facility in the Turkish language, and years earlier, when Toufiq's cousin, Sulti, hired a tutor, Toufiq took advantage of this opportunity to sit outside the open window to listen. The bit he learned made his stint in the Turkish army a little less burdensome.

Toufiq's careful approach to difficult decisions such as military service shows skills that, if he were alive today, would help him excel as a political consultant. It was his belief that his cousin Sulti, a Christian, should be elected to the position of *Basha* in the government of King Abdullah. A *Basha* is comparable to a member of parliament in the British system or a United States senator in America. Becoming the *Basha* was important because Al Husn was one of the largest Christian areas of

Jordan, and Christians at that time had very few government representatives. It was clear that Toufiq knew the politics of the country, but both men believed that Sulti would be a better fit, and he declared his candidacy. Many members of the Ayyoub tribe held good jobs in Amman, the capital of Jordan, so Toufiq inspired Sulti to travel to Amman and obtain promises of support.

This fledgling move into politics became more dramatic when another Christian candidate of the Inmura tribe in Al Husn chose to stand for election to the same office. The Inmura tribe was larger and their candidate was college educated. Sulti was not even a high school graduate. However, Toufiq began to work his political wiles.

Earlier in life, Toufiq had developed a close friendship with Mahmoud Rashdan, a Muslim. They spent hours visiting with each other. One day, Mahmoud said, "I have been praying constantly to have children and so far no luck. If you pray for me too, I swear that my firstborn son will be baptized in your church." The prayers worked, and his son, Saleh, was baptized in the Orthodox Church. Years later, he became a fine influence on young Ibrahim. Based on the strength of Toufiq and Mahmoud's friendship, the Muslim community cast their considerable block of votes in support of Sulti, which swung the vote.

On the day of the election, the tribe of Inmura felt certain of winning. Excited women and men gathered to celebrate their win with dancing and ululations. Meanwhile, Toufiq stayed at the county seat awaiting the formal decision. When the announcement came from Amman, Sulti Ibrahim Ayyoub was declared the winner and became Sulti Basha. He was recognized as a great leader of the Christian community and became a favorite of King Abdullah I, a Muslim. One reason for this favor was Sulti Basha's refusal to break his religious fast, even though he had to attend a feast where the king was present. Sulti politely refused the king's repeated urgings, when other Christians in the company yielded, and the king was impressed by this.

Throughout his years of service, Sulti Basha kept the welfare of Jordanians uppermost in his thinking and passed those concerns on to his family, and later, his son was tasked with re-forestation projects in the areas ravaged during Turkish domination. When we visited Jordan during the summer of 2005, we toured the lovely, reestablished forests in the surrounding mountains.

Today, in Amman, the Ayyoub families have built a hall to use for social gatherings of the tribe. On the second floor of the hall is a room dedicated to the honor of Sulti Basha. When we visited, the family prepared a dinner there in our honor. I was seated next to a lovely young woman and I mentioned how much I appreciated the efforts of Sulti Basha's son in replanting the Jordanian forests. She smiled with pleasure and said, "That was my father. I am Sulti Basha's granddaughter."

Following the original election of Sulti Basha, the priest of the Inmura tribe in Al Husn, Khoury Mershid, told one of his sons that he'd rather have Toufiq Suleiman on his side than all the men of his own tribe. His opinion of Toufiq carried much influence with the rest of the village, and his three sons were important to Toufiq. The eldest became a priest, Khoury Alexandrous. The other two sons were Farhan and Najeeb. Farhan was an especially dear friend, and Toufiq named one of his sons Farhan to honor him. This baby is the child lost to the family by a scorpion's sting when he was a toddler. Khoury Mershid's youngest son, Najeeb, became Ibrahim's first teacher.

Occasionally, Khoury Alexandrous loved to join Toufiq and friends in a game of cards. Before sitting down, he removed his *Khalouseh,* the headgear symbolic of his rank, set it down in the corner, and told it, "You sit there, Father Alexandrous; I'm going to play cards with my friends." This was his symbolic way of saying, "Now I'm not a Khoury. I'm just a friend." Usually, they played *Scambeel,* which is played by four men in pairs, like bridge. The partners would sit opposite each other on cushions around a large *girbaal,* a sieve for winnowing wheat, placed on the floor and turned upside down to create a sort of low platform surface for the cards. Each player slipped 5 piastres, a considerable sum during the Depression era, under the *girbaal* and the game began. It was a friendly affair, and when they finished, some of the money was used to purchase sweets or fruit.

In addition to Toufiq's close circle of friends, there were others in the village who sought his opinion. He was diligent in his effort to carry out his duties as a village leader. One of the persons who sought his advice was his brother-in-law Abdo, married to Toufiq's sister, Zaineh (affectionately described by Ibrahim as the "silly sister"). Early on, Toufiq discovered that Abdo had a strange way of taking his advice about serious decisions. Abdo was an obstinate man, but Toufiq was crafty.

Abdo would ask, "Brother, that piece of property is for sale. Do you think I should buy it?" If Toufiq said, "The price and quality of that land is not a good buy," Abdo could be depended upon to purchase it anyway. So Toufiq learned to say, "Yes, brother, I believe you would make a good purchase if you bought it." Abdo would then do the exact opposite. This, of course, was what Toufiq really thought he should do.

When Toufiq's cousin, Yacoub Assad Ayyoub, a local leader and long-time friend, was a young married man, he made arrangements for his wife and son to stay in Al Husn while he traveled to America to secure employment with Ford Motors in Detroit, building Model T Fords. After about nine years, he moved back to Al Husn and brought a Model T with him, the first car in all of northern Jordan. Yacoub had an entrepreneurial mind, which he used to improve the quality of life in Al Husn. He paved the road between Al Husn and Irbid, set up the first system of street lights, and established the first post office.

Mother Miriam

When Toufiq was ready to marry, he chose a local girl, Miriam Swidan.

Both tribes, Ayyoubs and Swidans, were native to Al Husn, and Toufiq was aware long before prospective marriage was discussed that Miriam was a fine young woman. He would have indicated his interest in Miriam to his tribal elders. They would then have met formally with her tribe of Swidan to request Miriam's hand in marriage. Her opinion would have been sought, and the decision certainly was hers.

Bride gifts of gold were bestowed upon Miriam. Ancient custom required that she wear these gifts fastened to a specially crafted chain which covered her head and hung down the back under her headdress. Many women kept the family fortune safe by wearing it in this way. Along with all the other duties of being a wife, it was surely a heavy burden to wear while caring for the household. But, placing responsibility for the family's fortune upon the head of the mother speaks to her status and the esteem in which she was held. Her opinions were valued, and her wishes were honored whenever possible.

Toufiq brought Miriam as a bride to the small home in which they lived their entire married life. Miriam gave birth to eleven babies. Her first two children were daughters, Aiedeh, who later died in childbirth, and Subha. Then came four sons: Suleiman, Nasser, Yacoub, and Ibrahim. After these, there was one more daughter, Naimeh, followed by another four sons: Farhan, Naim, Fahim, and Saad.

For all these, Miriam preserved, salted, and dried food. She cooked meals, baked bread, carried water, cleaned, sewed, spun, and knitted. Due to the lack of local professionals, she was also nurse and doctor. Saad, her last born, was the only child born in hospital because his birth was most difficult. He suffered damage which impaired his abilities throughout his life.

While Miriam and Toufiq were establishing their life during the first two decades of the 1900's, across the ocean my people were also occupied in the pursuits of family and home. I invested much thought in recording what I know about my family: my mother's side, the Popkeys, and my father's side, the Rigneys. At the outset, I assumed that their lives and experiences were very different from each other. The Rigney family came from Oklahoma and prospered when they arrived in Jerome, Idaho. The Popkey family came from Michigan to the same area, but suffered great privation. However, as their stories unfolded, I found many similarities.

My mother's father, William J. Popkey, was a first-generation American, born to William J. Popkey (a Prussian immigrant) and Adelaide Hill (an immigrant from Canada) in August 1880. They worked to clear their Michigan land and owned a good farm, free and clear. My grandfather, often called Bill, was the youngest of four, after his sisters Mary, Annie and Nellie Jane. When Bill grew older, his father encouraged him to help work the farm, but Bill was impulsive and strong willed. He made it clear to his father that he was more interested in horses and having fun. Later on, since he did not choose to settle into a trade either, his only option was to work as a day laborer.

But, Bill was charming and good looking. Those attributes served to his advantage when he made an effort to attract the attention of Miss Louise Edith Mason, daughter of Austin and Mary Mason. It is easy to assume that the Masons might have harbored concerns over Bill's attentions to their sweet daughter, because he had no prospects. But Bill was a dashing, playful joker and easily won her heart. Whether or not her parents approved of their romance, Louise married Bill, and they began their married life in a little wood frame house called "Lakeside Farm" in Montague, Michigan.

While they lived in this house, Josephine (Josie) and Dorothy (Dolly) were born. Dorothy wrote in her memoirs, "We lived in a big lovely home. My father worked as hired help and the home was part of the pay for his work." It appears to be the paradox in Bill's life that he was not willing to work his father's farm, yet he chose to spend much of his life working for other people on their farms.

Louise's parents were originally from Ohio. Dorothy remembered her Grandfather Mason rocking and singing to her. "He sang 'Sweet little Dolly with the blue dress on.'" Grandfather Mason loved music and played the violin. He once declared to Dorothy, "There is music all around us in the air but we can't hear it." Mary Mason took great

Bill and Louise Popkey Wedding

pride in her tidy house. Dorothy said, "My grandmother used to hold her hand under the cup when she gave me a drink so I wouldn't drop water on the freshly scrubbed floor." My mother, Josephine, spoke of her Grandmother Mason as a quiet, hardworking woman who could pluck a chicken in no time. Louise likewise took pride in caring for the little house provided by Bill's employer, and during the nine years that they lived there, she grew much of their food in her garden. Her children grew up with a love for music, good stories, and laughter.

Bill's father had already decided to take advantage of a government land offer and moved the rest of his family to Jerome, Idaho, during the early 1900's. Though Louise and the girls missed them, it was Bill who really felt the pain of their absence. His parents were a somewhat steadying influence for him, and that ceased when they left. Then, after a stable nine years in the lovely house, it was destroyed by fire, along with everything Bill and Louise owned. This disaster caused Bill to decide that it was time to move, so he uprooted his family and headed to Idaho, following his parents.

Both of the children had vivid memories of the fire. Josie understood the sorrow that the fire caused but did not see why it should force their family to pick up and head to Idaho. Dorothy remembered her mother's sad longing for home and Grandfather Mason's grave words as he watched the little family board the train: "We will never see our daughter Louise again." And they never did. But, Bill was a life-long adventurer, and heading west was a natural progression for him. Louise simply followed her love.

Their story makes me pause to consider the significance of my own choice of mate. I made it very clear to my mother that I would follow my love wherever our lives might lead. I even had the audacity to request the song, "Whither Thou Goest" to be sung at our wedding. It became clear to me that my mother was well aware of what could possibly occur: I might be faced with a decision to leave all my family to follow my husband back to his homeland. As Bill and Louise's oldest daughter, she had lived the consequences of such a separation. Looking back, it amazes me that she so lovingly accepted and supported my choice. Josie remembered how difficult it was as an eight-year old to say goodbye and climb on the monster-sized train for the long, difficult, tiring ride. And, four-year old Dorothy was heartbroken because her new red coat had burned in the house fire.

In the early 1900's, Jerome, Idaho, was a sagebrush steppe with irrigation just becoming available because of the Milner Dam and the Twin Falls Land and Water Company, which constructed an extensive system of canals. Irrigation attracted the new wave of homesteaders, such as Bill's parents. In 1912, when Bill stepped off the train with his wife and two young daughters, they were welcomed by family who assisted them in obtaining a humble, two-room house on a farm owned by the Hobaker family. Once again, Bill arranged to serve as a day laborer in exchange for rent. The house came with a garden spot and the loan of a cow to milk. There was also a place to house a few chickens, and Louise would be able to sell eggs, if there were any extra.

But even with irrigation, Jerome was still a very flat, barren land, and Louise hated the sagebrush. The hot summer wind blew; dust was everywhere. Summers were fearsomely hot and sticky, accompanied by flies that invaded the house, since windows and doors had no screens. Winters brought freezing wind compounded by heavy snows and ice.

Try as she might to keep her home and babies clean and well cared for, it was an uphill battle for Louise. Water came from a cistern with an outside pump, and it had to be hauled into the house for drinking, cooking, and bathing. With no inside plumbing, they had to use a chamber pot at night or walk in the dark and cold outside to the smelly outhouse. Of course, dumping and cleaning the loathsome chamber pot fell to the mother of the house. If warm water was needed, Louise had to chop kindling for the big, black cook stove and build a fire. Then the fire must be kept alive with larger pieces of wood hauled from outside. Bill would sometimes find the time to help with hauling wood, but this became Josie's chore as soon as she grew big enough.

Laundry was an all-day task, as it would have been for Miriam in Jordan, carried on outdoors in the summer. Louise boiled the white clothes in a cauldron over a fire and used a scrub board with home-made lye soap, which caused her to develop reddened, rough working-woman's hands. Josie was put to work stirring the wash pot with a sturdy long paddle, and she had memories of the strong, acrid aroma of the soap. If Louise were lucky, the laundry dried on the outside line before another dust storm blew up to defeat her. Winter laundry took place inside and was hung out on the line to freeze dry, further reddening and chapping her poor hands.

Louise was a good cook. But, on a day-laborer's wages, supplies for cooking were scarce. Milking and caring for the cow fell to her, but she took on the task gratefully because of the butter, cream, and milk it provided. After each milking, Louise carried the milk inside and strained it through a clean white piece of muslin. Then, it was set aside to allow the cream to rise to the top to be saved for churning into butter. Milk for drinking was boiled to kill bacteria. Josie, until the day she died, spoke with distaste of being required to drink the glasses of tepid, lukewarm milk. Leftover milk was set to clabber into curds, which were then dripped through a cloth bag to make a sharp, tangy cottage cheese.

The difficulties that arose with this Spartan farm life were compounded by the lack of real money in the family coffers. The children watched with eager interest as the neighbors butchered their hog, wishing that they could be so rich as to own pigs. The neighbor was a kind German woman who tried to be helpful to the young family. The day after her hog was butchered, Mrs. Marshall appeared at the back door with a dish containing something warm and brown. She smilingly offered it to Louise, saying in her broken English, "Here, ve haf make dis lovely dish of food for your wee ones. It is my special bluud pudding. I come back for my dish tomorrow. Ve hope you like?"

Louise was no snob. She valued this dear woman's friendliness and did not wish to hurt her feelings. A good neighbor was to be cherished as a source of social support in the often lonely life of a farm woman. Usually her man was off doing manly things, such as working for wages or hanging out across the fence shooting the bull with his male counterparts. Because Louise often felt the need of female companionship, she could not afford to alienate this good neighbor. But she also knew that there was no way any of her family would ever eat a smidgen from that bowl of blood pudding. Regardless, she took the dish and graciously thanked Mrs. Marshall. After Mrs. Marshall left, Louise set it on the table and did some careful thinking.

Then, she called to the family dog. Pete came running with tail wagging while Louise put the dish of congealed blood on the floor in front of him. Pete was beside himself with joy and lapped up its entire contents in no time. Then, Louise turned to her daughters and sternly commanded them never to say anything to anybody about what she had just done! The dish was scoured clean with soap and warm water and set on the drainboard for when Mrs. Marshall arrived to retrieve her dish. She immediately noticed the shining clean dish and burst into a huge smile. "Oh, you like my bluud pudding!" Louise gave her neighbor a kindly pat on the shoulder and replied, "It was every bit eaten!"

While Louise was practicing diplomacy, her rambunctious husband was marching to a different drummer. He had been assigned a fearsome, hateful task on the farm. Before new land could be cultivated, the stubborn sagebrush must be removed, and grubbing sagebrush was something that Bill detested. It involved dragging with iron rails and chains, or another device called a "mankiller," effective but dangerous.

Bill was convinced that any type of equipment used for the task was a "mankiller." Some days, he was given the control of the horses doing the rail-dragging, and that was not quite so distasteful since he had a great love of horses. But on other days, Mr. Hobaker assigned Bill to dig out the stubborn, leftover clumps with a hoe. It was back-breaking work, and he was soon sweating and cursing.

The boss was a demanding person and would not tolerate cursing from his employees. On the day that he heard Bill yelling some colorful expressions, he made a point of stopping beside Bill to criticize his choice of language. Bill was well known for his inability to accept criticism. He could explode in anger over the least little suggestion pointed in his direction. Instead, he simply said, "That's all right; I'll be leaving tomorrow."

He meant it. He headed straight to the house and told Louise, "Get our things packed up. We'll be heading out to the lumber camp in Ketchum tomorrow." Bill knew people up there, and he knew he could help out with haying and logging until school started again. If the truth be known, Bill was simply following a pattern of avoiding difficult situations. He chose, once again, to pick up his family and move on, rather than see a problem through. *A consistent pattern of heading out to find jobs in the hills during the summer and then back to Jerome in winter so the girls could attend school became their way of life.*

This characteristic of yielding to his quick temper and his propensity to act rashly was a constant, wearing drain on Louise. A close look at pictures of the woman Louise had become in comparison to the serene beautiful young bride of earlier days shows what her hard life did to her. She's tired, worn, and defeated. Her body sags and her shoulders droop

Sometimes, Bill left his family in Jerome during the school year while he lived in the logging camps. Ironically, Josie experienced a reverse form of this pattern in her adult years when it became necessary to leave her husband, Jesse, to fend for himself when school was in session, so she could teach in a distant school and provide education for my brother and me.

While he lived away from home, Bill spent jolly hours with ample opportunity to exercise his love of practical jokes. When he came home, if he had pulled off some particularly good antics, he'd regale the family with his stories. Josie, with a twinkle in her eyes, remembered many of these stories and retold them to me. His great good humor kept their household bouncing with laughter, even when times were difficult. Bill told his girls of one escapade:

> Our crew would come in to sit at this long trestle table with four sturdy legs. But the table wobbled a bit cuz of one leg bein' uneven. So I called out, "Cookie, after we eat our supper, I want you to turn this table upside down and measure these legs to find out which one is a bit too long. Get it fixed before we come in

for breakfast." Cookie answered, "Sure, Boss. I'll take care of it." After we ate, Cookie upturned the table, carefully measured and sawed the offendin' leg to make things even. So he left the cook shack convinced that he'd fixed it just fine. Then I sneaked into the mess hall; upturned the table; sawed off a bit of a different leg.

When we came in for breakfast and sat down, the table wobbled as usual. "Cookie," I yelled, "I thought I told you to fix this here table!" "Well sir, I did just that, Boss," he answered back, lookin' real perplexed. I complained, "You sure don't know nothin' if you think you fixed it. Get it fixed right." "Yessir, Boss," he nodded. "I'll get it done right this time." By this time the rest of the crew was in on the joke and they took up the complainin' and helped undo his work. You know, that dumb cook never figured it out, and the table kept getting shorter and shorter until we had to have a new table to get our legs under.

Another example of his prankish humor involved a cranky and very fat lady cook, who often had to cross to the other side of a shallow ditch to tend her chickens. The camp boss placed a board for her to walk across in order to get to the other side. The crew did not much like her because she complained a lot and sat down to rest more than they thought she should, instead of serving them promptly. Bill decided he just could not resist the temptation to go out one night and saw the underside of the board about halfway through. Then, he urged his joker friends to hang around casually to see what happened the next time she took off for the other side. Of course, her weight finished what he had started, and she took an unpleasant tumble into the ditch. They couldn't very well laugh in front of her as she tumbled, but they enjoyed many a "har, har, har" about it in private.

Yet another tale Bill told was even less funny and even meaner. For a time, he lived in a winter logging camp where one crew member always took off his heavy wool shirt and hung it outside on a peg before coming in to the over-heated warmth of the sleeping shack. In the morning, the lumberjack would pull on his pants, hitch up his suspenders over his long johns, reach outside to grab his wool shirt off the peg and come back in to stand with his backside to the fire until he was warmed up enough to start his day. Thinking it would be a good joke, one night Bill found a nest of hibernating wasps which he tucked up in the folds of the wool shirt. Next morning, the guy did his usual routine of grabbing the shirt and sidling up close to the fires. Of course, the heat woke up the nest of wasps, and they proceeded to sting the poor, unsuspecting fellow. Bill joined the other loggers in laughing uproariously at the dance the man did in an effort to escape his angry attackers, but he never confessed to being the culprit behind the trick.

It is easy for me to imagine my mother's reaction when Bill came home to tell these tales because she turned the same look on me many times during my childhood. She would have looked at him with her all-too-wise eyes and declared, "Oh, Papa, how could you?"

Wide-eyed Josie and sister Dorothy

Josie was a quick study and she had a repertoire of practical jokes she played on others when she was an adult. One happened when she was working out of the home as a servant girl for a family one year. It involved scraping the leftover morning oatmeal into the hired hand's boots. He always jumped barefoot into his boots each morning. That morning, he received a squishy surprise. Her excuse was that she didn't like the way he tried to flirt with her.

Long after my mother married, she taught a Sunday school class of high school students and decided to make a certain loud mouth student quit teasing when they came on a weekend outing to her home. She mixed up pancake batter and poured it on the griddle. While the cake was still wet on the top, she spread a layer of surgical cotton from her first-aid kit on it before turning it over to finish cooking. Of course, the cotton didn't show and the pancake looked delicious. The eager kid liberally slathered it with butter and syrup before stuffing the whole thing into his mouth. She delighted in describing how he could not chew, nor swallow, nor talk.

It's obvious that Bill's stories of his lumberjack days had a formative effect on his family. The tales brought levity into their lives and modeled a way to exercise their own sense of humor when the opportunity arose. Sometimes, his jokes crossed the line. They bordered on sadism, in some cases almost as if he harbored a desire to get back at a world which he believed had treated him badly.

While he was away from home and storing up tales to share with his girls, Dorothy and Josie attended school in Jerome, riding the horse-drawn wagon or sleigh in the winter. They carried their lunch in tin lard pails, which Josie used as a weapon to bonk another passenger over the head when she thought she had been ill-treated. Josie remembered one wagon driver who loved to race with other vehicles while the terrified children hung on for dear life. She said that once, her lunch pail jounced out of the wagon and was lost because she needed both hands to hang on to her seat.

Another school memory for Josie was her envy of a child who brought a daily orange in her lunch. Oranges in Josie's home came only at Christmas along with practical, bare bones items, such as new mittens or possibly a pair of shoes, if finances were going well that year. Josie's greatest desire was to be rich enough to go to school every day with pungent orange peel under her fingernails. She wanted to waft them under the nose of her nemesis, the privileged rich girl in her class.

The rich child gave them a hard time, because their clothing, though mended, clean and presentable, was very humble. Of course, the privileged child wore new store-bought dresses of the latest fashion. She had never, in her young life, experienced the need to make-do or to improvise. Louise's girls knew nothing else as the family struggled to deal with no cash. Maybe Josie had the same problem with her nemesis as Laura Ingalls had with Nellie Mae, the store-keeper's daughter in *Little House on the Prairie*.

Louise somehow managed to scrimp and save her egg money to purchase a new Singer treadle sewing machine. Dresses were often sewn out of flour sacks, and one winter, their coats were made from an old wool blanket with a bit of coyote fur as trim on the collar. Dorothy was envious because her mama was able to use the wonderful sewing machine while she, at first, was forbidden to touch it. Later, as she grew older, Dorothy exhibited an extraordinary talent for sewing, and Mama relented. Dorothy once sewed some pants for Josie, but their father thought they were too tight so he got out his pocket knife and cut through them to Dorothy's great distress. Her loving effort to make a gift for big sister was destroyed because of her dad's perverse behavior. Had he kept his knife in his pocket, Dorothy felt she had enough skill perhaps to alter Josie's pants to a better fit.

The sewing machine traveled with them whenever they moved, once tumbling over the mountainside when it fell off the wagon. This caused a certain amount of angry cursing from Bill as he clambered down to rescue it. Much later, Josie inherited the faithful old Singer, and I learned to sew doll clothes on it when I was a child. Eventually, it was given a complete restoration. It deserved to have its wood refinished to its original beauty and is a treasured piece of family history.

Through many hard years, my mother's family lived in places as varied as a tent or a lumber company house. One of their best places was with Grandma Popkey in Jerome when she invited them to move in after Grandpa Popkey died. They had a nice home, big lawn, and large barn for the horses. Bill got a job riding ditch, one of the few steady jobs he ever had, according to Dorothy. This job entailed riding his horse daily along the labyrinth of irrigation canals to check that no leaks or damage threatened to cause major disruption of irrigation flow to the thirsty farms. Louise was greatly relieved to have a monthly income which paid household expenses and provided groceries and other necessities. Not only did Bill have time to relax and play his practical jokes and create his stories while living on his mother's farm, but his children delighted in being there. Dorothy described the place as having lots of trees, which she enjoyed climbing, and saddle horses that she loved to ride. Her friends also had horses, and they enjoyed riding and racing together. Some of her most pleasant childhood memories were formed during this time.

Besides the pleasant physical surroundings that came from living with her grandparents, Dorothy treasured the chance to develop closeness with Grandma Popkey. She loved to watch her grandma carefully spread out her white nightgown before she knelt to pray. Her grandma had a carpet bag which fascinated the budding young seamstress, because it was filled with materials purchased at a rummage sale. She was willing to spend the time to help Dorothy learn to sew them into things, and Dorothy remembered making baby stockings out of Grandpa's old cotton socks.

Josie was less patient learning such skills. But, she had other strong memories of that period. One time, she spoke of peeking out from under the patchwork quilt on her bed to sniff the aroma of morning coffee wafting into the room. She was expected to wear long black stockings which were held up by garters dangling from a hated shoulder harness. She always wished it would magically become summer so she could stuff those dreadful stockings back in the clothes box and run barefoot. She hated the shoes just as much. She would exclaim, "Oh, fiddle! Another button is loose." She would then impatiently give a yank with the button hook and pop! Off rolled the shoe button across the floor! She knew she should go find thread and needle to repair it but decided, "Never mind, it won't show under my skirt." After she slipped on her long school dress over her muslin petticoat, she needed to seek help from Mother for buttoning the many buttons which fastened it up the back. Blast the buttons of the world!

Josie never did learn to make peace with the many buttons in her life. As an adult, when I helped her with laundry, I would find in her garments an array of safety pins, which she used for various emergency repairs but never bothered to mend. She delighted in telling about walking in downtown Boise during World War II. Since rubber, and therefore elastic, was not available, she was wearing underclothing which was designed to fasten with a button. All of a sudden, she stopped and exclaimed, "The button just now came off my underpants! They are falling down!" Dorothy, who would never have been caught dead in improperly repaired undergarments, asked, "Oh, Josie, whatever will you do?" Josie simply shrugged and replied, "I guess there is nothing else I can do. I'm going to kick them off and keep walking. Move along, and act like nothing happened." So Josie gave a mighty kick, causing the offending garment to skitter into the gutter. They held their heads high and walked on, only to burst into a cacophony of sister giggles when they were far enough from the crime scene.

While Josie and Dorothy were either learning or refusing to learn their required girlhood domestic skills, little sister Marie was born. Then, the following year, while they were still living in Jerome, a "blessed baby boy" was born and named William James after his father. Bill was really delighted, and the girls remembered walking all the way to town for a nice cradle for that boy. Until then, Bill had been the only male in the family constellation. It must have been a gloriously proud experience to realize that he now had his much desired son.

My mother tells of a superstition that caused the two little girls much fear and heart-rending pain after the birth of their baby brother. They had heard the old wives' tale that a baby under the age of one should never be allowed to see himself in a mirror. It would kill him for sure. The girls did not believe such silliness and purposefully held little Willy up to giggle and coo at himself in their only looking glass. As it developed, joy and confidence in his health were short-lived. Young William caught whooping cough, which developed into pneumonia. He died in December, 1917. His big sisters could not confess what they had done, and no one knew that they struggled for years with what they saw as the crime that killed their only brother. Of course, losing his son took a devastating toll on Bill. It is possible that this was when his alcoholism really erupted. By this time, cars were becoming popular, but Bill was a teamster, and it became more and more difficult for him to find work. Dorothy told me that when he did earn a little money, it was more than likely "given to help out some bum he befriended" or spent on booze for his drinking buddies.

Dorothy believed her dad was never the same after Willy died. Louise also became sick and perhaps had a nervous breakdown. The presence of Grandma Popkey in the home offered the steadying influence which pulled the family through this rough time. She took over to help with the work when Louise could barely face each day. She also contributed financially to purchase family needs. She was every bit the godsend her granddaughters remembered.

In 1920, a new joy came into the family's life when Ernestine was born. Dorothy wrote that she was "Such a blessing! Mother got better, and we all were so delighted to have a baby again. We all played with her and really enjoyed her." When Ernestine was 1½, Bill once more loaded up the wagon with his family and headed to Ketchum for the summer. In the fall, when it was time to move back to school, they found that Bill's sister Nellie and her husband had taken over Grandma's place, which left nowhere for them to live. Dorothy always wondered what he had expected would happen to that place while they were gone.

They rented what they could find for what they could afford to pay. Life was really hard for a man with no skills, and the next two winters were the hardest yet. Bill got tangled up with a bootlegger and nearly died from drinking. Josie was old enough to take over and managed to bring him around and sober him up. Bill's problems with alcohol were never discussed while I was a child, but their dad's difficulties with alcohol are surely the reason that both Josie and Dorothy had such an aversion to hard liquor in their homes.

As a budding young lady, Josie decided that she preferred to be called Jo. She was ready for her senior year of high school, but Bill found a job in Lowman, working to build a road, and he was not willing to stick around in Jerome waiting for her to graduate. So Jo arranged to stay with a family in Emmett for her last year of school. The mother of the family was expecting a baby and appreciated Jo's help and company.

While Jo was in Emmett, the rest of her family went through another hard winter. Bill took his horses and wagon to Wallowa, thinking to find work, which left Louise to manage as best she could alone. The younger girls did not remember any money coming in. Bill arranged for credit at a grocery store for while he was gone; however, that was cancelled when they could not pay the bill. Dorothy worked for a lady with a bunch of small children, helping to care for them on weekends, making enough to pay for Sunday dinner. The resourceful Louise provided a bedroom to a good friend of Jo's in exchange for fresh produce and meat from her family's farm.

Eventually, spring arrived and here came Bill with his wagon to load up the family again. He decided to move them all to Lowman, Idaho, where he could work the same road building project. This meant that Dorothy didn't finish her freshman year. Instead, she found a job in the cook shack where she was paid a good wage of one dollar a day. That spring of 1924, Jo graduated from high school with no one from her family at the ceremony. Somehow, she managed to scrape up enough funds to attend Albion State Normal School for the summer. That short session of training gave her the qualifications to be hired for her first teaching job. She boarded with a kind Christian family, George and Julia Sloniker, on their farm, and they taught Jo so much about living that they became friends for life.

I was a frequent visitor at the Sloniker's when I was growing up. I remember Julia's kitchen with its huge wood-burning cook stove with a built-in reservoir on one side for heating water. The rich homey smells in that kitchen were wonderful yeast breads, fresh churned butter, preserves, fried chicken, mashed potatoes, and gravy. George worked constantly with his cows and other animals so he usually came into the kitchen smelling of the barn he had just left. I played in a cart kept for hauling cream cans out to the road for daily pick-up by the Payette Creamery.

We visited the Sloniker's once when I was a pre-teen and discovered that they no longer needed to use the outhouse, because they had converted their bedroom closet into an area for a toilet. This really surprised me! How could you go to the toilet in your clothes closet? Their large family became my family, and I even had a young school-girl crush on their sweet, good looking son, Bob. Julia introduced me to the fine art of tatting to make delicate lace. I spent years learning how to do it and eventually made enough to edge a pair of pillow slips for my daughter. I owe all of these memories to the fortunate opportunity my mother had to live with them during that first year of teaching.

In the meantime, Jo's family was living in a tent at Five Mile Creek. Bill was hauling logs for a saw mill owned by a man who had a ranch nearby. Dorothy wrote about, "how pleased Mother was when Dad came home saying he had made arrangements to rent the ranch." Dorothy described it as a nice house "with running water, chickens to care for, cows to milk, and cream and butter to use." Dorothy was delighted to learn that she would have a bedroom of her own, something she had never had before. She felt it was perfect except that Jo would not be living with them.

When school let out, Jo joined them with an enthusiastic plan to make money by churning ice cream and operating an ice cream stand down by the road. She wanted to use the money so that she and Dorothy could both go to school in Albion. Dorothy could finish her high school and Jo could continue her teacher training at the State Normal School. By then, Dorothy was seriously interested in Walter March, but Jo and their mother wanted Dorothy to go to school to make something of her life. The plan to sell ice cream was hard to execute because obtaining ice was difficult; milking the cows and churning the ice cream in large quantities required a lot of effort; and they made a miniscule profit. Still, somehow they did manage to rent a one-room house close to Albion where they started their school life together.

The sisters caught a ride to Boise at Christmas and Walt came to drive them to Lowman. Dorothy had no intention of finishing high school but finished her sophomore year because her mother and sister wanted it. When Dorothy and Jo finished their year in Albion, Dorothy made good on her determination not to return. Soon after that, Walt presented her with a diamond engagement ring and they made plans to marry in the fall. Her folks were furious! This refers mostly to her father. Louise was saddened that Dorothy would not finish school, but Bill threw a hissy fit. Dorothy remembers his threat, that if she married Walt, she would never be welcome at home again. She told him she'd come anyway to see Mother and the girls and that he couldn't stop her.

Dorothy packed her "shabby little trunk" with what little she had. She and Walt headed to Idaho City where they got their license, located a minister, and exchanged vows. They had a "real love affair." Dorothy never regretted her decision. My own daughters believe that Dorothy deliberately chose such a hard-working and dependable man because he was the exact opposite of her flamboyant and irascible father.

While Dorothy was making important decisions for her future life, Jo also found she had a lot to think about. She had other beaus before my father, although she never mentioned anyone to us. But her photo album includes a picture inscribed, "Sincerest regards from George. Aunt Dorothy said he was "Jo's boyfriend," but she knew nothing else about him. I've studied his serious young face with great interest, wondering what kind of person he was and what Jo's life would have been like if she had married him.

Jo spent the next few years attending summer school at Albion State Normal while teaching in rural schools during the winter. During one session at Albion, she chanced to become reacquainted with a young man, Jesse Rigney, who was a student at the nearby university in Moscow, Idaho. Jesse remembered Jo as a member of his class during her first three years of high school in Jerome. He said that he admired her even then, because she was so cute and fun-loving, but she barely gave him a passing notice. Jesse was highly attracted to her and even sent her an invitation to attend his 1924 high school commencement exercises in Jerome, although we don't know if she accepted.

A friend gave her a memory book which she filled with her high-school activities, recorded in her own handwriting, including invitations, programs, photos, and letters. Her entries show that she was very busy with the friends she acquired in Emmett. She sang in the glee club, went to the prom, and attended square dances. Perhaps she was too preoccupied to pay heed to a former classmate from Jerome. But now, in Albion, she discovered Jesse to be very smart and sincere, though he seemed to suffer from some sort of inferiority complex. As they spent time together, Jo learned a great deal more about Jesse Rigney and his family.

His father, my grandfather, John Douglas Rigney, was born in Missouri in 1876.

John Rigney

Leoda Lycan Rigney

He was the fourth of eight children, only five of whom survived. Later, the family moved to Indian Territory in Oklahoma, where John met lovely Leoda Gertrude Lycan.

When John and Leoda married, they continued living in the area of Stroud, Oklahoma. During that period, John became deeply invested in the teachings of the First Christian Church and developed a strong desire to study for the ministry. However, his family did not support his beliefs, which caused many unpleasant rows. Rather than attempt to deal with further discord, John chose to leave the region.

When he learned that the Twin Falls Land and Water Company was hiring workers to develop irrigation canals and ditches in Idaho, it sounded like a good opportunity. So, in 1905, the couple boarded a train, along with their three children, the youngest of whom was my father. They had five more children, while living and working as tenant farmers on land just newly opened for farming in Jerome.

John Rigney, whom the children called Pop, held his large family to high expectations. There was his way of doing things, and then there was the wrong way. While still living in the Jerome area, he became a leader in the community and developed good rapport with other farmers, who elected him as their Idaho State Senator for three separate terms. Senator Rigney traveled to Boise to attend legislative sessions, which usually lasted two months out of the year, and then returned to farming during the remainder of the year.

One bill he wrote, promoted, and saw passed was a boon to Idaho dairy farmers. When margarine was just coming on the market, the competition became difficult for the creameries. Senator Rigney's bill required that only real butter could be served in Idaho restaurants. Later, the Governor of Idaho appointed John as Director of the Idaho Public Utilities Commission (P.U.C.), a position he kept until he retired. Because of that appointment, he resettled his family in Boise in 1929 and was instrumental in the decision to bring electricity to Idaho City.

The Rigney family first lived in a big two-story house on a high ridge of land called The Bench. At that time, it was way out in a rural area. Now, it's a developed, incorporated part of the city. As the Rigney children began to leave the nest, the house became too large for John and Leoda, so they moved to a two-bedroom home with a third small room in the basement. It was conveniently situated within walking distance of John's work at the State Capitol. This is where the family lived until John retired from the PUC, and it continued to be home for the rest of his life.

My memories of Grandpa John always revolve around him as an older, retired gentleman who sat in the corner of the living room in his leather Morris chair with its wooden arms. He smoked a pipe, and I can remember its sweet aroma when I visited as a child. There was an antique lampshade beside his chair, and I was allowed to use its fringe for braiding practice. Each time we headed back to our home in Oregon, all of the eight-inch fringes had been carefully braided into neat little four-inch braids, which Grandma then had to undo and straighten.

There was a unique, somewhat musty aroma throughout the entire house which I have never smelled anywhere since. It could have been traces of a light perfume that I associated with Grandma. I remember playing with the musical powder box in her bedroom and sniffing her bath powder. When I wound up the key on the bottom of the music box and lifted the lid, I was treated to a delightful, tinkling tune and an intense whiff of her perfume. It was the same odor that permeated her clothing in a more subtle fashion whenever I gave her a hug. The aroma also wafted from the old fashioned overstuffed chair where Grandma always sat or from its match-ing sofa. It may have also come from the slightly dusty atmosphere rising from the carpet. Grandma's home was kept meticulously clean and orderly, but her carpet was never exposed to a vigorous vacuum, since she always cleaned with an ancient carpet sweeper. Because windows were rarely opened to provide air circulation, perhaps the household aroma also contained traces of cooking odors mixed with coal smoke from the huge furnace in the basement.

Grandpa's basement was the first place I'd ever seen a stoker furnace. Whenever the thermostat clicked on, it automatically started up a screw-driven mechanism, which rattled a steady stream of small coal pieces from the stoker into the fire box. I loved to follow Grandpa down into that fiery-warm room to watch him use a big coal shovel to fill up the stoker from the large coal bin beside the furnace. One time, I also watched while the monster coal truck drove up on his lawn, and the driver unfastened a tiny wooden trap door leading down to the coal bin. Then he inserted a portable chute into the little door, turned on a motor in his truck and dumped a load of coal. About every other day, Grandpa had to manipulate long- handled tongs to reach into the furnace's fire box and remove the residue of burning red clinkers, which often lifted out in complete circles shaped like large, bumpy doughnuts. These he carefully placed in a metal scuttle pail to cool before he carried them out to the alley trash can.

I was in awe of Grandpa Rigney, and when I was in his living room, I would not have dreamed of attempting to sit in his chair or even to invade his corner. He did allow me, however, to open his smoking cabinet to retrieve his playing cards and build card houses on the carpet by his feet. I remember watching him use those same cards to engage in competitive family games of pinochle. Often, he held forth in argumenta-tive political conversations during the game.

But, Grandpa had interests beyond politics. He was an avid backyard gardener, and he grew the pickling beets, green beans, Concord grapes, leaf lettuce, and juicy tomatoes that I loved. Along the walk by the back door he always planted a showy, flowery row of pinks, which produced a heavenly cinnamon aroma that still lingers in my memory. Additionally, whenever he had the opportunity, he pulled on his chest-high rubber waders that were held up with suspenders, donned his pith helmet, slung his wicker tackle-basket over one shoulder and headed out to his favorite streams to engage in fly fishing.

My memories of Grandpa John all begin with our family visits in the early 1940's, and they are centered in that house. I stumbled out to the kitchen in the early morning to watch him pour hot water into his old fashioned two-piece drip coffeemaker with the green wooden handle. Then he turned to me and asked, "Doris, how do you want your toast?" He never ceased to tease me about my little-girl answer which was "burnt!" Of course, I meant dark brown, but he took it literally as burnt and reminded me of it during each subsequent visit. What he probably did not know was that I learned to like my toast that way out of necessity. My mother's somewhat rattle-brained cooking often required her to scrape a layer of burned crumbs from toast she had forgotten. After she applied butter to what was left, I thought it tasted great.

The whole family knew how much I loved the green beans grown in Grandpa's garden and, I made family history when he asked me one time what I wanted for breakfast, and I promptly answered, "Green beans." So, whenever our family arrived at Grandpa's for a visit, he would chuckle at me saying, "And here's our girl who wants burnt toast and green beans for breakfast."

Grandma Leoda would laugh right along with him and add her own joke at my expense. She kept a marvelously-full, green Depression-glass candy dish on the sideboard next to the kitchen table. She continuously teased that I was the quietest of all her grandkids when it came to lifting that clinking lid and sneaking out pieces of candy. Later in her life, she gifted that candy dish to me when she was distributing some of her keepsakes to the grandkids.

Grandma spoke with an old-fashioned Oklahoma dialect and some of her expressions are particularly sweet for me to remember. When she said, "Doris that is a very pretty waist you are wearing," she was talking about my blouse. Another expression caused me confusion at first. If Grandpa were heading out to the very first- Albertson's store, she would remind him, "Now John, be sure to get some cream for the kiddies." I knew I was one of the kiddies but wondered why they would be buying me cream. I made the connection when Grandpa came home with a hand-packed quart of ice cream. Grandma liked to share her recipes with daughters and grandchildren, but she always called them "receipts." And, if we could get her talking about the olden days, we could count on her every so often tossing in the phrase, "Well, now, I recalect."

The summer I turned eighteen, I came purposely prepared to capture Grandma's "recalections." By then, Grandpa had died and we granddaughters took turns staying with Grandma to help out in small ways. When I arrived, she had already harvested and washed a whole metal dishpan of baby leaf lettuce. I watched her as she opened the narrow, cubby-hole closet which housed the water heater and the short line upon which she hung her tea towels to dry. From where I stood I could sniff the distinctive aroma of that little cubby. It was a warm, damp smell of drying cloth confined in a small space. That particular odor was present nowhere else on earth except in my Grandma's tea-towel closet.

She also kept her Mother Hubbard apron on a hook in that closet. Grandma always wore that apron in her kitchen, and she gave me the pattern. As an adult, I have sewn many gifts from that pattern. The apron hangs down straight from the shoulders to below the hips and covers completely all of a person's front and sides. Then a separate half-moon flare of cloth is attached around the bottom which causes the covering to continue down to knee-length. I always wore one of her aprons when working messy projects with my kindergarten classes.

After Grandma put her apron on and tied the strings in back, she was ready to demonstrate a lesson in the preparation of one of my favorite dishes, wilted lettuce. She fried up a goodly quantity of chopped bacon which she poured, hot grease and all, over the lettuce. Next, she added chopped green onion, vinegar, salt and black pepper. Finally, she lightly tossed the salad with two long wooden spoons and carried it over to her round oak kitchen table. That, with a thick slice of her homemade bread provided a meal fit for royalty.

After we finished our gourmet repast, I retrieved a small notebook, sat back down at the table, and asked, "Grandma, what was it like to live on the farm in Jerome?" She continued to sit beside me in her tidy cotton housedress covered by her generous apron, and began to reminisce.

In 1905, at the age of twenty-four, Leoda climbed off the train with her husband and family in Twin Falls, Idaho. She was already the mother of three—Irene, Darrel, and Jesse— toddlers who constantly expected her to be at their beck and call. Soon after, Leoda became pregnant with her fourth, Nellie.

Pop obtained work from Mr. Ira Burton Perrine, who operated a farm and ranch operation in the Snake River Canyon. Although the canyon got plenty of water, the surrounding area could not be easily irrigated, so he convinced private financiers to assist in building the Milner Dam and subsequently founded the Twin Falls Land and Water Company. Pop was hired to help build irrigation canals after the dam was completed.

My cousin told me that Pop had at least one other source of income when they first arrived. He was a good hunter, and he spent hours out in the sagebrush shooting quail. These were packed whole, feathers and innards intact, into containers which he shipped to the big restaurants in Kansas. It would have been at least a two-day trip, and my question about the condition in which the birds arrived went unanswered.

The family's early living conditions in the desert heat were indeed primitive. They lived in a tent on the south side of the Snake River. The toilet was reached by following a path to an outhouse. It is possible that the company provided some type of portable cooking stove, since Grandma never mentioned cooking over a campfire. Mr. Perrine delivered a wooden barrel of water once a week, but it was never enough for a family of their size. Before the week was out, Leoda always found it necessary to carry baby Jesse and lead her two toddlers down into the canyon for a mile, then trudge back up the steep incline, retracing her steps, all the while trying not to spill any of the precious load in her bucket or lose track of her wandering children.

Their daily diet consisted of beans, rice, flour, salt pork, and bacon. If they were lucky enough to have some eggs, Leoda would deep fry them in several inches of bacon fat. To go with the eggs, the family sopped up the bacon grease with the lightest, most marvelous biscuits ever tasted. Whenever I visited her home, I marveled at Grandma's skill in making biscuits, and I remember the bowl of bacon grease next to her cook stove. My father said it was standard while he was growing up to have bacon grease available on the table in place of butter. Leoda gathered wild dandelion greens when she could find them and boiled them over a slow fire with lots of bacon bits for seasoning. I didn't hear her speak of a cow during their tenting days, so I don't know what she did for a source of milk. She spoke of coyotes which were brave enough to come right up to the tent. Leoda kept handy what she called a squirrel gun to frighten them off. A squirrel gun is any type of a gun (mostly a shotgun) used at close range which scatters the shot so that taking careful aim is not so important.

During that time in her life, Leoda was truly a pioneer. I don't know how long they lived in a tent, or whether the family found better lodgings before Nellie and Clarence were born. But, before Geneva arrived, the family was able to move close to Jerome on the north side of the Snake River and rent a farm. Pop paid rent and worked the farm for a percentage of the harvest to "Old Man Sergeant." Nobody liked Mr. Sergeant very much. Leoda described him as being nosy and fussy about getting his rent paid on the dot. He always seemed to show up when it was almost dinner time.

They lived there as tenant farmers while the land was still in the process of being "proved up," which means the people who filed claims under the Homestead Act of 1862 needed to meet all the requirements of the government before they could receive title to the land. Some of the stipulations included a maximum of 160 acres per family, building a house, improving the land, and living there for five years before the claimant could receive a patent on it proving ownership.

One of my cousins told me that there was much talk about the corruption that surrounded the Homestead Act. Large outfits, such as lumber barons or big landowners, claimed the land and then hired someone else to live on the property and make the required improvements until the five years were up. I suspect this was the case for the place where Pop lived, because he always rented and never did own any land in Jerome. Yet, my grandmother spoke of the land being finally "proved up." I believe that "proved up" also meant they had grubbed enough sagebrush to make it possible to plant crops. They spent years there, and they began to prosper from their hard work.

At least they had a real farm house, which was much nicer than where they had been living. But they still had an outdoor toilet with no inside plumbing and no electricity. Leoda spoke of the coal oil lamps with glass chimneys which required daily cleaning. Also, there were no screens on the windows, which meant flies, mosquitoes, and other flying visitors were always present. Leoda planted a garden, and she had chickens and cows. She spoke of ten to twelve milkers and had the daily, complicated task of washing the cream separator. The cream cans were picked up every morning, and the creamery left new cans for the next day.

By this time, Irene was old enough to be put to work, and work she did! Irene once complained to me about how much she hated washing all the tiny pieces of that cream separator. The younger children always spoke of Irene being the one in charge and complained of her bossy ways. However, a crew the size of the Rigney family required someone with a firm hand to give out orders. Irene capably filled that job description. As each young boy in the family grew strong enough, he was put to work helping with the monumental tasks of farming.

Leoda described the wheat harvest as a particularly trying time. The neighbors pooled their resources to hire a steam-engine thresher. The crew hitched the heavy, bulky threshing machine to teams of horses and moved it to whichever field was ready. Before it arrived, the farmer needed to use a horse-drawn binder to cut the wheat. Then crews of men and boys tied it into sheaves which were hauled by wagon to the threshing machine. My dad spoke of the sun beating down on the hot fields and of the snakes that lurked in amongst the wheat stalks. Dangerous hard work, indeed!

When the threshing crew arrived to work the Sergeant place, Leoda and Irene were required to feed a breakfast of bacon, eggs, potatoes, biscuits, and pie to this team of ten or twelve hungry men and then turn right around to begin cooking their noontime dinner. The quantity of food they prepared was mind-boggling. Every spring, Leoda bought at least one hundred baby chicks, which she raised to young fryer size in time for the harvest. For one meal, she needed to kill, pluck, and fry seven or eight Leghorns. Along with the fried chicken, she served biscuits, potatoes, beans, relishes, and pie or cake. Cake baking presented an additional and unusual problem. One of the hired hands had a propensity for taking nips of alcoholic beverages. Since Prohibition was the law of the land, his access to the "good stuff" was limited. Consequently, vanilla with its high alcohol content, needed to be hidden. More than once, Leoda prepared to bake a cake only to discover the vanilla bottle was empty.

If it wasn't threshing time, it was time to cook for the haying crew. The process of haying also required extra help to mow, rake, and stack the fresh-cut hay before it could be moved by team and wagon to the barn. They owned a tall derrick with a cable hanging down to the ground that could be attached to bundles of hay, which were then lifted into the loft. Once, when I was about eight years old, my brother and

21

I visited Uncle Darrel and Aunt Myrtle's farm in Jerome. I have strong memories of playing with my cousins, Billy and JoAnn, on a derrick just like Grandpa's. It became our swing.

On the Sergeant place, the folks also raised pigs, and in early winter after the first hard freeze, the men butchered six or seven hogs. Pop built a smoke house where they cured their own bacon and ham. Sausage meat was fried into patties and then sealed in crocks covered with lard. Leoda or Irene spent hours tending a kettle on the fire in order to render the pig fat into lard. The family rejoiced in butchering time, because they loved to eat the crackling leftovers after the rendering process was complete. Cracklings were the crispy, crunchy little bits of skin and morsels of meat which were strained out of the boiling hot lard before it was poured into stone storage crocks.

There was no such thing as cold storage, so other means of preservation had to be employed. Leoda knew how to make other great delicacies at butchering time, because nothing was wasted. One such treat was pickled pig's feet, which were boiled with spices and preserved in vinegar and salt. Also, the hogs' heads were boiled and picked clean of meat, which was then mixed with broth saved from the boiling process. Leoda made head cheese from it by adding vinegar, salt, pepper and spices to the mix. This was then poured into flat pans and allowed to cool until it formed into a gelatinous concoction.

If the chickens were laying more than her family could consume, she placed the raw eggs in a heavy-lidded crock and covered them with a mixture of saltpeter and water. Beets were pulled from the garden, boiled, and stored in a brine of salt, sugar, vinegar, and spices. A few boiled eggs were always dunked into the purple beet brine and left for a day or two until they turned a lovely purple and picked up the flavor of the pickled beets. These were items the children loved to squabble over. A beautiful purple pickled egg is a treasure worth fighting for. Carrots, potatoes and cabbage went into an underground root cellar. Leoda had a fifteen-gallon wooden barrel in which she made and stored sauerkraut.

Additionally, she gathered field corn which she covered with lye water made from the wood-stove's ashes. The corn was left to soak until it became soft enough to boil into hominy. Sweet corn was blanched, cut from the cob, and sun-dried on racks with a cheese-cloth covering to keep away insects. During these grueling, back breaking years, Leoda took time to pass her cooking secrets on to her daughters. There was always a pot of green beans simmering on the back burner and she never varied her recipe for those beans. She added bacon bits with plenty of salt, pepper, and bacon grease and then boiled them all day, removing every iota of vitamins before she thought they were fit to eat. I didn't care one whit about vitamins, and her way of cooking them was exactly why they tasted so good to me when, so many years later, I came to gobble them down for breakfast.

Leoda missed the company of other women because she was only able to see them if she could travel to church, which was a long four miles away from her home. Or, she might invite company for dinner after church. Sometimes other families invited the Rigneys to come to their home for Sunday dinner. Jesse remembered one such occasion when they visited a home with no screens on the windows, but the mother of that house was not as careful as Leoda. Jesse was excited when he noticed the dessert on the kitchen drainboard. He hurried over to admire the beautiful whipped cream cake that was decorated with what he assumed were raisins. That is, until he came close enough to discover that the decorations were actually flies that had flown too close to the cream and had become stuck. One of her children remarked, "Mother, some flies landed on your cake." She answered, "Oh bosh, I'll just pick them off!" Needless to say, all of the Rigneys found that they were just "too full" to eat dessert.

Throughout the years she lived in Jerome, Leoda was occupied with babies. Walter arrived, and last of all came Grace. During these years she continued to provide clothing, did the cleaning up, and saw to it that her large brood received schooling. Attending school regularly was very important, and a discussion about further education arose about the time that Jesse and his brother Darrel graduated from high school. Darrel was a year older than Jesse, but the Jerome High School Annual shows that they both graduated in 1924. Pop allowed his oldest daughter, Irene, to go into teacher's training, because by then, Geneva, whom everyone called "Sister," was old enough to begin helping Leoda. But, Pop wished that his sons would stay close to the family in order to work on the farm. That suited Darrel just fine, because he loved farming.

Pop was not convinced that Jesse should head off to attend college. However, Jesse wanted more education. He was intellectually curious and was a serious reader. He was selected to write the class poem for his school annual. The poem itself is nothing of great quality. But it does rhyme, has correct meter, and is full of complimentary descriptions of his classmates, written using somewhat flowery expressions, which seemed to be the accepted writing style of that era. His school activities listed next to his class photo state that he took part in debate and in the Athenians, which was described as a literary society.

There are hints in his high school annual which lend credence to Jo's suspicions that he suffered from feelings of inferiority. The nickname beside his photo is "Fat." And, he was selected to play "Amanda, Olivia's Black Mammy" in the senior class play. Most likely, he was painted up in blackface and dressed in a female servant's costume with a rag-head covering. During the 1920's in this conservative Idaho farming area, people of color were usually the butt of jokes. There is proof of this in the racial slurs found in the annual. His role as Amanda was probably that of a buffoon.

This must have been demeaning for a person with my dad's deeply sensitive personality, but he had a need to show a tough exterior at school. The motto he chose to have printed beside his picture reads, "Nobody molests me, unhurt." Also, there was a tendency for his father and siblings to be caustic in their criticism of each other and of other people in the community. My father, though kind, funny and generous, suffered from a fairly deep sense of pessimism on many subjects. It was common for him to say to my mother, "Jo, you know you can't do that." And, just as often, my mother would answer back, "Now, Jesse, don't fuss about it. I think it'll work out just fine." Mother served as his optimistic and can-do counterpart, which helped to keep their life together in a workable balance.

Knowing these details about Jesse's personality helps me understand the problems he must have experienced when he requested permission from his father to attend college. At first, Pop argued against it and then finally agreed that Jesse could go but only if Darrel went too. This is difficult to compute, and I suspect that perhaps Pop didn't have enough trust in Jesse's ability to succeed unless Darrel went along to serve as a supervising older brother. If that is the case, it would explain my father's lack of self-confidence, a characteristic with which he struggled for most of his life. Darrel already knew he wanted to farm, but he decided to try the college bit because Jesse wanted so much to go. There was really not enough money to send two boys off to school at the same time, but off they went.

Jesse did well in his studies, but he felt awkward because his clothing did not fit the norm. He was a large young man, and being short on funds, he often had only overalls to wear to class. As his friendship with Jo developed, he felt comfortable in sharing his concerns about staying in school. Jo came from a background where she knew what life would be like if she didn't advance her education. She urged Jesse to stick to his goal even though it was really tough for him financially. By then, Darrel had decided to give it up, and it was clear that Pop would soon withdraw his support.

After one year, Darrel went back to Jerome, married his wife Myrtle, and became a successful farmer. Jesse struggled through a portion of his sophomore year before finally deciding that college was a bad idea. When he headed back to Jerome, he needed to find useful employment. One of the jobs he found was cooking for a sheep camp.

Jesse comes a courting

The main lesson he remembered from that experience was a determination never to eat mutton again. He then found a job as a caretaker for the bus station in downtown Boise.

Though Jesse struggled to find his way, he always managed to obtain some sort of employment, a pattern which he maintained throughout the difficult years of the Great Depression. It was in these early days in Boise that he and Jo began to keep serious company. Photos demonstrate that he owned or had the use of a car and he often came to take Jo from her teaching job for outings.

My mother never spoke much of their romancing days, so I don't know the exact details of their engagement, but it was a pleasure to discover, inserted in Jo's class book, a handwritten letter on peach-colored stationery with a photo of Jo's mother pasted on it. It's addressed to Jesse and written in Louise Popkey's careful script:

Lowman, Ida- Dec 17, 1927

Dear Mr. Rigney,

We received your letter and we are not surprised at your news, as Josie has told us how much you are to each other and we see no reason why we should not give our full consent and approval. Come up and see us when Josie comes home. We are sorry you couldn't come for Christmas.

Sincerely yours,
Mr. and Mrs. Wm Popkey.

While the young couple began to make plans for their life together, across the ocean a new life was stirring for the Ayyoub family. In December of 1928, approximately one year after Louise Popkey in America wrote her welcoming letter to Jesse, the Ayyoubs in Jordan also welcomed a new member into the family, for that is the year Miriam gave birth to my future husband, Ibrahim.

CHAPTER 2

Our Childhood Lives

"Are you traveling to Irbid this week? If you do, please stop by the county seat and tell them that Toufiq Ayyoub has a new son." This is one version of Ibrahim's birth record. But, he had three official documents attesting to different dates: church baptismal records and his family bible; the registration in Irbid; and, the date shown on his first passport. When Ibrahim became a naturalized U.S. citizen the judge allowed him to choose his date of birth from the three options. He picked December 11, 1928, the date on his passport.

His early life was spent in the village of Al Husn, and he was curious and adventurous from the start. Ibrahim was still tiny when he discovered the chicken coop situated in the courtyard of the family compound. Often, he crawled through the opening into where the chickens had their nests. He then lay there to nap until he heard a hen cackle, which announced a fresh egg. He would eat this warm delicacy raw, leaving the telltale shells behind. The family worried that some predator was stealing all their eggs until one day an older brother caught the sneaky "animal" by his little legs and pulled him out.

Another of Ibrahim's early memories is of escaping through the courtyard gate, carelessly left unlatched, when he was barely old enough to toddle about. He wandered into the street to gaze at the big outside world, all on his own for the first time, at about two years old. There were probably some motorized vehicles buzzing about in the sandy, dusty streets. But, mostly, there were merchants sitting and visiting with each other in the shade of their shops, having a smoke or sipping sweet tea. There were donkeys braying and bullocks moaning as their drivers urged them on to deliver loads of produce to the market, and camels complaining with a distinctive bellow. The street provided plenty of potential dangers for the tiny boy.

At that time, his father owned a shop. Thankfully, it was not far, just around the corner from home. Ibrahim must have known that his father went there, because his baby feet led him in the direction of the shop. If he had no knowledge of all these people bustling about, there were plenty of folk who did know him. "Look, Toufiq's youngest has ventured out of his nest." Strong arms lifted the boy onto shoulders and proudly carried him to the shop.

I would have thought Toufiq might chastise his little one for wandering without permission into the dangerous streets, because that's what my father would have done. But, that was not the way of the village. Instead, his father said, "Son, since you are old enough to join the world, you must carry a gift of celebration home to your mother." Then, Toufiq directed Ibrahim's rescuer to carry a large box of soap with him as Ibrahim was escorted home, with the message to "Tell his mother that Ibrahim is bringing this gift home for the family."

The celebration of welcoming young Ibrahim into the world outside his court-yard is a good example of how family culture influenced the children. Miriam also trained her children to be responsible members of society. She accomplished this by example: to be kind; to have a sense of humor; to be honest; to be industrious; and, to represent the honor of the family in their actions.

The effect of her training was exhibited in small ways. One day, when Ibrahim was still quite young, he came running into the courtyard to find his mother sitting and working in the shade. "May I have some money? There is fresh apple for sale in the market." "I'm sorry son, your father did not leave any money with me before he left town on business." Ibrahim wandered discontentedly around the courtyard and noticed the large piles of wheat stored in the small room to one side of the courtyard. He glanced at his mother and decided that she was not looking. So, he gathered up a small quantity of grain in the tails of his *dishdasheh,* the long white garment somewhat like a nightgown worn by most village children. He checked his mother again and then carried the grain out of the gate.

As he headed towards the market, he began to think very seriously about what he was doing. "I see the other children bringing wheat or eggs to barter for what they want to buy. I can do it too. But what will the village people think when they see Tou-fiq's son bartering?" His pace became slower and slower. Finally, he stopped, turned, and retraced his steps to the family gate. He entered, walked to the storage room, poured the grain back on the pile, and ambled over to plunk down in the shade beside his mother. Only then did Miriam speak. "Son, I saw the grain in your *dishdasheh*. Why did you not buy your apples?" "Mother, I did not want the village people to think that my father did not have money. They would say, 'Oh look at Toufiq's son, he must barter for his treats instead of paying with money.' I did not think it would be right for me to make them think that."

Most probably, based on my brief experience with her, Miriam's face broke into deep smiles of pride. He didn't remember her saying anything to him, but we can be assured that she shared the tale with Toufiq when he returned. Miriam's face, etched in smile wrinkles, bore witness that she seldom felt the need to frown. Each of her eleven children had a personal story about the one time that child made Miriam frown. Ibrahim had a long-enduring memory of the time he received his "lesson from Mother."

When the children were young, they spent many hours playing nearby their mother while she worked. If the project was suitable for the roof, she carried her tools up the ladder and her babies went with her. Miriam was a thrifty wizard in the ways of make-do-with-what's-available. The roof was a breezy, sunny, uncluttered place to work as she provided for the family welfare.

Young Ibrahim was about six or seven at the time of his lesson. He was up on the roof with his mother and younger sister, Naimeh. He was restless and bored because not enough was going on to entertain his active mind. He noticed that Naimeh was engrossed in play with a little toy. Not that he liked the toy, but she had it, and he did not. So he began to chase and torment her to steal it. There was no big problem there, except they were on the roof eight feet above the ground with no guard rails. The chase quickly became perilous, and Miriam's orders for Ibrahim to desist were ignored. Naimeh was not fast or strong enough to avoid her brother, but she was clever. She ran to hide behind her mother's skirts where Ibrahim brashly followed. This was his undoing.

Miriam grabbed her young son by his thick curly hair and sat on his squirming body. Then, she proceeded to vigorously scrub his scalp with her fist, "and it hurt him hijjus!" The next part of this story leaves me breathless, and so it did for Ibrahim. Miriam knew that Toufiq was close at hand and able to help, but Ibrahim's memory has it that Miriam picked up her young son and dramatically threw him off the roof crying, "Here, take this child. I want nothing more to do with him!"

The miscreant was caught in the capable arms of his father, who placed him on the ground. Ibrahim remembered creeping off to his pallet and sleeping for the next ten hours. Never again did his mother feel the need for harsh discipline with Ibrahim. She continued to make her wishes known with smiles or meaningful looks, and Ibrahim obeyed. He took his place among the siblings who had each received "the one beating from Mother."

Ibrahim had plenty of older brothers who did not subscribe to a one-beating rule. One of Ibrahim's beatings from his family occurred when he proved his excellent stone-throwing by hitting and killing one of his Aunt Miriam's pigeons. Not only did the pigeon bite the dust, but one of the stones bounced off the wall and struck his aunt. Miriam, one of Toufiq's sisters, did not stop to reason with the child. She marched straight to his mother and father. "What shall we do with a child who is turning into a stone-throwing gangster? He needs to be punished for this misbehavior!" Unfortunately, one of Ibrahim's brothers was only too willing to oblige.

While Mother Miriam toiled in the home, Toufiq plied his skills as a businessman. He engaged in many partnerships with his friend, Mahmoud Rashdan and Mahmoud's cousin, Barakat. One such partnership was the establishment of a shop that sold a variety of dry goods and other household necessities. Toufiq was adventurous and traveled away from home a great deal, sometimes purchasing goods for the shop, sometimes carrying out missions for local people.

For a few harvest seasons he was employed as a purchaser of wheat. His cousin, Mousa, a resident of Haifa, Palestine was selected to manage the operation of buying wheat in Jordan for the British Steel Company. Mousa knew that Toufiq was acquainted with many of the farmers in the region and was influential in the area. He also trusted Toufiq to judge good quality wheat. So he hired Toufiq to buy wheat on consignment. During the time of this employment, Toufiq provided a good living for his growing family.

Toufiq also had the ability to understand the impact of international politics on the country. When it became apparent that World War II was about to break out, he saw the writing on the wall. In advance, he purchased quantities of rice and sugar to offset the coming shortages of war. All of Al Husn, and even customers from other areas, came to his shop because they heard that Toufiq still had supplies, so he carried on a robust business.

When he tired of running the shop, he turned it over to the husband of his sister, Miriam, and her son, Selman. This left him free to begin new ventures. He and Mahmoud knew that transportation by taxi cost a shilling or more, which was very expensive for most villagers. So they and a group of investors established a bus company which traveled to Irbid and back. It was successful because it reduced the cost of a one-way trip to two piastres.

Also, Toufiq came to understand that for generations the farmers in his area used only the top ten centimeters of soil. They needed to plow deeper to bring back productivity, but had no access to heavy equipment. The law allowed citizens to import a fancy Cadillac but were forbidden to import farming machinery. It seemed the government attempted to keep farmers from becoming self-sufficient, or perhaps it was an effort to break them so that they would be forced to sell their unproductive land. Toufiq felt the injustice and determined on a course of action to rectify it.

He and Mahmoud gathered a group of associates, and together they formed a partnership to invest in a black-market purchase of a tractor. They arranged to have it smuggled over the border from Palestine, and this was the first tractor in the area. They hired drivers and rented out the tractor to farmers. Things went well and the tractor was in operation twenty-four hours a day. Because business was so very profitable, some local people were jealous. The culprit is not known, but someone poured a foreign substance into the gas tank. When the driver fired it up, the material dispersed and gummed up the engine. Immediately, a strong jerk twisted the crank shaft and casing. They brought mechanics from Syria and Lebanon who were unable to fix it; it continued to spill oil. Parts were unavailable, and profits drained from the venture. To pay off debts, the partners were forced to sell the ruined tractor.

Toufiq had received little formal education, although as a child, he did attend a crude, primitive school in Al Husn where he was required to sit on the ground, balancing a notebook on his knee, learning to read and write. This accounts for his life-long habit of writing on his knee. The only books available for young Toufiq were the Bible and the Koran. But he read these extensively and became self-educated.

Toufiq valued learning, and all of his sons were offered education at school. Some of them flourished in school surroundings. Others chose a different route. Suleiman graduated first in his high school class in all of Jordan and went on to hold an important position with the government in the Land and Survey Department. Naim also joined the Land and Survey Department, and Nasser made a career in the Jordanian army. Fahim attended college in Egypt and became an engineer. Due to his developmental difficulties, Saad stayed at home with his mother.

Of the daughters, Aiedeh and Subha married early and received no formal schooling. Naimeh attended school through third grade and then stayed home to help her mother. She also married at a young age. All three daughters stayed in the village and were available to help their mother with family dinners and heavy household tasks. Although there was no formal school available for the girls, Miriam's daughters were well-schooled in the home skills. It was well known in the village that the best meals came from Miriam's hands, and she made sure that all of her culinary secrets were passed on to her daughters. However, reading and writing were not among the skills she was able to teach.

Likewise, my grandmothers didn't have much schooling before marriage, since it was common in both countries for girls to marry at an early age. Leoda Lycan and Louise Mason were young brides. American schools during the late 1920's and 1930's did offer more opportunities for girls. But, as we have seen in Jo's story, not every child was able to take advantage of that. It was Jo's persistence that saw her through until she finally came to believe that her level of education was adequate for the time being and that possibly her married life could begin.

But even after Jo and Jesse agreed in 1927 to marry, Jo's need to provide financial support for her mother and little sisters meant it was another two and a half years before they could wed. Jo continued to teach in rural valley schools near Boise. She preserved a photo of one of those schools where her class appears to consist of only five or six students. The building was very humble, just one room, and as a teacher, I wonder what kind of supplies she was given to work with and what her duties entailed

During her teaching years, Jo's mother, dad, and younger sisters were once more forced to move and left the ranch. It was the onset of the Depression, and Mr. Ort felt sorry about their leaving, but the ranch was all he had, and he had to make it pay. They found a place to rent for $10 a month in the little town of Star, Idaho. Once again, it was struggle time, and it is clear that Bill Popkey was not always living with his family. He continued to pursue his fascination with lumber camps, and he also tried his hand at mining for gold. Idaho was noted for placer mining, which employs sluice boxes or gold pans for washing grains of gold out of the mountain streams.

Among keepsakes stored in my family's basement were Grandpa Bill's mining helmet with a smelly carbide lamp attached to its headband and the big, tarnished copper pan he used when panning for gold. He always had a few samples of shiny rock in his pockets to impress my brother and me, but he assured us that none of them were valuable; he called them "fool's gold."

Grandpa Bill may have understood all about fool's gold, but he had very little understanding about the foolish and irresponsible way he behaved towards his family. I'm sure that Jo's teaching job was extremely important to the well-being of her mother and younger sisters, Marie and Ernestine, who were still at home. It must have frustrated Jo and Jesse that their marriage was delayed by her family's dependence on Jo's salary.

One of the times when Bill was home with the family in Star, Dorothy and Walt stopped by to announce they were expecting a baby. Dorothy went in, but Walt didn't. Then, Bill came out to ask, "Why in the hell don't you come in?" Apparently, he had forgiven them for getting married. Louise went to stay with Dorothy and Walt for a week or so after Roger was born, and Dorothy said her mother "was so happy to have a grandson."

The following spring, after Roger was born, Jo and Jesse were finally able to make plans for their wedding. Dorothy mentioned in her memoir that during this time she and her sister developed some sort of misunderstanding. My mother never mentioned the falling-out to me, so the comment in Dorothy's writing was a surprise. But it does answer a question which immediately struck me when I read the newspaper article about my parent's wedding. I wondered why Dorothy and Walt did not attend the ceremony. It is one of very few major celebrations during the entire lives of the two sisters where they were not together.

A newspaper article about my parents' wedding is charmingly written and describes the affair as "a very pretty wedding" on a Sunday in June. The bride wore a pale yellow satin gown with a white lace overlay and carried roses and fern tied with tulle. My father's mother prepared the wedding dinner, and there is no mention of Bill Popkey, father of the bride, who was probably already up in the hills on one of his "summer pursuits," what with it being June. I saw the dress when I was a child and peeked into a beat-up metal suitcase. I found the slowly deteriorating yellow satin dress covered with cream-colored lace and decorated with little rosebuds. It looked like the dresses I've seen in movies that a "flapper" might have worn. After finding the article about my parent's wedding, I realized this was my mother's wedding dress.

The next period in the lives of the newlyweds is a bit murky. I know that Jesse worked in Boise for some period of time, but there is no record of where they lived. It would have been a rental for sure, since my parents were never able to buy until I was twelve years old and we lived in Nyssa. It is possible that Jo taught at least one more year of school, but after my brother Jim was born, her teaching career was suspended. Women who were pregnant or mothers of young babies were not allowed to teach.

Since this was the period following the "crash of '29," money was extremely tight and they were existing only on Jesse's wages.

Jo would have been barely pregnant in February of 1931, when she was burdened with the worry of her mother's failing health. Louise had "female problems." Perhaps she had uterine cancer, and Dorothy wrote of how shocked she was to get a telegram that her mother was "sinking fast."

Louise died on March 16, 1931. Dorothy believed that she "didn't have the care she should have had. There wasn't any money for anything." The loss reconciled Jo and Dorothy, and they were always very close after that. Dorothy said, "Dad was really low after losing Mother. He told Jo to take the girls. Ernestine was about nine years old by then and Marie was fifteen." There is a strong possibility that alcohol was again influencing Bill's behavior.

My mother described how difficult it was to be pregnant, to grieve for her mother, and to take in a ready-made family. Marie was at an unruly age and was very interested in marrying an unsuitable man, who Dorothy said, "turned out to be a jail-bird!" Because Jo was at her wit's end in trying to deal with the situation, she called her cousin Ruth, who agreed to provide Marie with a home and education in Michigan, where she eventually married and raised her family.

Ernestine stayed with Jo and Jesse. She loved to tell one particular story about that period in her life. It is well known that Jo was not particularly gifted in the home-making arts, but she decided to sew a dress for Ernestine. I really can empathize with Ernestine's reluctance for this project, because when I was a child, many of my mother's sewing disasters became items of clothing that I was expected to wear. Whenever Jo attempted to sew, she laid the fabric out on the table, sort of held the pattern down with table knives and whacked away. Ernestine's dress didn't turn out too well, but Jo had worked very hard on the project and insisted that Ernestine would wear it to school.

Ernestine sneaked some other clothing out of the house and hid it behind a billboard that stood next to the street on the way to school. Dressed in the hateful outfit, she left home and headed down the street. When she got to the billboard, she slipped out of sight behind it and changed into her other clothing. Perhaps that sewing project is still behind a billboard somewhere in Boise.

October rolled around and it was time for Baby Jim to arrive. Jo was a small-boned woman married to a very large man, which created the possibility of producing a large baby. Jo's doctor put her in the Boise St. Alphonsus Hospital where her son, Jim, was delivered by Caesarean section on the 12th of October, 1931. A Caesarean delivery would have required a lengthy and expensive recovery period in the hospital, and Ernestine was only ten or eleven, but may have been all the help Jo had.

Jim had a difficult beginning; he cried all the time and could not seem to keep down any food. Finally, with the advice of friends and family, Jo and Jesse located a pediatrician named Dr. Trumain. He took one look at Jim and told them he was starving.

He told them to switch him to goat milk and to fry bananas in butter. My mother was appalled at the advice, but she followed it, and Jim began to thrive.

While she was dealing with her sick baby, Jo reached out to her in-laws for support and assistance. I know that she found comfort in Leoda's friendship, but even more in Geneva's. Although Jo was 26, while Sister was only 19, she already stood out as a mainstay of the Rigney family. Everyone in the family learned to depend on her as a capable, agreeable helper, which she continued to do until she became too frail to give any more.

Aunt Geneva became my life-time role model. She was smart, hard-working, kind, and she had the Rigney sense of humor which she exercised with humility and graciousness. She garnered all of Leoda's cooking skills and developed more of her own. She approached problems with common sense solutions which could be counted upon to solve difficulties. This was exactly the kind of supportive strength that Jo needed, and the two women formed a bond of sisterhood as deep as that which existed between Jo and her own siblings.

About the time that Jim began to thrive, Geneva had decisions to make which shaped her future life. She graduated from Boise High School in 1930 and continued to live at home while attending Junior College. Before finishing her two years, she chose to quit school in order to work. Pop wanted her to continue with her schooling, but he allowed her to make her own decision, and she began working for the Bell Telephone Company.

She was still working there when I came on the scene in July of 1935.

I was also delivered by expensive Caesarian section, because I was a ten-pound baby. My parents always threatened me with the need for good behavior because, "You are not paid for, and we can still send you back." I was a gullible child and very willing to accept that it could really happen. I was a healthy, happy baby from the get-go. No skinny starving infancy for me. Jo had plenty of milk to nurse me, and I had no need for fried bananas or goat milk. I have wondered if the trauma of grief which Jo underwent while pregnant with my brother could have influenced his poor start. Then again, he was always "Skinny Jim," whereas I started life at ten pounds and never lost an ounce of it.

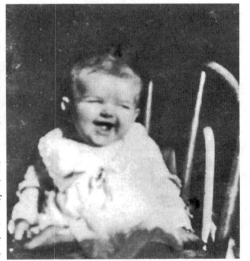

Baby Doris

When I became a teenager, my Aunt Geneva loved to tease me about my sedentary babyhood. She told me that I was perfectly happy to sit and watch the world go on around me. The whole Rigney family joined in the effort to teach me to walk, and they did it with bribery. "Come here Baby Doris. If you stand up and take a step, we'll give you this sugar lump." So, I'd stand, take one step, claim my bit of sugar, and then plunk back down on my diapered bottom until they offered another.

Several years before I was born, Ibrahim, over half a world away, also developed strategies to get what he wanted. However old he was at the time, he was young enough to lack any sign of embarrassment about throwing a royal hissy fit. Toufiq was about to make a merchant's buying trip to Damascus, where he had to purchase items used in weddings: velvet fabrics, good cloth for men's suits, shoes, and *Hattas,* a woman's headdress. He decided this trip would be a good time for Miriam and him to get away on holiday. Therefore, they asked the older daughters to care for the smaller children while they were gone and requested Abu Ghanem to drive them to Irbid so that they could hire a taxi for the trip to Damascus.

But, Ibrahim wanted to go. He began to scream hysterically and ran after them. He was a fast, determined child and jumped on the bumper of the old fashioned taxi. Abu Ghanem stopped the car, got out, set the child down on the street and climbed back into the driver's seat. No sooner had he started up the motor than there was frantic Ibrahim clinging to the bumper again, all the while yelling his bloody head off. This scene was repeated three times before Miriam said to her husband, "Oh, let him come with us." Having accomplished his purpose, Ibrahim immediately settled in for the trip of his life, the first time out of Al Husn, and alone with his parents! It was his lump of sugar.

Damascus was a jewel of a city. They stayed in a hotel close to *al Marjeh,* also known as Martyrs Square, which was built as a memorial to the 1916 revolt which sparked the end of Turkish domination over Syria. It was lined with trees and strung with decorative lights. They dined in their room eating *hummus,* bread, and *falafel,* or in restaurants famous for their skewers of *shish kabob.* They rode in an *Arabayeh,* the one-horse open carriage, where the hooves of the horse went tek, tek, tek, tek along the cobbled street. Ibrahim took in all the wondrous sights.

His mother and he whiled away their time with delight in the gardens and the comforts of the hotel while Toufiq chose the many purchases to be delivered to the shop in Al Husn. Miriam's opinions were consulted concerning the quality of goods. Ibrahim didn't know if his brothers or sisters were ever treated to such a trip, but he always valued the memory of that precious time alone with his parents.

Ibrahim was at the shop back in Al Husn when the shipment arrived from Damascus. His father immediately started to unpack the piled boxes and store the contents in the proper sections of the shop. The problem with this operation was Ibrahim. His little head and body were always two steps ahead of his father, pushing and peeking into the boxes. Ibrahim remembered chattering out loud, and marveling, "Oh, what wondrous shiny cloth! "Who will get to wear those big shoes?" "What will be in the next box?" "Let me see, let me see!"

Toufiq realized that no work could be accomplished until he resolved the situation with his over-eager, curious son. He stopped trying to work, looked down at the tot and said, "Son, we have been working very hard. It is time for us to rest. Come here and sit beside me on this chair."

So they sat, and they sat, and they sat. Ibrahim began to wiggle and squirm, but his father steadied him with a firm hand saying, "Son, we are not done resting. We must sit a while longer." "Aren't we done resting yet, Yaba?" "Oh, no. We are going to rest for a long, long, time."

Wiggle, twitch, and squirm. Ibrahim "rested" as long as his active little soul could take. When Toufiq saw that his son had reached his limit, he released his hold and pretended to be looking away at something very important. Ibrahim immediately decided that his father was distracted, slipped off the chair, and raced out of the shop!

This tale became one of the family stories told during evening courtyard gatherings. In later years, when he studied his first college course in psychology, it dawned on Ibrahim that there were very few new concepts for him to digest. He'd already learned them, first hand, sitting at the feet of his father.

When Ibrahim reached school age, he was a busy little boy running in the village streets. Teacher Najeeb planned his introduction to school and directed his friend, Toufiq, "You must buy gifts of pencils and paper and bring young Ibrahim to my school." As Ibrahim played, his father walked by and took him by the hand saying, "Come with me, Son." Ibrahim was happy to be going somewhere with his father, who led him to the classroom. Najeeb directed Ibrahim where to sit and formal education began. Najeeb soon recognized Ibrahim's abilities and told Toufiq, "Educate this boy, or I will!" Toufiq told him not to worry, that "If anybody is going to be concerned about my son's education, it will be me."

Najeeb reported to the family on how Ibrahim took punishment for school misdeeds. Any miscreant was instructed to hold out his hands. The teacher would then repeatedly strike the palms of each hand with a switch. This was done with vigor, aiming to make the child cry, but Ibrahim's teachers could never strike hard enough to cause tears. Instead, he just accepted the punishment and then cupped his hands together to blow on them. Ibrahim did not think the punishment unusual; this was the way of school. He wisely learned to hold his hands up high so that the blows landed there instead of on his face or body.

He did have opinions about some of the teachers or principals who carried their authority too far. Because he was the son of Toufiq, a village elder, he was sometimes selected to serve as a student assistant. The principal once requested him to help with the vision check for the first graders. He directed Ibrahim to bring each child out into the hall and wait until the principal tested the child's responses to the old fashioned eye chart. The child was to indicate with his fingers if the E was pointing left, right, up or down. One child was so frightened that he froze and could give no response.

Repeated commands produced no answer. In anger, the principal yelled, "*Ibin Kalb*," son of a dog.

Then he strode up to the little boy and bit him on the shoulder, lifting him off the floor. Thanks be to the cold weather, the child's several layers of clothing padded his little body so the bite did not break his skin. But due to his terror, he peed in his pants and managed to soak the principal as well. "Ibrahim, go fetch Selman, the janitor!" Ibrahim ran to the janitor's closet saying, "The principal wants you in his office!" The principal yelled at Selman, "Go to my home and tell my wife to give you a change of jacket, shirt, pants and shoes for me," exhibiting no concern for the welfare of the ter- rified child who received no sympathetic assistance.

Actions such as this, taken at school, never prompted complaints from home. Parents loved, coddled, and spoiled their little ones while they were infants, but a child was sent to school with the expectation that discipline would be strict. They had a saying: "Here sir, is my child. Yours is the flesh! Save me the bones!"

One punishment that Ibrahim well remembered occurred in fourth grade. This was the year that English instruction began. For homework, the teacher told each student to buy a new notebook with lines printed a certain way. They were to copy the first lesson of English words from their text. So each student went to buy the notebook and carefully copied all the words.

The following day, students were instructed to place their notebooks on their desk tops. The teacher walked down the row, picking up each notebook, checking its contents on the front page, and commanded, "Go to the front of the room!" indicating that the student should prepare for punishment. The teacher went to the next desk, checked the front of that notebook and repeated, "Go to the front of the room!"

This continued until all students were standing in the front of the room. "Hold out your palms!" Switch! Switch! Switch! Switch! Down the row went the teacher, delivering blows along the line of students who were attempting unsuccessfully to hold back their tears. Finally, their teacher reached the last of the row. One student, braver than the rest, requested permission to speak. "Please sir, can you tell us why we are being punished? We all copied our assignment."

Only then did the teacher explain, "In English, the front of the book has the spine on the left, and that page in your notebooks is empty. All of you wrote your assign- ment on the first page of your notebook with the spine on the right. In English, that is the last page of your notebook. You wrote in the Arabic style of right to left. That is not the English way. Words are written from left to right." Of course, they had not been instructed ahead of time, and the punishment seemed unfair, but the lesson made a permanent mark on Ibrahim's memory. Still, he often read greeting cards from right to left and therefore missed the punch line.

Some days, Ibrahim had an incentive not even to show up at school. There was a shoemaker in Al Husn who used the rubber of discarded tires to fashion shoe soles. As Ibrahim headed to class, his street buddies called out to him, "Come with us today to help the shoemaker soften the rubber for his shoes." Each boy claimed an old tire to roll down the hill, push it back up, and roll it down again. They thought it was great fun. Ibrahim made the mistake of allowing his tire to roll into the school yard where he was supposed to be sitting in class. Of course, his teacher caught him and that resulted in more punishment.

The boys were anxious for the shoemaker to remove the rubber from the tires because he would give what was left to the boys. During that time, tires were reinforced with two woven steel mesh hoops. The boys set fire to the tires in order to burn off the rest of the scrap rubber. This left precious hoops to play with. They constructed a tool made from a length of wire, the thickness of a metal clothes hanger. One end had a hook to control the hoop. The other end was bent into a handle. They ran for miles at a time chasing their hoops.

Once, Ibrahim ran with his hoop all the way to Irbid and back, about five miles each way. He became hungry along the way but did not have any money. When he arrived home at last, his mother was sitting in the courtyard with Aunt Fuddah. "Son, what did you eat all day?" He answered, "Fleyta." This caused both women to laugh because Ibrahim childishly mispronounced it. The real name of the plant was *ilfaitteh*, roadside rushes that have a juicy stem. He also ate the white inside part of orange peelings that someone threw away.

In addition to running after hoops, Ibrahim spent much time tagging along after the Candy Man. This person was an itinerant candy maker who came during summers from Damascus. He rented a small shop from the Ayyoubs where he plied his skill at making taffy and hard candies shaped in animal molds. Ibrahim spent early-morning hours watching him work and even learned how to make taffy. The Candy Man boiled sugar, water, and lemon juice to the correct consistency. Sweets such as taffy require a bit of acid to keep the candy from turning crumbly or "sugaring," which is why the Candy Man added lemon juice.

During my own childhood I learned a similar recipe for taffy which used vinegar as the acid. My girlfriend's mother was an expert with vinegar taffy. I loved it so much, that one day while still a pre-teen, I decided to make some. As usual, I developed this scheme while my mother was not there to intervene. Checking our supplies, I discovered we were out of vinegar. "No problem," I decided. "Pickle juice is made of vinegar and we have plenty of it. It'll work just fine as a substitute." Ah, sad to say, that was not so! The consistency was taffy-like, but the candy had a distinctive dill flavor. Ever after, my friend's family teased me about Pickle Juice Taffy.

However, the Candy Man did not tolerate innovative substitutions. As his mixture boiled, he tested it by first dipping his fingertips into cold water and then quickly dipping them in and out of the boiling mixture. He could tell when the syrup was ready for taffy by the way it cooled on his fingers. When he determined it was finished cooking, he poured it out on a large marble slab to cool. Deftly working the mixture into a molten mass, he was finally able to drape it over a hook fastened to the wall of the shop. Then it was time to begin pulling it, bunching it up, and pulling it again. The taffy turned porous and white as it was worked. To determine if it were finished, he pulled out a thin sliver and tapped it with his fingers. If it broke off cleanly, the taffy was ready. Then he stretched it into ropes and tapped it into serving pieces about eight to ten inches long.

Buyers came running as he walked down the street in the afternoons carrying a huge tray full of candies balanced on his shoulder. One piaster could buy two sticks of taffy or two candy animals. The hard candies were molded into red roosters, green birds, yellow camels, and other animals. All the creatures could stand up on their own candy legs, and children hungered for their sugary goodness.

The Candy Man also sold roasted salty treats such as garbanzos and pumpkin seeds, chanting "*Adami, bitsheel essin, wib tood awado.*" "The seed uproots your tooth and sits in its place." He could say this as a joke because there is nothing harder to chew than a handful of roasted garbanzos. Every day after selling all his wares, he bought a bottle of Araq and a hot meal of *kubiz,* the Arabic name for pocket bread, and roasted lamb which he carried back to his shop for an evening's relaxation. When winter arrived, he closed up his shop and traveled back to Damascus.

Ibrahim and Cousin Saad, his constant playmate, greatly admired the Candy Man and spent happy hours watching him prepare his candies or running after him with their piaster to buy a favorite treat. Cousins Saad and Kamel were Uncle Yacoub's youngest sons. Ibrahim remembered the old Ford car that Uncle Yacoub brought with him when he came home from Detroit. By the time Ibrahim and Saad were young boys, the wonderful Ford had turned into a rusty, broken-down relic. It sat beside Saad's house, and they spent hours pretending to drive it to parts unknown, well provisioned with their daily purchase from the Candy Man.

The two youngsters were cohorts in mischief at all times. Ibrahim recalled one incident when they were playing in the streets while their teacher expected them to be doing their homework. They knew that things would not bode well for them the next day at school if their teacher discovered them out "measuring the streets," their term for aimlessly hanging out doing nothing. When they saw their teacher walking down the street toward them, they ducked into their Uncle Salem's butcher shop. They chose to hide near a woven straw mat which was standing on end, rolled up at the back of the shop. Saad quickly wrapped himself in its folds and Ibrahim ducked behind it. They both stood like statues as their teacher entered the store, visited for some time, and made a small purchase.

Finally, he departed, and the boys could emerge from their hiding place. Ibrahim was startled to see Saad in tears and grabbing his chest. "What is the matter?" Saad's face was streaming with agonized tears as he replied, "A scorpion stung me while I was inside the straw mat." His hand clutched the crushed scorpion in the folds of his *dish-dasheh* next to his chest. Ibrahim rushed breathlessly to inform Uncle Salem. Uncle quickly came to the rescue, slashed the bite with his sharp butcher's blade, sucked out the poison, spat it on the stone floor, and then gently bandaged the wound. Saad was one very sick little boy for several days.

When Saad and Ibrahim were not chasing hoops, hiding from teachers, or driving imaginary trips in the broken car, they found plenty of other ways to be entertained. One day, they chose to sneak into the Roman Catholic Church to gawk at the beautiful decorations. Even though a mass was in progress, they wandered the aisles, hands clasped behind their backs, staring up at the statues and stained glass windows. Deeply engrossed, they didn't notice the nun coming up behind them until she grabbed them by their ears and dragged them out into the church yard.

They clambered over a stone wall and dropped down into the church orchard. Since the trees had no fruit, they decided to leave. But just then they discovered a path which led up to a cave dug into a little hillock. They crept into the cave's opening where they spied a very tall pottery jar large enough to hold at least twenty gallons of sacramental wine. Saad, ever the adventurer, suggested, "I'll bet I can find a stone heavy enough to break that jug." Ibrahim cautioned him, "You must not do that." He stood in front of the jug to shield it from Saad. "Move out of the way, or I'll hit you!" yelled Saad. Ibrahim moved. Swish, kerklunk! The stone made a direct hit! The jug shattered, and the wine gushed out of the cave and ran in rivulets down the path.

The two frantic young boys scrambled up over the stone wall to escape. In order to run unencumbered, each gathered up the ends of his *dishdasheh*, held it in his teeth, and scampered away. No one guessed that they were responsible. The church authorities didn't discover the perpetrators of the crime, and for sure, the boys never confessed.

Saad plied his skill with stones in another escapade with Ibrahim. The boys were about seven or eight years old when Aunt Miriam's son, Selman, decided to marry. The wedding home was situated on a hill. Guests arrived by walking up a rocky side road leading from the main street of Al Husn. Most of the village was invited to the wedding and it was indeed a very merry affair, seeming to emanate from a large wooden chest that was filled with bottles of Araq.

The two little boys curiously watched their elders become more and more joyous. They correctly determined it had something to do with the content of the bottles and decided they needed to experience this merriment for themselves. "*Problem One*," the box was closely watched by an older relative. They noticed, however, that as guests called him to bring another bottle to their table, the box was left unguarded.

At just such a moment, a small hand reached into the box and grabbed a bottle. Quickly the boys disappeared from the wedding celebration and ran out with their loot to a spot by the road. "*Problem Two*," the bottle was tightly sealed and they had no tool to open it. Saad quickly determined, "I can hit it with a stone and break off the top." Ibrahim wasn't so sure about that. "You'll break the whole thing and we won't get to taste it." "No, stand back!" commanded Saad. "See, I'll just do this!" He aimed his stone at the neck of the bottle and, sure enough, broke the top off cleanly, allowing the lovely scent of licorice-laced alcohol to waft out. Then, the two miscreants sat down to sample this wonderful stuff. It tasted nice, since they both liked foods flavored with anise. It also burned a bit as it slipped down their throats, and soon they began to feel somewhat dizzy. But they were determined to drink as much of their booty as possible.

They couldn't remember how much they consumed, because eventually *"Problem Three"* presented itself. They tried to stand up and discovered they could not. Ibrahim giggled at his cousin and said, "Okay, let's just roll down the hill." *"Lam bataal"* Good idea," agreed Saad. Two small drunken bodies rolled merrily over and over down the rocky road, landed at the edge of the street and curled up to sleep in the cool night air. Luckily, some adults strolled by and recognized that they were the sons of Toufiq and Yacoub. Since the two were obviously 'out for the count,' they were carried home to Miriam, who tucked them into bed. Ibrahim grinned at the memory and said, "When we woke in the morning, we were so sick! No further punishment was required."

When he was not busy with other forms of mischief, it seems that church property continued to offer a mysterious attraction to Ibrahim. On a day while Ibrahim played alone, he became curious about the Orthodox Church yard. He scaled the stone wall to see what wonders might be seen and was disappointed to see very little of interest. However, always a lover of apples, he discovered a low hanging branch of the apple tree with ripe fruit beckoning. He intended to pick only one for immediate consumption, but as he reached to pluck it, the weight of the fruit and his tug broke off the entire branch.

Worse luck, the Khoury appeared just at that minute. It was clear that the Khoury didn't recognize Ibrahim. But, he immediately discovered the broken apple branch, picked up a stone, and began to yell, *"Yal-an deenak,* Curse your religion." Ibrahim headed for the wall and made it to the top, one leg straddling each side, when the stone struck exactly where his foot had just been. Once more this lucky culprit escaped undetected. But then a new wonderment troubled him. He had never before heard such words come from a priest. Had he done something so bad that he was going to be cursed forever? He fearfully asked his father, "Yaba, do priests ever curse?" Luckily, his father did not pursue the reason for his son's question.

This does not mean that Toufiq chose to ignore Ibrahim's possibly incriminating behavior. He created opportunities for his son to practice honesty and responsibility. One day, Ibrahim was in his father's shop when a load of goods arrived. Since the delivery required immediate payment, Toufiq turned to Ibrahim saying, "Son, here is the key to open the cupboard where I keep our money box. Run to our house and bring it here. Come back quickly, and be very careful not to let anyone see the box or stop you on the way." Some of his older brothers were available for the errand, so it surprised Ibrahim that his father trusted him to carry out the mission. He hurried home, went to the locked cupboard, retrieved the box, hid it under the folds of his *dishdasheh*, and scurried back to the shop. In retrospect, Ibrahim believed his father was providing a "teaching moment" especially for his son's benefit. Ibrahim never forgot the impression that his father's trust made on him.

CHAPTER 3

———◆———

My Life at Owyhee

WHILE IBRAHIM WAS ALREADY learning about responsibility from his father, I had just turned two and was barely responsible for staying upright on my own feet! My brother was six and ready for school. Because my father's immediate need was to find a way to support us, he secured a job at Fort Peck Dam in Montana, working for fifty cents an hour.

The mighty Fort Peck construction project hired thousands of workers to build a huge dirt dam. At the time the Fort Peck Dam was constructed, it was the largest embankment dam in the United States, with the fifth largest man-made reservoir. Dad was put to work on the monster-sized dredges that sucked dirt, sand, and clay from the bottom of the Missouri River. The sludge was hydraulically pumped through miles of huge pipelines and used for fill along the length of the dam and settled to form the central core. Then, railroad cars of rock were dumped near the core to complete the embankment. In 1990, Abe and I drove across its four-mile width and nostalgia welled up within me as I visualized my dad helping to build it.

While Dad was in Montana, Mom stayed in Boise with us so that Ernestine would have family near and Jim could attend first grade. This was the first time our family lived apart, but it became a pattern in our lives for many years to come. Dad went where he needed to go to get work, and Mom was left alone in charge of our care. At that time, we lived in what my parents called South Boise and spent the summer of 1938 with Dad in Montana. I do know that I missed my Aunt "Nonnie" (Ernestine), who did not accompany us to Montana.

I have two memories of that summer. One is the dirt in front of the worker's shack where we lived. That area of Montana suffers extremes in weather, with rainstorms that turn the soil into a sea of mud followed by scorching blasts of heat which have resulted in temperatures as high as 114°F. I distinctly remember carrying a huge doll over dirt that was cracked into large, solid plates, and I remember wanting to pick them up to use as play dishes.

The other memory is really a story that was told about me so many times that it seems like I remember it. The area was being deluged in a heavy summer downpour while I was taking my nap. Mom was fretting that our shack was in danger of being flooded out or even carried off down the rows of shanty town. She said the water was up to the door sill and leaking through cracks in the wall and roof. I woke up to see my frantic mother and decided I needed to offer her some comfort, so I soothingly assured her, "Don't worry Mama. It's just sprinkling." Mistaken though I was, at least we didn't get washed away in a flood.

Dad worked long, hard hours, but his pay was not adequate to meet all our needs. Life was full of hard times while we were in Montana. Mom loved to tell a tale on him, which reminds me of the orneriness of which he was capable. I don't remember ever going hungry at any time in our young lives, but Mom said the only food left on the shelf one night was one can of pork-and-beans. Dad challenged her to a game of pinochle, and the prize was that can of beans. She took him on, but his cards were much better than hers, and he won.

Then, he sat there in front of her, she said, and opened the can, picked up his spoon, and slowly put bite after bite of beans into his mouth. He continued smacking his lips, grinning at her, and refusing to offer her even one tiny nibble until every last bean had been devoured. I always felt so sorry for my poor mother every time she told that story. I still hope perhaps she might have enhanced the story. It would not be the first time a Popkey was guilty of telling tall tales.

And yet, I am aware that Dad always retained some of that characteristic in his make-up. His position would have been that he won the beans fair and square, and Jo just needed to suffer the consequences. Such behavior is mean, but he would have laughed and thought of it as a fun way of getting even with his "pushy" wife.

Mom found a way to pay Dad back on a very hot day, when Jesse was in bed with nothing on but a sheet. The story goes that he moaned on and on that he was soooo hot, repeatedly calling on Jo to "do something" because he was soooo hot. A few more minutes went by and then in came Jo. She tore off his sheet and dumped a pitcher of cold water over him. "Whooooff," he roared. Jo ran out the front door and Jesse chased right after her. He was half way around the house before he remembered he was stark naked!

I don't know how long Dad continued to work in Montana, but Jim needed to be back in school by fall, and though there were schools provided for workers' families, we went back to Idaho. I'm also certain that our family would have wanted to be back in Boise for Aunt Geneva's wedding which was approaching. She was an employee of Ma Bell, and telephone operators were required to be single. When Sister met Clifford Austin, she was forced to choose. She could either marry the love of her life and stop working at the telephone office or give him up and continue sitting at a tall desk, plugging cords into little sockets, with the polite request, "Number Please!" There was no contest in her decision.

I was three years old when Aunt Geneva married Uncle Cliff at the Rigney home on the Bench. After their marriage, they maintained their close friendship with my parents and formed a happy foursome whenever Dad was home. Aunt Geneva was a skilled cook and often invited us for delicious meals, which were then followed by games of pinochle.

Uncle Cliff was a kind, loving man who delighted in devising little ways to entertain us kids. If he had a bit of heartburn, he would drop an Alka-Seltzer into water and then hold the fizzy glass under our chins so that we could feel its bubbles. He also loved to tell fascinating stories about his fear of snakes. Later on, when they acquired a gentle white horse, he spent hours leading it up and down the road so that all the children could have a ride.

Not too long after Aunt Geneva and Uncle Cliff were married, my mother went back to teaching at Linder, so that Jim could attend school there. The rural school board liked her work, and they made her principal of the two-room school. We rented a furnished house close to the school until Dad finished up in Montana, and when he came home, he took on the management of a small service station right beside the school on the main road leading west from Eagle. This allowed us to move into the one-room apartment in the back of the service station. I have a memory of my dad teaching me how to cook my own little pot of white navy beans on the service station heater and how good they tasted because I had cooked them.

Mrs. Bair took care of me, and I remember playing with a girl named Dorothy Myers, another child who stayed with her. We had tea parties on a small table set that my dad built for me. Those little wooden doll chairs traveled with us when we later moved to Oregon. We played in the grass alongside a shallow artesian stream that grew watercress and buttercups. We picked the flowers and held them under each other's chins to see if our chins reflected the yellow. If so, that meant we loved butter.

I thought Dorothy Myers sometimes acted strange, and I told my mother so. She was quick to give me my first lesson in being kind to people who suffered from disabilities. She said, "Dorothy has a sickness which causes her to have spells from time to time. If it happens when you are playing, just run and tell Mrs. Bair." I was too young to understand the consequences of epileptic seizures, but the experience instilled in me an early empathy for other people's differences. Dorothy never came to school when I grew old enough to attend, and I learned much later that she died while she was still a child.

During the time that Mrs. Bair was my babysitter, we continued to live in the little back-room apartment behind Dad's service station. But, it would be the last residence in Idaho where we all lived together, because Dad began to search for new employment opportunities. The Idaho and Federal road systems chose other routes west in preference over the highway on which Dad's service station was situated. He realized that his little business would soon have very few customers and would be forced to shut down. Eventually, there was no school and no service station on that corner. There was nothing but an empty field.

Once again, the federal government came to his rescue. Just as Fort Peck had provided our family with a living, the Owyhee Dam likewise offered a beacon of hope. At the time it was completed in 1932, it was the highest dam of its type in the world. Dad learned that a job was opening up for the position of gate tender at Owyhee in the remote red-rock canyon of Eastern Oregon. Following Jo's urging, he applied for the job and was hired in July, 1941. This sudden change in Dad's job presented problems, since Jo had already signed a contract to teach another year at Linder.

Mom and Dad decided we would make the move to the dam, and then Mom could come back with Jim and me to live once more in the rented house. I have vague recollections of the house, which was comfortably furnished and provided much more space than the back of the service station. As we prepared to leave our service station home, we all must have felt some trepidation about this new family project.

Just as John Rigney and Bill Popkey were enticed by the new water project in Twin Falls to emigrate as pioneers for work in the sagebrush lands of southwestern Idaho, so now Jesse Rigney prepared to resettle his family at a major water project to develop the thirsty, sagebrush-covered lands of southeastern Oregon. There is a strong connection between the women's experiences, too. While the men were always engaged in large public projects, the women did the similarly back-breaking work of keeping the home and of birthing and raising the children. They left beloved families behind and lived in tents; hauled water; endured child mortality; had no female companionship; struggled to feed the family; promoted education for their children; and were unwavering in support for their husbands.

Continuing this pattern, Jesse and Jo were about to embark on a new generation of experiences as they loaded their young son and daughter into the rumble seat of their Model A Ford and headed over the rock-strewn, bouncy-jouncey path which native Oregonians called "the road to the dam." At one point in the journey, they approached a threatening rocky tunnel. I am quite sure that Jo heard the echo of her mother's voice asking, "I wonder what happens to us next?"

Ten miles on the other side of the rock-strewn tunnel, along the washboard road, Dad drove "Old Betsy" around a bend and we caught our first glimpse of the Owyhee Dam. It was a smooth cement structure, tall, wide, and magnificent with a cement roadway and rows of lights running across its top. Even more impressive for my brother Jim and me was the sudden realization that this gosh-awful long trip from Idaho was ending. We were thirsty, dusty, and extremely tired of putting up with each other in the rumble seat.

We couldn't talk to Mom and Dad along the way since we were separated by the Ford's back window. They were sitting in relative comfort inside, while we were stuffed together in the little seat that folded out from the trunk, subjected to the torment of the sun. Even worse torment for me was the constant bickering and teasing from Jim, who was skilled at making my life miserable. I would not turn six until July, and Jim was ten, already behaving like an obnoxious teenager. When I fussed loud enough for the folks to hear, my mother turned around and chastised us both with gestures through the window. Not fair, of course, because it was always his fault.

In addition, all around our feet and sides were bags stuffed with groceries and personal items that Mom didn't trust to the truck driver, who followed along behind us, carrying our pitiful array of belongings. Mom and Dad knew we were promised a house with basics like steel sleeping cots and mattresses, a stove, and ice box. But we still required a table, chairs, sofa, Dad's leather rocker, washing machine and rinse tubs. We also had our dishes, cooking equipment, clothes, bedding, and many boxes of household paraphernalia.

As we drove over the last trestle bridge and approached the camp, we saw that it was surrounded by a chain-link fence separating the employees' compound from the public park, which was situated directly next to our new house. We were exactly one mile below the dam, and from our vantage point, it was no longer visible, but we couldn't care less. Our long drive was finished! We were here! Dad got out to open the gate and instructed Jim to jump out and close it again. He energetically did so with a loud distinctive clang which seemed to me to imply, "We have arrived and the outside world cannot get in to disturb us." Then, Dad drove on around to the front and into our very own driveway leading to a small garage beside the house. I can still visualize the driveway, because it was carpeted with a deep layer of crushed red shale taken from the canyon walls surrounding the camp.

Instead of carrying boxes, I was allowed to scramble out of the rumble seat, run all around, scream and giggle with joy, relieving pent-up energies in discovery of this new place. I remember strong first impressions of everything being extraordinarily green, fresh, and cool after riding through the hot sagebrush and rock-strewn canyon. Our parents told us that we were coming to a "camp," but to my little-girl eyes, it was a paradise!

I saw a huge area of carefully manicured green lawns with sprinklers spraying rainbow arcs. There were fruit trees and shade trees of all kinds, grape vines climbing on some of the fences, and empty garden patches beside each of the camp's four houses. A long, narrow sidewalk led from our back door past a row of bunkhouses, office, and on past two more houses just like ours until it ended at a much fancier house at the other end of camp. I slipped out of my hot shoes and prepared to run barefoot along the entire length of sidewalk to explore, but my father stopped me, commanding that we children must not go further than the office.

Beyond the office, the sidewalk led to the Stockham's house at the end of the line. This section of camp was off-limits to us, because Mr. Stockham was Dad's boss, the Superintendent of the Owyhee Dam Irrigation Project. His wife did not think much of children, and she owned two snappish little black Scottish Terriers who defended their territory with a vengeance. That limitation on our freedom didn't bother me too much, since we still had plenty of space left to explore.

Around the front of our house along the edge of the lawn, there was a row of cute little umbrella trees. I learned later that they were Catalpas, which grew long seed pods during late summer before the yard man cut off all their branches in preparation for winter. Beyond the lawn edge was a wide, sandy lane stretching the whole length of camp. On the other side of the sand, huge California Poplar trees swayed in the breeze. In the heat of the summer sun, they emitted a unique perfume and dropped sticky leaves and seeds which clung to my bare feet when I stepped over the sand at their base.

Directly opposite our house was a path leading down to the river with a noisy pump house built beside it. I learned that the pump house contained a huge, messy, black, oily-smelling pump which brought the river water up to spigots all over the lawns. Ralph Moore, the yard man, was responsible for maintaining the long hoses that connected irrigation sprinklers to the spigots. As I became better acquainted with him, I learned that he was a hard-working man who never smelled very clean. Ralph was a sort of lonesome, wiry, wrinkled man dressed in denim shirt and overalls with deep folded-up pant cuffs. He had just one arm and kept his empty sleeve pinned up and tucked inside the front bib of his overalls. His disability never seemed of any importance to me, because he was skilled at accomplishing all his tasks with one hand. When my parents invited him to our house for a meal or just to visit, he had a habit of tapping his cigarette ashes into his pant cuffs while he sat with us.

Ralph was a kind man, and I quickly learned to admire him because he tolerated my trailing along steadfastly behind him while he operated the large lawn mower which kept the lawns looking so beautiful. I have no idea why I found that to be a source of entertainment, but I spent hours as his young shadow on mowing day. He also never seemed to be upset when I moved his hoses around in the park to shape an imaginary play house for my dolls. He would not move my stuff, however, when it was time to turn on the sprinklers. As a consequence, my dolls and their household effects often had an unwelcome bath.

My little rubber baby doll, Toodlums, which I was given while very young, really fared poorly. From the outside exposure to sun and water, her rubber began to melt, and she didn't survive my childhood. My favorite doll was a cloth-bodied Mama doll named Nannette, who could say "Mama" when tipped forward. She also was not suited to such bathing. She was a WWII-era doll and cheaply constructed. Her painted face, neck, arms, and hands were molded from a hard material made of sawdust and glue. The sprinkler-soakings caused weather cracks unbecoming to her original beauty. Her pretty little mouth and fingernails wore completely away. But, I kept her and patched her up with dabs of red fingernail polish.

After I was an adult and had a little daughter who loved dolls, my Aunt Dorothy provided Nannette with a second chance at life. By then, my doll was not so lovely, being completely bald, and her little partially-destroyed cloth body was totally naked. Aunt Dorothy took her home and performed serious surgery by creating a new body and legs out of Uncle Walt's cotton long johns. Then she begged for a hank of my daughter's shiny, dark-brown curls with auburn highlights which she sewed into a darling old-fashioned bonnet. As long as Nannette keeps her bonnet tied, she looks like she has a beautiful head of hair. She was dressed in a red-checkered gingham and lace dress with a white petticoat and pantaloons and went to dwell happily in my daughter's home.

Though Ralph honored my desire to have a playhouse made of laid-out hoses, my brother did not. Jim delighted in offering to visit my "house" and then refusing to abide by the rules of entering through the designated doorway. I became infuriated when he stepped over the hose-walls to come inside my house. Now, I realize that was the only reason he offered to play. It was planned as a chance for him to tease and torment. Jim had his own games and dearly loved the heavy wooden picnic tables in the park. His imagination allowed them to turn into airplanes when he sat underneath them as a "Flying Ace," and he spent hours expertly shooting down Zeroes. He urged me to join this game, but it seemed silly to me. Consequently, both of us children learned very early on to be content with our own, separate, imaginary pastimes.

Another of my favorite activities turned the red-shale driveway into the Amazon River. We owned a long narrow bench which, when turned upside down, became my trusty canoe. Using a small board for a paddle, my dolls and I spent hours exploring the Amazon while sitting in our sturdy vessel. It was necessary to make frequent camping stops. Jim always showed up to tease me and pretend to be a vicious crocodile or a warring native tribesman as I sat beside my pretend campfire made of sticks to toast crusts of dried bread for my evening meal. He always did his best to ruin my fun. His favorite trick was to steal my bits of bread, and then run off chortling with laughter. Looking back, I suspect that Jim was attempting to interact with me, but he was a bit embarrassed to admit that my game could become more than just a childish little-girl fantasy.

On our first day in camp, I noted that there was a sour pie-cherry tree just beyond our garage, and it looked as if it offered tree-climbing possibilities. Sure enough, when we were settled into the camp routine, I discovered that I could climb it quite successfully, and Dad offered to cut a board just the correct length to wedge into its branches so that I could comfortably sit up there to daydream. It quickly became my property, my tree home. I do not remember ever having my ownership challenged by Jim, which was really quite unusual. I was dismayed by the sad discovery that, after I grew up and moved away, somebody cut it down.

Many years later, I was given permission to walk around inside of what had been our house but had become a vacation rental for fishing holidays. Although the furnishings had changed, it was amazing how all the memories of my childhood home came flooding back. It was just a humble, government-owned house. But as a child, especially after living in one room, it seemed comfy and spacious.

We always entered from the back door into the enclosed porch, and we needed to be careful to watch our feet, because on the left were steps leading down to the musty-damp earthen cellar with its spider-infested fruit shelves; overhead clotheslines; a swish-swish wringer washer with its ever-filthy rinse tubs, and the coal furnace with huge ducts leading up to grates on the main floor, where we children would huddle to dress on freezing winter mornings.

The porch led directly into the kitchen, with its linoleum that already had seen better days. The bathroom was to the left and the living/dining room was a jog to the right. That was where Dad established his corner, with his overstuffed leather rocker giving off its odor of sweaty overalls and cigarettes. To his right, his smoking stand held his prized shortwave radio and issues of *Saturday Evening Post*. Opposite his corner was Mom's horse-hair chair that matched the three-seater couch against the window wall. That is where the front door was, but it was only used when I ran outside to the tall chain swing that Dad constructed for Jim and me in the California Poplar. Jim didn't swing much, but I spent hours in that swing making up stories.

We had a wobbly, painted, drop-leaf table where Mom figured our bills and served meals. Once a month, she directed us to set the table with her best red dishes, ordered from the Sears Roebuck catalog. That meant we were to have a "Rigney Super Duper" dinner, where we had to say "please," "thank you," and keep our elbows off the table. Mom planned these meals so we could practice good table manners. We were required to chew with our mouths closed, and she tolerated no "muckling," our family term for noisy eating.

We sat on assorted wooden chairs, two of which were sturdy spindle-backs. I still own the one that Mom toted to the river whenever it iced over. She pushed it for support while she unsuccessfully attempted to ice-skate. Dad tried to convince her to let go and even offered to hold her up. But, most of the time, Mom just watched us as she sat next to the bonfire that Dad always built. I was a cautious, careful skater, while Jim raced to jump over the rocks jutting above the ice.

Usually, that chair stayed by the table to serve as Mom's office chair where she tallied and struggled with the multitude of charge accounts that followed us every time we moved. The effects of the Depression were still a harsh reality. We were making monthly payments on medical bills and charge accounts that were run up during our years in Idaho. My parents' salaries never provided enough income to see us through the month.

So, the first thing they did when they arrived in Nyssa was to establish an account at Wilson's Super Market. Nyssa, 35 miles from the Owyhee Dam, was the town where we bought our supplies. It was necessary to haul in enough food to last until the first government payday. The owners of Wilson's were kind to extend credit to us; however, they also had confidence in Dad's steady, government job.

The sad part of the arrangement was that the accounts were never completely settled each month. Expenses continued to outpace income, so Mom scribbled and schemed on her scratch pads to decide which bills absolutely had to be paid and which ones could slide for a little while longer. Then, each month she would look up and optimistically declare, "If we just manage things the way I've got them figured out now, by this time next year, we will be out of debt." We kids always believed her, but I'm pretty sure that Dad knew it was just another part of Mom's continuing pipe dream. Some sort of problem always popped up before the next month rolled around.

One problem requiring an immediate fix was the lack of adequate bedroom space in our little home. There was really only one true bedroom, which led off the living room. The family who lived there before us had renovated a sleeping porch beyond the bedroom by installing glass windows instead of screens. This served as a second bedroom, but it didn't work too well for us. We started out with Mom and Dad in the bedroom, and Jim and I were supposed to share the sleeping porch. That lasted no time at all, because of our constant bickering and fighting. It was obvious that Jim, soon to be in the sixth grade, needed his own space. The basement was out of the question, since it was just a hollowed-out dirt cellar.

Then, Dad hit upon the idea of renovating the garage into a room. The superintendent gave permission as long as Dad did the labor on his own time and paid for the materials. So, once again, the family resorted to charging what was needed at the hardware store in town, thus adding to our debt. But it was worth it. We all agreed that our Ford, "Old Betsy," didn't mind sleeping outside. Jim really enjoyed his privacy out there, and I was so delighted to have him out of my hair!

Soon after Jim moved out to the garage, Mom and Dad moved to the sleeping porch, and I was given the real bedroom. One end of my bedroom had a door with access to the living room, and on the other end there were a door to the sleeping porch and a door to the bathroom containing a classic, claw-foot tub. Actually, the floor plan was such that Jim and I could easily play indoor tag on cold winter days by running full circle from kitchen to living room, to bedroom, to bathroom, and back to the kitchen.

I was pleased to have my own room, where I could keep stuff: my dolls, library books, china tea set, and a cotton-filled box where I nursed a featherless baby bird that fell from its nest. I'd found it outside while playing, and I worriedly carried it into the house where I attempted to become its adoptive mother. Dad told me it died because mother birds chewed the worms first for their babies. Since I wouldn't do that, I guess I killed it. But, I gave it a nice funeral.

I spent more time playing outside than in my bedroom. Something that Jim and I both enjoyed was the ready supply of fresh fruit and garden produce. Soon after we moved in, Dad planted the garden with corn, peas, green beans, tomatoes, onions, potatoes, and squash. We arrived early in the summer, so not much fruit was ripe, but we didn't wait for ripe! Three of the trees along the sidewalk by the bunkhouse were early green summer apples, good in pies and edible while still unripe if we carried along a salt shaker when we attacked them. A bit of salt made the tartness bearable.

While we played, Mom toiled for hours in the small kitchen of our house with its linoleum-covered drain boards. There was a three-burner electric stove/oven, with a deep-well cooker in the fourth spot, an ice box, sink, and cupboards. I do mean "ice" box. In the early 1940's, we hauled huge blocks of ice from town and slid them onto the stinky bottom grate. Later, we sprang for a new-fangled electric fridge purchased from an appliance store in Nyssa, on a time-payment plan, of course.

Mom's reason for spending so much time in the kitchen was because she embarked on a new mission in life to preserve all available fruit and produce. This was probably a throw-back to her memories of food deprivation in her early childhood. It broke her heart to think of wasting any of the precious bounty which now surrounded her. She acquired a hot-water-bath canner and loads of blue-green glass canning jars. In the 1940's, canning jars came provided with glass lids, rubber rings, and either metal clamps which snapped down or zinc screw lids to hold everything tightly in place while the filled jars boiled in the canning kettle. Some of the jar lids came lined with a special plastic or ceramic material to insulate the zinc portion from coming in contact with food inside the jars, since zinc reacts badly with the acids present in fruits and vegetables.

During all the summers that we lived at the dam, my mom canned scores of jars of venison, corn, green beans, tomatoes, tomato juice, cherries, apricots, peaches, apple sauce, pears, jelly, jam, pickles, and grape juice. And, by the way, her grape juice always managed to scorch while she simmered the grapes before straining the pulp through a cloth drip bag. Many years later, when I became old enough to share in my first communion of good grape juice and wafer at church, I was amazed at how delicious it was. Until then, I thought the normal flavor for grape juice was scorch.

Whenever possible, Mom enlisted my help in canning. The jars were always stored down in the dirt cellar. Since housekeeping was not my mother's forte, the jars were, more often than not, stored unwashed until the following canning season. I became the unlucky one who was ordered to brave the spidery dirt cellar, carry the stinky, dusty, cobwebby jars back into the light and wash them. In addition, every year a few jars of food developed a leak and bubbled over with poisonous gook. I had to carry those up too, dump the contents out in the garden, and scrub the jars, since we could not afford to waste.

To these memories, I must add the fact that against all rules of combating botulism, Mom's green beans, corn, tomatoes, and venison were canned in a hot water bath just like her fruits, except that she left them in the bath for at least an hour longer, since she never had a pressure canner. It's just as well; she probably would have experienced an explosion or two if she had. How did she manage to keep us all alive? That is the unsolved mystery.

Mom's training in food preservation did not come from any high school home economics class. She must have learned the basics during the years she lived with the Sloniker family or by asking Grandma Rigney. Most available knowledge about food preservation was tucked inside the brains of these two estimable housewives, and they would have happily shared what they knew. However she managed to acquire her training, Mom was aware that there was more to canning than just harvesting produce.

Harvesting was no small job. Getting fruit off trees required climbing ladders, and Mom was a short, round woman who would have found that difficult. I don't remember doing much ladder work, but Jim was sent to the top of many a tree to pick. I was enlisted to help pick the Concord grapes. Their pungent perfume lingers even now in my memory. Of course, many of the sour-sweet morsels never made it to our kitchen. A ripe Concord grape has a tough purple skin which can be squeezed with thumb and index finger to pop the slippery insides directly into the mouth with a sweet, juicy squirt. The skin is also kind of fun to chew, before spitting out the tough part with the seeds, because it quickly becomes very tart. This, of course, left smears of purple all over my hands and face, but who cared? I only cared when Jim came along to help, because the insides could also be squirted at one another with that same deft, popping motion. Then the grape-popping war was on!

Over-ripe fruit fell on the sunny lawns, where it moldered into mushy rot. I have a strong memory of the hot summer smell of rotting fruit under all those trees and vines and of the many times I slipped and fell on it while carelessly running too close in my bare feet. The fermenting odor attracted fruit flies, yellow jackets, birds, and other hungry little creatures.

After the fruits and vegetables were harvested and carried to our kitchen, they required several water baths to remove dirt and insects, such as earwigs. Earwigs are wiggly little creatures that make their home inside corn, apricots, and other produce. Their name comes from the myth that they enter the human ear and bore into the brain, causing insanity or death. Of course, my family informed me that scientists said "There is no truth to that balderdash," but no one could convince me that, other than an occasional pinch, earwigs could not harm people. No matter what the scientists said, I still detested watching all of those wiggly insect bodies squirming up to the surface after I poured a load of fruit into the kitchen sink. They eventually drowned, and then I had to scoop them out into the trash basket along with the twigs and leaves.

I was expected to help with washing and cutting and seeding and stemming. But, I was still too young to deal with blanching. The kitchen became steamy hot and smelled of partially boiled vegetables, which Mom dipped out of the hot water and packed into the jars. Then, she filled the jar up to the top with brine or sugar syrup, depending on what food she was preserving. I quickly learned the importance of carefully wiping the top of the jar to remove any residue which might prevent the lid from sealing.

When Mom had seven jars filled and the lids fastened down, she placed them in the metal canning rack containing sections for seven jars. The canning kettle needed to be partially filled with lukewarm water. If the water in the kettle was still boiling hot from the last batch, the newly filled, cooler jars were in danger of breaking when they were plunged down into the kettle. I witnessed that disaster more than once. After the jars were in, Mom carried more water from the sink to fill the canner until the jars were under water. Then she covered the canner and set the whole thing to boil. The processing time depended on what food was in the jars. Our electric stove had a dinger-timer which let us know when the batch was done boiling. There was no rest for us during the processing period because that was when we needed to prepare the next seven jars.

Lifting finished jars out of the canner was also tricky. The rack partially lifted out and locked on the canner's edge. The jars were much too hot and wet to handle. A friend of Mom's gave her a metal contraption, which he invented and which I still have, with its little metal tag which says, "patent-pending." It is a noose-like system of wires bent in two half circles with a top wire device which slides up and down to make a rounded section snuggle firmly under the rim of the jar. That device is now over seventy years old, and I would be lost without it when I decide to do a bit of canning.

After lifting out each boiling hot jar, Mom carried it over to the drainboard where she had a cloth spread out to set the jars, making sure that no jar touched any other. It was important that the area for cooling should not be too cold or the jars could crack from the sudden change of temperature. Cooled jars needed to be wiped with a damp cloth in order to remove sticky residue, and they had to be checked to see if they were properly sealed. This was done by tapping the lid lightly with the handle of a teaspoon. If sealed, the jar made a distinctive ringing sound. If not, the sound was more like a thud. Jars that did not seal became food for supper that night and then the jar was washed for re-use. It is easy to guess who had to carry the sealed jars back down to their earthen storage room.

Mom's enthusiasm for harvesting and preserving all the available summer foods carried over into my own adult life. Both of my daughters witnessed my canning and enjoyed the results. I even attempted to enlist their help. I tried the same technique on them that always worked for my mother with me. She would set up her pear-canning station outside in the shade, sitting in her ladder-back chair with a huge pan of washed fruit placed on a little stool in front of her with a couple of bowls and two knives. Then she would start in to woo me. "Doris, let's have a race! I'll bet I can peel the pear halves faster than you can cut out the cores." It worked every time; I always fell for the challenge. It became a game to see who could work faster, and in no time we had seven jars of pears ready for the canner. I must admit that my daughters caught on to my scheming in no time.

The summers were never all work and no play, however. Something that Jim and I both enjoyed on a hot summer day was running through the sprinklers. The one drawback was that our wet skin attracted horseflies. The stinging bite of those horrible critters was always the price we paid for playing in the spray of the sprinklers. We also had fun sitting on the tiny front stoop in the afternoon shade eating watermelon and having seed spitting contests. Much to our delight, we would later see little baby watermelon plants spring up in the grass, but they never survived the next mowing day. That front stoop was also where we watched the huge, striped June Bugs that attached themselves to the screen door in an effort to enter the coolness of the living room. They made an interesting, distinctive loud buzz when they were stuck to the screen with no way to escape. I chose not to help them get loose, because they had a ferocious bite.

One of the garden chores assigned to us, both disgusting and yet the source of macabre entertainment was to pick the big, fat, green-and-black-striped worms from the tomato vines. No one wanted to kill them by squishing because their bellies popped green gook. Instead, we pulled them off and plopped them into empty pork'n bean cans to carry out to the large ant piles in the sandy strip along the front of the yard. A full-grown tomato worm is about the size of an adult's thumb, but it is no match for an ant hill. Ants swarmed up by the thousands to fight the green intruder, and the ants always won, while we watched in morbid fascination.

We were in a fisherman's paradise, and my dad was an avid fisherman. He never really enjoyed eating his catch, but he truly loved trying to catch "the big one." The lake that formed behind the tall dam was loaded with trout, perch, bass, carp, and even ugly old suckers. It was a great place for sitting on rocky outcrops and dropping in a line with bobber, hook, and worm. A favorite fish, because of its abundance and its delicate flavor, was the crappie (pronounced croppie).

Crappie is a freshwater fish in the sunfish family. Its body is flat with a middle section that is quite plump, with plenty of flesh for good eating. In the early evening, the crappie would bite on almost anything. Dad taught both Jim and me to catch them, and we brought home huge messes of fish for Mom to clean, dip in cornmeal, and fry in bacon grease. Yum! Mom loved to cook and eat all kinds of fish but she finally drew the line at cleaning them. She soon began to enforce the rule, "If you catch it, you clean it, and then I'll cook it."

When we couldn't go fishing, we rambled over the hills beside camp. This posed some dangers, since the Owyhee Canyon was rattlesnake country. Mom and Dad set the rule that we had to go together and stay together. This was done in case one of us was bit, then the other could run for help. It was drummed into our heads that the worse thing to do would be to panic and start running, which would pump the poison more quickly to the heart. We were taught to carry a bandanna, to be used as a tourniquet, and a pocket knife. Not that we would ever scrape up enough courage actually to cut open a snake bite and suck out the poison, but we thought we could.

Also, our family acquired a feisty little Fox Terrier named Spot, who was fearless around snakes, and we were required to take him with us when we hiked the hills.

Many times, I saw Spot run up and tackle a snake who ventured onto the lawns of camp. He always kept up the fight until he killed the snake. He ran around for days afterwards with a jaw swollen twice its usual size from the poison of the bite. After such an episode, I remember sitting beside Spot on the back stoop, petting and cuddling him. I had a handful of his favorite Friskies dog-bone biscuits which I fed to him one at a time. He crunched them so delightedly that I decided they must taste really good. So we sat together; Spot ate a dog-bone, and then I ate a dog-bone. One for Spot, another for me. Dog-bone flavor is a childhood memory that I relish.

Some of Spot's escapades made him not always so pleasant to cuddle. In the late summer and early fall, the water level in the river dwindled to a trickle, since the farms beyond the canyon drew it down for their irrigation needs. This low water level always stranded a large number of fish who died and rotted among the exposed rocks of the river bed, and Spot loved to roll in their stench. I will never understand why. I don't believe he was even welcomed to sleep on the foot of Jim's bed in low water time. He also willingly tackled any skunk who ambled into camp, and Mom would have to use some of her precious home-canned tomato juice to give him a bath. Dad was quite a tease, and each spring he brought out the red paint can and dipped Spot's white tail in it. Dad had no real reason for doing this. It just pleased his offbeat sense of humor, and maybe he did it as a symbol of juice baths to come. I don't think Spot minded because he proudly wagged his red-tipped tail for all to see.

Spot was the first to discover the dead steer about half a mile down river. I'm sure the rotting aroma is what attracted him to the carcass. We kids were fascinated, and we spent days observing its stinky, decaying process. I had an up-close observation post to watch squirming maggots work their wonders in reducing this poor dead animal back to nature. It amazes me, as an adult, how I could stand to hold my nose against the smell and go back again and yet again to see how the deterioration was coming along.

Granted, our childhood was bereft of social contacts with other children, but some of our experiences, such as monitoring the decay of that dead animal, compensated for not having playmates. However, when I was reluctantly forced into social situations as a pre-teen away from my wilderness retreat at the Dam, I never mentioned the dead steer story. I knew these two separate parts of my growing-up did not comingle in any satisfactory way.

My favorite places to hang out were up in my cherry tree or in that fabulous swing that Dad constructed for me. It was a long, strong chain swing with a sturdy board seat. Its chains were attached to the solid limb of the poplar, which swayed high above my head. The area below the tree was deep sand, so that even if I jumped out from quite high up while swinging, I landed softly in squishy sand. I loved to twist the two chains around and around as tight as I could get them before hopping onto the seat. The swing would then dizzily unwind at quite a speed while I whirled around in delight.

Later, in college, while studying children's literature, I was introduced to Stevenson's poem "The Swing," and I remembered swinging as "the pleasantest thing ever a child can do." I spent hours in my swing or in my cherry tree, making up stories modeled after the fairy tales I read in books which we checked out monthly from the county library. My stories were childish, but fun for me. I never wrote them down or told them to anyone else, but I remember them.

The more I think about the necessity of entertaining myself at such a young age, it becomes clear that the experience contributed to my imagination as an adult. It may have been the reason why I have always loved the richness of children's literature. I suspect it played a large role in my teaching success with kindergartners. During rest time, the children were required to spread out their resting towels, lie down, and close their eyes. I sat on the teacher's chair and closed my eyes too. Then I took them on what we called "dream walks," where we climbed into a magic flying contraption which carried us to wondrous places. The wiggles and giggles of the children would cease and all would become relaxed and quiet while I spun out fanciful adventures. Regrettably, I don't remember the exact details, but the kids lapped them up.

I later understood that I was not the only lonely kid there at the dam. Since we did more fighting than playing with each other, most of the time I really had no idea what was going on in my brother's head. But, imagination was possibly a contributing factor to Jim's development also. I remember that when he was an adult, he spent a lot of time telling my two little girls about traveling to places like Pie Island.

During one summer, when I was about nine, there were rare occasions when my brother and I did do things together. One such adventure, which took place in the hills surrounding our home, could have had serious consequences. Jim invited me to go rock climbing on the opposite side of the river. We had to cross the old trestle bridge at the base of camp to reach the cliffs he wanted to climb, which was much steeper than either of us imagined. I was my usual scairdy-cat self when the going got really steep, but big brother protectively reasoned, "I'll go first, Doris, and prepare a safe route for you. Just climb along behind and put your hands and feet in the same places you see me using."

I was bravely trying to follow his instructions when, up above my head, his foot slipped. This caused an avalanche of large stones and rubble to come tumbling down on top of me. I screamed, let go, and awkwardly slid back down the mountain to our starting point. There I sat, bawling bloody murder, while I surveyed my smashed and mangled thumb. Jim looked scared and very white-of-face while he tried to offer comfort. Finally, he convinced me to stand up and walk with him back to camp. I did it, but I kept up my loud screams all the way home.

When we arrived at the house, I heard him tell Mom what had happened and then whisper his real concern. He said, "I wanted Doris to keep worrying about her smashed thumb, because I didn't know what would happen if she knew about the hole in her head." Sure enough, I really freaked out then, as I realized how much my head hurt, and I looked in the mirror to see the blood pouring from the gigantic wound on the top of my scalp. Mom, expert as usual when faced with an emergency, applied appropriate first aid to both thumb and head.

Then, I was tucked into bed, so I could calm down. That adventure cured me from ever developing interest in rock-climbing. Many years later, I still felt squeamish about financing a rock-climbing lesson for my two teenaged grandsons, who begged me and who received permission from their mother. While they had a ball, I sat there on the visitor's bleachers, pretending to enjoy watching them. But, all I could see were mangled thumbs and cracked heads.

Since I had lost interest in mountain rambling, I felt fortunate when another opportunity arrived for fun. Not many children in the 1940's were privileged to have their own swimming pool. Halfway to town was Snively's Hot Springs, natural sulphur hot springs on land privately owned by old Mrs. Snively. While her husband Fred was still alive, they built a nice little swimming pool along with a row of wooden bath houses and piped the hot water from the spring to the facility. By the time we moved to the dam, Fred had died. But Mrs. Snively still operated the little picnic-and-swimming resort. On summer trips to town, Mom packed a picnic lunch, and Dad and she drove us as far as Snively's. Jim and I were allowed to stay there under the supervision of Mrs. Snively until our folks returned. I think the charge for the day was about ten or fifteen cents apiece.

Oh, how I loved that pool! At first, I didn't know how to swim, but over the summer months, I slowly taught myself to keep afloat and then I began to paddle about even in the deep end. Mrs. Snively sat under a shade tree along the edge as our life guard, but she never interfered in our water games. Swimming at Snively's was one of the few instances in our young lives when my brother and I truly enjoyed each other's company. When lunch time came around, we were not even required to get out of the pool. We sat on the steps at the shallow end to eat our sandwiches, and Mrs. Snively kindly brought us drinks of lemonade. I describe it as our private pool, because I don't remember any other swimmers ever coming when we were there. I'm sure she had other customers at different times, but during those long summer afternoons, the pool belonged to us.

After the long hours of swimming under the sun, a certain degree of punishment awaited us. By the time Mom and Dad came back to gather us up in the evening, we were both boiled lobsters. The sunburn never seemed to hurt until we dressed and started home, but then misery set in with a vengeance. Mom had a big jar of stinky, raw, sheep lanolin which she plastered over our tender skin and tucked us in to bed. It hurt so bad to be sunburned over such a large portion of my body! As I began to heal, great patches of skin flaked off. Jim and I often peeled skin off each other with much fascination. As gluttons for punishment, when another swim day was offered, we eagerly accepted to repeat it all again.

Over the years, I've wondered how I managed to escape developing skin cancer from those repeated sunburns. Perhaps the ozone layer offered more protection in those earlier years, or else I have just been extremely lucky. Soon enough, there were no more problems with sunburn, because chances to swim diminished as fall approached. As those carefree, sunny days wound down, my family began to make preparations for changes in our routine to provide schooling for Jim and me.

CHAPTER 4

———◆·❖·◆———

Our Grade-School Lives

WHILE I PREPARED FOR my first year of school, big changes were also happening for Ibrahim in Jordan. He stayed in Al Husn until he finished fourth grade, but at that time, he decided he didn't want to go to school in Al Husn the following year. So, he asked his father for permission to attend school in Amman where his cousin Essa would be. Amazingly, his father agreed to his wishes and contacted a relative to locate a school in Amman.

Toufiq requested help from his brother, Faez, to place Ibrahim in the Amman government school. Faez Ayyoub held an important position in the Jordanian government with a rank similar to that of the U. S. Director of FBI. Uncle Faez approached the principal of the government school, but the principal denied his request, saying there was no room.

However, Uncle Faez knew how to get things done. He went directly to a woman he knew who worked in the palace. She, in turn, spoke to a courtier, who told her to have the student stand in front of the King's *diwan malaki,* where the King holds audience with his citizens. Ibrahim went alone to the *diwan.* He was met by an enormously tall African man dressed in a red *gombaz,* a long-sleeved gown, which was open at the front and fastened with a shiny wide sash. The courtier took Ibrahim's hand and walked toward the school, which opened onto the same courtyard. Since he was very big and walked with powerful strides, Ibrahim had to reach high just to hold his hand and he was forced to scurry to keep up.

When the courtier reached the school, he kicked the door open, strode down the hall to the principal's office, and kicked that door open. The principal, who was sitting behind his desk, jumped up and saluted. When the courtier commanded that he wanted the boy in school, the principal protested that there was no room in the fifth grade, but he could place him in the fourth. The decision was left to Ibrahim. By then, Ibrahim was beginning to feel embarrassed for the principal. He decided that it would be satisfactory to repeat the fourth grade. So Ibrahim began his year in Amman living with relatives and attending the government school. In his classroom, he was seated next to Labeeb, the courtier's son, and they developed a friendship.

It was a difficult school year. The principal never forgave him for the embarrassing beginning and sought every opportunity to cause trouble or discipline him. He even suggested that Ibrahim should ask his father for money as a bribe, which Ibrahim refused to do. Also, this was the year his vision became a major difficulty. Before the school term, while still at home, he contracted Trachoma. One possible source of contamination was Lake Tiberius. His sister Subha's husband, Rajah, was an army officer stationed next to the lake. Whenever he was invited to stay with them, Ibrahim spent all his waking hours swimming.

The other possible source was in Al Husn, where he first learned to swim in the *Birkeh*, an ancient structure originally built for watering livestock. Ibrahim remembered one day, watching a small boy dozing on the cliff in the sun. The child's head dipped lower and lower until he tumbled into the deepest part of the pool. Ibrahim jumped in and pulled him to safety. He gathered the wet tyke up and asked him where he lived. The little one showed him his home, and it turned out that he was the son of Raji and Fadieh, who was Toufiq's niece. That one plunge may be when Ibrahim contracted the disease.

By the time classes in Amman began, his eyes were painfully crusted and red. Trachoma causes pimples to form on the inside of the eyelids; the motion of blinking then irritates and damages the cornea. Ibrahim could not see to the front of the classroom. Because light hurt his eyes, he sat at his desk with head down, memorizing his lessons by listening. His teacher, Toufiq Ammary, taught by asking a question as he walked toward a student. The student must answer correctly before Mr. Ammary arrived at the student's desk or be prepared for punishment. One day, he decided to catch Ibrahim because of his supposed inattention. "Ayyoub, if a merchant bought sheep at nine dinars a head and sold them at fifteen dinars a head, what is his profit?" While asking, he marched to Ibrahim's desk. Ibrahim answered the question correctly, but the teacher grabbed his hair, jerked his head up and demanded, "Why aren't you looking at the chalkboard?" Ibrahim answered, "I cannot see it, sir." Then the teacher saw his eyes, inflamed with Trachoma, and apologized.

One day, another teacher spoke to Ibrahim on the playground and urged him to ask for help if it was ever needed. Ibrahim thanked him and replied that he was doing okay for now. He interpreted that offer either as a way of saying that his teachers were aware of the principal's harassment or else they were concerned about his eyes.

Once, during that year, Ayyoub relatives accompanied an aunt to another town to see her off on the train. Ibrahim and other children his age were allowed to go along. The train station was situated close to the government's Arab Legion military camp where some of the clan were employed. While the adults were bidding the aunt goodbye, the young ones wandered away to explore the nearby Wireless Station.

After playing for a while, Ibrahim sat down on an available curb for a few moments of rest in the sun. All of a sudden a gang of youngsters approached them. The local kids carried shiny metal rods which they proceeded to swing around as if they were holding sabers. They began to yell taunts and challenge the newcomers' right to be on what they considered their playground. Ibrahim's group replied with determined voices, "This is not your home. This is the Arab Legion camp and our relatives work here. We can be here if we choose!" The local kids called them intruders and began to swing their shiny sticks and actually hit some of the littler ones.

Ibrahim looked around to see what he could use to scare the strange gang off. His eyes fell upon a good-sized stone by his feet. So, he picked it up, stood, and took aim at the back of their leader who was hitting a little kid with his stick. *Whiz, ka-pow* went the stone, hitting the leader directly in the middle of his back. The startled tormentor threw up his arms, his legs crumpled and he sank, unmoving, to the ground. His followers took one fearful look at him lying there and scattered in desertion.

Ibrahim's gang decided that the leader was dead, so they all took off running back to the safety of the Wireless Station. Knowing better than to report their mischief to their relative, they simply asked him for help in finding a ride back to Amman. Their uncle was relieved to see them ready to leave, because he knew that a roaming gang of kids in his hair and hanging around the camp would be frowned upon if his superior officer happened to show up. He called on a fellow soldier to put them into a pick-up truck for a ride back to Amman.

In reflection, Ibrahim decided the local gang leader was probably just stunned and temporarily winded. If there had been a death, it would have invoked a tribal court hearing causing serious trouble for the kids and the whole Ayyoub tribe. Since there was no notice ever about the death of a child near the Government Wireless Station, he must have recovered. What can be said about a half-blind kid who still is able to throw with such accuracy? Suffice to say, he might have gone far in big league baseball, if he had grown up in America.

Stoning the strange bully was not the only time Ibrahim was dead-eye accurate with his throwing. Before moving to Amman at the age of eleven, he spent hours roaming the streets of Al Husn. One day, he happened to pass by the home of a relative who had a calf wandering near the street. The calf looked directly at him as if he wanted to play. Ibrahim, without thinking, picked up a stone and threw it just to see if he could hit the young steer. Once again, Bingo! The stone struck directly on the animal's forehead, and for sure, this time the throw resulted in death. Ibrahim hung around, surreptitiously keeping an eye on what was going to happen to the animal, and soon he noticed beef being carried to the market for processing. He never did confess to that transgression either, but it weighed on his conscience for eighty years.

Despite these incidents, stone-throwing continued to be a common pastime for Ibrahim at that young age. Kids saved up their grudges until the end of the school year, since they would be in serious trouble if rock fights came to their teacher's attention.

But when school finished for the term, the kids found a spot away from town and each gang built stone walls a good distance away from each other, and gathered up a supply of stones. Then they set to it. Amazingly, either because they were quick to duck, or else the range was too far, no one was ever seriously injured. If an adult happened by, everyone scattered and warfare ceased until the next opportunity arose.

While in Amman, he lived at the home of Faez Ayyoub, whose younger brother went to house-sit the home of his sister for one night. Ibrahim accompanied him, and they spread their mattresses on the veranda under the open sky. They slept well in the fresh air, until Ibrahim began to experience a frightening dream. He dreamt that everybody was calling him *majnoon*, crazy. In his dream, he ran down the street with other children chasing him, banging stones against tin cans and calling out "*Majnooni! Majnooni!*" He stopped at shops along the street, begging for help, but the shopkeepers shooed him away saying, "*Itlah, Majnooni,* get out you crazy!" Ibrahim became very nervous in his dream, but he told himself, "I may be dreaming. I'll open my eyes and wake up." So he raised his eyebrows thinking he had opened his eyes. Still, the village children were chasing, chanting "*Majnooni! Majnooni!*" He thought, "Even when my eyes are open they are still yelling at me. I guess it is not a dream. I must really be crazy."

Then, it seemed almost as if a hand reached down onto his forehead and gently forced his eyes to open. He looked up into the starlit sky and beheld a radiant, golden full moon shining down upon his frightened soul. With a yell, he tossed his quilt aside and jumped to his feet. His startled cousin woke up, complaining about the commotion, and Ibrahim told him he'd had a very bad dream. Soon, they settled back down and finished their sleep.

As a child, the dream was very real to him, and he was bothered by it. One day at school, during recess, he sought out the advice of his teacher. He explained that he'd had a very bad dream in which he was crazy. He worried that it meant he really was going crazy. Mr. Ammary wisely answered that the fact that he was afraid of being crazy was a good sign that he was sane. Ibrahim thanked him and felt very relieved.

But still, the encounter with the moon was significant to Ibrahim. That beautiful moon burned a lasting impression in his memory. Ibrahim decided it was so strong because the moon was the first thing he set eyes on when he awoke. As he grew into adulthood, he absorbed all the feelings of romance which are ascribed to the moon, particularly the significance given to it in the movie *Moonstruck*. At the ripe old age of 83, he still identified deeply with that story line and had a love of the moon in all its stages. He was reminded by his brother, Naim, that the astronauts who landed on the moon proved it was just another hunk of dirty rock, which destroyed its mysticism and romance for lovers. But regardless of Naim's opinion, Ibrahim often walked out at night to see where the moon was shining in the wide dark sky and to remark upon its beauty to all who would listen.

When the fourth-grade year was almost finished, Ibrahim's father came to Amman on business and stopped by to visit. Ibrahim told his father that he didn't want to go to school anymore because his eyes were so bad that he could not see the board. Toufiq said he would get Ibrahim's eyes fixed and sent him to his brother Suleiman at his survey camp to ask for fifteen dinars so that they could go to Jerusalem to see Dr. Teikho, the *Rab El-eyoon*, the God of Eyes. Ibrahim also had to go to the officials and acquire a passport.

This was in 1940. Ibrahim was almost twelve years old, a young age for all these important errands. But it did not seem to faze him, perhaps because he had already been entrusted with such responsibilities as carrying the money box through the village to his father's shop. So, he rode a bus into the desert until he reached the Land and Survey Camp where his brother was working. He explained his errand, but Suleiman didn't have the ready cash. He sent Ibrahim to the next town to his friend's store to borrow the money. Ibrahim succeeded in following his brother's directions and headed back to Amman with the loan.

The next task was to secure the passport. First, he had to travel by bus to Irbid to obtain a copy of his birth certificate, and then back to Amman. He found the correct government passport office and entered. But everything was strange and new to the little boy. He stood wondering what he was supposed to do next. There was a man sitting at a table out in the hallway in front of the office door. "Little boy, what do you want?" "I am in need of a passport. Where do I go?" "Well, you have come to the right place. I can help you fill your papers." So Ibrahim sat on a chair in front of the table and gave his information to the scribe who filled out all the necessary paperwork.

When the scribe was finished, Ibrahim gathered the papers and stood up to walk into the passport office. "Wait a minute, young sir!" The scribe raised his voice. "You must pay me for my work." Ibrahim looked bewildered but did not reach his pocket for any money. The scene caused adults passing by to stop and stare at the scribe. Evidently this caused the scribe to feel sheepish for harassing a child, because he shook his head, shrugged his shoulders and returned to his table minus the few piastres he had expected to receive. Much later, Ibrahim figured out that the man was providing a service which required payment, and the scribe had assumed the boy knew that.

In Jerusalem, Ibrahim underwent the first of many procedures on his eyes. This first time required a stay of four or five days in the Jerusalem hospital. Dr. Teikho split and separated the eyelid skin from its layer of gristle to cut away the pimples caused by the Trachoma. With the pimples removed and the eyelids healed, the disease was arrested. Ibrahim's eyes were relieved from the inflammation and stopped being crusty-red. He regained some vision. Much later in life, an American ophthalmologist informed him that a series of penicillin treatments would have rapidly stopped the Trachoma in its tracks. Penicillin was not an option at that time for the "God of Eyes."

While in the hospital, he shared a room with a Jewish man, whose teen-aged daughter came to visit regularly and was very kind to Ibrahim. The hospital didn't serve meals to the patients, so relatives were required to bring food. When the daughter brought the man's food, he directed her to ask Ibrahim about what kind of food she could bring him. Ibrahim told the daughter that he would be pleased to have some of whatever she was bringing and that his father would give her money to pay for it. They knew Ibrahim was an Arab, and Toufiq was very grateful to the Jewish family for being so kind to his son.

Soon, Ibrahim's young body began to recuperate and his vision cleared up enough for him to read again. By then, his one year of schooling in Amman was completed, so his father took him back home where his family began to think about what would be best for the next phase of his education. They decided to keep him at home to attend the Christian Men's School (CMS) in Al Husn.

At the same time, I needed to face my own first school experience in America. My family was required to begin living in two separate households because, while Dad remained at the dam, Mom needed to fulfill her contract with Linder School. Linder was where I would attend first grade. The summer days ended, and as fall approached, Mom began to prepare for our coming year. She was able to rent the same furnished house where we had stayed previously, so furniture was not a problem. She and Dad agreed that we would commute to the dam on weekends whenever possible to resupply his grocery needs.

The commute was long, about sixty miles each way, so they both knew there would be weeks when Dad would have to send down to Nyssa by way of others or else borrow the government pick-up if he needed to go. No one in our family was aware of it at the time, but this year of family separation marked the beginning of many years of struggle to hold the family together while our parents each pursued what had to be done for survival's sake.

I have some poignant memories of that year. I was so excited on the first day of school. I rushed into the room where grades one-through-four held their classes and picked out what I thought was the most perfect desk in the row. The old fashioned desks were bolted to long wooden runners along the floor.

Since I was a large, sturdy first grader, it was a bit of a squeeze to get into the seat. I tucked my new tablet, pencil, and crayons deep into the back of the desk's shelf which was attached to the immovable desk top with its very pretty black iron grill-work. There was a funny hole up at the top of the desk with a little bottle stuck in it. I knew that was for ink if our penmanship skills ever advanced from pencil to ink pens. Then, since it was still early for Teacher to step to the door and ring the bell, I ran outside to play on the merry-go-round. I knew all about this school stuff, because my mother was the principal.

When our teacher did ring the bell, we filed into the classroom, and horrors, some other kid was sitting in my desk! I was totally stymied with no idea what to do. So I just lingered at the back of the room, making no attempt to sit down anywhere. Finally, Teacher directed me to a desk in the back row. I was close to tears by then because that other kid had my seat and my new school supplies. When Teacher told us to take out our pencil and tablet, I was devastated because I didn't have any. She finally noticed my distress and waited while I somehow explained my problem. Then, I had to walk up the row with all those kids staring at me and wait for the usurper to remove his stuff so I could have my desk back. An awkward beginning for sure!

Eventually school routines settled, and I once more felt comfortable. In fact, I made friends and felt so secure that I enjoyed writing little notes to them while class was in session, a strictly forbidden activity, of course. I remember nothing about Teacher's name or her looks. My one memory is that she had long, shiny red finger-nails which swooped down from behind me to snatch up my note. Being the daughter of the principal didn't cut me any slack; I missed recess over that infraction.

Next door, my mother taught grades four through eight when she wasn't busy be-ing principal, sweeping her half of the school, building the fire in the stove, or cooking a pot of soup for her students' noontime meal. There was benefit, however, to having a family member at school. I was allowed to join the big kids for lunch to get my hot soup. That was nice.

I also was allowed to hang around in the teachers' supply room after school until Mom was finished for the day. I loved to watch her cook the goop for the hectograph duplicating process, and pour it out into a large oval turkey platter to solidify. Then she and my teacher used a special hectograph pen to write a master-sheet for a student exercise or an art-paper. The copy process was complicated. A wet rag was applied to soak the hectograph platter, causing it to give off a heady, inky, school-teacher-thingy smell. The master sheet was then placed down on the platter and left for a period of time while the ink soaked into the rubbery surface. When enough time passed, the master sheet was lifted off, the surface re-dampened and copy papers were applied with firm pats one sheet at a time. The next day, we students would receive a lovely hectograph-smelling copy to color. Then, Teacher would direct the class teacher's pet (who was never me, by the way) to pass out scissors so we could cut out our work. Ev-eryone who passed by the school could then tell that we had just finished our art les-son for the week because she taped all the carefully-colored pictures on the windows: pumpkins in October, turkeys in November, Christmas trees or Santa's in December, and so on.

I remember one significant art project that first year. Every child was instructed to bring ten cents to school to purchase a white plaster-cast figurine which we were going to paint as a gift for our family. I was in my mother's room after school the day the salesman came by to make his pitch for the purchase of these figurines. I was so excited to see the lovely white and gold statues he exhibited: beautiful sculptures of biblical scenes and likenesses of historical personages. I was wiggling with excitement the day the shipment arrived, when we each received our own plaster piece.

Much to my dismay, all the first graders were handed the same thing, a small stat-ue of a little duck. It seems we were not to be trusted with anything more complicated.

We were instructed to paint them yellow with an orange bill. When they dried we were allowed to apply a coat of shellac to make them shine. That was it! Boring! I do remember the luscious odor of the shellac, but other than that, for me, the whole project was a bust. I decided at this tender age, if I ever got to be a teacher, I would not make every kid always produce the exact same copy of something during art class. This promise was one that I was able to keep.

Once, the teachers' supply room almost did me in. I was hurrying to close the ancient door because Mom was finished for the day, and I caught a huge sliver under my fingernail. I was aware of my mother's doctoring skills from past experience, so I knew she would poke and prod and pour dreadful iodine on the wound. To avoid all that misery, I decided to hide the sliver from her. About a week later, I was plagued with a monstrously infected finger, which she discovered when I refused to put my hand into the bathwater. Then all hell was to pay, because she attacked my wounded finger with diligence while I screamed and hollered enough to wake the neighborhood.

The pain of my healing wound diminished when Mom piled us into the car to commute to the dam for a weekend early in December. However, that particular trip brought with it a major change to the whole world. It was December 7, 1941. I happened to be the one to deliver the news that the Japanese had bombed Pearl Harbor. We had no phone in the house, so when the camp office blasted out two longs and three shorts, it meant our family had a phone call. I was available to go racing to the office on my scooter to discover who was calling. I was too young to understand the significance, but I could tell by the superintendent's dazed expression that it must be a very important message so I tore back home yelling, "Mama, the Japanese just bombed us." My Mom's face turned white with horror, and I had the first inkling that something had occurred which would turn our comfy life upside down.

And, upside-down it went. The war department began issuing orders. The lights on the dam were slated to go permanently dark; guards would patrol around the clock. Authorities were fearful that total devastation would occur for the Snake River Valley if the Japanese succeeded in breeching the dam. The deep lake behind its structure would inundate vast swaths of territory.

Mom became paranoid about such a possibility. We were made to sleep with clothes under our pillow, and she held actual training sessions where we grabbed and ran for the hills. This, of course, terrified me, causing nightmares and bedwetting to the point she had to ease up. After all, our camp was one mile below the dam; we would have had less than five minutes to make it up the hill. How could anything get out of the way of such a wall of water?

The hiring of guards brought a huge change in our family structure. Grandpa Bill was hired, and he settled into the bunkhouse with his second wife, Amelia. The bunkhouse was originally constructed and furnished to house workers who built the dam, and it contained at least fifteen sleeping rooms. The nice large room and the only kitchen were at the south end of the bunkhouse. This was where Grandpa Bill and

Amelia lived, while the other guards used the sleeping rooms. I have a vague memory that Amelia might have been assigned the task of cooking for all the guards, but the operation required only a few guards, and most of the remaining bunkhouse rooms, though furnished, were unoccupied.

Jim and I were delighted to have our Grandpa Bill come. Usually, Grandpa Bill came for just a short visit during Christmas. Now, he became a steady part of our lives. We loved him dearly, and in our eyes he could do no wrong. For our mother, it was surely a different matter. Not once during our childhood did she ever express how she felt about growing up with such a father.

I discovered the darker side of Grandpa Bill, after I reached adulthood, from reading Aunt Dorothy's diary. Just like Grandma Louise, who was long-suffering and who never spoke ill of her husband, Mom adopted that same silent model in dealing with her dad. After Grandma Louise died, Grandpa Bill sank into deep despair and resorted once more to alcohol to dull his pain. Hidden baggage, of which we kids were innocently unaware, traveled with Grandpa Bill when he moved to the dam.

He was fortunate to meet and marry Amelia, since she managed to straighten him back out. Strangely, it was Amelia that Mom and Dad gossiped about, because she was opinionated and much too thrifty. If she did become the guards' cook, she would have exerted military authority and exaggerated her superior cooking skills.

Everything she did seemed to rub my parents the wrong way. One story that they refused to let die dealt with a Christmas fruitcake that Amelia made for us. Dad declared that the candied fruit in that cake was the same that Mom had thrown out because of weevils. They were certain that Amelia rescued it from the trash to make their cake. Obviously, in their eyes, she could do nothing right. However, as a child, I had a whole different view, and I found her to be kind. She invited me for tea parties. She sewed a doll coat, which is still treasured as a family keepsake, out of Grandpa's green-plaid wool shirt. She gave me manicures and shared her joy in collecting salt and pepper shakers.

To us, Grandpa Bill was a warm cuddly man in wool shirts who smelled of cigars. We would huddle close and listen with rapt attention, believing every word, as he spun his tall tales. Grandpa Bill told us that one of the other guards was fearful of bears, so Grandpa began to warn him to be on the outlook. To our knowledge, the Owyhee Lake area was not bear country, but Grandpa began to drop scary hints to the contrary. Then, one snowy night, Grandpa said he contrived two poles with gloves the size of bear paws and stamped fake bear tracks along the entire length of the roadway going across the dam.

The next morning when the guard came on duty, Grandpa spun a long tale about how frightened he was last night with all the bears around. In Grandpa's version, the guard became so terrified that he refused to go on duty and soon quit his job. Since we were required to head back to school during the week, we were never privy to whether

Grandpa's stories were for real or just things he told us, which we believed as God's honest truth.

My brother was in fifth grade that year so he had his own mother for a teacher. He was expected to call her Mrs. Rigney at school. Mrs. Rigney was noted for her innovative school musical programs, which she wrote and directed. That year, one of the musical numbers involved acting out the song, "Bicycle Built for Two." Her idea was cute and original until she hit upon the plan that Jim would be the one who rolled the bike onto the stage and pantomimed the lyrics to a sweet young girl sitting all alone on the stage, while the chorus sang and swayed to the music on the main floor below them. Of course, Jim had cat fits and was in open rebellion because he truly did have a crush on that particular girl but was trying to keep it secret.

Mother prevailed, and on the day of the program, there was reluctant Jim in stage makeup and slicked-down hair parted in the middle, as was the style for handsome beaux, strolling across the stage pushing a bike while the audience heard the chorus singing, "Daisy, Daisy, give me your answer, do, I'm half-crazy all for the love of you." The production received rave reviews from the community, and Jim received merciless razzing from his friends. I got lots of mileage out of his discomfiture. Our family sang a lot, and I could count on his negative reaction if I started to croon, "Daisy, Daisy give me your answer true."

It amazes me how we managed to put up with such an original, energetic mother, since that was not the only time she pushed her ideas in our faces. She was always disappointed when we reacted disagreeably. I still have memories of an unsettling surprise sixteenth-birthday party for me where she invited boys. The guest list included the guy, a year older than I, whom I secretly carried in my heart with unrequited love during all of my high school years. She should have given me fair warning on that one, so I could have had time to practice a proper reaction.

Another time, when I was just thirteen, she was the brains behind my decision to invite a boy to a Job's Daughter's Dance. The kid said he would go but never showed up, while I waited at our house, all dressed up for the dance. Mom made me go dateless. Then, there was the time, at a high school function, when she accepted a ride home for me with a boy I detested. Luckily, I heard what she was doing and skipped out ahead of them to walk home alone. Later, she gave me a tongue-lashing for my bad manners. Horrible mother!

But, at Linder School, my mother's turn for razzing happened in the spring, and it happened as a result of my actions. We girls loved the boys to chase us, as long as it was the boy we wanted to be chased by. There was this little boy in my class who bugged me a lot. Size-wise, I was easily two boys bigger than he. He was definitely not my choice of guy, and yet, there he always was. One muddy spring recess, while we were running around and squealing in the hopes of attracting the right attention, he jumped on my back with an arm lock. I immediately "saw red."

With a twist, I had him off and onto the ground with his face in a mud puddle, and then I simply sat on him. The poor little fellow didn't have a chance. I continued to sit there while the kids circled around yelling, "Fight, fight! Doris took a boy down! Doris took a boy down!" Both teachers came running, and I was thoroughly chastised while they helped my attacker up and took him inside for a cleaning up. I felt somewhat embarrassed but, by gum, he had it comin'!

The rest of the story unfolded at the next school board meeting, which my mother, as principal, was required to attend. Before the meeting began, the chairman of the school board came over to Mom and with big guffaws began to give her a huge razzing. "My son came home to tell me that your daughter took a little boy down on the playground and sat on him. What kind of a wrestler are you raising?" Mom, ever quick with the repartee, replied, "Yes, but did your son happen to mention the part about him being the little boy that got taken down?" Then the razzing went in the other direction and the entire school board had a good laugh. My reputation was burdened with wrestling stories for years to come.

Finally, the year at Linder drew to a close, and we kids could get back to the business of real life. Real life! This is what being at the dam grew to mean for me, at least. In the spring of 1942, while I was finishing up first grade and struggling to avoid more wrestling matches, Mom and Dad decided that it was just too difficult to maintain separate households in order for Mom to continue teaching, so she did not accept another year's contract at Linder, and we made a permanent move to the Owyhee Dam. She gave a lot of thought over the summer to what would happen for schooling when fall arrived.

When we arrived at the dam, we were delighted to learn that our Grandpa Bill and Amelia planned to continue living there for the duration of the war. This meant that we could enjoy his company for the whole summer and beyond. Grandpa Bill fascinated us in many ways. He knew the difference between real gold and fool's gold and showed us samples of each. We were allowed to handle his pan for panning gold. I still remember the distinctive odor of the small working carbide lamp on the top of his miner's helmet! He was responsible for my interest in collecting quartz, because that was where gold could often be found, and I spent hours adding to my collection, which I kept in an old candy box throughout grade school and on past high school. I loved the sparkly white stone and the lovely clinking sound the word made in my mouth when I said it. "Quartz!"

Grandpa Bill became my rescuer when once I heard him quietly command, "Doris, get up on the porch right now!" His tone made me comply immediately. After doing so, I turned around with breathless relief to watch him chop off the head of a big old rattler with the end of his shovel. He was also able to convince me that I was safe from the danger of snakes if I kept Spot, our Fox Terrier, close by. He must have realized how deeply fearful I was, because he spun long tales about heroic exploits of other Fox Terriers he had known, possibly all manufactured for my sake.

He always carried a sharp pocket knife, which he used to whittle toys or wooden chains out of a solid block of wood. He turned a plain willow stick horse into a Palomino by stripping the bark away. I could travel ever so much faster on my Palomino than just by running on two feet. Grandpa Bill loved to have us kids as his audience while he ate raw hamburger and onions, making it look scrumptious but not so much that we dared to taste. While eating it, he always smacked his lips and complained that he needed a dab more hamburger, and then maybe a few more onions, because, "I just can't make them come out even."

Long after my grandpa died, I remember my brother Jim entertaining my children with the same kind of drama while he added sugar to his coffee and smacked his lips, adding a bit more coffee or a bit more sugar, complaining that he couldn't seem to make it "just right." All the while, they waited breathlessly for him to fix his coffee correctly so that he would tell them a promised story about "Skinny Dress Island." I doubt that any of us, especially Jim, were aware at the time of the similarity between his mannerisms and those of our Grandpa Bill from so long ago.

As an adult, I visited Aunt Dorothy, who told me other tales of the many practical jokes Grandpa Bill played while he worked at the Owyhee Dam. He recognized that bears were not the only subjects that evoked fear among others at the dam; some had a deep dread of snakes. This was a legitimate fear, because while the guards were on patrol, it was common to see the large reptiles slithering over the long cement roadway which crossed the top of the dam. Also, rattlers and less dangerous snakes, such as bull, king, or garter, often invaded camp to bask in the moisture of the green lawns.

There was one guard who loved to talk and who pretended no fear of snakes, often waxing forth long and loud about eating rattlesnake. Since it takes a braggart to know one, Grandpa Bill noted a somewhat different reaction when that guard found himself in proximity to a snaky visitor. So, Grandpa Bill began agreeing with him on how delicious rattlesnake meat was.

He waited until all the guards were in the bunkhouse and then began to spin a long-drawn-out lecture about the correct preparation of rattlesnake for supper. "First you whack off the rattles to keep as a trophy. Then, just grab that critter by its tail and slit it all the way up to his gullet. The skin will peel off as easy as peeling a banana." Then he dwelt on various recipes for cooking rattlesnake meat. "Some say that baking works fine, but I prefer to fillet it and fry it up all crispy brown in bacon grease." Finally he ended up with a description of how it tasted. "I've heard tell from some folks that it tastes like chicken. Others say it's more like a tasty little morsel of fried fish."

The next time they were all together, Grandpa Bill spun a tale about a huge rattler which almost attacked him the day before while he was on guard duty. He said, "Thankfully, I was able to kill the vicious thing, and now I'm thinking about what a good supper it might make." To finalize the joke, Grandpa fried up a batch of whitefish all crispy and invited the guards to come on over for a great meal of rattlesnake. He sat down in front of them and began to eat, urging them to join. The joke was in watching the braggart turn a dull shade of green and quickly leave the room.

Aunt Dorothy shared another story about one of Grandpa Bill's tricks that had nothing to do with snakes. It seems that one of the guards was very proud of his fine black moustache and was quick to bring out his bottle of moustache dye if he noticed white hairs appearing. I assume that the bottle came with a swab attached to the cap, like a liquid shoe polish applicator, so that one could dab a little bit of blacking on the offending white hairs. According to Aunt Dorothy's story, Grandpa Bill sneaked away the bottle, emptied it and refilled it with green ink. Then, he laughed hilariously at the consternation and embarrassment of the vain, mustached man who applied his correction fluid one morning and then was faced with the choice to go around in green or shave off his glorious moustache and start over.

It is quite apparent that Grandpa Bill had a well-developed skill in recognizing vulnerabilities in others. He saw it as humorous to prey upon those frailties; but he often went too far, and some of his jokes bordered on sadism. The tale he told of the fat lady who walked over the ditch on the partially sawed board comes to mind. I have decided that I'm no fan of those who play practical jokes. It is strange that I should say that, since my family seems to have been full of them. Grandpa Bill's saving grace was his charm, and he could apply it with ease. But, distaste for his tricks was surely shared by many who associated with him. His joking behavior towards others and his reaction to jokes when the tables were turned on him probably had a lot to do with why he was unable to hold a steady job.

Aunt Dorothy said that if a joke were played on Grandpa Bill, he took it as criticism and would burst into foul language or throw a sulky fit. My mother was aware of her father's quick temper. She was a first-hand witness to the many times he forced the family to pull up stakes and move on because he was embarrassed by someone, lost his temper, and refused to stay. It seems that his *modus operandi* was to deal with problems by running away.

Young Grandpa Bill

This gives me another insight into my brother's adult behavior. He surely must have inherited Grandpa's tendency to deal with problems in this way, since Jim also moved his family to a new situation on a regular basis. It usually occurred in the fall of the year, a pattern lived in childhood. Because I was busy living my own life, I never gave it much thought. But now, I see a definite similarity in their behaviors. Not only were they both fantastic storytellers, but they also handled personal distress in a similar fashion. They even looked alike.

Jim developed many of Grandpa Bill's same characteristics. Possibly they were learned from sitting at the foot of his elder. But, many of Grandpa's less desirable traits also manifested themselves as Jim dealt with his own family. If I could talk right now to my Grandpa Bill and to my brother Jim I would say, "Dear Ones, for your great good attributes of imagination, whimsy, intelligence, and charm, I thank you. As for the darker side, now I understand it better."

Adult Jim

Because Mom was so aware of her dad's flaws, she made sure that we kids were never witness to his temper. If Mom and Dad became upset with Grandpa Bill, while he and Amelia lived at the dam, they managed to turn their complaints toward Amelia. Also, Grandpa knew we were his adoring audience, and he most certainly attempted to control behavior that might have caused our disillusionment.

As Grandpa Bill and Amelia were settling into their life at the dam, other changes both large and small affected our life there. One such change, though not momentous in itself, left a lasting memory. It had to do with the lights mounted on tall cement pillars across the top of the Owyhee Dam. Until the war, those lights always shone out bright and clear to travelers making their way over the tiresome, rocky road leading to camp.

Sketch of lights on Owyhee Dam

When Mom, Jim, and I were returning to camp, we were often on the road until way after dark. We kids would be cranky and tired, so Mom invented ways to perk us up. About ten miles before reaching camp, we drove around a bend, and there would be the lovely lights shining like a beacon of promise that we were almost home. Mom invented the "I" game. Each of us tried to engage the others in some sort of distracting conversation or song to get our minds off the imminent light show. Then, the first of us to yell "I" upon seeing the lights was the contest winner. This little challenge grew in importance until we even began to keep score.

But for security reasons, soon after war was declared, the government decreed that the lights must go permanently dark causing the "I" contest to come to a heartbreaking halt. In our childish way, we blamed the Japanese for spoiling our game. Losing the lights of the dam was not a serious change considering the total devastation caused by the war, but it held prime importance in our minds.

We were children and not easily daunted by the daily newscasts of war atrocities. They slipped past our consciousness to be replaced with the joys of living in the paradise at the dam: swinging; running through sprinklers; swimming at Snivley's;

climbing hills; reading books; picking fruit; fighting each other; and, making up again, so that we would have someone to play with.

During the summer we were blessed with visits from my father's relatives, who drove up for a week's visit a few days before my birthday. It was late June, 1942, and on the first of July I would turn seven. I was wiggling with anticipation, even more when my parents told me that Daddy's Mom and Pop would be coming to visit us. In my mind, they were very old, and I wondered how they could drive all the way from Boise. It was at least ninety miles away. But, I learned that Uncle Cliff and Aunt Geneva would be coming too, and they would ride together in one car to save on gas-ration stamps.

Grandma Leoda, Grandpa John, and Uncle Cliff were avid fishermen, and the Owyhee Lake was an ideal place for them to spend July 4th holiday. Of course, the prospect of good fishing was uppermost in their minds, but in my heart I knew the real reason they were coming. It was so that we could have Aunt Geneva's fried chicken and Grandma's raised doughnuts for my birthday party.

Mom worked to make everything ready for their arrival and find sleeping places for everyone. The bunkhouse was put into use; we kids would sleep outside under the stars, and Mom and Dad commandeered Jim's garage room. When I heard our metal gate clang open and shut, I couldn't contain the excitement and ran out to receive my hugs and kisses. Jumping up and down with eagerness, I immediately quizzed, "Grandma, did you bring your doughnut recipe?" She smiled complacently down at me, pointed to her head, and said, "It's right up here." Her answer so puzzled me! How could something so big that belonged in a cookbook be up there among the curly gray waves of her hair?

I totally expected her to walk right into the house and prove that she had that recipe tucked up there somewhere in her head. Instead, for the next two days, she rode with the men up to the top of the dam and sat beside the lake to fish. I think I might have mentioned doughnuts to her once or twice, but she did nothing to reassure me. Despite my impatience, Grandma said not a word about them until two days later, after she caught the biggest fish, and all the grown-up visiting had settled down.

In the meantime, my mother wanted to know how the Boise in-laws were faring with the war rationing, and she explained in detail why the lights of the dam were no longer shining. Dad needed to hear Grandpa's opinions on the progression of the war. They both had gossipy tales to tell about Grandpa Bill and his new wife, Amelia. Aunt Geneva and Uncle Cliff were good listeners, and everyone else talked and talked and talked. I thought the subject of doughnuts was forgotten forever.

It was the morning before my birthday when Grandma came out to the kitchen dressed in her Mother-Hubbard apron declaring, "Jo, I reckon this is the day when I'd better make this Kiddy her birthday doughnuts." I "reckoned so" too and was ready with eyes, ears, and nose to take in every detail of the important activity. Many years later I was delighted to find her recipe, which I had later written in pencil with many spelling errors. I was much too young to record such details during that summer. I just absorbed by osmosis.

Grandma's capable hands moved with purpose and care as she filled a stew pan half full of flour, added salt, sugar, nutmeg, a piece of butter and two broken-up cakes of Fleischmann's yeast. She made a hollow in the middle of the flour into which she slowly trickled lukewarm water with vanilla added. My memory is vivid of her patient fingers working towards the outer sides of the pan until all the flour was incorporated and the dough was just right, not sticking. My little nose was right there, as close to the process as allowed, and I can smell the yeasty mixture as I write. She worked that dough, kneading it from the outside to the center again and again until I thought she would never finish.

Our kitchen was humble, with a linoleum covered drain board. But, it was clean to receive the dough when Grandma decided she was finished kneading. After she dumped out the ball of dough, she worked remaining bits from the pan and greased it with lard. Then back into the pan went the puffy, smooth dough with a bit of lard greased over the top. I was allowed to pat it with my freshly-washed hands. It was kind of like patting a little baby's bottom! When Grandma covered it with a tea towel, she sat down with her coffee cup for more gossip with the grownups.

Doughnut-making required way too much patience. I fidgeted for almost an hour until Grandma got up, checked under the tea towel, punched the dough back down and told me it had to rise again. All the while, I hovered on the outskirts of their conversation and our kitchen filled with the heady aroma of yeasting dough. When Grandma declared it to be ready, she rolled out the dough with our rolling pin. Then, she cut out doughnut shapes using a glass for a cutter and a bottle top for the hole. She laid them on a cut-open paper sack sprinkled with flour. I later wrote in the recipe, "a flowered paper." The "buttons" from the middle and small scraps of dough wrapped into "twisters" were also saved. Everything was covered with the tea towel to rise yet again. Sigh!

Finally, I was treated to the smell of melting lard in a heavy cast-iron fry pan. Grandma told me, "It has to be good and hot." Her fingers were expert at picking up the delicate pieces, without crushing, and slipping them into the bubbling grease. Never so much as a splash! At a safe distance, I was allowed to watch the dough first sink and then bounce back up to sizzle and bob while the underside turned a golden brown. Grandma turned them with a fork except that the buttons, the little devils, had to be teased to turn over.

As Grandma lifted out each golden-brown globe from the hot lard, my task was to swirl them in sugar. Yes, I admit to licking sugary grease from my fingers while I worked. With my family's assistance, few doughnuts remained by the next day. But that is to be expected; fresh is best. Now, I understand what Kipling meant when he said, "It was indeed a Superior Comestible . . . and smelled most sentimental." With the memory of my marvelous birthday doughnuts lingering, the rest of the visit from the Boise relatives took sort of a back seat in importance for me. But, there is one incident involving my beloved Uncle Cliff which begs to be shared.

I'd not heard this story until I visited many years later with Aunt Dorothy. She mentioned Uncle Cliff's deep fear of snakes, which caused me to remember watching Uncle Cliff's beautiful eyes grow large with horror whenever the subject of snakes came up. He loved to fish and spent hours up on the lake before coming back to camp for sleep in the bunkhouse. I'm not sure if the perpetrator of his snake scare was Grandpa Bill. It would fit the pattern if he were the one who pulled off this trick, but it could have been my own dad. He, also, was capable of a mean trick or two.

Regardless of who did it, we almost lost Uncle Cliff to heart attack right then and there when he climbed into bed to discover a coil of something wet where his feet were supposed to go. It turned out to be a snake-sized hunk of wet rope all coiled up under the covers. The story goes that he shot out of that bed with a yell that could be heard all over camp. I loved my Uncle Cliff, and I always felt he was treated in an unforgivable manner just because he was willing to admit his genuine fear. The cold, fake snake in his bed was no joking matter for Uncle Cliff, and we should not have been surprised if he declared the visit to be over after that incident. But, he was also kind and forgiving, so he graciously tried to be a good sport.

When the relatives finally said their goodbyes and headed back, we were left with that curious, empty feeling which often comes after loved ones have departed. The rest of the summer began to drag a little for us kids. But there were still plenty of chores required of us while Mom once more launched into harvesting every bit of food in sight.

Mid-summer is definitely not deer-hunting season, and yet both Dad and his boss felt that if a deer came within rifle range, it was fair game any time of the year, unless the game warden was prowling around. I can't begin to name the number of times that our dirt basement became a crime scene while Mom and Dad frantically worked to cut up and hide the evidence of the men's poaching. It became a game of challenge for them to keep from being caught. I can see now the twinkle in Dad's eyes and his laughing face as he sat in his leather rocker relating how they had a close call and almost didn't get away. All of us believed that the game warden knew what they were doing, but that he played along and made his presence known on several occasions while he searched for evidence of their kill.

I don't know how they hid the hide, head, and bones. But, I can still smell that warm wild meat and visualize the bloody sheet they used as it soaked in a sink of cold water. Also, I remember cut up meat being stuffed in canning jars, which Mom processed for interminable hours in our canning kettle. We had no way of freezing the meat, so canning was the only alternative. Though I was very young, I knew that canned venison could be dangerous to eat unless it cooked for hours after Mom removed it from a jar to make a meal. I never enjoyed the flavor of canned venison. It tasted "wild" and greasy no matter how Mom tried to disguise it in her stews or cottage pies. I'm sure this law breaking weighed heavily on my mother's honest, Christian soul. She made a great show of teaching us kids how wrong the whole thing was, but still she insisted that she must help to hide the crime to protect her husband.

Even with all the excitement that the whole illegal deer-meat venture created, we kids were becoming restless and tired of the summer activities, and so we began to wonder where we would be going to school when the vacation ended. Unbeknownst to us, Mom spent a great deal of her summer devising a plan for our schooling in the fall.

We were not aware how deeply concerned Mom was about it, because she remembered her own difficulty in obtaining an education due to her dad's choice to live in remote places. And now, here she was situated thirty miles from town with no school. She was determined not to repeat the same pattern for her own children.

The plan she came up with required permission, so she requested a meeting with the Malheur County Superintendent of Schools and drove to the County Seat in Vale to plead her case. She asked the county either to provide transportation to town, or, since there were two children of another family living close to us on a farm along the Owyhee River, she felt it reasonable that she be allowed to establish a school in our home.

This conversation happened during the early 1940's when the concept of home schooling was not as much in vogue as it is now. In fact, creating a home-based school for four children of two families was probably a rare occurrence for the Malheur County Superintendent. However, Jo Rigney was a persuasive supplicant, and she skillfully led the authorities to agree with her request. When she came home that day, she had consent to start the school, an offer to provide all needed textbooks, and also the promise of a small salary. She literally bounced into the house proclaiming her news.

"But Mommy," I protested, "We don't have a school house and desks and stuff like a real school." No problem! Mom's brain had been buzzing while she drove home, and she had everything already planned out. She declared that my bedroom would be our schoolroom during the day; she would move some of the small tables and chairs from the bunkhouse for desks. She had brought the textbooks and workbooks from the county plus library books. We learned that two other children from a farm downriver would be coming every day. She even found a real school bell to ring when it was time for recess to be over.

Thus, I began second grade. At first, we kids thought it would be a lark. Holding school in my bedroom seemed like it would be kind of fun. But Mom insisted that during school hours, we must address her as Mrs. Rigney. That was a tough order. And, speaking of tough, she really was! She allowed the proper times for recess play, but that school bell always rang promptly calling us back into the drudgery of books and papers. Mrs. Rigney demanded perfection from the two Rigney students. I hated the arrangement of using my bedroom, which required me to hop up quickly in the morning, make my bed, and tidy up my playthings. I've never been a cheerfully alert person early in the morning, so this caused me to feel resentment towards the two strange kids who attended our school.

It became apparent that Jim and I were much more capable students than the little kids from downriver. Because it was so boring while we waited on them to answer questions and to complete their assignments, Jim and I slipped into the habit of reading library books at a voracious pace. I believe that Mom was secretly delighted with that outcome. She also spent hours reading aloud to us, and one of the things Jim and I fought about was one or the other of us sneaking out the book she was reading to us and reading ahead. Some of those wonderful titles that are still prominent in my memory are: *Five Little Peppers and How They Grew; Black Beauty; Pollyanna; Girl of the Limberlost;* and *Beautiful Joe.*

Actually, I don't even remember the other students' names, and by the time Hallowe'en rolled around their parents explained to Mom that they wouldn't be attending our school any longer. I'm not sure if the parents or the kids were dissatisfied. Perhaps they just moved away. Whatever happened, Jim and I were not sad to see them gone.

We wanted to do Hallowe'en up in regular style, so Mom helped us dress in some homemade costumes, and we went tearing down the path to knock on doors and yell "Trick-or-Treat" to the other three houses in camp. Mom told us to take our time, and if we behaved ourselves, she would prepare a treat for when we arrived back home. Probably, our neighbors had not expected trick-or-treaters, since I don't remember much of any kind of treat coming our way.

When we ran back to knock on our own door, Mom met us with a plate of what she called fudge candy. Obviously, once again, Jo Rigney was not too successful in her attempt at the finer culinary arts. The plate contained little puddles of sticky chocolate goo that was never going to turn into fudge. But in the center of the plate were two huge pieces of candy that looked like fondant covered with the same messy chocolate.

I wondered at the time how she had managed so quickly to make such fancy candy. Of course, as she knew we would, Jim and I each chose to grab the big pieces. Jim eagerly popped the whole piece into his mouth and began to chew. I was a nibbler and took a tiny little lick off the corner of my piece. Then, Mom and Dad both began to chuckle as Jim choked with foaming soap bubbles escaping from his mouth. The centers were not fondant but rather large squares of Ivory soap.

This was Mom's idea of a Hallowe'en Trick. She had once again lived up to the reputation of being Grandpa Bill's daughter. When telling the story in later years to my daughters, she described my reaction. She said I looked up at her with disappointed eyes saying, 'Oh Mommy how could you?'" She also moralistically added that her reason for the trick was to teach us not to be greedy and grab the biggest piece. I might add that they were the only two pieces that could be picked up. The other so-called "pieces" were just gooey puddles of chocolate syrup.

School carried on, until soon it was time for Thanksgiving. Mom decided we must put on a Thanksgiving program. She wrote a script, invited everyone in camp, and turned our living room wall into a tiny stage. She helped me dress up as an Indian Maid with a wig made of silk stockings died black and a dress made from a gunny sack tied with a cord belt. Jim was Squanto with a bare chest and war paint. I don't remember much about the script but I have distinct memories of pantomiming and singing "Red Wing."

The song tells the fable of a prairie Indian maiden who loved a warrior bold. He rode away to do battle and died in the fray. Red Wing continued to wait and dream for his return. But when the braves returned, her beloved was not among them, "For afar 'neath his star her brave is sleeping / While Red Wing's weeping her heart away."

Our audience was kind and applauded with gusto. After our presentation, Mom served homemade Thanksgiving treats of cider, popcorn, pie, and coffee. I remember that program more than anything else about our little school. It is good that we had such a memorable experience, since that evening marked the beginning of the end of our home schooling.

After the other family pulled out, the county cancelled the agreement. They notified Mom that after Christmas, they would no longer support a school for just two children. We needed to make other arrangements. Never-say-die Jo Rigney scurried to find a solution. She soon learned of a school which was in trouble because they would be losing their seventh and eighth grade teacher/principal after Christmas. Mom applied for and was awarded the position. However, there were drawbacks. It was the dead of winter, and the school was situated fifty miles away from the dam. We would need to find a place to live during the week and once again commute to the dam on weekends.

Mom began to work out plans for all these changes, because her determination to provide for our schooling took precedence over all other problems. When Mom told us during the freezing cold days of late December that she had accepted a teaching position at Pioneer School, I was confused. How could we become pioneers now? I knew from reading Wilder's *Little House on the Prairie* that pioneers lived a long time ago when people traveled in covered wagons and camped out under the stars until they could build a little sod dugout to live in. That couldn't be us! But when I saw the housing provided for us next to Pioneer School, I began to believe that it did, indeed, describe us.

CHAPTER 5

⬥

Our Pioneering Lives

NOT ONLY WAS IT dreadfully cold and far away from the dam, but our December move to the new school half way through the school year meant that no adequate living quarters were available. The chairman of the school board searched hard to provide something for us, but could locate nothing except a deserted two-room tar-paper shack situated in a field beyond the school playground. Mother must have inspected the premises before she brought us along for moving-in day, because her voice took on a falsely cheerful tone as she described the adventure we were going to have in our new week-day house. Jo Rigney was truly a "make-do" woman when push came to shove, and getting her two reluctant young ones to accept these very humble lodgings took a lot of pushing and shoving.

Since we must begin school immediately after New Year's Day in 1942, Mom and Dad scheduled our move for the weekend after Christmas. Once again, we loaded up belongings and provisions in the Ford Coupe. We were met by the school board chairman with a key to the shack and a pail of water. The key, I understood, but why the water? I soon learned. The chairman knew we would need that pail of water, since the place had stood empty all fall and early winter. He instructed us always to save a portion of water each day to pour into the top of the outside pump in order to prime it. That thawed the works and removed any air pockets in the shaft. Then, the water would start gushing up from the well when someone pumped the handle. This would be our water source, since there was no indoor plumbing. We would need to carry water just as I had learned about during pioneer days, which seemed quite logical to my young mind. After all, this was Pioneer School.

After the long ride from the dam, we all needed a potty break. I was not surprised to learn that our new home fit the age-old expression, "two rooms and a path." I was familiar with outhouses, since our Idaho friends lived on a farm with an outhouse. But, I had grown accustomed to the comforts of indoor plumbing, and the icy cold outhouse seat was quite a shock for my little bottom. Mom secured a chamber pot for use in the middle of the night. The pot had a distinct drawback: someone had to dump it in the morning. Since I was still pretty young, I was not assigned that chore. It must have become another task for Mom. What an odoriferous smell came from that pot hidden under the bed until she found time to dump it!

Dad stayed long enough to help set up the iron double bed for Mom and me and the single cot for Jim in the shack's second room. Mom hung some old sheets on a line between the beds to allow for privacy. Our clothes were quickly hung up on nails pounded into the wall. Mom was a great fan of the wooden orange crates that could be had for the asking at Wilson's Super Market in Nyssa. They made great shelving for books, clothes, linens, and all sorts of household items. She used them everywhere in that little shack, as she worked to make it homelike.

In the main room, there was a linoleum-covered shelf fastened to one corner of the wall as a kitchen drain board. With orange crates stacked beside it, Mom organized her dishes and groceries. On the shelf, she made room for two buckets of water and a metal dishpan. One bucket was kept filled with clean water for drinking. That was a kid's job, and we regularly fought about whose turn it was to carry in the water. A metal dipper, which we all used for dipping up drinks, hung from a nail in the wall. The other bucket was for washing hands and dishes.

Sketch of orange crate

A slop bucket for dirty water was kept under the shelf. This had to be dumped outside, another kid's job. A mirror was placed over the shelf so that we could see to comb our hair. There was a crude two-burner electric hotplate fastened to a shelf on the opposite wall. There was no refrigeration. We drank a lot of diluted canned milk and ate tinned meats, such as Spam or tuna. Hot dogs and bacon were staples that kept well without refrigeration. We just made do, because it was winter after all.

Next to the only door, there was a working oil heater. When Dad showed Mom how to fire it up, the cold little shack began to glow with homey warmth. A table and chairs were placed along the wall adjoining the sleeping room. Mom covered the table with some nice, new, cheerfully decorated oilcloth. She even had a throw rug to place on the cold linoleum floor. That spot became a favorite place to huddle in the morning while I got dressed.

There were no cozy electric lamps, just plain-wire electric bulbs, turned on and off with a pull string, hanging from the ceiling of each room. Mom may have had an oil-burning lamp on the table where she sat to grade papers. In the 1940's, most homes kept these lamps for power outages. We had a small radio perched on a shelf above the electric hot plate. A radio was not really a luxury. Having a source of news was almost a necessity. I woke up every morning to the sound of Gabriel Heatter giving out the latest war news. His main news program was broadcast in the evening, so this must have been a morning repeat. He was famous for saying, "There is good news tonight."

The radio also became very important as our source of entertainment. In the evening hours, we were allowed to listen to programs such as *Blondie, Jack Benny, Bob Hope*, and *Red Skelton*. My brother particularly liked *The Green Hornet*, the tale of a masked vigilante and his faithful sidekick, Kato. Music was provided by The Andrews Sisters, Glen Miller, Bing Crosby, Vaughn Monroe, and Benny Goodman. I remember "Don't sit under the apple tree with anyone else but me, till I come marching home."

When all the moving and settling-in was finished, it was time to brave the scary world of second grade. I don't know how Jim fared in his sixth grade class or what effort my mother put forth to straighten out the disarray from the previous seventh-eighth grade teacher's sudden, midterm exodus. My interest was entirely self-centered. I was too tall for my age, a pudgy, loner who was now being required to socialize with strangers who had already developed friendship bonds during the first half of the year. Add to that the fact that I was once more "the principal's brat," and therefore expected by others to become the teacher's pet. This stigma did not sit well with me, and I quickly learned to hide my light under a basket. In church, we were taught to sing, "This little light of mine, I'm gonna let it shine . . . Hide it under a basket? NO!" But at my age, the lesson didn't take, and I decided the only way to survive with the other kids was to hide what I really knew or could do. Later on, during my teenage years, in an attempt to overcome this behavior, "This little light of mine" was one of the songs I sang to myself as I marched each day to school.

Being the biggest and newest kid in second grade, plus suffering from painful shyness, I seldom raised my hand or volunteered for anything. I have a strong memory of our class dramatization of *Ferdinand*, a story that I loved about a little bull who didn't want to fight the matador but chose instead to sit and sniff flowers. I would've loved the narrator's part, or even one of the flowers, but instead, guess who had to be the mother cow? That was the way my second grade went. When I became a teacher in later years, these early memories provided me with a particular empathy for the shy and awkward students in my kindergarten classes. When Judith Viorst's lovely book, *Alexander and the Terrible, Horrible, No Good, Very Bad Day* was published, I quickly shared it with all my classes, because I could relate!

Making friends came slowly. Again, as at Linder School in first grade, I wished the little boys would sometimes choose to chase me like they did the others. I particularly pined with unrequited love for the attentions of a very small boy named Donnie Trueblood. He was cute and quick and beloved by all the little girls. My brother teased me about him. How could I have been so willing to let my family know I liked Donnie? Big mistake on my part!

Slowly, by spring, I developed friendships with some of the other girls. One such friendship got me into a heap of trouble. A little girl named Joanne invited me to go home with her to play after school. I wisely knew that I must get permission, so I went to Mom's room after class. She was busy speaking with another teacher, but I interrupted to ask, "Mama, can I go play at Joanne's house?" Being preoccupied, she gave a cursory nod in my direction, and I took off. Joanne and I had such fun playing in her yard with her dolls and toys that afternoon. Mama had not said when I needed to come home, so I paid no heed to the time. It became evening, and Joanne's mother kindly invited me to eat with them. She probably didn't know what else to do with this little girl who stayed and stayed.

I was sitting down at the table to share their meal when a very upset Jo Rigney knocked on the door. It seems she was not even aware which Joanne's house I was going to. So, she was required to hunt among the homes of my classmates to find where I was. After deep apologies to the mother, she pulled me from the table, pushed me out the door, and headed towards the little shack. She had a strong switch in her hand which she applied forcefully on my bare legs all the way home as she berated me for not telling her where I would be going. Between my sobs and tears, I protested, "But Mommy, you said I could go and you didn't say what time I should come home!" "That makes no difference," she answered heatedly. "You should have known better than to go off without letting me know exactly where you would be. And no child stays and stays until the mother feels obliged to feed you. For shame!" I was grounded, and I've always believed that I was unfairly punished.

One other instance of invoking my mother's ire remains in my memory for that year. In the mornings, there was a huge scurry on Mom's part to get us dressed, my hair braided, Jim's neck and ears scrubbed, and breakfast in our tummies. Mom always had to leave before us, but we kids were assigned chores which must be done before school. Mom took time to rinse out the dishes, which usually included last night's supper dishes, as well. She was often too tired for that chore after supper, but would get up early to clean everything the next morning. My task was to dry all the dishes and silverware and put them away in their proper places. Our spoons and forks were made from some sort of cheap, war-ration metal that rusted if not dried carefully.

One morning, I was in a hurry to get to the playground, so I decided things could air dry. Off I skipped and was happily playing on the swings before the school bell. Suddenly, there stood my Mom in front of me. She had gone back to the shack to retrieve something and discovered the dripping silverware progressing towards its early stages of rust. I was so embarrassed to be chastised in front of my friends and sent home to dry those pesky spoons and forks! Such a small thing, but there it sits in my memory, right along with the resentment that grew as I worked to get the loathsome task finished and not be late for class.

All was not punishment and resentment. There was one bright spot in life every week. Since my mother determined that I should have piano lessons, she located a teacher in the nearby town of Payette, situated just a few miles beyond the Snake River, which formed the border between Oregon and Idaho. Immediately after school on Tuesdays, we loaded into the Ford and headed for Payette. Those piano lessons did not enter into the bright spot. I was supposed to practice every day on the school piano, but I rarely did it with full zest and was usually unprepared for the new lesson.

Also, the teacher had horrible bad breath, and she spent way too much time talking about triads and dominant chords. It was just so much mumbo-jumbo to me. I envied Jim's good fortune, because while I suffered through yet another hour-long session, he was allowed to accompany Mom as they did errands and grocery shopping.

Happiness began after the piano lesson, and we went to eat dinner at Maude Owens' Café. We almost always ordered chicken fried steak. What a meal! And that is not just the little Rigney girl's opinion. In 1986, I was delighted to read Robert Fulghum's book, *All I Really Need to Know I Learned in Kindergarten*. One chapter deals with his search for the perfect chicken fried steak, and with great aplomb, he singles out Maud Owens' Café in Payette, Idaho and offers a full five stars and flowers for the dish, which was "accompanied by parsley, a spiced peach, two dill pickles, and a fried egg. And free toothpicks AND free mints."

Several years ago, my friend and I drove back to Payette in search of that café. Mr. Fulgham would be just as disappointed as I to learn that Maud's no longer exists. But in 1942, that café was my reason to anticipate Tuesdays. That, and if Jim and I had managed to get through the day without quarreling, Mom would reward us by springing for a movie.

Who cares what movie we saw? It was just whatever was playing, a western, a romance, or a musical. Every movie was preceded by a newsreel full of pro-American propaganda about the war. Then, there would be a cartoon of the Roadrunner and Wile E. Coyote or Bugs Bunny and Porky Pig. Everything up on that magic screen was acceptable to us. It was often as late as nine or ten o'clock when we tumbled back into the Ford and fell asleep while Mom drove us back to the shack. I think the wonderful diversion of a night on the town must have more than compensated Mom for her loss of sleep.

Rest and sleep were also in short supply for our mother on Fridays. In fact, her whole weekend, which should have been a time for recuperation, was hectic. On Friday after school, we switched gears from living in our weekday home so that we could head back to the dam. During our years at Pioneer, we spent hours driving to and fro. With indefatigable energy, Mom put in a full Friday of herding seventh and eighth graders. Then, she marshaled us two cranky kids, loaded up laundry, and piled us into the Ford Coupe.

Sketch of Model-A Ford

Ah, the travails of travel in our family's Model-A Ford coupe.

It was a 1931 model and purchased second hand when I was tiny. By the time my memory serves, our car had seen better days. We named her Old Betsy. There is a reason for the motto "Built Ford Tough," because she was indestructible. She had to be, since the road we drove on was no real road. In 1927, the Bureau of Reclamation created a railroad through the river canyon to carry materials from town to the Owyhee Dam construction site. When building was finished, they pulled up the rails and did a bit of grading. Only a high-centered, tough old vehicle could negotiate that rocky, bouncy-jouncey trail they called a road.

Mom was an "I mean business," loving, worrisome nag to us. "Jim, did you fill the water bucket? We can't prime that pump on Monday unless we store some water." Jim would reply, "Nah, I told Doris to do it," and I would whine, "But I did it last time, and it's Jim's turn." While we argued, Mom lost patience. "Get that water and be sure you don't let that stray cat sneak inside. Hurry up, Joris!" When Mom was frustrated, she often called out a combination of both our names. That was a signal for one of us to jump to action, usually me. I got stuck doing the unpleasant chores because Jim was older, cleverer, and stronger. He regularly wheedled me into doing his work with promises made but seldom kept.

After stopping in Nyssa for groceries and loading them into the rumble seat, we finally started for the dam. Mom was short and round, and I also was round. Skinny Jim got the left-over space. We kids always fought to sit by the window, since the middle rider had to straddle the stick shift. Often, I feigned car-sickness to win the coveted window seat.

As we headed down the highway towards Skinner's Corner, Mom's nerves would settle down and she would coax us into singing. Some of our favorites were: "Turkey in the straw, turkey in the hay;" "Oh Susannah;" "Darling Clementine;" "I don't want to play in your yard if you won't be good to me;" "Oh, where have you been Billy Boy, Billy Boy;" "She'll be comin' round the mountain when she comes." We had fun making up new verses: "She'll be driving in Old Betsy when she comes; "She'll be eatin' Momma's cookin' when she comes," or "She will have to sleep with Doris when she comes." Our repertoire lasted long enough to eat up the miles.

Good behavior meant we could go with Mom into the store at Skinner's Corner, which was the last real bit of civilization with a telephone. Mr. and Mrs. Skinner welcomed us to share the latest gossip from town, and they loved to tease us kids. Sometimes, Mom bought a small treat to nibble as we headed down the road. She usually called Dad from there so he could start timing our trip. He knew exactly how long it took to travel from Skinner's Corner, over the jiggle-jounce road and into camp. Depending on the time of year, we sometimes had enough daylight left to spot our favorite landmarks in the red rock canyon, such as the one with the big rock protrusion that looked like the cartoon character, Andy Gump. Or the large "balanced rock" which I was sure would someday break off at its narrow neck and tumble down upon us. Though it never tumbled, others did. Believing we truly might be crushed, Mom put us in training. When she yelled, "Duck!" we were required to scrunch down beneath the dashboard. Supposedly, that would save our lives. All it really did was terrify me, so she gave up the drill.

The only disastrous rock tumble we ever encountered occurred early in 1942, soon after we began the weekly commute. It happened at the scary railroad tunnel, about ten miles from camp. The engineers had blasted the tunnel through a rocky outcrop, which was too close to the river to build a route around. One night, Mom forgot to phone Dad or he would have warned us not to come. We arrived at the tunnel, and our headlights illuminated what looked like a complete cave-in .A huge mound of rock blocked the tunnel entrance at least a quarter of the way up towards the tunnel ceiling. We were stopped and stymied. Since it was a narrow section of road, turning around was not a happy option.

Mom was plucky and undeterred. She knew Jim was fairly good at driving by then and asked if he could drive while she got out and moved rocks. Jim was pleased to be trusted with the task. So, Mom rolled away rocks while Jim inched the car forward bit-by-bit. Following Mom's command, he would let out the clutch very slowly and then hit the brakes while she moved more rocks. Sometimes she would yell for him to apply the emergency brake and get out to help with a boulder. Mom, Jim, and Old Betsy became a careful team, while I sat rigidly with teeth clenched and tears of fright streaming down my cheeks. I was certain that another cave-in would happen while we were inside.

The tunnel was a fearful place. I always flinched when, on other occasions, Jim or Mom teased the bats hanging in the ceiling by honking "ooga, ooga, ooga" as we rolled through. This night, after hours of inching, stopping, and creeping some more, Old Betsy worked her way up over the top of the slide and down the other side. All of us agreed that our coupe had a will of her own, and that night she was determined to find her way to camp for a well-deserved rest.

My tears evaporated into smiles when we reached the other end of the tunnel. We bounced on down the road in triumph to where we could spot the lights of the dam, which had not yet been ordered dark. They twinkled that night with an extra degree of delight to see us arrive. Our singing started up again, "We'll be singing Halleluiah when we come, when we come!" No one could believe their eyes when they spotted us coming up the road. They had received a phone alert earlier in the day from someone who stopped and turned back. Dad's ulcers were kicking up a fuss because Jo hadn't phoned ahead like she was supposed to. Worried for our safety, he griped and criticized once he knew we were safe.

Years later, my gruff, introverted, and often cranky father became more understandable to me after I was exposed to A.A.Milne's *Winnie the Pooh*. Dad was the epitome of an Eeyore, and my father's behavior flashed in front of me each time I read to my kindergarten classes about Eeyore's meeting with Tigger. When Piglet introduced them, Eeyore "thought for a long time and then said: 'When is he going?'"

Dad handled bad situations in much the same manner as Eeyore. I'd say that Dad sincerely appreciated Mom's optimistic "can do" attitude about everything, but I was a witness to way too many unpleasant Friday nights when we hit camp. After a week of stewing alone in that little house, Dad had all his worries bottled up and ready to drop on her the minute we arrived. Of course, it was the worst possible time. She, understandably, was exhausted and cranky herself, and so the turmoil began.

Their conversation usually developed from normal discussion into heated bickering. Dad always finished it off by blaming it on his "stomach" kicking up. He drank Alka Seltzer or warm soda-water like others would drink soda pop. We had sympathy for his ulcers, but not enough to hang around while he fussed at Mom. Needless to say, things usually ended up going the way she wanted, so we learned always to initiate our requests with her. She would then take our side and deflect his constant negativism. Dad loved to tease us but, in the earlier days of our childhood, he rarely gave either of us any positive reinforcement. He was quite willing to believe that in any given situation, the worst was always about to happen.

Usually Jim and I went off to our own activities to get out of hearing range. I'm sure that contributed to how I learned the beauty of solitude and the fun of imaginative play as an escape. But on the night of the cave-in, Mom just brushed off his ranting and smiled to herself. She must have felt justifiably pleased with the clever way she overcame an impossible situation. Jim and I were plumb tuckered out and sleepy. As I crawled into bed, I knew for sure that Old Betsy, sitting outside in the red rock driveway, was grinning.

But, it was no grinning matter for Old Betsy when we had another adventure, locked together in that Ford. For quite some time, Dad had been cautioning Mom always to fill the radiator before leaving Skinner's Corner, because it seemed to be using more water than normal. On this particular night, Mom heeded his advice and filled the radiator to the brim before calling to let Dad know we were on our way. It is certainly good that she did. We traveled about halfway home, not yet in the canyon, but down on the flats where there were isolated farms situated along the river.

Suddenly, the interior of the car's engine began to emit a strong steamy odor. It made gurgling noises, and we could see the radiator cap bubbling up and down with bursts of steam. Then, poor old Betsy came to a stop and refused to travel further. Mom knew enough to allow things to cool before attempting to check out the trouble, but she remarked that it was almost certain we had a radiator leak. After sitting for about ten minutes, she grabbed a rag, twisted off the radiator cap, allowed the steam to shoot out, and peered down into the interior. Bone dry.

Mom directed Jim to get out the bucket from the rumble seat and hurry down to the river to find a spot where it would be safe to dip up water. Jim headed off, and we sat silently watching his flashlight bobbing along while we awaited his return. When he came back, Mom quickly poured the water into the radiator spout, but it just as quickly poured out onto the road beneath the car. What to do? Mom was a great one for innovative ideas. She had heard that chewing gum placed on the outside of a hole was sometimes used to patch a radiator leak, but we had none. Her next thought was to put something into the radiator that would plug the hole.

Her great idea began to hatch! She pointed out the lights of a farm house over the way. Jim was directed to walk over there and politely ask if they would lend us a cup of cornmeal. Mom surmised that if she poured that down the radiator the grains would plug the hole and we might be able to limp on home. Jim agreed to do it and set off at once. I thought he was being much more patient than usual. Ordinarily he would have argued back, but he must have been worried about getting home. Meanwhile I offered my usual strong help by standing alongside whimpering.

I've always wondered what that farm wife thought as she listened to Jim's request, but after a while, back he came with the cornmeal. Mom carefully poured it into the radiator, added some more water to wash it down and said, "There, that ought to do the trick!" Some trick! Almost immediately, we heard "Glub, glub, glub" and out onto the road plopped a huge quantity of cornmeal mush. The engine was still so hot it just cooked it up and spat it out the hole in the bottom of the radiator. If I could speak to my mother today, I just might tease her about that fine kettle of radiator mush.

Later, in the retelling of this story over the years, Mom had great fun in elaborating on how funny the whole situation was. But, on the night itself, she was bone-tired and completely defeated. She could do nothing else but get herself and her kids back into the Ford and sit it out. Finally, Dad rumbled down the road in the company pickup to rescue us and tow the Ford to the dam. Later, I heard him say that the radiator hole was as big as a silver dollar.

Somehow or other, Dad managed to replace the radiator, and soon we were back on the road to endure the continued grind of weekday classes with weekend commutes. Eventually, the school term was ending, and the weather warmed up. Spring grasses and wildflowers spruced up the area around our shack; trips to the outhouse were less painfully cold, although considerably smellier; the pump tended to remain unfrozen; and delight of all delights, the stray cat that adopted us gave birth to a litter of kittens.

We kids discovered Mother Cat in the winter soon after we moved in. She was scruffy and starving. When we first saw her, we offered what we had, a few stale saltines. She snatched and devoured them so quickly that Mom took pity and poured out a saucer of canned milk, which the cat quickly lapped up. We never named her, and she was not allowed inside, but during cold nights, Mom relented and provided a spot for her behind the heater. Every weekend, Jim and I worried whether she would still be hanging around when we returned. Yep, she stuck it out and became a fixture in our lives. Mom constantly fretted that she might be left inside while we were gone.

With one week remaining in the school year, we discovered her litter of kittens tucked in a hollow under the shack by the front door. By then, Mother Cat was tame enough to trust us when we picked up her tiny babies for petting and cuddling. They were so cute and mewling with furry ears, tiny paws, stubby tails, and shut eyes. They were many colors, some grey, others striped or calico and not at all scruffy like their mother. I was ecstatic with love for them.

Evidently, Mom didn't much care for cats because she made it clear that my new kitten family was not going to move with us back to the dam during summer vacation. I implored her because Jim had a dog at the dam. Why couldn't I have the kittens? Mother Cat could catch and eat all those mice in our house. Mom refused, reminding me yet again of what the superintendent said about pets. This was her standard parental excuse whenever the subject of pets came up.

I tried a different tack and reminded her of how cold and hungry Mother Cat was when we first came. I asked if we were going to leave her babies all alone to freeze and starve. Mom replied that it would soon be hot summer and the cat could hunt for her food. All the babies needed was their mother's milk. Mom assured me that she was a wild animal and knew how to raise her babies to become wild too. They would get along just fine.

So, I gave up my argument. Besides, Mom kept us so busy that week that I barely had time even to check on the kittens. The end of the school year, for a teacher, is always hectic: grading final tests; filling out report cards; completing the attendance register; taking inventory; plus, there was the eighth-grade graduation and party. In addition to the school hullabaloo, our household belongings must be packed, because we were promised a lovely furnished house across the road from school for the next year. Mom was directing chores and issuing orders every waking moment.

Finally, the last day arrived, and Mom had us hauling out clothing baskets, piles of linens, and boxes of household equipment, which we were instructed somehow to stow in the rumble seat of the Ford. Periodically, Mom carried out a load and rearranged stuff to create more space. After one such trip, she marched back to the house all furious and holding a tiny kitten in her hand. "Doris, I found this kitten in the clothing basket and I distinctly said you could not take a cat to the dam!" "But Mommy," I complained, "I didn't pack that kitten in the car. You told me I couldn't." Mom turned her accusations toward Jim. "Nope, not me either," he replied. "Well, somebody in this family is not telling the truth," she asserted, as she tucked the tiny critter back into its nest.

The next load I carried out disclosed two more furry little babies nestled in the clothing basket. Just then, as Mom came out the door, we both watched Mother Cat, gently carrying another baby by the nape of its neck, leap up on the rumble seat and deposit her youngster in the basket. The cat was packing up too. One would think that would convince Mom to change her mind. But even with our renewed pleas for clemency, Mother Cat and her family stayed behind. We drove away sad and cat-less and there was no trace of cats near the shack when school began again that fall. That little girl deep down inside me is still brokenhearted.

Even though we were heading back to the Dam without my darling kittens, I couldn't be too sad. We had three whole glorious months of vacation stretching ahead. We sang as we bounced along the road and into camp. Dad seemed pleased to get his family back and the world was a rosy place. We quickly settled in to our lazy hazy days of summer, enjoying the same kinds of activities we remembered from the previous two summers. I was going to have another birthday soon, and that reminded me of the fun I had enjoyed while cooking with Grandma last summer. That experience emboldened me to think perhaps I could try a bit of cookery on my own.

Years later, as I peered out the window of a plane, I was inspired to write:

Mathematical Cream

Jet Props swirl cream clouds into blue-mint sky pudding.
Emerging in sunshine, I spy a whipped cream pie.
π in the sky?

Whenever I read the poem, I feel as if Mom should have been sitting beside me on that plane. She, above all others, would giggle at its silliness. This bit of nonsense about cream sends me back to my mother's kitchen, and a youthful solo cooking attempt which unfolded that summer at the Owyhee Dam.

A whole mish-mash of odors emanated from my mother's kitchen cupboard, where she stored Folger's Coffee, Hershey's Cocoa, Ovaltine, White Satin Sugar, Gold Medal Flour, Morton's Salt, Argo Corn Starch, Arm & Hammer Baking Soda, Calumet Baking Powder, and Old Fashioned Quaker Oatmeal. What is it? A trace of cinnamon? Vanilla for sure; pepper; Hunt's Catsup; Colman's Dry Mustard in its bright yellow tin and regular French's Mustard; bottles of Worcestershire and A-1 Sauce used to disguise the wild flavor of Dad's-out-of-season venison; stew spices like sage and bay leaf; burnt grease on the unwashed waffle iron; dust from the hard-to-reach high top shelf. Never have the odors from my own cupboards elicited that vivid sense of long-ago times.

Yet, in an unexpected moment, I find myself in a situation where a certain whiff brings memories flooding back. I become once more an eight year-old who is poring over *"Aunt Sammy's Radio Recipes,"* a book whose vegetable and meat sections are pristine, while the candy and cake sections are stained, tattered, and stuck together with spilled batter. I am once again pulling items from Mom's cupboard to concoct a fledgling attempt at culinary art. I see it as though it is happening right now.

First, you must realize that I'm all alone for my culinary escapade. Dad, Mom, and Jim drove to town. But because I didn't choose to ride for hours fighting with Jim in the rumble seat, I was allowed to stay home. Since they're gone, I choose without permission to bake a cake. I check Aunt Sammy's directions for plain yellow cake. She says to preheat the oven and grease a cake pan. That I can do. Mom allows me to use the oven. And, we always have a bowl of bacon grease sitting around.

Our kitchen is small. I tromp to the three-burner stove that has a deep well-cooker in the fourth spot and turn on the oven. Then three steps over the worn-out linoleum take me back to the low cupboard shelf by the sink to find a cake pan. The bacon grease can has black crumbs of bacon on the bottom, but I carefully pick out any bits that accidentally get rubbed on the cake pan and wipe them on the seat of my playsuit. Next, I reach on my tippy toes to get down two crockery bowls, since the recipe says that flour and stuff goes in one and butter and sugar go in a different one. I don't see the reason for that. It just makes more dirty dishes, but I started out determined to follow this recipe and get it right. I plunk the two largest chipped mixing bowls down on the linoleum-covered drainboard, pull out the wobbly utensil drawer and hunt around in its clutter until I find a big stirring spoon. Now I'm ready to get things out of Mom's cupboard and measure out the flour, salt, and baking powder into the bigger mixing bowl. I spill quite a bit, but it's easy to brush off onto the floor, wiping my floury hands on my belly.

Then, Aunt Sammy instructs something puzzling: "Cream the butter and sugar." I think, "That's strange. She doesn't say how much cream to use." Oh well, the butter part is easy. I wonder if I should use that much butter because it costs war-ration stamps. Maybe it'll be okay to use only half so Mom won't notice. Following the recipe exactly can't be that important, and I sure don't know how much cream to use. I decide to pour as much canned milk (what we call "cream") over the pat of butter as seems right and then I dump them both into the first bowl with the flour and other stuff.

This is so easy! Now, I need to crack the eggs, add the vanilla, and stir it all. After that, all I have to do is scrape the batter into the cake pan, carefully slide it in the hot oven and set the timer for thirty minutes. Things start to smell delicious! I eagerly await the finish of my glorious surprise for the family. When the oven timer dings, I am so excited to peek in the oven.

Oh No! That's not cake! This flat mess in the pan is all wrong. It's not how Aunt Sammy said it would look. I'm supposed to check it with a toothpick to see if it comes out clean. My toothpick gets stuck in it and won't even lift out of the glue! The kitchen is a mess and when Mom comes home she is going to send me out to the lilac bush to choose the switch she's gonna use on me! Last time I messed up, she sent me back to cut a switch larger than the one I brought. This time she'll expect me to bring in the whole bush! Then guilt sets in. I am very aware that flour, sugar, and butter cost lots of war-ration stamps. Dad even worries about driving to town because we're almost out of gas and new-tire stamps. Mom tells us to run barefoot all summer so we can save the shoe stamps for school. And here now, I've wasted our whole month's supply of food stamps. Dollar cost doesn't even register.

Then the solution dawns. We have nice soft dirt out by the garage because we are growing a Victory Garden to help the war effort. I do what any smart kid would do. I head outside with my ruined surprise, dig a hole, scrape out the sticky goo, and bury the evidence. All that's left is to wash the messy pans and slick up the kitchen. After that, I'm free to amble out to my tall California Poplar to swing, sing and dream up stories while I await the family's return. When they arrive, they bring me treats for being the good little lonely daughter left at home.

Since Mom was never very thorough in teaching me how to cook, I was forced to wait until I studied cooking in high school Home-Ec class to understand the different meaning that "cream" has. I never confessed to my mother. As a young child, I was far from innocent and was downright sneaky in my mischief. I quite often failed to confess unless I was flat-out-caught in the act by my parents.

But, I later learned that the mischief I did couldn't hold a candle in sneakiness to the misdeeds of young Ibrahim growing up on the other side of the ocean. I was an amateur. Ibrahim, while still very young, began to smoke. Since no one was aware then of the health risks caused by smoking, and though his parents might have wished that he would not smoke, it was fairly common behavior for a child of that age in Al Husn. However, Ibrahim was not allowed to have cigarettes with him at school, so he tried to hide them in the sleeve of his school uniform. His teacher always confiscated the cigarettes, but finally, Ibrahim developed a successful plan to hide them in the crack of a stone wall on his way to school.

In Al Husn, almost all of the men smoked. Toufiq and his friends often "rolled their own," using strong varieties of locally grown tobacco. To make it easier to roll, they added a small amount of moisture to the mix. Consequently, the cigarette did not stay easily lit if the smoker paused to carry on conversation, and his friends would tease him because his cigarette always went out. With great humor, Toufiq coined a witty Arabic rhyme: "*Ishrub heeshi, Meta keeshi,*" which loses its charm in translation but means "If you choose to smoke that kind of tobacco, do not take long to speak."

When commercial cigarettes became available, it was customary for a tray with various brands to be provided in the visiting room as a matter of hospitality. Young Ibrahim sat in the room listening to guests speaking of how this brand "tasted" better than that brand. So, of course, he needed to find out about that taste for himself.

Once, he and his friends pocketed some of the strong, locally-grown tobacco and some cigarette papers. They sneaked out of the courtyard, huddled against the outside wall, rolled the cigarettes, and lit up. His friends only lightly puffed, but Ibrahim knew how his father inhaled, so he pulled in the smoke as deeply as he could.

His little mouth filled up with saliva and he felt sure he would vomit. He became very dizzy and lay down at the side of the wall to sleep. Toufiq's friend, Mahmoud Rashdan, discovered him and carried him inside to Miriam. "I think your son may be ill!" Miriam was alarmed until she came close enough to sniff the aroma wafting off him. Parental disapproval did not prevent Ibrahim from continuing to experiment with cigarettes, but throughout his growing years, smoking was intermittent and more of a social activity until he became a habitual smoker while studying in the United States.

Another misdeed to which Ibrahim never confessed occurred in winter during his sixth year of school. An unusual snowfall created joy among the students, and unheated schools were still much warmer than the outside weather, so the teachers released the students to the playground while they all stayed inside for warmth. Ibrahim and his playmates were enjoying a great snowball fight in the school yard when a teacher dared stick his head out the door of the second story balcony. With deadly accurate aim, Ibrahim's snowball hit him smack in the face before he could duck inside. The teacher must have had no idea who threw the snowball, because Ibrahim got away with it.

Thankfully, during these years, Saleh Rashdan, Toufiq's Muslim/Orthodox godson, became a good influence on Ibrahim. Ordinarily, a person in Al Husn would never be both Muslim and Orthodox. Saleh was the exception due to the friendship between Toufiq and his father, Mahmoud, who honored his vow to baptize his first-born son in the Orthodox Church.

Saleh was a highly intelligent person, but while still a young man, he chose to stop formal schooling. Mahmoud helped him establish his own shop where he sold convenience items such as cigarettes, notions, candies, and magazines. While he waited for customers to come by, it was Saleh's custom to sit in the shade at the front of his shop and read from quality Egyptian political magazines containing prose and classical Arabic poetry. When Ibrahim was released from school for the day, he went to sit with Saleh as one might do with a beloved older brother.

Saleh is responsible for introducing Ibrahim to the beauties of poetry. Their favorite pastime was reading aloud a line or two of Arabic poetry. First, Ibrahim read and then waited for Saleh to finish the stanza from memory. Then, they reversed roles. Saleh read the beginning lines and gave Ibrahim opportunity to finish the stanza from memory. In this way, Ibrahim advanced his powers of memory, developed a life-long love of poetry, and Saleh continued his rich self-education.

Sometimes, Toufiq woke from his evening nap and strolled down to join them at the shop. He smiled at the two with their heads huddled together over a magazine. Saleh would offer *Ishbini* a cup of tea. This form of address surprised Ibrahim, because "*Ishbini*" is what one calls a Godfather. Until then, Ibrahim was not aware that Saleh, a Muslim, would have a Christian Godfather, never mind that it was his own father.

Ibrahim often reflected on the loving care offered to him by his mother and father. Once, when all the sons were asleep on pallets in the courtyard, Toufiq attempted to wake them up for the day. He would go to the pallet of older brother, Yacoub, and kick it with his toe saying, "Get up, you lazy, the sun will strike you in the face! It is almost noon! " But, when Toufiq went to Ibrahim's pallet, he would pat him gently on the shoulder and say, "Son, get up now. I have just brought cool, fresh fruit from the market. You must wake to eat some before it gets warm from the sun."

Ibrahim thought all this special attention and loving kindness suggested that Toufiq saw himself in Ibrahim. Toufiq, during his younger days, also had high abilities which he often wasted on mischief or were denied fulfillment due to circumstances. When Ibrahim's own children were asked to consider why their father seemed to receive such special attention, the answer came quickly. "You must always love the bad kid the most!" Though Ibrahim was full of mischief, his teacher urgently insisted that Ibrahim must be allowed to further his education because of his obvious abilities.

So, Toufiq and Miriam consulted family and village friends, who recommended Miriam's brother, Ibrahim, who had converted to the Seventh Day Adventist religion. He became a professor of Arabic language at the Adventist Middle East College in Beirut, Lebanon, and the college program was highly structured to conform to religious beliefs. The family decided that Ibrahim, a graduate of the sixth grade, should spend the next period of his education at Uncle Ibrahim's school in Beirut. Ibrahim began his seventh grade year in a Catholic school in Al Husn while his family prepared his application papers, and when his acceptance came through, the family energetically began to prepare for his going away to school.

When our daughters were leaving home for college, there were many trips to the variety store to purchase basic needs. But Miriam hand made everything. She spent long hours sewing new sheets from sturdy, quality muslin. When finished, she labeled the corner of each sheet for identification. She would be amazed to find one of those sheets still in his family eighty years later. It traveled with him to each of his destinations and now rests in a bottom drawer of the kitchen where we make use of it as a "bread sheet" when baking *Kubiz*, pocket bread. It is now very thin and much mended. But we can still see his Anglicized initials, *AA*, embroidered in red, at the corner, and we always pause to remember the hands that made it.

With tears streaming down her worn cheeks, Miriam kissed him goodbye, "*Trouh wa tiji bissalameh.*" Go and come back safely. Bidding farewell to his loved ones, Ibrahim set off on his new adventure. This was by far the longest trip he had yet taken, about 250 miles. He traveled with two other Arab students from his home town, planning to attend the same school. They made the trip by passenger car, and their route took them first to Irbid, on to Tiberius, and then northwest through Palestine to Haifa on the Mediterranean Sea. The next day, they drove farther north until they reached Lebanon.

Middle East College was an English-speaking charity mission, sponsored by leaders from America. The land for the campus was formerly a World War II military camp, and the purchase included books, machinery of all kinds, trucks, and cars but no dormitories. Ibrahim's travelling companions probably set him straight on what would be expected at Middle East College. This new school was very strict. Students were not allowed to smoke. The sect is vegetarian, so did not serve any meat. Ibrahim absorbed this information and determined that he would do his best to abide by the rules. He did not want to be sent back home in disgrace.

The new arrivals were directed to a small hamlet called Beit Mary, above Beirut, situated on a mountain overlooking the Mediterranean Sea. Since students could not yet live on campus, they were housed in large villas rented by the Mission until dormitories could be completed. It was a co-ed school, which was a new experience for Ibrahim. He remembered that some women students were in his classes and at religious meetings. Men and women also shared the cafeteria, but the rules were very strict about association with the opposite sex. Besides, he was too busy with work and study to take much part in social activity.

Students came from Arabic speaking countries throughout the Middle East. Most came from low-income families and were expected to work on campus to pay their way. As soon as Ibrahim settled in, he was placed in classes and assigned to outdoor manual labor. He toiled energetically, digging foundations for the new campus, helping to maintain the machine for drilling the well, sometimes working in the machine shop.

Ibrahim's English was still very weak, but since the language of mathematics is fairly universal, math became his subject of choice. The course textbooks for Math, Physics, and Chemistry also were purchased from the military and were self-teaching, brief, and concise. Ibrahim felt confident of his success. Mrs. Branson, wife of the President of the Middle East Mission, taught in the Department of Math. When Ibrahim came to sign up for courses she told him he would need to take Algebra before he'd be allowed to take Geometry. Ibrahim struggled to make her understand that Math was his strong subject. He hoped to take both courses simultaneously. She didn't think that it was a good idea, but she agreed to try it for the first two months.

Mrs. Branson gave a test to determine student progress at the end of each month. Ibrahim worked diligently and was well prepared for the first test, which consisted of ten questions. He answered all ten rapidly and was the first student to place his paper on her desk. As he prepared to leave the room, he had a doubt about the meaning of an English word. He turned around, walked to the desk of another student who was his friend, and asked for clarification on its meaning. When he learned the meaning, he realized that it made a difference in his answer. So he went back to the desk, retrieved his paper, and made the correction. He was still the first person finished.

All the while this was transpiring, Mrs. Branson monitored the class from the corner of the room. When she observed what he did, she marched to her desk, grabbed up his paper, scrunched it in a wad and threw it into the waste basket. All the class looked up in awe. Ibrahim didn't protest. He knew the subject; he'd answered correctly; he did not cheat. What she did with his paper was her choice. He walked out of the room.

Later, his friend went to the library where Mrs. Branson was grading the papers. He told her Ayyoub did not cheat. He just asked for the meaning of a word. When she heard this, Mrs. Branson told him to go back to the classroom and retrieve Ibrahim's paper from the trash. He did this, and she graded the paper. Every answer was correct. The next day, she handed back the students' work. When she handed Ibrahim his paper, she paused to tell him all the questions were answered correctly and that she had given him half credit.

At the end of the class period, Ibrahim took his paper to her work station in the library. He trembled as he laid his paper on the shelf and asked nervously that she either give him a zero or give him full credit. It was very important for him to know if she thought he cheated. His tone of voice probably angered her because she gathered up the paper, once more scrunched it into a ball, and threw it away. Paradoxically, she allowed him to stay in the Geometry class, and he did well.

In addition to math, Ibrahim continued his struggle to master English and was exposed to his first courses of mandatory religious education. He thought seriously about his religious beliefs and began to accept the philosophy espoused by the Adventists. Easter approached. Ibrahim discovered he would be allowed enough holiday time to make a trip home. He set off by passenger car via the northern route which went through Damascus. It should have been simple then to travel south to Irbid and Al Husn. But officials stopped him at the border between Syria and Jordan because he did not have the correct entry visa stamped on his passport. The officials sent him back to Damascus to obtain the correct stamp. Bad luck followed him. When he arrived in Damascus, the office was already closed for the day. He and other travelers huddled around a woodstove in a hotel to stay warm until the office opened the next morning. This meant he lost an entire day of his very short vacation. By the time he arrived in Al Husn, it was already Easter Eve.

His family was delighted to see him. He spent the evening visiting with them and his buddies until it was time to attend the Easter ceremony at the Orthodox Church. Hearing his dramatic memory of Easter, it was clearer to me why he was not very impressed when I invited him to a more staid Easter service many years later in the United States. At the stroke of midnight, the head Khoury banged on the church door three times. After each knock the Khoury called out, "Open ye gates for the Lord is risen!" After the third knock, he kicked the gate open and began to sing the anthem that goes with the resurrection. The Lord Jesus is risen! When the ceremony finished, the Easter celebration began.

Finally, it was time to sleep. Early the next morning, little children woke up and found Easter eggs. They cracked their hard-boiled eggs against their opponents' eggs to see whose would crack first. The first to crack had to be offered up to the winner, who then gobbled it down. Ibrahim spent the early morning getting a little more sleep. Toufiq eventually felt the need to tap his son gently on the shoulder and hesitantly ask, "Are you really going back to school, son?" "Yes, Yaba, I will get up right away. Thank you for waking me." It was only later that Ibrahim learned the reason for his father's hesitancy. It seems that when the family saw him climb out of the taxi upon arrival, Ibrahim's uncle said to Toufiq, "See, didn't I warn you? We knew that before we could see his head disappear down the road, we would see his feet returning." Miriam and Toufiq's unspoken concern was that he was expelled from school, coming home in disgrace. But that fear evaporated, and with hugs and kisses, they proudly waved him off on his journey back to school.

Back at school, Ibrahim continued his efforts, both at his studies and work for the college. He put in many hours of manual labor, and he began to log some financial credits which were applied toward his school expenses. No money changed hands, but the work credits paid for tuition, food, and housing. Ibrahim also found time to have some fun. He met a student from Syria who was skilled at playing the *Oud*, an eleven stringed instrument similar to a lute. The Syrian student wished to make some needed repairs on his *Oud* and invited Ibrahim to go with him to the home of an Armenian family in Beit Mary whose father made the instruments.

The visit was very friendly. Members of the family were smoking and drinking *Araq*, a licorice-flavored alcoholic beverage. Ibrahim happily accepted both cigarettes and drink while listening to the two performers take turns playing their lovely stringed instruments and walked back to his room that night with pleasant thoughts of the evening. However, even pleasant memories can turn sour. It is difficult to understand how news could travel so fast. Perhaps it was the small campus or its conservative climate, but soon Ibrahim was summoned to the office of the Dean of Students.

"Mr. Ayyoub, it has been reported that you smoked. Is this true?" "Yes sir, I have smoked." "Students at our school are forbidden to smoke. If we hear again that you have smoked, we will give you your passport to return home." Ibrahim heeded the warning and did no more smoking while he was a student of Middle East College. This incident, however, was not the end of trouble during the first year.

For most of the year, Ibrahim found it necessary to make his own way. Uncle Ibrahim Swidan, his mother's brother, was a professor at MEC, but his family was large and lived in a villa off campus. Ibrahim was not taking any classes taught by his uncle that year, so they had very little contact. One day, Uncle Ibrahim had reason to seek out his nephew to issue a warning that strong rumors were being circulated that Ibrahim was going to be accused of thievery. Ibrahim was astonished. His uncle told him that items were missing from the student living quarters in Beit Mary and that some students being questioned had named Ibrahim as the culprit.

Ibrahim knew of those students because he had heard about some of their actions. Since it was not his habit to carry tales, he had reported nothing of the things he knew, even when asked. But now, this situation colored his whole opinion of the Adventist scene. He knew he needed to speak out in order to clear his name. It was late on a Friday afternoon, almost time for the weekly celebration to welcome in the Sabbath. But, justice could not wait. Ibrahim immediately went to the Dean of Students' home and asked for permission to speak with the Dean. The Dean's wife ushered him into the living room and stayed to listen to the conversation. The Dean was seated and did not offer a chair, so Ibrahim stood in front of them and began to speak of his pent-up frustrations.

Ibrahim explained that his parents had sent him to the school in the hopes that he would learn good behaviors for living, but the examples set by teachers and other students taught him the opposite. He reminded the Dean that sheets made by his mother, with their distinctive red initials, had been borrowed and never returned. Now, the Dean would not look him in the eye when they met on campus. Ibrahim said that he had honored his promise not to smoke and had chosen not to tell tales on other students whom he had seen stealing, even though his silence had caused him to be under suspicion. Then, he spoke of events which could be proven by asking other students. He ended by agreeing that the school could choose to expel him, but if he went home, he would make it no secret that he had seen little to admire among Adventists.

The scandal was investigated. When other students were questioned, their information supported what Ibrahim had said. Soon after that, Ibrahim's sheets were returned. Three students were given their passports and sent home. Ibrahim learned the difficult lesson that there are times when even relatives will not or cannot intercede, when it is necessary to step forward for oneself. He realized that the way he dealt with the experience proved he was growing in maturity and independence. Both faculty and students appeared to be more cordial to him, and he once more felt comfortable in the religious community.

As the time for year-end finals approached, Ibrahim found that he was too busy with the outside labor assigned to him and missed Mrs. Branson's class. That day, she directed her students to study the sample exercises at the end of the text. Since Ibrahim missed the class, he asked a fellow student what went on. He was told to answer the questions at the end of the text.

It was the weekend, so Ibrahim had time to do the assignment. He neatly printed out each question and carefully illustrated each answer with its necessary geometric drawing. He ended with more than twenty pages of work and created a title page with his signature surrounded by small drawings of bunches of grapes. On Monday, he came to class and placed his papers on the top of his desk. Mrs. Branson walked past his desk and picked up the work, scanning through the pages. "Mr. Ayyoub, may I make copies of your work for use by the entire class?" He consented, saying it was hers to use as she pleased since it was his homework assignment. Mrs. Branson told him she hadn't assigned it for homework, but it would be a very useful tool as a study guide. She copied it for everyone and made sure to credit Ibrahim on the title page.

One of Mrs. Branson's final assignments for the year was given a week before it was due. She directed each student to create a large drawing incorporating geometric figures into a beautiful design. They could use the square, circle, triangle, parallelogram, rectangle, and ellipse. All the figures in the drawing should stand out and yet be an integral part of the whole. Ibrahim was keenly interested in this assignment and spent two or three days entertaining himself with its production. He decided it would be even more beautiful if he colored the different shapes so that they truly stood out. He finished his project, turned in the assignment, and headed off to work. He hadn't understood that Mrs. Branson had posed it as a contest among students.

That week, Ibrahim's physical work was particularly messy. Mr. Johnson, the shop superintendent, had constructed a primitive machine to drill for a new irrigation well. The drill was created from a used gasoline engine, a flywheel, and assorted moving parts. It went ka-klunk, pound, ka-klunk, pound, deep down in the hole. Regularly, all the moving parts required a gooey coating of grease. That was Ibrahim's job; he was the grease-monkey. After only a few minutes of work, he became as well-greased as the drill.

Shortly before noon, a student came running down the hill and yelled over the din of the drill that Mr. Johnson and Mrs. Branson wanted Ibrahim immediately. Ibrahim shouted back that he'd have to shower and change first, but there wasn't time. "They want to award the prize!" Ibrahim had no idea what he was talking about, but he knew he must obey a summons from his boss and his math teacher. So, he shut down the drill, wiped off as much grease as possible, and trudged up the hill.

He entered the Math department where all the Geometry class was assembled. Mrs. Branson did the honors. "Mr. Ayyoub, your geometric design has been judged the best of the contest. We wish to award you with this prize. Congratulations!" She reached out to shake his hand, but Ibrahim could not offer his greasy hand. Instead, he bent his arm so that she could shake his wrist. The prize was a book, which Ibrahim said he never did read. Reflecting on the occasion, he decided the true prize was in knowing that Mrs. Branson finally found a way to show that she valued his efforts. Besides, she gave him an "A."

CHAPTER 6

⊰•◈•⊱

Our Summer Lives

SHORTLY AFTER HE WON that prize, it was time for Ibrahim to head home for his first summer vacation since the beginning of his boarding-school experience. He felt great relief in being back with his family to enjoy the slower pace, and he luxuriated in freedom from the stresses of school and studies. He quickly settled back into his family's routines and customs, and he brought with him a new interest in religion, determined to share his new-found knowledge. He felt quite confident that his year of Bible study would become a "source of enlightenment" for his father.

"Yaba, do you know about the beautiful psalms and proverbs found in the Bible? I think these religious people in the Adventist Church are really good. The things they are teaching me will help me know how to live a good life." Toufiq smiled and quietly asked, "Did they also teach you about Lot and his daughters?" "Oh yes, the people of Sodom and Gomorrah were very sinful. God decided to destroy the city, but first he saved Lot's righteous family except for his wife who chose to look back and was therefore turned into a pillar of salt." Then Toufiq said, "There's more to the story. After they left the city, Lot's daughters managed to get him drunk so that they could behave badly with him. The Children of God are not always free from sin." Ibrahim sat there in silence thinking, "My father is so far ahead of me. I'd better shut up."

Toufiq did not push his views, but Ibrahim's estimate of his wisdom was correct. He was a learned student of political and religious thought, and he formed his own views about most religions. The story is told that the teachers of the Government school often said to each other as they walked to Toufiq's home, "Things are too quiet today. Let's go and visit with the Modern Old Man." Ibrahim's brother, Suleiman, also listened to Ibrahim praising the goodness of the people at Middle East College, who were trying to share their beliefs with others. His advice was much more specific, "Yes, that is a commitment they may have, but it would be wise for you to keep your eyes open and see what else they are capable of doing." Ibrahim kept this counsel in his thoughts and continued to enjoy his summer at home.

In addition to talks with his father and brothers, Ibrahim spent some of his vacation days watching and helping his mother. She was a genius at using the sun, the air, and salt to preserve food. When tomatoes were in season, she removed seeds and skin and slowly cooked the juice down to a thick salty paste which was stored in huge brown, rough-cast and unglazed pottery jars. A heavy layer of crusted salt kept the air from entering to cause spoilage. One or two spoons of the tomato paste reconstituted with water would season an entire meal. The same process was used to preserve meat. Rendered fat from the lamb was used to seal the tops of the meat containers. These food storage containers are still cast by potters and fired in villages throughout Jordan. We saw huge stacks of them in a marvelous variety of shapes and sizes offered for sale along the road when we drove from Amman to Al Husn.

Certain food preservation tasks were accomplished in the spring, long before Ibrahim's vacation. Cheese, butter, and yogurt were already prepared for his enjoyment. When the sheep were lambing, milk was abundant. Ibrahim remembers going with his father while still a small child to where the shepherds were tending the flocks. Toufiq used a stick and his mantle to prepare for the little boy a small tent, out of the dusty wind. The shepherd always carried in his pouch a container of rennet. He would milk a bowl of fresh milk, sprinkle in a pinch of rennet, and Ibrahim would dine on the fresh sweet curds which formed.

Milk was carried to the shepherd's compound in quantity, made into yogurt and placed in a churn. A traditional village churn was created from a sheep skin from which the wool had been removed. The skin was then cured and sewn into a bag. Rocking this bag back and forth separated the *zubdeh,* butter, from the *shaneeneh,* whey. The whey and butter were then carried to Miriam's compound. The whey was salted, dripped through a bag, shaped into small balls, and spread on a white sheet up on the roof to dry in the sun and become *jameed*, hard-as-stone dried yogurt. Miriam could soak the balls of *jameed* overnight in water and rub them, using a special brown pottery bowl with rough interior, to reconstitute it into cooking sauce. Jordanian women still cook with this unique ingredient, and so do I when it is available, but now we use an electric food processor to speed up the reconstituting step.

The butter was simmered over a slow fire with a small handful of bulghur wheat. As it boiled, Miriam skimmed off impurities until nothing was present except beautiful golden *samneh,* clarified butter. *Samneh* will keep without refrigeration in a covered jar. Our daughters and I regularly use this process. The aroma of eggs being fried in *samneh* always evokes savory memories of Miriam's cooking. However, if *samneh* is not stored correctly, it won't taste right. The year in which Ibrahim's older brother, Nasser, prepared for his wedding, Miriam sent Toufiq to purchase 50 gallons of *samneh* for use in cooking the wedding feast. It arrived in ten five-gallon containers. Miriam checked its quality and felt somewhat worried about it. So, she prepared a family meal using the *samneh*. She asked the family to taste and offer opinions. Each person gobbled up the offering and pronounced it good until it was little brother Naim's turn.

Naim was not more than six or seven at the time, but he was known for his excellent sense of taste. As he ate, he moved the food around his tongue, sniffed deeply at his plate and told his mother, "There is something wrong with the *samneh*. It does not taste delicious as it should." Miriam asked Toufiq to return it to the seller. She wanted the very best for their son's wedding and used only the best ingredients in her cooking. Later, she discovered the *samneh* had been stored in a damp cellar causing it to absorb moisture, and giving it a slightly musty flavor which only she and Naim had detected.

Each spring, Miriam and her daughters also prepared *jubne,* sheep milk cheese, in huge quantities. Milk was warmed to "baby-milk" temperature; then rennet was stirred in and left to clabber. Next, it was salted and dripped through a bag. With all the whey removed, the cheese was placed on a tilted surface to drain, then covered with a clean wooden board and weighted with stones or bricks to press out all remaining liquid and form a firm block of cheese. When finished, the cheese was cut in squares the size of brownies and stored in water "salty enough to float an egg." In later years, I learned to make a fairly successful *jubne* from cow's milk.

To serve the *jubne,* the cheese was soaked in fresh water over night to remove the excess salt. This luscious, somewhat chewy cheese can be fried and popped into a piece of fresh baked *kubiz,* Arabic pocket bread, or it can be eaten separately with olives. This delight was Ibrahim's favorite during his summer at home. He shared many breakfasts of *shai*, sweet tea, with *jubne*, olives, bread, olive oil and *za'ter,* a lemony-flavored spice mixture made from ground sumac and oregano mixed with crunchy whole sesame seeds.

After such a delicious breakfast, Ibrahim felt fortified to offer help to his brother Suleiman. His sister's husband, Rajah, decided during the summer to construct a new building on his land. Rajah requested that Suleiman mark the square corners for the foundation, and Ibrahim offered to help. Suleiman sent him back to the house for his survey tools, telling him to bring a tape measure at least 12 units long. Ibrahim turned back to the house and found the correct tape but wondered why the tape had to be at least 12 units in length. When he asked, Suleiman raised his eyebrows in surprise and said surely Ibrahim, who had just won a prize in Geometry, must be aware of the Pythagorean Theorem. To design a proper right triangle, one must have a measure that is at least 12 units in length. While in class, Ibrahim drew many diagrams illustrating that same simple theorem. But now it dawned upon him that textbook geometry had little value if he did not know how to apply it to a practical situation. Once again, during his first summer home, 14-year-old Ibrahim wisely decided to close his mouth and pay attention to his elders.

Ibrahim spent many hours observing, listening, and learning from his elders. On most evenings, Naimeh and her husband, Abu Adeeb, came to take part in the conversations. Abu Adeeb liked to farm and was highly successful in managing his large tract of wheat land. Toufiq greatly admired Abu Adeeb's expertise in caring for the land since it was not something he could do. Toufiq reminisced about his own childhood when he was assigned heavy farming chores and how he hated it. He could always expect laughter from his audience when he joked about his feelings with this story. "If a brother of mine should be murdered, I would chase the murderer to the end of the earth to seek revenge. That is, unless the killer happened to run onto a piece of farmland. Then, I must refuse to follow, and the killer will be allowed to go free."

On lazy, quiet summer days in Al Husn, many people came to visit, family and friends who traveled to Toufiq's door whenever possible. They were influential people, including Abu Adeeb's brother, Majid Ghanma, a lawyer who later became a judge and his elder brother, Dr. Amjed Ghanma, who worked in Beirut for the Iraq Petrol Company. Another important guest that summer was Amjed's relative, Khaleel Ah Salem, a graduate of American University of Beirut. Khaleel served in the Jordanian Ministry of Education and later at the Ministry of Finance. He was a brilliant mathematician, Harvard educated at government expense, and a contributor to Jordanian textbooks.

When Dr. Amjed visited, his wife and two little children accompanied him. Ibrahim remembered a beautiful example of medical common sense practiced by Dr. Amjed. Dr. Amjed's wife dressed her children in their very best clothing, freshly laundered and ironed to make a good impression on the village relatives. Since visitors came in and out at various times, it was her hope to keep the children looking fine throughout the day, which is a reasonable wish for a mother when she takes her children visiting. But when her children arrived in the humble dusty courtyard, they immediately began to chase around, playing happily with their many little cousins. Their mother found it difficult to see them soiling their good clothing and began to chastise them for getting dirty. Dr. Amjed stepped quietly aside to suggest to his wife, "We should leave them be! They need to be exposed to the dirt so that they develop immunity. It is very healthy."

The story of children happily playing in the dirt begs for the telling of a story about Ibrahim's younger brother, Naim. This would have taken place much earlier and was joyfully retold every year when family gathered. Naim, himself, never tires of sharing the humor of it. He was just a small tyke at the time and did plenty of chasing around in his little *dishdashi*. Naim's Godfather stopped him to say, "Naim, look at your *dishdashi*! How did you manage to get it so dirty?" Naim stopped to look down at his very soiled front and replied, "No, I'm not dirty!" Then he turned his backside to his critic saying, "See, I am very clean on this side."

When guests arrived, it was time to prepare a feast. Miriam had a reputation for excellent cooking, and she began the task of preparing *Mensafe,* a special Bedouin meal of lamb, rice, and sauce. She was joined in her labors by her two married daughters, Subha and Naimeh, who lived nearby. An important aspect of family life is the sharing of work among the women. It is a time when many hands, accompanied with visiting, gossiping, and laughter, make work easier while they prepare a meal which requires hours of elaborate preparation.

For the feast of *Mensafe,* an entire lamb is slaughtered. Nothing from the sheep is wasted. The hide is scrubbed with a curing mixture, such as saltpeter and alum, wrapped in a cloth and tucked away in a cupboard. Months later, the cured hide will be given as a gift rug in memory of the feast. We received such a rug after our visit to Al Husn. My children agree with me that a sniff of that soft wool evokes loving memories of times spent with our Jordanian family.

All the meat of the lamb is carved into bite-sized chunks of meat with smaller bones left intact. The meat is simmered until tender with onions, salt, pepper and *bahar,* a spice mixture of cinnamon, allspice, nutmeg and cloves. Miriam kept close watch on this pot and on the pot of *mlehiyeh,* reconstituted *jameed,* simmered with garlic, *samneh,* and *bahar.* Cooking *jameed* smells like good, strong cheese when it is melted. *Mlehiyeh* requires stirring and checking for taste and consistency. It must be thin, but not watery, have a salty tang but not be briny.

Another huge container is used to cook the short-grain rice seasoned with turmeric, which turns it golden. Thin pasta, toasted brown and similar to vermicelli, is combined with the rice. When tender, the meat is added to the pot of *mlehiyeh* for the final hour of simmering. One daughter would chop bits of lamb and pan braise them in *samneh.* Imagine the aroma of meat sizzling in butter! Another daughter would toast a large quantity of *snobar,* pine nuts, in *samneh* to be used for garnish.

All these items were cooking at once on one or two-burner propane appliances. Perhaps Miriam's daughters brought their propane burners from their homes. The other women could offer opinions on the meal's progress but Miriam was the smiling queen whose directions and decisions were followed. In her full-length black robe and headdress, Miriam would reach out to the pot with her long wooden spoon to stir and taste. When finished to her satisfaction, she said one word, "*Kwaiseh.*" Nice. There is more to the experience that is *Kwaiseh* than simply the cooking food. It is the beauty of her hands and smiling face, the smooth cooperation between mother and daughters, the simplicity of the cooking arrangements and the knowledge that they are making all this effort to honor the guests. Indeed, there was an abundance of *Kwaiseh!*

Miriam, Queen of Kwaiseh

Delicious aromas would float throughout the compound. Everyone knew that Ayyoub was preparing a feast. Portions of such a feast were always carried to the homes of elder relations. Ibrahim remembered being sent with servings of the food to relatives who lived alone and were no longer able to cook for themselves. Miriam sent him to an old woman who lived very close and who had lost all her family. When he handed her the dish of food, she cried, "Wait! I have something for you." She brought from her cupboard a small pot of cold boiled rice. "Hold out your hands." She dipped into the pot and piled a scoop of cooked rice into his outstretched hands, which Ibrahim ate as he walked back home. He understood her desire, as a matter of pride, to reciprocate with a gift of her own.

When cooking was completed, the meal was spread on a huge flat pan three or more times the diameter of my largest pizza pan: first, a huge mountain of rice, then carefully arranged servings of the stewed lamb, then the *mlehiah* was dipped over it, and last the daughters sprinkled on the garnishes of browned lamb bits and *sno-bur*. A side bowl of piping hot *mlehiah* would be close at hand for those who desired more sauce. The ancient Bedouin way to serve the meal was in the reception area with guests seated on mattresses. They sat around the *mensafe*, and each guest carefully ate with only one hand from a specific area of the tray. Balls of food were formed in the palm of the hand and deftly popped into the mouth with a flick of a thumb. However, for large numbers, Toufiq's guests were offered plates and utensils, and they often ate at small tables. The Bedouin arrangement was inconvenient for a crowd.

When a guest finished eating, Ibrahim's task was to attend the guest by pouring a thin stream of water from a small-spouted pitcher over outstretched hands, and offering a towel for drying. Younger members of the family waited in the kitchen area for the guests to eat their fill. They stood around a tiny table loaded with an abundance of leftover food and served themselves buffet style.

It is a rich meal which requires a counter-balance when the meal is finished. Therefore, dessert is often a huge tray of fresh-washed *khiar*, baby cucumbers. The best *khiar* come from the valley of Jerash about 25 kilometers from Al Husn. My family always considered pie, cake, or ice cream to be appropriate dessert, so the offer of cucumbers struck me as strange. But one bite into that cool, juicy crunchiness convinced me that it was exactly what was needed and desired. In later years, on the farm in America, Ibrahim learned to grow a cucumber similar to those and always called them Jerash cucumbers.

On other occasions, instead of cucumbers, the guests were offered fresh fruit. When the season for pomegranates arrived, Toufiq bought large quantities of them and stored them on high shelves in the house walls. When it was time for dessert, Toufiq directed Ibrahim to climb to the shelves and bring the fruit to the family. Miriam usually commanded, "Son, select the ones which must be eaten immediately before they spoil." Ibrahim was amused when she said this, because immediately Toufiq countered her direction, "No son. Pick the nicest ones. For once we should enjoy eating a perfect fruit, instead of being forced to save the worst ones from rotting."

Sometimes a guest could not stay long enough for a feast to be prepared. But there was always time to share a cup of coffee. The grinder of the coffee beans, be it father, son or nephew, beats a personal rhythm. Tek, tak, teka, teka, tek, tek, dunk; or dig, diggety, dig, dig, duk, duk, donk. He flings his arm up and down, pounding the *Mehbash,* the mortar and pestle, as if it were a musical instrument. Onlookers feel the need to clap or dance to the music while they drink in the aroma of freshly roasted coffee wafting from the mortar.

Coffee grinder

Ibrahim with Mehbash

In my house, the family's ancient brown *Mehbash* is displayed as a work of art, and it is no longer used.

Over a hundred years ago, it was carved from the trunk of the *Bootum,* the Gum Arabica, which is a Jordanian hardwood. Tiny age cracks have formed along its sides, but the intricate triangles and niches of carved decoration still capture the eye. Years of handling and polishing with restorative olive oil have given it a dull brown sheen. Toufiq or one of Ibrahim's brothers roasted and cooled the coffee beans before they were placed in the *Mehbash.* The raw beans were placed over a charcoal fire in the *Mehmaseh,* which is a steel pan with curved sides and a very long handle, something like a wok, stirred with a narrow steel bar attached to a steel disk, something like a spatula. Once Toufiq was asked to roast and grind the coffee when the King of Jordan came to Al Husn to attend a feast prepared by Toufiq's relative, Sulti Basha. He remembers the King stopping beside him to remark on the marvelous aroma pouring forth from the roasting coffee. Any friend passing by the home could smell the pungent roasting beans. Omar al Farrah, the poet of *al Bedia,* citizen of the desert, wrote of Arab coffee culture and "the *hadith,* the talking that goes on in the presence of the *hail wa dalleh,* cardamom and the coffee pot."

Coffee is brewed using a set of three unpolished brass coffee pots with graceful handles and pointed spouts. Ground coffee is added to water in the *dalleh,* largest of the three pots, and set to boil over a charcoal fire in the *mankal,* a brazier made of clay. The pot must be removed for cooling several times to prevent boil-over. Meanwhile, whole cardamom seeds release their sharp scent as they are pounded in the *Mehbash* and placed in the second pot. After the coffee grounds settle, the brew is carefully poured from the *dalleh* over the cardamom in the second pot, leaving the residue behind. The second pot is set to keep hot until guests arrive. At that time, coffee is poured into the *barjack,* the third pot, which is smaller and more decorative with scroll-work designs. Its spout is on the right side and the straight handle is arranged to allow a tip of the left hand to pour the strong, dark liquid into three tiny cups held in the right hand.

During Ibrahim's summer at home, he was often the one to make the rounds of the room, carrying three tiny cups and the *barjack.* The server offers the first three guests a cup containing a small sip of coffee. The tiny amount washes over the tongue and trickles down the throat, providing an instant caffeine buzz. The first time I was served this drink, I immediately thought, "Now that is coffee!" Custom dictates that the first three drinkers each take a cup, consume its contents and hand it toward the server. If one wishes another sip, it will be poured. If not, one gently shakes the cup to indicate "enough," and the server will move to the next in line.

Later in the evening, hot sweet tea was served, flavored with a touch of mint. Usually, Miriam or her daughters would arise to set the water to boil, add sugar, fresh mint, and a sprinkle of tea leaves. When properly steeped, it was poured into small glasses and served on a tray. So, with good food, strong coffee, fresh fruit, and sweet tea, the summer evenings slipped away. Ibrahim spent precious hours enjoying family, friends, and guests from out of town. With much laughter, old stories were retold, and good conversation lasted into the wee hours. Kerosene lanterns, sparkling stars, and glowing moonlight illuminated loved one's faces as they sat around the courtyard in the cool of the evening and on into the night.

On any given evening, there would be the retelling of favorite stories about Joha, the legendary Arab joker who performs mischief in village folk tales. If someone had a story to tell, he would often choose to provide the perpetrator with the name of "Joha." Our family fondly remembers a trilogy of Joha stories which undoubtedly were retold during Ibrahim's pleasant summer at home after his first year of being in Beirut. The first story has Joha hungering for *Halawa*. In most Middle Eastern countries it is sold as Halva, crystalized tahini paste of crushed sesame seeds and sugar. Joha entered the sweetmeat shop and asked the shopkeeper, "How much will you let me eat from one of these gallon tins of *Halawa* if I pay you this shilling?"

In those days, a shilling was a great deal of money, and the shopkeeper was delighted to reply," I'll let you eat as much as you can hold." So the bargain was made, the shopkeeper brought Joha a knife, and placed the tin of *Halawa* on a rug in the corner of his store where Joha sat down and began on his first huge slice. Since this confection is quite crumbly, crumbs fell on the rug as Joha ate, which he carefully picked up and placed in his mouth. The watching shopkeeper asked, "Why are you eating those crumbs when you have all that good *Halawa* in the tin?" Joha answered, "I am very hungry, and I must eat all of this tin and the crumbs, and I will also need another gallon tin to eat." The merchant became fearful that this big eater would ruin him so he yelled, "Stop! Here, take back your shilling and leave my store before you eat my whole supply." So Joha managed the good trick of eating his fill and getting all his money back too.

The second tale also has Joha hungry, but he has his own bread and just wants some shade in which to eat. He entered a shop full of the enticing aroma of Kababs roasting on a grill and asked the proprietor if it would be permissible for him to sit within its cool interior to eat his bread. The owner agreed, so Joha sat down on a rug and thoroughly enjoyed his bit of bread as he sniffed the rich aroma of Kabobs. When his bread was consumed, he stood to thank the shopkeeper but the cook grabbed his arm and demanded payment for the smell of his food. Joha thought about that for a moment and agreed. He reached into his pocket and jingled his stash of silver coins through his fingers. "There sir, is your pay. The sound of my money easily pays for the smell of your food."

The third tale is one Toufiq particularly loved to tell, not only because it spoke of the greed of merchants, but also because it spoke to his experience as the father of a child with afflicted eyes. Joha's son was suffering from an eye infection, so he went to the pharmacist, who reached for a large bottle and poured a bit of its liquid into a small container. He placed it on the counter and asked for a shilling, but Joha had only one piaster, so he placed his coin on the counter, grabbed the bottle, and ran. The owner ran after him, but Joha ran faster. Finally, the pharmacist gave up the chase and turned back to his shop exclaiming and cursing, "May God punish you. I'm still making 100% profit on that bottle."

Whenever Ibrahim thought on this sweet time of storytelling, which he spent in the pleasant company of his family, he knew that he was blessed. However, summer began to wane, and suddenly it was time for him to travel back to Middle East College. Once again, his family gathered to wish him well and a safe journey. But they felt much better about his departure this time. They had spent the summer in careful observation of his growth in maturity and his development toward adulthood. Though tears still streamed down Miriam's cheeks, her heart was more at ease as she waved her son goodbye.

Although Ibrahim's Jordanian summer was enjoyable for him, I suffered and fretted during my long American vacation. Perhaps it was the difference in our ages. Ibrahim was almost fifteen years old, while I had just turned eight. Almost an adult, he was able to relish the entire summer at home, visiting with family and friends while consuming his mother's excellent food. Meanwhile, I was still a child enduring the fact that I could not have my heart's desire, a bicycle. To alleviate the situation, I decided to become an entrepreneur.

I had dreams of owning my own transportation. Other kids had little peddle cars, but I was too big to fit in one. Or they had a real horse, but we were allowed no pets except a dog. Grandpa Bill helped out by teaching me to strip bark from a long willow stick, turning it into Trigger, my Palomino horse. I spent hours galloping on that stick horse with its string halter. Then, Dad bought me a second-hand push scooter, and I rode my trusty scooter constantly on the narrow cement walkway that stretched the length of the camp, often carrying messages to camp employees.

Even with my stick horse and my scooter, my desire for real transportation remained unsatisfied. I wanted a bicycle. Of course, when I approached my folks with my request, their answer was a given: "We have no money for it." But Dad thought seriously about my wish and proposed a way for Jim and me to earn money. He reminded us of how great the Owyhee Lake is for fishermen, and that they always needed bait. Ralph, the yardman, told him that the lawns were so rough because of the many night-crawlers that lived in them. Dad told us, "There's nothing better than a fat, juicy worm for catching a big old lake trout. You kids could start a worm business."

As usual, Jim was "gung ho" for the idea, while I was hesitant. I had no fear of worms. But night-crawlers, basking in the wet grass at night, are as long as young snakes, and we did have rattlesnakes that came into camp on occasion. Besides that, worm-catching must be done after dark! Worms were slippery and stretchy, and I experienced proof of that from walking over them barefoot after dark. The sensation of a slimy, frightened worm slithering into its hole under my bare feet sent me hopping and squealing to the house.

My brother had already terrified me the previous summer by persuading me to attend the movie "*Frankenstein and the Wolf Man*," when we visited family in Boise. He promised it would be funny but I spent the whole movie with my head under my coat. I peeked out just enough to register a hearty terror of full moons and dark nights. In addition to that hovering fear, it was obvious that we were headed for many a row over this joint enterprise.

Even so, with Dad's offered help, the partnership went forward. He dug a hole in the sandy riverbank under the row of California Poplars. Then he sank an old galvanized wash tub, filled with fluffy garden loam. "Now you kids will have to keep this loam damp, but not soaking. And you must mix in cornmeal and coffee grounds for worm food." Then, instructions for catching and selling the worms were doled out. "Jim, you're the fastest. You'll do the catching. Grab fast and hold on gently but firmly. The worm will try to stretch out and fight back because a bit of it is always still in the hole. Pull too fast and you'll break it. Too loose a hold and it will slip away from you every time. Doris, your job is to shine the flashlight ahead of Jim and hold the can. The biggest sales days will be the weekends, and when you put up your "Worms for Sale" sign, fishermen will be knocking on the back door as early as 5:00 a.m. I think they'll be willing to pay a penny apiece for good worms."

Immediately, I calculated that buying my $25.00 bicycle would require selling 2,500 worms, and that was just my share! Even so, amidst much bickering about who was doing what wrong, our venture began. I hated digging out my old shoes, "cuz they don't fit me no more but I'm not goin' out there barefoot!" Jim discovered he'd miss radio programs and complained about going out before they finished. Our mom started in each night, "It's getting late and you still have to catch your worms. Get moving, Joris!" Jim would moan, "Ah Mom, can't Doris do it by herself tonight? *Dagwood and Blondie* is about to come on," and I'd resist, saying, "Mommy, I'm not going out there alone, and I can't hold the flashlight and the can and have a hand to grab the worms."

We'd eventually get out the door, but then the real bickering began. "Dang it, Doris, shine the light in the right place! And quit stomping; you made a whole tangle of worms slip away." "I didn't stomp! You just go too fast for me to keep up. Slow down, and the light will be where it's sposed ta be." Sometimes Jim would get really angry and hit; I'd cry; and no worms would go into the tub that night.

Somehow, we developed regular customers who counted on us to supply their bait. Jim liked getting up early enough to sell the worms. Then I realized that he pocketed the payments with a promise to divvy up later. A promise seldom kept! Finally, we faced the July 4th disaster when I sleepily trundled out early to find the tub empty of worms. Working hard, we had prepared a large supply. But the worms had vanished and we faced angry fishermen, now thirty miles from town without bait! Later, Dad dug up the tub to discover the bottom was rusted out, which accounted for the great escape. I didn't earn enough for my bike that summer.

The next year, Jim opted out of the business, escaping much as the worms had done. But I plodded on. I learned to hold the light with one hand, while I used the other hand to grab that worm in a tug-o-war. I always felt triumphant when I won, and plopped it into the can sitting nearby on the ground. Working outside alone in the dark meant I also had to keep the Wolf Man at bay. But, I reached my 2,500-worm goal!

I had to settle for a "junior-sized" bike, all I could afford, which was almost too small for me. Dad taught me to ride, allowing me to solo around the block by our town apartment in Nyssa where we lived during my fourth-grade school year. He forgot to teach back-pedaling to brake, so I ran directly into a slow-moving car and scared the "bejezus" out of us all. There was no damage to my precious bicycle, though, which served me well until I completely outgrew it.

My dad strongly supported the worm business. I believe he was pleased to see me stick to the project until I reached my goal. Many years later, I learned that other kids in the family received his help for money-making projects. Judy and Sandy, two of my Boise cousins, visited Mom and Dad one weekend when, as a teen-ager, I was away at church camp. They remembered being excited about riding to the Dam in the Ford rumble seat. On the way there, Dad stopped at Skinner's Corner and bought several cases of soda pop. My cousins were allowed to sell those bottles of cold soda, packed in a large ice-filled galvanized bucket, to the people in the park on the 4th of July! The girls stood on each side of the bucket and carried it around the park, offering bottles to thirsty folks. Judy told me, "We had a variety of flavors to offer; I remember Orange Crush, Grape Soda, Coca Cola, and Root Beer. We sold every bit of the pop and could have sold more. Uncle Jesse let us girls keep the profits!" Dad had a soft spot in his heart for helping out little kids, and perhaps this was my Dad's quiet effort to teach his values of work and responsibility.

Another little kid caught my Dad's attention that summer. It was in late July. With nothing much exciting going on, lazy-day doldrums were settling in, and one morning, Dad came home to tell me, "Doris, there is a little blind girl, Ralph's niece, visiting at his house. You oughta go on up there to see her." I could tell from the way he spoke that this was not just a suggestion. It was an expectation. Not being socially adept at meeting new kids, the whole prospect seemed rather daunting. Besides, I had never before set foot inside Ralph's house. I really liked him, but since he never smelled too clean, I was a bit afraid of going into his home.

But, I went. The door was answered by a slender, pretty young girl about two years older than I. I told her who I was and that I lived in the house down the way. She said her name was Gennie and invited me to come in. I noticed the house was kinda dark, dingy and, indeed, smelled just like Ralph. I wondered why she didn't have the lights on to make everything more cheerful. Maybe I even bluntly asked why she was sitting in the dark. Of course, she made it clear that she didn't need any lights. And, as I grew to know her, I discovered she had the capability to create her own light from within.

I asked if she would like to come to my house to play. That seemed like an agreeable idea to her, so I took hold of her elbow to give the assistance I thought a blind person would need in order to walk to our house. That was when I received my first indication that she had a strong, independent nature and was prepared to teach me the correct way to do things. Gennie said, "Don't ever try to lead or guide me. Just hold out your arm and I will take it to walk beside you." So we headed off to my house. From then on, she became an important part of my childhood. We remained friends and think of each other as "Sis."

Gennie introduced me to a whole new world of experiences. Of primary importance was my newfound appreciation for what could be accomplished without sight. I found myself attempting to emulate the skills that Gennie exhibited while she moved about the house without smashing into things. After once being given a tour of our home, she had the layout memorized and moved with confidence wherever she wanted to go without holding on to my arm. Because she did it so well, I tried to do something similar with my eyes shut but always failed miserably, bumping into furniture, knocking over items and quickly opening my eyes again. Our family learned to leave the furniture arrangement unchanged, because anything out of place confused her.

My solitary mode of play quickly underwent a dramatic change, and I do mean dramatic! Gennie was light years ahead of me in imaginative play. She was an astute listener to radio and could suggest a whole repertoire of drama possibilities. We sat for hours on the edge of my bed talking the parts we chose to play in radio dramas. We each chose pretend names that changed daily, depending on our mood, and then acted out what would now be labeled improv theatrical radio programs. Also, she was well-read, having spent hours poring over thick Braille books at her school. She already knew most of the books I had read and filled me in on ones she thought I should read. When we weren't producing radio theater, I discovered that I enjoyed reading aloud to her from our county library books, and Mom also took time to read to us.

But our play was not always sedentary. Gennie was game for any outside activity I could come up with. We swung, climbed my tree, picked grapes and apricots, walked in the park, swam at Snively's Hot Springs, slept outside under the lilac bush and played tag. We even got my dad and brother involved in that game. Her sense of hearing was so acute, it was impossible to get away from her if she were "It." Any slight movement of ours sent her chasing skillfully after us.

I don't remember how long Gennie stayed that first summer, but visits during following summers were eagerly anticipated by both of us. Mom enjoyed spending time with Gennie and quickly became deeply interested in her educational progress. Gennie told us that during the school year she attended the Idaho State School for the Blind which was a boarding school in Gooding, Idaho. She freely stated that she hated it and thought it was a terrible school.

When summer came to an end, Gennie headed back to her hated school in Idaho, and we once more packed up our belongings to live near Pioneer School on week days. I started third grade, and Jim was in my mother's seventh grade class. Poor fellow! I have strong memories, later during my sixth grade year, when Mom was my math teacher. It was easy for me to turn around in our old-fashioned row desks to help the girl behind me understand long division, but I felt like I'd die if asked to solve a problem on the blackboard, because I had to stand there with everyone staring at my backside. My thinking froze, and even concepts that I understood just flew out the window. I developed a permanent aversion to the subject, because Mom's expectations and impatience with my performance were inhibiting. If Jim's experience was similar, he must have agreed that having your mother for your teacher is pretty rough.

During the school week, our living quarters at Pioneer were luxurious in comparison to the previous year. We had a comfy, cozy, furnished rental. The item that stands out in my memory was the large cabinet containing a wind-up Victrola and a collection of records. I can still hear "Barney Google with the Goo-goo Googley eyes" and "If I Had the Wings of an Angel, over these prison walls I would fly. I would fly to the arms of my true love and there I'd be willing to die." There may have been other records, but those two were significant because I loved the silliness of Barney Google. And, the poor guy in prison sounded so lost and hopeless. I was certain that, somehow, he needed to sprout those wings.

My penmanship folder from that year shows some appalling copy assignments which definitely imprinted prejudicial messages in our minds. I carefully wrote out all of the song lyrics for "Old Black Joe." Granted, Stephen Foster was a revered composer of American folk tunes, but "Gone are the days when my heart was young and gay / Gone are my friends from the cotton fields away" conjures up the image of the "happy darky" and of course, we have finally accepted that happy gaiety in those cotton fields was an illusion. There were other misguided, thoughtless selections, but my teacher was a product of her time. In 1943, in that community, racial superiority was a given.

As I grew older, I realized that my dad employed racist slurs and told racially offensive jokes. My mother always went out of her way to speak up for the neglected, the needy, or the child with challenges. Mom never spoke the way Dad did and chastised him. My present feelings against racism were planted during childhood by my mother. Given the large blocks of time when we kids were away from Dad, Mom was our primary adult influence.

One of the ways she directed our development was through storytelling. Leading up to Christmas that year, Mom took time on winter school nights to tell us stories of the frugal Christmases during her childhood. She would mimic her mother's voice as she cried, "Josie! Dolly! Hurry up now! Eat your oatmeal. Children must have a warm meal in their tummies before all this excitement begins." Mom told us that she frowned at her own untouched bowl and glowered at goody-two-shoes Dolly spooning up her last few bites. She remembered craning her neck around to catch a glimpse of the front room where a tiny fir tree covered with popcorn-cranberry strings and delights tucked in its branches beckoned to her.

Josie invented devious ways to avoid eating what she considered slimy stuff, such as forcing her little sister to eat it or slipping it to the dog, while her mother just as slyly taught her to eat it, knowing they were very lucky to have even the oatmeal. My grandmother would sit down in the rocker with a mystery pot on her lap from which she spooned up bits of something. Josie sidled up and repeatedly clamored to have a taste. Her mother refused, smiled and continued nibbling. After much begging, Mother eventually handed over the pot for Josie to finish up. Of course, the pot contained leftover breakfast oatmeal which Josie delightedly gobbled up saying, "Ummm, this is so good."

For them, gifts were practical, bare-bones items. Each child received a Christmas orange. Mom reminded us again of her greatest desire to be rich enough to go to school every day with pungent orange peel under her fingernails, so that she could waft them under the nose of the privileged rich girl in her class, Josie's nemesis. Because of these "hard-times" memories, my mother contrived to create different Christmas traditions for us. One change, the opening of gifts, occurred on Christmas Eve. And no oatmeal! We gathered for a dinner of ham and potato salad before we set upon the abundance of gifts piled around the tree. I now realize that the ever-present family debt must have increased by at least one hundred dollars from buying gifts on credit.

Christmas 1943 was memorable for us because Pioneer school was closed two weeks prior to Christmas due to an outbreak of Scarlet Fever. Mom piled us into the Ford, drove to Nyssa where she charged a large box of holiday food at Wilson's Super Market, oversaw the tie-down of a small fir tree in the Ford's rumble seat, and claimed packages from the post office that Santa delivered via Sears catalog. Then, she telephoned Dad that we were on our way. He monitored our travel time because, more than once, he needed to drive the government pickup to our rescue when we were in trouble. We sang songs led by Mom while we chugged along the bumpy, snowy road, driving past the haunted house where we kids always held our breath until we passed (because that keeps the ghost from following), past Snively's Hot Springs, hurrying through the rocky railroad tunnel before any rocks could tumble down, and on into the warm welcome of the camp.

Our arrival was punctuated with badgering started by Dad, who was often a bigger kid than we. He began while we unloaded the car, "Jo, you're home two weeks early. Everything is ready. Let's celebrate Christmas this weekend." Of course we kids loved the idea! She insisted we must enjoy a proper Christmas at the proper time. But Dad had spent a lonesome week without his family and would not let up. It was three against one, and Mom eventually gave in. "Okay, I'll prepare the food while you children set up the tree. But remember this well: if we have Christmas early, not one thing special will happen when the real Christmas arrives."

We decorated the tree with zeal, ate a quick late supper and tumbled into bed. The next day, we ate our ham and potato salad and squealed over our gifts. Mine was a much beloved doll, which I quickly named Nannette. Jim received a real submarine that would submerge and reappear in the bathtub water. The family gift was a glorious game called "Pieces of Eight" played like anagrams in which players earned gold and silver cardboard coins by correctly arranging letters into words using clue-cards. There were bags of candy and new books. I remember receiving at least two new *Nancy Drew* mysteries. Over the next two weeks, we delightedly enjoyed our gifts and listened while Mom read to the family.

The calendar alerted me to the fact that December 24th had arrived. My thoughts began to stew. "I know Mama said that Christmas won't come again because we celebrated two weeks ago. But I think Santa might not agree. Tonight I'm going to hang up a stocking on the heat register anyway. Santa will come like he always does." So I hung out my "hopeful stocking" and trundled off to bed.

Alas, I woke in the early morning to discover nothing. Nothing! My limp sad stocking sagged on the cold register. I have often thought about the lesson my Mom was trying to teach. She surely must have been tempted to satisfy my little girl longings. But in the end she opted for helping me learn something much more important. All choices and actions have consequences. I know it did not destroy my faith in Santa. He still arrives in regular fashion. My own little girls were often commanded to halt beside a closed bedroom door when they heard a hearty "Ho, Ho, Ho" which meant, "Don't you dare enter. Santa is busy working in here!"

But after Christmas vacation wound down, we had to resume the drudge of weekly trips to Pioneer School with all its lessons, chores, and wishes for the year to be over. And finally, it was over. We were delighted to learn that it would be the end of our Pioneer days, because Mom was promised a sixth grade teaching position in Nyssa for the following year.

When the school year ended, we once again headed to the Dam to enjoy the summer. I was hoping to see Gennie again if she could come for a visit with her Uncle Ralph, and I carried on with my worm business. I finally seemed to get the hang of it, and I was quite pleased to collect all the profits for myself. Jim was also happy to be out of it. Since he no longer had to share the burdens of a partnership, he was free to roam the area and to follow his own pursuits. Little did I realize that he also harbored dreams the same as I. While I was resigned to having a stick horse as a pet and concentrated my efforts towards earning a bike with my worm profits, Jim wished for a horse and actually made an effort to fulfill that dream.

When I became reacquainted with Tony, Jim's son, I was surprised to discover that Jim told his children about the pet horse he had at the Dam. For a while, I thought that perhaps Jim had followed in Grandpa Bill's footsteps by spinning exaggerated tales to his kids. But after reflection and after hearing more details from my nephew, I began to piece together how Jim could really have had a pet horse.

At the base of camp, after crossing the river on the trestle bridge, one could choose to turn left and drive on up to camp, or turn right and travel back downriver on the opposite side of the canyon. I seldom went far along that road, except to visit the dead steer when I wanted to watch the maggots at work. But I knew that road led to a farm. I knew about it because it was visible as we drove the main road into camp. I paid particular attention to it because it had a large working wooden water wheel. I was glad that we were forced to drive slowly, because I loved to watch the river turn the wheel to fill the attached tin buckets with water, which then poured into a tin-lined wooden trough. Mom told me the farmer used the water wheel to provide stock water and also to irrigate his pasture. I loved that water wheel, but not enough to walk downriver to see it up close.

Obviously, Jim checked out the farm many times. He was, after all, four years older than I and more adventurous. He was known to roam independently over much of the terrain surrounding the Dam. Tony said that he was like his Dad in that respect, because he also took off by himself to explore all over the many towns and countries they lived in while he was growing up. Neither of his parents ever knew about all the places he went.

Jim told his son that he wandered down that road to befriend a horse who grazed in the farmer's pasture. Tony remembered that his dad named the horse "Star," because it had a white star on its forehead. Tony remembered being very young and confused about a horse having a star on its head. I suspect that Jim was admiring the horse at the same time I was gawking at the water wheel. I have a vague memory of animals in the pasture, and one looked something like a brown and white spotted pony. Jim was highly interested in Indian horse stories while we were growing up, so maybe the object of his desire was indeed a paint. It really isn't surprising that Jim kept his interest in the horse a secret. If Dad had known Jim was hanging out at the farm, he would have been forbidden to go. Dad would have thought that no farmer wanted a kid hanging around and causing a nuisance.

So, Jim must have set about planning how best to make friends with his horse. Tony said that his dad decided to give the horse some sort of treat. Our entire family knew that our household supply of sugar was a very dear commodity due to war rationing. Jim would have needed to sneak a fistful from Mom's sugar canister before hiking several miles to the farm. He must have felt exultant when his new friend fi-nally trotted over to the fence and decided to lick up the sugar.

Taming a real horse was more interesting than galloping about on a make-believe Palomino stick horse. But then again, I enjoyed undying loyalty from my trusty horse, and I didn't need to sneak sugar from Mom's scant supply. I don't know how long the friendship lasted, nor do I know how much sugar disappeared in order to tempt the horse. Tony said the ending of the friendship was not happy. For some reason, whether out of perverse curiosity or lack of sugar, Jim one day decided to see if a handful of salt would work just as well.

Maybe he was thinking of the salt-lick blocks which farmers put out for their stock and that the horse would enjoy a little lick of salt. Or, knowing Jim, he might have decided that offering salt instead of sugar would be a good joke to play on his four-footed friend. Tony told me that the salt was held out in the same manner as the sugar. To Jim's great disappointment, the horse snorted at the taste of salt, trotted off, and refused to come back. On later visits, no amount of sweet talk ever enticed the horse to come close to Jim again.

After that, we two kids once again fell back on our usual solitary pastimes. Jim, in his loneliness, continued to be a pest by teasing and taunting me. And I spent all my free time daydreaming in my swing. Thankfully, this state of affairs was often in-terrupted with family excursions which didn't require a trip to town. The distance plus gas and tire rationing meant that we couldn't go driving down to town whenever we chose, even though our kitchen provisions were sometimes in short supply. Also, the folks limited the trips to town, because our grocery bill was always in arrears at Wilson's Super Market.

One excursion was great fun for us. Dad enjoyed giving us all a ride up to the Dam on the way to his work for the day. Sometimes, he allowed us to accompany him down inside the Dam, which was always a thrill. There was a locked elevator shaft that let out creepy groans and clangs when we rode down into the depths of the Dam to where the huge motors and pumps hummed loudly and the air smelled musty, damp, and mildewy. It was cool inside the passages, and we kids enjoyed playing hide-and-seek with Spot while we waited for Dad to do whatever maintenance sent him down there. Every once in a while, the passages would open on lookout platforms where we could stand to marvel at the tremendous height above and below us. If we stepped out on a platform close to the Spillway, we could stand under the spray, which felt just like being under a waterfall.

When it was time to head home, Mom often organized hikes, just for the exer-cise, back down the mile of winding, rocky road. She could usually entice us to ac-company her on the long walk if we were going downhill. Hiking from camp uphill to the Dam was difficult and seemed like pure torture to my sedentary way of thinking. But I enjoyed the walk down as long as Mom was there to keep Jim from being too obnoxious in his jokes at my expense. One tease which he invented scared the bejezus out of me every time he pulled the stunt. Just before we left the cement pavement to start down the road, Jim would scramble up to stand on the wide wall which served as a railing all across the Dam. He'd stand there, causing shivers in me just to see him. Then he'd yell, "Good-Bye Cruel World" as he jumped off the other side. He always did it at the edge of the Dam, where he could land safely on an outcropping of rock which was hidden from my view. But I fell for it every time, envisioning my brother leaping the full height of the tallest dam in the world.

Another family outing was a drive on up the road along the lake behind the dam and past the "Glory Hole," which is a structure built to deal with overflow when the lake is full. Beyond that was a boat ramp that worked on a winch to raise and lower fishermen's boats into the lake. It was my Dad's job to operate the ramp during the summer season. When he had no customers, he sat in his camp chair, wearing his pith helmet, which he had spray-painted with aluminum-colored paint to help reflect the sun, and dropped his fishing line off the edge of the boat ramp. In the late afternoon, Mom often packed an early supper, and we joined Dad for a picnic. If there were not many fishermen, he lowered the ramp down into the water about waist deep, and we were allowed to swim off it. I will always remember the delightful thrill of paddling out into the icy cold lake as I imagined how deep it was to the bottom. Perhaps overcoming any fear of that deep water was a great lesson for me, because I've always felt comfortable in water, no matter its depth.

The "Glory Hole" is built separately behind the Dam proper. It has been called that since the Dam was first constructed and refers to the round deep structure which can be raised or lowered to accommodate irrigation needs. The water that rushes down it flows out the other side of the Dam in huge quantities through the spillway that is now hooked to turbines. The rim was not too narrow and only visible during the fall when lake levels were low, but it could become slippery and was definitely off limits to all tourists. However, stories abound of stupid kids trying to dance or play around the ring. Jim's son, Tony, heard his father tell stories about playing tag with friends along the rim. And I'm sure that my brother was just dare-devil enough to try it. If he lost his balance and fell into the lake, no problem, because he swam like a fish. But falling down the hole would have been the end of him.

I believe Dad truly enjoyed the task of operating the boat ramp. It gave him opportunity to "shoot the bull" with the fishermen as he helped them raise and lower their boats into the lake. He came home with lots of gossipy stories garnered from his day's work. But another required summer assignment was painful for him, and it was sure to set his ulcers afire. We kids hated that time of year, because he was so cranky, and yet we knew he was suffering.

Inside the "Glory Hole" all the way to the bottom of the lake, and also inside the Dam itself, there are areas which must be scraped and painted each year. Dad was assigned this horrible painting job. First, all equipment had to be scraped free of rust using a wire brush dipped in a solvent containing naphtha. After that, he applied a

thick coat of steel gray or black paint. Air circulation in the depths of the tall structures was very poor, and the fumes were dangerously oppressive. Dad arrived home
each night upset and wheezing from congested lungs. It is amazing that he didn't
contract cancer from this yearly exposure to such potent chemicals. Throughout his
life, he did have a terrible cough, bringing up mucus which he constantly spit into his
large cotton handkerchiefs. But, we just thought it was due to his incessant smoking.
This terrible part of his job at the Dam is one of the main reasons that he finally opted
to quit work at the Dam and move to the tiny apartment in Nyssa, where he worked as
night watchman at the Sugar Factory.

We spent two more summers living at the Dam before Dad decided to call it
quits. And, we had some good times together when Dad was not toughing it out with
the painting. Our family often piled into the Ford and headed down-river through the
sagebrush for an unplanned picnic or an overnight sleep-out where the fishing was
best in the early morning hours. Mom gathered up a loaf of bread, left over lunchmeat
or hot dogs, if we had some, along with mustard and catsup. And, of course, she always packed the huge blackened camp coffee pot, the can of Folgers, some Carnation
canned-milk and a bit of sugar. We had blue enameled steel cups and plates that we
always took along.

Mom loved to help me scour the chosen campsite area for pieces of sagebrush,
while Jim carried a bucket to the river for water. Dad created a fire pit with the camp
shovel and ringed it with stones. My memory is strong of the marvelous odor of a
sagebrush fire with coffee perking on a flat cooking stone set near to the blaze. I sal-
vaged Mom's tall grey graniteware coffee pot when I cleaned out the family home the
summer after my parents' deaths. Because its outside was blackened from campfires,
I wrapped it in newspaper when we carried it on our own camping trips. Whenever
the newspaper was unwrapped, the strong burnt-sagebrush odors mingling with the
stale perfume of long-ago coffee-times wafted up to remind me of how Mom did love
a good campfire. Even as an adult, whenever I took trips with her, she asked to stop
the car out in the desert somewhere, because she spied some pieces of firewood that
she wished to pick up and save for later occasions.

Camping trips were the only time I was allowed to drink coffee. Mom poured
a large amount of canned-milk into my cup, added some sugar, and then filled it to
brimming with strong hot coffee. Good camp coffee had the ground coffee scooped
right into the pot which was filled with cold river water. Then it was set to boil for
a long time while its pungent odor whispered past my nose. Before serving, Mom
pulled the pot further away from the heat of the fire and dashed in a bit of cold water
to settle most of the grounds back to the bottom. Part of the joy in that steaming cup
of java served on a cold frosty morning, after I'd just struggled out of my bedroll, was
the piping hot cup in my chilled hands, with a few coffee grounds that always managed to float to the surface.

Those were not my only vacation pleasures. Gennie did come back for a long visit, and our friendship took up right where it left off the previous summer as if no time had passed. We once again played out our imaginary personas while we sat on the edge of my bed to create our radio programs. And, we had many happy hours swimming at Snivley's Hot Springs where I convinced her to jump into the deep end before she had really learned to swim. But it was a small enough pool that she bounced back up safely to the surface with a little help from me. Gennie wasn't much for playing with dolls, so I tucked my babies into their cradle and ignored them in favor of reading with Gennie. She was hungry for books but had limited access to Braille books in the summer.

Another exciting adventure became available while Gennie was still with us that summer. Mom learned of a wonderful church camp being held in Pilgrim Cove at Payette Lakes, Idaho. She arranged for Gennie to attend with the three of us, Mom, Jim, and me. In an early scrapbook, I discovered an essay titled, "The Story of My Life," which convinces me that documenting my family's history began early. I included "church camp in the summer with my mother and brother to a beautiful lake." Beside the story was a coupon assigning us to Cabin 4 in the United Church of Christ Conference Grounds at Pilgrim Cove, Payette Lakes near McCall, Idaho. This was the cabin which Mother, Gennie and I shared with other women with younger daughters, because I was not old enough to be in the girl's cabins. Jim hung out with boys his age, and we saw little of him.

The week before camp, Mom took a break from canning and preserving to prepare. She mended our play clothes and took us to town for purchases of new pajamas and underwear. Then, Mom took me to the grocery store and allowed me to choose my own bar of soap. I saw Lux on the shelf and quickly answered, "Oh, I choose this one cuz I heard on the radio that '9 out of 10 movie stars use Lux.'" I still associate the perfume of Lux hand soap with going to camp.

I also was pleased to receive a new toothbrush and my own little can of Pepsodent tooth powder. Because of this earlier love of Pepsodent, I was delighted when advertisers introduced the 1950's radio jingle, "You'll wonder where the yellow went, when you brush your teeth with Pepsodent!" It brought back great memories of my camper days.

Dad helped tie up bedrolls, since we did not own sleeping bags, and checked the flashlights for batteries. Then, he waved us off as we climbed in the Ford coupe and headed to Boise. From there we joined other families for a ride on the church bus to Pilgrim Cove. It seemed like a very long ride to my nine-year-old way of thinking, and I felt great delight when I finally caught sight of the lovely timbered shoreline of the lake.

Mom worked in camp to help pay our way. I know that sometimes she cooked. Also, she may have taught some of the classes. That first year, I felt secure about going away to camp with no homesickness, because I had my Mom and Gennie right there with me. Still, the routine of camp life had its ups and downs. I remember the impatience I felt from being required to attend long morning chapel services or interminable Bible classes, which contrasted with the pleasant enjoyment of sitting next to Mom at the evening campfire song fests, followed by a flashlight-trek through the forest back to our cabin. I loved cuddling into my warm bedroll while listening to the night sounds of wind stirring the branches of the Douglas fir trees with a soft swishing music.

The resinous odor of sun-toasted timber lingers in my memory and reminds me of sitting in the sweltering after-lunch craft class braiding plastic strings into necklaces and waiting impatiently for the camp bell to ring, calling us to water activities. The tolling of that early-afternoon bell signaled the real reason for going to camp. Religion had not yet touched my heart, but when my young sweaty body felt the delicious shock of plunging into the cold lake water, it was about as close as I could hope for a religious experience. I expect that Gennie felt that way too as we continued efforts to swim skillfully, but I was pretty much still at the stage of dog-paddling. I watched Jim with envy, seeing him dive off the end of the dock and swim clear out to the float.

In subsequent summers, both Gennie and I did accomplish the swim out to the float, and we even were able to jump off the high diving platform. Gennie remembers her first terrifying climb. Because she was afraid to climb back down, I told her the only other option was to jump. She did. What a fearfully brave solution to her predicament!

There was a certain amount of tingly fear involved in swimming in that lake. It was difficult for me to control my fright because rumors abounded about the sea-monster that skulked in its depths. It was different from tamer waters. Of course, whenever Jim felt like paying attention to us "littler" kids, he'd swim close and inquire, "Have you felt any nibbles on your toes today? They say the sea monster is out and about right now." Of course, there were nibbles on my toes, because the little lake minnows loved to swim up and check us out. So, I'd wince and head to shallow waters for a bit. But then, my desire to play would take hold, and out I'd paddle to the deeper waters by the dock. Fear or no, I was not about to be denied the joy of that luscious afternoon play in the water because of some old sea monster that maybe didn't even exist.

To my knowledge, we never tattled to Mom about Jim's teasing us. It didn't do much good to tattle on Jim. Mom was skilled as a parent and kept discipline of one kid in that youngster's lap without allowing stuff to slop over to the whole family. And for sure, an admission of my fears would just add fuel to the fire for further teasing, including from my Dad when we arrived back home. Both Jim and Dad shared the common pleasure of teasing about such things. I had so many fears, but I kept them pretty much tucked inside, which was probably not something that added to my overall emotional health.

Besides, we didn't want to allow our fears to keep us off the lake when the dock-side guards offered instruction in rowing a boat, I remember the pride I felt when I successfully negotiated one of the small rowboats out to the float and back to the dock. Gennie also worked at learning to row, and as long as we were far enough away from traffic, it didn't matter that she couldn't see where we were headed. She always tended to row around in circles because she exerted more effort with her strongest arm. Of all our family, I believe I was the one who had the most confidence in what she could do. We often engaged in trying out new skills, which the adults would have frowned upon if they had known. Boating was one of those skills. Later in life, when I was discovered *The Wind in the Willows,* I could relate to the conviction that "there is nothing–absolutely nothing–half so much worth doing as simply messing about in boats."

Our family, with Gennie and another girlfriend, made the pilgrimage to Payette Lakes for the next several summers. Even after I was baptized in our church in Nyssa, and though I witnessed Jim catch a serious case of religion when he was baptized at camp during our last year there, the influence of churchly activities never held a candle to the attraction I felt for that beautiful lake. So, during the summer after I finished eighth grade, when our pastor announced that a new camp opportunity was offered at Cove, Oregon, I was gung-ho to go. It was "Cove," after all, and my heart leaped to learn we had an Oregon version of Pilgrim Cove. I was fourteen that summer. Gennie spent the vacation with her Mom, and my big brother had developed other interests which did not include church camp.

But, Mom was interested and she once more offered her services as cook. We prepared easily, because we were experienced campers. Transportation was a big old school bus which one of the valley churches owned. I had to earn my fee, and I spent many weekends babysitting to save the required $25.00. When August rolled around, we loaded our gear into the back of the bus and off we went, singing camp songs such as "We're 100 miles from home; a hundred miles from home; we'll ride a while and walk a while; we're 99 miles from home." *Et cetera, et cetera ad nauseum.*

Imagine my deep disappointment to arrive at the camp and learn it was just a large mess hall with a huge top-floor girl's dormitory. Guys were in tents. No lake. A few scraggly pines. A creek. And, a public swimming pool in the town of Cove! It was hot and dry, with none of the gracious amenities of Pilgrim Cove. Predictably, Mom joined the camp spirit and enveloped me with her contagious enthusiasm. I learned from her example that it is not facilities which make camp successful, but the people.

Mom often joined in with the joking, but she also came in for her share of strong ribbing when she served terrible baked eggs on huge platters for breakfast. One of the special persons there was Rev. Gene Robinson from La Grande who clowned with the campers, telling a fantastic story in a German accent about meeting a skunk.

Gene became my mentor. His passion for the gospel and for living a meaningful life caused me to see him as my model throughout my college years, and he was the pastor who performed our wedding ceremony many years later.

I went back to camp with pleasure every year of high school. Due to Cove summer camp and the experiences I encountered there, I finally developed the deeply religious outlook that my parents had been wishing I would acquire. I can attribute much of my adolescent character to the influence of camp at Cove.

CHAPTER 7

⟞⟐⟞

Our Lessons in Real Life

MOM BECAME EVER MORE entranced with Gennie's abilities and began to talk seriously about making an effort for her to move from the horrible Idaho State School for the Blind. She began writing letters to people she knew to see what would be required for Gennie to move to the State School for the Blind in Salem, Oregon. At this stage in her teaching career, Mom was quite certain that she wished to pursue more training in speech correction and other aspects of Special Education. She began to develop contacts with state and county officials who could direct her towards her goal. Along the way, she discovered that Salem had an excellent school for the blind and that the main hurdle for Gennie was Oregon residency.

When Mom talked with Gennie's Uncle Ralph, she learned that Gennie's father did live in Oregon and could possibly help her claim residency. Although he did not have legal custody, there might be a way to work it out with the cooperation of the Salem school. With that bit of information, Mom developed a "bee in her bonnet" to make things happen. First, she checked with Gennie. No convincing was required there. When Mom mentioned that she would like to find a way for her to attend a better school in Oregon, Gennie's answer was immediate and definite. "Jo, I hate my school! I will do whatever it takes to make the change." With that agreement sealed between them, Mom set the wheels in motion as we prepared for our new life in Nyssa.

Mom managed to rent a cramped little apartment in the Bennett complex, and once again, we launched into living away from Dad during the school week and traveling back to the Dam on the weekend. There was one major change, though. Because Nyssa was so much closer than our previous schools, Mom discovered that she could enjoy Sunday evenings at the Dam, rise early on Monday mornings and make it to school in time to start the week. The Bennett apartment was cheerless and lonely, and she enjoyed Sundays with Dad. It made the weekend that much better to spend the evening in what we all considered to be our real home.

I definitely had a big problem with the plan, however. I have never, to this day, been an early-morning person. I was literally yanked out of bed by my mother, thrown into one of my two dresses, fed some kind of hot cereal, and stuffed into the car, where I immediately fell back into a stuporous doze as we bumped down the road. If we were behind schedule, I had to ride in my pajamas and get dressed when we reached school.

Usually, that early breakfast caused bouts of nausea for me on the way to town. And worst of all, my sleep-fuzzy hair was left untended because Mom never had time to braid it until we reached school. I resented being forced to sit in the staff room while Mom gossiped with her co-workers and yanked my hair into braids before I could meander out to the playground where the normal kids gathered. "Normal" meant those who were not cursed with having a teacher for their mother.

At the time, being the child of a teacher did seem like a curse. However, as I reflect upon my mother's story, I discover that I'm blessed with a totally new viewpoint. I am now proud to describe Jo Rigney as my most important teacher and also as a provider of music for my soul. My mother carried a song in her heart throughout life. I don't mean to imply that she was an accomplished musician. She never had music lessons, but she sang with us kids during the long hours of commuting and sang hymns while I sat beside her every Sunday and Wednesday during church.

We children were solely her responsibility on schooldays and her sidekicks during the long commutes. Because of this constant single-parent contact, we learned our values from her example. Even as a youngster, it was obvious to me that she harbored dreams of my becoming skilled in music. I suspect she had these hopes because of her own difficult childhood struggle to receive an education due to her will-o-the-wisp father moving the family around so much. Also, her mother and grandfather came from a musically gifted and cultured family. Jim had already exhibited very little interest in obtaining musical skills. I was her only daughter, and her dreams were heaped on me.

Mom had high expectations for the success of her children and consequently was an "I-mean-business" disciplinarian who constantly wrote detailed to-do lists. She refused to allow us to slack off on study, chores, behavior, or manners. If her efforts at gentle persuasion produced no progress, she resorted to what I came to think of as "nagging to the Nth Degree."

Her campaign to develop my musical skills began when she paid for my piano lessons in second grade. Ingrate that I was, I seldom practiced, because I really disliked my teacher. Then, when I was in fourth grade, she smiled with joy to learn that all students were required to learn to play tonette, a cheapo plastic instrument played like a recorder. I still remember the particular stink of that wretched, black, pointy tonette. I learned where to put my fingers, but the sound that came out was usually somewhere between a high-pitched squeak and a loud screeching squawk.

What a pain I must have been to my mother! I exerted great effort to maintain my status as a glum, resistant child. I've come to think that my taciturn ways were probably because I admired my mother's skill and her outgoing nature too much and was convinced that I'd never be able to be like her. For proof of that, I just need to remember when it came time for our tonette class to play for a school assembly; I was the only kid who had to stay sitting on the bleachers, watching my classmates perform up on stage. My outcast status was the result of my refusal to memorize "When the Caissons go Rolling Along."

Oh how I hated that song! Strange that now I can recall it in detail and am able to sing it with gusto! As I look back, I wonder what it must have done to my mother to see her stubborn, uncooperative offspring sitting alone on the bleachers during the program. After all, she was the sixth grade teacher and the one to whom everyone looked when planning musical events. When it came time for school programs, she was always at the center of planning the musical productions so that children had an opportunity to act out whatever songs fit the theme.

That dismaying program was only one of many times I let her down, musically. In fifth grade it was the clarinet. Another disaster! My dad had changed jobs by then and moved to town with us. He worked nights at the White Satin Sugar Factory and could not abide my squeaking and shrill whistles, which were about all I could produce from that reluctant instrument. For one thing, I hated the odor of that spit-soaked reed that I was supposed to put in my mouth. That instrument quickly became another failure.

During those school years in Nyssa, I heard constant positive comments about Jo Rigney's musical and teaching abilities from her co-workers and community members. They'd say how clever she was and what wonderful ideas she had. I knew I was a disappointment to everyone. When I was caught in mischief, my teachers frowned at me saying, "Doris, Mrs. Rigney would not want to know about your misbehavior. Do I need to report it to her?" This was part of the problem that created my attitude. While at school, Jim and I were expected to exhibit excellent behavior and also call our mother "Mrs. Rigney." Being a teacher's kid was about as bad as being a preacher's kid, and I behaved accordingly.

I was smart and capable but worked very hard not to let it show. For example, in fifth grade, we were required to put our heads down on our desks while we listened to the Standard School Broadcasts playing classical music. This type of music was a brand new experience for me. I was absolutely thrilled with it but quickly realized I was the only one who seemed to enjoy it. I groaned and moaned along with my classmates when the listening-hour was upon us, while secretly relishing every second.

In sixth grade, Mrs. Rigney became my math teacher and my music teacher. My only saving was that I had the other teacher for everything else. By then, I'd taken enough piano lessons for my mother to decide I should be put to work. Her pushing for me to "shine" was overpowering. I often felt her pressure unbearable. Of course, it was her desire to see me happy and successful, but to me it seemed like she just wanted me to develop skills she had always wanted to possess herself.

For a while, she forced me to be the accompanist for the class while they sang. I was terrified the kids would laugh at me. Since Jo Rigney never took "no" for an answer, I found myself at the piano fumbling along for several sessions until she finally realized that I really could not do it and asked clever little Barbara M. to take over. Of course, Barbara played splendidly. I was once more humiliated by my mother while she was, again, deeply disappointed by me.

Towards the middle of sixth grade the high school music teacher, came to our class and sought out beginner string students. With her usual bouncy enthusiasm my mother approached me with her idea that I should learn to play the viola for the high school orchestra. The instrument and lessons would be provided—a no-cost musical education.

I still don't know why I agreed to take it on, but this time I was really hooked; I wanted to play a stringed instrument. Perhaps it had something to do with being allowed to go over to the high school for the lessons. I still didn't practice enough, and I had a terrible time learning the viola clef. By then, I had enough training to read the treble clef and now I was expected to give new names to the notes in order to play the viola. I remember being embarrassed one day when Mr. Lawrence stopped the class and asked, "Doris, what note are you playing in the second measure?" I was forced to answer, "I don't know." I knew it was the note played with two fingers down on the "D" string, but I did not know its name.

I also began to understand why my mother wanted me to succeed in music. With all her musical ability, she never learned to read music. She leaned on me for that. Mother was skilled at playing piano by ear and listened to songs she liked until she could pick out the melody, adding chords for accompaniment. When our family was finally able to move into our own house, one of the first items of furniture she acquired was a second hand upright piano. It remained in our living room until the day she died, and then I prevailed upon my husband to move it to our home.

One of my mother's greatest pleasures was finding time to sit down at the piano and play while our family gathered around to sing. I had a clear soprano voice; she was gifted at harmonizing. Dad was a great bass, and even Jim seemed to like joining in with the melody. Dad and Mom loved all the old-time hymns and the songs from their younger days such as "My Blue Heaven" and "Just a Song at Twilight." My choices were songs like "Lonely Little Petunia in the Onion Patch," "Galway Bay," and "Mairzy Do-ats and Dozy Doats." Often, the songs my mother wished to sing were a not-so-subtle hint that I needed to keep improving my ability to smile. We almost always sang, "Smile the while you kiss me sad adieu" and one of Mom's favorites, which declared that "When you're smilin', keep on smilin' / The whole world smiles with you."

I struggled to find my smile at the same time I was sawing away on that viola. In the meantime, my mother cooked up a really big surprise for my fifteenth birthday. Unbeknownst to me, she quietly spirited the pieces of her Grandfather Mason's violin out of the house and sought out a violin-maker who glued, polished, varnished, and restrung to make it my birthday present. She beamed with delight as she presented me with that brand new violin case. When I opened it up, it was lined with bright pink fur, nestling the most beautiful violin I had ever seen. There was a new bow, a shoulder rest, and a tiny little pitch pipe to help me tune the strings.

I loved it. The significance of the gift stemmed from her memories of listening to her grandfather play this same violin when she was still a child in Michigan. When her family immigrated to Idaho, she never saw her Grandfather again. So, it was sentiment that prompted her to say, "Doris, you have shown enough interest in strings that I think you are ready to receive your great-grandfather's violin. I've arranged with Mrs. Fisher to give you private lessons." I was close to tears in the depth of my thanks. Also, I quickly realized that if I studied violin instead of the viola, I would be back to treble clef, a big boon to my confidence.

By then, I was old enough to realize that my mother didn't have the money to pay for refurbishing the violin. She probably paid by installments, as we did with all other purchases in our family. I was very grateful, and I truly appreciated her gift. That appreciation bore fruit, too. As I began to blossom into adolescence, I really put effort into the violin. I found I did have musical ability, as Mom had known all along. I continued with orchestra throughout high school and even played from memory a complicated violin duet for high school graduation.

My mother had an indomitable spirit that she developed by overcoming the hard knocks that life dealt out during her own childhood. She was determined that her children would fare better in life than she had. Jim, due to his hot temper, often had angry outbursts when she pushed too hard. I was more passive-resistant, dragging my feet rather than showing open rebellion. Both of us must have caused her many sleepless nights; nevertheless, she never gave up.

Being too tired to get a job done was not an option. She approached life with determination, making it clear that when she chose to accomplish something, she would find a way to do it. In the process, she leaned upon her deep sense of humor and her religious faith to carry her through the rough spots. I know now that she yearned to find ways to pass this determination on to us.

Doris graduate playing violin

For sure, my mother's efforts did succeed. Somehow, through hard spells and good times, she managed to see that both my brother and I earned college degrees before she finally completed her own B.A. in Education. I know, for a fact, that acquiring that degree was a highlight in her life. It didn't happen until after I was married and had a child. She lived with us that summer in my college town and posed in her cap and gown, proudly holding her grandchild.

My mother had a joy in living and a fantastic sense of humor. She laughed a lot and felt the day was not complete if she found nothing to laugh about. I know she learned this from her mischievous father, who regaled the family with his long tales of practical jokes, whenever he was sober. Because of her sad memories of his drinking problem, Mom allowed no alcohol to come into her home, while we were growing up, and proved that lack of drink did not mean lack of fun.

Her concern for the child troubled by poverty, physical disability, or speech impediments is the reason that she worked so hard every summer until she earned her Special Education Certification and convinced the Nyssa Public Schools to allow her to establish the first Special Education Department in Malheur County, Oregon.

The last day of school used to mean loading up for a car-trip to our summer home at the Owyhee Dam, but in the summer of 1947, Dad changed jobs to work night shift at the sugar factory in Nyssa, and Mom went off to summer school. It was a rough transition for me. I think Dad made the change so our family could be together during the school year, and it was a good decision for us. But, the move to Nyssa caused us to lose the summer at the Owyhee Dam. I no longer could hope, on that last day, for hours of daydreaming, tree-climbing, fishing, swinging, and swimming in that paradise.

Our summer was spent in Bennett Apartments with one dark, windowless bedroom. It was filled to overflowing with my parent's double bed and a set of bunk beds for Jim and me, plus a cupboard which served as our closet. The bedroom led into the dinky front room furnished with our couch, chairs, radio, Singer treadle-sewing machine, and an old oil heater. Around the corner was a small kitchen with barely room for table and chairs, electric stove, refrigerator, sink, tiny drain board and an inadequate few cupboards. Off the kitchen, was the bathroom, a little closet with toilet, sink, and a moldy metal shower stall.

As usual, I brought home an adequate report card on the last day of school. Because I was able to anticipate what teachers required, academics were easy for me. It was nothing special, since Mom was my math teacher that year and participated in writing the report. This year, she had no time to ooh and ahh over my efforts. No special meal or family outing was offered, such as we'd enjoyed in previous years.

Mom needed to attend a special four-week summer school clear across the state in Salem, Oregon. At the end of the session, she would qualify for a Special Education Teacher's certificate. Therefore, she explained that I must stay home to be woman of the house. I was eleven. Mom was an inveterate list-maker and sat me down at the little kitchen table, forcing me to listen while she made her list of expectations for my summer.

1. Laundry.
2. Keep the house clean and quiet so Daddy can sleep.
3. Prepare meals for Daddy and Jim.

Laundry meant I had to learn how to use the local 'washer-teria' across town. Mom assured me that on Monday mornings when Dad got off work, he could drive and leave me there with the dirty clothes before going home to sleep. In 1947, a public place to do one's laundry was quite innovative. The business was situated in a large store-front building containing several washing stations. Each patron was assigned the use of a "swish-swish" ringer washer and two adjacent rinse tubs. Little wooden stools were provided so that laundry baskets could sit at a convenient level for catching wet clothing as it was put through the wringers. Only one tub of hot soapy water was allowed for the fee we paid.

The owners of the establishment were kind enough, but they probably had as many doubts about my eleven-year-old ability as I did. Of course, I'd helped Mom with laundry when we lived at the Dam. I was somewhat aware of the need to sort it into piles to be washed in the correct sequence: whites first; good colored clothes next; then Dad's denim work-shirts and overalls; and, last of all, came his pile of cotton handkerchiefs. These required a separate cold-water soak and rinse before all his snot and spit would release and I could wash them in the swish-swish. Oh, how I detested those handkerchiefs! My stomach still churns remembering the wretched, slimy task.

During my first trip to the washer-teria, I expected to do the sorting on the floor in front of the machine. But what I discovered was a steamy, wet, public facility with water spills and a floor that was far from clean. There were no laundry carts available as in the modern laundromats, so I needed to do my sorting into bundles at home before piling everything into the bushel fruit basket Mom used for laundry. It was fitted with a special plastic lining that Mom bought for that purpose.

The suds became progressively filthier with each batch. By the time the snot rags went in, the water was already scummy and not so warm. Thank goodness for Oxydol! I'd listened to Charlie Warren on the *Ma Perkins* radio program and knew all about Oxydol's "Hustle Bubble Suds" and how "those pudgy fellows lifted out dirt and helped to wash white clothes "white without bleaching." However, the little bubbles were not equal to the challenge of Dad's handkerchiefs.

Then, there were my Dad's huge work-stained overalls. He was not especially careful about checking his pockets, and nor was I. Often, soggy matchbook packets floated up to the surface of the wash water. Worst of all was an overlooked slimy handkerchief, which then had to be fished out of the soapy water and plopped into the bucket where all the other disgusting things were soaking. If I was careless while inserting the overalls' bulging metal buttons and big buckles through the wringer, they'd catch and grind the rollers, so I had to pop the emergency release on the top of the wringer. More than once the owner hurried over to rescue the machine before the buckles chewed the rubber roller to pieces.

Thankfully, the managers allowed me to leave behind the wet stuff sitting in its basket until Dad woke and could drive to pick it up. That freed me to walk to the apartment after my struggles. When he brought the basket of wet clothes home, I had to hang everything up to dry on the outside clothesline, where I was certain all the neighbors peeked at me to see if I did it correctly.

I was aware of the rules for clotheslines. First, I had to wipe the line, so it wouldn't soil the fresh wash. Then, I had to hang clothing in the correct order so that neighbors would not gossip about undies being displayed. A person must never hang clothes out on a Sunday and must get everything off the lines before dark, including the clothespins. Leaving the clothespins out on the line was tacky! Our family was definitely tacky since the clothespins always stayed on the line while they slowly deteriorated from the sun, wind, and rain.

Chore 2 on the list meant I needed to stay quiet during the day while Dad slept. It also meant I had to stay out of my teen-aged brother's way because he had quite a temper when crossed. I was not even allowed to play the radio until Dad woke up. I experienced terrible loneliness.

Chore 3, meal preparation, was the most daunting chore of all. My disasters in cooking were numerous, and Aunt Sammy's Radio Recipes were, as usual, unhelpful. I remember with particular pain the day I made croquettes. The recipe suggested a mashed-potato base mixed with egg yolk, pepper, and onion salt. It was supposed to chill before being fashioned into individual cone-shapes. The directions said to "egg, crumb, fry, and drain." I had to guess what all that meant. I tried hard to make the darn things stay clumped together while they fried but most disintegrated into scrambled moosh. Not only did I burn my hand but also the croquettes! Several dropped on the filthy floor. By the time Dad woke up to prepare for work, I was in tears. He was kind and chose to not criticize the waste of precious food, but he didn't eat any of them, either.

As the weeks stretched on, I decided that my position in life required that I should never smile or laugh again. I purposefully practiced going around the house and town wearing a somber, unsmiling countenance. I know that I worried Mom when she finally came home from summer school, because she devoted the last half of summer to providing freedom and encouraging little-girl pursuits. She brought with her a baby doll, which I had requested for my birthday present. She helped me begin to learn how to sew doll clothes on our Singer. She gave me sole control over the empty milk bottles, which I could sell back to the corner grocery store for a nickel each. Two milk bottles paid my way into the Saturday matinees, which were mostly shootem-up bang-bang westerns; not my favorites, but they provided cheap escapism for a kid.

There was also a road construction project in front of our apartment, and Mom didn't object when I climbed into my swim suit and used the hose to pour water in the ditch the workmen had dug. Then, I was allowed to play in that lovely cool, squishy mud. I liked to pretend that I was making mud pies in the Panama Canal. There is a song about, "Mud, mud, glorious mud! / Nothing quite like it for cooling the blood!" After my wise mother's return, smiling became something I once more allowed myself to enjoy. The memory of that terrible summer prompted me to provide a better end-of-school experience for my own little girls many years later.

When our life settled into a more stable family routine, Mother began attending church on Sunday mornings and prayer meetings on Wednesday evenings. Living full-time in town instead of commuting back and forth to the Dam allowed her to establish some much-desired social contacts with the little congregation of the First Christian Church on Ennis Avenue. Mother believed in the proverb that advised, "Train up a child in the way he should go, and when he is old, he will not depart from it." It worked for me! I was anxious to be wherever Mom was, so I willingly accompanied her to services. Cuddled beside her warm chubby body with her arm often around my shoulders, I was exposed to all the old gospel hymns sung at every service. The lyrics are locked in my subconscious. My thoughtful daughter searched until she found a copy of the First Christian Church hymnal and presented it to me, and now I am able to page through it to recall those song fests with Mom.

I remember how she began to model the way to sing the second layer of notes in the hymnal, the harmony line. I was so pleased with myself when I finally caught on and discovered that I possessed the ability to sing well. At first, the music meant more than whatever our pastor was preaching. But with constant exposure, his messages became internalized. Those teachings are imbedded deeply within me, even though I am no longer a participating member of any church. If I hear the lyrics of those old hymns, surprising, unexpected emotions rise to the surface, and I find myself choked-up and teary-eyed.

Music has the power to touch a portion of our being and unexpectedly bring forth long-buried feelings. Perhaps those old hymns evoke in me a longing for my mother's arm once more to enfold me or maybe it is a desire to return to the kind of certainty and safety I felt while snuggled next to her. I can almost smell her. My youngest daughter, who spent hours in her Grandma's bedroom exploring all her finery, clothing, shoes, and cosmetics, remembers a blend of pressed powder, Jergen's lotion and spit. She remembers the smell of grandma-spit because Mom had a habit of spitting on a handkerchief to scrub off a lipstick-kiss or clean up my little daughter's face, dirtied from eating the candy she found while exploring Grandma's purse during church service.

My daughter also has memories of communion in the Nyssa church. That part of church was the highlight for her; the shiny tray with all those sparkly crystal jiggers meant 'snack time!' A shiny sparkly snack was what church was all about! However, communion had a much deeper meaning for me. In the practice of the First Christian Church, serving the Lord's Supper is done every Sunday. Dad was a Deacon and later an Elder in the church, so he often took part in passing communion up and down the aisles and over my head. Only baptized believers were allowed to partake, which means the tray of crackers and the lovely round rack of dainty little communion glasses always zoomed past me to the next adult in the row.

They believed that twelve years old is when a child reaches the age of reason, which happened for me during my nightmarish summer. No one pushed or suggested

I should do it, but one Sunday in the early fall, as our pastor offered the invitation to come forward at the end of services, I began to think about stepping out into the aisle and walking down to the front. Perhaps the draw was more towards being allowed to take communion, to sip grape juice out of a tiny cup rather than any heartfelt religious conversion. My deeper religious understandings did not begin to develop until I started attending summer camp during junior high and high school.

Whatever the motivation, with the church full of loyal parishioners, Reverend Whipple offered the invitation to come forward to accept Christ as personal savior. I'd heard him give that same invitation every service since we started attending church. But somehow, this time, he seemed to be speaking directly to me. It was fearful to imagine how I could ever walk all the way to the front with the entire congregation staring at me. Then they started to sing, as they always did, "Just as I am, thou wilt receive / Wilt welcome, pardon, cleanse, relieve."

With no warning to my parents or even to me, I stood up and started the long walk down the aisle. Our congregation was small and struggling in an unfinished basement in a building with a flat, tar-papered roof. Normal attendance averaged between 30 and 40. New converts were few and far between. So everyone had huge smiles of encouragement aimed directly at me as I trundled down the rows of wooden pews. Even those pews were quite new, since the church used to sit on rows of folding chairs.

I felt very much alone standing up there in front of all those people, but Rev. Whipple took my hand and I overcame my fright. There is no messing around or waiting in the First Christian Church. They kept the baptismal tank full at all times, hidden behind a velvet curtain. Everyone waited while I was robed and led into the tank where Rev. Whipple was already standing knee deep in water. He gave me a cloth to hold over my nose and directed the velvet curtain to be opened to the congregation's view. Then he held me tight and dunked.

I know the members of the congregation were thrilled for me and my parents were proud. I don't remember any particular celebration after church. Baptism was a time of quiet happiness for families, but no big whoop-de-do happened for anyone. My brother was not even there, but he did experience a deeply religious period during summer church camp after his junior year in high school. However, when I was twelve, he was too interested in his girlfriend to join the family at church so I didn't even consider it out of the ordinary that he was missing from the occasion. I have little memory of how I felt after the baptism. I suspect that I had the blasé thought, "So, okay, that's taken care of. I must be saved now."

The best result happened the following Sunday when they offered me a piece of cracker and one of those tiny little cups of juice. It tasted so sweet and not at all like my mother's homemade scorched grape juice. Communion became satisfying and religiously important to me. I remember the liturgy shared by my father or one of the other elders each Sunday. They sat in front of the church, facing the congregation, on each side of the communion table where the trays of juice and crackers were covered with a lovely embroidered white cloth. The deacons passed the communion trays from row to row. After communion and the offering, Dad would come to sit with us for the sermon.

I remember being very surprised and somewhat intimidated by my Catholic cousin who argued with me that after prayers were said and blessings given, the juice and crackers really turned into blood and flesh. This went against what I was taught that the entire ceremony was just symbolic; it became one of the many things which disturbed me as I delved deeper into what my beliefs should be. Another disturbing religious teaching caused difficulty for me while I listened to preachers at Payette Lake church camp. They held forth loud and often concerning the sinfulness of attending movies, and they especially warned against dancing.

Both of these teachings gave me great trouble during my formative years. I loved going to movies! But I spent most of my eighth grade year abstaining. Worse, the PE teacher in Junior High required boys and girls to line up on each side of the gym where kids marched to music until all were matched up, boy-girl. She expected the partners to assume dancing positions which involved holding hands and placing the other hand on shoulder and waist. Then she taught the fox trot, "slow, slow, quick, quick."

Since I was already painfully shy, at first it was easy to claim religious beliefs which allowed me to be excused to sit on the bleachers and watch. Soon, though, I began to suffer from ostracism which didn't help my naturally low self-esteem. Mom came to my rescue once more. She spent hours discussing the pros and cons of what we had learned at church camp and slowly brought me around to her much more liberated viewpoint. It was like a great weight being lifted off my shoulders when I finally decided to attend movies once more. However, the business of dancing was much more difficult, because it meant I actually had to get out there on the gym floor and touch a boy! Horrors!

While I struggled with my religious convictions during my awkward adolescence, Ibrahim, already a young man, was also grappling with his religious beliefs. After his summer at home, Ibrahim returned to Beirut and a more settled second year at Middle East College. The dormitories were finished and students could live on campus. His English skills became more polished because he learned to appreciate the beauty of the library. Often, when he went there to fulfill an assignment, he would discover a book on an unrelated subject and sit down among the stacks to read.

One of these discoveries was a beautiful English translation of the Koran. He often wished he had stolen it for himself, since he never found another copy of the same edition. In Arabic, the Koran flows with poetry that is almost impossible to translate into English preserving the meaning and beauty. Ibrahim found the more well-known Pickthall translation quite ugly, but he memorized portions of Surah 96 from the unknown poet-translator. He was struck by the "blood coagulated" in the creation story.

Another book Ibrahim found caused him a great deal of worry. It was a medical reference, and he spent hours poring over its pages. He read the description of each disease and immediately began to feel sick because he had the same symptoms. When he read on to the next disease, the same thing happened. With so many symptoms of such terrible diseases, he decided he must be getting ready to die, so he took the book to Mrs. Krick, who managed the school dispensary.

"Mrs. Krick, I must talk to you. I believe I must be very ill." "Tell me your problem, Mr. Ayyoub." "Well, I was reading in this book about this terrible disease, and I must have contracted it because I have the same symptoms." She looked at the book's cover and told him the book was written for the use of medical students and not meant for his eyes. She told him to take it back to the library and never open it again. There was nothing wrong with his health. Ibrahim felt very sheepish but did as he was directed. From that day on, he told folks that Mrs. Krick was responsible for saving his life.

Over the next couple of years, as he worked his way through school, Ibrahim had a series of jobs. The task of digging the well was abandoned because the mountain contained an underground shelf of hard stone which destroyed their machinery. Another job he remembers was that of monitoring the noisy college generator. He enjoyed that task because the generator was warm. He carried his books with him and lay down beside it for many hours to study. Often he fell asleep next to its warmth, but the prolonged exposure to such loud noise probably contributed to his later severe hearing loss.

Another of Ibrahim's responsibilities was the milking in the college dairy. During their initial instruction, Mr. Mall said, "These are the healthiest cows in Lebanon, but I want you to drink all the milk you want because it will help you develop immunity to anything you might catch from your close proximity to the animals." It might have been an "old wives tale," but the students took his direction to heart. Each daybreak, they stopped by the cafeteria kitchen to pick up empty milk cans and a large baguette. Their first task was to build a fire in the dairy's stove to heat water for washing the cows' udders.

They always milked the Jersey first and poured her milk into a large, three-pound tin set in a pan of water on the stove. While they milked the other cows, the rich Jersey milk heated until a good two inches of cream rose to the surface. After they finished milking and hosing out the dairy, the two young men stood around the tin to scoop dollops of heavy cream onto their bread. They consumed the bread and cream and gulped down all of the hot milk. Then they rushed to deliver the Holstein milk to the kitchen. They needed to hurry as they showered and changed clothes so they wouldn't miss breakfast. It's a wonder Ibrahim couldn't hear his arteries clogging from all that fat, but he remained exceptionally healthy.

In fact, the only true illness that Ibrahim experienced while at Middle East College happened close to the end of his first year, long before he had any association with the dairy. He had an extreme drop in appetite. Ibrahim always had a problem of forgetting to eat if he were engrossed in study or some other serious interest. He probably forgot to eat and was not consuming the balanced diet required for a healthy lifestyle. Ibrahim headed to the infirmary and spoke to Mrs. Krick about his lack of appetite. She sent him to Beirut for an exam at the medical school. While he sat on the examination table, the head physician asked the students surrounding him, "This patient has anemia. What do you suggest for the appropriate treatment?" Each student recommended that he "Take vitamin such and such," or "Take this kind of iron pill," or "Take that pill." The head physician simply said, "Eat meat, especially lots of liver."

Eventually, Ibrahim's anemia was brought back under control during his visits home. He told his mother what the doctor had prescribed. She cooked thinly sliced lamb and special meals of liver. Then, she closed the door to the kitchen and sat him down in front of a plate of meat much too large for him to consume. When he had his fill, he would sneak the door open and invite Naim and Fahim to gobble up what he couldn't. The next year, after he began his work in the dairy, he experienced a reawakening of his normal young man's appetite.

Since Ibrahim was not a vegetarian, yet was required to follow the vegetarian diet while at school, he knew the only way he would be able to eat meat was to visit Beirut. Members of the college did that. In fact, he once witnessed an Adventist instructor wolfing down a huge meal of lamb shish kabab. At the time, he was surprised, and in his opinion, it was hypocrisy for an Adventist to eat meat. But eventually, he concluded that even these good people were not as perfect as he had assumed them to be. Actually, it salved his troubled conscience a bit, because he now planned on doing the same whenever he could get to Beirut. Such opportunities were rare, given his class and work schedule.

One trip involved a perilous journey in the college's old, standard transmission pickup with a student from Syria. Abe knew how to drive, having learned as a boy during the days of his father's tractor business. However, on this particular jaunt, his companion was driving. Middle East College is situated on a mountain up a narrow, steep and winding road. On the way down, the driver didn't have the truck in first gear so it picked up speed much faster than could be controlled. The brakes were weak and it was too late to attempt shifting down. Ibrahim gritted his teeth and tensed for disaster as they approached a sharp right turn. His companion twisted the wheel hard right but to no effect. If they had been able to negotiate the turn, the next curve would have sent them off the road and down into a deep ravine. Providence was watching over them. The pickup refused to turn and tore straight on ahead. Emitting frantic yells, the two boys hung on for dear life. Deep within Ibrahim's soul rushed the certainty, "I'm a goner." As the truck flew over a gully, it somehow reversed direction, sailed through the air and landed with a crash to the ground. It came to rest on a hillock with its nose facing back up toward the college. Needless to say, they were rattled and shaky as they clambered out of the precariously positioned pickup and walked up the hill for help.

Ibrahim chose not to make any more of his trips to Beirut in that truck, but there was always bus transportation, if he had the time and energy to hike down the mountain to the bus route. It was less dangerous but more expensive than the truck. He and his roommate agreed to meet at the open air market to eat and then go back to school together. The market was always enjoyable. Each shop owner displayed his wares and loudly proclaimed the value of his merchandise. As Ibrahim wandered the aisles, absorbing the cacophony of sounds and smells, he saw displays of cheap knick-knacks to entice tourists, racks and tables piled with clothing, displays of leather goods, long cords strung across stalls with glittering gold bangles and necklaces, fabulous Persian rugs hung on racks and walls, cages containing chickens and ducks, assortments of spices, stands full of fresh produce, fruit, fish, and cheeses. Freshly butchered lamb and chickens hung from the butchers' shops. Heavenly aromas wafted from the food stands serving sizzling meats, hummus, *tabouleh*, bread, tea or coffee, and a variety of sweets.

As he strolled along, stopping to admire or touch an item here or there, he checked his watch and realized it was way past the time he had agreed to meet his roommate. Ibrahim was so late that he chose his lunch and ate. Heading back to the bus stop, he passed a shop displaying woolen trousers and stopped to feel the cloth to see if it was good quality wool. Knowing that he had no need for more clothing, and seeing no one manning the stall, he walked on. A few steps down the aisle, he felt a finger tapping his shoulder. It was a shopkeeper.

"Why are you messing with my merchandise? You are not a buyer!" Now, Ibrahim really was not planning to buy anything that day, but he did not like the merchant's accusatory tone, so he answered, "I am too a buyer, but there was no one in the shop for me to speak with." "No, No, No," said the merchant. "I say you are not a buyer. If you are a buyer, you must prove it to me. How much will you pay for those trousers?" "How much are you asking for them?" countered Ibrahim. "60 livre," answered the merchant. Ibrahim had learned from his family in Al Husn that when bargaining from positions of ignorance about an item's true value, always offer half of the asking price. Since he really did not wish to buy, he decided to cut it short and offer one fourth of the price. "60 livre is too much. They are not worth more than 15 livre." "Ha," exclaimed the shopkeeper. "I knew you were not a buyer. You don't even have 15 livre. If you do, show me."

Indignantly, Ibrahim pulled out his money and answered back, "I do too. See, here it is." Immediately, the merchant grabbed the notes and pocketed them. "Good, you are a buyer. Now let me help you pick the correct size and we are done." There was no provision for trying them on at the shop. The merchant checked his waist size, held a pair up against him to measure length and said, "These are just right. Here, take your purchase." Feeling foolish for being suckered into buying, he tucked the trousers under his arm, rode the bus back to the end of its route, hiked up the hill to campus and tossed them onto his bed.

When his roommate returned, he saw Ibrahim's trousers and said, "Oh, you bought from the same shop I did. How much did you pay?" Ibrahim reluctantly answered, "15 livre." His roommate scoffed, "You paid too much. I only paid 7½ livre." "Well, it can't be helped now." said Ibrahim. "Let's just try them on to check the fit." Ibrahim was pleased with his and decided the day's expenditure was not too bad after all. But when his poor roommate tried on his trousers, he discovered that the left leg was way too baggy while the right leg was narrow and skimpy. Many years later, Ibrahim heard a lecture on the philosophy of *caveat emptor,* "Let the Buyer Beware," which reminded him of this experience.

Because he was operating on a very limited budget, Ibrahim learned to take good care of the few items of clothing he possessed. During work hours, the college provided heavy duty coveralls, but he had to have proper attire for attending classes and other school or church gatherings. This required him to own a good white shirt, tie, jacket or sweater, and decent trousers. He had a favorite white shirt which he wore constantly whenever it was clean. When it became too soiled for another wearing, he sent it to the school laundry for washing, starching, and ironing. This work was performed by girls attending college on work scholarships just like his. The unique part about the shirt is that it was totally worn out except for the front and collar. Its sleeves and tails were in tatters. But after the girls finished their efforts and sent it back to him, he could dress with it; pull on a sweater or jacket, and none of the tatters showed. Surely those in the laundry who knew his secret must have giggled among themselves when they saw him walk into church wearing that "special" shirt. Only they knew the truth.

Ibrahim may not have allowed himself time to attempt much social contact with the girls on campus, but he did come in contact with one woman who caused him some stress and worry. He mentioned to one of his teachers that he wished to learn to play piano. His teacher mentioned that the history teacher's American wife taught piano. Ibrahim appeared for his first lesson. The lady was exceedingly beautiful and wore excellent perfume. She sat beside him on the piano bench and began to instruct him saying, "Your wrists are too stiff. Here is how they should be." Then she took hold of his hands to loosen them up into their proper position on the keys.

Her close proximity was overwhelming to innocent, young Ibrahim. He felt he was headed for big trouble. He thought, "What did I get myself into?" He was not at all sure how to deal with the situation. Thankfully, a way out appeared. His piano teacher informed him, "For every hour of instruction, you must practice five hours." Ibrahim quickly answered, "I do not have time in the day for that kind of commitment. When I'm not in classes I must work to pay my fees. I'm sorry, but I will not be able to study piano after all." He thanked her for taking the time with him and hurriedly terminated his only brush with a musical education.

Not only did his job rescue him from the danger of piano lessons, but Ibrahim found his work to be a source of satisfaction as he learned new skills in the shop. Dr.

Krick, president of the mission, often came to the shop with challenging tasks. One of these involved finishing a hardwood bedside table for Dr. Krick's daughter. Since Ibrahim knew nothing about working with wood, Dr. Krick showed him how to begin by smoothing the wood with the straight edge of a broken piece of glass. Then he began sanding, always working in the direction of the wood grain, with medium grade sandpaper. After that he was taught to rework it with finer and finer grades of paper. Ibrahim spent hours sanding diligently until he felt it was very smooth, but when his teacher came to inspect, he was told, "That's coming along nicely, now graduate down to a finer grade paper." This went on for hours and days.

When the stand felt totally smooth, Dr. Krick checked again saying, "You almost have it as smooth as glass, but give it a little more work." He felt a great accomplishment when the table was finally pronounced ready to varnish. The experience came to mind when we watched the movie, *Karate Kid,* which portrayed a young boy waxing and polishing for hours to satisfy his teacher's demands. Ibrahim not only learned woodworking but also received a lesson in patience.

In his spare time in the machine shop, Dr. Krick worked on his Plymouth. Once, he crawled out from under the engine holding a small copper piece which had broken off. He showed the piece to Ibrahim and asked if he could fashion a piece exactly like it. Ibrahim knew the shop had a sheet of copper that appeared to be the same weight, so he offered to try. He drew around the part on the copper sheeting. After carefully cutting it out, he smoothed and shaped it. Then he took it to Dr. Krick, who crawled back under his car. Obviously it was satisfactory because Dr. Krick poked his head out, grinned up at Ibrahim and asked, "What are you doing here in Middle East College? You should be in Detroit!" Ibrahim knew about Detroit! His uncle Yacoub did well in Detroit and came back to live a successful life in Al Husn, so Dr. Krick's praise left a deep impression. At the ripe old age of 83, he still loved to share the story. The glow on his face while he talked let us know how important that memory was.

As success began to build with his manual work, Ibrahim also became more secure in his academic classes. One quarter he took Arabic composition from his Uncle Ibrahim, who praised his command of written Arabic. His English was becoming stronger too. During the opening assembly of students for his fourth year, he was selected to make a welcoming speech in English to the new students. Public speaking did not come easily. In preparation for the talk, Ibrahim found an isolated section of campus where he paced back and forth, practicing for several hours. By the time he stood at the podium, every sentence was carefully rehearsed and memorized. Uncle Ibrahim sat in the audience beside President Geraty, newly appointed head of the college. President Geraty asked, "Who is that young man giving the talk?" "He is my nephew, Ibrahim Ayyoub." President Geraty was impressed and said, "His English is better than that of some of our faculty members." Uncle Ibrahim was kind enough to pass on the praise and told him, "You know, nephew, I might be able to secure a position for you as a translator." This recognition coming from his uncle pleased him greatly.

At that time, George Keough, founder of the college and a skilled Arabic linguist, was in Beirut producing Adventist radio broadcasting. Uncle Ibrahim thought there might be interest in hiring his nephew to assist with their translation efforts, and he began to do some quiet lobbying in that direction. After Uncle Ibrahim talked about his nephew's ability with language, Mr. Keough staged an impromptu interview. One day while walking on campus he saw Ibrahim with another student and stopped to engage them in conversation. Speaking Arabic, he asked their names and inquired about their home towns. Ibrahim knew who the gentleman was and answered, "I am Ibrahim Ayyoub from Al Husn, Jordan." The other student also introduced himself, but Mr. Keough gave his attention solely to Ibrahim and asked a surprising question, "Don't you have a small lake in Al Husn? What do you call it?" Ibrahim was amazed that this important man would know about his little swimming hole. "We call it a Birkeh," he replied politely. Mr. Keough raised his eyebrows quizzically, "I thought you said you were from Al Husn. People from that town would pronounce it Bircheh." Ibrahim smiled, "You are correct, sir, but I chose to use the formal term because I wished to speak correct Arabic with you."

Meanwhile, Ibrahim was enrolled in a class on "The Life of Christ," which required extensive Bible reading. The more Ibrahim read, the more troubled he became. He was stopped cold when he came to the passage which urged, "Be ye therefore perfect, even as your Father which is in heaven is perfect." This passage caused him to spend days in serious reflection. He pondered on the concept of perfection because he was very aware that he was not perfect. He spent hours recalling how others around him often compromised rules, such as eating meat. They took great care to appear perfect, even when it was not so.

He began to believe their behavior simply proved that they were human. He knew that the Bible taught that Christ was perfect, the Son of God, conceived by the Holy Spirit. He mused, "If Christ were a normal human being like me, I would be more successful in my effort to emulate him." Finally he conjectured, "Perhaps I have missed something in my reading. Maybe somewhere in the Bible there is a section that says Joseph slept with Mary. That would make Christ human and I could willingly attempt to be like him." After spending more time mulling over the problem, he decided to ask his teacher. Even then, he waited for several weeks before seeking advice.

If Ibrahim had truly understood the depth of Adventists' belief, he would have known that in their eyes such doubts bordered on blasphemy. But, he was not aware of that. He needed clarification and finally decided to ask. His teacher's wife, as deeply devout as her husband, was visiting in the office and became a witness to the conversation. His teacher welcomed him into the office and offered him a seat. Ibrahim laid out his problem and explained his central concern: "because I am a human, I know I am not nor ever will be perfect. Yet I am asked to be like Christ who was perfect. This seems impossible for me to do if he was born by Immaculate Conception. That makes him all powerful like God. What I really need to know is this. Is there any place in the Bible which says that Joseph slept with Mary? If that were so, then Jesus would be human like me, and I could hope to become like Him."

The atmosphere in the room turned cold. Ibrahim's glance showed that the wife had stiffened with shock. His teacher's lips compressed tightly and his complexion turned ashen as he answered, "No, Mr. Ayyoub. I am not aware of any such passage in the Holy Bible." No one said anything for a while. In the ensuing silence, it dawned on Ibrahim that there would be no interesting intellectual debate. Questions on such basic beliefs were not open for discussion. He left as gracefully as possible, but his soul searching did not abate. He continued to refine what he believed and what he did not. The meeting taught him a difficult lesson. He now knew that he would need to keep doubts to himself. Who knows what took place among college authorities after that office conversation, but the translation job never materialized. When the school year ended, college officials came to Ibrahim saying, "We have secured a teaching job for you in Amman. You will be welcomed there at the beginning of next term."

At the time, Ibrahim suspected that this placement was an easy, quiet way to remove him as a non-believer from the campus, but this could have been an unfair assumption. Regardless of the reason behind the job offer, he was pleased to accept. It took him back home and offered employment. He was grateful to his teachers and leaders at Middle East College and was determined to abide by the rules to fulfill their expectations while he taught in the Adventist school in Amman.

CHAPTER 8

⟨━━━⟩

Our Young Adult Lives

MOVING TO AMMAN WAS a joyful experience, yet slightly intimidating, since Ibrahim was now preparing to begin his first job. When he reported to the Director of the Amman Mission, he was introduced to members of the school staff and discovered that he was to be the only male teacher. His arrival was a welcome addition, since the school needed a man to serve as a chaperone for the boys. He was lodged in a furnished room in the home of an Adventist family, on a hill next to the compound of an English diplomat and advisor to the King. Every day, Ibrahim walked up from school and passed through a high-walled alley where Bedouin soldiers smoked and guarded the compound's gate. On the other side of the alley, a set of cement steps led up to Ibrahim's private entrance.

His lodgings were clean and included a small bathroom and a set of steps which led up to a rooftop overlooking many roofs holding water tanks, but Ibrahim could not peer down into the closely guarded Basha's compound due to a heavy canopy of trees. There were no cooking facilities, but the room did contain a small circular heater which had a tiny flame like a simple kerosene lamp. It stood upright on out-spread legs and had a flat surface on top where Ibrahim could heat water for tea. He sometimes would simmer 5 or 6 *shamandar*, beets, all night, and then eat them with a little salt for breakfast.

The room was plain and cold, more like a monk's cell, with no curtains at the window. There was not even an adequate reading light, just a bare electric light bulb suspended on a cord from the ceiling. The walls and floor were grey cement, plastered over stone. It was sparsely furnished with a steel frame cot, chair, and table. His family in Al Husn provided bedding, a small carpet, and a few cushions, but it was far from being homey.

The lack of amenities made little difference to his relatives. To them, this residence in Amman was welcome news. At separate times during his first year of teaching, he was able to offer hospitality to two of his cousins and to his brother. They valued this assistance, because they needed a place to stay while seeking employment in Amman. Bus fare and food costs quickly exhausted any funds they had. His room allowed them to stay in the city longer, and they were all successful in obtaining work. Ibrahim remembered that each job hunter brought his own pallet from home and spread it out on the roof to sleep. Their company was welcome and made the place seem a little more like a home.

It was a happy time when his older brother Yacoub finally found a job. One Friday afternoon, he came swaggering up the steps carrying two liters of beer, singing "I found a job! We are going to drink this beer and then go downtown for a good meal." Ibrahim found two glasses, and Yacoub filled them. Ibrahim sipped his one glass while Yacoub polished off the rest. When his brother was ready to head for supper, Ibrahim declined, admitting, "I'm sorry, brother. You will have to eat your celebration meal alone. I cannot walk or even stand." From the age of eight, he was well known not to hold his liquor well.

For that reason, drink never interfered with work. His teaching job was successful, and several times during the years he taught there he was given raises. He taught Arabic poetry, algebra, and history to the seventh and eighth grade classes, which were co-ed. The school used government-approved textbooks purchased by the students.

Two sisters taught at the school and were very kind to him. The younger sister developed quite a liking for him and knitted him beautiful sweaters. They engaged in playful banter, which sometimes got Ibrahim in hot water. Once she complained to him that she was not very strong or healthy. Ever a gallant with the ladies, he replied, "What do you mean? You're very healthy! You have the legs of a camel." Needless to say, that did not go over well.

Ibrahim's own health took a turn for the worse early in his second year. His eyes again became a problem, and his vision was cloudy and blurry. Acting upon the advice of friends, he sought out a famous eye physician, Dr. Gayyaleh, who had been on the medical staff at the University of Beirut before coming back to Amman to set up his own practice. During his first appointment with the doctor, Ibrahim detailed his previous treatment for Trachoma. Dr. Gayyaleh assured him that the disease was no longer present. However, when the infection was rampant, scar tissue formed, and now an opaque film was developing over the cornea.

The doctor told him that he could treat the condition but cautioned that it would be painful. Eye pain was something with which Ibrahim was well acquainted, so he agreed to treatment knowing what was in store for him. The treatment required Ibrahim to lay his head back while a special powder was applied under the eyelid. Dr. Gayyaleh gently wiggled his eyelid until tears began to flow freely. Then Ibrahim was required to sit in the office waiting room for almost an hour until he could see well enough to walk home.

Of course, it hurt terribly, and Ibrahim would leave the office with reddened weeping eyes. After a few days of recuperation, he was expected to come back to the office for a repeat treatment. Ibrahim didn't remember how long he continued the treatments, but it seemed like an eternity. As he walked to appointments, he was already anticipating the excruciating pain he would soon be enduring.

Over time the cloudy film disappeared, and some of the corneal scarring smoothed out. Treatments were suspended because his doctor noticed that blood spots were forming on the eyeball. Ibrahim remembered Dr. Gayyaleh saying, "You have the healthiest eyeballs I have ever seen to tolerate this much extended treatment." Finally, he was prescribed new glasses, and his vision returned to satisfactory levels. His healthier eyes, and the improved prescription, allowed Ibrahim to function with no further difficulty for many years, including after he was living in America.

While his vision treatment was in progress, Ibrahim moved to an apartment, which he shared with a friend. This person was skilled at writing and often submitted articles anonymously to a famous newspaper column called *"Min Aina Laka Hatha,"* "Where did you get all this wealth?" This column was often critical of the socio-economic conditions in Jordan and espoused views which were not acceptable to the government. Ibrahim delivered the articles to the paper, because the safety of his friend could be jeopardized if his identity were known. Due to his roommate's influence, Ibrahim began to explore new areas of political thought.

Another friendship also contributed to Ibrahim's political awakening. Saleem Abassy, who was employed by the Jordanian government, wished to go to college in America and needed to pass an English proficiency test in order to obtain a student visa. When Ibrahim offered to help him study, Saleem told him about an Arab club where they could meet for tea or coffee and play chess. Ibrahim began to smoke again while he spent time at the Arab club, which was so different from the Adventist atmosphere.

The founders of the Arab club were dedicated to teaching youth how to read and write. The students were children from poor families who worked on the streets polishing shoes or selling gum and papers. Some were Jordanians, and others were Palestinian refugees. All of these children belonged in school, but Jordan was strapped for cash to build enough schools. The government understood the need to educate the street kids, so they allowed the Arab club to use school rooms during evenings if they promised to provide qualified teachers. Ibrahim joined with doctors, lawyers, and other professionals volunteered to teach in the night school. Doctors also volunteered their time for two days a week establishing free clinics to treat the sick. The associates who taught with him provided role models that he chose to emulate throughout his adult life. He admired the fact that their beliefs were followed up with humanitarian actions. Because of the influence of these associations early in his career, Ibrahim consistently spoke up for the underdog and supported causes which helped those unable to help themselves.

In his day job, Ibrahim taught a particularly brilliant young Palestinian refugee, who was fortunate to find a place in the mission school. One day she was absent due to illness, so Ibrahim walked in the rain to her home to deliver assignments. Her mother met him at the door and insisted he remove his *kofeya*, Arabic head covering, which was dripping wet. She dried it, ironed it, and offered him cigarettes while he waited. She recognized him from the Arab club.

Ibrahim knew that all of her children were bright, capable, and in need of education. He decided to try to find them a placement in the government schools. But when classes were full, Jordanian officials often operated on a system of influential favoritism and *Baksheesh,* or, grease my palm with silver. Ibrahim knew one person who possessed the necessary influence, but, the official said he had no jurisdiction in the area of schools. Also, Ibrahim was very short on the where-with-all to provide *Baksheesh,* so he was unsuccessful. He was saddened when he lost track of the family and never discovered if their children received an education.

All of these activities filled his schedule. In addition, the head of the Amman mission came to depend on him to translate his weekly sermons into Arabic during Saturday worship services. One week Ibrahim was asked to deliver the sermon to the congregation, because the mission leader was out of town. Ibrahim politely refused saying, "I'm not a strong believer in everything taught by the Adventist church. I would not be able to stand and preach in front of the congregation." Someone else was chosen to preach that week, but the episode made it clearer to Ibrahim that life within the Adventist fold could not be a long term commitment.

His understanding was confirmed during a school field trip to visit sites of Biblical importance. The head of the Jordanian mission, teachers of religion classes, and their students went on the trip, and Ibrahim went along as a chaperone. They stopped in Jericho for lunch at a dig site where workers were operating deep down in the ground. The archeologists climbed up to meet the students and answer questions. Curious students asked, "Where are the walls that Joshua knocked down?" The archaeologist explained three walls at successive depths, pointing out the discovery of stores of grain at each level, which were carbon-tested to determine structural age. The tests proved that the top wall is two to three thousand years old. The second level existed four to five thousand years ago, and the deepest level is approximately seven thousand years old. The students saw a handful of the grain, black like charcoal.

The head of the mission, who was paying for the trip, became more and more nervous and impatient. "Come now, we don't have time. Let's go! Let's go!" Then the mission leader quickly gathered up the stragglers and ushered all the curious onlookers away to the bus before any more inappropriate information might be offered. Ibrahim realized that lectures such as that given by the scientist are close to blasphemy to devout followers of the Adventist doctrine. Adventists believe that human history computes to the hour, and the magic number is three thousand years. It is impossible for a devout follower of the faith to accept that Jericho had at least three stone walls over a period of seven thousand years.

Once again, Ibrahim's faith took a leap toward a different view. He wondered about the church leaders who were determined to believe the world is only three thousand years old. Ibrahim became convinced that it was an inaccurate interpretation. He had never known about carbon-testing before this trip, and the leadership's refusal to consider such scientific proof made them seem phony. Mr. Keough at Middle East College had refused to consider Ibrahim's earlier questions about Mary's Immaculate Conception. Because of that, Ibrahim lost a good job as an interpreter. His thoughts codified, "And now the Mission leader asks me to volunteer as an interpreter for church services but will not allow me to explore with our students the evidence of Jericho's stone walls. Definitely phony!" His skills were welcome, but his intellect was not.

When Ibrahim discussed this experience in later years, he would rant in amazement over the way religious leaders spoke to their followers. He thought it obvious that scientific discoveries didn't jibe with the views they were preaching. Yet, in their eyes, science had it all wrong. Millions of people still believed that they would be lifted up beyond the world until they could touch the hands of God who was reaching down from the heavens to embrace them.

He pointed to the episode in *Elmer Gantry* when the evangelist preaches "I am the morning and the evening star." Ibrahim saw Elmer Gantry as a real phony, pretending to speak for God, while he was actually out to grab the money and the beautiful babe. That film helped to clarify Ibrahim's religious opinions. However, at the time he was teaching in Amman, he thought he should just keep quiet. He wouldn't debate with a missionary about his belief, when it was clear that he would not accept any other. But he knew he must begin to plan how to move on with his life. He knew he could not live for long within the atmosphere of the Adventist philosophy.

The way forward presented itself. A letter arrived from his friend Saleem Abassy, who had passed his English proficiency test, finished his papers, and headed to America. He landed in Walla Walla College, a small Adventist school in College Place, Washington, which offered a four-year college degree. Now, he wrote to Ibrahim urging him to follow the same path. Ibrahim replied that he must first save money, and Saleem quickly answered with a second letter in which he enclosed a bank draft for $200. He explained, "You don't have to worry about money once you get here. It is possible in American colleges to work while you are a student and earn your way. Your English is so good. You helped me improve mine. Come join me and we will study together."

With this encouragement, Ibrahim began the effort to secure his papers. The first step was simple. He went to the U.S. Information Center and easily passed the English proficiency test. By then, his third year of teaching had begun. He spoke with his principal, explaining that he wished to complete his college degree in America and that he hoped to attend Walla Walla College. She was very supportive, probably because he planned to attend an Adventist college. So, he gathered his Middle East College transcripts, completed the college application forms, and waited.

During that same fall, a huge problem of the heart arose. It became very clear that the young lady who knitted sweaters was hoping for something much more permanent from Ibrahim. Perhaps she felt she needed to capture his commitment before he headed off to America. He struggled with how to deal with this concern. He knew that if he allowed the relationship to progress any further, marriage would surely need to follow. She was beautiful, intelligent, and kind-hearted. But, she was also deeply devoted to her religious beliefs. He was convinced that they could not reconcile her strong faith with his ever stronger doubts. He knew if he stayed in Jordan and married her, his life would become enclosed by the Adventist circle. If he followed that scenario, it would be impossible for him to live a happy life.

With this struggle settled in his own mind, he determined to resolve the situation. One day, she urged him to sit down beside her while she made an effort to express her strong attraction to him. Ibrahim became a man of few words. He took her hand, smiled lovingly at her, stroked her face, and simply said, "I cannot. This is not for me." He could see the disappointment in her eyes, but she seemed to accept his decision and said nothing more. They continued to be friends, at least on the surface, and she exhibited no more indications of her desire for romance. Later, when Ibrahim arrived in America, her beautifully-knit sweaters came with him. Perhaps, her heart came with him, too.

With affairs of the heart resolved, Ibrahim was free to pursue the tasks still needing his attention. While he was waiting to hear from Walla Walla College, he decided to go to the United States Consul's office to begin his application for a student visa. His principal arranged to have his classes covered by other teachers so that he could go during working hours. He entered the waiting area of the Consul's office and approached the desk. Behind it sat a stern, prim, and proper middle-aged Arab lady. The card attached to her desk declared her name to be Miss Khoury. "What is your name and your business?" she asked officiously. "I am Ibrahim Ayyoub and I need to know what I must do to receive a student visa to attend college in America," Ibrahim answered. She sniffed and directed, "Sit over there. I will call you when it is your turn." She pointed toward a row of chairs on the far side of the room.

He sat down and began the first of many long waits in that office. Miss Khoury seemed to ignore him completely while he sat for more than an hour. Finally, she called his name. "Do you have an acceptance paper from an American college?" she inquired. "I have applied to Walla Walla College, and I'm expecting to hear from them very soon." She frowned, "You must first have this document in your hand. Go, and come back when you have received it." Ibrahim thanked her, but as he walked out he felt distressed by his wasted day.

This was just the beginning of his trials with Miss Khoury. Each time, after he carefully prepared lesson plans for his substitute teacher and made the lengthy trip to the Consul's office, she would require him to cool his heels in the row of chairs. After a long wait, she would call him over to her desk, give him one small direction to fulfill and send him away. "You must have a health exam." "You need a clearance report from the police." "Bring us" this. "We need to see" that. Ibrahim grew frustrated; every new demand meant another missed day of teaching. On his next visit, Miss Khoury once again demanded an item he had not known was needed. This time Ibrahim lost all patience and exploded. "Miss Khoury, it seems you are making every effort to prevent me from obtaining a visa!" His voice rose louder as he continued, "I am a teacher. I miss a day with my classes each time I come here. Would you please just give me a list of all that is needed? Then I can fulfill the requirements at one time in one visit!"

About that time, the inner door opened, and the United States Consul himself appeared. "What's all this shouting about?" he inquired. Miss Khoury replied stiffly, "This person is disrupting our office because he wants to obtain a student visa." The Consul eyed Ibrahim and turned to Miss Khoury, "Give me his folder." He shuffled through the pile of papers and again looked up at Ibrahim. Speaking to him in Arabic, he directed, "Come with me young man," and ushered him into his office. "Have a seat while I check over your file." Ibrahim sat down in wonderment that such an important American official would be speaking such excellent Arabic.

"Mr. Ayyoub, I believe that all your work is in order. We need just one more item and that is proof that you have enough funds to pay for your education in America. Do you have the necessary amount of money?" "Yes sir, I do," Ibrahim answered with a straight face knowing that it was not true. "Good. Bring us a copy of your bank statement, and your visa will be issued." Ibrahim stood to shake his hand saying, "Thank you so much for taking the time to help me. May I ask how you come to speak such excellent Arabic?" The Consul smiled and replied, "I had plenty of time to polish my Arabic while I was stationed in Egypt. I wish you luck with your studies in America. Good day." This time Ibrahim left the United States Consul's building in a much happier frame of mind. All that was left for him to do was produce a large amount of money, which he did not have.

After leaving the Consul's office, Ibrahim traveled back to school to check on how his classes had fared for the day. He sat in his empty classroom ostensibly checking lesson plans, but really stewing over the money issue, when his principal stopped by the door. "How did it go at the Consul's office this time?" She was aware of his frustrations during the past visits. "It went very well. I actually received an audience with the U. S. Consul himself, who studied my file and determined that all is in order. He needs only one item more, but that requirement creates a huge road block. I must prove that I have enough funds to pay for my education in America."

His principal paused and then said, "Mr. Ayyoub, I am going to write a check made out to you for 3,000 dinars. Use it to open a bank account. They will issue a receipt to present to the Consul's office. Pay me back when all is finished."

Ibrahim could not believe his ears; "I cannot take that kind of money from you!" His principal replied, "Oh, you are not taking it from me. I know how these things work. This requirement of proof is just a formality." Ibrahim was speechless with gratitude. Unable to express how he felt, he just shook her hand, and nodded agreement with the plan.

It worked. The Consul's office issued his visa, and Ibrahim was able to return the 3,000 dinars to his principal. Again, her generous spirit showed itself. She handed back 350 dinars for his fare. With grateful tears welling up, he said, "I don't know how to show my thanks to you." She continued to show her kindness by saying, "When you get rich in America, you can pay me back."

It was now nearly the end of October, which meant leaving his teaching job at mid-term. Due to the long delays at the Consul's office, he was already terribly late to meet the acceptance deadline scheduled by Walla Walla College. He finished up loose ends at school, thanked all his associates, and promised to keep in touch. He purchased a boat ticket and scheduled his departure for early in December from the port in Beirut. He went the rounds of his friends at the Arab club one last time, saying goodbye and thank you.

His brother, Suleiman, traveled from his surveying camp to wish him well. As they were visiting, Suleiman observed, "You will probably marry in the United States." Ibrahim answered with a vehement shake of his head, "Oh no, never! I've seen in movies how the American women behave. They 'do this' and 'do that.' They are not morally strong." Suleiman's reply was one that lodged permanently in Ibrahim's psyche. "You should not judge people by your standards. You should attempt to know something about them and try to understand their position. Perhaps they are doing what conforms to their standards of morality." With that excellent piece of brotherly advice, Ibrahim packed up his few belongings, said his last goodbyes to all, and traveled to Al Husn.

Ibrahim was pleased to discover his father's home to be very calm. Only his mother and father and Saad were at home. He spent several quiet days with them. He did not wish a big fanfare or goodbye feast to honor his departure. Miriam helped him replenish his clothing and bedding in preparation for living in a colder winter climate than that to which he was accustomed. He spent long hours looking around his home attempting to plant a permanent image in his memory, because he knew he might not revisit it for a long, long time.

He sat quietly in the cement-covered courtyard enjoying the fresh open air. Remembered occasions of laughter and chatter among guests and relatives came rushing back to him, as did the imagined aroma of his mother's many meals prepared there. He particularly wished to remember the feelings of security he felt while sleeping on a pallet under the stars and his beloved moon. Of course the moon would travel with him to America, but would it ever be as beautiful?

He wandered into the tiny kitchen with its single table and shelves piled high with stores of food as he attempted to fix in his memory the hours he spent there in the company of his mother, father, and siblings. Then out he went again to the courtyard corner where he carefully examined the well, which had become such a boon to his mother in eliminating many of the trips she previously made to carry water from a distant neighborhood well. The courtyard well was really a cistern, with its round hole covered with a cement plug under which hung a rope and bucket to haul up water when the cistern was full. Ibrahim remembered watching during the rainy season as the first rain washed the flat roof, and after that, all the cool, fresh rainwater was captured and piped into the cistern.

He checked out the family's dark storage area which had been the total living space when his father and mother were first married. He remembered the piles of wheat stored there when he was very young and of his plan to barter wheat, before he thought better of it. Then he studied the two rooms adjacent to one another which were added before he was born. One room was used for family activities and sleeping, containing mattresses on long rugs. He also printed in his mind the beautiful wooden bureau used for storing the family treasures. He caressed its smooth sides and was reminded of being trusted to retrieve the money box from within its locked doors.

Finally, he spent a good deal of time peacefully resting in the reception room whose walls were lined with chairs to accommodate the many visitors who made their way there. The most important corner of the room was always saved for strictly Arab-style comfort, where the best mattress was arranged for people invited to sit in the place of honor with Toufiq, head of the family. The mattresses were placed over long woolen carpets on the cement floor and piled with brightly colored cushions to provide comfortable arm and back rests. He stared up at the roof of these two rooms, which was crafted of timbers covered with creosote-treated thatch, and he stroked the cool plastered walls which were two feet thick and hollow with openings at the top for storage of wheat or other food items. He chuckled as he remembered climbing to the openings to retrieve the best pomegranates instead of the oldest, nearly rotten ones.

His eyes traveled up the bare reception room walls to rest on its only decorations, two portraits placed very high, almost to the ceiling. One was a portrait of Farhan, Toufiq's dear friend and a leader of the village. The other was a recent photo of himself taken as he prepared for departure. The recent placement of that photo was important to him, because its message was clear. Toufiq and Miriam were bestowing blessings on their son who would soon be heading out to seek his way in far-off America. Ibrahim knew his leaving brought them heartache. Still, even though they would miss his presence, they validated his choice by displaying his photo in their place of great honor.

The day for departure arrived. Miriam felt as she always did at leave-taking while she watched her son venture off. Her feelings must have been multiplied a hundred-fold this time. In addition to her sorrow, there was strong anxiety about the unknown, the great divide of an unseen ocean, and a foreign land with new customs and new dangers. He would be absent for a very long time. Her heart was heavy and her tears flowed freely as she kissed and hugged, then kissed some more, this adventurous child of hers who was once more setting off on his own.

Miriam stood at the courtyard gate and watched Ibrahim and Toufiq walk away until they were out of her sight. Toufiq wished to spend a little time alone with his son before seeing him off. Earlier in the day, he had offered Ibrahim money. But, Ibrahim held his arm saying, "No, Yaba. You must keep your money for things needed here. I have plenty." He felt sure the contents of the money box were barely sufficient for their needs, a new pair of shoes, or a piece of good meat. He had some of the principal's loan left after buying his ticket, and he was determined to accept no more financial assistance from his family.

Now, as they walked along, Toufiq stopped, took hold of his son's shoulders, looked him in the eyes and gave his blessing. "We have raised you. You have lived with us until you were an adult. We trust your judgment and we wish for you only a happy life. We have confidence that you will succeed in everything you attempt. *Salaam Alekum.* Peace be with you." Ibrahim was shaken to see tears in his father's eyes. It was the only time he had ever seen his father cry. He realized what a responsibility was being placed on his shoulders by those firm hands. He must live up to the pride and expectation he saw in his father's face.

Then he looked up to see some women they knew standing close by. So Ibrahim told his father, "I must go now to say goodbye to those dear souls." This allowed Toufiq to take his leave. He said he had something he wished to do and walked away in a different direction. Ibrahim watched him go, knowing that Toufiq could not face other townsfolk while he was so emotionally vulnerable. As Ibrahim set off on his journey, his mind kept going back to the sight of his father's tears. He thought, "During the years I spent with the Adventists, I worked my tail off to live up to what my parents expected. I know I can do it again."

The first portion of his journey covered very familiar territory, the taxi to Irbid and the car to Beirut. There he would stay overnight with his Uncle Ibrahim. Although young Ibrahim had been a student at Middle East College for four years and had even taken Arabic classes from his uncle, he had never been invited to his uncle's home. He marveled at his uncle's comfortable, spacious villa. They spent a pleasant evening, and Uncle Ibrahim gave him messages to carry to Uncle Gabe, his brother, who lived in Detroit, Michigan.

The next day, Ibrahim carried his luggage by taxi to the dock and boarded a small ship to Italy. The Mediterranean was calm with smooth sailing, and this respite from all the leave-taking gave him time to reflect on his decision. Of course, Saleem had initiated all this by writing the letter and sending the $200. But Ibrahim knew that his reasons for leaving Jordan went deeper than that. He had no ill feelings towards the Adventists. They had been very kind to him, and he was deeply grateful. At the same time, he knew that his changing beliefs created impossibilities for continued life among them.

It made him second-guess his decision to apply only to Walla Walla. It was another Adventist school, so he was not really leaving their environment. He justified the choice because they offered a degree in engineering. He could return to Jordan and easily be hired with that training. Also, Saleem was there. And, the truth was, he didn't know any other colleges in America. He was excited to dock in Italy, because it meant he was one stage closer, but the authorities instructed him that he must stay on board, since he did not have a visa to enter Italy.

The following day he transferred to the large, three-year-old SS Constitution. It was the beginning of December, 1954, and as they traveled the North Atlantic sea route, winter storms were ever present. Ibrahim's bunk was deep in the bowels of the ship with no windows, so he spent as much time as possible up on deck. There, the storms would send the rain towards him as if it were falling horizontally instead of from above. He saw many sailors in uniform bending over the railing or ropes in spasms of sea sickness, but he was not affected at all. He marveled at the walls of water approaching in mountain-high waves, which made it look as if he would be engulfed and carried to the ocean depths. Then, the ship would rise above, glide over the crest and sink into the canyon of water below. He never tired of watching and loved the thrill of experiencing a roller coaster ride on the waves of the ocean, while breathing in the exhilarating fresh sea air.

At night after dinner, entertainment was provided in the large ballroom. Pretty girls came up to him asking to dance. Although he knew nothing about dancing, it was great fun to pretend he did and slowly shuffle around the floor in some semblance of musical rhythm, holding one sweet young thing after another in his arms. As the long voyage neared its end, he began looking forward to seeing his Uncle Gabe in Detroit. He watched on deck as they sailed past the Statue of Liberty, which has welcomed so many others to America. His thoughts were not on its significance so much as they were filled with relief that he had come this far with so very little difficulty. He was beginning to feel confident that he had made the right decision to attempt this biggest of adventures.

Although he did not know it at the time, his ship was one of the last big ocean-going vessels to land immigrants at Ellis Island. Soon after his arrival, Ellis Island was closed. But Ibrahim has a vivid memory of the huge immigration hall with the lovely domed windows. And many years later, he was thrilled to visit it again with our daughter Laila after it had become a historical landmark. He was even able to locate his name on The American Immigrant Wall of Honor.

After disembarking he stood in line waiting for his turn at one of the tables of investigators to have his passport and visa checked. When it was his turn, of all the questions asked by the immigration official, the one which amazed him was, "Are you a communist?" He replied somewhat flippantly, "Do you really think if I were a

Communist I would say yes?" The official replied, "You would be surprised how many do say they are communists. We allow them to enter and keep a close eye on them all the time they are in the country. But if you say "no" and we later find out you are a communist, we will throw the book at you." Ibrahim quickly assured him that he was not now nor had ever been a communist, so the official stamped his passport and waved him on.

At that time, Ibrahim was unaware of America's concerns about communism. It was much later when he learned about the harsh Internal Security Act of 1950 which barred members of communist or fascist organizations from immigrating to the United States. However, in 1952 changes to immigration law caused policies to soften, and very few were being detained by 1954. If he had known about the McCarthy era brouhaha taking place in America, he would not have spoken so carelessly to the immigration official.

As he walked over to claim his luggage, he was stopped by a stranger who asked his name. The man was sent by Mrs. Branson to bring Ibrahim to visit her family. Ibrahim knew that Mrs. Branson, his geometry teacher at Middle East College, was now living in New York. Her husband transferred back to America to become the head of the entire Seventh Day Adventist New York Conference. Since they were aware of his coming, he had been invited to be their guest when he arrived. Ibrahim was touched by the kindness but was very late to reach his next destination. He asked the man to convey his best regards and explain why he must travel on. He asked instead that the messenger assist him in locating the bus depot. What he did not say was that he had another reason for declining the invitation. He knew they would notice that he had resumed smoking and he did not wish to cause disappointment for his teacher.

The Branson's friend obligingly drove him to the Greyhound depot where Ibrahim used some of his diminishing funds to purchase a ticket to College Place, Washington, with a stop-over in Detroit. Thanking the kind man, Ibrahim soon boarded a bus headed out of New York and west. He saw none of the sights of New York. He didn't visit the city again until years later when he rode across the country in an old VW bus with a group of college teachers to attend an American Federation of Teacher's Union convention. Even then, he was not much for sightseeing and was teased because he slept through most of the trip. "Well Abe, how did you see America?" he was asked. His teacher buddy answered for him, "Like a pair of eyelids."

It was most fortunate that Ibrahim was not asleep when the bus made a stop at an inspection station. An official climbed into the bus asking, "Is there anyone on board traveling on a passport?" Ibrahim raised his hand, and the official came to his seat to look at it. Then he said, "Please get off the bus and come with me." Ibrahim did so, wondering what trouble he was facing. When they reached the station office, the inspector asked, "What is your final destination?" Ibrahim answered he was traveling to attend school at College Place, Washington. "Well sir, right now you are about to cross the border into Canada. This bus travels part of its route in Canada before swinging back down to enter the U.S. when it reaches Michigan. We will be very happy to welcome you into Canada, but your passport carries a single-entry visa to the United States. You will not be allowed to re-enter the U.S."

Ibrahim realized he was in a big predicament, but the official did not seem to be worried. He said, "We need to get your luggage off this bus, and I will put you on a different bus which will take you to a nearby city with a bus depot. I will send directions that the bus company must cut you a new ticket to carry you to Detroit on a route which does not enter Canada." Ibrahim thanked him gratefully and complied with the directions he was given. After not too long a wait, he boarded the new bus and headed on with his trip.

He arrived in Detroit at about 3:30 a.m. and carried his small suitcase into the bus terminal. He knew it was too late at night to arrive at his uncle's, so he decided to wait out the night where he was. He remembers naïvely thinking, "When it's daylight, I'll find a bus and tell them to take me to Allen Park and drop me off at the home of Gabe Swidan."

Ibrahim started walking around the terminal, which was full of people even at that hour. The surroundings included many rows of shiny wooden benches filled with tired passengers, both adults and sleepy, cranky children. All just waiting for the night to end and for their departures. His eyes fell on a young man of about his same skin color, and there was room beside him on the bench. The young man smiled and indicated that Ibrahim would be welcome to sit there. He asked the usual questions of Ibrahim, "Where are you from?" and "Where are you going?" Ibrahim shared his information and learned that his companion was originally from Pakistan and was now doing graduate study at a nearby university. He was waiting for a bus to take him to Canada for a visit with some of his family during the holiday break.

They fell into conversation about the political situation in the Middle East, and time passed enjoyably. After a while a blonde, blue-eyed man dressed in a good suit got up from the bench behind them, walked over to their side saying he had overheard their conversation and asked if he might join them. They moved over to make room and the new person sat down between the two of them. Ibrahim felt a bit uncomfortable in his presence, because he had heard stories of how secret police, wearing plain clothes, would act just like this fellow in an effort to discover information to use against someone. Because of this worry, he kept quiet, just listening to their conversation. But the new guy seemed to be quite knowledgeable about their subject of conversation, so Ibrahim began to relax.

It was almost 5:00 a.m., and Ibrahim could see daylight showing through the terminal windows. That was when their newest companion turned to him and asked, "What is your name and where are you from?" Ibrahim answered, "I am Ibrahim Ayyoub; I just arrived from Amman, Jordan and I am waiting until morning to contact my uncle Gabe Swidan in Allan Park, Michigan. I did not want to disturb him while he might still be asleep. The blonde man asked, "Why don't you telephone him?" "I don't know if he has a telephone," Ibrahim replied.

The man led him over to a row of phone booths, and the man picked up a directory, searched through it, reached in his pocket for coins, inserted them into the slot, and dialed. After just two rings a man's voice answered. "Is this Gabe Swidan? Good. I have a young man here who wishes to speak with you." Then, he handed the receiver to Ibrahim who excitedly spoke into the mouthpiece, "Hello Uncle, this is your nephew, Ibrahim. My mother Miriam is your sister." "Oh, my blessed, darling young man! Where are you?" shouted his Uncle Gabe. "I am here at the Greyhound station in Detroit." "Well don't move. I'll be with you in fifteen minutes." With that command, he hung up.

Ibrahim reached into his pocket for coins and turned to speak with his assistant, "Let me pay you for the phone call." "Oh no, it was nothing. Keep your change." Then Ibrahim took a small notebook from his pocket and asked, "Will you please write down your name so that I can thank you properly for this great help you have provided?" The man grinned, "I was afraid you would ask for that information, and you will be very surprised." He took the notebook and wrote his name in perfect Arabic, Tareq Kammash.

"I am a professor of nuclear physics here at a university in Michigan. I am from Amman, Jordan. I know all your family and I served in the same division of the army as your brother, Nasser." Ibrahim was floored! Tareq had none of the usual physical characteristics of an Arab. Ibrahim realized he must be Circassian, an ethnic group that tends to be blonde and blue-eyed, who migrated to Jordan from the Caucasus centuries ago. He vigorously shook Tareq's hand, and they walked back to the bench to wait for Uncle Gabe. What had been unknown to Ibrahim was the close proximity of Allen Park to downtown Detroit. He quickly realized that he would have appeared very foolish indeed if he had asked a bus driver to take him to his uncle's house. After living in America for fifty-eight years, he still felt so very grateful for this serendipitous turn of events and he always remembered with pleasure the name of the kind, blue-eyed, Tareq Kammash.

Uncle Gabe arrived quickly, causing Ibrahim to feel rushed in saying all he wished in thanks to Tareq. As his uncle came hurrying up to greet him, there were kisses, hugs, exclamations of *al hamdu lillah,* praise God, *Ahlan wa saahlan,* welcome, and more kisses and hugs. Ibrahim introduced Uncle Gabe to Tareq and quickly explained what a great help Tareq had been.

Then, it was time to head out to the car and drive the short trip home. Aunt Gertrude, Patsy, and Eleanor were already up, dressed, and preparing a deliciously warm breakfast. This was Ibrahim's first meeting with Gabe's family, and he was quickly impressed with their warmth, friendliness, and welcome. Aunt Gertrude was an American whom Uncle Gabe met when he immigrated to America. She was an elementary school teacher, and their two daughters were attending college close by so that they were able to live at home. Their home was comfortable, but not nearly as spacious as Uncle Ibrahim's villa near Middle East College in Lebanon.

There were two bedrooms on the main floor. One was for his aunt and uncle. The other was shared by Patsy and Eleanor. A comfortable cot was prepared for Ibrahim in the basement with plenty of warm covers, since Michigan winters can be very cold. After their welcome meal together, Ibrahim was extremely grateful to be allowed to curl under those covers and drift into a long and peaceful sleep.

His visit with them lasted slightly over a week. Ibrahim gave his uncle the letter he carried from Uncle Ibrahim, and they found time to visit every evening about the family back home. On the weekend, Ibrahim rode around Detroit in the family Ford with his uncle while Gabe ran errands for the family. Uncle Gabe was so excited to have him there that he did not drive as carefully as usual.

Once, he ran a red light while he was busy talking, and a cop pulled him over. Allen Park was such a small suburb community that everyone knew Uncle Gabe. So when the policeman leaned on the window, he exclaimed, "Hey Gabe, what's going on? Is there an emergency? Do you need a police escort?" Uncle Gabe grinned and replied, "Oh no, my dear friend. Do you see this darling boy beside me? He is the son of my dearest sister and just arrived in America. I am drunk with happiness to have him here. Please give me my ticket." The policeman gave his greetings to Ibrahim and said, "No, Gabe. No ticket today. Be on your happy way."

During the work week Ibrahim couldn't help but be aware of how hard this family struggled. Uncle Gabe woke up early each morning in order to reach the Ford factory where he worked. Aunt Gertrude was also up at the same time, preparing lunches for the family and leaving food for Ibrahim. Then she caught a ride with a fellow teacher to make it to her school on time. Both girls were early risers in order to catch a bus to their morning classes.

Ibrahim slept late in the mornings and woke to find a nice breakfast waiting for him on the kitchen table. It was often an Arabic breakfast of boiled eggs, flat bread, cheese, *za'ter,* his much beloved spice mixture from home, and olive oil. After eating, he washed up his dishes and stuck his head outdoors, thinking to explore the neighborhood. But he quickly changed his mind due to the extreme cold. Instead, he explored his Uncle's magazines and experimented with their small black and white TV. But it didn't offer much of interest due to his limited English skills. Also, at that time, television was not much more than a technological novelty.

He luxuriated in his quiet days alone after the rigors of his travel and he rested up in anticipation of the long bus ride still awaiting him. In the very late afternoon, the family arrived home, prepared dinner, visited with him, and retired early to do a repeat performance the next morning. During their visits, Aunt Gertrude learned that he had a December birthday, so she took the time to describe how birthdays are celebrated in America. Later when Ibrahim arrived at Walla Walla College, he was surprised when she sent a birthday cake in the mail. This was his first ever birthday celebration, one of the many new American holiday traditions he would encounter.

During the last few days of his visit in Detroit, there was respite for the family because the Christmas holiday arrived. Ibrahim delighted in watching them decorate their home and put up a Christmas tree, also a first! He had seen one stiff little fake Christmas tree when he was a child in Al Husn. It was placed one year in the Christian Men's School, but Christmas at home had always meant church, feasting, and visiting. In Michigan, Aunt Gertrude trotted out her favorite holiday cookie recipes and traditional foods from her culture. Uncle Gabe prepared Jordanian *Kibbeh,* a mixture of seasoned meat, onion and bulghur served both raw and baked. That was a welcome taste of home to Ibrahim, and he was so very grateful to enjoy it with them. Friends in the community dropped by the house to meet him and to wish season's greetings. Mainly, they just shared in their quiet joy of being together. When he realized that an exchange of gifts around the tree was in order, it distressed him that he had nothing to give. This made no difference to the family though, and they reassured him until he felt comfortable.

He hated to leave this gracious, loving family and head off into the cold Michigan winter-scape traveling to places unknown. His aunt and cousins gave him their good-bye kisses and hugs at the house. He tried to fix in his memory the sight of these three wonderful people as they stood waving to him while he drove off with his uncle. On the way to the terminal, Uncle Gabe tried to press some money into his hand. Ibrahim was not at all sure if he was doing okay, but he was certain that this hardworking, dear uncle needed every penny he had for his family, so he assured Gabe he had plenty.

Ibrahim found himself back on the bus and heading out of the terminal. He saw his uncle standing on the loading platform and waved. As he rode off, he reflected on his dear mother and felt a new appreciation for her family from having this opportunity to become acquainted with her brother Gabe.

Ibrahim had very few memories of the countryside during his bus ride across the United States. He was amazed at the size of this new country and bewildered by the unbelievable distance he was required to travel. When he rode to school from Al Husn to Beirut, the entire trip was accomplished in a few short hours. He began to think he might not have chosen Walla Walla College if he had realized how far he would need to travel to get there. To him, scenery outside his bus window did not offer much of interest. It all looked flat, cold, and endless, a stretch of two or four lane highways. He was surprised at the way drivers stayed in their proper lanes and drove quite sedately. There was none of the frantic weaving in and out while "laying on the horns" that he was accustomed to in Jordan.

It was more entertaining to "people-watch." Americans were interesting. They were much more open to sharing their stories with total strangers than his countrymen. Jordanian travelers, especially women, were reticent to divulge information about themselves. These American passengers carried on long involved discussions about their destinations, their families, and their views. He did not enter into conversations, so much as he listened to other passengers while attempting to understand the meaning of all the new words he was hearing.

New words were particularly bothersome at the rest stops. He got off the bus with the others and watched to see where the smokers were standing so he could light up a quick puff or two. If folks headed into a café, he would follow, knowing he would have time to order something to eat. But then, he was faced with deciphering the strange words on the printed menu. Early on, he found his limited English to be useless in a restaurant. He asked the waitress, "Please give me a cup of milk." She asked, "What?" His request was so simple, "A cup of milk" he repeated. She still didn't get it. Finally he pointed to his neighbor's glass, tipped his hand towards his mouth to pantomime drinking and said, "Milk." "Oh," she said, "You want a glass of milk?" He nodded and tried to understand the difference between "cup" and "glass." He knew to ask for a cup of coffee or a cup of tea, why not a cup of milk? On later stops, he learned to flow with the tide by pointing to the food that the person seated next to him was eating. "Give me some of that." This behavior became firmly entrenched. Over the years, even after his English was much improved, Ibrahim always chose to wait to see what others were ordering and then say, "I'll have the same thing."

The trip continued uneventfully until he reached Salt Lake City. It was evening, and some passengers left the bus, and some passengers boarded. He was in a seat by himself, but his former seatmate had left pillows. His new seatmate had plastered her face with cream and lipstick and began to doze off. Since there were extra pillows, he asked if she needed one. To hear him tell it, she threw herself in his lap! Unbeknownst to him, her lipstick smeared his pale jacket, his necktie, and his white shirt.

When he reached Walla Walla, he was met by the Dean of Students and his teenage son. He rode in the back seat, and every once in a while the son would look at him with interest. Ibrahim thought maybe he was admiring his necktie or jacket, but then the father was doing the same, and Ibrahim thought they were a strange pair.

When they reached the campus, the Dean took him to the President's office, where there were already guests. The president looked at him, and the guests looked at him. Finally, the president asked if he knew anybody on campus. He told them about Saleem Abassy from his home town, so they sent for him.

When Saleem arrived, he wouldn't go near Ibrahim, who was puzzled by his behavior, because he could have come close at least to shake hands, if not hug. Then the president asked if he wanted to room with Saleem, and when he accepted, they were excused. They walked out, Saleem Abassy in front, and Ibrahim said, "What the hell Saleem! How come you're so cold?" Saleem replied, "Don't talk to me. I'll tell you later." They arrived at his room and he practically lifted Ibrahim off his feet and placed him in front of a mirror. The shirt, the necktie, the jacket—all painted with lipstick and cream and whatever. Not even the dry cleaner could get the stains out of his clothes.

Ibrahim felt the incident caused prejudice based on assumptions, and as a result, he had no help selecting classes. He stayed about a month and began to know some Arab students. Dawoud was from Iraq and told Ibrahim about Eastern Oregon College in La Grande, seventy miles away. He knew the foreign student advisor, who had been a Fulbright scholar teaching in Baghdad. So Ibrahim traveled to La Grande and located the professor teaching a biology class. Ibrahim crossed back and forth in front of the door until he was noticed. Professor Quaintance came out to ask if he could help.

After class, they walked to the Registrar's office, where Ibrahim presented his unofficial transcript and said he was looking for a college that would put him in classes immediately. The Registrar not only agreed but also offered him a scholarship. He wouldn't have to pay fees, and he would have a campus job. The structure was similar to his schooldays in Beirut, and that was all Ibrahim needed to hear. The next day, he was off to Walla Walla to get his things.

He started classes in January, 1955. Everyone at the college was helpful and kind; especially Mrs. Miller, Director of Student Housing, who gave him a job washing pots and pans and mopping the kitchen floor. He also cleaned and polished floors in the residence, Hunt Hall. These jobs allowed him to earn some money and some high praise from the cooks. When Ibrahim went through the cafeteria line, the cooks would heap his plate and sing his praises. They said they had never seen the floor so clean.

Dr. Quaintance was also very attentive. He invited Ibrahim to attend civic organizations and churches with him to share a little about Arab culture. For those meetings, Ibrahim prepared a short talk about his life at home which seemed to impress everyone who came to hear. At one church, a woman thanked him for coming and said, "We are so ashamed of what we have been doing in our church. A collection plate has been passed many times with the request to 'Pay a dollar to kill an Arab.'" He didn't know how to answer such a statement. It was the first time he had come in contact with anti-Arab sentiment, and he did not know how to deal with it. It made him believe that it was a good plan for Dr. Quaintance to take him around to groups, if it would help change such thinking.

One day, he was called to the Registrar's office. He thought he must be in some kind of trouble. Instead, he was invited to sit and was handed a letter with a sparse address: Ibrahim Ayyoub, Hunt Hall, USA.

The envelope seemed to have traveled to every Hunt Hall on every campus in America and each time was marked: 'Not at this address.' He opened it, and it was from Yaba! Dr. Johnson chastised him for neglecting to write to his parents. He gave the lame excuse that he wasn't much of a letter writer. Toufiq must have learned from other students at Walla Walla College that Ibrahim had moved to Hunt Hall but he did not know any more of the address. Dr. Johnson wanted to keep the envelope as a testament to the efficiency of the U.S. Postal system.

One reason Ibrahim had not written home was because he wanted first to assure himself that he could do well. After that, he relaxed a bit and began to enjoy his new friends, who made it their purpose in life to Americanize him. His roommate, Bill, took particular pleasure in teaching him American expressions. Two of these caused him confusion. Ibrahim walked into their room and Bill yelled out, "Abe, stick a board in that hole!" Ibrahim started looking around for a board or a hole but saw nothing. Bill realized then that this guy knew nothing. He meant close the door. He also confounded Ibrahim when he said he was going to hit the sack. Ibrahim turned around in his chair to see what sack Bill planned to hit. Instead, he just crawled into bed under his quilt. Finally, Bill sat down one afternoon and said, "Abe, you and I could talk with each other for hours and you wouldn't understand anything I said. I think I need to teach you how we talk in America." He began taking pains to point out what various expressions meant, and Ibrahim worked hard to pick up what he was taught and use the new terms whenever possible. It was becoming clear to him that learning this American slang was just as necessary as being able to speak proper English.

The other person who was an important influence during those first months in La Grande was a cowboy character named Roger Tiller. Roger was interested in a friendship because they both were older than most of the students. Ibrahim was twenty-seven, and Roger was a year or two older. He had been working in his home town of Burns, Oregon and kept hearing other townsfolk brag about their sons going off to college. After a while, he noticed the same kids back in town. Roger was never one to mince words, so when he met the parents in the coffee shop he asked what happened. He heard excuses about the kids not liking school. Then the parents would turn the tables on him and criticize by saying, "You couldn't cut it either if you went to college." That became a challenge to Roger, and he headed off to prove them wrong.

Ibrahim never saw anyone work harder than Roger, who woke up early to eat breakfast, and then headed back to his room to study. After another break for lunch, he'd go back for more study. He started out earning "C's" with one or two "B's." The following quarter he pulled his grades up to "B's" with one or two "A's." The instructors admired his determination and enjoyed his ability to josh everyone. One day, he ambled into the library and called the fearsomely prim and proper Miss Bliss by her first name. Roger had no fear and called out, "Helen, ain't you got no good books in this here place?" Miss Bliss pretended to be shocked and then grinned, "Oh Roger!"

Ibrahim could never tell when Roger was telling a true story and when he was "pulling his leg." They all had to write a term paper for their very demanding and highly respected History professor. Roger wrote on the history of soap and declared that in former times, soap was made from urine. No one believed him until he produced a picture of a chamber pot accompanied by a description of how urine was used. He added that bit to his paper because he loved to grab every opportunity he could to shock. Dr. Johnson accepted the paper and gave him a good grade. Roger's term paper reminded Ibrahim of the story that, long ago, Bedouin women collected urine from their animals, which they then used to shampoo their husband's hair.

Roger took time on the weekends to teach Ibrahim how to play. He loaded up his car with college students and drove them all to the local bar. The other guys could manage quite a few beers while Ibrahim struggled to drink one. When it was time to leave, he was the wobbly-legged one that could not walk unassisted, requiring support from strong shoulders on each side just to walk from the car to the dorm. On one of these outings, he sat at the bar and, when his glass was empty, he just reached over and helped himself to a refill from the tap. He ignored the fact that the tap was still flowing and started to drink. Luckily, the bartender, who had become a good friend of Roger's, roared with laughter. Roger was turning into a long-time friend. He had an ability to pull Ibrahim away from his tendency to be shy and show him a glimpse of American life.

Spring quarter ended, and Ibrahim didn't know what was coming next. He was not earning enough with his work in the dorm to save for the next year's expenses. Then he got a scholarship offer from the Registrar's office. He wanted to know who was paying the scholarship so that he could say thank you. The Registrar explained how scholarships work and assured him he was not like those who "think that America owes them an education." Reassured, Ibrahim enjoyed his classes during that first year and also was well-liked by his new friends, but he struggled to settle in to college life in America.

CHAPTER 9

⸻◆⸻

My Blossoming Social Life

WHILE IBRAHIM GREW UP with the self-confidence to embark on such an ambitious undertaking, I grew up a self-conscious mess. Throughout much of my girl-hood and early adolescence, my self-image was in the dumps. I was fat.

Our family described it as being "heavy" or "large-boned for my age," but they added to my problems by allowing unkind discussions as they compared me with my slender cousin. I remember once being gifted a whole box of chocolates and then being criticized for eating them. At the same time my ornery skinny brother was encouraged to eat everything in sight with no ill effects. I became a somber-faced child, hiding my abilities and personality behind that façade so that others, except for one or two special friends, could not know the real me.

My mother worried about my attitude and constantly strove to help me improve my social graces. During the year I was twelve, she encouraged me to join Job's Daughters. This was a girl's organization whose mem-

Dumpy Doris age 12

bership was exclusive to relatives of Masonic Lodge members. I qualified since both Dad and my Uncle Walt were Master Masons. In our little town, "Jobies" offered a social alternative to the strong pull from an active Mormon youth program. Neither Mormons nor Catholics were allowed to join Job's Daughters.

Job's Daughters is based on the story of Job, and includes secret passwords and a ritual with lots of memory work for officers, who wore white Grecian gowns tied with a cord over the breast and waist to accentuate a young girl's figure. Members marching into meeting looked like angels without wings. The Honored Queen wore a white satin gown covered by a long, royal purple, velvet cape and a beautiful jeweled crown. As a dumpy twelve-year-old, I sat on the sidelines to watch these angels strut their stuff.

But, I didn't remain on the sidelines. The guardians of the Bethel, which is the name given to a chapter of Jobies, realized that I could sing, and they put me to work in the choir. Soon, I was appointed to fill an office. Younger members usually started as inner or outer guards for the door. I soon graduated to hold one of the five messenger stations, where I was required to memorize long speeches telling the story of Job. Folks discovered I also had a good speaking voice with an excellent memory for the ritual.

My mother was particularly determined that I take part in the social aspects of membership. There were cake walks, dances, and box socials where boys were invited. The dances were a special trial for me, because I was required actually to touch a boy. At box socials, I lived in fear that no one would bid on my lunch and then when they did, I had to eat and talk with the winner. I'd rather hide in the bathroom!

On top of that, Mom began a determined effort to help me lose some of my pudge by talking me into trying one more diet. This one was completely vegetarian and because Mom was not really a successful cook, she left out protein and iron, so eventually I became anemic. There was not even any bread! She stoked me with watery soups loaded with bits of carrot, soggy boiled onion, and cooked celery. It was vile.

I still don't know if my mom's many diet attempts worked or if it was the result of maturation, but by the beginning of tenth grade I finally developed a figure that looked nice in my new store-bought clothes. Mom told me her principal had observed, "You know, Doris would be really pretty if she could ever learn to smile." This tidbit caused me to rethink my attitude, and I renewed my efforts to smile. I began to repeat a jingle in my head as I marched to its rhythm on the way to school each morning: "Put a song on your lips, a smile on your face, and make friends, make friends."

And, I did make friends. I loved being in plays and speech club. We had a gang of giggling girlfriends who did everything together. Wonder of wonders, during my eleventh grade, the Jobies elected me to the highest office, that of Honored Queen. My parents were ecstatic! Masonic participation was important to our family, and my achievement was a real "feather in their cap." That year, our guardians took the unusual step of inviting the DeMolay chapter from Gresham, Oregon to travel across the state for our installation ceremony. DeMolays are the boys' counterpart to Job's Daughters. Their coming was not a special tribute to me. It was just my good luck they came at that time.

I was feeling pitty-pats over the DeMolay hitting town. The high school gymnasium was reserved for the occasion, and friends and relatives were sent invitations. I purchased small gifts for each of the officers and for our guardians. Special music and flowers were prepared. There was ritual to memorize and marching formations to practice. One would think it was my wedding, instead of a simple installation of officers in a club.

Our gymnasium had high walls with rows of bleachers crammed with relatives from Boise, members of our church, and Mom's friends from all over the valley. My brother Jim was absent because by then he was in the air force, but Mom and Dad sat proudly in the first row. We lined up nervously out in the hall until we heard the singing begin, "Open, Open! Open the gates of the Bethel." That was our cue to march in, escorted by the marvelous DeMolays. We were seated in a triangle formation in front of the altar. As officers were installed, they were escorted out of the triangle to their stations and their chairs removed until I was the only one left seated. My costume was the plain white satin gown, bare of cape or crown. The installing officer from the De-Molay then escorted me to the altar where I knelt and placed my hands on the Bible. That good-looking boy intoned the virtues of an Honored Queen, her generosity and grace, her taste and leadership, "the beauty of her young womanhood."

Oh Joy! I took it all to heart. He was talking about me! Then he picked up that fabulous velvet cape and draped it over my shoulders. I crossed the cords over my breast and tied it around my waist, and then came the crown. After that I was helped to my feet and escorted to my station where he announced "Doris Rigney, who has been installed as Honored Queen for the ensuing term" and presented me with the gavel.

Everyone applauded as the solemn ceremony end-ed. I realized that I was now responsible for the well-be-ing of all the new dumpy twelve-year-olds in Jobies. My path toward leadership had begun. After all that pomp, I rattled off my thank-you speech almost without a hitch. I thanked everybody, guardian, officers, DeMolay but the Honored Queen was expected to introduce her parents, and Doris, the excited, self-centered young woman, for-got even to mention them. My heart has ached over that omission ever since.

Failing to offer public recognition towards my par-ents is especially dismaying when I pause to reflect on the tremendous effort Mom and Dad exerted to give us a stable home, even though for most of my early child-hood, our family lived in places owned by others, either rentals or government housing. Wherever we resided, in a very short time after we moved in, my mother man-aged to make it more than a house by carefully arranging our furniture, throw rugs, knick knacks, and books to

Honored Queen

make the empty rooms become cozy and welcoming. My brother and I never had cause to feel doubt about where home was.

Deep in my mother's psyche, there must have been a strong yearning for more stable roots due to her own childhood experience of being pulled from hither to yon by her restless dad. Never did her family enjoy permanence, and after she married my father, the country sank into the Great Depression, which forced our family to follow the jobs. In this respect, Dad was always successful. He took pride in the fact that not once was he unemployed, even during the deepest years of economic downturn with bread-lines and Worker's Progress Administration jobs for countless numbers of America's workers. Dad often accepted employment which did not match his abilities. During one period, he even took on a second job of sweeping floors every evening in the school where Mom was teaching. That must have been damaging to his self-esteem.

Years later, during the fall of 1947, Mom learned from the other teachers that there was a re-possessed house for sale in the new Stunz subdivision of Nyssa, situated across from the small city park and only two blocks away from the First Church of Christ. Mom came floating home from school full of dreams about homeownership. She bounded into the cramped living room of our little apartment, rented from Old Man Bennett, and announced to Dad that she wanted to go see the house being of-fered for sale at 223 S. 7th Street.

Dad was always cautious about any new venture and asked, "Why on earth would you want to do that? We don't have any money to buy a house." "That makes no-never-mind," she answered. "They are holding an open house, and we at least need to go see." On the following Saturday, we walked across the threshold of what was to become Mom's dream home. By today's standards, the house was quite humble. There were five cement steps situated smack dab in the center of the house leading to the front door. The sidewalk leading up to the steps was bordered on each side by a poorly-maintained lawn full of weeds and anemic grass. There was a driveway, also full of weeds, to the left of the house but there was no garage. And the huge backyard was piled with dirt, un-landscaped.

The realtor ushered us into the empty living room with walls painted a dirty, off-white. It had a hardwood floor in very poor condition with no filler in the cracks between boards and badly scratched from careless use. Our footsteps echoed in the emptiness as we toured the two small bedrooms, the one bare-bones bathroom, and the miniscule kitchen. There was only room for a tiny two-seater table, plus the cup-boards, sink, and spaces for a stove and refrigerator. There was no dining room.

Steps led from the kitchen down to a full, unfinished basement with a cement floor. A huge stoker furnace and coal bin dominated the area. Directly below the up-stairs kitchen there were two plumbed stationary cement rinse tubs. From the ceiling, a light bulb hung on a cord containing a plug-in socket for connecting the electric cord of a wringer washer, also not included. The basement walls were rough cement, and a bare stud wall partitioned a space that would have made a nice-sized room, if finished.

Dad was silent while in the presence of the realtor. Jim and I didn't offer opinions either, but Mom gushed to all of us about how she would arrange her furniture and which bedroom could belong to whom. It must have been obvious to the realtor that he had "hooked a live one." But when we returned to the apartment, Dad held forth with his many negative opinions on all he had seen. He fumed that we had no down payment worth anything. He tried his best to convince Mom that committing to such a major purchase was unwise. Mom's answer was one I would hear many times in the coming years, "But if we don't buy now, I'll never have the pleasure of owning while I am still able to enjoy it." She held firm with her argument, and Dad gave in. They signed the papers, and we moved in.

I was too young to follow the ins-and-outs of the real estate deal. I constantly heard the name of Lawyer Henningson but understood no details. I vaguely knew that we were required to pay double monthly payments for a long time to make up for no down payment and that we would need to save for a huge balloon-payment which would become due sometime down the road.

In order to make the double payments, we gave up the front bedroom so that it could be rented out to a single male teacher. He was not allowed to cook in his room and Mom did not provide board for him, so I wondered where he ate. He was a real loner with many idiosyncrasies. He didn't smoke, but while he was there, a strange odor wafted from his room every time his door opened. None of us ever figured out what caused it.

He always marched into the house to greet us with "Hi Ho!" Mom started returning his greeting with "Ho Hi!" but he never cracked a smile or indicated he had even heard her. He immediately disappeared into his room and stayed there except to visit the bathroom before retiring. We gossiped about him, and none of us liked his being there. The renter probably thought we were the strange ones. But his rent helped make the mortgage payments, so we put up with the awkward situation. This meant that both of us kids were relegated to the basement.

The renter left after a year which allowed me to move upstairs to the back bedroom while my parents disinfected and scrubbed out the front bedroom so they could move in. I remember the thrill of leaving the dank basement where sheets were hung to provide some privacy for me. In my new room, I had a steel-framed camp cot exactly like the government-issue ones in the bunkhouse at the Dam. Perhaps the bed came from the dam. I had orange crates for shelves. But it was my very own room, and I was ecstatic.

After I moved upstairs, Mom employed creative use of orange crates to make a real room for Jim in that shell of a basement. We had no funds whatsoever for real contractors, so Mom stacked orange crates to create a wall between the laundry room and Jim's sleeping quarters. She then lined each box with wallpaper, of all things. Some of the crates faced into Jim's room and some faced outward to the laundry room to serve as utility shelves. That orange-crate wall stayed in place until I cleaned out the house in 1978. She nailed flattened cardboard boxes on the other bare-stud wall and wallpapered over them, also untouched forever. Then, beyond the furnace and next to Dad's workbench, she re-organized what had been my bedroom into a jury-rigged sleeping area for guests.

Other renovations and improvements went on, with Mom constantly pushing and Dad always dragging his feet. It didn't take her long to begin wielding a paint brush to spruce up the walls and throw rugs to cover the worst spots on the floors. We were required to endure the poor condition of the hardwood floor for many years, but occasionally Mom valiantly rented a floor-polisher from the grocery store. I helped, and we worked on our hands and knees to apply paste wax and then polish.

I remember one occasion when Mom was required to go to a long evening meeting, and Jim generously offered to help me wax and polish. Mom was pleased with the offer, so of course, I agreed. After she left, he got out the can of wax to begin applying it. He was in a hurry to finish because he planned to meet his friends at the movies. I threw a hissy fit because I knew the correct procedure. The floor was filthy and it needed to be scrubbed on hands and knees, the stuck-on dirt scraped away with a spackle knife, and then allowed to dry before applying the paste wax.

We got into a huge fight over it, until, in exasperation, I exclaimed, "Oh go on to your darned old movie. I'll do it all by myself. Shades of *Little Red Hen!* "Really, are you sure you don't mind?" he asked. I fell for it. Of course I minded, but I became the martyr and sent him off. I shall always remember that long lonely struggle. The floor seemed huge to me, but I did it properly and it was shining and beautiful by the time Mom arrived home. I tattled because I wasn't about to allow Jim any credit for his false promise to help.

The floor stayed lovely for about one day and then, as usual, shoe scuffs and tracked-in dirt took it back to its former condition. Mom never did manage to refinish it properly so that it would hold a shine. Eventually, she sank us deeper in debt and purchased wall-to-wall carpeting. This was her *modus operandi* for each new purchase made for the house.

Again and yet again, we kids witnessed the same basic confrontation that went on between Mom and Dad. "Jesse, if we delay Wilson's bill until your next paycheck, we can afford to make time payments on the lovely new sofa I saw." To which Dad replied, "Jo, you know we're not able to make monthly payments on the things you've already bought." So she would sit back down at the table and do some more figuring and present her case again. Each time they had such a discussion, she kept at it until Dad gave in. He knew full-well that the decision was unwise, but it was not in his nature to stand firm until he won such an argument with her. He would just sit back in his chair and engage in a roaring bout with his ulcers while Mom committed to the new purchase.

The table where she sat to figure out the monthly bills was one of Mom's earliest splurges after we moved in. It was a beautiful, second-hand, oak table with six matching chairs. She placed it in the living room adjacent to the kitchen doorway. Thinking about that table elicits strong memories. It had a slight jiggle while she sat to do her writing. That jiggle was a small but daily irritation if I was sleepily trying to consume my eggs and toast while she energetically wrote out the list of chores I must accomplish after I came home from school.

Two extra leaves were stored in a compartment under the table. For breakfast guests, it became the place where Mom directed waffle-making production. I still own and use her ancient electric waffle iron. That and two other items in Mom's kitchen also played important roles for waffle-making. One is a beat-up, cream-colored, melmac spoon which saw too many hot times and is therefore mostly burnt brown; the other is an oval, chipped, grey graniteware serving platter.

The platter was loaded with crisply fried bacon, at least a pound or two. She fried the bacon in her cast-iron pan and then cracked about a dozen eggs into the hot bacon grease. Because she often became distracted with chatter, the eggs were often over-cooked with crispy brown bottoms and edges. The overcrowded eggs had to be separated with a spatula. I ate many a rubbery egg with yolk turned to stone because it sat too long on the hot stove.

When the eggs and bacon were prepared and set aside to keep warm, Mom made the waffle batter. She dumped Aunt Jemima waffle mix into a large mixing bowl, poured in water and oil and beat in an egg with that treasured Melmac spoon. This was carried to the table and placed beside the round waffle iron, which was sitting on a thickly-folded newspaper. Even as an adult with my own kitchen, whenever I arranged these items at our table on top of a flowered plastic tablecloth, I began to smell breakfast cooking before I even started, and I could almost hear my mother's voice as she spooned batter and shared gossip she'd heard at her school, her church, or read in the *Gate City Journal*.

The ELECTREX waffle iron was a present when my parents were married in 1930. While I was growing up, it was always a skuzzy black, inside and out. Layers of crusted oil and bits of leftover burnt waffle mix dripped down the outside onto the narrow rim at the base. In its newer days, it had a legitimate handle, but that broke off long ago. So the iron had to be opened and closed by sticking a metal nut-pick into the hole where the handle should have been. An ancient and scary electric cord, with some of its wiring exposed, plugged into two prongs protruding from the base. The plug had an on-off switch so that Mom didn't have to remove it from the wall between waffles.

Years later, I searched hardware stores until I found a new cord. I confess to attacking the outside with an S.O.S. pad and shining it. Antique hounds would have a fit. Don't mess with the original patina of an ancient object! For sure, Mom never messed with it. Her waffle-making routine reminds me of the way a queen would reign supreme over a proceeding. When the batter was properly mixed and the table set with plates, coffee cups, cutlery, butter and Aunt Jemima Pancake Syrup, she carried in the fry pan full of eggs and the platter of bacon. Beside the waffle iron she also assembled a small dish of bacon drippings, a fork, a nut pick, and a rolled up piece of waxed paper that she used repeatedly to grease the iron. In later years, the wrapper was replaced with a *bona fide* pastry brush. She sat down, summoned the family, and waffle production began.

The little iron always was quite efficient. Shortly after it was plugged in, everyone could smell it heating up with an odor of previous grease and batter. When it was hot, Mom poked in the nut pick to lift the lid. This required dexterity, because the lid would not stay up independently. One hand held the lid while the other dipped the waxed paper in oil and brushed top and bottom of its 5½" diameter. Little puddles of oil always dripped out and onto the newspaper below. After greasing, she put the lid back down to reheat for a second or two and then again lifted it to spoon batter into the smoking interior. Almost immediately, our nostrils were filled with the delicious promise of waffles. It was a delight to see the iron top rise as the waffle began to puff up. Mom often misjudged the amount of batter, and we watched the excess trickle down the sides.

Too much batter

Mom kept up a patter of conversation until she could fork out the finished waffle. Dad, at the other end of the table in his denim shirt and overalls, always got the first one. The Queen of Waffles served herself last. Along with overdone eggs and scads of bacon, our wait was finally rewarded with a crispy golden waffle. We slathered on butter and syrup and tucked in with delight. Pleasant times around that table are prominent in my memory of childhood days. If the company was my Aunt Dorothy and Uncle Walt or Aunt Geneva and Uncle Cliff; we could expect long drawn-out conversations among the women as they sat over the remains of the meal and nibbled on the left-overs: a little bite of the last piece of bacon, or a quarter piece of cold waffle with just a touch of butter patted on to go with another cup of coffee. While their talk carried on, they often consumed another entire meal from the left-overs.

The men always left the table to the women and relaxed in the easy chairs to hold rather loud political discussions about the terrible state of affairs now that Truman was leading us towards ruin and Old Lady Eleanor was out stumping around the country making whiney-voiced speeches about human rights. Even as a youngster, I privately felt disgusted with the way those men talked so rudely about our national leaders. I chose to sit with the women until Mom told me it was time to begin clearing up the table.

Washing dishes was still considered a daughter's role with no expectations of help from Jim. Rarely did my brother stay long in the living room after a meal was finished. He either headed downstairs to his room or found an important reason to leave the house. After all, he was a busy high school student involved with acting in high school plays and training on the boxing team. He was developing into a good boxer and won important roles in the plays. When I wasn't fighting with him, I secretly admired his acting ability. The example of his skill led me to take part in drama as soon as I was old enough.

But at that time, drama wasn't offered in junior high, so I had to be content with music. I developed friendships with a gang of girls, and we often worked on singing duets or trios with the hope of performing for school assemblies. I don't remember actually being on stage in junior high, but we thought we were good enough to be. In my last year of junior high, our family came up against a huge bump on the road which knocked all thoughts of stage performances out of my head. After my parents struggled to make steep payments for two years, I was frightened to learn that Lawyer Henningson served foreclosure papers, and we were going to lose our house.

I do believe that it was a deceptive loan policy which the lawyer encouraged my folks to do. They really had no business taking on the burden of home-ownership, although the total purchase price was a mere $8,200. But, there must have been small print which they failed to read carefully, since neither of them was skilled in "law-yer-ese." Possibly their situation was similar to that of the struggling families during America's 2007 housing bust. My parents became victims of the same shady lending practices that put people in untenable debt positions then.

Of course, Dad was furious, but his anger was not directed towards Mom. In his mind, the entire fault lay in the lap of that devil Henningson who had "snookered us into a rotten deal." If the truth be known, it's more likely that Mom's way of managing the family finances caused the difficulty. It would not surprise me if she missed some payments or sent in partial payments, since that was her way. She always justified her actions as being necessary in order to buy what she thought the house needed. There must have been some breach of the contract, or Lawyer Henningson couldn't have begun foreclosure. I know the folks had long worrisome arguments about bills, but we kids were never included in the discussions, so we just hung around the fringes and were kept pretty much in the dark.

Dad was ready to throw in the towel, but Mom was determined to find a way out of the difficulty. That ratty little house had been owned at least once before, and it had so many things wrong with it when we first moved in. Mom had exerted two years of effort to create a comfy home, and she refused to allow it to slip away. One day, I was surprised to learn that Mom took a day off from school and drove alone to Boise to plead her case with the mortgage company. I distinctly remember my fear while she was gone.

I do not know the details that she worked out, but I do know that she came bouncing back with a twinkle in her eye that told us she had somehow managed to save our home. Jo Rigney rides to the rescue once again! Abe later suggested that she might have played the old "It's all in who you know" card. He believed that she just might have mentioned that her husband, Jesse Rigney, was the son of Idaho State Senator John Rigney. Mom was not above name-dropping if she felt it to be useful.

With the fading fear of losing our home, our family settled into the routines of home ownership. Mom kept after Dad until he leveled the back yard. Some poor-quality, high-alkaline topsoil was delivered, but it was all that Dad was able to obtain. He raked it over the gravel, spread the grass seeds, and watered it carefully. It produced a lawn which was even more anemic than the front, but at least it cut down on constant wafts of dust sifting into the house. Not much other landscaping ever happened out back; Dad planted one lone green-apple tree smack-dab in the middle of the lawn. We mainly went out there to take out the garbage, to burn trash in the burning barrel, or to hang out laundry on the sturdy clothesline which Dad constructed from rusty steel T-shaped poles set in concrete.

I didn't mind that our yard was scruffy, because we had a nice park right across the street. Every winter, fog rose up off the Snake River, and surrounded every tree, bush, and weed in that park and froze it into a delicate white hoar-frost. When I skipped out the front door to trek the two blocks to school, I entered a fairyland. Engulfed in frosty mist, the silence and beauty was broken only by the raucous calls from my friends, the big shiny black crows who cawed their morning greetings to me. I felt a real affinity to them and answered with my returning caws. I was pretty good at it, and I believed they thought I was one of them because they never failed to answer. Perhaps the neighbors wondered if the Rigney girl might be a little teched in the head to be talking to crows.

The fog had a slightly suffocating moistness that caught the breath in a pleasant way. It was such a pleasant relief from the sugar beet factory. Even worse than the cloying odor of cooking beets was the sour smell trailing from the trucks which zoomed on the highway just a block away from our house, carrying beet pulp out to farmers' silos. During the winter, processing the sugar beets into granulated sugar dominated the economic life of Nyssa. Locals called it "the campaign," and we were all pleased to see the trucks rolling again because of the work it provided our community. So, I did my best to ignore the odor and spend my walking time communing with the crows.

This behavior is why I was often late for school. We lived so near school that I could hear the first warning buzzer from our street. Then, I increased my speed and charged through the school house door just as the second buzzer sounded to inform me that I was about to be late again. Once, during my senior year of high school, when I was late to first-period English, Mr. Attebery, whom I highly-respected, demanded that I write an essay in apology. I really liked my teacher and believed the feeling to be mutual; so, I took a chance on the clever idea to write a whimsical piece entitled, "'Twasn't My Fault." I filled a page with outlandish excuses beginning with "Sompin simply awful happened to me the other day. It ain't never happened before. I was late to school. You see, 'twasn't my fault. I feel sompin' turrible about it." I ended each paragraph with "'twasn't my fault." I was fairly certain that Mr. Attebery would accept it, and that proved to be the case. He gave me a high grade on the paper and then wrote "and it ain't my fault" across the top of the paper,

Tardiness became deeply ingrained and carried over into my adult life. As a teacher, my co-workers often teased me by joking, "Well, school can start now, Doris is here." Dawdling in the morning was one of the ways in which I exhibited passive resistance to my mother's early morning energy, as I lay abed ignoring her calls. I knew that if I got up the first time she called me, I would be subjected to her litany of plans on how the day was supposed to go. She would finally give up on me and head off to meet her morning duties. As soon as I heard the front door slam, I moved with lightning speed to dress, gobble down the cold, greasy eggs she'd left on the table, and rush out the door with my books under my arm.

Throughout my high school years, I carried those books home each day with the expectation of doing all assigned homework. However, I am now ashamed of the many times I carried them back to school with the homework untouched, knowing that I could sit in the back of first-period English, pretend to be paying attention, and do the algebra assignment for second period. I believe the teachers were much too easy on me, or else I was really good at bluffing my way through, because my grades were always excellent and I graduated among the top ten students academically. School work was never something that I remember sweating over until I reached college. There, I discovered to my surprise that instructors wouldn't allow time during their lectures for me to sit in the back of the room and catch up!

Social situations were another story. I constantly felt the odd-person-out as I walked down the halls between classes. Even after my body slimmed down and I became rather pretty, I never felt free to chatter and flirt with the boys. I had my share of girlfriends, and we enjoyed the usual stuff that teenagers cooked up to have fun. But not so in the boy department. I later came to see that I was much too serious a young lady to understand how to go about the casualness that school flirtations required.

Participating in high-school plays helped. My previous envy of Jim and my determination to be on stage finally paid off. I took part in every drama activity offered. Nyssa High School had a tradition of staging three major productions a year. The first, which usually occurred in October, was set up as a one-act play competition. Each class chose and prepared a play. All four were performed during the same evening. Then the audience judged and voted the best performance. I turned out every year for every possible audition and usually landed a part.

During my freshman year, the play was titled *Aunt Miranda's Will;* I was assigned the part of Aunt Miranda. One might assume that made me the lead player. But not so! Aunt Miranda did not appear in the story till the last scene and then, I had just two lines. But obviously, those lines must have carried great importance, because we won the competition! We also won as sophomores the following year with *Wilbur Minds the Baby.* Once again I was cast as the mature female, Mrs. Maxwell. Something about my demeanor, or possibly my size, always got me that type of role. However, by then, I had managed to find my smile.

Juniors and seniors were allowed to perform three-act plays. As a junior, I played the lead as Toasty, proprietor of Poison Pot Café, a local kids' watering-hole in *Love is Too Much Trouble*. I held forth with motherly opinions on all the teenagers' love troubles. Our senior three-act was a mystery-comedy, *Tiger House*. Again, I played an elderly lady, Aunt Sophia. It was a fun part with lots of scary suspense from jewel thieves and mysterious visitors. Aunt Sophia managed to lose her false teeth and became hysterical. Other members of the family tried to calm her down with a little nip of brandy. It turned out that she decided to help herself to more than a nip, and I brought down the house with my drunken behavior. As I threw down the last drink in one gulp, "I need strength—lost my teef, you know—Hot, isn't it?" When the wind slammed a window, I called, "Aash, 'ish too bad. Let the little wind moan—nice little wind. Blew 'way Sophie's teef!" I exited unsteadily, singing, "Oh the wind blew high, o'er my old Kentucky Home."

In reading through my senior high school annual, I found myself laughing at comments of friends about the sight of Aunt Sophie getting drunk up on stage. One of my best friends wrote, "'member the drunken scene–we were going to do something to your 'cider' but decided not. Can't even 'member what we were going to do." I've reflected on why I enjoyed playing these roles. I believe it allowed me to be someone other than the self I was reared to be. For sure, this is what makes role-playing so valuable for persons seeking therapy. I also know that the ability to put myself into another role easily is what made kindergarten teaching such a delight. It was so easy to think like a five-year-old and play up the drama of the story I was reading to the children, or to manufacture activities which not only served an educational objective but also were just plain fun for the kids. Also, there was enough of my mother's goofy sense of humor in me to make it possible to assume a different character, such as drunken Aunt Sophie.

When not on stage, I spent hours working with the stage crew, as we painted scenery, sewed costumes, and searched for props. In that more relaxed atmosphere, talking with the boys seemed natural. Perhaps the guys also relaxed while working with me backstage when they became aware of this other side to Doris. She was definitely not the serious student they knew in the classroom.

But nothing ever led to my being asked out on dates. I went stag with my girl-friends to the school dances. My memory-program for the Senior Prom provides a space for me to list the name of my date. I filled in, "Me, myself, and I." It was a delight if someone asked me to dance. In those days, girls didn't ask the boys unless it was a "Sadie Hawkins Day Dance."

If I had been closer in age to my brother, he might have been helpful in offering advice while I struggled with my social development. Making loads of friends and being popular were always so easy for him. But he was four years older and therefore graduated from high school just as I was ready to enter. I felt that I was on my own. Happily, change soon came to our family structure and altered those feelings.

Before I entered high school, the spring and summer of 1949 became significant in many ways for our family. Immediately after his graduation, Jim left the family nest to enlist in the Air Force, and I was feeling sort of at loose ends with him gone. Then we learned that Gennie was ready to attend public high school. Mom's determination to help Gennie improve her educational opportunities had produced results. In 1947, Gennie was allowed to transfer to the Oregon School for the Blind, where she completed eighth and ninth grades. Gennie no longer needed special schooling and was prepared to be in public school. But, she was required to attend an Oregon high school in order to continue receiving services through the Oregon State Department of Rehabilitation.

Gennie needed to live with an Oregon family in order to attend public high school. It was easy for all of us to agree that Gennie should come to live with us and attend her last three years at Nyssa High School. The state was willing to hire someone to read her lessons aloud, and she had a talking book which was like a phonograph with records.

Also, she was proficient in typing and took notes skillfully and rapidly in Braille. I was fascinated by the sound of her little hand-held stylus peck-peck-pecking away on her slate. She inserted special thick paper between the hinged metal sections of the slate and secured them with four pins at the bottom. Away she went, every bit as fast as I could take hand-written notes. She punched in the Braille symbols from right to left creating bumps in the paper. When she was ready to read what she had written, she removed the paper, turned it over and read from left to right with her fingertips. I expressed interest in learning to write in Braille, but it required more work than expected, so I quickly gave up. I regret to report that, later in life, I exhibited the same lack of dedication when I attempted to learn American Sign and Arabic.

Gennie was always full of fun when we had gotten together during the summers, so I looked forward to having her live with us. Finally, I would have a sister! I was sure it would be lots more fun than living with my rascally brother. Because we agreed to share a bedroom, Mom moved the double bed upstairs from the basement and put the old camp cot downstairs. I was a restless sleeper and tended to kick Gennie a lot, and she said that she often woke up just as she was being pushed out of bed. I, on the other hand, remember nothing about that, except that twin beds soon replaced the double. She also recalled that since I complained loudly about having to listen to *David Copperfield* on her talking book, she finally moved the machine into Mom and Dad's bedroom in order to finish her assignments.

We soon discovered that sisters could have just as many petty disagreements as brother and sister. Gennie was relieved to be offered the basement bedroom, and she spent the Christmas holidays getting settled into Jim's old room, with the double bed. I kept the twins so I could invite my friends for sleepovers. Our adjustment difficulties didn't end there. Mom had the great idea that I could become Gennie's reader and earn a little pocket money. I initially agreed to do it, but I'm ashamed of my on-the-job performance. I thought her reading assignments were boring, and since Dad had earphones on his short-wave radio, I figured that I could read the lessons aloud while listening to the radio with the earphones. Consequently, I read in a listless monotone and didn't even pause if she asked me a question or needed something to be repeated. She was very upset when she discovered what I was doing, and when Mom found out, I was fired.

The new reader, Janet, was only ten years old when she began reading for Gennie. But she was great at her task and kept the position until Gennie graduated. Janet walked over to the high school every day after classes and read the day's work while Gennie took notes in Braille. Then, Janet walked with her across the busy highway until Gennie was safely on the sidewalk of our street where she was able to walk the rest of the way independently.

We walked to school together every morning. Since we had taken a private preschool tour through the building during the summer, finding her way around the building was easy. She was a master at memorizing doorway entrances and counting steps. If she had a chance to walk through an area once, her brain imprinted the layout. People were seldom prepared for how independent Gennie was or how much she expected to do things for herself. She patiently explained what she did or did not need when anyone approached her with eager offers of assistance. She quickly developed friendships among her classmates in the sophomore class, and they enjoyed walking with her when moving between classes. She easily moved between classes, but her isolation bothered her when she ate lunch alone, when her friends had different schedules from hers. It was lonesome when others didn't make the effort to come and visit with her while she ate.

Her most serious logistical problem involved the stubborn hallway lockers with poorly-constructed combination locks. All new students suffered in our effort to master those difficult locker combinations. Finally, the school arranged for her to have a locker on the end of the row and allowed her to close it with a padlock and key. One of my lasting memories of high school is the mingled hallway noise which erupted between classes; laughter and teasing, serious discussions, clanging locker doors, and frustrated wails when the locks failed to open.

During the summer before her senior year, Gennie went to training camp for Guide Dogs for the Blind and came home with Thunder, a Dalmatian. After that, she had far more independence and no longer had to put up with my slow-poke morning routines. We loved that dog! When he was wearing his working harness, he was all business, not to be petted or played with, carrying out his responsibility of guiding Gennie wherever she needed to go. Thunder did have his idiosyncrasies, however. Gennie loved to attend concerts, and he could not be trained to stop howling obnoxiously during the performance. She often found it necessary to get up and leave or else just leave him at home and go with a friend. We thought perhaps he was just a very musical mutt who thought he was singing along with the music.

Gennie was game to try any activity. She was even determined to learn how to bowl. Now, we live in a time of beepers in pucks, so that blind kids can play hockey, but this was in the days before the advent of such technologies. Her effort was a valiant one, but we won't discuss her bowling scores. When she took part in the physical education classes, her teachers discovered she had a natural grace for dancing, so Mom insisted she take private dance lessons at a studio in our neighborhood. Gennie was grateful that Mom urged it and credits those lessons with improving her posture and teaching her to walk more gracefully.

Soon, my parents discovered that Gennie had a cousin who was a Mason, which qualified her to join Job's Daughters. Her initiation ceremony was unique, because she required someone to walk with her as she traveled though the ritualistic marching from station to station. I had been expected to walk her through the ceremony. But, I learned that if I worked very hard, I would be allowed to sing Handel's soprano solo, *I Know That My Redeemer Liveth.* I was determined to master this difficult piece of music, which is important in Job's Daughter's ceremonies because the lyrics come from the biblical story of Job. Mrs. Wilson, our talented guardian of music, patiently worked with me for weeks. Instead of me, Janey, Jim's girlfriend, offered to be Gennie's escort. Since Gennie didn't know her at all, she felt a bit uncomfortable at first. But Janey was very kind, and they got along. Jim and Janey were married several years later and Janey became a part of our family.

After Gennie's induction, Job's Daughters became a major social outlet for both of us, and we were both appointed to several offices. Gennie was Chaplain more than once and amazed everyone when she managed to learn the complicated marches to and from the altar independently. Nothing in Job's Daughters was ever simple about the way officers must move around the room, and the official ritual book describes everything in detail. We had to "march" a prescribed number of paces from point A to point B, then turn a square corner to face east, and march to point C and face north, south, west, or whatever. It was all a complicated rigmarole designed to make us look mysterious and important to onlookers. Gennie had to count her steps and practice over and over to execute a proper square corner. But she persisted until she could do it well. Once again she employed her marvelous navigational skills which always stood her in good stead.

Mom and Dad were so proud of her accomplishments. Dad displayed a particular gentleness in his dealings with Gennie, and she felt he was more of a father to her than her own. Dad loved to tease her and gave her the nickname of Squeak. Who knows why? Once, she came upstairs all upset because she knew she had failed miserably in her attempt to paint her toenails. No one else was home, so my dad got out the polish remover and patiently cleaned up each of her toes.

Still, Mom and Dad both had a tendency to underestimate her abilities. She was forbidden to operate our wringer washer, but she really wanted to be able to do her own laundry. Consequently, we waited until one day when both parents were out of the house, and I taught her how to use the wringer without catching her fingers. We were so proud of our accomplishment. But, it backfired! After Mom became convinced that Gennie could do it safely, she was written into the to-do list for her turn at the laundry. She suffered over Dad's overall buckles and the horror of having to wash his handkerchiefs, the same as I did. She continued to learn more about cooking too. Her hearing was so acute that she could listen to a pie in the oven and determine when it was done by the sound of the bubbling juices. However, she got tripped up occasionally. We all teased her mercilessly one Thanksgiving while Mom was stuffing the turkey, and Gennie innocently inquired, "Jo, how do you stuff the turkey legs?"

In addition to domestic skills, she learned important academic skills, too. The Biology teacher, Mr. Steffans, had very demanding ways, and he expected us always to pull top grades. "Eachus, you scored a '2' on that last test instead of your usual '1!' Shape up!" Our grading system began with '1' as top mark and went down to '5,' which indicated failure. Mr. Steffans taught Gennie to take extensive and accurate notes, a skill that paid off throughout college. I also enjoyed his challenge for me to do well, and dissecting a frog in college was no trouble at all due to his meticulous instructions.

Charlie Steffans played piano in a dance band for high school functions. The student body was rolling in the aisles with delight whenever we could convince him to play and sing for an assembly. Since he was such a fearsome personality in the classroom, we could scarcely believe it was our same Mr. Steffans, as he sat up on stage, during an assembly, singing: "So you met someone who set you back on your heels, goody, goody!" The kids roared their approval of this grumpy old man who was willing to let his hair down. But, he did do one disturbing thing. Some of his advice demoralized me and did not meet with my mother's approval. It created in me lasting doubts about my abilities.

During my junior year, the school administered aptitude tests. The questions all dealt with our preferences. "Would you rather collect and classify butterflies or attend a social tea party?" "Are you more comfortable reading a book or going out with your friends to the Friday night dance?" Since I was raised as a loner, all my answers reflected my preference for solitary pursuits. Mr. Steffans met with me to assess my results, and I shall never forget hearing, "Rigney, the results of your test definitely show that you will never be successful in any profession that requires you to work with people. You need to become a research scientist or a librarian." By then, my mother had already begun the gentle pushing to point me towards teaching. After my advising session, I told her I would never be an effective teacher because Mr. Steffans said I didn't have the aptitude." Needless to say, Mom was visibly furious that an advisor would say that to a student. In one hour, he managed to discourage me and destroy years of her efforts to strengthen my self-confidence.

Soon after that, Mom approached me with a need at church. Our new pastor and his wife, Rev. and Mrs. Hollingsworth, were expressing worry over lack of a Sunday school teacher for the three to five year-olds. Mom thought I should offer my help.

Since I'd spent many hours babysitting, I decided it would probably be okay to try teaching the little kids. After all, it was more like babysitting while parents attended their own sessions, but I was pleasantly surprised at how much I enjoyed it. The tiny ones were sweet, and we got along just fine. I even taught them to sing, "This little light of mine, I'm gonna let it shine" for the all-church program. The more success I experienced, the more Mom must have secretly gloated, knowing that Mr. Steffans was definitely wrong. I had no way of knowing it at the time, but that first class of Sunday school children became the harbinger of things to come for my future successful career as a kindergarten teacher.

Looking back, not only did babysitting provide me with the confidence to know that I could work well with kids, but it also was the way that both Gennie and I paid for extras that the folks couldn't provide. It paid my way each year to church camp. But, it didn't provide enough for me to buy some of the neat clothes the other high-school girls had, so I tried other, more difficult, summer jobs, like working the belt in the potato sheds. That didn't last long because my motion sickness reared its head. I was absolutely no use at working a moving belt. But the job did require a social security number, and that's when I started paying into the fund which now provides my monthly retirement checks.

During the summer after Gennie graduated, we both hired on at the corn cannery. She became a whiz at folding cardboard boxes and wore out endless pairs of rawhide gloves. Gennie saved her money for when she enrolled at the University of Oregon. The State Department of Rehabilitation paid for books and tuition, but she needed personal funds, and this job helped fulfill her needs. Gennie's graduation and move from our home to embark on her college career marked the beginning of a long period of separation from "Sis."

She came home for holidays, but neither of us was very good at letter-writing, and we began to go our separate ways. Gennie majored in literature and trained to become a high school teacher. After college graduation, she moved to St. Louis where she spent her working years teaching English to sighted students in a Catholic high school.

When Gennie left our home in Nyssa to attend college, I experienced mixed emotions. While I missed her fun companionship, it was also nice to be an "only child." Jim was off pursuing his life, Gennie was away at school, and I confess to luxuriating in being the center of attention in the family. I looked forward to my last year of high school, and the summer before my senior year, I was thrilled when Fred Bracken decided to hire me to come in part-time to fold clothes, gift wrap

Gennie and Thunder graduate

and do the "flunky chores" that needed to be done in his dry-goods store. Bracken's Department Store was, by far, the highest quality menswear and shoe store in town. Two full-time shop ladies worked for him, Pearl and Irma. They were alternately kind and tough on me, but I learned a work ethic that served me well over the years.

Bracken's installed one of the early Fluoroscope Shoe x-ray machines. It was a shoe-fitting machine touted by *Parents Magazine* and advertised as a scientific method of fitting children's shoes. Of course, at the time, no one was concerned with the fact that using a shoe-fitting fluoroscope meant standing on an x-ray tube. The only barrier between the feet and the tube was a thin aluminum filter. There should have been warning notices, according to government regulations, detailing exposure limits, but I do not remember any warning placards on our fluoroscope. I was charged with keeping little kids entertained while Fred, Irma, or Pearl sold shoes to the parents. So, I played with the children by letting them look at the bones of their feet in the fluoroscope. Neither Fred nor the sales ladies ever suggested that I shouldn't operate it, and the machine was situated in full view less than six feet from the check-out counter.

That's not the only guilt I've endured concerning my job. I was hired at Bracken's the summer that Jim and Janey got married in Portland because Jim was on furlough from the Air Force after returning from his tour of duty in Korea. Janey was in Portland, finishing up her nurses' training. I was so newly employed that I chose not to ask for time off to travel with Mom and Dad to their wedding. I'm sure it would have been okay for me to take off the two days, and I'm positive that Jim and Janey's feelings must have been hurt, but I chose to stay home. Shame on me!

Those first paydays were so special. I soon discovered that I could open my own charge account at Bracken's and buy Jantzen sweaters and a beautiful Jantzen swim suit. Jantzen from Portland, Oregon was the "in" brand name for all the girls in our school. I lusted after the beautiful products that I folded and stacked every day. All my wages went to pay for the sweaters and the green knit swimsuit. However, they continued to serve me throughout my college years and beyond. They were well worth the cost!

I continued to work for Fred Bracken throughout my senior year of high school, which was abundantly full of other exciting activities. I served half of the year as Honored Queen of Job's Daughters and at the same time threw myself wholeheartedly into that fun senior three-act play. Since I was working downtown, I was appointed co-business manager of our high school annual. My partner and I divided up the business community and garnered over 75 sponsors to support the cost of publishing. Going from shop to shop to plead for donations was really scary, but I persevered.

Being elected to the court for the Cinderella Ball was a big deal for me. This was basically a popularity contest, because all high school students had the opportunity to vote for ten senior girls and ten senior boys. I was exhilarated to be elected, but then reality set in when I realized I would be expected to attend the Ball, and of course, I had no date. Thankfully, I had a great girlfriend with more than one admirer. She cornered a sweet, friendly guy who was smitten with her, and he offered to be my escort as a favor to her. That took care of my dating problems for that one glorious night.

I was also in charge of the program for the Ball. I wrote and directed a script, scrounged live music from my violinist buddies, selected songs for singers, and obtained a troop of little ballerinas from Wilson's School of Dance. We even convinced a faculty quartet to sing one of the songs. Things all came together to create a nostalgic story based on the song, "'Twas Just a Garden in the Rain" which we chose as the theme for the Ball. My team and the decorations committee worked very hard to create a theater-in-the-round setup. The music and dance numbers went off without a hitch. But, acoustics in the huge gym were horrible, and I doubt that even with a microphone the audience could hear the narrator as she read my script.

My participation in the Cinderella Ball activities causes confusion for me to this day. My scrapbook shows a very different picture from the way I saw myself. Perhaps those very real feelings of social inadequacy were so deeply ingrained that I overcompensated with a whirl of activity. I know that by then I'd developed a winning smile and had learned how to let my fun-loving sense of humor shine out. But, it was still not easy. Also, I based my lack of social success on the fact that boys never asked me out on dates. However, I got along splendidly with all the girls. The girls were probably the ones who voted for me. After all, by the time of that vote, my performance as drunken Aunt Sophie had already debuted.

As graduation approached, my mother's not-so-subtle nudging led me to decide to attend Eastern Oregon College in La Grande to train as a teacher. The payoff for that decision came when I won a four-year scholarship from the Oregon State Parent Teacher's Association (PTA). They wrote me a very nice award letter offering a full-tuition grant of $300 a year. Considering today's costs for college, the amount seems pitifully small; but it was sufficient. I knew I'd need to work for my board and room, and I hoped that my parents could provide small amounts whenever they were able.

The greatest excitement during my senior-year occurred when I won third place in an International Christian Endeavor essay contest sponsored by *Lookout Magazine*. This is a conservative Christian publication with a focus on "true-to-the-Bible teaching." The prize was $75, and in addition, it included an all-expense-paid train trip to Denver, Colorado. Rules for the contest stipulated that I submit a 1000-word paper typed in triplicate. The topic was "A Letter to My Congressman" on the subject of "I Speak for Christian Citizenship." The essay needed to deal with "the responsibility which youth has to combat the evils of Communism, narcotics, liquor, gambling, and prejudice."

Since Christian citizenship was the subject of my junior-year term paper, my opinions on all of those issues were well-entrenched. I also had something to say about racism, even though racial subjects were not openly dealt with in my family. Dad had quite a repertoire of racial slurs and jokes that he felt comfortable using on certain occasions. Mom never agreed and would gently chastise him. But, the feelings existed in the family. I remember going to Boise when I was about sixteen to meet Rigney relatives who came for a visit from Chicago. One aunt started in about the terrible problem with the "N. . .s" in Chicago and how lazy, stupid, etc. they were. It was not my nature to speak up in conversation among adults, but I did that time. I told her it isn't fair to label folks as she did. She got all huffy and put me in my place saying, "Young lady, you have never been there, and you don't know what you are talking about." I believe I embarrassed my Grandma and Grandpa for being so forward as to criticize my elders.

The concept of overt racism had not yet hit our area in the 40's and 50's. Nyssa had few African-Americans, some Japanese, and just a handful of Mexicans. The model for my thinking was my mother, who always went out of her way to speak up for the neglected, the needy, or the disabled. Her example instilled in me a consciousness of human differences and the desire to place myself in a position to walk in another's shoes.

So, I began my essay by laying out my concerns that the people of our state were troubled by the problems of hate, vice, and fighting. Then, I zeroed in on a specific example of discrimination, praising a Christian man who refused to patronize a restaurant because it posted, "We do not serve colored people." The citizen told the owner that "the Good Book says that we are all God's children and believe me, if God pays no attention to physical differences, we shouldn't either."

In the next section of the essay, I described an imaginary group of citizens making plans to confront their city council on the problems of too many saloons and gambling houses. My last point was an ecumenical call for churches to seek better agreement with each other. I suggested that young people be allowed to form interdenominational youth organizations to work together on community projects and solve mutual problems. As a conclusion, I addressed Senator Morse, asking him to "Work with us and pray with us."

The entire essay, no doubt provided by my mother, was printed in the *Nyssa Gate City Journal*. She always broadcasted every bit of news about me that she could. We teased her that we must be cautious about what we said in front of her for fear she'd rush down to the paper with it. One summer Sunday, our pastor turned over the sermon time to me so that I could read the essay to our pleased and enthusiastic congregation. At the time, I labored under the adolescent assumption that the members of our church were quite in awe of my shining light—"*This little light of mine, I'm gonna let it shine.*"

Confronting the perspectives I held at age seventeen is rather disconcerting for me as an adult. I was so full of religious zeal. Life's experiences have caused major changes in my thinking. My present views are more inclusive, and they impact my philosophical, social, and political actions in many different ways. However, it is enlightening to see that my concerns about racial discrimination were articulated succinctly at such an early age. I have always been deeply offended whenever anyone does what Carl Sandburg described as "monkey with the buzz saw of race." I can't remember a time when such talk did not set me on edge. And now, from re-reading my essay, I'm pleased to see that I made early attempts to speak out and act on my concerns. The effort of thinking it through and getting my words written down probably afforded more benefit to my long-range development than the exciting trip to Denver with its cash prize.

But, do not underestimate the glory of traveling solo on my first long-distance train trip. I was honored at the conference, photographed for the front cover of *Lookout Magazine,* and treated to all kinds of inspirational meetings and convocations. Also, I was given responsibility for my first expense report. The magazine sent me a check for $175.00 with a letter of instructions requiring careful accounting for all expenses. I was directed to return all unused funds. I still have a copy of the record showing that train fare was $81.42, hotel charges were $7.00 a night, and after meals and registration, I was able to return $23.00.

I remember how grown-up, and yes I must confess, how very wise I thought I became on that trip. Mother's efforts had finally paid off; although, she probably felt they had backfired and must have found me difficult to live with. I vividly remember that she quietly chastised me one day when I popped off a particularly sarcastic remark. "Doris, you probably think you are teasing and funny when you speak like that, but you need to know, it hurts my feelings." That softly-spoken criticism has lived in my heart for over fifty years.

I maintained that sense of self-importance for the rest of the summer and on into my first week of college. I was feeling pretty secure about college plans until I learned that Mom would be attending a full summer session of college in Eugene, Oregon. It began in late June and she was not finished until the end of July. After a month at home, her teaching year started. But then, she was required to attend some sort of conference in Portland during the third week of September. She would be gone when it was time for me to leave for freshman-orientation at Eastern Oregon College. Because she was still working to earn her college degree and permanent certification, she could not skip the conference. That was when my self-confidence began to erode. My Mommy would not be home to see me off!

Not only was she not around much that summer, but Dad changed jobs again. He once more worked for the North Board of Control which operated Owyhee Dam. He stayed in our old house at the Dam during the week while irrigation season was on. If he couldn't come down for the weekend, Mom drove up to stay with him. Sometimes, I was the only one at the Nyssa house, and she always left a to-do list on the dining room table. Before she went to Eugene, she left detailed instructions on care of the house: when to mail payments and a reminder to ask Dad where the grocery money was hidden. She had the beds all made up before she left so that my cousin, Shirley, and my friend from high school could each have her own bedroom when they stayed with me during part of the summer.

While Mom was in summer school, she wrote to me almost every day with encouragement and helpful suggestions. Dad did what he could on weekends, but he was at the Dam during the week, and it was just not the same without Mom. But the summer settled in to quieter times. I quit working at Bracken's and during the early part of summer, I worked with the girls in the potato-packing sheds. We drove up to visit Dad on weekends.

When Mom arrived home in late July, she encouraged me to carry out my desire to go to camp. My buddy agreed with me that even though we were high school graduates, we deserved to collect one more year of church-camp memories. So once again, we scraped together the required fees and enjoyed our week with all our old friends from the other churches. By the time camp was over, the corn cannery started up, and I started working the night shift. I usually arrived home about 2:30 a.m. and slept late into the morning. I spent my days preparing for my college venture.

My folks purchased a second-hand portable Royal typewriter for me, and they also gifted me with a brand new portable turntable that played 78 rpm, 45 rpm and LP records; this satisfied my hardware needs. Many of these things, plus my bedding for the dorm, were bulky, so Mom and Dad scrounged up a trunk and suitcase to transport all my loot. We hired a church friend to sew two new skirts for me, and we agreed that my high school blouses and Jantzen sweaters would be okay for classes. My dressy clothes from all the Jobies' functions would also serve. The last year of Home Ec included tailoring, where I'd made a classy wine-colored wool jacket, which went well with the new skirts. My college wardrobe had taken shape.

The day of departure loomed. Mom took the bus to her conference in Portland while I packed all by myself and spent lonely hours stewing about what lay ahead. My friends were going through the same turmoil as they headed off to school, and we commiserated over the phone. One friend was even heading to La Grande, but her parents were going to drive her to school. That didn't help to soothe my frazzled nerves.

I remember receiving a big boost of assistance from Dad. He somehow managed to drive down from the Dam to give me a ride to the train station. It seemed imperative for me to put on a brave appearance in front of Dad. I set my violin down on the station platform and gave him a huge bear-hug along with a grateful "thank you" before clambering up the train steps. Later, I realized that he was probably feeling as rattled as I was. I found a note tucked inside the phonograph when I unpacked at school. In it, he sent "all my love" and then wrote something which he could not say directly to me. But over the years, he repeated it in several letters, "Just remember, Dear, that Mother and I are betting everything we have on you."

I don't believe that I went all teary-eyed in front of him at the station, but after we heard the final "All Aboard," and I was in my seat, looking out at him, I saw him as a big, lonesome guy standing on the platform waving his only little girl off to her new adventure. For sure, I had a lump in my throat, and I'll bet he did too.

CHAPTER 10

━━◦◦◦━━

Our Lives Intersect

As I READ THROUGH letters I received from my parents during the fall of 1953, it is difficult to determine who was more lonesome. Mom wrote from her hotel room at the Portland conference and mailed it to La Grande, so that I would have a letter waiting for me when I arrived. She wrote that she would be praying for me "to choose wisely between right and wrong," that she had faith that I would because of my own deep Christian faith.

Three days later, she wrote that Dad kept calling her from the Dam saying that he wished I hadn't left and suggesting that as soon as the irrigation was shut off, "Let's you and I go down to La Grande."

When I arrived at the station in La Grande, I was met by upper classmen who had volunteered to assist bewildered freshmen. They helped me claim my luggage and hauled me up to the college. I was immediately escorted to Dorion Hall and assigned to Room 4 in the basement. The room was a quarter the size of my bedroom at home, and I had to share it with two other girls who'd already arrived and were settled in. Consequently, I got last choice of the three narrow beds. Beside each bed was a tiny desk which also served as a bedside table. There was one closet and a pigeon hole containing a toilet and sink. That was it! My roommates were welcoming and showed me which drawers along the closet wall were mine. After I unpacked, they helped me locate the storage area for trunks and suitcases.

I was just getting settled when an announcement came over the intercom that we were expected to be at a welcoming convocation over in the auditorium of the Administration Building. At that meeting, we were informed that students seeking campus work should report to the lounge of Dorion Hall immediately following this gathering. I scurried back to the dorm and showed up at the meeting. The only job still available was scrubbing out the community showers, toilets, and bathtubs on every floor of the girl's dorm. No one else seemed too eager to apply, so I got it and became gainfully employed. The facilities had to be thoroughly cleaned and disinfected daily.

Of course, I wrote of my good luck to the folks, and Mom quickly answered that the "extra $1.50 per day will help ever so much, honey."

Finances for college were a huge concern. Early that summer, the folks accompanied me to the bank where I opened my very own checking account at the First National Bank of Oregon. It was Dad who made me practice writing checks and taught me how to record everything carefully in the check register. He was the nit-picky treasurer for the Masonic Lodge, and he knew exactly how it should be done. Over the years, Dad just gave up on Mom's inability to maintain accurate financial records, but he turned it all over to her to save himself from more squabbling. I'm sure the "bean-counting" skills I've employed over the years for various organizations all come as hereditary gifts from Dad.

I didn't really discuss scarcity of money with Dad. It wasn't necessary, because we all knew how hard it was going to be, despite the fact that I had a bit saved from my jobs and my tuition was covered. In her letters, Mom urged me to attend any meetings the college offered about job possibilities. Somehow, our family needed to come up with $75 a month to cover books, board and room, and incidentals. One of her letters asked me to take $10 from my essay prize for the room deposit, and she promised to pay me back as soon as Dad's check arrived.

I remember how difficult things were. Mom took private speech pupils after school hours, and once again the folks rented out a bedroom. Mom and Dad put up with the renter for my entire freshman year. She only left then because her teaching contract wasn't renewed. Mom's letters that first year were full of details on how I should budget my funds. She rarely had the whole $75 to deposit in one lump sum. I became part of her very familiar financial juggling act. In late September 1953, all of the money she deposited needed to go to pay the month's board bill, and there was only $20 left for my books. She suggested I try to charge them, but I did not attempt it. I really did not learn good budgeting skills until much later when Ibrahim Ayyoub came into my life. However, at the beginning of each new school term I dragged my heels on purchasing books until I discovered if a professor was really going to use the book extensively. I also spent study time in the library, where texts were placed on hourly reserve.

I was so tight for money, Mom once deposited two dollars in my checking account, cautioning, "Don't spend it unless you really need to." While Mom's practical letters dealt with money, Dad's emotional letters touched me as he wrote of how much he missed me. I learned that both of them waited impatiently for my first letter. Mom was spending the weekend at the Dam, when the renter called to say my letter had arrived. Dad immediately suggested that they drive the thirty miles to town, and he would catch a ride back the next morning with his boss.

My dad teasingly wrote about trying to visit soon, although "I don't see why I should want to, tho, cause I really don't like you 'very much.' Ha Ha." He also teased me to watch for somebody who looked rich, but he brought the "letter to a sorrowful close. With all my love, your Daddy." I was still very much attached to home, and I was quite dependent on my parents for advice. I may have been more homesick than I was willing to admit, and I knew they were homesick for me. One day, I bubbled over with excitement when I found an advertisement in the La Grande paper about Manchester puppies for sale. Since I knew how much my parents wanted a new little dog, I walked to the owners' home and promptly fell in love.

Back at the dorm, I made an expensive phone call home to secure permission to buy him. It was my thought that perhaps if Mom and Dad had a new baby to love and care for, they would not miss me so much. I had managed to save the purchase price from my earnings as a bathroom scrubber. The folks were delighted with my offer of such a gift and suggested that I could ship him home on the train. I closed the deal, and the breeders helped me crate and ship him. Then, I waited nervously to hear that he'd arrived safely. The folks immediately wrote of his arrival and decided to name him Chester. That toy Manchester offered a pleasant substitute upon which Mom and Dad could heap loving attention to salve their loneliness after their girl left the nest. I've always felt pleased about my gift.

Even though I was aware that my family missed me, I was mainly absorbed in figuring out how to keep my head above water. During that period, the folks did most of the letter writing, and I responded with short little notes which just described my immediate needs. I felt like a hurricane had struck as I tried to settle into living in Dorion Hall. Approximately 30 freshman girls were assigned to the ten basement rooms. Most of us were away from home for the first time and free from the watchful, controlling influence of parents. Consequently, there were often noisy late-night parties with much giggling, screaming, running up and down the hall, and slamming doors. Rules prohibiting booze and men in Dorion were rigidly enforced by our dorm mother, Mrs. Thornburg, aka Mama T. Quiet study hours were also supposed to be observed, but Mama T could not be everywhere at once. There was no keeping the lid on this gang of girls.

However, the atmosphere inside Room 4 developed into something like a calm in the eye of a storm. I'm sure this was because we three girls were enfolded with a thick blanket of religiosity which caused our fellow classmates to avoid too much contact. Somehow, Mama T had managed to room me with an earnest young woman in her early twenties. She was attending Eastern Oregon College as a freshman with the firm goal of becoming an evangelical missionary to China. She was very shy but spoke out when her strict religious beliefs were being challenged.

She voiced her strong disagreement in class to Dr. Easley, our general science instructor, when the subject of evolution came up. At the same time, Dr. Easley helped me mature in my thinking by asking, "Who is to say if the Bible means that it took a literal seven days to accomplish the creation? Could it be possible that each day was a figurative description of an entire era?" Dr. Easley was a respected elder of the church

I attended in La Grande, and his answer soothed my soul. My missionary roommate vehemently rejected his suggestion.

Our other roommate was also deeply religious and not too successful academically or socially. I don't remember much about her, but I have a vague memory that she didn't remain in school after the first year. Both girls immediately bonded with me, since they saw me as a kindred spirit. Even so, they must have recognized that I also had a much less serious bent to my personality, and they seemed to enjoy my jokes and breezy attitude. We went to meals together and shared some classes. All three of us read a lot of Bible, said our prayers, and did our best to shrug off the noisiness of our neighbors. We didn't win any hearts when our aspiring missionary complained to the dorm mother about the constant noise on the basement floor.

The placement was probably a good fit for me at the time. It allowed me to concentrate on learning to study without so much push to socialize. A good number of the party-girls began to wash out, and our ranks thinned as kids found they couldn't make the grade and left school. In contrast, I developed a late-night-study habit, which remained the rule for me from then on, and I experienced success in my freshman courses of General Science, Biology, American History and English Composition.

I also continued with music, joining the choir at the First Christian Church and the Grande Ronde Symphony Orchestra. I signed up for a private-study class in violin because I realized immediately that I was over my head when the orchestra assigned me to the last chair in the second violin section. The music was wonderful, and I faithfully sat through all the practice sessions, faking the notes when things got technically difficult. Lack of time and dedication meant violin practice quickly fell by the wayside, and my skills diminished rather than progressed. Mom was full of praise for all I was doing and didn't fuss much when I dropped the individual violin lessons.

During my freshman year, I was delighted to be given a part in the fall play, and I immediately wrote my parents that they now had an excuse to visit me. Dad's reply expressed pleasure that I was involved in church, joked a bit, and then repeated his previous comment, "Just remember, Dear, that Mother and I are betting everything we have on you." I felt obliged to do my best and live up to family hopes and also to my self-expectations. I was a competitive kid, anxious to excel, and I knew he was pleased that I was heading down the college path.

Mom and Dad did drive up to see me in the play. I was so excited to have them arrive that I waited for several hours at the top of the hill that morning, looking to see their car. Actually, if they really came just to see me in the play, they were probably disappointed. The play was Ruth Gordon's autobiographical comedy, *Years Ago*, and my part was an almost inconsequential comical character. I realized later that Gordon is attempting to portray the pressures a young girl must withstand when she chooses to pursue different life goals than those planned by her parents. While performing in the play, it didn't occur to me that I was headed straight down the path that Mom blocked out for me long before I was even aware of a need for life goals. Up to this point in my life, I didn't feel as if I had withstood much of anything. I still needed to learn how to do that.

I remember how empty I felt right after my folks left, but not for long. Although it was great that my folks came to see me, I found that school, work, drama, and friendships filled my hours. I was happy to be where I was and not back in Nyssa. Drama once more took precedence during the spring of my freshman year when I was awarded a satisfying role in Shaw's *Arms and the Man*. I'm quite certain that my parents traveled to La Grande to watch me perform, since Dad kept spewing out fake complaints about having to come see my plays.

I wasn't interested in all the boy-crazy activity going on outside our room, because I still harbored a secret love for a boy from my home town. He had been a member of our high school drama club. He displayed a serious demeanor, was sweetly full of fun, and was a good-looking blonde with twinkling blue eyes. His family raised bees, and he kept very busy helping his father with their business. I remember the heady aroma of honey which permeated his clothing and wafted my way whenever I was near him. For years, in my sewing kit, I kept a small wad of fragrant beeswax, which I begged from him, because I swore it helped untangle sewing thread.

During our high school years, his church had a much more active and interesting youth group than our boring little group at First Christian. My desire to create an ecumenical young people's group in Nyssa stemmed from the fact that I was attracted to his influence. Due to my maneuvering, our two churches held joint social events for the young people. One time, though it was obvious to everyone that he brought a sweet girl as his date, I still chose to plop myself into the front seat to ride beside him when he offered to drive everyone home. I remember the huffing and hawing of his date because she was forced to sit in the back seat. Needless to say, I was the first one to be dropped at home. I still squirm in embarrassment at the memory.

I guess my bad manners didn't disturb him, because when he headed to college a year ahead of me, he agreed to be pen pals when I suggested it. And once, during my senior year, he came home from college and invited me out for our one single date. I remember he drove me to a church function in Nampa, Idaho. On the ride home, we spent the entire time in serious philosophical discussion about our differences in religious belief. He did give me a thrilling kiss before saying good night. The following day, I broke out with a case of rubella, so-called three-day measles. I wrote to him for fear he would catch my illness, but he wrote back that I need not worry because he'd already had the measles. He cautioned me to take care of my "beautiful eyes."

I believe his parents liked me, because I received congratulatory cards from them for my various high school successes and a lovely graduation gift. However, I never experienced the same comfortable level of affection from their son. I felt the problem was due to the differences in our religious beliefs and in the fact that I chose to argue those points with him. After all, he belonged to a different denomination and planned to go into the ministry. He grew away from our friendship when he went off to college and met other girls.

During my first year of college, I poured all my extra energy into writing clever letters full of great wisdom designed to impress the future minister. I remember clipping out poems and philosophical vignettes which I thought he might one day use in his sermons. As the year progressed, my letters pointedly began to reflect how I felt about him. But the tone of his letters continued to stay on the level of just a friendly pen pal.

During spring term of that first year, I prepared an educational exhibit as a science fair project for biology class. Of course, I chose bees. I wrote to my secret love's father to ask for help. He offered to construct and loan to me an observation hive with two frames of honeycomb containing bees and a queen. I created posters depicting the life cycle of bees with hand-drawn illustrations of workers, drones, and queen.

For spring break, I traveled to Nyssa to pick up the hive. It was beautifully made of freshly varnished, golden-colored wood, with glass sides. He told me to find a place for it outside so the bees could fly in and out freely. Back in La Grande, I chose a grassy meadow right below the dorm and deposited the hive. The next day I walked down to check on my bees. Alas, no hive in sight! Some horrible person discovered my pretty little hive and stole it!

I was frantic and heartbroken. My biology professor notified the authorities, but it was never found. However, a local bee man heard of my plight and loaned me an observation hive. It was definitely not as beautiful as the special one made just for me, but it did help me earn my "A" for the project. The hardest part was confessing the loss to my heartthrob's father, but he was very gracious about the whole thing. After all, he raised that wonderful son, so he must have possessed Christian understanding and forgiveness, right?

It was a relief when my freshman year came to an end, because I was beginning to feel a bit fidgety in the basement room. I remained friends with my determined missionary, and I knew that she wanted to be my permanent college roommate, but Mama T took a real interest in the girls, and she was pleased when I began to blossom socially. Consequently, when I began my sophomore year at college, she wisely assigned me to a different roomie up on the second floor, which allowed me to stretch my wings a little more.

I did have a couple of dates. One was a girl-ask-boy Sadie Hawkins Dance, and I was supposed to make this guy a boutonniere. For some deranged reason, I decided it would be fun to make him one containing a miniature fishing pole and line, with a real fish hook to mimic the cartoon of a man who had been caught. It was one of my least clever ideas because my date didn't see the joke. The fish hook tangled up in his suit jacket, and he never exhibited any interest in me after that. Another guy asked me out to a school game and later drove me up into a secluded section of woods behind the campus where he tried to make out. I firmly explained that I was not that kind of girl and asked to be driven home. He avoided making eye contact with me after that.

Despite my less than stellar success at dating, I continued to write to my special hometown boy. When I let my feelings show too clearly in the letters, there came a fateful day when I received my "Dear Doris" letter. He sounded just like a minister giving advice to a recalcitrant member of his congregation. He believed that my letters were beginning to be a little too serious, and he then informed me that after much prayer and discussion with the girl he was dating at his school, they both decided that the pen-pal letters should cease. He told me that he and this girl were seriously interested in each other and were going steady. He also offered the opinion that I was a very intense, focused young woman and suggested that I needed to lighten up if I ever wished to have a satisfactory relationship with someone else. He implied that, otherwise, I would scare off all the boys.

I shall never forget that letter. A dear friend later pointed out that he was scared by my intensity and wanted me to change. As a consequence, I accepted his implication that there was something wrong with me. Nevertheless, I failed to "lighten up." Until I met Ibrahim Ayyoub, my college social life involved very little flirting or dating.

However, I chose not to mope and moan. No letter of rejection was going to keep me down or dilute the challenge of college. I was excited by the opportunity to join Sock and Buskin, the college drama club. As part of the initiation for new members, we were told to prepare some sort of dramatic stunt for performance during class time. Previously, someone had mentioned that when I grinned in a certain way, I looked like Liberace. So I dressed up in a dark suit, slicked back my hair, borrowed a candelabrum, found a Liberace recording of "I'll Get By" and presented myself to our demanding history professor, Dr. Lee Johnson. He, being a good sport, allowed me to do my lip sync of Liberace singing that song. It was a great success and lots of fun. Kids all over campus began to hail me as the new Liberace.

In addition to drama, I began to develop an interest in writing poetry. As I walked the tree-lined streets between campus and across town to attend church, I was struck by the lacy beauty of the weeping birch trees. Descriptive phrases began to form in my mind, which I wrote down when I reached the dorm. I tucked the phrases away in a file until my sophomore year when Dr. Clarke, my English composition instructor, mentioned an anthology competition. Always up for a challenge, I pulled out the poem, polished it, and submitted it.

Autumn Impressions on a Sunday Afternoon

Silver-spun spiders' web floating through the breeze
Dancing sprites, gold and bronze bouncing where they please
Weeping birch, dainty grace, leaf-speckled strands still firm
Sleepy smoke, woody smell, sun soaked air still warm
Busy folk, happy folk, yet blissfully unaware

Daily tasks, self-centered cares leave nature's beauty bare
We pause to look, breathe deep to live, seek beauty in detail
Our eyes awake and thoughts uncurl, our simplest tasks can't fail.

Dr. Clarke liked it and submitted it to the competition. Much to my surprise, it was accepted for the 1954–55 edition of the *Annual Anthology of College Poetry*. The other student winner from our college, Ron Bayes, was already a "big man on campus," noted both for poetry and prose, so I felt I was in high-class company. The campus newspaper, *Eastern Oregon College Beacon*, included a piece on me, and I grabbed up copies for all my friends and family in Nyssa. Once again, people on campus made a fuss over me, and I basked in the attention. It felt lovely! The actual printed anthology did not come out until spring of 1955. However, my life was so full with new experiences that I didn't sit around waiting for it to appear.

College was causing some deep changes in my attitudes and outlook, which affected how I felt about going home. Vacation back in Nyssa seemed almost unreal. I longed for quiet and release. Though many school experiences were filled with fun and excitement, my basic impression of those first two years was a sense of constant pressure. I was no carefree co-ed. There was pressure from my instructors, pressure on myself, worry about money, desire to meet my parents' expectations, and desire to fit in socially. Pressure, pressure, and more pressure! I worked late at night and sometimes all night. Once, the power went off at 2:00 a.m. and I had the audacity to wake up Mama T because I needed light to study for a History exam. She lent me a flashlight.

When I arrived home for a break or vacation, the letdown manifested itself in an unremitting need for sleep. By that time, my parents had each claimed separate bedrooms upstairs because Mom said she slept better when not subjected to Dad's loud snoring. I was relegated to the basement. That was fine with me, since it was cooler, darker, and quieter, unless Dad began to stomp around and bellow, "Well, what did she come home for if all she is going to do is sleep?"

When I came home, I was less than successful in reconnecting with my old high school buddies. We were all coming from different experiences and we didn't seem to have the same "giggling" interests which bound us in high school. As usual, Mom implied I just needed to try harder because we had been such good friends. She would push me with reminders that I should return calls from friends. Dad said nothing, but on that first Thanksgiving vacation, I found a beautifully penciled note, in which he wrote that happy memories make for pleasant reminders but will never fully return. He said that I shouldn't brood but instead eagerly anticipate tomorrow, that "time marches on." Once again, his ability to speak to me in written form filled me with respect and appreciation. In the years to follow, I often forgot his deep-felt comments, but his love and concern meant more to me than I can ever express.

Longer vacations, of course, were spent working. One summer, Mom arranged for me to be a cabin counselor at a Girl Scout camp, and I got a good taste of how difficult it could be to work with teenage girls, which helped me decide that I was not interested in teaching adolescents. I knew that I was more skilled at working with younger kids. During the last month of each summer, I worked long hours at the corn cannery and saved up for the next year's expenses. When the cannery closed its season, there were always just a few days left to wash the corn goo out of my hair before it was time to head back to La Grande.

One benefit from the brutish, slug-bug work of canning corn cannot be measured in monetary rewards. I always knew that the job would end, and I was going to be allowed to clean up and get back to my different world. I rejoiced each fall that I'd been given the chance to experience messy hard physical labor for a few dollars, but that it would not have to become my life's work. There was this rainbow called college that offered me a promise of better things if I could just persevere.

Happily, my second-year college job was easier. I worked the desk at the library after dinner. In those days, students still wrote their names on check-out cards, which they removed from the book pockets. These cards were piled into a check-out basket until I arrived in the evening to sort them alphabetically by author using a special card-sorting folder. I was instructed to stack them into a bundle fastened with a rubber band for the head librarian to file in the date-due card box. At times, I struggled to stay awake over the dull task of alphabetizing, but one refreshing aspect of the job was that I sat at the desk close to the entrance and was therefore privy to the social comings and goings of students. Sitting behind a library desk was a very interesting place to be, because I was able to interact with kids. It was much friendlier than scrubbing showers!

One particularly interesting person who came and went from the library that winter was the handsome foreign student from Jordan. When he arrived in La Grande, his determination was strong to concentrate on his studies, earn his engineering degree and retrace his steps to Jordan. But, I caught sight of him as soon as he set foot on campus. Although neither of us was totally aware of what happened, for me the light dawned rapidly. When Ibrahim later became embarrassed about describing the meeting, he'd say "we'll skip the music." But, when I saw him for the first time, I heard it.

My home town of Nyssa was a conservative, rural community situated less than 150 miles from Eastern Oregon College in La Grande. My parents helped me choose it because it was the closest Oregon teacher-training institution to our home. I believe their hope was that I'd meet and marry a home-town guy. I'd always been too studious and too earnest with no clue about how to flirt. My dad kept joking in his letters that my job was to find a rich man to marry so that he could retire.

I had the dream that I would one day marry a dark-haired man who looked good in a white shirt. Our college cafeteria was co-ed, so my girlfriends and I were able to keep an eye out for prospects while we dined. One Saturday night, I chanced to look up. There he was. Abe, as he came to be called, was a guest of Dr. Quaintance, the foreign student advisor, so I knew he must be important. Very few foreign students attended EOC. Quick and careful snooping revealed that they planned to attend a concert at a local church after dinner. So, I suggested to my girlfriend that the concert sounded great, and off we went. I innocently observed that we'd have a better view of the stage if we sat up in the balcony. While the audience enjoyed the concert, my attention was focused elsewhere, on that black-haired fellow below.

As days passed, I continued sleuthing and developed a mysterious urge to volunteer for the campus newspaper. My first assignment was to interview the new foreign student. I learned that he was proficient in Arabic. Coincidentally, I realized that I had always wished to speak Arabic. Abe kindly offered to be my teacher. Lessons began, and we spent many pleasant evenings in the semi-private, glassed-off women's lounge. As a bonus, I even learned some Arabic. I learned how to write the alphabet and make the sounds for each letter; how to ask "How are you" (*Kaif Halick?*); how to reply "I am fine, thank you" (*Mabsoota*); and the studious "I am going to the library" (*Ana thahiba ila al-maktaba.*) And, I learned a most useful Arabic phrase—*Kam shubback fi darkum* ("How many windows are in your house").

I wrote a poem for my charming teacher friend, carefully signing it in both English and Arabic:

I have learned these past few weeks something good to know.
It seems that I have found a friend the finest here below.
Refinement, humor, pleasing grace of these he's rich in store.
Besides, his patience has no end while teaching me his lore.
I'm grateful for the time he's spent; there's no way to repay.
I wish I had some splendid gift to show what words can't say.
His native language I will learn in some far distant time.
And then much better say my thanks than with this weakling rhyme.

Doris دوريس

One evening, instead of language lessons, Abe started talking about himself, his arm casually draped over the back of our couch. I looked up into his shining dark eyes, his hand settled on my shoulder, and there were no more lessons in Arabic. Not long after that momentous last lesson, I wrote a short meditation on my teacher:

Changeable
always black
sparkling with mirth
or quiet with thought
His eyes.

My affection for Abe developed into mutual interest shortly after the tutoring was put on hold. The following week, our choir, along with my Blue and Gold Singers group, went on a three-day tour to high schools in Eastern Oregon. When we returned to campus, Mama T, sporting a huge grin, met me at the front desk. A young man had been constantly inquiring for me and worrying because I was not there. The next time Abe appeared at Dorion Hall's front desk, I was delighted to greet him.

Although I was immersed in this new friendship with Abe, I tried out for and landed the part of Tituba, the slave from Barbados, in Arthur Miller's play, *The Crucible*. This was an exciting accomplishment, and I threw myself wholeheartedly into the part. I had to learn to speak in dialect and successfully become a fearful enthusiast of everything Godly in order to save myself from persecution as a witch. My costume consisted of bare feet, head-rag, plain peasant blouse, and long skirt. Since I was already dark-complexioned, a bit of stage make-up browned me up to fit the role. In La Grande during the 1950's, it was considered acceptable to put a white-skinned woman in black face. Our college had just one African-American student. He sang with me in the Blue and Gold Singers, and we were dance partners in our square dance class, but he did not participate in drama productions.

At the time, it was obvious to me that Tituba's hysterical excuse, employing the age-old adage, "The devil made me do it," was a result of the atmosphere in which she existed. The play was a story about the religious hysteria, during 1692, concerning witchcraft in Salem, Massachusetts. However, Miller purposefully wrote *The Crucible* because he saw the same pattern in the Salem trials and the McCarthy hearings: the accused should make public confession, damn confederates, and swear allegiance.

As a young college student, I was aware of this hysteria over Communism and felt disgust as I listened to radio-broadcast snatches of the senate interrogations where people were jailed or black-listed for refusing to cooperate. I was too naïve yet to see Miller's connection between those dark periods. One reason for my ignorance was that my beloved history professor never allowed himself to speak in class concerning current American history. He stuck to the revolutionary period, the War of 1812, and the Civil War. If someone asked a question about more current history, he always stated it was not his area of expertise and would not comment.

But, of course, even though Abe had been questioned about it during his entry into the United States, communism was not a topic of conversation as we were becoming acquainted. He was just getting settled into classes while the play was in rehearsal. He told me he did attend a performance. But, I don't remember if my parents came. If they did, they wouldn't have caught Miller's metaphorical intent, either. They would have thought, as I did, that it was solely a commentary on the insanity of religious fervor against witchcraft. My conservative parents were outspoken in their dislike of ungodly Communism. Regardless of who was in the audience, I thoroughly loved performing in *The Crucible*. My program is covered with cast comments and autographs. To tell the truth, it was difficult to come back down to earth for the mundane business of attending classes and going to work.

But, I realized that stage life is far removed from the real work of college. Soon, the winter term was winding down, and I looked forward to heading home for spring vacation and some uninterrupted sleep. I mentioned to Abe that I would be going home, but it obviously didn't register with him. This is a trait that was always present in him. He rarely processed details for an upcoming activity the first time around. While I could have a meticulous plan working away in the back of my head for what was going to happen, it required more than one repetition to apprise Abe. He sometimes leapt or fell into a situation and he took off, on his own, during that first spring vacation break.

He knew that I was going to Nyssa for the week while he stayed in La Grande. However, it finally registered with him that all students went home for the week when the dorm supervisor asked him if he had somewhere to go while the dorm was shut down, including meal service. Since he had no family to visit, he was allowed to stay and have a key to the kitchen's walk-in cooler in exchange for scrubbing down the bathrooms and mopping, waxing, and polishing the hallways, and so on. He worked quickly with no distractions around and finished the to-do list early in the week. Time began to drag because it was too lonely and quiet in the empty dorm.

He had heard about Portland because it had a large Arab population. So, he packed a few necessities, bought a ticket to Portland, and climbed on the next bus. Only when he had been travelling for a couple of hours did he begin to realize that this might be a foolish idea. He hadn't thought how he'd find the Arabs in a city where he knew no one. He couldn't just walk up to strangers and ask, maybe getting arrested for making unwanted advances. He understood that he shouldn't have gone to Portland when he didn't know anyone there.

But he did know Arabs in San Francisco. His cousin Kamel was going to school there and Uncle Joey Ayoub, whose surname had a single "y" thanks to immigration officers, owned a factory there. So, Abe purchased a ticket to San Francisco. It was an eighteen hour ride, much longer than he had expected, since he always underestimated distances in America. Finally, the bus arrived, and he found Kamel's name in a directory. Abe explained that he got lonesome to speak Arabic. Kamel was surprised and pleased and rounded up some other Arab students to go get Abe.

They went to a pizza place owned by Kamel's relatives, laughing, joking, and eating this delicious new food called pizza. The smell, the taste, were similar to meals at home. It was such joy for him to visit friends and family who spoke his own language. While speaking Arabic, they could express their thoughts freely and Abe had been thirsting for just such a chance.

Towards the end of the week, the Greyhound took him back to La Grande. He didn't even notice the length of the trip this time because he could savor all of those rich memories of the fun he'd had. Somehow, with no careful planning, he was refreshed and happy to be back on campus ready to start spring term with all the other students. Soon after I arrived, Abe came to visit, and we shared stories of our holidays.

But, after that, I didn't see him for quite some time. Eventually, I asked Mama T if she knew anything of his whereabouts. She thought I knew Abe was very sick. When I asked his friend Roger Tiller, I learned that Abe was discovered by his roommate sick in bed with a very high fever.

The school nurse came and moved him to an isolation room. He began to think that it was such a tragedy that he had traveled all the way from Jordan just to die in La Grande. Finally, the fever broke, and he began to feel better and realized how many days of classes he must have missed. So, he shakily got dressed and headed out in the cold spring morning to his class with Dr. Easley, who took one look at him and sent him back to bed. Abe had been dangerously ill with diphtheria, never having been immunized.

I was relieved when I learned that Abe was recovering and ecstatic when he felt well enough to visit. Thankfully, by the time Easter rolled around, he was able to accept my invitation to attend services at my church. After church as we walked back to the dorm, I mentioned how much I had enjoyed the Easter Sermon. Abe hadn't realized until then that it was Easter. " You mean this is Easter! Then I shall be dining downtown. You can come too if you wish." I wished! That was our first real date.

Abe must have been just as nervous as I about carrying on mealtime conversation. He solved it by launching into an elaborate description of the mathematics problems he was working on in his classes. He had no idea how really ignorant I was in math. I managed to get through high school with just two classes of algebra, and so far I'd escaped all math courses for college. I remember that he used up several paper napkins writing equations and explaining their meaning to me. It was not what could be called a romantic interlude, but it worked fine for us. He could hold forth on something he really understood, and I was a good listener; anything he had to say was interesting to me.

My parents received my letters with glowing description of Abe. My father held a stereotypical view of Arabs and teased me by mailing a magazine photo of a dashing Bedouin in flowing robes galloping his white horse across the desert. That was the sum total of his knowledge. Later, my parents drove to La Grande and brought along my Grandmother to do inspection. She, of course, immediately asked, "Young man, have you been baptized?" He assured her he had indeed been baptized. I heard him tell her that it was in the River Jordan. Later, I learned he just said that to win her stamp of approval.

Formal dating was sporadic. Neither of us had time or money. We both worked to earn room and board, and Abe carefully counted and recounted his pennies (a math major, after all). When enough were collected to spring for a movie, out we would go. Our friends could usually guess what movie we had seen, because Abe polished his English by constantly practicing the phrases he picked up from the movies. If a Western was playing, we were treated to his newly acquired greeting, "Howdy there pardner!" *Anna and the King of Siam* produced a favorite of his, "A bee can travel from flower to flower, but flower must never go from bee to bee to bee." No problem there for me! I was one flower perfectly content to stay right where I was.

Besides the shortage of funds, we were way too busy to do much dating. All our free time was spent with the International Relations Club. We learned that the Model United Nations for college students was to be held in San Francisco during the first week in May. Abe was interested, because it would allow him once more to visit his relatives in San Francisco. I was ready to join anything of importance to him. Since Abe was our only resident Arab and had studied social issues while teaching in Amman, he was a natural source of inside information on our assigned nation—Egypt. He knew Arab thinking and knew what citizens of the Arab world wished for their countries.

Abe understood why Egypt overthrew King Farouk in 1952, and he had great respect for the new leader, Gamal Abdel Nasser. Abe helped us to become aware that colonialism must cease. Nasser had just come to power in 1954 with a vision for the "Egyptianisation" and modernization of his country. Nasser needed financial assistance to build his dream of an Aswan Dam, but because he railed against British/French control of the Suez Canal, any hope for funds from the western powers was disappointed. Consequently, he turned to Russia which was only too eager to gain a foothold in the region. That move convinced Western fearmongers that Egypt would embrace Socialism or worse yet, Communism.

Abe explained that Nasser was the first leader of an Arab nation who dared to challenge Western dominance of the Middle East. We learned that Nasser was a highly revered figure in the Arab world. Members of our International Relations Club were smart kids who were expert at parliamentary procedure and behind-the-scenes negotiations in the political arena. We studied the issues affecting Egypt and developed resolutions representing the Arab point of view. Both Abe and I saved frugally to afford the expense of the trip. My parents managed to contribute a little for me, and Abe was given assistance from the college petty-cash fund. Also, Dr. Easley offered to pay him for grading student papers, as a way to cover the expenses.

I kept a diary of that trip filled with my nineteen-year-old thinking and concerns. It reminds me that I didn't sleep the night before we left. As we departed, Don Starr, who was one of the brightest students in the club and a good friend to Abe, kept teasing me about Nyssa's sugar beets, jack rabbits, and green velvet hills. Three members of the group were from Nyssa, so we stopped there for a picnic prepared by our parents.

We enjoyed Mom's delicious "tater" salad and Mrs. Yoneyama's wonderful fried chicken and chow mein, among other things. The kids could not see how I could be my mother's daughter because I was so serious and she so full of nonsense. I made a vow to change that because I saw that my true inner nature had not been showing. Still, in spite of my resolution, our overnight stop in Reno prompted judgmental observations in the diary. I wrote about people spending their lives and souls, "old women, young people, hard, soft, disillusioned, drunk, bored."

I felt I had seen Reno in thirty minutes and hoped never to see it again. When we visited the Catholic cathedral, Ibrahim wanted to know where the "slaughter" machines were, as he called them, since they were in every other public building in town. He made a dollar playing nickels. Some of the others lost money, some won, and I self-righteously declared that I wouldn't be able to spend a penny of any winnings.

When we stopped at Lake Tahoe, we all skipped rocks across the lake. I was most impressed that Ibrahim thought the country looks exactly like Lebanon. Anything Abe shared, giving me a glimpse into his life before La Grande, always registered deeply with me. After my impressions of Reno, I was even more struck by Sacramento and its capitol building. I also commented in my journal on the campanile tower at the University of California at Berkley and the bells playing their six o'clock melodies. The long Oakland-Bay Bridge impressed this small-hick-town girl.

We stayed at the Whitcomb Hotel, and the assembly was held at California State College, starting in the stadium with various welcomes by dignitaries. The school Air-Force ROTC displayed the flags of the nations while the bugles sounded and drums rolled. It was impressive. I was interested in the caucus for the Arab states, because it provided my "first views of Arabs (real foreign students)." Somehow, I didn't see Abe as Arab in the same way. There was one idealistic and enthusiastic hot-blood who disappointed Abe.

According to him, the idealist was just seeking publicity and trying to show how he would like the Arabs to feel instead of how they really feel. His resolution was not accepted while the one which Abe believed in was approved and sent to the floor of the general assembly. Abe held many discussions with our team leaders concerning the kinds of resolutions which would be of real benefit to the average Arab citizen. The resolutions presented by our group were all aimed toward that goal.

Whenever possible, Abe and I slipped out of the sessions to explore. That first night out, we went for a walk on Market Street and bought hamburgers and ice cream. When we went to lunch in the cafeteria, we sat at the same table "with a real communist," a Chinese student from Shanghai. I was not impressed with his conversation and ended up arguing with him because he started in on a Capitalistic America with its one-sided viewpoint and propagandist newspapers.

Attending the long, drawn-out sessions was not really Abe's forte, so he contacted his relatives, who happily came to get him. He even convinced me to skip a session or two in order to visit the home of his beloved Uncle Joey. Abe explained that Joe Ayoub was the younger brother to Yacoub Assad Ayyoub, his father's cousin. Uncle Joey and his dear wife Aunt Betty were early family emigrants and had prospered as owners of a lingerie factory.

This was my introduction to Arab hospitality, and I was greatly impressed. They served the most delicious paté that had the texture of deviled ham, a tinned meat paste my family purchased from the grocery store. But this had an entirely different, rich flavor. I helped myself to several servings from the beautifully decorated platter by dipping up portions with lovely soft flat bread and biting strong dark olives along with it. Only then did Ibrahim inform me I was eating Kibbeh Nayiah, a raw meat dish. That took me aback a little, but not enough to keep me from eating more.

I also listened to Arabic music for the first time, enjoying the unusual melodies and instruments. Other guests arrived and Uncle Joey exuberantly introduced us, "Come in and meet my beloved nephew, Ibrahim, who traveled all the way from Oregon to see us, and his beautiful young friend from school." This graciousness made me feel so accepted, and I grew to love Uncle Joey and Aunt Betty.

Our advisor criticized us for skipping meetings, even though we apologized and explained how important it was for Abe to see his family. I felt thoroughly chastened and determined to conform after my experiment with living dangerously.

"Egypt" did not manage to get any of its resolutions passed. I was dismayed with the disorder and wrangling over technicalities that consumed the sessions. It became clearer to me that the real UN probably functions the same way, with resort to procedural tricks. We came with high ideals of what should happen, and then reality set in, illustrating how things end up much differently.

That evening, I requested permission once more to go with Abe. This time his Uncle Joey treated us to a fancy restaurant dinner. We had barbequed spareribs as an appetizer and ate with our hands. I was delighted by the hot, wet napkins provided to wipe our fingers. After our meal, Uncle Joey drove us up to the heights to see the lights of San Francisco and even took us on a quick drive through Chinatown. We stopped long enough for me to buy a few trinkets for gifts. I was gratified that we got back on time, as required by my commitment to compliance.

This trip was life-changing for me. Our return route led through Muir Woods and I saw my first redwoods. Since it was Sunday, I found one little quiet nook among the ancient trees and had my own little simple moment of worship. We saw Mount Shasta in the afternoon, but I slept most of the way, since I was worn out from the odd hours we kept at the conference. Also, I was sitting beside the love of my life, and that interest took precedence over views out the window.

That night we stayed in Klamath Falls and went to see *East of Eden*. It was a powerfully moving story and even then I thought Steinbeck was a master at depicting human nature as it really is. The next evening, we arrived in La Grande and the director of dormitories had saved a hot supper for us. Tired as I was, I went to orchestra practice and was in bed by 11:00. It was the softest, nicest bed that I'd slept in all week.

The rest of spring term is hazy, but we both continued to work and study very hard. Abe was deeply concerned about earning money during the summer of 1955 and undertook a serious search for work. I suggested he might investigate information that a pea cannery in Milton-Freewater was offering jobs and housing to college students. My girlfriend from high school and I had permission from our parents to live and work there during the summer.

So, Abe signed on also. However, it was a bad year for peas; there just was no crop, so work hours were sporadic or non-existent. Abe found himself spending the small store of cash he'd saved during the school year. Following Abe's recipe, I cooked our first meal there, a stew of canned garbanzos and onions sautéed in olive oil. It was a new dish to me, but a taste of home for Abe. Aside from that, ordinarily he allowed himself a daily-food ration consisting of a loaf of bread and quart of milk.

Abe told me he'd go back home if he could find the price of a ticket. Late in July, we girls did go home in defeat. But Abe and two other Arab students from Walla Walla College were hired at the Pendleton Lumber Mill because they knew the Adventist owner. Thankfully, Abe earned enough for another year of school.

One evening, he and his friends were walking in Pendleton when they were accosted on the sidewalk by three burly, drunken guys coming out of a tavern. One of the drunks looked at them and snarled, "Too many damn Mexicans in this town!" This was how Abe became aware that dark skin and hair evoked prejudice in America. On a different occasion, a new student arrived from Jordan and Abe took him to a local coffee shop. They were conversing in Arabic when a nearby listener interrupted their conversation to declare, "This is America. We speak English!" Abe politely explained that they were speaking Arabic because his friend was new to this country and not yet fluent in English." Another customer then kindly spoke up, asking them to continue to speak Arabic because she loved the sound of the language. The disgruntled complainer stood up and left.

While Abe struggled to earn his way back to school, I had less difficulty, because I was once again able to join the corn cannery night shift. However, before the cannery started up, I remember pining away in Nyssa as I listened with a lovesick, lonesome heart to Doris Day's "Secret Love" and Bobby Hatfield's version of "Unchained Melody," which can still bring a tear to my eye. It certainly was "a long, lonely time."

My romance was not much of "a secret love" to my family. However, I did keep secret the contents of the one letter which Abe mailed to me while he worked in Pendleton. Sadly, the letter was eventually lost, which is strange since I kept it close for years. It was rich with sweet loving expressions, and I was greatly impressed with his ability to write so beautifully.

It would be splendid if the story of that letter could end right there. But, years later when we moved to a new home in Yakima, I came upon a box of items saved from Abe's college days. Big mistake on his part! Among his many math books was a small volume titled *How to Write a Good Letter*. I paged through it idly and was thunder-struck to discover a page illustrating a sample love letter. Word for word, it was Abe's one and only love letter written so many years ago. Of course, I confronted him with the evidence. He grinned sheepishly but made no apology. He said that the sentiment was how he felt, but since he knew he'd never come up with words written as well on his own, he just copied from the book.

Whatever the real source of my love letter, it served its purpose. While Abe was working in Pendleton, I begged to be allowed to go for a visit. My parents reluctantly gave permission, as long as my girlfriend went along. So we rode the bus from Nyssa to Pendleton. One of the other Arab students had a car and the gang of boys drove us to the mountains to Emigrant Park for a picnic of tabouleh which they chopped and made right there on a picnic table.

Abe and I walked off into the forest for a private visit. He gave me a particularly long, sweet kiss and said, "I have made the decision to stay in America." I really don't know what I said back to him, because his words were burning their way into my happy heart. I'm sure I must have said something quite agreeable. When it was time, I climbed back on the bus, headed to Nyssa, and began to can corn with exuberance!

It seemed that before I could blink, it was time to head back to La Grande to start my junior year. This term, I was invited to share a neat room on the second floor with three friends. Two were from Hawaii, and the other was from Vale, a town close to my home territory. We girls valued that room because of its location. It was situated over the men's lounge and served as a bridge between Dorion and Hunt halls, since the two dorms were connected to form an "L" shape.

I took advantage of the overlook it provided of Hunt Hall to keep tabs on Abe's comings and goings. His friendship with Roger Tiller had deepened, and I was dismayed to discover that Tiller and Don Starr were initiating him into the delights of "men's night out." Abe's inability to hold his liquor stems back to early childhood, and the story of his jaunt to a downtown bar for beer has already been told. That night, he had to be supported by his friends to get back to the dorm. Of course, I saw the three of them when I looked out from my room. My beloved was staggering between these two heathens who had completely corrupted him! For sure, he heard about it from me the next day, while his good friends stood by chuckling.

When he wasn't out with his new pals on a Saturday night, Abe continued to scrub the kitchen floors, study for his classes, and perfect his English. My time was taken up with classes and work in the library. Also, I got a job for two hours every school day slinging hash for a lady who prepared short-order lunches in a little shop behind her home. Her customers were noon-time high school students from right across the street. She specialized in hamburgers, hot dogs, French fries and chili. She paid me fifty cents an hour and provided my lunch. That cut down on my school board bill, and I thought the arrangement would work out just fine.

The problem was with the owner. She was erratic and easily flustered when too many kids all came in at the same time. If she ran out of an item, instead of telling the kids that she was sold out for the day, she told them she needed to go back to her kitchen and bring more. Except, she didn't come back! I was left behind the counter attempting to placate the hungry teenagers impatiently awaiting their orders. Needless to say, her business folded quickly, and I was forced to begin paying for dorm lunches once more. This was the only waitress job I ever had, and it fostered my special sympathy for folks who do it for a living.

In addition to all this, I took part in one more play, *Sing Ho for a Prince!* in May of 1956. I had done costume design for *Time out for Ginger*; acted in *The Crucible*, sung in the choir and in Blue and Gold, and played in the community orchestra; and, for *Sing Ho*, I acted, designed costumes, and topped it off with a song lyric, "Land of Make Believe." The program calls it "the prettiest song in the show:

Land of Make Believe

In my land of make-believe,
There's no room for hearts to grieve.
Sunshine beams and shadows hide.
There's happiness all around and inside.
Here I'll dwell the whole day through,
Dreaming dreams all filled with you.
Come with me to this dear land.
Just find your smile and then hold out your hand.
We will live so happily,
I'll love you and you'll love me.
Hand in hand we'll waltz through the years,
While the stars beam from above
Here our hearts will dwell in love.

CHAPTER 11

⁂

Our Newlywed Lives

As MUCH AS I enjoyed the plays, the developing relationship between Abe and me was of most importance during my junior year. By that time, Abe had visited our home in Nyssa, and it was quite clear that our commitment ran very deep. My father wrote to say he wasn't "so overly pleased" about my announcement of a son-in-law. He acknowledged that Abe "probably is a nice fellow" and that I loved him, but he urged me to consider before doing "anything rash." He stressed "religious differences, citizenship—and a foreigner's attitude towards their wives and treatment they give them." He had sincere but misguided concerns that persist within our country to this day. Still, in the end, Dad stressed that it was my life, and my parents wanted me to be happy.

Ibrahim's father also wrote us a letter. Because news traveled slowly, and Toufiq was required to secure a scribe for translation into English, we received the letter long after our wedding took place. I was touched by my father-in-law's loving acceptance of me and was struck by the contrast between Toufiq's words and the stereotyped and slightly xenophobic comments in my dad's letter. Toufiq had no way of being certain that he would ever see his son again, and yet he made every effort to welcome me. He blessed us with a wish that every year of our married life would find us happier than the last. It was a wish that was fulfilled during our fifty-six years of marriage.

When we decided to marry during the summer after my junior year, it is significant that Mom and Dad went out of their way to embrace Abe and welcome him into the family. I was provided with everything I could desire as a bride. When Dr. Quaintance learned of our plans, he pulled Abe aside to say that mixed marriages usually do not work. Abe thanked him for the advice, but we continued planning for our special day. We worked it out just fine over the years, and I'd like to simply say to Dr. Quaintance, "Neener, Neener, Neener." His was the only negative comment received from any of our associates in La Grande.

We married on July 1, which was my twenty-first birthday. I've always relished the statement which that made concerning my coming of age. Also, it made it simple for Abe to remember both anniversary and birthday celebrations. Most of our friends attended the wedding. Gene Robinson, the pastor of my church in La Grande, char-tered a small plane and flew to Nyssa to perform our ceremony. Roger Tiller's entire family traveled from Burns, Oregon. Looking back, Mom must have feared that I would fly off to live in Jordan. Except for the new wallpaper in the living room falling down, because Mom didn't know how to ap-ply it correctly, and the hand-made party mints forgotten in the freezer, our wedding came off without a hitch.

Wedding Photo

During the reception, folks came up to Abe and asked permission to touch his hair. Needless to say, this startled him. He later learned that the barber who gave him his wedding haircut had gos-siped to the town, "You know, that Ay-rab has the softest hair. It's not like them Mexican heads."

Our married life began in a cramped apart-ment for $45 a month, including all utilities. Our landlady, Mrs. Sherman, ran a very clean, tight operation. She rented us a front apart-ment on the second floor, which included use of the attached porch. We had two furnished rooms, a living area, and a large bedroom. A section of the living room was a tiny, windowless nook for a kitchen. There was no ventilation to remove odors from my novice cooking. We had a sink, cupboards, refrigerator, and a four-burner stove with an oven.

Down the hall, we shared a bathroom with three other college couples. Mrs. Sherman kept it immaculately clean. In the basement, there was a sturdy Maytag wringer-washer, two rinse tubs, and overhead drying lines. Very strict rules were en-forced giving us access to the laundry facilities on our assigned day only, with no extra charge for its use. Mrs. Sherman liked us and often invited us down on Saturday night to watch *The Lawrence Welk Show*, since she owned the only TV in the building. She also owned the only phone, but she would allow us to make calls if really necessary, as long as we reversed long-distance charges.

I had just a few required classes left, plus a full three terms of student teach-ing. My folks were so determined to see us graduate that they offered to send us $50 a month, money they really could not spare. We both still worked on campus; Abe scrubbed floors while I worked in the library preparing new books for circulation. We ate Campbell's soup, twelve cans for a dollar, and a very dead deer covered with pine needles that a friend dragged down off the mountain. At first, we rented a frozen-food locker. Later, we saved that expense by turning the refrigerator on high, packing the meat around the ice chest and eating our way in. Abe filled the remaining space with oranges, which probably accounts for our good health.

Our first dinner guest was Ismaatt Dawoud, the Iraqi that had pointed Abe towards La Grande when he first arrived in America. I was determined to make a good impression by cooking an Arabic meal. Abe had mentioned several times how delicious his mother's meal of freshly slaughtered kidneys always tasted. "You just wash them carefully and fry them in butter," were the only directions he provided. "Okay," I thought, "That sounds easy enough." No one explained that kidneys purchased in a local store were probably not the same fresh quality that he was remembering. And, no one told me to soak them or how to clean them. Our guest arrived to the horrendous odor of fried urine-saturated kidneys in our tiny unventilated flat. He tried to be polite; and Abe was a gracious host with good stories to tell for entertainment, but it was a difficult affair all around. I'm sure Mr. Dawoud loved the conversation, but none of us could eat the food.

After my disastrous first attempt at a dinner party, we settled into our struggles to finish the school year. I began my first quarter of student teaching, and Abe continued his junior year. I found that I was quite successful with my student teaching assignment in a kindergarten class. My master teacher was complimentary and my singing ability seemed to work well to capture the kindergartners' attention. So, I focused on developing skills to teach at that level.

In the meantime, Abe engaged in some important thinking about his career plans. He had originally chosen engineering, because of advice from those he trusted. Engineering graduates were easily hired in Jordan, but he had decided to stay in America. He realized that he didn't have the eyesight to read and create the graphs and diagrams required for a degree in engineering. Also, there was way too much reading for his slow English-reading skills. The vocabulary he knew best was the language of mathematics. These symbols were universal, and he had a good grasp of the subject. He closed his eyes at night and enjoyed solving math problems just by thinking about them. He was certain that he wouldn't be happy spending his life grappling with engineering problems and drawing neat little diagrams.

So, he spoke with Dr. Easley, his advisor, about changing his major to become a secondary-level mathematics teacher. Dr. Easley agreed with his decision and determined that Abe would need just one quarter of student teaching, since he had already taught more than two years in Jordan. He also promised Abe a good placement for doing his student teaching. This encouragement caused Abe a great sense of relief. It meant that he would need to complete another year at Eastern Oregon College, but we both agreed that could be accomplished easily. I was certain that I could find a teaching job close to La Grande, and we could continue living at Mrs. Sherman's apartment house.

So, our future was looking rosy. But then, we discovered that a baby was on the way! We were slated to become parents before I could finish my degree requirements.

Needless to say, that kink in our plans caused much stress. The responsibility was daunting for Abe! I spent fruitless hours worrying and weeping. I was nervous about attending classes after my pregnancy began to show. And, if I had to take off too much time, would I be able to graduate with my class? And how would we pay for a baby? I remembered how my mother had always joked that since I was a child of the Depression era, I was not yet paid for. I was determined that our baby must be paid for upon arrival.

When emotions settled down, I moved on with my earlier determined attitude, and we started planning. We learned that babies cost about $350, so Abe started saving his pennies, nickels, dimes, and dollars in our trusty little red glass jar. He was sure he would have time to save that amount. And, the wonderful administrators at Eastern Oregon College came to our rescue. They helped me plan my coursework so that it could be finished in a summer session. Also, because they were pleased with my first quarter of student teaching, they agreed that I could practice teach with extra responsibilities during my second quarter, allowing me to satisfy all the requirements.

I was very healthy, and my pregnancy progressed easily. I remember not liking to drink coffee during the entire time, and I remember becoming so sick after eating a can of kipper-snacks that I still refuse to touch them. I also found that chewing on a piece of chalk was very tasty and worried that maybe I had a calcium deficiency. Since we had no car, we walked everywhere, and all that exercise did wonders for my physical well-being. I continued with college classes until the last few weeks and I managed to ignore the strange looks when I appeared on campus in maternity smocks. In the late 1950's, very few pregnant women attended college, and I suspect my appearance caused discomfort. But, I held my head up and continued about my business.

Finally, it was possible to take some time off to prepare for our new arrival. Mom was delighted to help and managed to find us an old-fashioned black baby buggy that rolled smoothly and jiggled comfortably like an English perambulator. The folks also helped us buy a lovely new crib. Janey, my brother's wife, had baby stuff that our nephew had outgrown, such as a neat folding canvas changing table, a bassinette which was great for the early infant period, a multitude of baby clothes, and patterns for making new things. I had fun sewing the little flannel gowns and kimonos using the second-hand portable Singer that my parents bought for me while I was still in high school.

Janey showed me her favorite type of cloth diaper and gave me all her old used ones. I knew that laundry was going to be a problem, so we scrimped on other things to buy extra quantities of brand new diapers, rubber lap pads, and receiving blankets. Friends dropped by with cute little items that cheered us up amid our stress. My favorite gift was a small fuzzy brown teddy bear with a bright red bow which I propped in the corner of the crib. Our apartment began to fill up with stacks of cloth diapers, diaper pail, the crib, and the changing table. It was a blessing that our bedroom was actually larger than the living-kitchen room.

When I informed Mrs. Sherman that we were expecting, she told us that it was fine for families with babies to be in the apartments, but she reminded me that she would still strictly enforce the rule about only one wash day per week. I'd done enough babysitting while in high school to know that tiny babies soil lots of clothes and diapers in one week. Also, I was worried about rinsing out the dirty diapers in a toilet shared with three other apartments. But, I knew of a marvelous new disinfectant called Pine-Sol, and I learned that old fashioned washing soda was cheap and would keep down the diaper-pail odor. Things began to look as if we might be able to pull this off, this new baby thing.

La Grande is a mountain town with late long winters. Wouldn't you know it? A heavy deep snow fell the night before my labor pains started. The next day, Abe walked as usual to his morning classes and then on to his work in the kitchen. My delivery time was imminent, and I was certain that I didn't have enough cans of food purchased so that Abe could heat up a meal while I was in the hospital. So at about noon, with labor pains beginning to make their presence known, I trudged off through the deep snow to lay in some cans of tomato soup and other things I thought Abe would be willing to cook for himself.

It was several blocks to the store, and the deep snow made walking a weary effort, but I made it there okay. By the time the storekeeper had the heavy canned items sacked up, it was obvious I wouldn't be able to carry them home. So I requested delivery for the groceries, but not for me. I again trudged all the way back to the apartment house. By then, it was late afternoon and beginning to get dark. I realized I didn't feel like climbing up the stairs to our flat, so I sat on the first step in the downstairs hallway and decided that maybe I should call a taxi to take me to the hospital.

That was where our neighbor from across the hall, found me. He was startled and asked what I was doing on the stairs. I told him I was just resting a bit while I waited for the store to bring my groceries, and then I was going to ask Mrs. Sherman to call a taxi because it was time for me to head up the hill to the hospital. He turned pale and asked if I had gotten hold of Abe. I replied that he was at work and hard to reach while cleaning the kitchen. My kind neighbor told me not to worry about anything, that he'd take care of everything, and he took control. So that is how I arrived at the hospital, due to the assistance from my neighbor.

Things were out of my hands after that. I was given something in my arm that allowed me to relax and later they put a mask over my face. My baby doctor had explained to me earlier that he planned to use a sedative called "the Freiburg method," also known as "Twilight Sleep," that would make me able to deal with severe pains. Mainly, all I felt were insistent and prolonged periods of ache, like a strong menstrual cramp. It caused me to have visions of a deep comfortable snow bank into which I seemed to sink with every heavy contraction. It was not a bad experience at all. In fact, I suspect my doctor sedated me more than I really wanted because I wasn't alert when my lovely little daughter was born.

Abe saw our baby before I did. I woke up in the early hours of morning to see a smiling nurse holding this beautiful little doll with inches of curling black hair so long the nurse had tied a pink ribbon in it. Abe was grinning proudly right behind the nurse. Somehow, because of all my sedation, it seemed as if the two of them had managed to find this warm, bundled, wonderful baby from somewhere else and were now giving her to me. Then, we experienced a sweet period of cuddling our tiny infant and getting acquainted. She was a peaceful, sleepy baby and absolutely perfect in every way. I sang some soft little nursery-rhymes to her, and we quickly became friends for life.

Abe told me that he'd called my parents and that Mom would arrive in La Grande as soon as she could. Dad was laid up with a slipped disk and would need to stay in Nyssa. In the meantime, because we were in a Catholic hospital, a firm "I-mean-business" nun came in to record the name we had chosen for the baby. Abe spent much of my hospital time hanging out at the coffee shops with Roger Tiller and was not there at the time, but we'd already agreed on her name. I told the nun, "Her name is to be Laila Jo Ayyoub." I knew that Laila meant "the special night or the special occasion" and Jo was my mother's name. But obviously I was no match for this powerful woman. She looked up sternly from her writing and said, "Oh, you don't want to call her just plain Jo. That is a nickname." I knew I did want to call her that, but I was intimidated by the nun's authoritative manner, so the name became Laila Josephine Ayyoub.

I rested all that day, drinking hot Jell-O which was brought to me by a very kind nurse. I spent precious moments cuddling with my baby whenever she was carried to me from the nursery. Then, a most surprising occurrence really shook me up. The nurse came to me with a story, and I didn't know what to think! It seems the hospital had received several calls from different people asking if they could adopt the little Ay-rab baby girl whose parents didn't want it. Each caller was assured that we doted on our baby.

This mystery really upset me, and I was in tears about it by the time Abe visited me that evening. He was fairly certain he knew the reason for the phone calls. That rascal, Roger Tiller, took Abe for coffee at a local restaurant in downtown La Grande while they were waiting through the long night for Laila to be born. Roger, in his usual form, only worse, chatted with the waitress. He could make everybody believe anything he said. "You see this guy having coffee with me? He's an Ay-rab. And he's drinking coffee with me tonight while we wait for his first baby to be born. And do you know something; he sure hopes it is a boy. Because Ay-rabs don't want baby girls and they have to take them out and bury them in the sand." Abe just laughed at his joshing because he knew what a joker Roger always was. But, the waitress believed Roger; it was hard not to believe him.

Later, Roger explained the rest of the story as if it were a great good joke. It seems that Roger went back to the same coffee shop the day after Laila was born. When the waitress saw him come in, she rushed over to ask about the baby Ay-rab. Roger put on a long solemn face and answered her, "You know it is such a sad story; he had a baby girl, and they don't know what to do. They need to bury her in the sand, and they can't find any because of all the snow." That was the end of his so-called joke, he thought, until he learned that the gullible waitress was spreading the tale to all of her customers. I can laugh about it now, but at the time, I struggled with my feelings. However, Roger began to invite me to come along when they went somewhere, and that was how Laila had her first outing. We took a lovely, sunshine-on-snow drive up the mountain towards Pendleton, almost as far as Emigrant Springs Park. Laila loved her ride, and I began to develop new appreciation for Roger.

Mom arrived while I was still in the hospital, and Abe took her out to dinner to celebrate. He really didn't know what was expected of him as a new father, so Mom suggested that he buy a small gift of flowers for me. They went to the hospital gift shop together and bought a sweet little china baby shoe filled with fresh pink roses. His thoughtfulness made me cry. I seemed to be doing more than my share of weeping during those days. That little vase was treasured for years and finally gifted to Laila when she was an adult.

Cultural differences, of which I knew nothing, caused some bumps in the road during our first days of parenthood. When it was time for Laila and me to be dismissed from the hospital, Mom stayed with us at the apartment to help out until I was settled in with caring for the baby. The first thing I noticed when I came into the apartment was that all the canned goods I'd purchased for Abe were still in their grocery sack on the kitchen counter. I turned to him and asked, "You didn't cook anything, and so what did you do for food?" His answer was one which would be repeated many times during the next few difficult days. Roger and he picked up something at the restaurant. It was obvious that during my confinement, Abe had learned to depend heavily on this friend who had caused me so much grief.

If our life could have returned rapidly to our normal routine, I might have handled things better. But now I was faced with the demands of our infant, the need to appease my mother who was constantly hovering, and a deep worry because Abe was very much an absent member of the family. I realized that having my mother there made him feel awkward, because she was a talkative dear who seldom listened. She had a nervous habit of asking a question and not waiting for an answer, already forming the next question in her mind. I knew that she often drove Abe crazy, but he was much too polite ever to let on. However, that was no excuse for him just to take off and be gone all the time! My vision of our happy home pictured him there with us, being the loving husband and new father.

My mother began to worry about his long absences, too. Finally, she asked if everything was all right with Abe and me. Of course, the new mother with a touch of the post-partum blues broke into tears. Mom gave me some very good advice, saying I needed to have a serious talk with him and tell him I needed him home.

When he came home, Mom wisely went out for a walk so that we could have some time for a private talk. Again, I broke into a weeping fit while I laid out my case. I didn't understand why he was never home, why he was always going off with Roger, why he didn't stay with me while we learned to care for the baby. Abe was totally mystified and dismayed. He thought he was doing what new fathers are supposed to do. In his village, bringing a new baby into the home and settling her is a woman's task. The men must leave the house and stay out of the way. I broke into a hiccupping smile and wiped away my tears and assured him that I very much needed him with me.

This mutual revelation called for a goodly amount of hugging and cuddling. When I calmed down a bit, I said maybe it was time to thank my Mom for her help, and suggest that we were ready to handle things on our own. Abe hoped it could be done without hurting her feelings and said it would be the best thing we could do. That statement was what made me realize how much Abe had been feeling like an outsider in his own home. I don't remember how I explained it to Mom, but she seemed to understand, and she soon announced she needed to be getting back to Jesse. She helped with the laundry one last time and packed up to go home. Abe joined in the baby care from then on.

Since Laila soon went on the bottle, Abe could share in feeding her. I'd tried to do well with breastfeeding, but it didn't work. Also, he took his turns staying with her when I needed to be out. Once, while I was gone, he started to worry because she was randomly waving her hands and scratching her face with her sharp little fingernails. When I came home, my frightened, white-faced husband confessed he had

Abe gives his baby a bath

tried to trim her fingernails and due to his poor vision, had nicked her tiny fingertip. Baby blood flowed freely and got all over her nightie. He was sure he had damaged her severely and that I would accuse him of child abuse. But, since Laila didn't even cry, I wasn't concerned. Abe was the one in need of comfort.

Soon, it was time for me to head back to college to tackle my spring quarter of student teaching. Usually, final-quarter student teachers were expected to travel to outlying valley schools. Once again, the college considered my situation and assigned me to half days in a third-grade classroom right on campus in the Ackerman Lab School. I was very appreciative of this, because it meant that Abe and I could stagger our mornings and afternoons so that one of us was always home with Laila. The arrangement made it possible for me to give her an early morning bottle, leave a prepared bottle in the fridge, change her diaper, and get her cleaned up for Daddy before I went off to school. Abe was deep into his first course in calculus which required a lot of study time. We were blessed with a child who took a long morning nap and was quite content to lie in her bassinette beside her daddy to watch the goings-on of the world when she awoke. Abe never mastered the art of diaper-changing, so she was always in need of some serious attention by the time I reached home at noon.

In the afternoons, Abe went to his classes and to his work in the dormitory kitchen while I stayed home. I wrote lesson plans when Laila napped. But, when she was awake and ready for playtime, I began very early to read to her. She couldn't yet hold up her head when I acquired Marguerite de Angeli's *Mother Goose Book*. I propped Laila up on my chest, held the book in front of her, and we would have a singing, bouncing great time. She never had a chance to dislike reading. I felt sure that Abe had no knowledge of, nor interest in, children's poetry and stories. When he came home from work, we ate our evening meal, and Abe went back to his studies. If I began singing or reading to Laila, he apparently paid no attention to what we were doing. But years later, with our family grown and gone, I often heard him humming and singing some of those nursery rhymes which I'd sung so often.

Nursery rhymes did not fit with third grade curriculum. I found that teaching this level was very different from the free-flowing atmosphere of the kindergarten, and I had much to learn. I was expected to plan and execute a complete unit of social studies with integrated activities involving language arts, math, reading, drama, music, and history on the subject of American Indian culture. It was a fun unit, and I plunged into doing my best. My new supervising teacher was just as supportive as my mentor had been for kindergarten. The third grade kids were eager and fun to work with, and that helped me feel successful. The kids knew I had a little baby and kept pestering me to bring her to school. Since the unit required a culmination program, I promised them that Laila would come to school that day. I knew that Abe wouldn't be able to dress her up in show-off frills, so I asked friends to help.

On the day of the program in early June, the classroom was full of parents who had come to see their children perform in their Indian costumes. My friends walked in with my wide-eyed, curly headed baby all dolled up in her very best outfit. The school children could barely do their program correctly, because they were so eager to cluster around Mrs. Ayyoub's baby girl. I felt very pleased with the whole occasion and extremely proud of Laila. It was a great day! It was spring. My grades were good. And, all my degree requirements were finished in time for me to graduate with my class!

Long before graduation day, I submitted a carefully written application through our excellent Eastern Oregon College Placement Service. They sent to me a notification of an available position in the small rural school of Island City, about five miles outside of La Grande. The school employed four teachers for eight grades, each assigned a two-grade split class. The school board was seeking a teacher for their third-fourth grade room.

Abe asked one of his friends to drive me to the school for the interview. I remember being very nervous as I prepared, but I'd received lots of drama training, having participated in every available play, both in high school and college. I took several deep breaths before heading into the interview, just like we were trained to do before going onstage. The school board didn't detect my nervousness and offered me the job. The annual salary would be a whopping, huge $2,500. Abe and I both wondered how we would ever spend that much money!

Graduation day with all its pomp was upon me, and the folks once more drove to La Grande but chose to rent a motel room since our quarters were so crowded. After the ceremony, we posed for happy pictures of the graduate plus more photos of Abe holding Laila, and the grandparents holding Laila.

As we went for a celebration dinner, Mom told me of her desire to come to La Grande for summer session. She needed just one summer of credits in order finally to earn her BA after all her years of struggle. As the four of us discussed the possibilities, we decided that Abe would live in Nyssa for the summer, because Dad could arrange a night job for him at the North Board of Control at the pumping station. Abe's main goal was to earn enough money to buy a second-hand car, since I needed transportation to my school. Mom would live with Laila and me in our apartment while I took graduate courses in education, and Mom finished her degree. I had no idea how hectic the summer would become, or I might not have agreed.

It was terrible! It had seemed to be a good plan, until Mom began to embellish it. The Rigneys were just as strapped for money as the Ayyoubs, so Mom decided that she would accept a live-in client during the first four weeks to help pay her fees. The child was six years old, and she behaved like a "Kid from Hell." Ostensibly, her family hired Mom to teach her how to talk, but the child was afflicted with behavioral problems. From what I now understand, she was probably autistic, but we didn't know what that was at the time.

Mom agreed to stop on the way from Nyssa to pick up the little girl from her isolated, rural home and bring her to live with us in the La Grande apartment. Ever the optimist, Mom was certain that we could provide a loving environment that would foster wonderful changes in the child. I was not consulted before this arrangement was made, and I quickly came to resent Mom for making this plan for our already complicated summer.

Mom was a master at taking over the affairs of the whole family. She failed to recognize that I was now a married woman with new allegiances. For years, she'd assumed the role of my confidante, and it was a real bone of contention between us when I turned to Abe instead of to her. I shed many a tear in front of my patient mate while I ranted about being forced to walk a tight rope between her plans and my wishes. I didn't want to hurt her feelings, and I still wanted her to feel my love, but I believe that she interfered in my married life without even being aware of it. She was wrong to interject such a troubled child into this summer of separation for Abe and me. Yet, I didn't know how to stand my ground and object.

All of Mom's training had focused on Special Education. Every problem child she ever met presented a challenge that she attempted to fix. After countless summers of training, she was qualified to become Director of Special Education in the Nyssa Public Schools system. Even before that, she'd worked with special needs children on her own time while carrying a full load as a regular classroom teacher.

The Nyssa school board was ahead of the times when they recognized her efforts and established the very first full-time Special Ed department in Malheur County. She specialized in speech therapy but also worked closely with the county health nurse to assist every little kid who needed help. She was noted for bringing home a child from the local labor camp for the night to provide a bath, clean clothes, and a good hot meal. When I was a high school student, I remember helping to scrub a little girl who was terrified because she had never before been stripped and dunked into bathwater.

In the eyes of the community, Mom was a guardian angel of the downtrodden. And that she was! But my perspective, seen through the distance of time, finds it possible that she did not always understand the psyche of the families she was attempting to help. I have since read about and visited with enough people who've been on the receiving end of such charity to understand that it can be resented. I do remember that Mom was disappointed to see the little kid that I'd scrubbed come to school dressed in dirty rags again the next day. She couldn't understand why the parents would refuse to let her wear the new clothing that Mom had scrounged to provide.

Knowing what I did about my mother's *modus operandi*, I should have put an early kibosh on her latest scheme. When we picked the little girl up from her home, she was so unruly that I was afraid she might harm Laila. She wouldn't sit still, and she erupted into a loud outcry when she realized she had to come with us. We were strangers, after all. How could we expect her to behave any differently? I suspected the child could be destructive and decided that I would need to watch her carefully around little Laila.

Instructors pile the work on during the short summer session, so Mom and I both had heavy daily assignments while also assuming full time supervision of this strong, willful stranger. Staggering our courses as Abe and I had done wasn't as easy during the concentrated summer session. Also, I missed my husband. Dealing with both my mother and this difficult child was trying, and I needed his support.

Abe was not faring much better. He was assigned the night shift at the pumping plant. Situated on the banks of the Owyhee River, this was a large cement building which housed huge, noisy motors for pumping water out of the river into various irrigation canals. The job required Abe to make the rounds every hour, from midnight until morning, recording the expenditure of power from each gauge. He was also expected to clean the river screens of dead fish and debris, sweep up the shovels-full of dead moths attracted to the night lights and try to stay awake in between rounds. Dealing with the constant droning of the loud engines must surely have affected his hearing, plus it was so unremitting that it invited drowsiness. Abe spent his time studying calculus, because it had been a difficult course during spring quarter, and he really needed to understand it.

Dad gave him rides to work whenever he had use of a North Board pickup. Sometimes, Abe caught a ride from another employee. When he arrived back at the house in the morning, he spent a short time over breakfast with Dad. Because Dad was the cook, they ate many a meal of hot dogs and Kraft Dinner, or Dad would fry up a pound of bacon and dump some eggs into the hot grease. Their diet was definitely geared to Dad's liking. Abe hungered for fresh tomato and cucumber salads or summer fruits. He also learned to steer away from anything political when conversing with his father-in-law. It was easier to beg off by claiming his need for sleep and head down to his basement bed.

The weeks ground on. Mom's little client was more a cause of tension than a creator of any specific destruction. She did scratch up a window screen, and she managed to find my leather manicure kit and play with the scissors until she cut all its little leather loops. When it was my turn to be at home with her, there was no chance for me to relax, because she required constant supervision. She had no ability to entertain herself and could not sit still to listen to stories. Her voice was loud, and she became easily frustrated when I could not understand what she was saying. Surprisingly, my fears for Laila's safety were groundless, because the child was quite gentle around the baby.

Mom did her best to improve her speech and behavior but neither of us felt the undertaking was successful. When the contracted four weeks were finished, we gratefully delivered her back home. Although we were both certain that we earned every penny the family paid, Mom was truly disappointed at not being able to accomplish more. The lovely part of the drive was that her home was fairly close to Nyssa, and we had the July 4th holiday to enjoy. What a celebration that was with Daddy reunited with his Laila and her mommy again!

Following the break, Mom, Laila, and I headed back to school knowing we could complete the rest of the summer with ease. I picked up many credits to be applied toward my later goal of a Master's degree, and Mom earned her BA. Even though Mom could be bothersome and often rattlebrained, she was smart and knew the ropes when it came to good performance in her classes. She easily polished off the final requirements for her degree, and soon it was time again to celebrate a graduation ceremony.

Jo Rigney Graduates

It was such a milestone for Mom, and we were so proud of her accomplishment. She'd started teaching right before she and Dad were married, after only one summer of training. She taught for over twenty years without her degree, taking summer courses whenever possible in an effort to acquire the needed credits. Now, she had made it! She wore that mortar board and gown with great pride.

Dad and Abe came to La Grande for the ceremony and once more we enjoyed a celebratory dinner. Then we packed up, put in a request for the larger apartment next to the bathroom, and headed to Nyssa for September break.

Abe left his job at the pumping plant so that he could make a short visit to Roger Tiller's family in Burns. They were like family to Abe. They had treated him with such kindness during the previous summer, and he wished to see them all again. I chose not to go, because I wanted to stay in Nyssa with Laila until the corn cannery started up. While Abe was in Burns, he told them he'd saved enough to buy a secondhand car, and they gave him some good pointers on what to look for. They also reminded him that he needed to secure a driver's license. Roger picked up a copy of the driver's manual from the small cubby hole which served as the Department of Motor Vehicles in Burns. Abe studied all the questions until he was prepared to take the written test.

Burns was a very small community, and the license examiner came to the office just one day a week. Roger drove him to the DMV late in the afternoon of the appointed day, and Abe took the written exam, passing easily. Then, the examiner looked at his watch and said he had to leave. He assumed that Abe knew how to drive, so he took the $3.00 and issued a license. No one, not even the Tillers, was aware that Abe's most recent driving experience had been when he was a student in Beirut. When he came back to Nyssa, he made the mistake of telling Dad he was given his license without having to take an actual driving test. Dad was floored! 'Til the day he died, Jesse Rigney was hesitant about handing his car keys over to Abe.

When Abe arrived back in Nyssa, he and Dad went car shopping. Dad knew of a green two-door Buick for sale. Abe amazed Dad by the way he bargained until the price was one that Abe thought was fair. He was very proud to drive home in his first-ever car. We didn't learn until much later that the thing guzzled oil.

Meanwhile, I once more secured my old job in the testing lab at the Nyssa corn cannery. I had worked there each fall since I was seventeen. The testing lab required some skill with figuring percentages and reading technical instruments, so when they learned that Abe was a math major with a science background, they hired him to work with me. Mom was delighted to have time to be Grandma to Laila while we concentrated on corn. We both agreed that it felt good to completely ignore the rigors of school and books for a while. One intensive month of manual labor in the cannery was a welcome change from student life.

For some reason, I was always assigned the night shift. The first year, I worked on the main floor below the sorters, and it was sloppy, cold work. All the ears of corn with worms were tossed down a shoot to land with a splatter in front of us, the trimmers. I was required to stand on a wet floor and use a machete to chop off the wormy ends of each ear and toss the cleaned-up cob onto a moving belt.

There was no chance to talk with my co-workers while chopping, because of the constant rumble of falling corn and the grinding of machinery. I had to work fast or be inundated by falling corn. I wore jeans, work shirt, head rag, rubber boots, rubber apron and gloves. In fifteen minutes, after starting work, I was totally splattered with wet sticky corn bits. Every two hours a relief-worker came to take my place for a ten-minute break. Those two hour stretches of work made me long for a chance to sit and rest my weary legs.

But, there was never time to do much sitting. Most of the break was consumed by getting the corn cleaned off in the cold night air at a large, round, cement fountain. The outside breeze wafted a mixed scent of cooking corn, soured corn juice, and the constant sickly-sweet odor of wormy corn. I shall always remember those odors: wet raw corn mingled with the steamy perfume of cooked corn.

Standing at the fountain, I had just enough time to wash all the corn from my face, hands, and apron. Then I would make a quick visit to the latrine before it was time to go back to my station. Around midnight the whistle blew, and we were given a thirty minute lunch break. Once again, I had to clean up before heading out to the front lawn to eat. There was a cafeteria where I could spring for a hot meal of chili and cornbread, but too much indulgence there cut into my efforts to save for school. After that short rest, it was back into the slop until things shut down around 3:00 a.m. I was given the loan of the family car for transportation, but they would not have appreciated it if I had messed up the interior with corn, so yet another session at the fountain took place before I could climb in and drive home. By then, my feet and hands felt frozen. It took a while at home to warm up enough to drift off to sleep.

The summer after my sophomore year at college, I was assigned to cardboard-box folding. One day the cannery foreman came looking for someone to work in the testing lab. He picked me and placed me there each year from then on. One co-worker weighed a large tub of corn that had just been pulled off a truck and run through a husking machine. After the weight was recorded, she laid out the sample on a long, flat counter according to size, texture and color. She counted and recorded how many ears were standard, (tough and old); fancy (tender with high moisture); and, unusable. Then, she gathered a proportional ten ears, selecting some from each category, and handed them to me.

My task was to slice the kernels off the cobs, just so. I could not cut real deep, which added too much cob to the sample, nor could I slice just the tip tops of each kernel. Then I cranked the kernels through a food mill into creamy mixture. The flat pan was handed to the next coworker, who scraped a few spoonsful into a special test tube placed in a device to cook the moisture to be measured. The moisture content and the percentage of useable corn was factored and recorded beside the lot number for that sample. This information became vital to the farmers waiting out by their trucks, because it determined how they would be paid. A standard-quality load paid less, even though it weighed more. Also, the cannery used the information to determine what quality corn they were canning on the line.

As I progressed in skill, I was assigned the job of laying out and recording the quality of ears. Then one year, the cannery installed an electric corn slicer and grinder, which standardized the cutting. They also eliminated the cooking step in favor of a new, delicate instrument which could determine glucose versus starch ratio. With just a drop of corn juice placed on a slide, we looked through a microscope eyepiece. The test results provided a number for starch/glucose ratio. That number was converted into percentages and recorded. With these improvements, the test lab workforce was reduced to two people for each shift plus the husker man.

The fall after our hellish summer session, Abe joined forces with me to run the test lab. He also convinced the foreman that he could work both shifts. Abe was able to compute percentages in his head, and I knew the whole process except for figuring percentages so was able to cover the lab by myself while Abe rested when things were slow. At the end of the night, Abe would bring the records up to date and record all the percentages while I hosed out the lab. When all was ship shape, we climbed into our car and wearily drove home.

We would tumble into bed for Abe's short bit of sleep before Mom called me to drive him back to the cannery for the eight a.m. shift. Then I could come back home to cuddle with Laila while we both took a nap. I didn't get long periods of sleep during that month, because Laila was a bouncy, happy baby who required lots of attention. I did my best to squeeze in as much mothering as I could before time rolled around for me to pack a lunch for Abe and drive back to the cannery. Most of the laundry, cooking, and childcare fell to Mom.

We did experience difficulty with the cannery because of Abe's propensity to side with the farmers. He and I believed that the cards were stacked against them. They were required to sign on with Idaho Canning Co. early in the spring, promising to sell their crop to the company. Then they were guided and dictated to throughout the growing season on how and where to plant, when to water, and most importantly when to harvest. The farmer must cut on the day ordered by the company, drive the trucks into line along the cannery road, and wait in turn to dump at the scales. Until the truck was dumped, the responsibility for corn quality lay with the farmer.

Most days, the trucks would sit for hours in the sun, losing moisture and cooking in the swelter of heat. Of course, that showed up in quality when the test sample hit our lab. Farmers came into the lab, wiping sweat off their worried brow to ask for their percentage number. Since Abe read the machine and figured the percentages, if there was the slightest doubt, he tended to decide in the farmer's favor. Abe listened politely during extra training sessions, but whenever possible, he continued reading the tests in a way that benefited the farmers.

He never regretted running the test lab the way he did. The cannery produced quality corn which was distributed nationwide, and the company continued to make a profit. They continued hiring Abe for as many summers as he chose to work there. It was convenient that the canning season usually closed down about the third week in September, the same time that college began. We had enough time to get our little family packed up and moved back to La Grande.

That fall, we could move independently in our own car. Abe was so proud of owning that Buick! Before we headed out on our trip, he decided to take a photo with the folk's camera of the two things in life which gave him the greatest pride. He placed his little girl, who had learned to sit up by herself, on the hood of the car and walked far enough away to photograph them both. Laila still has the photo of the howling baby on scary green car.

On the way to La Grande, we quickly discovered the problem with our lovely Buick. When we looked out the rear window, we could see a trail of blue smoke curling out of the exhaust. During the 150 mile drive from Nyssa, we needed to stop at a service station, not for gas, but for a quart of oil. After reaching La Grande, Abe bought a case of oil which we put in the trunk, and he checked the oil every time we planned to drive the car more than twenty miles.

We were allowed to move into the larger apartment down the hall. The rent went up to $50 a month, but hey, we were a family with an employed person under contract; we could afford it! The new place had a large kitchen with a cheery red countertop which stretched the length of the wall by the sink, providing a handy bath area for Laila. There were ample cupboards above and below the counter. The appliances were in good condition, and there was a window looking out onto the street leading up to the college. We actually had a real table in the kitchen for our meals.

Furnishings in the living room were clean and good quality. The rug was a combination of dull browns and beiges which complemented the plain brown sofa and the comfortable overstuffed rocker. In the corner, between two more windows, there was a nice-looking wooden desk and a new, unfinished wooden bookcase. Not knowing about unfinished wood problems, I soon set a vase of flowers on it, creating an irremovable water ring. I covered it with a doily and didn't confess to Mrs. Sherman.

The bedroom was ample, though not as large as our previous apartment. We had just enough room for the changing table, crib, and bed. Other baby equipment was stored in the large kitchen. The folks gave us a bouncy swing which fit nicely over the door frame between kitchen and living room, and Laila spent happy times playing in it. We still had to share a bathroom, but we already had that routine down pat.

The next important issue was quickly resolved. Mr. and Mrs. Hatcher were more than willing to provide child care for Laila. They charged fifteen dollars a week, but it was an amount we could handle with our new budget. Laila was much loved by this dear couple. I suspect they spoiled her rotten, but she thrived, and we were relieved that she was safe and well cared for. Laila always remembered that her favorite treat from Mrs. Hatcher was a piece of toast slathered with butter.

Over the years, my working outside our home as a teacher caused me to miss many mountain-top mothering experiences, and I'll always feel a certain amount of sadness because of it. While I was teaching other people's kids, Laila learned to crawl, spoke her first words, and then took her first steps, all under the tutelage of the Hatchers. Knowing that someone else became the primary witness to all her accomplishments caused a feeling of emptiness deep inside me.

That distress level was comparable with how I felt when I learned that Abe and the hospital staff greeted her as a newborn before I did. I believe my girls understand, though, that I never regretted my choice to teach instead of being a stay-at-home mom. In many ways, I feel my busy life was a benefit to the girls since it helped them learn to manage responsibilities which might not have happened if I had been there to do everything for them.

During her first fifteen months, Laila's goal in life was to reach the door knob leading out into the hall. When I came home one night, I was greeted with Mrs. Hatcher's pronouncement that from now on they would need to keep their door locked, because Laila accomplished her goal. She made it out into the hall but then timidly decided to venture no further.

With Laila settled in with the Hatchers, and with me busily preparing for my first year of teaching at the Island City School, Abe was free to give some serious thought to his last year at La Grande. During the summer break, he managed time to see *Blackboard* Jungle. It is a very disturbing Glenn Ford film about the difficulties of teaching in an American inner-city school. It really alarmed Abe, and he headed directly to his advisor, Dr. Easley.

As soon as he entered the office, he declared that he wanted to change his major to something other than education. He knew he would not be able to teach classes with wild students behaving like that. Dr. Easley's face burst into his characteristically wide grin and he invited "Ī-brim" to sit down. He explained that the movie was just Hollywood's version of a high school in America. and not true. He assured Abe that he would have well-behaved students serious about mathematics.

Knowing Abe's concerns, his advisor assigned him to advanced algebra at the La Grande High School with Mrs. Quinn as his supervisor. She was respected as an excellent teacher, and she was thorough and demanding of her student teachers. She expected good behavior from her students. During his first week of observation, Mrs. Quinn presented Abe with a challenge. She wanted him to create a simplified explanation for addition, subtraction, multiplication, and division using the slide rule. Abe neatly printed out a self-teaching model with examples and instructions which explained what she wanted. When he gave it to Mrs. Quinn, she thanked him and took it to make copies for students and other members of the faculty.

Abe was gradually introduced to the actual teaching of algebra and he found Mrs. Quinn to be very supportive. This was not the case for a very bright fellow student teacher who was assigned to teach her Geometry class. The student knew his math, but he spoke in a distinctive vernacular which was sprinkled with grammatical errors. He came to Abe to complain about his treatment, but his story was full of dropped g's, "the" became "da," and his verbs were a hodge podge of tenses and forms. Abe didn't find an easy reply for his complaint. So many times, he had been in trouble trying to communicate with Americans for the opposite reason. His English training had come from people formally educated in England. And though his use of English probably impressed Mrs. Quinn, he struggled to learn American idioms. Consequently, he just nodded in sympathy.

Abe experienced a daily struggle to write lesson plans and stay on top of his supervisor's expectations. During this period, I often heard him softly singing "the wayward wind is a restless wind, a restless wind that yearns to wander." I was aware of Abe's early story, and as I listened to him singing, I understood how his adventurous spirit must relate to those lyrics. Knowing his previous experiences of wandering, I appreciated him as a steadfast husband, daddy, student, and teacher. I thought there surely must have been times when he wished to toss it all away and follow "the wayward wind." But he said he just liked the way the girl sang that song.

He kept working hard to fulfill all of Mrs. Quinn's demands. Soon it was time for his final observation. By then, the course work had progressed to algebraic story problems, and the class struggled as they always do when faced with story problems. Abe wanted them to understand that the ability to solve such problems was the practical reason for learning algebra.

He told the students that if they knew the English sentence, then they had to believe that there is a corresponding mathematical sentence to match it. The story of the problem describes the relationship between verbal language and the mathematical equations. He provided the students with many, many examples of how that worked, and then he assigned homework avoiding some of the more lengthy problems just to make life easier for the students. His final observation was scheduled to take place the following day. So he sat at home, that night, solving all the problems in the textbook dealing with that section. He even worked through the ones which he had not assigned until he felt well prepared.

The next day, he stood in front of the class and asked, as he always did, if anyone had a difficulty with the problems. Hands went up, questions were asked, and Abe patiently worked through the questions on the chalkboard. Class was almost over when a student, who was noted for his ability to be a troublemaker, raised his hand and asked for the solution of #16. This particular problem was lengthy and wordy. Abe suspected he picked that question in an effort to cause embarrassment for Abe in front of the observers. Immediately, another student raised his hand to say that problem was not assigned. Abe thanked him for reminding them of this but said, "He is a student, and I am assumed to be a teacher. He has every right to request an explanation of any problem, and I must stand in front of you and deliver assistance."

He called on them all to be participants in helping to solve the problem. He read the first sentence and asked them to translate it to a mathematical sentence. When they completed the translations, they worked with the equations to arrive at a solution. When Abe turned around to begin, he happened to glance at Dr. Easley and Mrs. Quinn sitting side-by-side at the back. All he could see were big smiles of approval for the way he handled the situation. From that point on, the students began to understand what to do with story problems, and they relaxed. It was close to the end of the quarter, so Abe relaxed too. And Mrs. Quinn gave him an A for his final grade. It was a rare occurrence at EOC for students to earn an A in student teaching.

Unfortunately, it was not so easy for me to relax into my teaching job at Island City. If I were grading myself, I would say that, during my first year as a real teacher, I earned a weak C-minus. I approached the school year with great anticipation. After all, I was one of the chosen who had received A's in student teaching! I had a diploma and mortar board tassel in my dresser drawer. I knew what I was doing and felt on top of the world. But, on the first day of school, the kids tromped into my classroom, and all of my self-confidence flew out the window.

Until then, I'd spent my life striving to be an excellent A+ student. The real world of student behavior in public schools hit me with a jolt! I was prepared to believe that most students would behave under my superior management abilities as they had done at the college lab school. But, I was hired by a rural school board for a tiny school situated in close proximity to the college. Board members were always able to hire willing, freshly-graduated teachers who needed to stick around in the area for another year, which was my case exactly.

Therefore, the staff turnover was high, and program continuity was practically nonexistent. Only one of the four teachers at Island City had been teaching there longer than two years. She was an experienced teacher of the first-second grade class. I was the wet-behind-the-ears teacher of the third-fourth grade. The man hired for fifth-sixth grades also was brand new and the seventh-eighth grade teacher was only in his second year. He was also the designated principal.

There was scant orientation for us. I was handed a key to the building, shown my room, and assigned the additional task of teaching music to the four upper grades as a trade-off while those two teachers taught PE to our four younger grades. My classroom was very old fashioned with oiled-wood flooring, row desks fastened permanently together, slate chalk board, and large slide-up windows reaching to the ceiling. Ceilings were high and created quite an echo when my students became too noisy, which was often.

A long hall ran the length of the building from the main front door by the upper grade classrooms, past an office and lavatories on one side and a gymnasium on the opposite side. The hall continued past two primary grade classrooms and ended at the back door leading out to the playground equipped with a swing set and a marvelously dangerous whirling contraption with rings attached to chains. Children grabbed the rings and ran around the circle until centrifugal force flung them into the air for a flying ride. There were a few more pieces of playground equipment, but my third and fourth graders preferred the large open field for tag, soccer, softball, and the occasional settling of disagreements.

The building reminded me of the ancient Linder School where I attended first grade in 1941. Both of these buildings must have been from the same era. Linder was also an eight-grades school but with only two teachers. Island City School was a great deal more modern than Linder, because our lavatories were in the hall instead of outside, and we had central heating piped from the furnace room. We also had a strict janitor who convinced me that he owned the building. I was guilty of raising his ire, since I didn't know better than to rinse the residue from Plaster-of-Paris projects down the drains, royally clogging the plumbing.

I came to Island City fresh from the EOC Laboratory School, which specialized in integrating all subjects into unit-based curriculum with all kinds of special books, audio-visual materials and a state-of-the-art student library. Now, I was dumped into a room where last year's teacher had ordered a workbook for each child in every subject. I found them all stacked and ready to distribute. I suspect that this was her solution for keeping one class busy while she worked with the other. Not knowing any better, I believed I was expected to use all those workbooks.

I quickly learned that it really does not matter how many pages a teacher assigns in a workbook, if the students don't understand the concepts being practiced. They can whiz through ten pages in five minutes and answer all questions incorrectly. Whether the mistakes are intentional or not, they believe they are done, and that leaves them ripe for mischief. Because the desks were connected, there was no good way to separate a mischief maker from the group. By and large, the kids had my number for most of the year while I struggled to find my way. One of my constant issues involved the checking of all those pages of workbooks, since I believed that students needed to discover and fix their errors. Not a day went by when I didn't carry home huge stacks of workbooks to correct. What I needed was a chance to relax at home with my family and that was next to impossible.

There was no school lunch program at Island City. Each student brought lunch from home, but boxes of milk were delivered daily. I had to collect milk money and keep records. My mentor, the first-second grade teacher, explained that some children would be attending school from low-income homes and would not be bringing adequate lunches to school. She told me to establish a tray by the teacher's desk where children could place unwanted items from their lunch pails. Then anyone in the room was free to help themselves without stigma to whatever was on the tray. That worked fairly well, except there was always an array of food left over at the end of the day. By the time the kids scattered for home, I was always tired and hungry while I graded workbooks at my desk. So, I snacked on unclaimed leftovers. Because I hadn't slimmed down from pregnancy, my poor body eagerly piled on more fat because of those ever present munchies sitting right beside me. I gained many pounds during that school year, and my previous weight struggle during childhood once again reared its ugly head.

Adding to my fatigue was the bothersome task of attendance accounting. It wasn't just a simple matter of present or absent each day. In larger schools, a central office kept the registers for teachers. But in our little school, we teachers were required to enter daily attendance, in ink, and reconcile the numbers, much like a check book, at the end of the month. No errors could be allowed, because county funds for our school were determined by attendance records. The demand for error-free recording caused me to learn another little trick from my next door mentor. It is possible to erase an incorrect entry using bleach, and after it is thoroughly dry, the mistake can be corrected. Therefore, part of my teaching paraphernalia was a box of cotton swabs and a tiny bottle of bleach. I have always been a detail person; things need to be right! So, I sweated blood and tears over that register and often sat at my desk wondering if this was what teaching was all about.

My class was a mixture of sweet students and absolute rascals. Of course, I remember the antics of the rascals the most, especially one burly little boy with an explosive temper. One day, we were having a discussion about how to deal with family disagreements. He interrupted the discussion by standing up to declare, "Well, that never happens at my house. When I get mad at home, I just ups and throws my boots in the gravy!"

One of my students came from a Jehovah's Witness family, and I was prepared for his refusal to say the Pledge of Allegiance or to sing any patriotic songs. I also knew to provide other activities for him when our art project was based on a holiday theme. But, his mother explained to me that he was not required to follow the teachings of the church because their belief stated that even very young children were allowed to follow the dictates of their own conscience. However, if a child chose to stray from the religious tenets, the parent was expected to tell him that he was guilty of sinning against God's will.

When Hallowe'en rolled around, this little guy declared that he had decided to take part, so I distributed his share of the treats brought by other parents for the party. Right in the middle of the festivities, he experienced a dramatic change of heart. He jumped up, headed to the front of the room screaming, "This is pagan! You are all sinners! You will all burn in hell!" Then he ran from the room and out to the playground. My mentor covered my room while I rushed to the principal to report a runaway.

I also struggled with two of the older grades. While another teacher took the lower grades for PE, I took the upper grades for music, with a colleague along to play the piano. Since I loved to sing, I expected these sessions to be rather enjoyable. But I was unaware of the way older kids attempt to haze the new teacher. Since they respected my mentor, things always went smoothly as long as she was in the room. They were not enthusiastic about singing, but at least they behaved. The problem arose on a day when she was absent, and I was faced with a truculent bunch of students and a timid substitute piano player.

It was apparent to me that it was going to be a bad day when the kids came in noisily after their PE class and refused to settle down. Two of the biggest boys continued to stand up and would not take their seats. I directed them, using my very firm teacher voice, to sit down. The first boy stood there and said, "Make me!" So I went to him, placed my hand on the top of his head and pushed him into his chair. He was disgruntled, but he did remain seated. However, the large muscular boy behind him stated, "No teacher is going to push me on the head!" I realized I was being challenged and knew I had to act.

I shall be forever grateful for the rough treatment I received from my older brother while growing up. He had taught me the pain of an arm lock. Without saying a word, I quickly grabbed this kid's arm and twisted it into an arm lock behind his back. He was so startled at the power it gave me that he quickly sank down in his chair. I politely told both boys, "Thank you for being seated. Now, let's get ready to sing." As I walked back up the aisle to the front of the room, I heard the student grumble that he "didn't know they were hiring lady wrestlers for teachers these days!" Come to think of it, my lady-wrestler skills were apparent even when I was a first-grader taking down the superintendent's little boy and sitting on him.

Modern-day parents might have charged me with assault. But in 1957, corporal punishment still took place in schools. In fact, the boy was probably not inclined to go home and tell his father for fear of letting his family know that a female teacher got the better of him. Plus, in many families, such a story would likely cause his parents to mete out further punishment. I did report the incident to the principal, but he didn't seem perturbed and indicated that this particular student required a firm hand. I had found mine.

Other kids from the older classes were also determined to test me. One morning two of them appeared in my classroom before the morning bell and said, "Look teacher, what we found!" Then they held out a fairly large, live, bull snake in front of my face. Again, I did some quick thinking. I'd grown up in rattlesnake country and had a respectable fear of rattlers, but I knew this one was harmless. It was just being presented to see if they could get the new teacher to scream and jump on top of her desk. I quickly decided to hide all signs that I was startled and asked if I might hold it.

Their jaws dropped open as they handed the reptile over to me. I had never held a snake before, and I was quite surprised at how smooth, dry, and lithesome it felt. "Isn't it pretty?" I said, as I felt my face turning several shades of green. But, the kids didn't notice because they were so amazed to see this lady holding their instrument of terror. I handed it back with instructions for them to release it out on the edge of the playground, since it would not be happy in captivity. As they headed outside, I knew that, once again, I had earned an inch of respect from these country kids.

The school was accustomed to presenting a winter program for the community. Since I was reading Dumas' *The Nutcracker of Nuremberg* to my class, I suggested that each room take a section of the story and develop it musically around a script which I volunteered to write. I had done something similar for my senior class Cinderella Ball, basing the script on popular songs, which my classmates acted out accompanied by the music.

The other teachers agreed, so we divided the story into sections. The littlest kids could learn a circle dance based on "Waltz of the Flowers," which I taught to them. My class wanted to act out the battle of the Mouse King. That was very appropriate, since my kids were always eager for rough and tumble battles. I agreed because the scene obviously would enable them to allow their real skills to shine. The fifth-sixth graders developed a great Chinese Mandarin dance, and the oldest class provided the principal characters of Clara; her grandfather, Herr Drosselmeyer; and the Nutcracker. They also produced costumes and dancers for the Sugar Plum Fairy section.

We developed the production as theater-in-the-round with the audience seated around the walls of the gymnasium. Except for the raucous noise emanating from my classroom while we rehearsed the mouse battle, things came together quite well. One colleague was forced to step into my room more than once to ask us to quiet down.

Each room created its costumes as part of the art lessons. I found a good recording of the music and our principal worked the sound system. The program was well received by the parents, who praised the production and said that nothing of that quality had ever been done in the past. The students felt a renewed sense of pride. In retrospect, working on this production was one of the highlights for me during my year at Island City School.

As the school year slogged along, I began to develop some classroom control, but I'm still quite puzzled about whether my students learned much of anything. Part way through the year, I finally gave up on checking all those workbooks myself. Consequently, I fell back on the age-old technique of having the children trade workbooks and check each other's work while I read out the answers. This creates its own set of difficulties, because kids will argue. I had no way of knowing if the skill being practiced was also being learned. I do know it filled minutes in the day with kids being involved and not getting into mischief. In later years, with more training under my belt, I learned to assign short written assignments for which I could go down the row of students and place a beautiful red marker dot on their paper, which stood for correct, immediately after they finished the work. Kids went home having been given immediate feedback.

In the fall of 1957, the Russians launched Sputnik, and America went crazy to catch up. By January of 1958, our county delivered the edict that we must spend more time on science in the classroom. I did my best, but I didn't have much in the way of materials to work with. I remember designing a bulletin board with everything mounted on a background of black butcher paper to simulate space.

That science unit coincided with the week that the County Supervisor came for my teaching observation. The kids behaved while she was there, and I thought the lessons came off quite successfully. However, when the kids went out to recess, she proceeded to evaluate my efforts. She walked over to the bulletin board and held a light meter up to it saying, "You must remove all this black paper. It is robbing needed light from the children." I agreed to take it down, although her criticism seemed strange to me. It would have been much more helpful if she could have provided feedback on my teaching techniques, but I heard nothing from her in that respect. It seemed trivial at the time.

Over eight years later, my husband and I considered moving to a city where he had been offered a contract. By that time, many glowing reviews had collected in my record, and I felt quite confident about finding a job. But when I applied for a teaching position in the town, the interviewer brought up an item in my permanent record written by that novice County Supervisor. He told me that the report indicated that I had created an ill-conceived black bulletin board which was harmful to student vision because it robbed light from the classroom. The ignorance of the young and inexperienced has a long reach!

It surprised me that the principal, who interviewed me, even brought the subject up. It is very unusual for an interviewer to relate to you the statements, written by others, in your permanent record. The entire episode left me with a bad impression, and by the time I left the school, I was suffering a migraine. I knew from a doctor's diagnosis that my migraines usually came on due to stress, and it was clear to me that I had not done well in the interview. Therefore, it was no surprise to me when I wasn't offered the job. In the meantime, my husband developed nervousness about moving to such a congested city atmosphere with crazy traffic, and he knew we would miss all of our good friends. We agreed to stay where we were.

For sure, I experienced my share of migraines during that first year of teaching, but one bright spot offered respite. I was secure in the knowledge that each day would surely end, and I could drive back to our little home and gather up my tiny daughter. Laila thrived in all the love and attention heaped upon her. Before I knew it, she arrived at the ripe old age of one. Grandma and Grandpa drove the snowy roads to be there for her first birthday party. We made two cakes, one small layer solely for her and a larger cake for the adults. Grandpa insisted that she must be seated up next to the table and given freedom to dive in. He delighted in seeing her plastering frosting on her nose. When she didn't get messy enough to suit him, he insisted we strip her down to her diaper so she could really go at it.

The end of my first year of teaching at Island City School arrived just as rapidly as had Laila's birthday. I packed up my belongings and prepared to follow my husband wherever he might land for his graduate work; after all, I really meant "Whither thou goest, I will go." I gave notice to the school board that I would not be signing a contract for the following year, although they did offer me one. If the truth is told, I must relate what I said in later years to every student teacher who trained under me: "Be patient with your first year out. I was convinced after my first year of teaching that if I could have afforded to quit right then, I would never have signed another contract."

While I began to fold up the tent of my first school year and quietly steal away, Abe was doing the same thing with his last few weeks of college. Though he was done with his highly satisfactory student teaching experience, he still needed to finish some coursework. He was asked about his plans after graduation and replied that he wanted to go to Oregon State University to major in Mathematics. He hadn't applied for a graduate assistantship because he didn't think his spoken English would suffice, but he was encouraged to try.

I helped him complete the forms, and we mailed them off to OSU. Even before Abe could go through his graduation ceremony, we received a letter inviting Abe to Corvallis for an interview. Since I was finished with teaching for the year, I was free to drive with him, but we did not know what to do about Laila, and we had no money for such a long drive. Mrs. Hatcher blessedly offered to keep the baby, and Abe did something he swore he would never do. He went to a lending agency downtown and borrowed $50, promising to pay it back plus interest in monthly payments. In 1958, that was rent for a month or groceries for five weeks, but we needed to stay in a motel, buy gas and oil for the Buick, and have something left over for food.

Abe drove while I, supposedly, was the navigator. As long as we stopped every so often to add oil, we had no trouble getting to Portland, since Abe was familiar with the road via Greyhound. Trouble came when we reached the outskirts of the city. I naïvely expected to see a road sign saying, "This way to Corvallis." But the more we wandered the streets and byways of downtown Portland, the more confused and frustrated Abe became with me. Obviously Mrs. Navigator was failing. I had a road map, and I knew we needed to travel south, but that was no help in finding the way out of a city with no signs for Corvallis.

Finally, I spotted a sign directing traffic to Salem. I told Abe, "I'm certain that Salem is south of Portland. Take that exit to the right and let's head for Salem." Thank heavens it was the correct decision, and harmony was restored. However, to this day, no one in our family has confidence in my navigational skills, because I stubbornly refuse to learn how to use a GPS. I don't want some strange voice constantly interrupting to tell me where to go.

We wasted over an hour being lost, and by the time we passed Salem and reached Albany, it was turning dark, plus, a thick, heavy fog settled in around us. I know now that Corvallis is just ten miles from Albany, but the way was a winding road next to the deeply fogged-in Willamette River. If we wanted to check a road sign, we were required to pull off the road and stop to peer up at the writing. It is a wonder that some other car didn't smack into us. That was the longest ten miles of the entire trip, and we were totally exhausted by the time we finally arrived in Corvallis. We still had to locate a cheap motel before we collapsed for our well-deserved rest. It wasn't a very auspicious introduction to the place we later called our real home.

Since the Corvallis economy was centered totally around the university in those days, Abe had no difficulty finding his way the next morning. Everyone was happy to offer directions. Abe arrived at the correct building and entered where he approached a group of men chatting in the hallway. They were so casually dressed that he assumed they might be custodians enjoying their break time, and Abe was surprised to meet professors without three-piece suits and ties.

During his interview with Dr. Lonseth, who was head of the math department, Abe had the distinct impression that the main concern was if Abe's English was good enough to be understood in a classroom. Abe was informed that a committee would decide who would be selected and that he could expect to be notified by letter. He learned that a graduate assistant usually taught two courses in the fall when all the freshmen arrived, but by winter and spring terms, so many were weeded out that Abe would probably teach only one class. Dr. Lonseth also stated that the salary would be $150 per month plus tuition. With that and a hand shake, Abe left and returned to the motel where I was waiting.

We felt good about the way things had gone so we decided to find our way downtown for a celebratory lunch. That was when we discovered Burton's Café and ate our first bowl of clam chowder at their establishment. Abe marveled at the prospect of $150 a month income, and once again we wondered how we could possibly spend so much. We sat at the cheerful window-side table and allowed our heads to fill with schemes and dreams. In later years, Burton's Café became our memory-place for dining-out occasions.

Retracing our route to La Grande posed no difficulties, and I eagerly embraced my little daughter. I'm sorry to report that she didn't miss us at all. Mr. and Mrs. Hatcher completely charmed and spoiled her all the time we were away. Soon after our return, it was time to celebrate Abe's graduation. Yet again, my parents drove up from Nyssa, and we all relished the successful culmination of our long days of struggle at school. Now, we could proclaim that Ibrahim Ayyoub, Doris Rigney Ayyoub, and Jo Rigney were all college graduates. It was an accomplishment brought about by the concerted efforts of our entire family, and we felt exultant.

The folks collapsed the crib and packed it with the other baby furniture into the back of their car to take Laila back to Nyssa with them for a bit of loving and spoiling, while Abe and I stayed in La Grande for the first half of the summer. He worked on major cleaning projects in the college dormitory, and I attended a six-week summer session to earn a few more graduate credits. Soon, it was time to pack the rest of our belongings into the Buick, which was easy to do since we owned no furniture. It was time to bid good-bye to La Grande.

I remember scrubbing the apartment till it shone. Leaving a rented home cleaner than I found it became an item of pride for me. But Mrs. Sherman's housekeeping skills were meticulous, and it was hard to surpass her cleanliness. I suffered through her careful inspection of the premises and was forced to face the music for the bottle of ink spilled on the carpet and the water mark left on the cabinet. She was quite upset with me over that, saying she would have been able to remove it if I had told her immediately. My mistake caused her to charge us a small damage deposit. Later, when we were the landlords, I was in for a rude awakening to discover that my infractions were minor in comparison with what some renters can do to a place.

I felt nostalgia about leaving this first home. It sheltered our young family through many a turmoil and periods of quiet joy. This was our sanctuary as we developed our early understandings of how to live agreeably with each other. Here is where we welcomed our little daughter into the world. Here is where Abe struggled through his student teaching while I cut my teeth out in the full-time world of teaching. Here is where I first learned the valuable skill of separating my two lives of work and home. While teaching, I was able to put concerns about Laila out of mind, because she was so lovingly cared for during my absence; when I came home, I left school at the door.

And, here is the place in which we spent lovely hours enjoying the shade of that upstairs porch. Out there, Abe played three-handed pinochle, which he always won, with Mom and me. He eventually confessed that because the game was boring to him, he cheated so as to win and make the game end faster. We honest ladies never suspected until he showed us what he was doing.

We left that world behind and traveled back to Nyssa. It was good to be with Laila again, and to be done with summer school. Our baby had trained Mom and Dad well. They indulged her every demand and jumped whenever she peeped. By the time I arrived, she was not easy to live with. When I began to enforce rules, it confused her for a while. I didn't respond to all her demands, and I reinstated our time-out practice, when she was required to stay put until she was finished with the tears. Soon, since she was bright and normally agreeable, we could enjoy each other again.

There were still a couple of weeks before the corn cannery started up, so Abe made a quick trip to visit Roger Tiller's family. About the time that Abe returned, my brother Jim and his wife, Janey, arrived with their little boy, Tony. It was nice for us all to renew family connections, and it was obvious that Jim and Abe enjoyed each other's company.

Abe complained to Jim about the way our Buick burned oil, so when Jim heard about a 1954 Ford Crestline Coupe offered for sale, the two of them checked it out. Abe sat in the driver's seat and revved the engine while Jim checked the exhaust. Jim pronounced the engine to be sound, so Abe decided to buy. It embarrassed Jim to watch Abe's hard bargaining. He told us later that he would have paid the asking price. But since the dealer must have really wanted a sale, Abe got his price and also traded in the oil-guzzling Buick as part of the bargain. After that, Jim loved to speak of his wily Arab-trader brother-in-law.

Soon after, the cannery started up with round-the-clock hours and very little sleep for Abe. Once again, Mom watched Laila while I worked the night shift. One night, in a flurry of excitement, I carried a letter out to the cannery. Abe beamed with delight to learn that he was granted a Graduate Assistantship and was instructed to report to campus in late September. Now that Abe's plans were settled, I knew that it was time for me to find a job, too.

CHAPTER 12

─── ◆◇◆ ───

Living Our American Dream

ONCE ABE SECURED A Graduate Assistantship. I phoned for an appointment and learned that there were openings in the Corvallis School System. Mom drove Laila and me to Corvallis for the interview, and the principal of Harding School offered me a position teaching third grade. Harding was the school where many professors enrolled their children, and it was within walking distance of OSU. Mom and I immediately started seeking an apartment close to the college. We found a furnished three-room place on the main floor of an old, ramshackle apartment house on NW Orchard. It was humble and not very clean, but the rent was only $60 per month. And, it included our own bathroom!

The other apartment on the main floor housed a graduate couple who managed the apartments for the owner. The second floor contained two units, and in the basement, there was a one-room hovel occupied by two students from Korea. They received free rent in exchange for keeping the wood furnace operating during winter. The basement was rank and dirty, and all its corners were chock full of discarded junk and trash. That was where the swish-swish washing machine was set up beside rows of lines for drying. There also were clotheslines out back in a thistle-choked yard not much larger than a postage stamp. Of course, I soon discovered that Corvallis has a long rainy winter, when drying outside is impossible.

As Mom and I drove back across the state to Nyssa, we decided that I shouldn't go back to work at the cannery, since public school in Corvallis started much earlier than the university, plus I needed time to get settled into the apartment and locate daycare for Laila. I had to do the moving without Abe's help, and it wouldn't be the only occasion when this happened during our marriage!

In order to get our personal belongings moved across the state, I once more needed help from my folks. Mom and Dad loaded the crib and other baby furniture into the backseat of their car, and I stuffed boxes of everything else into our Ford. We moved on a weekend when Dad was off work and Mom was still on summer vacation.

After the long drive, we unloaded all the boxes, and set up the crib in the tiny cramped bedroom, which was really just a remodeled porch. There was barely room for the crib; the bed, closet, and dresser. The bed had a very poor mattress and springs that sank down with a discouraged squeak when anyone sat or lay on it. Laila had the best sleeping arrangements of the family!

I was glad I'd made the trip a whole week before school orientation because I needed that extra time to apply hours of elbow grease, along with scads of Pine-Sol and bleach, to scrub the whole place. Before they headed back to Nyssa, the folks and I checked out a wonderful store called Bi-Mart. It was a membership discount store and after I paid my one-time-only five-dollar fee, I received a lifetime card for the family. I had to show my card each time I went shopping, but I found excellent prices for all the household supplies I needed. That five dollar investment really paid off, because the Bi-Mart chain spread all over the Northwest, and my card is still good.

I asked a neighbor for advice about daycare, and she offered to fill in on a temporary basis until I could make more permanent arrangements for Laila. That resolved my immediate concerns and allowed me time to find the best situation.

Our apartment began to look livable as I worked it over that week.

The kitchen was by far its best feature, since the tiny little sitting room right off the entrance contained just a lumpy old couch, a scratched-up coffee table, and one easy chair. At Bi-Mart, I found some cheap throws to dress up the furniture, but the large, roomy kitchen was still the best place to hang out.

Not much can be said about the bathroom except that it was there. I scrubbed the filth from the old fashioned tub, toilet, and sink but couldn't do much to remove the rust rings or to smooth chips in the porcelain. I used bathmats to hide the damaged flooring, hung some towels, and simply felt grateful that we didn't need to share it with three other apartments.

One side of the kitchen had cupboards with a sink and a badly deteriorated drainboard. I covered the rotted area with contact plastic as a temporary fix. The outside wall had two windows covered with very dirty kitchen curtains which looked okay after I gave them a good bleaching and ironing. That wall also provided space for a desk, kitchen chairs, a little-girl table, and the two wooden play chairs saved from my childhood. Grandma and Grandpa gave Laila a little rocking chair which was arranged alongside her play table. The stove and refrigerator stood side by side on the wall facing the sink. The fourth wall had plenty of room for a kitchen table and several chairs. When I stopped to survey the total effect, I felt satisfied that Abe would arrive to a homey place.

Before I knew it, the time arrived for the huge, all-school orientation meeting of all Corvallis teachers. The size of the faculty was daunting to me after coming from a small rural school with four teachers. The Corvallis school system consisted of seven elementary schools, two middle schools and two high schools. The total staff from all these buildings converged on the high school auditorium for opening ceremonies, and I was overwhelmed.

Throughout the meeting, I sat there worrying how I could ever fit in and become a contributing member of such a large organization. In the afternoon of that first day, I went to Harding School, where I was introduced as the new third grade teacher. The staff were welcoming with offers of help in explaining duties, arranging my classroom, locating books, and acquiring supplies. This made it possible for me to relax a bit and roll with my new situation. The rest of the week was spent preparing for that all-important first day of school.

In 1958, Harding School was entrenched in the three-track organizational scheme for student placement. Each grade had three classrooms; an advanced, a medium-skilled, and slow-learner. I, being the new kid on the block, was assigned the group of slow learners. During my two years of struggle in that system, I learned that my students were not necessarily slow learners at all. They were just the bunch of kids that teachers found difficult to teach for one reason or another. I quickly discovered that my bag of tricks for their behavior problems was woefully lacking.

The sad reality of such a system was the fact that, of course, my students knew who they were and suffered its stigma as they advanced each year together through sixth grade. On the other end of the continuum, by the time advanced students reached sixth grade, they were so full of themselves and so intolerant of the slower kids that they became a classic example of false superiority, definitely afflicted with what Carl Sandburg called "burst bladders of the puffed up." But I was very green, with just the one year's experience behind me, so I struggled valiantly to cope.

The bright light of that first week was in meeting a fellow teacher who was seeking employment for her mother. Mrs. Beuler was an elderly widow who still needed to work to qualify for social security. Her daughter offered to drive her to my home each morning to serve as an in-home nanny for Laila, and I agreed to give her a ride home after school. With this agreement settled, we were ready for Daddy to arrive, inspect his new living arrangements, and begin our family life in Corvallis.

My school was in session about two weeks before corn season finished and Abe arrived on the bus. It was with great excitement that Laila and I prepared for his homecoming. I knew he was pleased with all the decisions I'd made when he said that we could be very comfortable in the apartment and with our in-home care for Laila.

He headed straight over to the college to check out the lay of the land. He had a few days before registration and the routines required of a graduate assistant. He barely set foot on campus before he met some Arab students and was able to strike up new friendships. It must have been so refreshing for him once more to speak Arabic with these guys. He was particularly pleased to connect with two Iraqi brothers. They immediately began teasing him because they said he was speaking Arabic with an American accent.

One of the brothers was a brilliant student struggling to finish his Mathematics degree during the six months before the Iraqi government, which was paying his tuition, would insist that he return home. Since he had been on campus for several quarters, he understood how registration worked on the huge college campus and offered to go through the lines with Abe. Everything was strange and new, so Abe was grateful for the help.

I'm sure the registration experience was just as bewildering to Abe as my orientation had been for me. The size of Oregon State University dwarfed anything he had known before. The lines and masses of students were mind-boggling. Thankfully, he just had to follow and copy his friend's example. He found that with his new friend's help, it was relatively easy to sign up for his classes and discover what he was to teach.

Finally, they approached the last desk with their papers. The clerk kept her eyes on the papers as she asked Abe's friend to pronounce his name and tell where he was from. When he answered that he was Iraqi, she stared up in wonderment to see this tall handsome young man and exclaimed that he looked "just like one of us," to which he immediately replied, "What did you expect, a monkey?" Suitably embarrassed, she found his name, stamped his papers, and sent him on his way.

Then it was Abe's turn. The clerk looked over his papers and asked for forty dollars. Startled, Abe told her he didn't have any money. She looked him up and down and then thought to ask him if he was doing anything for the university. When Abe answered that he was a graduate assistant for the Department of Math, she was visibly relieved and told him he didn't owe anything. He got his papers stamped and was free to follow his friend.

Soon, all three Ayyoubs were well launched into Corvallis life. Laila's challenge was learning how much she could get away with in the care of Mrs. Beuler. I think they quickly learned to love each other, but our dear old lady was not much of a disciplinarian. I had to intervene and really lay down the law to Laila when I learned that she had more than once scooted out the front door and run off down the sidewalk because she could move faster than her caregiver.

Mrs. Beuler was not expected to do any housework, but she soon offered to prepare lunch for Laila and Abe, who walked home from the college at noon. According to Abe, she knew only one lunchtime dish. It consisted of hamburger mixed with a bit of prepared mustard, chopped onion, salt and pepper, which she dipped in egg, coated with cracker crumbs, and fried to a crispy golden brown. He ate it so often that we labeled it Mrs. Beuler-Meat. When I'm short on ideas for supper, I sometimes still prepare it and we always think of dear old Mrs. Beuler.

Mrs. Beuler's daughter, my fellow teacher, seemed pleased that her mother had such a useful occupation, and I was relieved to have confidence in Laila's good care. I needed all the confidence I could muster just to handle my job at school. I was not doing at all well with classroom management skills and was often discouraged about ever getting a handle on the obnoxious behavior exhibited by those third-grade kids.

Early in the fall, my mom traveled to a Thursday meeting in Salem and afterwards drove the thirty miles to Corvallis to visit with us. Since she had an extra day, I asked her to visit my classroom on Friday to offer pointers from her years of experience. Sad to say, the class didn't behave any better with a visitor in the room. They were noisy, inattentive, scooting their desks over to sit by friends, and constantly hopping up to request bathroom passes. I knew that no real learning was going on. I attempted inane tricks such as announcing, "Now, everybody look up here at me, and if I see you are watching me, I'll wink at you." I can't believe that I have the temerity to confess, even now, how poorly I was doing.

After school was dismissed for the day, Mom sat in my classroom to offer her evaluation. I was dismayed to recognize that same steely look in her eyes that she had used when she disciplined me as a child. I thought, "Oh dear! I'm in for it now." She was blunt. She said the classroom was out of control, and I had to make some serious changes, or I'd never get them back. She outlined a specific plan to reorganize the friendly semi-circular, conference-style seating.

Over the weekend, we marked the floor with masking tape where each leg of every desk must be kept at all times. Desks were aligned far enough away from each other so students would find it difficult to talk or reach across aisles. Mom instructed me to keep a firm, straight mouth with no smiles, and to refuse all requests for bathroom privileges. Such business must be attended to during recess. I was to demand absolute silence during class and load them with heavy assignments. All day, I would patrol the aisles, and if anyone dared to squirm, I'd bark at them.

I planned brutishly long writing and math assignments, ready for Monday and the entire week. She said that if I held the line for a week, the class would be ready to negotiate better behavior in exchange for a friendlier teacher and less onerous classwork. Thanks be to my wise mother, it worked. I cleaned up my act and so did the kids! By the time of my evaluation, things were under control. After that, I followed Mom's suggestions in many classrooms. It was really Jo Rigney who made it possible for me to succeed during those two years. I even relaxed enough to participate in the teacher-talent assembly. Once again, I donned my Liberace persona and brought down the house.

In the meantime, Abe was also struggling. He did well with his teaching but had difficulties in his own course work. Differential Equations was really beyond him, and he pulled a final grade of "D" during his first quarter. He was deeply concerned about doing so poorly in the course because it was an undergraduate course, plus it was not part of his graduate requirements. He could have ignored the grade with no consequences, but he felt that such a grade was unacceptable. Besides, he really wanted to understand the subject, so he chose to repeat the course. Interestingly, when he later interviewed for the Yakima Valley College position, one of the questions was if he could teach Differential Equations. Repeating the course became a boon.

When not tied down with the difficulties of Differential Equations, Abe especially enjoyed his new friendships. Once, I was invited to attend a party where we met a Palestinian refugee family, Mr. and Mrs. Zacharia. When we invited them to our house for coffee, I learned that Mrs. Zacharia made Arabic pocket bread. She invited me to come to her house sometime to watch her make it, and I eagerly accepted. When I said that the only time available for me was during the weekends, she quickly explained that she could not invite me for a Saturday since that was the day she cleaned her house, but she named an early morning hour for the following Sunday. I have often described to friends that Abe dumped me on the doorstep of an accomplished bread-maker, and that's how I learned to make pocket bread. I've been making it ever since.

I arrived at her shining, spit-spot house which put my humble cleaning efforts to shame. Mrs. Zacharia had arranged several large bath towels and a clean folded sheet on the counter in her toasty warm kitchen. We started the project at her kitchen table with a huge mixing bowl into which she measured flour and a bit of salt. She added yeast and a bit of sugar dissolved in water, and then she patiently began to mix and knead until she was satisfied, just as my grandma had done with my birthday doughnuts. She explained that it would not stick to the hands when it was the correct consistency, and yet it must not be too stiff. After she turned it out on the counter top, her capable hands worked the dough, folding it over and kneading it again and again. Finally the dough was placed in the oiled bread bowl and covered to rise until it doubled.

While I watched her, I decided that a good bread-baker must have considerable upper arm strength. And, being a watcher was definitely my assigned role. Mrs. Zacharia treated me graciously as a guest but did not provide any opportunities for me to take part in the process. I took out my trusty pen and notebook and made detailed notes of the entire, complicated process. During the rising time, we sat to visit for about an hour, enjoying coffee and sweets. She spoke in carefully pronounced English, with a strong Arabic accent, of her pride in her children and the good life they were enjoying since their immigration to America. I shared my memories of making yeast doughnuts with my grandma, which also required long periods of waiting for the dough to rise.

When the dough was ready, she spread a layer of oil on the kitchen counter and divided the dough into about twenty-five small balls. These she rolled out in a bit of oil until they were about half-an-inch thick. Each was gently set on the sheet with space to expand. Then she covered them with the rest of the sheet and several layers of towels. After that, we had time for more coffee while they were left to rise for another hour.

I loved the baking process. She gently placed 4 of the pocket breads on an oiled pizza pan which was popped into the extremely hot oven. It was a delight to peek inside and see the bread puff up into a round ball which formed the pocket and then watch them turn golden brown. After removing each batch, she again covered the small loaves with towels to cool. When all were baked, she offered several of them for me to carry home to Abe. She told me that her family would eat them quickly but that she could also freeze them in plastic bags after they were completely cool.

I thanked her profusely and went home feeling great respect for this hard-working woman who so graciously spent most of her day in an effort to teach this American stranger how to feed her husband in proper Arabic fashion. Since bread has always been considered "the staff of life," I firmly believe that Mrs. Zacharia became, on that Sunday morning, a major contributor to our lasting and healthy married life.

It is impossible for me to describe Abe's delight when I triumphantly arrived home with what he considered to be the first real bread in our home since we had married. In the years that followed, I learned that even my worst cooking mistakes were accepted cheerfully as long as Abe had his bread to eat with them. The standard lunch that he carried to college included pocket bread, yogurt or oil, carrot sticks and fruit. Once, he had an officemate who would ask every day what Abe was eating for lunch and then tell him he'd be sorry for eating such healthy food when he was ninety years old.

After my pocket-bread lesson, my weekend tasks always included baking the family bread. Wherever we lived, the kitchen had to accommodate that project. If we had no counter-space, our bread was laid out on a card table. As our daughters grew up, they each were initiated into the mystery of bread-baking. I started their training by allowing them the fun of pounding and spanking the dough and taught them at a very early age about safe use of an oven. Eventually, baking pocket bread was in rotation as a weekly task that fell to me only every three weeks. We all loved having our own good bread, but I must admit, in my busy life of teaching, it helped tremendously to be free from doing it myself every single week.

Sometimes, though, I also felt that this additional weekly baking chore was something which Abe took for granted. It seemed to me that he began to expect that I would always provide good bread without any need for him to praise my efforts. During our early years, I often felt that he didn't appreciate anything I did. But I was wrong to make that assumption. He quickly dissolved my discontent on the day he purchased a record album of *My Fair Lady*.

One day, I came home from school to find a grinning husband who insisted that I stop in our front room to sit beside our phonograph. He placed the needle on the brand new record and sat back to watch my face. From that little machine floated my introduction to Professor Higgins declaring "she almost makes the day begin." The song describes moods, mannerisms, facial expressions, and ends with the implication that life would never be the same without seeing that special face.

I reacted as he hoped and began to weep sentimental tears because Abe's message was so very clear. He was attempting, as best he could, to say that he had grown accustomed to my face. In those early years of marriage, there were not many times where Abe found a way to express his feelings for me. But this was one of those times. He told me he'd heard the music at college, walked downtown, and bought it. A few years ago, he reminisced that he'd meant it as a compliment but had not been sure how I'd react. We learned to love all the songs on that album, but as far as Abe was concerned, he was hooked on Rex Harrison singing, "Damn! Damn! Damn!" As for me, I basked in the affection of my song.

Our front room and kitchen became tremendously improved towards the end of the school year, because our landlord made some changes. He bought us a new little couch for the sitting room and installed a new kitchen countertop. Finally, I had a convenient counter for baking bread.

Our lives continued to change in small ways. When the Korean students moved out, we spent our free hours cleaning the basement and working to landscape the back yard. The boxes and clutter surrounding the monster wood furnace had always concerned me due to its potential fire hazard. We asked and received permission to clear everything out and haul it to the dump. At the same time, I tackled the filthy little downstairs apartment. I can't begin to describe the layers of crud and grease I removed from stove, sink, table, and walls. When we were finally finished, Abe told Mr. Dunn that he would feed the furnace in return for the use of that shined up little room as a study.

At the same time, I complained to Abe that the laundry facilities were always filthy whenever I tried to wash. I scoured the machine and the rinse tubs before and after I used them, but the next time I went down, the other tenants had left them filthy again. So, Abe went shopping for our first major appliance at a local used-furniture store. He found a Faultless brand wringer washer whose previous owner had yanked the cord from the motor. The wringer rollers were missing, but Abe sorted through the junk pile at the back of the store and found two rollers that fit. He asked the proprietor for an electric cord with loose wires, and when he connected it to the motor, the machine ran with a comfortable hum. It also had a working pump to suck dirty water out into the drain. With these repairs in place, Abe was ready to make an offer. The owner agreed to sell it for five dollars and even deliver it to the apartment. This seemed like a reasonable bargain to Abe, and he drove home in triumph. It was our very first major household acquisition. From then on, with the hose attached to the kitchen faucet I was thrilled to wash in our own apartment.

With the issue of laundry under control, I also attempted to create some order in the tiny patch of back yard. In an effort to give Laila an outdoor play space, I started digging out the masses of thistles until I was able to mow with the old push mower we'd discovered in the basement. On days when it didn't rain, we could spread out a picnic blanket to enjoy some fresh air. The area also sported some wild sweet-pea vines which I carefully trained to grow over the fence, hoping for some flowers when the weather warmed up.

Laila was growing as rapidly as the weeds in that back yard, and soon it was time for her second birthday. I shined up the kitchen, made a cake, and organized some simple games. However, all the kids really wanted to do was "help" Laila tear into her presents. I could barely get them to sit still long enough for a photo. When Abe arrived home on that happy day, he posed with his little girl while at the same time showing off his car.

Soon after the birthday excitement, the weather began to promise the coming spring. Since there was less danger of being soaked in a Corvallis downpour, I found it pleasant to walk the eight or ten blocks to my school. During those walks, I noticed that Corvallis gardens barely finished with late fall flowers before the first tender spring blossoms began to appear. One early-blooming shrub that particularly caught my attention was Daphne. Not only was it beautiful, but it released a heavenly perfume. Consequently, I appreciated the bouquets of Daphne brought in to the classroom by my students.

However, during that period, I was plagued with almost constant migraine headaches. At first, I decided I was just too tense from the effort to control my unruly classroom charges. But even when class behavior continued to improve, the headaches increased. Next, I blamed it on the florescent lighting, a variable I couldn't control. Then, one morning as I arranged the latest bouquet of Daphne, another migraine struck with ferocity. I finally suspected the potent, lovely perfume emanating from the blossoms. Sure enough, as soon as the flowers were removed from the classroom, my headache began to ease. I knew about some migraine triggers, including too much cheese or an over-indulgence in chocolate. Now, I realized that certain perfumes belonged on my list of culprits. Daphne was no longer welcome in the classroom.

Another problem that spring, though not necessarily a trigger for migraines, became a constant nagging thought. Abe was in the United States on a student visa and therefore he was required to be registered in classes. In fact, he had decided to retake his course in Differential Equations during summer session because it helped him maintain his student status and, at the same time, allowed him to teach a class as a graduate assistant which provided some employment.

However, we knew he expected to finish his Master's degree in one more year. After that he could not legally remain in the country unless he attended school, even though he was married to an American citizen. The idea of becoming a career student was not appealing. We constantly discussed our options, and Abe inquired at the college for some direction. He was referred to the immigration office in Corvallis.

Abe prepared a folder containing his Jordanian passport, college transcripts, and all the papers he'd acquired when he entered the United States. Then, he requested an appointment with the immigration officer. In contrast to his experience with the secretary in the Jordanian Consul's office, this officer was very pleasant in his dealings with Abe. He simply asked the basic questions, such as whether Abe had a job. Abe replied that he taught part time as a graduate assistant for Oregon State University while attending classes. The next question was about assets, and Abe listed the Ford. Finally the officer asked if I had a job, and Abe told him I was a teacher with the Corvallis

Public School System. The officer explained that the government is concerned that immigrants are capable of self-sufficiency and will not become a financial burden to the community.

Abe came home with forms to complete, and the news that since he was here on a single-entry student visa, he might be required to leave the country and re-enter as an immigrant married to an American citizen. Thankfully, he would need only to go to Canada, rather than travel all the way back to Jordan. I was pleased that things had gone so well, yet concerned that he might have to leave the country and wait to receive a re-entry visa. I had visions of him being stuck somewhere in Canada while Laila and I were in the United States.

Such a trip and indeterminate stay was far beyond what we could manage financially. But, since my role in the family included the task of official "form-filler-outer," I set to with a will. As all government forms go, this one was a doozey! It required hours to work on the draft. I carefully copied the final version onto the forms and went with Abe to a notary. When the forms and necessary accompanying documents were in order, we tucked them into a huge manila envelope and said some fervent prayers.

Then came the most stressful time of all, the interminable wait for a reply. With customary government pace, we received no answer until well into the summer. When the official envelope finally arrived, we were almost too nervous to open it. Much to our joy and relief, Abe was granted permanent resident status and informed that his green card would be sent by separate mail. Nothing was said about the possible requirement to leave the country, and we asked no questions. I cooked a celebration dinner and decorated the table with a bouquet of wild sweet peas which did, indeed, clamber all over the back fence. Sweet peas have been a special flower for us ever since.

A few years later, after we moved to Yakima, Abe applied for citizenship. Again, I was called upon to help fill out a long and complicated set of forms. But this time, as we mailed off his completed application, we didn't feel tension. Abe was already a legal permanent resident with no danger of being deported. He felt that gaining citizenship was a way to become a fully-participating member of his new community and country.

We were warned that he must pass an oral exam in front of an examiner at the United States Federal Court House. Abe didn't feel too worried about that requirement since he was well-schooled in American history from his class at Eastern Oregon College. Consequently, he just did a quick once-over of the Constitution and the Bill of Rights.

When the day arrived for his appointment at the court house, he was greeted by the Yakima Superintendent of Schools, who served as his witness and declared that Abe was a mathematics teacher at Yakima Valley College. After that, Abe was ushered into a separate room with the immigration official. I waited on a bench out in the hallway.

The examiner looked over Abe's papers and then asked him to name the most important document in America. That was easy: the Constitution. Then, he asked the three branches of government. Again, that was easy: Legislative, Executive, and Judicial. But then, he asked how Americans govern themselves. Abe didn't understand the question, but the examiner assured him he did—"by voting, by voting!" Smiling, he looked back down at Abe's paper and asked if it would be alright if he gave Abe 100%. Abe grinned. That was very much alright with him.

With the formalities concluded, the examiner rose to shake his hand and tell Abe that he'd soon receive his citizenship but also said it didn't imply that he must sever relationships with his family in Jordan. Abe was filled with a comfortable, happy feeling. The examiner asked if he'd be willing to speak a few words at the November 16th ceremony. Congresswoman Catherine May would attend, and the examiner thought Abe was a fine candidate. Abe was not at all sure why the examiner asked him to speak, unless it was his desire to showcase an educated new citizen with a position at the college. Perhaps he wished to impress the congresswoman. Whatever the reason, Abe agreed.

Even though the talk would be only a few sentences, I knew his preparation would include pacing, meditating, and practicing as he walked up and down the streets on his way to and from the college. He never felt comfortable speaking in front of a crowd unless he had his words carefully chosen and memorized to perfection. Citizenship day arrived. Our daughters and I accompanied Abe to the Federal Court House. Laila was five, and Tammy was just two months.

To begin the ceremony, an immigration representative requested a "Motion for Admission of Applicants for Naturalization" to the presiding judge, who then affirmed the motion. It was with a great deal of pride and a deeply secure satisfaction that I watched Abe raise his hand as the judge administered the oath of allegiance. Then, we all stood to recite the Pledge of Allegiance to the flag before Congresswoman May gave a welcoming speech, and each new citizen stood in turn during a roll call.

When Abe's turn came, the presiding officer asked him to tell a bit about himself. Abe stood and said, "I am Ibrahim Ayyoub from the country of Jordan. I earned my BA at Eastern Oregon College in La Grande, served as a graduate assistant at Oregon State University, and now I'm teaching mathematics at Yakima Valley College." As he sat back down, we all burst into applause. At the conclusion of the ceremony, each new citizen was handed a packet which included citizenship responsibilities, a copy of the Constitution, voter registration, and a miniature American flag. Of course, Laila grabbed hold of the flag and waved it vigorously for most of the next few hours.

After an informal reception, our friends treated Abe, our daughters, and me to a celebratory lunch. After that, everything immediately returned to normal, and Abe went back to teach his afternoon classes. My parents were relieved to know that Abe was now an American citizen. This became just one more proof to them that he could be counted upon to provide a stable home for me and our children.

My parents had begun to develop confidence in Abe about four years earlier when he successfully bargained to purchase our first real home. At that time, we were still living in Corvallis. We were concerned that as Laila grew, our apartment on Orchard Avenue was becoming cramped. Laila wanted to run and play, yet there was no room inside or outside. In later years, Abe accused me of scheming to call his attention to the problem. He implied that I exerted unusual effort to assure he was in a good mood before I made my request.

He came home from the office one noon to eat and head back to the office, and the house was clean. Laila was clean and well behaved. Something that smelled delicious was cooking. He sat down and ate, thanked me, and stood up to leave. I stopped him and said he couldn't leave yet because I was not through with him. I reminded him that we had a two-year-old and always had to tell her don't run, don't shout, don't play because we lived in this confined apartment house. I asked him to inquire of the other teachers where we could rent a house with a yard.

One of his friends knew someone who owned a vacant house in North Corvallis, so he took Abe to meet the fellow and look it over. It was built from split logs and situated on nine acres of forested land. Three sides of the exterior were choked with wild blackberries. The interior was finished in knotty pine with a beat-up fir floor. It looked like there was possibly a water problem, since the ceiling sagged in places. But it had a small kitchen, living room, dining area, two tiny bedrooms, and a bath. A wood-burning Franklin stove provided heat. Rickety stairs led down to an unfinished daylight basement.

The house was built into a hillside with at least a nine foot drop at the back of the house. Half of the basement was separated from the hillside with a wall and a creaky old farm door with a broken window. When we looked through that door, we discovered that the house was resting on sloping bare dirt with just four layers of cinderblock to serve as a foundation. The dirt was damp and musty, like a convenient nesting area for rats and snakes.

Abe asked the owner if he would rent to us and promised to take good care of the property. But the guy firmly insisted that he would not rent; it was only for sale. Abe learned that the property was mortgaged with a GI Loan at 3% interest. The owner wanted him to pay the $3,000 equity and assume the balance of the loan which was another $3,200. Loan payments were $45 monthly. Abe had no idea how lenders in this country operated, so he said he'd like to visit some banks to learn if he could borrow to pay the equity.

The next day, he found just one bank that was even interested. After all, other than our jobs, we could offer only a second-hand Ford and a $5.00 washing machine for collateral. But this bank said Abe was good for a thousand dollars, so he did some careful thinking and decided to make an offer. The meeting took place at a coffee shop, and Abe explained his proposal.

Abe could assume the mortgage and make the monthly $45 payments. The $1,000 from the bank would be paid up front. The other $2,000 of equity would wait with no interest until we finished paying off the bank. After that, Abe promised to pay $50 a month to him until all his equity was paid. Unbelievably, he accepted the offer! He must have really needed out from under that mortgage.

After they reached their agreement, they sought the services of a lawyer to draw up the papers. As they explained the proposition, Abe suddenly realized that such a major purchase was daunting and became fearful of putting us under such a debt. So, he began to look for options that would allow him to walk away from the deal. The opportunity presented itself when the lawyer asked who would pay his fee. Abe quickly pointed to the owner and said, "He is." Just as quickly, the owner pointed to Abe and replied, "No, he is." Abe saw this as an impasse and stood up to walk out of the office.

The lawyer then asked to speak to Abe privately. He had not seen the property nor did he even know where the nine acres were located. But, he said this unconventional deal was a must and that he'd forgo his fee. Abe responded with relief, grateful for this kind of encouragement. He signed the agreement exactly according to the plan he had proposed, plus he paid the lawyer's fee. The next day, we went to the bank, co-signed the $1,000 loan papers, and then we signed the purchase agreement at the lawyer's office. When the closing day arrived, we became owners of a tumble-down-house and nine acres of forested land at 3085 NW Deer Run.

By the time we received the key, our new school year had begun. We continued to live at the apartment house for the first month of school and spent our weekends making arrangements for moving. One of the first times we went to inspect our new home, it was raining. We unlocked the front door and stepped inside to discover that it was also raining on the inside! The light began to dawn as to why the previous owner had been so eager to strike a deal.

I was dismayed by the soggy wet ceiling and puddles of water everywhere, but Abe tried to cheer me up by saying he'd just climb up into the attic and place some cans to catch the leaks. Famous last words! When he clambered up through the tiny opening, he was alarmed to discover that the entire attic was dotted with cans that were overflowing with rainwater. Quickly, he climbed back down and promised me that he would call his Uncle Gabe in Michigan to ask for a loan so that we could put on a new roof.

Uncle Gabe was so pleased to learn we had purchased a home that he responded almost immediately with a check for $200. We searched through the phone book until we found a roofer who turned out to be a Seventh Day Adventist and was therefore willing to work for us on a Sunday. Abe struck a bargain to pay him $60 for his labor plus shingles and supplies. The roofer came early the next Sunday and climbed up to tear off the old shingles. He called down to explain that the roof had been put on upside down by an amateur who left every nail exposed.

Abe was concerned that the roofer would require more than one day to finish, so he began to haul bundles of shingles up the ladder to help save time. With this assistance, the job was completed that Sunday. As he climbed down the ladder, Abe pulled out the cash to pay and was told he owed just $40. He protested that the bargain was for $60, but the roofer replied that the other $20 went back to Abe for being a good assistant. Once again, he had reason to feel grateful to a kind Seventh Day Adventist.

With this saving, we had enough left over to go shopping at second hand stores for our furniture. We were able to furnish our entire house for a little over $100. For that, we bought a table and four chairs; a blue velvet couch with a broken back that would fold down into a bed and looked just fine as long as it was propped up against the wall; a bed with a firm mattress, which we named the "good old '54," because of its width; a refrigerator; and, an antique Westinghouse electric range.

In the morning, I could preheat that oven to its highest temperature, place a roast with vegetables inside, and then turn it off. Believe it or not, when we arrived home from school, the food would be cooked just right and still hot. Many years later when we visited Franklin Roosevelt's summer White House in Warm Springs, Georgia, we were amazed to discover the exact same stove as the one we used for so long. We wondered if his cook prepared roasts the same way I did.

Westinghouse Stove

With the struggle of resettling resolved, we could focus on the new school year. I was again assigned the same level of third grade students, but I was much more adept in maintaining discipline. I also developed a special interest in language arts and was asked to serve on the district-wide curriculum development committee. This made it necessary for me to attend after-school meetings, and I needed to find good care for Laila.

Since we lived farther out of town now, Mrs. Buehler was no longer an option. So, we were pleased when we became friends with the large, warm, and friendly Swanson family, who lived across the road from us. They hailed from Oklahoma, and Mrs. Swanson used many of the same idioms in her speech as my Grandma Rigney. I often sat for a visit in their kitchen at the end of my school day. It was so easy for me to slip into the Oklahoma dialect that I'd learned from Grandma. In a way, it seemed like I was coming home to my childhood again. Mr. Swanson was a part-time minister who provided support for his family by doing contract demolition and saving the materials for resale. Consequently, their comfy old home was clogged with bits of salvage in various corners.

I noticed that Mrs. Swanson cared more about the children than cleanliness, and that didn't bother me. She welcomed Laila into the nest as if she were another chick joining her brood, and the arrangement worked out fine for all sides. Our monthly payments added to their income. Laila had playmates, plus she could run about getting gloriously dirty and came home at night cheerful and thriving. I remember asking each day as we walked over to our little house, "Laila, what did you have for lunch today?" She happily grinned up at me to answer, "Bread and gravy." Since the remains of it were obviously smeared all over her face and down her front, there was really no need for me to ask. But that was okay too. She was washable. Also, more than once, Abe had expounded on the need for little kids to run free as he had done in his own childhood. He was pleased to see this happening for Laila.

Each morning we bundled Laila up, usually still in her nightclothes, and walked her across the street where she was fed breakfast and began her day. Abe and I climbed into the Ford and drove the three miles to town where he dropped me off at Harding and drove on to the college. If I had an after-school meeting that day, I kept the car and took him to the college. He often begged a ride home from his student or faculty friends. Abe liked to come home early, if possible, to clear brambles away from our little house.

By using clippers and a machete, he kept at it until the entire area all the way down to our little creek was cleared. He learned that when he burned the piles of brush, the berries were slower to grow back. Then he was able to mow the wild grasses down like a lawn. Eventually, toward the end of that first year, we had a lovely little picnic area beneath the wild plum trees. We even had a spring gathering of Middle-Eastern students for a cook-out, and we broadcast loud Arabic music using our phonograph with an amplifier. I've often wondered what the neighbors thought, because such music would have been new to them.

Abe's coursework was slated to be finished by spring, and he just needed to write his Master's thesis in order to graduate. A professor in the math department suggested the thesis topic because he knew that Abe had a high proficiency in the Arabic language, and he wanted Abe to do a translation of Al-Khwarismi's original *Algebra of Inheritance*. Al-Khwarizmi was an Arab mathematician, astronomer, and physicist who lived in the House of Wisdom, a group of scholars in Baghdad. His work on the algebra of inheritance, published in 830 A.D. is noted by scholars as the basis for innovation in algebra.

I helped Abe spend hours of research at the OSU library, and we wrote many letters to libraries in the United States and overseas in our attempt to locate the original Arabic text. We found plenty of Arabic translations taken from earlier works, and we learned that a Latin translation was available. But, Abe's professor said none of these were acceptable because they were not from *the original* Arabic text. One Middle Eastern authority suggested that the original must exist either in someone's private collection or else in heaven.

Abe became discouraged, and I even wondered if his professor might purposefully be blocking his success. Abe was aware that he and the professor held disparate views about the political situation in the Middle East, and it was possible that discrimination had a role. Abe became convinced that the proposal would never come to fruition, which caused him despair about ever receiving his degree. He began seeking alternative solutions. Perhaps earning his Master's Degree should be put on hold while he sought employment. After all, he had his permanent residence status and no longer needed to be a registered student.

I was not aware of his slow change in thinking, and I felt sure that we would be in Corvallis for an additional year while Abe struggled to finish his thesis. So, I signed my next year's contract and enrolled for a summer course at the University. As it turned out, these plans went unfulfilled. Late in the spring, Abe was in the office and noticed a recruitment letter seeking a math instructor who could also serve as a foreign student advisor for a group of Arab students attending Yakima Valley College in Washington State. He brought the notice home to me.

We wrote a letter of inquiry and received an application packet. In late July, we received a phone call requesting Abe to come for an interview, so once again, we climbed into the Ford and headed out to seek what might lie ahead. I have one succinct memory of that trip. My family always teased me while I was growing up that I must hold on tight to my seat whenever we crossed a state line, because we were going to go over a big bump.

As we crossed the bridge over the Columbia River, I played the same game with Laila. It was a warm day, and we drove with the windows down. She was disappointed when we passed the state line mark in the middle of the river and felt no bump. But then she made a horrendous face and cried, "Oh Mommy, Washington sure stinks!" In those days, there was a cattle feed lot at the bridge, and I had to agree with her.

The interview at Yakima Valley College was successful. Dr. Bailey didn't seem concerned that Abe had not yet earned his Master's degree, and he accepted Abe's explanation that a search for the original text was still ongoing. What interested Dr. Bailey more was Abe's proficiency in mathematics and his fluency in Arabic. He explained that the influx of students from the Middle East was causing practical difficulties.

Later, we discovered that Arab students first learned about Yakima Valley College through a connection with somebody's older brother who attended Washington State University. When that student was invited to spend Thanksgiving in Yakima, he found that YVC was less expensive, smaller, and offered introductory English. That student told his younger brother and a friend, who applied and were accepted. From there, it just spread by word of mouth. By the time Abe interviewed, the former advisor was overwhelmed with so many needs from students with whom it was difficult to communicate. He was more than willing to turn the assignment over to someone who could speak Arabic.

Dr. Bailey and Abe talked salary and benefits, and Abe expressed his one stipulation. He was willing to accept the offer of a job if we could also locate a position in one of the elementary schools for me. This was a huge concern for me, since I would have to break my contract in Corvallis. But, Dr. Bailey thought a position could easily be located. He knew that positions in the Yakima system were all filled, but he felt sure that vacancies were still available in nearby valley districts. He suggested that I send my credentials to him, and he would get back to us within the week.

Our overnight visit in Dr. Bailey's home was pleasant. They were charmed with our little girl and she was, for the most part, on her good behavior. One faux pas, however, worried me that they might change their mind about wanting us in Yakima. They had a young peach tree in their front yard which had produced just three almost ripe peaches. Laila ran outside to look around and came bursting back into the house exclaiming, "Look what I found!" She was clutching the largest and ripest peach from the tree. I was horrified with what she had done, but Dr. Bailey just chuckled and said we shouldn't worry about it. Fruit could be found everywhere in the valley. We never allowed Laila to forget that she almost jeopardized her daddy's new offer of employment.

Traveling back from Yakima was a time for discussion and plans. I needed to notify my principal of our possible move. We had to find a renter for our house, and we must find a house to rent in Yakima. As soon as we arrived home, we sprang into action. The Corvallis school district agreed to release me from my contract, so my credentials and application were fired off to Dr. Bailey, and we soon learned that I could have my pick of three positions.

We placed a rental notice on the students' union bulletin board and got tenants who agreed to keep their furniture in storage and use ours until we were able come back for it. With that settled, we prepared for the move. Abe decided to stay in Corvallis to try his skill at a local beet plant during August, while Laila and I once more trekked to Nyssa to visit the folks and for my annual job at the cannery. After a short time of messing in red beet juice, Abe decided to join us because the pay was poor, the other workers seemed lazy and silly, and also, he missed his family. Soon after he arrived, we both secured jobs in the corn-testing lab for one last stint.

In the meantime, I called to set up an interview with the East Valley School system for their first-grade position. When the appointment was set, my mother, Laila, and I drove to Yakima for two whirlwind days. We often boast about the miracles we accomplished on the first day. I was offered the job, and I accepted. We found a tiny, sparkling clean, furnished apartment right across the street from my school. And, when we located a good child care situation just a quarter of a mile away, the lady had a cute black dog that she wanted to give away.

Mom and Laila fell in love with the little dog's friendly, wiggly manners and immediately named her Mitzi. Mitzi became an important member of the Rigney household and lived with them to a ripe old age. In later years whenever the folks came to visit us, the first question our girls asked was, "Did you bring Mitzi?" At the close of our success-filled day, I told Mom it was time to celebrate our accomplishments. For supper, before falling into our motel beds, we went out for banana splits. Mine was so sticky sweet and gooey, I've had no desire to eat one since!

Our two years in Corvallis had been very productive. Abe succeeded in his course work and teaching. I developed vital classroom management skills. Laila bloomed into an inquisitive and happy three-year-old. We became owners of a beautiful property which is still an important part of our lives. The rent that we received from the many tenants, who lived in our little house over the years, covered the mortgage so that debt was never a burden. Yakima, Washington became our permanent home, but we held Corvallis, Oregon in a special section in our hearts.

CHAPTER 13

———◆———

Our Expanding Lives

WE MOVED TO WASHINGTON in 1960. We were well situated in the town, or so I thought. As soon as Abe saw where we were going to live, he felt uncomfortable. Yes, it was very tiny, but his real problem was the eight miles he had to drive every morning to campus and the return trip each evening. He was also required to deliver and collect Laila, since her babysitter was on the same route. He had free hours during the day, but he wouldn't be able to come home between classes due to the distance.

I, on the other hand, was selfishly pleased with our location. I could kiss my family goodbye in the morning and walk across the street to work. Of course, being an elementary teacher with playground and lunch duties meant I had no free time during the day even to think about home or its proximity. My life was a busy one, and I was forced to learn to compartmentalize my thinking. When at school, I gave no thought to home, and when at home, my time was taken up with Laila, meals, shopping, laundry and (occasional) housecleaning. Actually, it is accurate to say very little housecleaning. Once, Laila discovered me scrubbing the bathroom sink and inquired, "Mommy, is it Saturday, or are we having company?"

In the first two months, Abe began to seek a place near the college, which would be more amenable to his needs. He found an unfurnished house situated on 16th Avenue about a five-minute's walk from campus. I was agreeable with moving because the place was larger and nicer, but we needed to find a way to retrieve our furniture from Corvallis. We decided to rent a U-Haul trailer and tow it with the Ford. We planned to make the trip over the three-day Veteran's holiday.

The drive went smoothly until we were almost in Corvallis. Then, the Ford began to act up. We lost power and barely made it to a service station. The mechanic took one look and told us we'd burnt out the bearings. He quoted a high price for the repair and said he couldn't get to it until the next week. Abe learned that he should have driven the freeway in overdrive instead of third gear.

Needless to say, we were dismayed, but Abe came through with flying colors. He took Laila and me to a restaurant and told us to order some clam chowder while he went off to bargain for a new car. We sat for a long time in that restaurant, but he finally came back with a big grin on his face. "Well, Laila, we've bought a brand new Chevrolet." Laila's face lit up as she asked, "What color is it?" He answered, "It's the color of your soup." I was pleased that we were going to be driving a lovely new white car home, but Laila told me later that she was really disappointed because she was hoping for a red car. I guess we should have ordered tomato soup.

Everything fit well in our new house, and Abe was once more comfortably close to his school. But, the burden of commuting was now on my shoulders, and I began to develop some resentment. Abe was now able to play host to his new Arab friends at our house during his free hours, while my day became longer and more difficult. I drove facing the sun in the morning, had the responsibility for Laila's transportation, and faced the setting sun as I headed back home to prepare supper. Also, it was necessary always to leave the kitchen and living room in presentable condition, since I never knew who would be coming in during the day.

However, I did enjoy coming home to listen to the stories Abe shared with me about funny things happening with the students. One particular Arab student, who had just arrived from the West Bank of Palestine, was bright and self-confident, but prone to making language errors. Soon after he arrived, Abe took him to Jordan's, a nearby drugstore, which boasted an old-fashioned soda fountain, so that they could get acquainted. The waitress smilingly approached them and asked, "What can I do for you?" The student looked up at her and said, "Shake well." Her smile was immediately replaced with a frown and a look of affront. Abe quickly spoke up and said, "I think he means milk shake but he got it wrong because he is new to America." This explanation brought the smile back to the waitress's face, and she hurried off to shake up the milk and ice cream for her embarrassed customers.

This same student also had strong feelings about the political situation in the Middle East, and one day he was ranting in front of several students to declare firmly, "The beeble want the beace!" Abe stopped him to explain that the English language makes a distinction about when to use "b" and when to pronounce a "p" sound. The young man gave that some careful thought and continued his conversation. When it was time for him to leave, the other students asked him where he was going, and he confidently answered that he was going to "the pook store."

I appreciated the levity of these funny stories because my entire school year was difficult and not much fun. My principal turned out to be rather disorganized, ineffective in providing needed supplies, and I struggled with learning to teach a new grade. My experience, so far, had fluctuated between kindergarten and third grade. Not even during my student teaching days had I been assigned a first-grade class. Starting little kids on the serious path to reading was totally new for me, and I suffered having to teach the less than exciting Scott Foreman series, *Dick and Jane*. "See Spot run. See

Dick. See Jane. Oh, Oh! OH! "I'm not sure how we accomplished it, but somehow, most of my little charges learned to read that year!

And finally, it was the last day of school! Abe drove me to school in the morning, and Laila was already with the folks for a visit in Nyssa. The classroom was sweltering, and I had to box up all my teaching paraphernalia, collect my paycheck, and be ready when Abe came to pick me up and help load my stuff. I would not be coming back to East Valley the following year, because Yakima Schools had offered me a contract.

Of course, I was not ready when Abe arrived. Books and equipment had to be inventoried, desks washed, and everything checked by the principal. I was wearing sandals and my feet hurt, my head ached, and I was short tempered when Abe impatiently started piling my boxes into the back of our new Chevy. He had hoped to be done in time to deposit my check before the bank closed, but we were already too late. Obviously, he was also feeling cross from having to load my collection of heavy boxes full of "junk."

Finally, everything was in the car. I handed him my check and felt relieved to be done. Abe sat there studying my pay stub with a puzzled frown. It didn't seem to be correct, and I should have been forewarned. We had been down this same path many times. Federal tax, SSI, and other deductions always seemed to be changing, and he usually distrusted the bookkeeping. Not that I remember ever having to confront the school business office, but pay day was important to him. In fact, the only time he visited me at school was on payday so that he could get our checks in the bank.

To Abe's way of thinking, it was obvious that I'd failed to give proper attention to the amount I was earning. He looked over at me to ask, "What is your annual salary?" This kind of detail was the furthest thing from my mind, and I answered that I had no idea. I asked him just to drive and that we'd look it up when we got home. By then, my dander was rising over being grilled about inconsequential deductions over which I had no control. And especially, on this last day, it would have been nice to receive a bit of recognition from him that I'd successfully weathered the year. Instead, he frowned and exclaimed, "Why on earth can't you keep that kind of important information in your brain?" I had no answer and was frankly too exhausted even to care.

Abe became furiously silent and started the car with a jerk. He drove too fast for a bit, then pulled over, got out of the car and started walking down the highway, leaving me sitting there in astonished anger. I called to him, but he ignored me and kept walking. After about five minutes of just sitting there, I finally crawled over to the driver's seat and began to drive while tears of frustration rolled down my cheeks. I came to the cemetery situated about a half mile from the school and pulled into the wide entrance to think things over.

Life seemed just too hard! And, it appeared that I was being deserted by my angry husband. Paychecks and numbers were not important according to my scheme of things. Family and concern for each other were the things that really mattered. In fact, if Abe could abandon the car while I'm still sitting there, I decided that I'd just clear out too. Hang the whole car and all the stuff in it! And, that is what I did. I stepped out onto the hot pavement, grabbed my purse, rolled up the windows, locked the car, and started walking down the highway.

Bad decision! My dress was thin, and my sandals even thinner. My feet soon began to burn and swell from the blistering heat. I knew I was getting sunburned and I was having trouble keeping my face looking calm whenever a car sped past. Several kind persons stopped to offer me a ride, but I wanted to make my point dramatically. I was the "suffering one." So, I turned them all down. If I gave in and accepted a ride, I would arrive home too soon, and he would not have had enough time to begin worrying about me. I wanted him to worry in a big way! I stubbornly kept trudging west, into the heat of the late afternoon sun.

I have no idea how long it took me to walk all the way home. It was a long eight-mile tramp, and I moved slower and slower. By the end, I was dehydrated and so exhausted I could barely place one foot in front of the other. But, I made it. I walked up the front steps and into the relative cool of our little house. Abe was lying down on the couch. He looked up at me but said nothing. I went to the bedroom and lay down on the bed where I sank into an exhausted doze.

I'll be forever grateful to Laila for causing the two of us to begin speaking to one another again. The phone rang, and Abe answered. My mother told him that Laila had come down with chicken pox. She asked us to come, because she was going to be teaching summer migrant school and couldn't care for a sick child. I sat up when I heard Abe say we'd drive to Nyssa to get Laila. That was when I finally told him that if he wanted his car, he'd have to get a friend to drive him out to the cemetery to pick it up. Then, I gave him my little prepared speech about what I thought was important in our life together. Things like paychecks and cars were not. Love and caring for one another in a considerate manner were. I handed him the car keys, washed my face, pulled on my nightgown, and went back to sleep.

Later, during the drive to Nyssa, we once again began to converse. I learned that he had not walked all the way home, because he accepted the first offer of a ride. When his Arab student friend drove him to get the car, neither of them discussed why the car was locked up and left at the cemetery. Abe felt it was nobody's business, and the student was wise enough to not ask.

Many years later, we held a conversation about that day. I mentioned to Abe that both of our children learned early on that he would get very silent and walk away when they told him about something they had decided to do, or worse yet, if they asked him for some new privilege such as being allowed to go on a date. He said that he refused to answer because he might say things that couldn't be unsaid later. He explained that the word "temporary" is derived from temper. If he walked away until his temper cooled, he was always grateful for the shortness of that feeling. We all wish he had explained this earlier in our marriage because it would have provided far better understanding throughout our years together.

I discovered that silence and walking away were learned behaviors modeled by his father. Abe said that when his father was under a verbal attack from his mother, he always put a grin on his face, turned silent, and walked away. He never in his life resorted to hitting or slapping his wife. Abe also mentioned that Toufiq didn't allow himself to become physical when angry because it could be dangerous. He told me that Toufiq had once required a badly behaving camel to kneel down on the ground, while the camel kept viciously swinging his head back and forth and bellowing ferociously. Toufiq lost his temper, struck the camel's forehead with his fist, and the poor beast immediately slumped over dead. Abe said that, "If you have a temper, it doesn't matter who you are facing. You are in danger of killing."

These stories shed light on Abe's occasional periods of prolonged silence. I also believe that he used those silent times to sort through how he chose to behave. I know for sure that after the long-ago last day of school fiasco, he developed more patience when I failed to remember something having to do with numbers. For me, to this day, numbers are to be stored on paper records and in computer spreadsheets. I see no reason to fret about carrying them around in my brain. And, I still have no idea if that final paycheck from East Valley was correct. We never discussed it again.

It is a blessing that Abe and I discovered ways to work around my abysmal lack of interest in numbers, because we had other concerns of more importance. As I observed Laila developing her own little personality, I mentioned to Abe, probably more often than he wished, that being an only child was not ideal. Although both of us wanted another child, neither of us felt confident that this was the correct time for another pregnancy, since we depended on both incomes. But, I seriously lobbied for a second baby and regularly brought up the discussion. Abe worked out our family finances and finally agreed that we could manage. We decided that I could teach my first year in the Yakima schools while pregnant if the new baby were planned for arrival during the summer.

By then, we were living in a larger rental on 26th Avenue, but still within walking distance to Abe's college. In fact, until 1966, we lived in a different rental almost every year. We were good tenants, and we took pride in leaving the houses in better condition than we found them. In most cases, the owner either wanted the house back for personal use or planned to sell it. But since we were not yet prepared to purchase another place, we kept renting.

Things could not have been rosier when we discovered that our second baby was on the way and due to arrive in July, 1962. This was exactly the way we planned it. Of course, one never remembers to plan for the accompanying difficulties of pregnancy. Morning sickness was part of most every day for the first few months. Thank goodness the classroom at my new school contained an individual bathroom. I learned to keep a huge stack of mimeographed worksheets close to the bathroom door. When nausea surged up, I directed the class monitor to hand a sheet to every student, and

I instructed them to work on it quietly. After my nausea passed, I stepped back in to take control of the lesson.

My other strong memory of early pregnancy was my difficulty with cigarette smoke. Abe was considerate enough to smoke outside, but during that winter his older brother, Yacoub, came to stay with us. He hoped to find work, save money, and bring his family to America. If anything, he was a more dedicated smoker than Abe. I came home each night to a smoke-filled living room that really caused problems with my well-being. However, being proper Arab hosts, neither of us felt we could ask him to change his ways.

Except for the cigarette smoke, we were pleased to have Yacoub visiting us. Laila loved her new uncle. He was kind with a funny sense of humor. His English was not strong when he arrived, but small children have ways to communicate in spite of language barriers, and they hit it off splendidly. We put up a tree and shared our Christmas traditions with him much in the same way that Abe experienced his Christmas with his Uncle Gabe's family.

It felt good to be able to come full circle with America's newest Ayyoub immigrant. But Yacoub lacked education and was unskilled except for driving cars, since he had been a driver for officers in the Jordanian military. In the middle of winter, locating work in Yakima seemed impossible. Finally, after a valiant effort, he headed off to see Joe Ayoub who could offer excellent help for him in San Francisco.

The other concern for Abe that year, besides attempting to help his brother, was his desire to finish his Master's degree. Though we continued efforts to find Al-Khwarismi's original text, no leads surfaced. So, Abe's interest was immediately captured when he received a brochure describing a grant program offered by the National Science Foundation. After four summer semesters of concentrated work at the University of Illinois-Urbana, graduates of the program could earn a Doctorate in Math Education if they followed the coursework and wrote a dissertation.

The grant generously included transportation, full tuition, board and room, and a stipend for books and supplies. Although applicants must already hold a Master's degree, Abe optimistically brought home the forms, and we filled out the application. When he demonstrated that all requirements, except for the thesis, were completed, they accepted his explanation.

However, all the positions had already been filled, so he took a different tack, and accepted a National Science Foundation grant to study during summer at Oregon State. In addition, we made some plans for him to make a quick trip home to see his parents. None of these plans materialized.

Suddenly, Abe received a Western Union wire saying there had been a last minute cancellation at Illinois-Urbana, and they could now offer him a stipend. This meant a college education during summer while being paid close to $1500 for going. He'd be gone three months, and it also meant he had a strong chance of going back for three more summers, so he'd get his Master's and have a long head start on his doctorate. I was so happy for him.

He learned later that he was the only member in the group who did not have a Master's degree. But, he also discovered that he was better prepared than many who attended the institute. Ultimately, he opted to complete the four summer semesters and be content with earning a Master's degree plus forty-five hours beyond. This placed him at the top of the salary scale, and earning a doctoral degree would not have increased that. He decided there was no measurable benefit from enduring the extended time, effort, and expense to complete the dissertation.

This sudden development meant I'd be needing some help for a few days in the middle of July when our baby came, and I planned to make arrangements with Laila's babysitter to get her when my labor started. Laila would be perfectly at home there, until I came home from the hospital, and I hoped my folks could come until I got back on my feet, telling them I knew a lady I could get to come in and help, but I was afraid she would drive me to nervous distraction. My parents immediately rejected my idea of staying in Yakima alone. Instead, they suggested that Laila and I stay with them in Nyssa for the summer.

After all, in 1957, Dad wrote a letter to welcome Laila's birth and invited Laila to come live with them. He promised to "keep the house nice and warm and Chester [the dog] will help too. He can keep her face & hands clean by licking them." He said he'd "have a box with a pillow in it all ready" for her, as if she were a barnyard runt. Needless to say, my response in 1957 to Dad's invitation was a sputtering refusal. Although, in later years when we laughingly remembered the offer, it came to mind that we often called our second daughter "Tammy Lammy." Perhaps Grandpa's offer to bottle feed baby Laila like a "bum lamb" had something to do with Tammy's nickname.

But in 1962, Laila and I were grateful for the new invitation, and we agreed to move in with them for the summer. We discovered that we would be allowed to sublet our house on 26th Ave. while we were gone. And, Mom arranged for Dr. Danford in Nyssa to take over my obstetrical care. She also learned that Malheur Memorial Hospital in Nyssa would be available when it was time for delivery. My school district insurance would cover some of the expense.

As soon as the school year finished, Abe was on the train. His sessions would last from the time he turned in his student's grades at YVC in the spring and not finish until it was time for him to report for fall registration. He remarked each year about his enjoyment of the leisurely cross-country train trip, since it was his only vacation. He loved spending hours in the Vista Dome of the train, smoking and watching the beauty of the land as he rolled by. It must have been a totally different experience from his bewildering bus trip when he arrived as an immigrant.

I was nearly eight month's pregnant when we waved goodbye to Abe at the train station, but still I was able to drive to Nyssa in the white Chevy with Laila. I don't remember where she slept in Nyssa, but I do know it was not in a pillow-lined box.

The folks fixed up my old room with a double bed and a rocking chair for me. I wrote to Abe that Laila seemed to become more clingy and babyish in her behavior while we waited for the baby's birth. Grandpa didn't help at all when he asked her, "Laila, which do you want—a new baby brother or a baby elephant?" I suspect his question was prompted by my big belly which looked like it held an elephant. Laila answered, with no hesitation, "I choose a baby elephant."

Grandpa would not let up on his teasing, repeatedly describing how ornery her new baby brother would be, which provoked even more uncertainty in Laila about the prospect of a new baby. When we went for walks in the evening, Laila always wished on the first star of the evening that the summer would hurry up and be over so that Daddy could come home and go walking with us as we had done in Corvallis. She missed holding our hands while we played the arm-swinging game of "one, two, three, woopsy-daisy."

It was a hot June in Nyssa, and I trundled down in my bulky maternity clothes to watch Laila cool off in the municipal pool. Of course, looking as bulgy as a pregnant woman can, I ran into my old flame from high school. He'd come home with his wife and family to visit his folks. I have no idea how he felt, but I know it felt awkward to me. I'd had no further contact with him since his disheartening "Dear Doris" letter from college days. I pointed out my splashing young one to him and waved at his son who was also in the pool. After a few minutes, we each went our own way, as we had all those years ago.

On most days, while awaiting our new baby, I slept late, read, and just lazed around. We had new infant clothing and diapers already prepared, so not much else was required of me. Dad went to work at the pumping plant every morning, and Laila went with Mom, who was teaching Migrant Summer School. My reading material was not at all a wise choice. My sister-in-law stored her nursing texts at the folks' house, and I found one on pregnancy and delivery.

It was filled with details of the entire process, including everything that could go wrong. There were graphic photos of excessive bleeding and Caesarean sections. I began to worry about each symptom and wondered which ones applied to me. My fascination with this book reminds me of Abe's experience in Middle East College, when he read a medical book and decided that he had acquired every ailment described in it. I finally had enough sense to lay the book aside and concentrate on developing a more positive outlook.

And, a positive outlook was difficult to come by. I wrote to Abe on our anniversary that it was fortunate for him that he was not around to put up with my impatience. My stomach swelled tighter and the baby kicked harder all the time. I reached my due date and there still was no baby. Two weeks later, I was in labor for two days without success. The birth pains came regularly but no baby. They kept me in the hospital for two days and then gave up and sent me home. I was so very discouraged. I felt that baby was stuck inside of me for eternity. I stayed home for an afternoon and a night still suffering birth pains.

The folks tried hard to be helpful; I must have caused them so much worry. At 5:00 a.m. I called Mom to take me back to the hospital. But, nothing had changed. I thought I should go home because the hospital was charging me for staying and I was getting nothing done. However, Mom disagreed. She had to go teach and she knew I was too weak and too tired to drive myself there later on. She made me promise to stay until she finished teaching for the day.

All of a sudden everything happened at once and the baby was here in three hours. I wrote to Abe that there were no difficulties, that I was awake every moment without pain, that I felt her being born, heard her first cry, and saw her before she was one minute old. I assured him she was normal in every way and eagerly took the breast when they brought her for feedings.

What I wrote to Abe soft-pedaled the pain part. In the beginning, I must have had Braxton-Hicks contractions, sometimes called false labor. I remembered reading about them in the nursing book. I was determined to not be as sedated during my second child's birth, but I was definitely confused about how much pain I could expect. The other patient who was in labor spent most of her time screaming. I told the nurse that I was not usually a screamer, but I needed to know if things would get so bad that I would be yelling as much as that one. The nurse assured me that I was progressing nicely and that everyone approached childbirth differently.

So, I made an effort to employ the mental processes I had used to relax during Laila's birth. I tried to recall those visions of deep comfortable snowbanks which I sank into whenever a heavy pain came. The only problem was that this was July, and it was much too hot for easy snowbank imagery. But, I truly did attempt relaxing into each contraction and was fairly successful, until the screamer in the next bed belted out another hysterical call for someone to come get her out of it all.

I distinctly remember feeling excitement when I heard the doctor say the baby's head was crowning, and then, swoosh, the blessed relief of feeling her slip into the outside world. I was so grateful to be alert and able to welcome my wet little red-faced baby. She immediately started crying lustily, and I cuddled her on my tummy and told her, "Don't cry little one. It's okay if your daddy isn't here. We love you already and you are most welcome to our world." Abe and I had previously determined that her name would be Tamam Lameese Ayyoub. Her first name, in Arabic, means "complete" or "perfect," and the meaning for Lameese is "soft." As I cuddled her in my arms, it became clear to me that this perfect, soft, little bundle of baby was well-named. Remembering my dad's teasing when Laila was newborn, I was certain that our little Tammy Lammy was no "bummer lamb."

It was almost nine in the morning when Tamam was born. While they carried her off to the nursery for cleaning, weighing, and dressing, I was wheeled back to my room and offered some breakfast. I remember what pleasure I experienced while drinking the first cup of coffee I'd had in nine months. Coffee made me deathly ill while pregnant, but was most welcome now. As soon as Abe received the news of Tamam's birth, he sat to write her a letter.

He told her that her birth was "the happiest piece of news" and that he hoped she would "grow to understand and forgive" him for being absent. He knew "it might have meant a great deal" to me for him to be with us, and he closed with the hope we would "all learn to love and respect one another." And he was right—it would have meant a great, deal, but it was even more a great deal that he understood that. I cried, of course.

He also wrote to me, to say "well done, my lady," but at this stage of our marriage, verbal expressions of love were unusual for Abe. Not that he didn't receive these words from me! My letter written about Tammy's birth was signed, "Know that I love and miss you." I asked Abe why it was difficult for him to express his love in words. In our early years together, I rarely heard that he loved me. Abe replied that it was never a model he heard at home while growing up. His parents were non-verbal in such matters and if Toufiq ever said to Miriam A*na bahibbak*, I love you, it would have been in privacy away from the children's ears. Yet, his loving care for his wife and large family was always in evidence.

Abe believed that such outward expressions of love were somehow kind of phony. He knew that his father always lived in a way that demonstrated his love for wife and family. Definitely, Abe did the same in his actions for our family. With serious problems, it was always Abe who quietly carried out what needed to be done. Once, I left the hose running outside all night, and by the next day, the entire basement was flooded with over an inch of standing water on our new rug. I expected to hear harsh words as Abe struggled to drag that sopping, dripping rug up the stairs to dry out on the patio. Instead, he quietly labored to clean up the mess and never once voiced a word of criticism. No I-love-you was required. His actions did the speaking.

If the truth be known, Abe often drove me crazy with the way he reacted to small things said or done. On little things, he could get very hot-under-the-collar and spew criticism, and, on occasion, he retreated into his silent treatment. But with huge mishaps, there was never any of that. He just pitched in to do the best he could to alleviate the situation. Abe said he did his share of stupid things, and his parents never came after him with a stick. To him, it would be a crime for him to tell his children or his wife they are no good when they do something stupid. They feel bad, they know it is a mistake, and do not need him to say anything more. They are in the same position in the family as they ever were, and that does not change.

Consequently, Abe's letter after Tammy's birth, where he joked of almost forgetting himself and expressing love, became a precious keepsake for me. I am deeply aware that this letter was written by a father and husband thousands of miles away from the center of a major occurrence in our family story. He must have felt every bit as lonely as we felt by not having him with us.

Happily, it was not a time of loneliness for Laila. Friends and relatives in Nyssa flocked to see Tammy, and all of them brought new-baby gifts plus gifts for Laila. She managed to maintain her "princess" status with ease and relish all the attention she received as big sister. She had her problems, of course. She said she wished she were a baby again, but I told her she was lucky. She could pretend to be a baby if she wished and still grow back to a five-year-old whenever she wanted, while the baby would always be wishing she was as old as Laila and would never be able to be. Laila was entranced with the thought and complained no more.

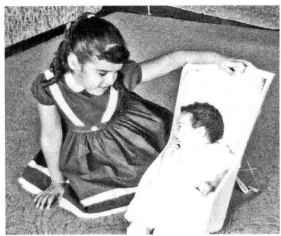

Laila and new baby sister

We stayed in Nyssa while I recuperated and while Mom finished her summer school job. Then in the heat of early September, we loaded up the kids and all our trappings for the drive back to Yakima. Mom and Dad followed in their car, and we caravanned the four-hour drive over the desert hills between Nyssa and Yakima. Because our car had no air conditioning, Baby Tammy fussed and developed heat rash.

As soon as we came over the hot sagebrush hills and down into the Yakima Valley, we stopped to cool off in the shade of a roadside park. We pulled off Tammy's shirt and diapers and allowed her to lie on a blanket in the cool grass. We chuckled at her as she stretched out her little arms and legs and gave an audible sigh of pleasure, "Ahhh." It was exactly how all of us felt. When we finally reached home, Mom and Dad helped us get settled, rested overnight, and returned to Nyssa.

The students were aware that we were coming home and had moved out, but I'm sorry to report they hadn't left the place at all clean. I had my work cut out for me to get things ship-shape to welcome Abe back to see his three girls. Always a glutton for punishment, I cleaned house, irrigated, mowed, and trimmed, while also trying to pacify a fussy baby and attempting to keep Laila happy.

In addition, I baked a batch of pocket bread and prepared *Malfouf*, cabbage rolls stuffed with meat and rice. I invited seven of his Arab student friends for a picnic. Preparing Arabic food in the heat for that number is daunting for one woman to accomplish, not to mention the stress of caring for the girls, but I pulled it off and we were ready to provide a proper welcome on the day he returned. It was some party!

Immediately after his arrival in Yakima, Abe headed back to teaching at YVC. I opted to be a stay-at-home mom for awhile, but that made our finances really tight. When the school district called in February asking me to come back to finish out the year in a first grade class, we decided I should do it. Mrs. Meade was happy to welcome both children into her daycare. She also suggested we might like to rent a lovely modern home nearby. The owners were going to travel for a few years, and we jumped at the chance, since our additional income allowed us to manage the higher rent. The beauty behind the move proved to be that we would both be within easy distance of our work and Mrs. Meade was right across the street. So once again the Ayyoub family moved! And from then on, I taught in the Yakima School system every year until retirement.

I remember many years later, attempting to justify my decision to work when one of the girls asked why I didn't stay at home and be a full-time mother and house-wife. I justified my choice by explaining that in some ways a working mother allowed children to learn more responsibility for their contributions to the family well-being. They were expected to assume chores for the good of us all, which might not have happened if I were home all the time to be at their beck and call. I reminded them that my mother had done the same thing for me, and it didn't seem to warp me too much. I ended my argument by saying, "Besides, I find my teaching career to be rewarding and fulfilling. I enjoy doing it."

Who knows if they were convinced? They detested their chores as much as any child does. On Friday nights before bedtime, I always filled out each kid's "to-do" list that must be done on Saturday mornings before cartoons or playtime. They quickly discovered that I loved to sleep in on Saturdays, and they could pretty much do what-ever they chose as long as they kept quiet enough not to awaken me. Their infractions were so obvious, although they believed their "dimwitted mother" never caught on. But I was aware of their procrastinations and gamely kept trying to get them to follow my rules. We usually did our work together, after I woke up to supervise. I eventually gave up trying to change that routine. My need for a morning off to sleep was just as important to me as was their desire for some unhindered free time.

It became even more urgent for me to have that Saturday morning respite when I decided to finish my Master's program while Abe spent his summers in Illinois. The girls' routine of going to the babysitter continued each summer as I joined a carpool and commuted thirty miles to Central Washington University. During the school year, I undertook an experimental study of a new set of teaching materials called the SRA Reading Lab. I designed a regime of teaching and testing my first graders using the materials and had a control class across the hall. I worked very hard to be accurate and as scientific as one can be with the variables inherent in teaching small children.

My professor urged me to set up my hypothesis to read, "There will be no statisti-cal difference between the two methods of teaching." Good thing that he did, because it proved to be exactly the case with the final outcome of my two-year effort. This professor, a jewel of a man, had just earned his doctorate, and I was his first Master's candidate. When he learned that numbers were definitely not my forte and that I had no knowledge of statistics, he ran the statistical analysis for me.

However, I found that I was skilled at the actual writing of the thesis. I did all the charts and graphs supporting the statistics and created a carefully-written description of the study. I later discovered that my chapter review of related literature was recommended to other Master's candidates as a model for correct form. My oral exam was a snap. When I met the committee, my professor asked me to give a short synopsis of the study. Then he asked, "And, are you satisfied with the results?" I answered the question, and he said, "Fine. Let's all go have a celebratory cup of coffee." So much for difficult oral exams!

I was not alone in experiencing celebratory times. Soon after I first began work on my thesis, Abe had an even more important reason to celebrate. When Laila was in first grade and Tammy was a rambunctious year and a half, I secretly began planning a surprise for his Christmas gift. He came home one evening in December, 1963, to hear me playing Bing Crosby singing, "I'll be Home for Christmas." Then, I handed him an envelope with a ticket to Jordan. I knew how much he missed his family and friends at home. He had not seen them in nine years.

Obtaining the ticket was no small feat for me. At this stage in our marriage he held the purse strings tightly, since I was still my mother's daughter and not yet secure in operating on a cash-only basis. In deference to Abe's better business sense, I consulted with him on everything before spending money, including my proposal to spend $10 on a new mattress for our baby! And now, here I was, brazenly dipping into our pitifully small savings account to purchase an airline ticket for halfway around the world! I was really not certain whether he would be pleased or upset with my actions.

Also, I found it rather daunting to arrange the details with a travel agency, which meant mapping out the schedule and checking to see that his new passport was in good order. Abe had applied for and received the passport before Tammy was born, because he'd hoped to make the trip during the summer of 1962. It seemed to me that going home for Christmas might be the next best alternative. He had sixteen days free before classes resumed. I was both delighted and relieved to see that he was surprised and touched by this marvelous surprise. Tammy and Laila were in on the secret and clambered all over their daddy with giggles and hugs while he sank down on the couch to soak it all in.

By the time we bid him goodbye, I had just a few days remaining until elementary schools let out for vacation. Then, I loaded the girls into the car and drove to Nyssa to spend Christmas with my folks. I chose to go because it kept my mind off missing him while he was gone. This plan meant that all members of our little family got to "be home for Christmas." Never mind that "home" meant opposite sides of the ocean!

We made one huge mistake in planning the venture. We notified the dear ones in Jordan of his arrival time, and things didn't work out as planned. Abe's plane was delayed in Rome, which caused a late arrival in Beirut. Because of this, the airline put Abe up at a luxury hotel, and he continued his journey the next morning. Although word of his delay was sent ahead to Amman, his waiting loved ones didn't receive the notice.

Abe explained that the problem dealt was the nature of the airport. Jordan's only airport at that time was a military airport situated quite a long distance from Amman. Civilians were required to wait for arrivals outside the airport proper. A large group of eager family and friends waited anxiously with no word from Abe for hours before giving up and going back to sleep in the city. Only his brothers toughed it out and waited for over a day outside the airport gates. When the wandering son finally walked through the airport gates to greet them, he told them that on future trips he would just arrive without notice and find his own way. His sisters and their children were all waiting at his brother Nasser's home in Amman where tears flowed abundantly with much hugging, kissing, and ululation.

From there, they drove for another hour to reach Al Husn where his parents stood beside the courtyard gate. I can only imagine what it must have been like for them to see and touch their child after nine years of absence. For Abe, it was a fulfillment of a dream once more to kiss his mother's soft face, which was bathed in tears as she expressed welcome, "*Ahlan wa Sahlan, Ahlan wa Sahlan,* You have come home and may your path to us have been easy. *Ahlan wa Sahlan!*" Abe's heart was overflowing with emotions too deep to express or describe. His yearning for this moment had dwelt in his heart for years, and now here he was.

On this trip home, because two lambs were killed, his mother had to prepare for the arrival of the many folk who came to welcome him, but on the following trip, all others went to sleep while she sat beside him throughout the night as they visited. His task was to answer all her questions about his life in America, describe the girls and me, and tell of the life our family lived in Yakima. Mother, in turn, detailed all the happenings of Jordanian family members.

Predictably, Abe remembered details of a poker party that his brother Nasser put on for him in Amman the day before his departure. The relatives who had been disappointed not to see him at his arrival were now invited. All of his old playmates, now grown men in the army or employed by the government, were there. They had a great time laughing and joking as they remembered stories of the mischief they had caused.

One particular anecdote had to do with the fact that by then Abe was beginning to sprout a few gray hairs among his waves of black hair. He noticed that several of his friends were still just as dark-haired as they had ever been. He remarked to the group that life in Jordan must be kinder on the men that they could remain so young in appearance. His friends looked rather sheepish but said nothing. Later, in private, they admitted they were dying their hair to hide the gray.

Abe found it difficult to describe how happy it made him to connect with cousins. He remembered that trip for the rest of his life. On that first trip home, the days flew by much too quickly, and soon it was time to say goodbye. Abe witnessed again the sorrow in his parent's faces as they bid him safe journey. And once more, he left the family home with no promise of when he might be able to return.

The return flight left Jordan on New Year's Day. We arrived home from Nyssa in time to greet him at the airport. Of course, the women of his family had tucked little surprises of candy and knick-knacks for the girls into his suitcase along with some packets of *jameed*, sun-dried, salted, fat free yogurt, and *farika,* green cracked wheat roasted for soup, as gifts for me. Abe took great care in instructing me how to cook these specialties. With all that excitement, we agreed the Christmas of 1963 was indeed memorable, and we felt refreshed as we headed off into the new year.

It was a blessing that we enjoyed that respite, since the next two years were full of turmoil for me. I was teaching first grade in a new building, and, therefore, once again was new-kid-on-the-block. The other two first grade teachers were set in their ways and often exhibited their opinion that I knew nothing about how things should be done. I tried to be agreeable and follow their lead, but I often found solace by just shutting my door and teaching the way I thought would best serve my students. This was the building where I needed cooperation to do my experimental study for my Masters, so it was a strain to walk the tight rope between building expectations and my determination to succeed.

Abe was gone both summers to Illinois, and during the year he became involved with a group of fellow teachers who were attempting to organize a college local of American Federation of Teachers. This created a great deal of conflict among staff who considered themselves "too professional" to stoop to joining a union. It became a power struggle between AFT and the NEA, National Education Association. Thus, Abe was under heavy strain, also.

Laila finished her first grade year in relative ease because she pretty much knew most of the first grade academics before she started. We requested testing by the school counselors to see if she was in a correct placement. The advice we received was that she should skip second grade. At the time, we thought that was the best decision. However, later in the course of her schooling, she always felt behind. Her classmates matured faster and seemed to be quicker in social skills. If we had it to do over, we probably would not choose this option. During these two years, 1963 and 1964, three of us in the family experienced a heavy load of strain.

During that same time, rambunctious Tammy was ushered across the street every morning to Mazie Meade's. Tammy was a happy, inquisitive child who loved to explore her territory whenever she was given the chance. In fact, she was so prone to taking off that she ran away once too often while on a vacation visit at Grandma's. So, Grandma bought her a kiddie harness and leash. I decided the idea had its merit and I used it too. It left both of her little arms free, and she could walk without being yanked around while reaching up to hold my hand. Tammy didn't remember the leash, and during a phone call with her sister after they were both adults, Tammy commented scornfully to her sister that she had seen a toddler on the streets in a kiddie harness and thought it was a rotten thing to do to a poor little kid. Laila mocked her right back—"Tammy, you were a kid on a leash!"

Actually, I needed all the help I could get. When Laila was very young, I felt certain that I was quite skilled in parenting techniques, because they worked with Laila. I instructed toddler Laila to hold my little finger as we walked in public places, and she would do it, never letting go. Not so with Tammy. She'd wiggle loose and take off running. If young Laila threw a hissy-fit tantrum in a store, I found a quiet out-of-the-way place, required her to sit there until she was done crying, and she would stay there while she wailed away! I went on about my shopping and checked on her unobtrusively every few seconds. When she was calm again, I invited her to come and join me. Laila later used a similar ploy with her first born. I still remember his little voice calling out from his place of banishment, "Done, Mommy, Done!"

That never worked with Tammy. She just got up and followed me while screaming bloody murder. I wish I'd known ahead of time that what works with one child may not necessarily work with the next one. My second-born also challenged my self-image of being a "perfect parent" by refusing to go quietly to sleep and stay where we'd put her. While she was still a toddler, Mazie reluctantly told me she had resorted to tying barriers across Tammy's bassinet during naptime to keep her from climbing out. This was before she could even safely negotiate the climb-down without falling. That posed a real danger for Tammy, so we asked Mazie to put Tammy to nap on a floor pallet and eliminate the bassinet.

But, we could understand Mazie's problem. During that year, we discarded the crib and bought low twin beds for the girls' bedroom, since we worried about Tammy climbing out of her crib and taking a serious tumble while we were all asleep. We couldn't keep her in bed. Every morning it was quite a family hunt to find her. She was a wanderer and chose strange places finally to fall asleep. The most common place to find her was in the closet nestled on top of the shoes.

An Arab student gave Abe a set of tiny decorated brass slippers which were designed to serve as individual hand-held ashtrays. Tammy spent hours trying to force her toes into them.

When visiting Grandma's house, if we couldn't find Tammy, we knew she would probably be holed up in the closet struggling to stand up and walk in Grandma's high heels.

Our house on Logan had a basement, and Tammy considered the stairs to be an attractive challenge. Rather than constantly worrying about her falling down the stairs, we supervised climbing lessons. Consequently, she could negotiate the stairs soon after she learned to crawl. We stacked pillows at the bottom to provide a soft landing in case she missed a step.

Brass slipper ashtrays

I was pleased to teach cooking skills to Laila, and she learned to turn on the stove and make pancakes. While we worked in the kitchen, Tammy was right there to "help." I placed plastics and kettles in a lower cupboard, which she knew was hers to get into whenever she chose. So, not only did we have a baby to step over, but also myriads of cooking utensils.

It felt productive to be taking time with the girls in the kitchen. Laila loved the cooking lessons and Tammy thought she was cooking, too, with all her kitchen toys. But, I was so absorbed with teaching during the year and commuting to attend summer school that I found it difficult to make time even to read to my girls. At that age, Tammy lost interest unless it was bouncy nursery rhymes with good illustrations, but I believed that Laila had the maturity to enjoy chapter books.

It would have been a correct assumption if I had paid more attention to her choice of books. But, the literature course I was taking required me to read *The Wind in the Willows*. We read right before bedtime, and Laila squirmed, a captive audience, while I read off long segments of Toad and Mole's adventures. I fell in love with the book, but it was boring to Laila. She usually drifted off to sleep rather than listen.

However, when the Master's was almost finished, I was gratified that Laila brought home *Minn of the Mississippi*. It was a long, beautifully illustrated story of the adventures of a three-legged snapping turtle traveling from the headwaters to the mouth of the Mississippi River. Laila really wanted to know about it and cuddled close to listen each evening. Now it was my turn to "yawn" when reading time approached, but I managed to stick with it. We finally finished reading it during our vacation week after my thesis was finished.

Reading and language development were important in our young family. Laila and I had good discussions on a variety of topics. Shortly after the end of her first grade year and after we put Abe on the train for his third summer in Illinois, Laila and I were driving downtown past the Liberty Savings and Loan building. It was being remodeled, and in the process, they removed a very large, heavy, old Statue of Liberty from the corner of the building. Laila had always loved that statue, and she moaned and groaned all the way home about its removal.

In her opinion, "They didn't have to go and take down all the old and beautiful things just to make something modern." She even quoted from a sermon she'd heard Billy Graham give on the evils of modern living. She seemed ready to go down to the site and do hand-to-hand combat. I told her that the way we could protest was to write a letter to the editor of our newspaper. I thought it was a good opportunity for her to practice our family's convictions that one must make one's voice heard.

As soon as we got home, she took me up on it. She sat down and composed her letter. I gave her help with spelling, but the choice of words was hers alone. She justified, with rather hot argument, why she said what she did

Dear Editor,

I was listening to a preacher the other night. He was complaining about modern devices. I don't think it was right to take down the Liberty Statue. It's just like burning the flag. If they want it down, they can just go back to England.

Sincerely,
Laila Ayyoub, 7 years old

I wrote about this to Abe and said, "I questioned her on the England bit. She knows that America got its independence and liberty from England. She just figures that anyone who will not respect the Liberty Statue deserves to be back under the powers of Old Mother England." On Saturday, there was an editorial about her letter. I commented to Abe that it was the first time that year that the paper has been worth buying.

Tammy's language skills were also developing that summer. Mom was there to help while I attended summer school. On the weekend, we'd decided to can some of the apricot harvest. We sat in the living room with pans on our laps, pitting the fruit. Tammy would come toddling by, and we prompted her to say "Thank you" when we popped a bit of fruit into her little mouth. We felt justly rewarded when she would grin and reply, "Ta Too." It was just like me with my sugar lump.

During that same summer, it was an absolute necessity that I stay for a week in the campus dorm to organize and check every page number of the sources for my "Review of Literature" chapter. Mom offered to care for the children during that time, and alas, on one day of that long week, she managed to lock the whole family out of the house. She was desperate and finally hit on the plan to break and enter. She found a tool from the garage and managed to tear open the screen by the kitchen window, force the window open, and send Laila crawling through to open the back door. Tammy, in the meantime, sat happily on the grass totally unaware of the crisis. I didn't hear about the adventure until I arrived home on the weekend, tired but exultant because the chapter was finished. The window screen wasn't properly repaired until Abe came home from Illinois.

I once again experienced regrets that I was an absent mom for so much of my children's baby years, either physically absent at work or college or at least mentally distant while I struggled to finish my Master's. The proof of that came home to haunt me many years later when Laila called to ask advice about potty training her young son. When she asked how I had gone about training my children, I was forced to admit I had no idea. The babysitters trained both of them. As I look back, I realize that I was operating under the strain that burdens all over-stretched, working mothers, wanting the best for my kids, knowing what I should be doing, yet not finding enough hours in the day to accomplish everything. It still bothers me that I depended on others to do so many of the important tasks of raising our girls.

After I finally finished the horrendous task of writing my thesis and getting it approved, it was ready for the typist. I felt numb. It could be likened to the feeling I experienced after Tamam was born; exhaustion, exhilaration, peace, release. I tried to call Abe and share my contentment, at least over the telephone wire, but he didn't answer. Why were we so far apart at times when it would mean so much to be together? I wrote to *Barhoumy*, my Ibrahim, if it still was alright with him if I took the girls to the ocean for a week. It would cost, and I had been laying out money heavily on the thesis. Staying in the dorm, buying expensive paper, five cents a page for a long thesis. I thought the typist would charge ten cents a page on tables, and I had twenty-three statistical tables. My salary increase to the Master's level had already been spent for the first year. Still, I needed a week of sand and sea before I tried to teach any more first-graders. I didn't know how much money we had.

As it turned out, we never made it to the ocean, since we discovered a lovely laid-back place which opened up promises for future vacations. We escaped to the nearby mountains and hibernated in a rustic cabin at American River Lodge for a week. The cabin had indoor plumbing and electricity, so I was able to take along my little portable Singer sewing machine and finally keep my promise to Laila to sew doll clothes. I built wood fires for heat and we filled the long lazy days with forested silence and relaxation.

I engineered another happy celebration for the girls and me. In the college bookstore, a print of Renoir's *Irène Cahen d'Anvers* caught my eye. That print has been prominently displayed in our home ever since. I've always referred to it as La Petite Irene, and I love it because it reminds me of my own two beautiful girls. When I brought the print home from college, I told the children that we were going to buy beautiful La Petite Irene dresses for them and splurge on a special dinner out at The Dragon Inn.

Both children have memories of how important the occasion was. Laila has reminded me that the dress I bought for Tammy was so large, it took years for her to grow into it, but I photographed Laila on the day of our special dinner. When Abe came home to begin his next year of work at YVC, he too brought the girls beautiful dresses which were much too large, practically down to their ankles. I put a deep hem in each dress and the girls wore them with pride because Daddy had chosen them.

CHAPTER 14

—————◆—————

Our Maturing Lives

THE GIRLS WERE HAPPY to have their daddy back home, but they were still too young to be aware of what was happening in their parents' social lives. While they were occupied with school and daycare, Mommy and Daddy embarked on new adventures. This was the year that Abe began to develop close ties with his department colleagues and was pleased to accept invitations to their parties, where he met interesting new friends. At first, I was shy about attending, because there was a lot of smoking, drinking, and long, loud, conversations about social and political issues. I didn't drink or smoke, and I wasn't knowledgeable on current events. Plus, I felt awkward with the casual chit chat that also went on at such affairs, so I found it easier to stay home with the girls.

But, Abe's friends began to question him about why I didn't come. Eventually, I realized that these people were important in our lives, and that I'd better make an effort. They welcomed me into their circle. Thus began my education on how concerned citizens went about trying to make a difference. And, make a difference we did! This was the 1960's when racial issues were omnipresent in America. Our group of dedicated souls worked diligently both in political action and in grassroots efforts to form coalitions in Yakima. At the invitation of the new friends I met at the parties, I found myself swept up in the Mayor's Committee on Human Rights, which convened at City Hall. J.C. Morrison served as chairman.

J.C. and his wife, Mamie, were respected leaders of Yakima's African-American community, and they set-to with a will to bring about change. Ostensibly, the Mayor formed the committee in an attempt to prevent racial unrest in Yakima. But, we believed the Mayor expected us to become a committee of do-nothings, satisfied to have a seat at City Hall and not much else. Instead, he was confronted with much more than he bargained for when we proved to be activists who immediately formed sub-committees.

Roho Shinda, a Los Angeles realtor, moved to Yakima during this time and received a cold reception from the community when she attempted to practice fair housing principles. So, she and her husband, Fundi, became active in the Housing sub-committee, working alongside Pat Haas, a quiet-spoken woman, who was warm with grace. Nancy Faller took a leadership role in the Employment Discrimination sub-committee, and I became chair of the Education sub-committee. I held meetings in our home to determine what could be done to eliminate racial disparities in our schools.

Throughout the rest of my years in Yakima, our sub-committee efforts have remained vibrant, even when the Mayor withdrew his support. We formed the Yakima Valley Human Rights Scholarship program, which now has charity tax status and awards scholarships each year to (primarily) minority high-school graduates. It has served the valley continuously since 1966.

Every time I came home from meetings, engrossed in my concerns about what was happening with the Mayor's Committee, Abe was ready to listen and offer his suggestions on what else I could do. But the reverse didn't really happen, and I was left out of the loop as he supported his friends, Dick Lord and Mauno Saari, in their efforts to form a college teachers' union.

Abe's way of dealing with his college concerns was to zone out in front of the television. We usually ate the evening meal in front of that screen, and the girls learned early on that Daddy owned the TV. My task was to keep them from interfering with whatever he was watching, and they learned to carry on their conversations during commercials. I didn't understand what caused his long periods of withdrawal from the family evening scene. I thought he was just addicted to his news programs on the tube. He later told me, "When my wife came home from school tired and still faced with all the needs at home, dumping my worries on her was not my idea of comfort to my family."

Among his worries was the fact that Abe knew ten signatures were required in order to establish the union, and even if that happened, he thought that their efforts might not achieve the goals they had in mind. He was apprehensive that nothing could be accomplished in this conservative community. He was not about to voice those doubts to me and especially not to his friends. Abe recognized in them the same qualities that he had so admired among his associates when he volunteered in Amman for the Arab Club. They had deep concern for the injustices heaped upon those least able to withstand such hardships.

Abe valued Dick Lord's friendship for many reasons. His sense of humor was marvelously witty, and he was well-read. In addition, he was a painter, whose work we purchased for our home. Whenever Dick attended a gathering, he carried his sketch pad and made ink drawings of what was going through his mind as a result of the conversations swirling around him. Since Dick had been a member of a teacher's union in Idaho, he provided valuable input.

Mauno Saari loved to come to our home and relax with a brandy while proclaiming his latest unconventional ideas. He championed causes which seldom took root, such as his wish for the college to build a swimming pool. I listened to him expound on the grave error the city was making to grant cable franchises to corporate conglomerates. He championed for millionaire families to purchase the franchises for city use. Of course, his ideas went nowhere because of the push-back from corporate interests. He was branded a socialist.

Another dedicated soul, RK Smith, arrived from Seattle the same year that Abe joined the faculty. He was hired to teach art, manage the gallery, and produce the annual. He agreed that instructors needed to receive grievance rights, fair wages, and collective bargaining to improve the climate on campus. RK brought with him his connections with the Seattle American Federation of Teachers where he had been a member.

All these good friends worked tirelessly to garner the necessary ten signatures. When not in class, they were in the coffee shop networking with other teachers to explain the advantages of union membership. It was not easy, and there were many after-hour gatherings at RK Smith's home. Finally, on October 9, 1963, the American Federation of Teachers, Local No. 1485 was established. Abe was given a plaque naming Ibrahim Ayyoub as a charter member.

Abe's buddies loved to tease him, because he was not vocal in promoting the union. At one weekend meeting up at Central Washington College (now Central Washington University), RK shared a room with Abe. As they were relaxing before bedtime, RK asked, "Do you know what this is all about?" Abe grinned and answered, "No." Many years ago, I discovered an anonymous quotation which I saved because it perfectly described Abe's union activities:

His thoughts were slow, his words were few and never formed to glisten.

But he was a joy to all his friends. You should have heard him listen.

After the union was officially chartered, the real work began. Abe finished teaching his classes at two in the afternoon. Then, he often accompanied Mauno, RK, or Dick on door-to-door leafleting excursions. Abe felt that the guys always had brilliant ideas of how to approach people, but that he didn't have their eloquence so he just went along as moral support and let them do the talking. But, one time, someone asked that if they didn't like the way Yakima was, why didn't they just leave? Abe replied, "If you send out all those who are trying to improve things, who do you have left?"

Once, during the early years of union activity, the new college president summoned Abe to his office to urge him to reconsider his union activities. Abe was being "hot-boxed." Basically, the president suggested that Abe's association with union activities would be a detriment in the hiring process if he became interested in moving on to employment at some other institution. To Abe's eternal credit, he answered that these were his friends. He believed that they were working for just causes, and he had no interest in abandoning them in order to advance personal ambitions. Eventually, this particular president became supportive of the AFT's efforts.

This was also a time of great political effort to strengthen the Democratic Party in our conservative valley, so as the guys went from door to door, they actually carried out two missions, signing up AFT members and organizing Democratic precincts. During the next few years, both efforts paid off. Enough teachers joined AFT so that they could hold an election, which the union won, to become the negotiating body for the college. The union and the college administration hammered out a collective bargaining agreement.

To this day, the American Federation of Teachers is the representative body for the college staff. In fact, professors learned that it was to their advantage to join the union because of its quality assistance in cases of due process. During the years before Abe retired, thirty-six cases were satisfactorily concluded. At one time, Abe served on the negotiating team, but again he never spoke up during the sessions. When they broke for caucus in the hall, the other team members could count on Abe to tell them what he had observed while watching and listening.

Our daughter, Laila, has experience on a bargaining team, and now team members are trained to do just that. She notices body language and records everything so that she can contribute during caucus time. Her father's model, set for her while she was growing up, is now a skill she employs.

Both daughters have reminded me of other actions which also influenced their adult lives. We organized the first Yakima march for human rights after the assassination of Dr. Martin Luther King Jr. We honored the grape boycott and picketed stores who sold grapes during the United Farmworkers push for rights. I traveled to Washington, DC, as a representative of AFT, to attend the White House Conference on Racism, and then came home to give speeches around the community about what I'd learned.

These activist causes and people were an integral part of our family life. Our children all played together, and as an adult, one of those children said, "We always knew we were the kids of very politically active parents. I'm not sure we really understood the meaning of 'political,' but we knew you all were fighting for human rights." There was always some sort of publication in process at Dick and Mary Jean's. Tammy loved to help collate and staple.

Throughout all of this reaching out to the community, my responsibilities as homemaker and teacher continued, which caused me to feel like I was leading a double or triple life. Most of the staff members in the various buildings where I taught were probably aware of my political-social leanings, but they pretended to show no interest, and I rarely voiced my viewpoints at school. Once, however, I was forced to speak.

I discovered, to my deep disappointment, that my principal openly expressed his racial prejudices. I was standing in the hall with another teacher when he came out of his office to share what he thought was a joke but included the use of the "n" word.

I was shocked, but said nothing. Instead, I went back to my school room and stewed about it for the rest of the day.

After discussing my distress with Abe at home that night, I decided I must speak up. I knew that if I tried just speaking to my principal, I wouldn't have the courage that Abe showed when he confronted his accusatory geometry teacher at Middle East College. Instead, I would melt into a trembling mess and probably burst into tears. So, I wrote the principal a carefully-worded letter saying that I was deeply concerned about his so-called joke. I said that it was not funny, and it reinforced racial stereotypes.

I also wrote that a leader of our administration should never set such a poor example of racial thinking or speech to the teachers under his direction. The next morning, before classes convened, I asked for a private consultation in his office. He invited me in, and I carefully closed the door. I was, indeed, shaking and nervous, but I stood in front of his desk and handed him the letter. He read it and appeared to be upset, as people often are when called out on something for which they are being criticized.

He offered the usual platitudes about not meaning the joke to be a slur against another race, and "some of my best friends are Negro." I thanked him for his time and left. I suppose it didn't change his thinking, but at least he never again shared such language in front of me. His written evaluations, which went into my permanent record, were always laudatory. This incident was definitely an exceptional experience for me. Usually, home concerns stayed at home, and school concerns stayed at school.

Along with the constant necessity for multi-tasking between home and school, suddenly we were faced with the added distraction of needing to find another home. We learned that our traveling landlords wanted to move back into their house as soon as the school year finished. Once again, we packed up our second-hand furniture and found a place to store it. Abe had one summer left in Illinois, so we decided on a marvelous plan for the girls and me. We had loved our week during the previous summer at American River Lodge. This time, the owner of the lodge offered us a cabin with two little bedrooms where we could live and help to earn our keep by cleaning all the other tourist cabins when vacationers departed.

There was enough room to invite all three of my brother's children to spend the summer with us. His wife, Janey, was more than agreeable with the plan, so we loaded up the old swish-swish Faultless washing machine, purchased a galvanized washtub for baths, and headed to the hills. Abe had time to help us hook up the washer under the trees, using a long outdoor electrical cord, at a spot within hose distance of a cold-water faucet. I found a good detergent for cold-water laundering.

When we were settled into our new domicile, I drove with the girls to Eugene to pick up Tony, Karen, and Krissy. It was on the way home, with five kids in tow, that I began to wonder about the wisdom of the task I'd laid out for my summer "vacation." Tony was about 11; Karen and Laila were 7 or 8; Krissy was about 5; and Tammy was just two and still potty training.

The kids had a ball, and they still all speak of the summer in glowing terms. The older girls helped me with cabin-cleaning, and Tony got a job helping with the horses at the corral. He played guitar and was offered gigs to entertain customers in the main lodge. He was paid in candy bars. My girls remember being jealous of his superior status. I was cook, commander-in-chief and laundress for our little crew. I remember a bucket of dirty socks constantly soaking outside the door, because after the first bleeding stubbed toe, I insisted they wear socks and shoes, instead of running barefoot on that rough terrain filled with exposed tree roots, rocks, and pine needles.

Once a week, we drove into Yakima for shopping and a movie. It seems I was repeating the role my mother had modeled for me with that excursion to town. The thirty-mile distance from civilization was even the same. Once during the summer, my parents came to visit and brought Janey and my beloved Aunt Geneva with them. I barbequed shish kebob out under the pines.

I have a warm, lovely memory of walking with little Tammy along the American River in the night-time to watch the moon cast its reflection on the silvery waters. We would sing, "I see the moon, the moon sees me. The moon sees somebody I long to see." At that point, Tammy always chimed in, "I wanna see Daddy." I wrote long letters to Abe telling him of all our adventures. I'm sure he loved my description of riding a reluctant horse up along the trail and then having to hang on for dear life when it was time to head back. That horse was much too anxious to get back to the corral and rid himself of his burden.

Abe's letters were full of concern about where we would live in the fall. He felt it was time to begin searching for a place to buy and urged me to seek out possibilities. Nothing turned up, so I contacted Roho, who knew about real estate. She took me to a pear orchard in the small rural community of Gleed outside of Yakima. The place had a rental on it that would be available about the same time that we needed to move back down from the mountains.

I struck a deal, and based on my description, Abe agreed, so I sealed the bargain and paid our deposit. We had friends with a truck who helped me get the furniture settled in, and Laila was enrolled in the Lower Naches elementary school to begin her fourth grade year. We found a loving family nearby for Tammy's child care.

During the process of moving, we stopped one day at a service station where the owner offered the girls a free German Shepherd puppy. I don't know why I agreed. The girls named him Rebel, and he was well-named! By the time Abe finished his summer school and arrived home, we were ensconced in our new house, Laila in a new school, Tammy at a new babysitter, and with a new gangling half-grown dog, whom the girls adored almost as much as they did their daddy.

It was a good year. Country-school living suited us all. Laila's teacher loved physical education and ran the legs off her students around and around the track. At first Laila complained, but then she began to see how much stronger and more limber she was becoming, and we heard no more about it. In fact, Laila became so physically fit, her friend and she decided to see how far each of them could jump from one picnic table to another in the tiny little park close to our house. Her friend came to me yelling that Laila was bleeding and I'd better come. Thank heavens, Abe was home, because when we rushed to Laila, it was clear that we needed emergency assistance. Her leg right below the knee was split open, and I could see the white of her bone amongst all the blood. I'll never forget that desperate trip! We wrapped her leg in a clean towel and Abe told me to drive while he held Laila. To this day, I can't be sure who cared for Tammy during the excitement.

When we reached the hospital, the staff took charge. Laila was crying a bit, but not too badly. Perhaps she was in shock. I was allowed to stand at her head to pat her face for comfort when they began to insert a huge needle-full of pain-killer into the torn flesh. I was vaguely aware of a nurse yelling, "Get the mother!" The next thing I remember, I was ungracefully sprawled on the floor. It's the first and only time I ever fainted! Laila managed better than I.

Just because I was not prone to fainting, it must not be inferred that I was never faint at heart! The spring of that year was filled with nights of creeping, freezing cold, and our landlord had to fire the smudge-pots in his pear orchard throughout the night. We left the back door open so he could come sit in the warm kitchen with a bit of hot coffee until time to go back out and add oil to the pots. Not only was it dark and mysterious in that smoky haze, but I made the mistake of starting to read *The Lord of the Rings* while lying in the creaky upstairs bedroom of our rented house.

The girls were asleep in their room across the hall; Abe was asleep in front of his TV downstairs, and I was surrounded by Ringwraiths, Dark Riders! These were nine nearly-immortal men bound to the power of the Ring. They were Sauron's "most terrible servants." We know that I was an impressionable child when it came to full moons and the Wolf man, but who would believe that grown-up Doris found it necessary to get up and check out the dark closet to be sure nothing supernatural was lurking inside? Later, when the girls asked me to read the trilogy to them, I was reluctant, but I agreed to read *The Hobbit,* sure that the later books would terrify them. But, no. It seems I am the only scairdy-cat of the family.

However, we were all alarmed one morning when suddenly we heard a screech, bang, crash! We were preparing for the day when we felt the entire house jolted off its foundation. The force was strong enough to crack the living-room ceiling and to knock the children's little ceramic kitty-cat dishes off the shelf. A Lower Naches school-teacher, who was late for an early-morning meeting, tried to take the corner too fast. She lost control, plowed across our yard, and smacked into the corner of our house.

Normally, it was Tammy's habit to play in the yard while she waited for us to get ready to leave. The gods were watching over us that morning, because she was still inside and Rebel Dog was already fed and fastened to his clothesline-run for the day. Abe rushed out to check on the driver, who was pretty smashed up. While Abe grabbed a blanket to cover her, I called the sheriff, but we didn't attempt to move the driver from the car and waited for emergency help to arrive. None of us was hurt, the house was quickly repaired, and the main damage for us was ruffled nerves. The teacher's car was totaled, and she recovered in the hospital.

Our family was becoming very comfortable in this sweet little two-story bungalow, so we approached our landlord with an offer to buy. He wanted to sell but firmly insisted that we must also buy the orchard. We knew we were completely ignorant about managing fruit trees, so there was no deal. We continued to be on the lookout for other rural properties, spending many a weekend driving from one place to another, until Abe brought home news that a friend had approached him with an offer to sell us his house at 221 S.18th Avenue. It was ideal, except for the obvious fact that it was located smack-dab in the middle of town. No wide-open fields, no freedom for the kids to roam, no meadow larks singing to us in the early spring.

During spring frost season, just as had been the case while living near the pear orchard, there would be no fresh air. Yakima Valley is shaped like a bowl and suffers from severe inversions similar to Los Angeles. Yakima was often thought of as "smog central" during springtime when orchards had to be heated. On particularly frigid mornings, we struggled to deal with a choking haze. We knew of one family who even shut their central heating off on cold nights so that their furnace fan wouldn't suck smudge smoke into their spotless house.

Homes on the heights surrounding Yakima got more wind so the smudge was not so thick, and the outlying Gleed and Lower Naches areas had breezes that kept the mosquitoes at bay. But, in town, oily, smoky clouds of smudge penetrated everywhere. Orchardists use smokeless heaters or wind machines, now, but in the '60's and 70's, many farmers even burned old tires, and residents were forced to endure greasy nostrils and grimy clothing.

We had already experienced smudge problems in the pear orchard, and that house was situated right next to a busy highway. The prospective house was a short walk to YVC, Roosevelt Elementary, and Franklin Junior High. The lovely Franklin Park with its swimming pool for summer and steep hill for sledding was just around the corner. The house was no more than five blocks from Davis High School. The asking price was reasonable, and the owners wanted to carry the mortgage.

When I toured the house for the first time, I was struck with the similarity of its floor plan to my Aunt Dorothy's house in Boise where I spent happy hours and days during all of my growing years. I remarked that the builders must have worked from the same blueprints. The kitchen and bathroom were small but adequate. The main level included a dining room, a living room with a fireplace, and two bedrooms, all with hardwood floors. There was an attic with a finished bedroom under the eaves.

Steps by the back door led down to an unfinished utility room with two stationary laundry tubs, a small storage room that could serve as another bedroom, and a large unfinished area containing a monster-sized coal stoker-furnace and coal bin. In the front yard, there was a huge black walnut tree and an even larger evergreen with a low hanging branch just made-to-order for a rope swing. A tiny garage bordered one side of the large back yard, with grape vines on the other, and there was adequate space for a garden at the back.

There must have been a sale on dark industrial-green paint, since all of the rooms were that color. But that was cosmetic, and we became convinced that our family would be very comfortable in this house for many years. By the time our school year came to a close, we had signed the deal. We once again called on friends to help us move all those ratty, second-hand pieces of furniture we'd purchased in Corvallis. During Tammy's younger years, 18th Avenue was a kid-friendly neighborhood where she felt free to play hop scotch and roller skate in the middle of the quiet street.

There were some major differences, though. Rebel Dog and our five-dollar swish-swish washer would not be moving to town with us. Neighbors in Gleed wanted to have Rebel Dog and also offered to buy our sturdy old washer for fifteen dollars. I couldn't believe our good fortune. The washer served us through the diaper-years for both girls, and we were selling it at 150% profit! The deal included a used button-hole attachment, for my sewing machine!

Rebel had become such a trial. If we let him run loose, he came home with buck-shot in his rear end from chasing someone's chickens. I had to keep him tied when I hung the washing out because he was prone to pulling clothes off the line. Laila was not particularly consistent in pooper-scoop patrol, and even though both girls loved him dearly, none of us knew the first thing about training an adolescent German Shepherd. When Rebel moved to the ranch, they trained him and reported to us that he was the smartest, best-behaved pet they'd ever owned.

The first of many purchases for our new home on 18th was our spanking new "suds-saver" Kenmore automatic washer. The soapy wash-water could be pumped into one laundry tub and saved while the machine continued through rinse and spin cycles. Then the sudsy water was pumped back into the machine to wash a second load. It seemed unjust to acquire this luxury appliance only after both children were done with diapers! We still didn't spring for a dryer, though, and I hauled heavy loads of wash up the steps and out to the lines in the back yard, or else I made use of the bad-weather clotheslines strung up all over the big basement room.

Really, I didn't mind it too much. This system was all I'd ever known, and I loved the fresh odor of line-dried sheets and towels. Laila hated the wrinkled tablecloths, however, because ironing them became her chore. I can remember her trudging up from the basement complaining that she was suffering from "cloth-o-phobia." That chore probably explains why, to this day, neither Laila nor Tammy use tablecloths. I also resorted to my mother's earlier scheme of sprinkling down the ironing and storing it in our freezer until it was needed.

Of all the areas of the new house, the large basement room became the one Abe envisioned as his eventual place of refuge. The family cooperated in helping him achieve that goal. Abe saw past its dusty, dark dinginess and began to scheme. We needed new wiring for better lighting and large storage cupboards on the side wall where we could hide all our clutter. After the first year or so, major renovations began.

The laundry lines came down, and we replaced the coal stoker with a gas furnace. This allowed us to finish the room with siding and ceiling tile. I loved teasing Abe and a buddy for installing the ceiling tile without using a plumb line to determine if the house was correctly square. Of course it wasn't, and they were forced to remove a large section, measure, and start over. In the meantime, I read the directions, which were explicit on how to approach the project. I couldn't resist the comment, "When all else fails, why not read the directions?"

We purchased a large rug, and I set to with my trusty Singer to fashion Arabic mattresses and large throw pillows. I studied how to craft Roman Shades out of upholstery fabric for the high casement windows, and our faithful RCA TV with its rabbit-ear antenna was moved to Abe's lower sanctum. This lovely comfy room became the favorite hang-out for the whole family, but it was always made very clear that Daddy controlled the TV when he was stretched out on his mattress.

We developed quite a routine of preparing our meals and carting them down to what we dubbed our Arabic Room, where we sat to dine on the mattresses with low coffee tables in front of us. We carried it to such an extreme that I eventually moved the table into the living room and turned the dining room into a music room with a bean bag chair that I sewed for lounging. It was the middle 60's after all, and the girls wanted a place to listen to The Beatles with their friends.

Soon after settling into our new home, my parents drove from Nyssa to inspect and admire. This was the first of their many eagerly-anticipated visits to the house on 18th. The first thing Tammy always asked as they climbed out of the car was, "Did you bring Mitzi and Tootsie?" Grandma and Grandpa were welcome, but for sure they had better bring along the dogs. Tammy spent hours with Tootsie, dressing her up, putting her inside a bushel basket and telling her to "Stay!" The poor little pup was a beloved, compliant, friendly playmate.

From that very first visit, my mother became enamored with the fireplace, and she eagerly looked forward to building fires every time she came. She had always dreamed of living in a home with a fireplace. Laila was in sixth grade, and we had been living on 18th for several years, when Mom really flubbed her fire-building. We were not home at the time, but she decided she wanted to have a cozy little blaze.

Blaze it became, but not so cozy! She neglected to open the draft vent and ended up with a smoking, dangerous fire. It ruined the living room paint, scorched the floor in front of the fireplace and filled the entire house with foul-smelling smoke. We were lucky she was able somehow to smother the fire, or we would have lost our home. She was devastated and traveled back to Nyssa in tears.

After the repairs were complete, I sent my Mom a bouquet of roses with a little note saying, "Thank you for being my Mother." She never caught on to the double meaning behind that note and she kept it pinned above her dresser until the day she died. I didn't have the heart to explain that I was grateful for her carelessness. Because of her actions, we received an insurance check which paid for a new paint job and dry-cleaning that needed to be done even before the fire.

By the time we finished the home improvements, we were able to afford some new living-room furniture. Until then, our living room sported the blue velvet "Early Second-Hand" monster with its broken back propped against the wall. In replacement, Abe and I chose a brand new easy chair, a cocoa-brown couch, matching loveseat, and a coffee table from the Bon Marché. We requested delivery, but failed to pre-determine the day and time of delivery.

Obviously, we also failed to include the girls in the information loop because Tammy, a kindergartner, was surprised when she hurried to answer the doorbell. I was hosting a meeting of the Human Rights Education Committee in our living room, and Tammy served as my door-lady. When she opened the door, a strange man asked her, "Would you like to buy some new furniture?" She was amazed that one could buy furniture from a street vendor who just came knocking on the door. But she answered, "Sure!" and invited him into the house.

At that time, we prominently displayed one of Dick Lord's paintings over the fireplace. It was a bright, bold, acrylic showing a wild, hungry-looking man wearing a clerical collar, juxtaposed against a gravestone inscribed with the Lenny Bruce quotation about, "any man who calls himself a religious leader and owns more than one suit is a hustler as long as there is someone in the world who has no suit at all." Several members of our committee were deeply religious, and one pastor had just finished remarking that the painting offered real food for thought. Then, the Bon Marché delivery guys tromped in with our spanking-new furniture. I could have died! I felt as if I professed certain beliefs while doing something entirely different. New suits, new furniture, same difference!

Not only were we doing well enough to buy new furniture, we were beginning to sock away a bit of savings, and that feeling of financial security was gratifying. But in the back of Abe's mind there still festered the problem of my parents' constant debt because of my mother's propensity to buy most everything on credit, and her scheme of partial payments every other month to the businesses that were the most demanding. She was constantly at the mercy of her many creditors, and over the years continued her old habit of "juggling" finances. Most every time our families were together, she would proudly inform me that if she were just able to do this and this and maybe that, by next year they would be out of debt. I'd heard that since I was five.

It bothered Abe tremendously that it didn't ever happen. After ten years of marriage, by holding tightly to the family purse-strings, Abe finally managed to teach me proper household finance to the point that he could loosen up to buy some of the new items we needed. Now, he sat down for a serious conversation with me about my parents' difficulties. He urged me to travel to Nyssa during summer vacation for a visit with them to explain his plan.

He wanted me to carry our check book with me and offer to pay off all their creditors with the understanding that they would not charge anything again and would begin operating on a cash basis. In addition, I was directed to explain that he wanted to assume their mortgage payments. I was to emphasize his concern that they were approaching retirement and multiple accounts with accompanying interest charges would not provide a worry-free, comfortable life for them. I agreed to do it as soon as I finished the school year.

There is a distinct contrast between the last day of school for me as a child and the same occasion when I was an adult with my own young children eagerly waiting for Mama to get home. That last half-day of school was a time of celebration for them and a time of near collapse for me. Sending my antsy class out the door on time, each student clutching a report card and a sack full of personal belongings, required the organizational skills of a general in the Marines.

After the feat was accomplished, I rushed home to hear about the day's experiences of my two daughters, "ooh and ah" over their sacks of art work, and praise them for their good grades. Then, leaving Daddy to fend for himself, we climbed into the car, which I'd packed up the night before, and headed out for our "girl trip" to visit Grandma and Grandpa, who lived three hundred miles away. In addition to his wish for me to have a private discussion with my parents, Abe really didn't enjoy frequent visits with his in-laws and was delighted to see us head down the road, leaving him with a respite from fathering and husbanding.

Though I was exhausted, the girls' anticipation was contagious, and I soon caught a second wind. They each had their favorite sections along the way. The first of these favorites was the old "Horse-Heaven" highway beyond Prosser. The area was wheat country with steep hills, and we called it the "roller coaster road." The girls pretended to be exasperated with me when I insisted on reciting an old finger-play rhyme about Mr. Wiggle and Mr. Waggle going up the hill, and down the hill, and up the hill and down the hill. But, I knew they expected and anticipated my silly routine, just as my brother and I expected our mother's songs and games when we were children.

We always enjoyed our picnic, sitting in the footprint of a house which had burned down, leaving just its solitary stone chimney and fireplace. And, we made the mandatory stop for ice cream at the "48-Flavors" as we drove through La Grande. Finally, in the early evening, we reached Nyssa, where the girls were usually more excited to greet Mitzi and Tootsie than their grandparents. Grandpa's grin was contagious as he beckoned to the girls to come into the kitchen to admire the many cans of black olives and the two pounds of bacon he'd purchased just for them. Thus began a busy, happy week for the girls, while I spent the time answering all my mother's questions and catching up on news of the town.

During the visit, I found a private time when the girls were asleep to explain Abe's offer. I was a little concerned about how they would take it, but after my mother's grateful tears, they both willingly accepted. They had one condition: we must agree that the Nyssa property would be deeded to us, reserving a lifetime use for them. Mom dug out all the various accounts, and I wrote checks paying everything off.

After we headed home, they traveled to the county seat and wrote up a legal document for the deed. In the same document, they deeded the shares of Oklahoma oil property, which paid my dad a tiny royalty each month. That property was Jesse's only inheritance from his parents, and he always joked that someday the oil well would strike a gusher so that he could finally afford to run away and live on a showboat traveling up and down the Mississippi.

At the time, it bothered me that my brother was not part of this arrangement. But Mom and Dad assured me that I was to be named executor, and when the time came, after Abe recovered all that he had paid, the remaining balance should be equally divided with my brother. In later years, that is exactly what happened. At the end of our visit, I drove away with the girls, secure in the knowledge that my folks would be better off financially than they had ever been. And, they stuck to the bargain, living the last few years of their life debt free.

It is impossible to emphasize adequately the deep respect I feel for Abe's commitment to the welfare of my parents. This same feeling of responsibility also applied to his family. While we were helping Mom and Dad, he was also sending $50 per month to his younger brother, Fahim, a college student in Egypt. That amount seems a pittance, now, but in the early 70's, that money made it possible for Fahim to live quite comfortably.

During this same period, Suleiman's oldest daughter, Hana, graduated with honors from high school in Jerusalem and was ready for college. We discussed how best we could assist and decided to offer our little basement room to her so that she could live with us and attend YVC. Hana and Suleiman gratefully accepted the invitation, so we set about preparing for her arrival.

The room itself was as comfortable as most dorm rooms would have been. We laid carpet, and there was space for an easy chair, a bed, and a desk. One wall was lined with closets and shelves. However, since no toilet facilities were available downstairs, we knew we needed to do some more construction. Abe bargained with Sears so we could build a small bathroom off the corner of the laundry room. I think our own two daughters probably felt a bit jealous about the new shower, since the upstairs bathroom had only a tub. They soon began to pester Hana for shower privileges.

Hana stayed with us for two years and became a dear member of the family. I immediately scheduled her into the duty roster for baking pocket-bread. She became a loving older sister to Laila and Tammy, full of fun and a good example for them in how to deal with hard times because she was a teenager during the Israeli-Jordanian conflicts. At one time, she was forced to flee across the Jordan River to safety.

Subsequently, she could not receive an entry visa back to the Israeli side to visit her family in Jerusalem.

After YVC, Hana moved on to Washington State University in Pullman where she graduated and moved back to Amman to work for Chase-Manhattan Bank. This left the little student room in our basement empty until a nephew, Fuad, came to stay with us for a short time. When he left, Hana's younger brother, Soubhi, arrived. We bustled with noise and merriment created by these great kids and they introduced a unique cultural aspect to our household. I will be forever grateful for the experience they gave to our own two children.

I felt strongly about offering varied experiences to our girls. This was probably deeply ingrained in me due to the model my mother provided while I was growing up. However, whenever I fell into the trap of over-organizing activities for them, I tried to pause and remember the resentment I felt as a kid when my mom pushed me in uncomfortable directions, such as the Job's Daughter dances or the box socials where I actually had to talk with a boy! I was aware that my happiest early memories were of the unstructured days during the summers at Owyhee Dam, and I wanted that same freedom for my girls.

Although both girls approached new experiences with gusto, sometimes I was guilty of pushing in exactly the same way Mom had done with me. I remember listening one summer, when Laila was about twelve, as she whined about being bored. My unsympathetic answer to her was, "In our family, there is never time for being bored. If you think you have nothing fun to do, it's time to choose something new." Laila took that statement to heart and decided she would like to try acrobatics.

She had a friend who did acrobatics at the St. Claire School of Dance, and she begged permission to join the class. We investigated the school and decided her plan was viable. Laila turned out to be quite good at it, and the following year, Tammy began lessons there too. Mr. St. Claire was a very demanding teacher and was quickly nicknamed, "Mr. Bear." Tammy was exhilarated the day she could accomplish a backbend!

We were happily surprised the next year, when Laila decided she would like to give up acrobatics to study ballet. I went to speak with Mrs. St. Claire to explain that we were not interested in dance-show recitals, because it required extensive extra rehearsals and costuming. She assured me she didn't ever consider her students accomplished enough for recitals. She was exacting, and she gave her students quality classical training. Laila became enamored with ballet and stuck with it through high school and on into college where she majored in Psychology with a minor in Dance. Mrs. St. Claire finally had to admit to being pleased when she traveled to Seattle to attend one of Laila's college recitals.

Tammy wanted to learn piano, an interest probably sparked when Mary Jean Lord babysat her while she was in kindergarten. Mary Jean played piano beautifully, and Tammy often would have heard her playing. This meant we needed to approach my parents about our need for a piano. Mom willingly offered to give us the piano that had been in my family home since I was twelve years old. Abe enlisted his many Arab students to get it up the steps and into our dining room where it stayed all the time we lived on 18th Avenue.

We checked with the Wilson School of Music and learned that Tammy needed to be able to stretch her thumb and little finger an octave before she was really old enough to profit from lessons. She could just barely do that when she turned six, and so her lessons began. Of course, Tammy was not interested in regular practice any more than I had been during my days of studying violin, and we had our share of rows. But the piano was situated directly next to the kitchen where I could see and applaud Tammy's early efforts while I prepared the evening meal. She became quite accomplished and continued lessons through high school. Wilson School of Music did require recitals, and I remember the scary times while she prepared for her performances, but she was a real trooper and did well.

The piano took up a lot of room and didn't really fit well in that room, which we designated the music room. I confess to being the culprit who desecrated my mother's piano. I chose to do it while Abe traveled to Jordan during the summer. He had hoped to take us all home to meet his family in 1967, but in June the war between Egypt and Israel broke out causing us to cancel our plans. By the summer of 1969, we decided he must go home, but we believed that it might still be too politically unstable for all of us to go with him.

So, I kept the girls at home and threw myself into all kinds of household renovations to keep my mind off worrying about him. I refinished the kitchen cupboard doors with a process called antiquing, which required the removal of all doors and application of layers of dark-brown finish. I also boxed up all the dishes and kitchen supplies for well over a week in order to paint the insides of the cupboards a light, creamy, orange-sherbet color. All that upheaval caused difficulty in preparing meals. We ate a lot of scrambled eggs, canned soups, and sandwiches. We also went out for hamburgers far more often than our budget or figures could tolerate.

Conveniently, our good friends Aziz and Kitty Jubran were living close by. Aziz taught at YVC, but our families had been close from our earliest days in Yakima. Aziz, from Palestine, and Kitty, from Alaska, shared common experiences with us. Just like Abe, Aziz immigrated to America and married an American wife. Kitty is the one who noticed the photo in *Sunset Magazine* which put the bug in my brain to redo our ugly dining room.

I started on that project by removing the wallpaper, since it was an old-fashioned floral green to match the rest of the industrial green of the house. In the middle of a very hot summer, I spent hours with a rented steamer attempting to strip the wallpaper. Laila remembers my grumpiness, because whoever applied the wallpaper had not pre-sized the walls, causing the plaster and paper to fuse into a single layer that resisted steaming and peeling. Laila had a vivid memory of me "so fixated on steaming wallpaper" that I gave no thought to dinner. She felt very much "a poor waif" but marvels now that she was too helpless to "make a sandwich or open a can of soup."

I painted the walls a creamy antique-white and changed the window treatments. Aziz was very skilled with tools and constructed wood frame valances just like ones in the magazine, and I covered them with the same cream-colored burlap I'd purchased for the draperies. When he came over to install the valances, we both agreed that these new trappings took up too much room, causing the piano to be even more out of place. I hit upon the idea of pushing the piano back into the alcove where a hutch was supposed to go. But there was a big problem. The old-fashioned piano lid had a crown molding on each end which made it just that many inches too wide to fit in the designated space.

Aziz is a problem-solver, and he had no reservations about suggesting that we amputate the edges. It was just an old piece of furniture which could be made to fit. So I agreed that he could saw off three quarters of an inch on each edge of the piano lid. Success! The piano slipped into place. I covered the top with a nice runner, and nobody was the wiser. No one seemed to mind until Tammy grew up and began to learn the value of truly old furniture. As an adult, she often criticized me for what I did to our piano. She said that it could have been restored if I had saved the pieces. But, I didn't have the sense to do that. After all, I was the one who'd sawn them off in the first place!

The projects were completed and the messes cleaned up before Abe's return. We were so relieved to have him safely home, and he was complimentary about my efforts. He suggested that we should complete the renovations by installing wall-to-wall carpeting in both the music room and the living room. I was delighted at the thought of being done with keeping hardwood floors properly shined. We chose a sculptured design in rich burgundy with tiny flecks of dark-green which complemented all the creams and browns of my summer improvements.

The children didn't suffer unduly during that arduous process. The two of them, along with their friends, practically lived at Franklin Pool. It was just a five-minute walk from our house and cost one dime. Abe left a bowlful of dimes on the mantel so they'd always have money to swim. It was possible to splash away every afternoon from 1:00 to 4:00, come home ravenous, and head back for the evening swim from 6:00 to 9:00.

When not swimming, Tammy and a friend spent hours playing Barbies. There was much changing of doll clothes and all kinds of make-shift contraptions for Barbie furniture. Their non-stop dialogue for the dolls reminded me of the "radio" dramas that Gennie and I produced up at the dam. When not playing Barbies, they were roller-skating or playing Monopoly. They were together for at least eight hours daily most of that summer.

Laila and Tammy also read a lot. I remembered my long, lazy, childhood hours of devouring books from the county library and was pleased that both of our girls were self-motivated readers. They were allowed to read any book that they could understand. Laila read *A Patch of Blue* while still quite young. This story deals with racism and tells the tale of an abused, blind girl and her first love. I happened to be in the living room as she was finishing it and noticed the startling impact it had on her when she reached its revelations. She closed the book quietly and sat there with a shocked expression on her face, then stood up and left the room.

Only once did I take a tough stance on one item Tammy had planned to read. She came home with a stack of bargain books. When I glanced through what she had chosen, I put the kibosh on one that I considered to be purely pulp-pornography. I acknowledged that I had said they could read anything they could understand, but that one was trash, and I didn't want her to read it. Parental supervision took precedence over liberal-mindedness that time.

Kamly Jubran was Tammy's constant playmate during that long summer while I was preoccupied with renovations. They spent great times playing around that sturdy tree in the front yard. It had a perfect rope swing that Abe constructed for them soon after we moved in. He fastened a thick, strong rope to an old rubber tire and firmly attached it to a high branch. The kids loved to twist each other up as tight as possible and then let go for a dizzying, whirling ride as it unwound. It reminded me of the wonderful swing at the Dam which was so important in my childhood. The tree was "home base" for hide-and-seek with six or seven neighborhood kids most every night in the summer. Curfew was when the street lights came on each evening.

This was our home during most of the years our girls were growing up. From Tammy's first day of kindergarten, when she came home asking, "How many more days of school do I have to go to?" to Laila's senior year in high school, our lives revolved around 221 S. 18th Avenue. This was where we lived when Yakima schools finally offered public kindergarten to all students, and I stopped teaching first grade to begin my fifteen years of kindergarten. It was the refuge to which I returned after burying each of my parents.

Our beloved Grandma Jo was the first to go. During Labor Day holiday in 1971, the girls and I met Mom and Dad for a weekend of camping in the hills above Baker, Oregon near the historic gold-mining community of Sumpter. As we drove to our camp spot, we were impressed to learn that this area was the location for filming the musical, *Seven Brides for Seven Brothers*. It was a pretty spot, conveniently halfway between Yakima and Nyssa.

During that trip, Mom and I went for a long walk while she confessed that she had taken a bad fall off the back of the camper while packing it up for the trip. Thinking the tail gate was fastened securely, she depended upon it to climb up. Instead, it gave way and she fell backwards on to the driveway giving her head a good smack. She mentioned that she had been dealing with a nagging headache ever since. I urged her to get to a doctor for a good check-up when they reached home.

A few days after driving back to Yakima, we received a call from Dad saying that Mom was so bad by the time they reached home, she was dazed and throwing up. He got her to the doctor who rushed her to the hospital in Boise. She was diagnosed with a hematoma on her brain and was in need of immediate surgery. Because my school year started that week I needed to call for a substitute. Abe arranged for me to fly to Boise where I stayed with Aunt Geneva. By the time I reached her, Mom had already undergone surgery and was in a coma. I do not know how many days I stayed with her while Aunt Dorothy, Aunt Ernestine, and Aunt Geneva also hovered by her bed, and we all waited for her to wake up. She never did.

I decided to whisper my goodbyes to my silent mother while she still lay in her coma and then I flew back to Yakima. Mom hung on until September 12 before I received the dreaded but expected phone call. Tammy was outside playing hide-and-seek in the early evening and was called home to find Abe, Laila and me sitting together on the Arabic mattresses downstairs, crying. I told her that Grandma was gone, but Tammy didn't know what that meant. She thought I was telling her that Grandma had gotten up and left. It wasn't real to her, and she didn't understand that she wouldn't get to see her Grandma again. Death and funerals just didn't register for her. It didn't become clear to her until the next time we all went to Nyssa and "Grandma really and truly wasn't there."

Of course, my dad was devastated, and I locked my feelings into neutral. I just coped. Abe and I left the girls with friends in Yakima while we drove to Nyssa to be with Dad and help work out the funeral arrangements. We both agreed that the girls need not experience this pain, but we used the excuse that they shouldn't miss school. Looking back, I suspect they regret not being given an opportunity to say their goodbyes.

I know that the decision I made not to view my mother's body didn't sit well with Nyssa friends, but in my mind, she was not there anymore. I wanted to remember her as the fluffy, white-haired, laughing, teasing Jo that I had seen during the camp-out. Every spring since her death I've held my own little memorial when the white irises come into bloom. Their lovely, ruffled, frivolity always reminds me of Mom.

Friends and relatives descended on the house with countless offerings of food. There was a bizarre flurry of dividing up all those pies, cakes, and casseroles into serving-size portions to freeze for Dad. He promised to come for a long visit with us soon, but insisted he first needed some time alone. Dad did come, as promised, almost a year after my mother's death.

I drove to Nyssa and brought him back to stay with us clear through the fall until after the presidential election. He loudly proclaimed that he would cancel my vote for McGovern and was gleeful when Nixon won. Because he was very heavy and suffered from arthritis, he found it painful to move about. Since I was trying to be a good daughter, I waited on him hand and foot, bringing food to him to eat from a TV tray while he sat in the recliner. I didn't fuss when he chose to sleep there all night instead of going downstairs to his bedroom.

My solicitations were not good for him, and he became so stiff he could barely move at all. Wisely, he finally asked Abe to drive him back to Nyssa. It was the first time he ever trusted Abe to do the driving, but he was anxious to get home, knowing he needed to get himself moving and become responsible for himself. Abe realized the steps had no hand-rails, and Dad had become so weak that he was going to have trouble getting into the house.

So, he offered, "Let me help you, Dad." But my father refused to rest all his weight on Abe's shoulder. Abe said he would never forget Dad's realization, "Oh God, there is nobody who loves life more than I do, and just look at me!" Finally, Dad had to crawl up the steps. He didn't want Abe to stay and urged him to turn around and drive back to Yakima before the daylight was gone. Abe left him sitting in his easy chair where he was already making a phone call to his good friends, who planned to stop by with milk and eggs. This was the last time that Abe saw my dad alive.

Back in his own safe surroundings, Dad did improve, and we felt things were looking up for him. In fact, shortly after school let out in June of 1973, he mapped out a driving trip for us. Laila had other plans and chose not to go, but Tammy and I drove to Nyssa to join Dad on a cross-state trip to visit places he had gone with Mom. We left the car in his driveway and rode in his camper, carrying the new tent and folding cots he'd bought for us, and a sleeping bag. I can't say "bags" because I forgot to pack the other one, so Tammy shivered with a bed-roll which was none too warm.

While I rode up front with Dad, Tammy stayed back in the camper, lounging on a giant mattress at the elevation of our heads. She could open up a little set of curtains and see us, but there were two layers of window with no opening between. She remembers being a little dependent on the toilet and leg-stretch stops for company, but she read comics and books for hours, made up stories, and slept a lot.

It was early June and rainy on the west coast so we had a great many picnics in the rain. Grandpa and Tammy would sit in the cab, eating pork-and-beans out of a can while I wrestled with a weak little fire to make coffee or to heat other food. Tammy thought I was "determinedly cheerful." Grandpa was "inclined towards resignedly pessimistic," while she, herself, could be either "whiny or bubbly," depending on her handler.

We drove to the Oregon coast and stopped in Newport. I can still picture Dad, a lonely old man walking with his cane clear out to the end of the pier where he and Mom had taken a boat to go salmon-fishing. Later, we drove south on Highway 101 to the redwoods in Northern California, alternating between motels and camping. I'm sure that Dad relished this memory trip of times long past, and I felt very good that we were able to do it. Abe believed that he was saying goodbye to the world by revisiting these happy places he had previously enjoyed with Mom. That is probably true. A couple of times during that trip, my father forgot himself and called me Jo.

The trip was not without its humor. This was the summer of the Arab oil embargo with long lines at the gas pumps, and Dad worried about running out of gas. Sometimes, after interminable waiting, drivers discovered the station had shut down because it had run out of gas. To avoid this, Dad installed a second gas tank and kept both tanks full at all times. He often stopped to refill even if he'd used only a quarter of the first tank. Finally, I decided to chide him about his obsession. I said, "You know, Dad, the gas in that second tank might become stale if you never use it." His answer was, "Oh, bosh! Gas doesn't get stale." But, I watched him stew over it. No further than thirty minutes down the road, he pulled over and silently switched to the second tank.

On the way home, we would be going right past the turn to Crater Lake. Since I had never seen it, and it was my turn to drive that stretch, I made the turn. Dad had a fit! Not enough gas, too winding a road, he'd already seen it. I stubbornly insisted on continuing. It was, indeed, a twisting, steep ascent, and when we finally reached the top, the entire mountain was fogged in. Dad sat in the camper and fumed while Tammy and I got out and peered into the blanket of mist where Crater Lake would have been if we could have seen it. We've joked about the list of things we've almost done. Crater Lake is at the top of that list!

After leaving Dad in Nyssa, Tammy and I zoomed to Yakima while my head was abuzz with all I needed to accomplish. I was determined to get the yard in shape, and that meant tackling the back-lot weed patch which I optimistically called my "garden." I had an abundance of grandiose ideas which rarely came to fruition. However, I was seldom lonesome while struggling away out there. Laila's friend Catherine enjoyed hanging out with me and helped a great deal as I battled the weeds in the mud, pulling up masses of thistles and chickweed. She liked to garden and was very helpful with this activity that neither of my girls enjoyed. Tammy was grudgingly pressed into duty to gather our piles of weeds and haul them to the compost heap.

While we worked, Catherine and I had great conversations. She was an original! Her thoughts and interests were unique as she conjectured about how things were as opposed to the way they ought to be. She was far ahead of her time in fashion, skillfully designing and sewing many of her own clothes. I loved to hear about what she was constructing and what she was reading. Catherine helped me set out the little Forget-Me-Not plants after we cleared the weeds, and we were very pleased with how the little plants seemed to thrive. Quickly, the bed became so overgrown that I decided to thin them out and share with my friends.

I offered some to Ginger Mansour, who grew up in Yakima and married Nasser Mansour, a Palestinian. The Mansours became the third member of our fearsome-threesome of American wives married to Arabs. By the time I offered to share my Forget-Me-Nots with her, they were settled in a house of their own with a huge backyard. Ginger was even less enamored with gardening than I, but she did want something to fill in a big barren patch in one portion of their yard. So, I dug up all my plants that needed to be thinned and carried the cumbersome box, heavy with muddy soil to her home. I was quite matter-of-fact and definite about the quality of the plants, so she gratefully accepted my gift, and I left.

Sometime later, I watched with dismay as my so-called "Forget-Me-Nots" began to blossom and evolved into just another weed patch. Obviously, I hadn't identified them correctly. Soon after that, at a picnic, I casually informed Ginger, "Oh, by the way, I probably should tell you that those plants I gave you weren't Forget-Me-Nots after all. They turned out to be an invasive weed. I hope you didn't ever get around to planting them." Ginger was thunderstruck because she, who hated to garden, had spent hours on her hands and knees setting out each tiny little plant, and they were thriving.

Happily, Ginger remained a staunch friend. One day, Laila managed to end up with the sewing machine needle jammed completely through her finger. I wasn't home, so she desperately called Ginger, who drove over, applied first-aid to the bloody, bruised finger and rushed Laila to emergency. By the time I arrived home, Ginger had everything under control.

Once, during that summer of 1973, someone reported to me that Laila was seen in Franklin Park, standing under a tree being kissed by a young boy. Laila never mentioned it to me, and I loved Ginger's observation that it was, "Better to be open about it for the whole world to see, than huddled in the back seat of a car."

During that same summer, when Laila was sixteen and Tammy was almost eleven, we finalized plans for our entire family to make our long-postponed trip to Jordan. Our niece, Hana, agreed fly to San Francisco to manage Yacoub Ayyoub's corner grocery, which freed his family to meet us in Chicago, so we could all travel home together.

CHAPTER 15

❖

The Homecoming of a Lifetime

After the June drive to the Oregon coast with my Dad, and after my frantic effort to get some of the backyard garden under control, our attention focused on passports, tickets, and shopping. We filled an entire suitcase with treats such as Lifesavers, Pop Rocks, gum, and other little gifts such as colored pencils, sketch-pads, and children's books that we thought might be appreciated by the many young relations we were about to meet.

Abe knew cash would be the best gift, and he'd saved for two years. When we traveled, he wore a money belt containing over $3000. It would be the equivalent of five or six times that today. That was a significant amount of money, especially considering average incomes in Al Husn at the time. It was extremely important to Abe to be able to share it with his family. During our stay in Jordan, I observed him discreetly slipping twenty-dollar bills into the clothing of tiny children and hundred-dollar bills into the pockets of his beloved elders.

Each of us thought we packed lightly, but when all our clothes and personal things were assembled, it looked like enough paraphernalia to go on safari for two months. In particular, we carried an over-abundance of shoes and later discovered that in the heat and dust of the village, we only wanted a comfy pair of sandals.

We boarded the bright yellow Hughes Air West commuter flight to Seattle knowing we had a tight connection in order to join Yacoub's family in Chicago. It was the girls' first time flying. However, it was a short flight! We circled the airfield twice before our captain announced that the landing gear would not retract and we must return to Yakima. Not a propitious beginning!

Of course, I was frantic. We would miss our connection! The girls were white-faced and silent. Abe immediately took charge to locate some other way to get to Seattle in time, and his efforts paid off. A former student of his had chartered a private plane with enough room for us also. We were so relieved to get our luggage loaded into the six-seater. In no time, we were back in the air, and thirty minutes later we landed in Seattle. After our luggage was checked straight through to Amman, I began to relax.

We had no difficulty finding Yacoub's family in Chicago. They'd arrived earlier and were waiting to greet us at our gate. I renewed acquaintance with Yacoub's wife, Nihad. She and her sons, Khalid and Majid, had been to Al Husn quite often to visit family. Even though I'd met them previously, I immediately began to feel ill-at-ease, realizing that I was the green-horn-Americani who knew nothing!

Before too long, we were all settled on a huge Alitalia airliner and began our long trans-Atlantic flight. Such a long flight was a new experience for the girls and me. I'd come prepared with homework from the beginner conversational Arabic class I took at YVC the previous winter term. All the Americans married to Arabs, along with Tammy, had enrolled together. But Tammy didn't like the teacher, because he had little white balls of spit constantly forming at the corner of his mouth, and she felt like gagging. She often excused herself to go to the restroom where she would while away the class hours by practicing gymnastics on the bars across the top of the ladies' toilet stalls. She said that she got pretty good with her dismount.

Although Tammy didn't profit directly from the class, I knew that I did, and I loaded up all of my notes for study on the plane. I planned to be able to speak proper phrases of greeting when we arrived. Since Nihad was a native of Al-Husn, I kept asking for help with proper pronunciation and attempting to collect new words. She no doubt tired of all my questions, and as the flight droned on, we settled into our own silence, and finally to sleep.

Alitalia served delicious but unfamiliar food. I remember the excellent hard rolls which I felt compelled to defend to our nephews, who thought they were just stale. The girls were tired and numb and knew there was nothing to do but suck it up, because Abe and I were thoroughly stressed in every airport. There was an edge of warning in every look and word from both of us. Tammy loved the Alitalia flight. Anytime she wanted a soda or peanuts, someone would just drop them by. On the other hand, she was totally freaked out by the raw fish or carpaccio they served, but Laila enjoyed the lemony freshness.

Our route was Seattle, Chicago, Milan, Rome, Athens, Cairo, Amman, but not every stop required a plane change. However, we were required to disembark in Rome and wait for a connection. It was a long, tiresome wait, and we saw none of the Roman wonders. The girls and I marked up another item on our "almost got to do" list. Yes, we've been there, but we never left the airport.

When we were finally called to board, there was nothing orderly about it. From our experience in US airports, we thought that a few rows at a time would be called according to pre-assigned seats. I expected that everyone would line up to wait their turn, so I wasn't prepared for the chaos. Passengers pushed and shoved to get through the door, rushed up the ramp, and grabbed the first seats available. We were surprised and alarmed. When I finally realized what was happening, I grabbed the girls' hands while Abe pushed ahead to claim four seats for us. The Yacoub Ayyoubs had to fend for themselves.

It was well over twenty-four hours of total travel time before we finally landed in Cairo where we were to take our final flight. While the other adults handled the officials and documents, Nihad ordered the kids some beautiful-looking lemonade. It looked so refreshing, but it turned out to be strangely bitter and icky sweet at the same time.

It was late evening as Abe presented our carefully organized flight documents and passports. The official shuffled through them, leaving all in disarray, and declared we would have to stay in Cairo overnight. Not only that, he insisted upon keeping all our paperwork. Once again, I was frantic. The heat and humidity felt like I was trying to breathe in an overheated steam room, and we were all so exhausted. I was close to tears as the officials guided us to a dank room with no windows and hard cots. I was so dirty, and we couldn't even change our underwear. I remember trying to wash out my undies, but they didn't dry in the humidity, and I was forced to put them back on wet in the morning.

Still suffering from swollen legs and jet lag, we were relieved the next morning to be given back our documents and allowed to board a flight to Amman. I still don't understand our treatment in Cairo. Abe finally slipped someone a bit of *baksheesh,* and thought that bribe might have been what the officials expected.

I have very little memory of our arrival at Amman International Airport. I do know that we had no trouble going through customs, because members of the family had connections with airport officials, so we sailed right through. Once outside the terminal gates, we were met by Suleiman and all the family of Abe's older brother, Nasser. Tammy felt her cheeks were positively tattooed with kisses. Everyone urged us to come immediately to their home, but Abe wanted to press on to Al Husn. He promised to come back later for several days, and before we knew it, we were piled into taxis and heading down the expressway through Amman and onto the quieter highway leading to Irbid and Al Husn.

I thought all of that study had prepared me to meet my mother and father in-law. After all, my Egyptian professor had been very articulate in teaching what I should say. Hadn't I spent long hours on the plane practicing my very formal greetings? After Nihad gave up on me, I wrote the phrases phonetically in English and pestered Ibrahim to correct me. Never mind that he thought no Jordanian would understand my Egyptian dialect. I was prepared! One of my first decisions during all this preparation was that, while on this trip, I would call my husband by his true Arabic name. Ibrahim was the name by which he was known in Al Husn, and I was determined to fit in by using it.

As our open-windowed taxi drove through the dusty streets of Al-Husn and rolled up to the gate of the Ayyoub family home, we were greeted with the sound of women's ululations. As we stepped from the taxi, I heard *"Ahlan wa Sahlan," "Ahlan wa Sahlan."* "You are welcome." *"Ahlan wa Sahlan."* Grandma Miriam met us with tears streaming down her cheeks, and all the practiced greetings flew from my brain. We entered through the courtyard gate and were enfolded in her arms.

She was dressed all in black, with a soft wool crepe robe, a *shursh*, to her ankles. Her head was covered with a crepe scarf called a *shamber,* which did more than cover her hair. It wrapped firmly around her hair and chin, exposing only her face, and tucked down into the bosom of her robe. From Ibrahim's many stories of her, I was expecting a tall imposing matriarch. Not so! For some reason it surprised me to discover that she was round and short. She had to reach up to clasp my face as she kissed each cheek multiple times.

Most memorable was the beauty of her smile lines etched in the soft folds of her face. There was also a unique aromatic essence to her embrace. It is difficult to describe. Perhaps it was complemented by the odor of lanolin from her wool clothing. There was an aroma of *jameed*, a cooked sauce made from yogurt, which wafted about her and gave us a hint of the meal to come. But I also detected a slight hint of moth crystals. I discovered later that best clothing was always stored away with careful application of moth treatment. Of course, this day would surely call for breaking out the best of everything.

When Miriam could finally allow herself to release me, she enfolded Laila and Tamam with the same embraces. The girls were exhausted, sticky hot, and bewildered. But they did their best to absorb all the newness with grace, and I was very proud of them. Laila was confused by the costumes of her relatives, the ululations, and the multiple kisses, but I couldn't tell by her expression at all. She looked like a tired young lady doing her best to be brave. But later, Laila wrote of her arrival experience:

> Al Husn looked like a monotone of golden beige, domed with a hot blue sky, stone buildings, stones along the roadway, and stone-colored dust in the road. Buildings were small, single-level. I probably would have been scared if I'd had enough energy. When we got out of the car, we were surrounded by women ululating. I had never heard this before, and it frightened me. We were surrounded by large women in long black crepe coverall-dresses, and I wondered how they could bear the feeling of dust and heat. Every stranger I met seemed to need something like six to ten kisses on each side of the face. I was prepared, somehow, for one or two, but all the extras took me by surprise.

Tammy was immediately embraced as the beloved little daughter of Ibrahim who could do no wrong. She was entranced with all the attention heaped upon her by a host of young girl cousins. The younger Jordanian relatives had a fairly good grasp of English, which made getting acquainted much easier for Laila and Tammy. It worked well both ways, because now the cousins had real live Americans with whom to practice their school-book language.

During all this time, Ibrahim was lovingly greeting his father, brothers, sisters, sisters-in-law, nephews, and nieces with hugs and kisses. The courtyard burst with family all talking, smiling and weeping. I received my share of kisses and hugs from Toufiq. He struck me as a beautiful elder. He was taller than Miriam but slightly frail and bewhiskered. He wore a *koufiya* and *agal,* the traditional men's head covering made of white cotton and held in place with a circlet of black rope, and he was dressed in layers. His first visible layer was a black *dishdashi,* a full length gown with mandarin neck, pockets, and long sleeves. Over that was his *meznuk,* a long-sleeved, striped robe made of cotton or soft wool which hung open down the front. Ibrahim was weeping as he kissed his father. Arabic culture is not shy about expressing strong emotions during such a long-awaited occasion.

Greetings continued for a long time. I was finally able to call up one word of Arabic, *"Marhaba,"* Hello. It was a truly pathetic performance, but no one seemed to mind. Language differences created no barriers. We could not speak Arabic, and they spoke no English, but it didn't matter. Their long-lost son with his Americani wife and children had finally come home.

With emotions finally calmed, I was able to notice my surroundings. The cement-covered courtyard could be compared to a family room in the United States except it was in the open air. I learned that this was the place where guests were greeted and entertained; meals were prepared and eaten; and pallets were spread in the late night for sleeping under the stars. It was a walled area suitable for keeping toddlers from wandering, but it also contained a tethered lamb, for our welcome-home feast.

We were ushered from the courtyard into the reception room, urged to be seated, and offered the first of many tiny glasses of hot sweet tea. With the tea, we were served a platter piled high with pastries imported from Damascus, baklava and other delicate sweets whose names I did not know. Both Laila and Tammy fondly remember that the huge stash of baklava was stored in Grandma Miriam's pantry cupboard, because they freely dipped into it whenever they passed that way.

One of the young men made the rounds of the room carrying three tiny cups and a lovely carafe full of coffee. He first offered the American guests a cup with one small sip. This was my first experience with Arabic coffee, and I noted that it contained a trace of cardamom and no sugar. I watched the others and saw that I would be invited to take a cup, drink, and hand the cup back. If I wished another sip, he would pour it. If not, I shook the cup from side to side to indicate "enough," and then the server moved to the next in line. Because we were all "beloved family," immediately it occurred to me that there was no need for washing cups in between servings, Every time visitors arrived from the village, the coffee ceremony was repeated. The supply seemed to be inexhaustible.

Whenever a new group of well-wishers appeared, everyone stood while the guests went around greeting us all. Since we were the reason for guests to be there, we received extra kisses and hugs. Conversation came to a halt and we listened respectfully to the greetings from the new arrivals. At last, we would sit back down, and the visiting would resume. Lacking Arabic to follow the conversation, I was free to observe faces, mannerisms, and surroundings.

I could discern the general ages of the guests by their choice of clothing. People of Toufiq and Miriam's generation dressed as they did. Some of the really aged women had tattoos on their foreheads, cheeks, and hands. Men of Ibrahim's generation came in suits and ties, while the women wore their best dresses. The next generation wore T-shirts and jeans or short dresses.

The older men all had their *misbaha*, a little string of beads on a strong cord. The beads were worked with the fingers of one hand around the circle. When the beads came to a central fastener, the fingers deftly flipped the circle and started back in the opposite direction. *Misbaha* look somewhat like a rosary but are not for prayers and get little attention. It is just something to do with the hands. I could relate personalities to their choice of *misbaha*. Quiet, shy, listener types often had very tiny wooden or metal beads. The brassy talkers who tried to dominate the conversation usually preferred large, showy colored-glass beads.

I sipped my tea and looked around. In America, it could have been the waiting area of a doctor's office. Three walls were lined with twenty or more comfortable, high-quality chairs. The many chairs were needed in order to accommodate a constant flow of visitors who arrived every day and evening. From Ibrahim's memory of this room, I could see that little had changed. Although he'd come back after years in America, it was clear that time had stood still for the physical surroundings of his family home. The fourth corner was still arranged for comfort in Arabic style, and I immediately related it to the cozy nest we had created in our Yakima basement.

The same flat mattresses were there with brightly-colored cushions. And Toufiq, as head of the family, held forth in the place of honor. As an honored leader of the village, there was no need for him to dominate conversation. But his words were always treated with deference, since most guests who were there had, at one time or another, benefited from his wise leadership and advice.

The creosote-treated thatch and timbers of the ceiling were exactly as Ibrahim had remembered them. I was pleased to recall the stories he'd related to me of all the happenings which ocurred on that roof. There were the two-foot-thick plastered, hollow walls with their openings for wheat storage. The walls were still bare of decoration except for the two portraits placed very high, almost to the ceiling. One honored Toufiq's dear friend, and the other was of my husband just before he left for the United States.

In 2005, I was given the opportunity to revisit the family home. Of course, Toufiq and Miriam were both deceased by that time, and the complex was rented to other tenants. Nevertheless, I was astounded to discover Ibrahim's dusty portrait still attesting to the blessings his parents had bestowed upon their son so long ago. Using a long-handled rake, we worked to lift it off the wall and brought it back across the ocean where it could occupy a new place of honor.

That first day of our visit stretched into evening, and after a good meal prepared by Miriam and Naimeh, we were ushered into the sleeping room for much-needed rest. In preparation for our arrival, the women of the family had taken apart, washed, and left to sun-dry all the family comforters. These marvelous coverlets were made of wool encased in white cotton covers, and loosely quilted. Comfy floor mattresses were spread invitingly around the sides of the room, and they beckoned to our travel-weary bodies. Nihad, Laila, and I were grateful to sink into them, and we quickly slipped into deep sleep. The men and children took over the courtyard, and Ibrahim could once again fall asleep beneath the night sky. Tammy remembered a special comforter with a blue satin back that stayed cool to the touch despite the weight of the cover. She claims it was the best sleep she ever had in her whole life, ever.

Over the next few days, we settled into the family's routine. Mornings greeted us with hot sweet tea and marvelous *khubiz*, pocket bread freshly baked in the early morning at the homes of Naimeh and Subha, Miriam's daughters. With it we ate *labneh*, which is yogurt dripped through a cloth, formed into balls and packed into jars of olive oil, and *jubne*, a sheep's-milk cheese preserved in salted water. The *jubne* and *labneh* were stored in huge glass jars on high shelves that lined Miriam's little kitchen. Cheese and yogurt are made only after spring lambing when the sheep are being milked, and Miriam and her daughters worked long hours, days, and months to prepare extra stores in anticipation of our arrival.

After breakfast, we had time to prepare ourselves for the day. In a separate area of the family compound, there were a very small dining room and the kitchen with a two-burner hot plate, a sink with a cold water faucet, and a pantry cupboard. There was no refrigerator until Abe purchased and installed one during this visit. Adjoining the kitchen was the modern bathroom which had recently been constructed with toilet and shower in anticipation of our visit. The area which was rebuilt into the bathroom used to be the chicken coop where baby Ibrahim committed his egg-stealing crimes so long ago. Outside these buildings, in the courtyard next to the tethered lamb, was an ancient hole-in-the-floor toilet house, which was still useable.

The new shower was fed from a tank on the roof filled with water piped from a city reservoir and warmed by the sun. Prior to our arrival, there had been no piped water into the home. Laila remembers that I vigorously admonished her to use water sparingly. "Get wet; turn off water quick; lather with soap; shampoo; quick, quick, quick rinse-off." She was enchanted by the bathroom, which was a simple concrete room, complete with a drain, toilet, sink, and a high window. The shower was a spout and faucets in the wall. There was no enclosure, no curtain. She says that remains her favorite, the most wonderful shower of her whole life. She found it hard to stop and follow the rules about water conservation but understood and took pride in doing her best. She was grateful for the chance to rinse off the sticky dust, and also was grateful for the solitude.

It was unrealistic of me to expect them to understand, but I knew that the tank had to be refilled slowly with some sort of siphoning technique, and then time had to pass for the water to be warmed by the sun. So as our family used the bathroom to clean up in the morning, I patrolled the area to be sure the girls only used the water that was absolutely necessary. I even required Tammy to share the shower with me so that I could control it.

Soon after I had seen to the morning needs of my family, it was time to prepare for the daily influx of visitors who began arriving in the early afternoons. The girls were free to head off with their cousins, while Ibrahim and I spent time with each group of friends. Of course, it was a time of great joy for Ibrahim, and he luxuriated in renewing past friendships. I, on the other hand, was dependent on translators. Usually there was someone in the group who took pity and sat down beside me to explain what was being said.

I quickly discovered where my husband's ability to tell a great story had originated. His father was a master! We spent late afternoons and evenings in the shade of the courtyard or under the stars while conversation flowed. There was never a need for TV or other electronic amusement. Although stories were related in Arabic, someone always made the effort to translate for me. Family tales were repeated with gusto and punctuated with laughter. Then, there would be a pause for translation and we would all enjoy the laugh again. This was how I learned much of the mischief caused by young Ibrahim. Also, I heard the fabulous Joha stories that had been shared during Ibrahim's college vacation summers.

One afternoon, some of the young people remarked that they would like to go to America so that they could experience the things they saw on television. Ibrahim and I answered back, "Why would you? You have such wonderful evenings with good conversation right here. Who needs television?" It was quite evident that they didn't agree with our viewpoint. When we visited again in 2005, we noticed that in most Al Husni homes the television now plays a major role in daily life. Consequently, evenings of storytelling and good conversation have diminished in the same way as happened in America.

There was another noticeable change during our 2005 visit. The *misbaha* were replaced with modern technology. Just one or two of the older men were moving beads through fingers while visiting. Instead, almost every man had a cellphone in his shirt pocket, with its distinctive ring tones sounding off, beckoning its owner away from the conversation. But in 1973, that lovely old courtyard was awash in rich conversation, sharing what was happening in present-day lives and fondly remembering days gone past.

The courtyard had a lower room, the oldest of the complex. I never went into that room, since it was being used for storage and seemed to be somewhat like a basement where one tucks out of sight all of the necessary items of the household. I learned that this older room was once the family living area. Toufiq brought his young bride to live there. But when we arrived in 1973, it had been relegated to a storage area. I saw Saad or Naim carry items down those steps and bring out other containers of foodstuffs, which they handed over to women in the kitchen. Ibrahim told me this was where he went, as a young child, to fill his dishdashi with stored wheat that he planned to trade for apples in the market, but then thought better of his actions in order to show respect for his father.

Unwittingly, I contributed to the convenience of that storage area. I'd noticed that over by the lamb there were a few small tins containing household waste. Thinking the family must have need for a garbage can, I went with Ibrahim into nearby Irbid and insisted he purchase a tall plastic garbage bin. Miriam took one look at it and immediately put it to use as a container for storing foodstuffs away from cats, rodents and ever-present insects. She was amazed that I would think it should be used for garbage!

Other new things also came Miriam's way. Suleiman's wife, Um Omar, purchased some strong paper towels in Irbid. The first time Miriam used one, she carefully rinsed it out and draped it over a line to dry, asking if these "towel-papers" cost too much money. She appreciated their wonders and hoped it might be possible to own more. I'm quite sure that she never purchased more for herself once she knew they were disposable. Her thrifty re-use of the ones she had explains why I've often seen Ibrahim washing out paper towels and drying them in our home. Like mother, like son!

In 1973, pottery, glass, or bags were used for storage. However, during our later visit in 2005, I was dismayed to see everyone using plastic bags, disposable diapers, and other throwaway conveniences, as most Jordanians seemed to be unaware of what was happening to their environment. As these products became available, they welcomed them enthusiastically. But, as happens in emerging economies, it requires time and effort for the majority of citizens to embrace effective waste disposal. No framework for recycling had yet been established. As a result, we looked out on vacant fields and roadsides that bloomed with thousands of discarded plastic bags. Our relatives saw the plastic disposables as a scourge descended upon their country.

But during that first visit in 1973, I was full of admiration for Miriam's skill in re-using every small item, and I marveled to discover many similarities between her household management and that of my homesteading grandparents in Idaho. Miriam was a master in preserving food stuffs without modern conveniences. She employed the same techniques as my Grandmother Leoda. Both Leoda and Miriam spent their lives preserving food with salt or with sun-drying. Refrigeration was not yet possible for either of them, and ice was a rare and dear commodity.

When Ibrahim had the refrigerator installed, Miriam was not too comfortable with using cold as a means of preventing spoilage. We often saw her carefully cover left-over food and place it in her pantry cupboard just as she had always done. Keeping things cold during a hot summer day was a new concept for her. Also, she remembered an earlier experience of eating her first cold food. During a rare visit to the city, someone served ice cream, and she found the cold on her tongue such a shock, she couldn't decide whether to spit it out or let it slide painfully on down her throat!

When I contemplate all of Ibrahim's stories about Miriam's food preparation and preserving, it doesn't surprise me that the refrigerator was regarded with suspicion. But, with all the visitors that summer and the mountains of food that needed to be safely stored, it became a useful appliance. For sure, Suleiman's wife, Um Omer, and Naim's wife, Siham, appreciated its convenience as they assisted their mother-in-law. Um Omer was caring for busy little three-year-old Maha and baby Omar. Their Aunty Siham was like a second mother, so both women had their hands full. I tried to be of help and make friends with Maha, but I had no success at all. She wouldn't come near me, and told her mama that "Aunty Doris doesn't know how to talk right."

That situation came full circle when we returned in 2005. By then, Maha, now a research scientist with a doctorate in pharmacology, and I had become the best of friends. It was Omar's little girl, Natalie, and his even younger son, Samer, who would have nothing to do with me. I had brought all kinds of books and toys in an effort to entice them with not much luck. Again and yet again, my life has experienced unnecessary obstacles because I've never learned Arabic.

Tammy was mistakenly enchanted that her new-found Grandma Miriam had obligingly provided her with a pet lamb for the visit. Neither the girls nor I were fully aware of the lamb's future when we arrived. But soon, the lamb was no longer tied in its accustomed corner. Long before we awoke, the lamb had met its fate. It was killed in preparation for our welcome feast.

Tammy remembered the lamb's disappearance as personal. I had to coach her to accept that the lamb had been killed in honor of our visit and that we would likewise honor him for fulfilling his lamby destiny. The way he was so completely consumed was respectful. I can still see Tammy's sad little face as I tried to make her understand, and she was very noble about not showing her dismay in front of her Jordanian relatives. But for one who falls so completely in love with all animals, it was a difficult life-and-death lesson.

After that, Tammy focused on taming the many *bissas* who roamed the compound. They were feral cats, tolerated by the family because they controlled the rodents but were never considered pets. Our Jordanian family was amazed to watch Tammy coaxing "Here kitty, kitty, kitty," for them to come close to her so she could give a quick pat or slip them a morsel of food. Saad, Abe's youngest brother, took special notice of her interest in the cats and would follow her around repeating, "*Bissa, Bissa, Bissa.*" We learned later that after our visit, Saad continued to give special attention to Tammy's *bissas* by petting them and slipping them leftover bits of food. We were told that one little cat was even named *Bissat Tamam,* Tammy's cat.

Attention to details such as caring for the *bissas* was characteristic of Saad. He was the last-born of Miriam's eleven children. A young man with special needs, he was kept close, loved, and sheltered by Miriam as long as she was alive. Older siblings urged that he be allowed to attend a school for specialized training, but Miriam refused even to consider sending her beloved Saad away. His vocabulary was limited, and he required assistance with many daily tasks. However, his memory for detail was acute. If Miriam needed to know where a certain item had been stored, Saad could immediately fetch it.

At first, our girls were fearful of his unusual behavior, louder than usual laugh, and constant repetition of words. Laila found him a little scary, but she remembers his repeating aloud the names of what was being prepared for dinner, such as the green bean, meat, and tomato stew called *fasoulia*, and then giggling with delight after each repetition. Uncle Saad really enjoyed his food. Laila understood then that he wasn't scary, but very happy, enjoying simple things all day long. After all these years, remembering him say *jelly* or *fasoulia* "provokes a great lump of joy" to fill up in her heart. Everybody has a gift and a lesson to teach, and Saad's was joy.

While Tammy was occupied with the *bissas,* Miriam began portioning the lamb. The first morning, we breakfasted on the liver, kidney, tongue, and testicles chopped fine and sautéed in *samneh,* clarified butter, along with fresh bread for sopping up the juices. Next, Miriam began the major process of preparing *Mensafe,* a special meal of lamb, rice, and sauce, for our celebration feast. To accomplish this time-consuming preparation, Miriam was joined by her two married daughters, Subha and Naimeh, who lived nearby.

Suleiman's, Naim's, and Yacoub's wives also came to help. The preparation and serving of *Mensafe* had not changed a bit from the days when Miriam reined as Queen of Kwaiseh so long ago during Ibrahim's college summer vacation. Consequently, special memories revisited him while the aromas, flavors, and cooking techniques were all new to me. I was not allowed to become part of the work crew. As the Americani guest, I was onlooker and note taker, rapidly scribbling all the details in my diary.

I described the preparation of many meals in that little diary, and the majority of them required hours of elaborate effort. For sure, the preparation of *Mensafe* was an expression of the Ayyoub women's artistic abilities, so I felt a bit of dismay to see how quickly the culinary beauty disappeared. We sat down to a spread of artfully arranged and decorated dishes. We smiled, thanked the hands which made it, "*tislam adeki,*" and then proceeded to destroy it all. Since that first feast, I have been treated to Mensafe on many occasions and have even prepared it in my own home. But the memories of sharing it that first time will always have precedence.

All edible components were eventually consumed. The ears and leg knuckles were tucked away for a future meal when they were cooked along with the head, which was roasted and scraped to remove all hair and impurities. Also, the stomach and intestines were meticulously cleaned, stuffed with bits of meat and rice, and simmered with a huge pot of *Warak Dawali,* stuffed grape leaves, and stuffed *Kousa,* zucchini.

The hide was scrubbed with a curing mixture, wrapped in a cloth, and tucked away in that mysterious lower room. Months later, it arrived in the mail as a gift in memory of our feast. All I need to do is bury my face in the soft wool and sniff to bring back the memory of our treasured visit.

On a different day during our visit, I learned how to prepare *moghrabia*. I had previously eaten couscous, but I had no idea how it was made, so we watched one afternoon while Miriam prepared it. Her feet were bare and, she sat on the floor with her back against the wall of the little dining room.

My girls huddled around her as we all watched the miraculous motion of her ever-moving hands. Finely-ground bulghur was soaked for several hours, and then excess water was drained. In the meantime, she prepared a bowl of unbleached flour and another bowl of salted water with yeast and turmeric.

Miriam makes Mograbia

Miriam placed the bulghur in a flat pan on the floor, sprinkled a small amount of flour over it and began to rub it with her hands in a careful circular motion. Then she added a tablespoon of water and rubbed again. This process continued with alternate applications of flour and water which begin to coat each kernel of bulghur. Since she had no English, and we had very little Arabic, communication was carried on with smiles and nods. She saw that I was writing down notes, so she told one of the cousins what I needed to know, and they translated.

The process seemed to go on for hours, but her gently moving hands never slowed or faltered. Finally, each kernel had built up to the size of a lentil. When she was satisfied, she rose and carried the pan out into the courtyard to dry in the hot sun. Only then did I see her stretch her back and indicate that now she would relax. It was such a hot afternoon, we all agreed to join her in taking a bit of rest.

While we were resting, the sun shifted, and the shade covered the grains. Later we noticed a long trail of ants, one by one, marching our *moghrabia* up the courtyard wall and away from the drying basin. Insects will not disturb foodstuffs in the heat of the sun, but food must not be allowed to rest in the shade. We heard Grandma Miriam begin to shout, "*Nimli, Nimli, Nimli,*" Ants, Ants, Ants. She quickly moved what was left out of harm's way.

My daughters thought it was hilarious and we immediately made up a new version of "The Ants Go Marching One by One":

Nimli go marching *wahad be wahad,* one by one — Hurrah, Hurrah!

Nimli go marching *wahad be wahad,* — Hurrah, Hurrah!

Nimli go marching *wahad be wahad,* the little one stops to grab *moghrabia*

And they all go marching up the wall to have a ball.

After much giggling and translating, the younger nieces and nephews joined in with our singing. Grandma Miriam must have thought we'd all lost our minds.

The rest of a couscous meal consisted of boiling lamb or chicken in salted water with tomato juice, whole small onions and what we dubbed "Grandma Spice," which is a special blend of spices that Miriam created with equal parts cinnamon and allspice, with a touch of clove and nutmeg. The *moghrabia* was placed over the boiling meat in a large, flat sieve like a double boiler, and covered with a damp cloth.

The grains steamed for an hour, emitting the aroma of a heavenly stew. After that, Miriam quickly stirred in butter, salt, and two cups of stock. This time, she covered the *moghrabia* with a lid before placing it back over the simmering meat for another hour. When it was served, we were treated to a bowl of savory, tender meat and vegetables, surrounded with delicate golden grains floating in the broth. Ambrosia! Once again, a work of art rapidly disappeared in many mouths.

When I returned to Yakima, I taught a Social Studies unit about Jordan to my kindergarten class. Every little child had a chance to rub the grains, using the same circular motion as Miriam's to form the kernels of *moghrabia*. I showed them the photos of Grandma Miriam and watched them giggle as they imagined the thievery of the ants. Their finished product was somewhat lumpy compared to that of the expert, but it cooked up okay and smelled delicious. For the unit culmination, we served *moghrabia* to their parents, retold the story of the ants that stole our food, and raucously belted out the song.

While in Al Husn, I was treated as a guest and therefore I was not given much opportunity to cook. One day, I happened to pass through the kitchen while the morning milk was being pasteurized. I realized that it was about to boil over so I turned off the burner and went to report to Miriam. Having such limited Arabic, the only thing I could think to do was exclaim, "*Haleeb!*" the word for milk, then wiggle my fingers and say "bub, bub, bub!" She burst into a wide grin, and soon everybody present was teasing me about bub, bub, bub. But I'd made my meaning clear and the *haleeb* was rescued.

In fact, I had only one truly successful cooking experience during our time there. I was given the opportunity to prepare a meal for Toufiq, who had undergone gall bladder surgery earlier in the summer. Saad loved to display the jar containing the huge grey gall stones that had been removed from his father. As a consequence of slow recovery, Toufiq had not felt much like eating when we arrived. The family kept pressing him with small delicacies to tempt his appetite and most were refused.

One morning, Ibrahim approached me with a problem. He needed to take Miriam and most of the other family members to a notary in Amman to sign land transfer papers. Toufiq didn't need to go, so the girls and I would be left alone with him all day. Ibrahim asked if I could manage to prepare some sort of meal for his father. I did a quick mental inventory. I knew how to light the propane burner with a match, and I had noticed a jar of red lentils, some onions, and a plate of chopped lamb meat on the pantry shelf. There was plenty of fresh-baked *Kubiz* under the bread sheet, and I also knew where the spices and lemons were stored. So I replied that I could cook *margat adas,* a lentil and meat soup.

Needless to say, my confidence was superficial. But, I knew that Toufiq would be resting on his mattress in the courtyard shade and my girls could offer encouragement. No one else would be there to make me feel nervous if I fumbled a bit. So I talked myself into believing that I could do it. When the family took off by taxi for Amman, I began to cook. I sautéed the meat and onions in *zeit zeitoon,* olive oil, a little salt and Grandma Spice. Then, I added a large quantity of water and lentils and covered the pot to simmer. I checked regularly to be sure nothing boiled over and worried how it would turn out. I found myself checking the taste more often than usual, adding a bit of pepper or salt then stirring some more, maybe a touch more Grandma Spice, perhaps a small glug of olive oil. I felt just like a bride might feel, attempting my first meal for the in-laws. No room for mistakes today!

The soup continued to cook until the lentils began to melt. Then I seasoned with more salt and pepper, and added a flour paste to create a golden brown, slightly thickened porridge. There was a lot! When the meal was prepared, I went to Toufiq and said, *"Tafadalou."* Come to eat. This was an important word in my limited Arabic vocabulary. Toufiq left his mattress and came to sit at the tiny table in the dining area.

I poured a large bowl of soup, provided bread, and cut a fresh lemon for him to squeeze over the dish. He said nothing but proceeded to eat noisily until the bowl was empty. I offered more and he accepted a second bowl. Then, still saying nothing and giving no indication of his opinion, he returned his spoon to the bowl and went to his mattress. My only indication of success rested in the amount he ate. The girls and I ate our share, cleaned the kitchen and stored the remaining soup in the pantry.

In early evening, the family returned. Toufiq asked if there was any more of that soup. His womenfolk, happy to see him ask for food, heated it up and he consumed another two bowls full. Then he called Ibrahim over to sit beside him on his mattress and asked very seriously, *"Ala ta'rifu anna hadik el-akleht shatwiyeh?"* Don't you know that this is a winter meal?

It has become our delightful family story. A man so sick he had not felt like eating, consumed four bowls of hot lentil soup on a scorching summer day and said nothing of praise except to note that I should have known this was a meal to be served only in winter. From that day forward, we chuckle every time we sit down to "a winter meal" even in the summer.

Soon after my culinary triumph, we began a series of short trips to visit other areas of Jordan. We spent three days with Nasser in Amman. Their home was close enough to allow us to visit the 2000-year-old Roman Theater situated in the middle of the city. Nasser's daughters escorted us, and we learned that it was built by the emperor of Philadelphia, as Amman once was known. As I climbed the steep stone steps to its top tier of seats for 6,000 people, I tried to imagine what it must have been like to sit there long ago and watch a play. The theater is still a venue for performances.

Ibrahim stayed with Nasser while we toured, but he remembered how close his school was to the Roman Theater during the year he attended fourth grade in Amman. Directly to the left of the stage, the exit emptied into a large paved courtyard in front of the King's *diwan,* where citizens could have an audience with the King. It was where Ibrahim had been escorted to the government school. I marvel that he studied so near this ancient Roman structure. I asked him if its magnitude ever filled him with awe while he was there as a young boy. He said he was used to all those places, because he went to see them on school trips.

During our short stay in Amman, I was intrigued with the morning ritual of bread vendors cycling past the house balancing huge platters on their heads piled high with a special kind of flat bread. The vendors confidently wheeled in and out of traffic at quite a speed as they called out, "*Ka'ek, Ka'ek.*" Householders would come out to buy their wares. One morning, Nasser went into the street to purchase some of the bread for us.

It was shaped like a large flat donut which was puffed up and hollow within the ring. Some *Ka'ek* had spices inside or sesame seeds. It was chewy and quite different from the regular *khubiz* we knew. I found this new bread quite tasty, but I was most impressed with the skill the vendors exhibited in balancing those gigantic trays on their heads while negotiating Amman traffic. In fact, Amman traffic is so congested I couldn't imagine attempting to drive there, let alone ride a bicycle and tote a burden of bread on my head.

Nasser's wife and daughters were gracious hosts. When they learned that Tammy would be celebrating a birthday while we were guests, they baked two lovely birthday cakes for her. Tammy just glowed from all the attention. Both Laila and Tammy were impressed with the skill with which the younger set of Ayyoub relatives spoke English, and it bothered them that they couldn't reciprocate in Arabic. They were even more bothered by the way that I, their mother, lapsed into speaking what they described as stilted, pidgin-English when conversing with them. I made a conscious effort to speak slowly and choose my words carefully since they were non-native English speakers.

Both girls were highly critical of my language on one occasion. During our visit in Amman, we were invited to lunch at the home of Saad Habjoka. Mr. Habjoka had previously been a guest in our Corvallis apartment when he studied at Oregon State University. His family wanted to return our hospitality. Now, he was president of the Bank of Amman and a close associate of King Hussein. Mr. and Mrs. Habjoka both spoke perfect English. To her credit, Mrs. Habjoka did not in any way indicate that my stilted responses were poorly executed. I was not even aware of what I was doing, but my children were dismayed. When the visit ended, I was raked over the coals for sounding like an uneducated country bumpkin. I didn't do them proud, and they let me know it.

I was not prepared for what an Arabic "lunch" really meant. Our family was overwhelmed with the five-course meal containing at least three entrees. Mrs. Habjoka served us *Warak Dawali*, grape leaves stuffed with meat and rice, *Kefta*, a roasted meatloaf of ground lamb, onions, and parsley, and *Sesan Mhammara*, chicken roasted with onions and spices. The meal also included appetizers of tiny individual T-bones seasoned with cardamom. We picked them up with our fingers, rather like eating ribs, to chew the thin strip of meat around them. We also had rice pilaf, and tomato-cucumber salad. Laila was especially impressed with the slices of cold melon served as a final course, since both children longed for vegetables and fresh cold fruits.

When I reflected on our humble surroundings in that Corvallis apartment where we entertained Saad Habjoka so long ago, I felt shy to be a guest in his lovely home. All I can think is that during Mr. Habjoka's lonely stay in Corvallis, Ibrahim must have offered a friendship and hospitality that meant a great deal to him. For sure, my effort to serve him authentic Arabic food couldn't have been much more than baking up some fair-to-middling homemade pocket bread. However, Mr. Habjoka kindly told me that he remembered being served some delicious homemade pizza.

Shortly after our lovely afternoon, we went back to Al Husn. The young men of the family were pleased to learn we toured the Roman Theater and began to urge Ibrahim to take us to more of the ancient wonders in Jordan. Although reluctant, Ibrahim finally agreed to be a good husband and arrange for us to see Petra. After all, how could he deny his family the opportunity to view what has been described as one of "the seven most amazing human creations on the planet."

To reach Petra, we needed to make a long, 300 kilometer drive south across flat desert to *Wadi Musa*, Valley of Moses. Ibrahim bargained for a private taxi to take us from Amman to Petra and back. It was a hot, exhausting trip across land that seemed to contain just one type of low-growing green plant. Our driver explained, in broken English, that camels were the only animals that would eat its spiny, bitter leaves.

The driver agreed to wait around for hours while we climbed on horseback and traveled the narrow path between steep rock walls to reach the ancient site. What a thrill to end that dark, winding path and see it open into the marvelous vista of The Treasury!

At that time Petra was not yet heavily developed into a tourist facility. Because of this, there were no guides with long speeches explaining the history and wonders. We walked around and marveled at the hillsides carved with

Sketch of camel

dwellings. I did learn from our driver that Petra was populated by the Nabataeans. They devised a water system which drew camel caravans and encouraged commerce. The driver also told us that Petra fell under Roman rule for centuries and that major earthquakes had caused heavy damage.

Since our head guide was Ibrahim Ayyoub, the world's least interested tourist, he soon pushed us to begin our journey back to Amman. By then, our driver, who was becoming more comfortable conversing with the lady and girls in the back seat, began to urge that we also must be sure to see Jerash. I replied that we had begged Ibrahim to stop there each time we drove between Amman and Al Husn. We complained that our request was always denied. So the driver turned to Ibrahim, his seatmate up front, and asked him in Arabic if he had ever been to Jerash. Ibrahim had to ask in Arabic, "What is Jerash like?" The driver ratted on him to us in English, and then we really made a fuss and vowed to report him to the folks back in Al Husn.

After that, thanks to the driver's influence, several of the young Ayyoub men arranged for us to spend an afternoon in Jerash. Once again, Ibrahim chose not to go. He was adamant that he had gone to Jerash with a school group while still a child and that he was not impressed by "just a bunch of old Roman columns and fallen-down buildings." When we were begging him to stop and see it, he had no interest in repeating his earlier experience. This would not be the only antiquity that Ibrahim refused to re-visit that summer.

We discovered that Jerash was even older than Petra, going back to prehistoric times. Although earthquakes and battles wreaked great damage during its long history, we were able to identify the Triumphal Arch and the Street of Columns, the main street of the city. Many tall columns still stand that lead to the Forum. We were awed that ruts made by the wheels of passing chariots can still be seen in the paving blocks. As I stood sheltered from the afternoon sun, beside one of the columns, I imagined I could hear the chariots' rumbling wheels rolling towards me.

The Forum, erected some time during the second century AD, was definitely a highlight for the girls. Laila was studying debate in high school, and when she learned that it was not only a marketplace, but also a gathering place for political discussions and debates, she marched to the middle of the huge paved space, climbed up on the centre plinth designed for a statue and loudly proclaimed the opening of Mark Antony's speech from *Julius Caesar*, "Friends, Romans, countrymen, lend me your ears." Tammy and I sat on the stone risers to serve as her audience. Tammy thought her sister's speech was so cool that she mimicked sections of it after that whenever we came close to another Roman ruin. I couldn't help feeling sad that Ibrahim had not come with us to enjoy his daughter's Roman debut

CHAPTER 16

———◆———

In the Thick of Regional Life

AFTER OUR VISIT TO Jerash, we accompanied Ibrahim's brothers and their families to the West Bank in Jerusalem and Bethlehem. Subha and Naimeh also joined us, so we became a large group gathered to cross at the border. This journey became the most difficult travel experience that we encountered during our entire visit to the Middle East. Before we could start, we had to obtain entry visas for Israel, which meant traveling by taxi to Amman. Also, we had to be sure that we got special papers instead of our passports for the Israelis to stamp, since an Israeli stamp in our passport would prohibit us from returning to any Arab country that does not recognize Israel.

From Amman, we hired taxis to take us to the Allenby Bridge, the sole designated exit/entry point for Palestinians living in the West Bank. It took about an hour to reach the "Crossing Point" east of Jericho along the Jordan River. There, after paying an exit tax and ensuring that our paperwork was in order, we loaded ourselves and our belongings into a shuttle. We were charged a transport fee plus extra for each piece of luggage for the five kilometers to the Israeli terminal.

It was just a lot of hassle up to this point, but then something happened which really disturbed me. When we presented our papers to the Israeli authorities, Ibrahim, the girls and I were directed to queue up in a much shorter line situated in a cleaner, sheltered section of the terminal, while all our relatives were herded towards a long, unshaded line of Jordanian and Palestinian travelers. The official explained that we did not have to be in that line because we were Americans.

Many years later, after September 2001, dividing airport queues into Americans and foreigners was often repeated in the United States. Of course, the division was a foolish and ineffective attempt at security in the aftermath of the World Trade Center attack, but in 1973, as I stood there with my family, I felt the Israeli authorities were intentionally determined to humiliate the Palestinians.

When I finally understood what was happening, I maintained my outward composure, but I seethed inside and adamantly refused to follow the official's directions.

I insisted that we remain in the same line as the rest of our family. Because of this, we underwent the same degrading experience that happened to all Palestinians at this crossing. The luggage inspectors tore through my carefully folded clothing and personal items, leaving our cases in shambles. I was required to go into a private inspection booth with a female guard, and one of my sisters-in-law told us she was made to strip down to bra and underpants. My nephew had the chunky heel of his stylish boot sliced open because the guards suspected it might be used for smuggling.

Knowing that we would be staying with our relatives for about ten days, we had packed only what was needed, leaving the remainder of our luggage in Al Husn. Our family told us that for some unknown reason certain items like newly purchased lipsticks or small household appliances could cause difficulty at the border. Because of this, my sisters-in-law requested that I pack their purchases in my luggage, since they would be confiscated if discovered among Palestinian possessions, but would be allowed in the suitcase of an American.

Our whole party was held up for over two hours, because the inspectors were suspicious of the book that Laila had with her. It was a high-school textbook, *Strategic Debate*, she needed to study. When they discovered it, the inspectors called in supervisors, and we wondered if we would need to wait around while they read the entire thick book.

After a lengthy wait, they brought her book back with the admonition that she should not attempt to smuggle contraband literature into their country. Who knows what alarmed them about it? Perhaps it looked suspicious because it had an official look about it, or their English was not strong enough to understand that it was simply a textbook. The whole episode deeply embarrassed our young daughter, and I kept thinking that it could have been avoided if we had been less naïve. The entire experience had dangerous potential. We would not have been the first to be arrested for innocent transgressions.

In fact, during the summer of 1969 when Ibrahim traveled across this same border, he easily could have been arrested. That was the summer when the girls and I stayed in Yakima while he visited his family, and I anxiously threw myself into the work of remodeling the 18th Avenue house to keep my mind distracted from worrying about his safety. There was good reason to worry about him, since it was only two years after the Six-Day War, and border security was extremely tight.

There is seldom any room for levity at that border, because Palestinians feel very much "under the thumb" of authoritarian oppression, but when Ibrahim came home, he told us of his confrontation with the Israeli soldiers, and we laughed uproariously at the comic situation. When Ibrahim arrived at the terminal on the Israeli side, the soldiers told him to sit down at their table for questioning.

It was obvious that they spoke little English and no Arabic. They asked him, "Do you have money?" As Ibrahim answered, "Yes," they asked, "Show us the money." So, he stood up to unbuckle his money belt. The alarmed soldiers misunderstood his actions and yelled, "No, No, No! Sit down!"

Ibrahim stopped and sat back down. Then the two soldiers, looking at him closely, asked again, "Do you have money?" Ibrahim stood up as he answered, "Yes," and began to remove his money belt. Their response was the same, "No, No, No, sit down!" Once again, Ibrahim complied with their command and sat back down. For the third time and speaking with vehemence, they repeated their question, "Do you have money?" This time when Ibrahim heard, their "No, No, No, sit down," he just continued to pull his money belt from his pants-loops against their orders. Then he unzipped the pockets inside the belt and laid everything on the inspection table.

By then, the soldiers were obviously angry, as was Ibrahim. The soldiers heatedly discussed in Hebrew what to do and they finally called their superior. The officer spoke with them and then turned to Ibrahim and said in precise English, "We are going to teach you a lesson. When we say to show us your money, you just show your money!"

Ibrahim answered, "The problem is communication with your officers and misinterpretation of my actions. The money is in my belt. When I stand up to remove the belt, they do not understand and shout, "No, No, No, sit down!" The superior asked the soldiers if this were true. When they affirmed it, he turned to apologize to Ibrahim and instructed him to put his money back into his belt and allowed him to continue on his way.

Ibrahim knew that it is common for travelers at most borders between nations to be questioned about the amount of money they are carrying. What was scary about this incident was the harshness of the soldiers while they were dealing with him and the original intention of the officer to "teach him a lesson." But our family was relieved at how things turned out that time, and we relished seeing the soldiers portrayed in such a poor light over a simple lack of communication. One would think that after this incident in 1969, we would have remembered the difficulties inherent at this border crossing. We should have exercised more caution. But, obviously, we hadn't anticipated the brusque, oppressive, authoritarian manner in which the Israelis treated us.

However, our ordeal was eventually over, and we were allowed once more to pile into taxis for the last leg of our journey to Jerusalem. After such a long, grueling experience, it is difficult to describe the relief we felt in arriving at our brother's beautiful home with its cool polished stone floors and soft beds which beckoned to our tired bodies. Inside that lovely home there existed a sweet feeling of safety and peaceful repose.

Ka Krinng Ting Ting! Ka Kronng Tap Chip! Through the haze of my exhausted first night's slumber in Jerusalem, I slowly awakened to this repetitive and rhythmic clatter of metal-against-stone outside our bedroom window. I peeked out into the cool dawn to discover stonemasons already at work. Our brother's house was situated next to a craftsman's yard with huge mounds of stone awaiting the skilled hands of masons to carve limestone into decorated building blocks.

Timber is at a premium, which is the reason that most homes are constructed of local limestone. I remember following noisy, sturdy trucks that spewed smoky, diesel, exhaust fumes from their tail-pipes while lumbering along the highways of Jordan and Palestine. Their cargo was huge chunks of limestone lifted from the mountain quarries. Throughout the stay at our brother's home, I never tired of listening to the sounds of the simple sledge and chisel or watching the workmen's artistry.

After watching from the window for a while, I decided I would really enjoy a warm bath. Um Omar, my sister-in-law, had anticipated my desire and had already lit the fire beneath the water heater next to the tub. When I went into the bathroom, I was entranced with the fuel used for burning. It was beautiful, odd-shaped bits and pieces of olive-wood. Many of the pieces were missing perfectly-cut circles, as if they had been cut with thimble-sized cookie cutters.

When I asked Um Omar about it, she explained that their friend in Bethlehem owned a factory that fashioned olivewood objects from Palestinian orchards. The main items they created were beads, and the holes were created in the scraps as the rough beads were cut out. I was dismayed that they collected the scraps for fuel because I thought the pieces were too beautiful to be burned. Um Omar laughed when I asked for some to take home. She promised that we could tour the factory when we visited Bethlehem.

Before the visit to Bethlehem, our nephew drove Subha, Naimeh, Laila, Tammy, and me to the Muslim and Christian holy places in Old Jerusalem. On the way to the Church of the Holy Sepulcher, we drove down the winding narrow street known as the Via Dolorosa, the way of grief. I reminded the girls that this was believed to be the route which Jesus walked, carrying a cross, on the way to his crucifixion. It was not as long as I expected, only about 2,000 feet, ending at the huge stone doors of the church. I experienced an upsurge of emotion to realize that this was the actual spot that had become sacred to me during all my years of church involvement. Tammy still recalls the awe in my voice as I explained the significance of the Via Dolorosa.

There were swarms of little boys who descended upon us whenever the car slowed. They were hungry kids trying to make a penny or two from tourists who might buy the packs of gum they were hawking. Although I understood their need, there was something incongruous about this commercialization in the midst of such a holy spot. Our nephew urged us not to buy anything, because it would only encourage even stronger and more exuberant solicitations.

Other than my biblical upbringing, I was quite ignorant concerning the Church of the Holy Sepulcher. I discovered that it contained a beautiful rotunda supported by tall columns above polished stone floors, which led to ornate altars and shrines. We didn't linger inside nor climb down into the area containing the actual caves which are believed to contain the tomb of Christ. I was actually somewhat dismayed to see all the gold-plated trappings of the many shrines. It didn't fit with my mental image of a simple tomb with the giant stone which was rolled away on Easter morning. It made me think of Christ's anger when he felt the need to cleanse the temple of all the money-changers and hypocritical scribes and Pharisees.

I was amazed later to discover that the huge, three-ton stone doors are locked with a key entrusted for a millennium to descendants of a Muslim family who supervise the locking and unlocking each day. I wish I had known that fact as we left the church and prepared to tour the Dome of The Rock. When I consider the animosity exhibited in the United States towards Muslims today, it is meaningful to contemplate that a site so sacred to the Christian tradition has been a site of cooperation between Muslims and Christians for such a long time.

For me, it is a matter of courtesy to honor and follow the expected behaviors at each holy place. We didn't experience that at the Dome of the Rock. First of all, it upset me to discover that the entrance to the shrine was under strict guard by armed Israeli soldiers. It was difficult to reconcile their presence and their guns with my understanding of holy sites. Secondly, I was appalled by the casual, disrespectful behavior of other tourists. In a Muslim place of worship, it is appropriate for visitors to cover the body, remove shoes, and speak in hushed tones because others are praying. Yet tourists of all sorts were wandering about, dressed in shorts and shoes, and talking loudly.

Although this behavior was deeply distracting, I did my best to soak in the significance of this magnificent holy monument. We knew that it was constructed over a sacred stone which is believed to be the place from which the Prophet Muhammad ascended into heaven. Despite the raucous noise of tourists around the fringes, we still felt a hushed reverence that settled over us as we stood inside.

The building is an octagon designed with beautifully balanced dimensions. Each outer wall is exactly sixty-seven feet long, equaling the diameter of the glorious dome, which is covered in gold leaf. We saw a lush red carpet in the interior that encircles the central area containing the sacred stone. Where we stood, the carpet was a deep green and was where worshippers knelt in prayer between columns of varying shapes and designs which rose up to support the dome. The height of the dome rises up that same balanced sixty-seven feet. Walls are covered with intricate mosaics of Koranic verses, but there are no mosaics of people. I learned later that Muslim law forbids depictions of humans in its art. The many vegetation designs evoked an exotic garden.

I felt saddened to learn of the deep disagreements surrounding the Dome of the Rock. Faithful Jews believe that the rock is where Abraham prepared to offer Isaac in sacrifice and that the rock is the site of Solomon's Temple and Herod's Temple. In their eyes, this disputed spot is where their Temple must be rebuilt. I began to have a clearer understanding of the tensions between the two peoples.

From the Dome of the Rock, it was just a short walk to the third holiest site in Islam, the 1300-year-old Al Aqsa. Our nephew told us that the silver-domed mosque also sits on territory which is under dispute and that Jewish citizens wanted it to be destroyed so that the Third Temple, known as Ezekiel's Temple can be built. After we were there in 1973, many attempts have been made to damage it. Even now, tunnels are being dug beneath it which weakens its foundation. It is a large rectangle with four minarets and a dome constructed of wood plated with lead enamelwork. In the courtyard, there is an unused fountain, known as *al-Ka's*, the Cup, where worshippers once performed ritual washing before entering into the mosque.

Leaving Al Aqsa, we came to a section of the Temple Mount which overlooks the Wailing Wall. Our nephew wouldn't allow us to go down to the base of the wall because, since we were a party of Arabs, we would not be welcome, and we might even find ourselves in trouble with nearby guards. The wall is believed, by devout Jews, to be the Western Wall of the Second Temple, whereas some Arabs dispute that it is really part of the Al Aqsa Mosque. We watched as worshippers nodded their heads and prayed. Most left little pieces of paper containing prayers slipped into the cracks in the limestone wall.

As we finished our tour and headed toward our much anticipated meal in Ramallah, I had mixed feelings. How could beautiful places of such religious significance be so important to so many cultures and at the same time be the source of so much anger and territorial hatred? For me, some of the "holiness" became diminished in this "Holy Land."

The beautiful garden and food that we enjoyed in Ramallah were in great contrast to the tension and conflict I felt while visiting the holy sites. At the time of our visit, Ramallah was not the hotbed of political uprisings that it would become during the Intifada. It was still a quiet, peaceful village. Our large family party was ushered into a lovely garden restaurant. I remarked on the tall blooming bushes that surrounded the area and was amazed to learn that they were geraniums.

Ayyoub family dines in Ramallah

We were seated at long tables and served a Mezza, an array of small hot and cold appetizers. There seemed to be more than sixty little dishes ranging from hummus, baba ghannouge, falafel, and tabouleh, exotic then, but now well-known in the West. We ate with gusto, and after being completely satiated, the servers brought in the main course! It was broiled chicken that had been marinated and seasoned with sumac, a deep red, lemony herb. It was so excellent, I couldn't resist, even though it seemed impossible that I could hold another bite.

However, finding it impossible to hold another bite was the norm during most mealtimes while we were in the Middle East. I repeatedly was reminded of the story that Ibrahim told me about Justice Douglas being urged to eat "for my wife's sake. . ..

and for my mother's sake . . .. for my uncle's sake." Everywhere we went, I found myself being plied with second helpings and even more.

Most memorable was the huge quantity of excellent *Sphiha, a* pastry topped with seasoned ground meat, which Ibrahim's sister-in-law, Um Omar and his sister, Naimeh, baked one day. It was as Rudyard Kipling described in his *Just So Stories*: a "Superior Comestible." We carried the Sphiha to a wonderful picnic at the natural pools of Beit Shiheen. Not only was the food delicious, but it was a delight to swim in the marvelous warm waters of the hot springs. Ibrahim usually was more inclined to sit on the sidelines and just enjoy visiting with his family, but even he could not resist the lure of the warm waters and was soon encouraging his little niece, Maha, to take a dip. Feeling ravenous after the swim, we made quick work of the Sphiha.

Another occasion of dining well and in excess happened when we drove to visit Aziz's home town of Rameh. Aziz was there visiting his family that summer, so it was an excellent opportunity to meet his brothers and sisters. They saw to it that we went away extremely well fed. On the way to Rameh, we stopped at Nablus to see Jacob's well, where Jesus stopped to drink and where others traveling with Jesus criticized him for drinking from a well belonging to Samaritans. Jesus rebuked them for their prejudice. We were pleased to follow an example set by Jesus, so Ibrahim's brother, Suleiman, drew up a bucket fastened to a very long rope and treated us to a cold, refreshing drink of the water.

While on the Rameh excursion, we took a side trip to visit Nasser Mansour's village of Safad. Nasser particularly requested that we go to see it since he was forced to flee with his family when he was a teenager during the 1948 war between Palestinians and Israelis. They had no time to gather any possessions and just ran for their lives. Safad is in high country overlooking the valleys of Palestine, and is strategically close to the Golan Heights of Syria.

Because of this, it became an important military city for Israel and was carefully guarded. A carload of Palestinians slowly driving around the streets was sure to become immediately suspect. Suleiman asked us to take out our U.S. passports in case we were stopped, but I'd left them in our suitcase back in Jerusalem. Since Suleiman wasn't willing to subject us to a military interrogation as undocumented tourists, we quickly drove around a few streets and left before we found ourselves in trouble.

We knew that we had not successfully fulfilled our promise to Nasser, which made it all the more important that we visit Nasser's mother and father in Damascus, and we made plans to travel to Syria later. Fortunately, many years later in 1995, Ibrahim went back alone for a visit and he was able to photograph the beauty of the area for Nasser who, as a Palestinian refugee, has never been allowed to visit his home.

Before we left the West Bank, we visited Hebron to see the Tomb of Joseph. Jacob and Rachel, Isaac and Rebekah, and Abraham's tomb are there also. Jewish men were praying against the stone wall of the tomb, and we were told that the site is holy to all, Jewish, Muslim and Christian. Close by was an ancient oak tree, called the tree of

Abraham. Although still alive, it was propped up with painted poles and a covered roof.

A guide explained that the tree was where Abraham is said to have offered his son for sacrifice. Since this biblical event is also attributed to the Dome of the Rock, I realized how many different places lay claim to the same historical stories and relics, even though they conflict with each other. There is no way to be sure where the actual honest-to-goodness spots are. But all claimants are sincere in their effort to carve out their own special connection to these historic events. We noticed this same phenomenon occurring several times concerning places where parts of John the Baptist's body lay buried.

After seeing Hebron, we were treated to our promised visit to Bethlehem, stopping at the home of Siham and Um Omar's father, Abu Beshara. We sat in the shade of his grape arbor and enjoyed sweet tea and servings of refreshing tabouleh. While strolling in the yard of the Huzainah family home, I was entranced to discover their ancient clay *Taboon,* a dome-shaped outdoor oven. It was no longer being used, but the family took time to explain how it operated. Although I never had opportunity to taste food baked in it, we were treated to other Bethlehem bread prepared in ovens like this one, and I can attest to its delicious flavor.

When we finished our visit, it was time to move on to Manger Square, which is the central square in Bethlehem. Naim was personal friends with Elias Mitri Freij, the Mayor of Bethlehem since 1972, who remained in that post until 1997, shepherding his citizens through the many political upheavals which have befallen Bethlehem.

Mayor Freij took us on a tour of industries that he owned along the square. There was an olivewood factory that specialized in making beads, figurines and decorative boxes, many of which were enhanced with mother-of-pearl mosaics. I purchased figurines of a shepherd and his wife and also received a nice sampling of the loose beads. Then, we visited a pottery factory where I was given some tiny replicas of the larger vases.

After the tour, Ibrahim and Naim sat drinking beer with the mayor in the shade, while Subha, Naimeh, the girls, and I toured the Church of the Nativity. I urged Ibrahim to join us, but once again he refused, so we made the pilgrimage without him. We had to stoop to enter the church, because the entrance is just a tiny wooden door. Being a tall woman, it was not easy for me to go through.

I learned that it had been purposely constructed small to prevent horsemen from riding into the interior to wreak destruction. Over the centuries, the edifice was built, destroyed, and rebuilt many times. The doorway was an effort to protect it from further invasion. What struck me first as we moved inside, were the tall rows of magnificent red stone pillars, forty-four in all, leading into the rectangular basilica. I was told that the first construction was octagonal to resemble Christ's birth in a cave, but now just a few remnants of the octagon are still visible in the Armenian chapel.

Once again, the ornate marble and mosaics were overwhelming. Instead of what I'd pictured in my mind as a simple manger, the floor was white marble, with the silver fourteen-pointed Star of Bethlehem surrounded with a Latin inscription which translates, "Here Jesus Christ was born to the Virgin Mary." Above the star hang fifteen burning lamps. Six lamps belonged to the Greeks, five to the Armenians, and four to the Romans. Even in this holiest of shrines, I recognized divisions within the Christian faith! Stories abound concerning the territorial fights for control between sects.

It became crystal clear to me that our very own family was a splendid blending of two of the religious sects represented in the church that day. While Naimeh was Greek Orthodox, whose daughter would eventually marry an Orthodox priest, her older sister Subha had married into a Roman Catholic family, and her daughters became nuns. Yet, burned into my memory is the image of those two dear souls kneeling side by side in devout worship at one of the altars during our visit.

While growing up, it always bothered me that members of religious groups in my community were each adamantly convinced that they held the one and only truth. Here, it was even more disturbing to discover that three sects of the Christian faith insisted on laying claim to this holy place and that each group had built its own chapel as they continued to carry on the conflict with each other. I was told that every year there is a huge argument over which group will be allowed to clean the one remaining section of original ceil-

Naimeh and Subha kneel in prayer

ing before Holy Week. This sense of territorial pride was evident when I learned from Ibrahim's family of the great satisfaction they felt over an honor given to their relative, Abu Beshara, who was assigned the task of ringing the church bells for over fifty years, and people reported that the quality of sound became greatly diminished after he was no longer in charge.

When we finally emerged into the sunshine of Manger Square, we were greeted by Mayor Freij, Naim, and Ibrahim, who had chosen during our absence to devote no effort at all towards worship. Pleasant quaffs of cool beer, accompanied by an ever-present cigarette along with friendly conversation suited them just fine. Since this was Ibrahim's standard practice, it would have been unusual for me to throw a hissy fit about his non-participation. But, it opened up a fine opportunity later in Al Husn, to criticize my errant husband for ignoring all the holy sites. The girls and I were called "Haji," pilgrims. When I came to understand their meaning, I caused much laughter when I replied in my broken Arabic, "Nam, ana Haji, but Ibrahim La Haji." Yes, I am Haji, but Ibrahim is no Haji.

Following our visit to Bethlehem, the time soon arrived for us to say our tearful farewells to Naim, Suleiman, and others who would not be going back to Al Husn with us. It was very difficult for Ibrahim to say goodbye. Once again, he had no way of knowing when he would see them again. Subha and Naimeh traveled with us, again by taxi, through the difficult crossing at Allenby Bridge over the Jordan River and on into Amman. There, we hired a different taxi to transport us to Al Husn, where we planned our trip to Damascus. I expected that the trip to Damascus would be easy and enjoyable, because it was just slightly farther than a drive to Amman. We planned to stay overnight in a nice Damascus hotel, visit Nasser's family and return the following day. But no.

Ibrahim negotiated for a taxi while I packed a light overnight case for the family, and we set off very early in the morning. As usual, the girls and I rode in back while Ibrahim sat up front beside the driver. We were fortunate to have a very courteous driver who took care to see that his Americans in the back seat were well entertained. As we saw things of interest along the way, he would answer our questions with Ibrahim serving as translator.

Although it was only seventy miles, assuming a direct route, there was one segment of the trip which made it seem much longer than that. The driver stopped at an inspection station to show officials our passports, and I realized that we had just passed the northern border of Jordan. Consequently, I assumed that we were now in Syria. Not so! We continued to drive, drive, and then we drove some more, but still we didn't come to the Syrian border. We were traversing a wide swath of dry, desert land between the two countries. Perhaps this is not unusual between two nations, but it was definitely unknown to me.

Finally, our driver pulled into another parking lot which was obviously the Syrian border inspection station. This area was glutted with cars, trucks, busses and several convoys of military vehicles. Our driver explained that the Syrian border had been closed and was just now re-opening. He planned to curry favor with the officials and be allowed to go to the head of the line because we were Americans. Ordinarily, I would have resisted such an action, but I held my tongue.

He was gone for quite a long time and came back with such a sad story to tell as we pulled out of our place in line, drove past the convoys, and headed into Syria. I had noticed him conversing with two huddled, forlorn people who were standing in the parking lot. They turned out to be a distraught father with his frantic wife holding a wailing baby. The family had crossed the same Jordanian border that we did. They'd just learned that they weren't going to be allowed to enter Syria because they didn't have proper documents.

Compounding the situation, Jordan wouldn't allow them to re-enter. Their child was seriously ill, yet the inspection station had no doctor. Ibrahim and the driver surmised that they were probably displaced Palestinian refugees. It appeared to me that they were permanently stuck in No-Man's-Land. And we drove off, never knowing what happened to them, the memory of that little lost family still haunts me.

As we entered Damascus, I tried to imagine how Ibrahim must be feeling, having traversed this route so many times. Whatever changes he noticed in the city, it appeared to be another huge bustling Middle-Eastern metropolis filled with cars, trucks, bicycles, and one-horse open carriages, *Arabaiehs*. I was reminded of young Ibrahim savoring the sound of horse's hooves going tek, tek, tek, tek along the cobbled streets.

There were throngs of people milling about in the streets and shops. Curbs along each side of the street were unusually high, frequently causing shoppers to stroll in the street proper, dodging traffic as needed. Since our windows were rolled down for a breath of air, we could hear the screech of vehicles, the whistles of traffic police, and the shouts of vendors. Odors wafted in, predominantly of exhaust and manure, but occasionally of simmering spices or coffee from street vendors.

Since we were arriving at the Mansour's home unannounced, Ibrahim had no intention of knocking on their front gate until we were well established in our overnight quarters. Otherwise, the family would be pushing for us to stay with them, even though our arrival was unexpected. Ibrahim knew Damascus well, and he felt confident that with transportation help from our willing driver, he would soon be able to secure comfortable lodging.

He directed the driver to take the girls and me to a lovely outdoor café garden. I now wonder if it could have been the same tea garden he remembered from his childhood visit. There is no way of knowing, because his story happened so long ago, but it's nice to think so. It was a pleasant, secluded, walled garden filled with grass, trees, and flowers. We were invited to sit at a comfortable table, and Ibrahim ordered cups of hot sweet tea for us. I don't know what other directions he conveyed to the servers before leaving, but we were definitely left in the care of the proprietor while he took off with the driver in search of a hotel.

And there, I am sorry to report, we remained. As soon as first cups of tea were consumed, a polite waiter promptly refilled them, not once but many, many times. The girls restlessly explored the garden, and I nervously examined my watch while time passed slowly by. Of course our host spoke no English, and I was limited to *Na'am Shukran*, yes, thank you. Eventually those replies changed to La Shukran, no thank you, when we couldn't possibly consume another sip.

We were ensconced in that garden for over two hours, and I really began to worry. I had no money, so I couldn't pay or tip our servers. I spoke no Arabic, and most importantly, I didn't even have our passports. Ibrahim carried these with him in order to secure our hotel. Although I did not want to upset the girls, I began to try to map out some sort of action plan in case a terrible accident had befallen their father. It was a fairly weak plan, since I really felt out of my element. Who knows what I would have done if he hadn't come back? I must have kept all worries to myself, because my daughters were totally unaware of my concerns.

Eventually, and much to my relief, our errant head of family returned with his driver at his side. He was much too frustrated to listen to my tearful complaints. It seems that the border closings had securely locked down the city for tourists. No traffic was going in or out between Syria and Lebanon. Consequently, not a single room in any hotel was available. After futile searching frantically from one establishment to another, Ibrahim made the decision to ask our driver to turn his taxi around and immediately take us back to Al Husn.

This upsetting news didn't suit me at all. With the driver listening to our heated conversation, I reminded Ibrahim of our commitment to Nasser Mansour. How would we ever explain to him that we drove all the way to Damascus but turned around without ever seeing his family? I saw the driver check his watch and make a guess at what our argument was about. Finally, he offered to take us to the Mansour home and then wait all the rest of the day in Damascus so he could drive us home in the evening. Ibrahim was hesitant, but now he had both the driver and his family against his plan, so he relented. I'm sure the tea room proprietor was generously paid and tipped for his kind care of us, and we climbed back into the taxi.

Nasser's family lived on a hill, and we climbed the many steps leading up to the gate of its front wall. When Ibrahim knocked, a young man came to the door and was most surprised when he discovered who was there. We were ushered into the guest room and surrounded with beaming hosts all exclaiming, "*Ahlan wa sahlan*," God welcomes you, while others were proclaiming, "*al-hamdu lil-lah*," praise God! We were immediately engulfed with smiles, hugs, and kisses from Um Nasser, Nasser's mother, a short, round woman with pink cheeks and twinkling blue eyes, robed all in white from head to toe. We were urged to be seated while the family explained that Abu Nasser, Nasser's father, was at his prayers and would join us shortly. When he arrived, everyone stood, and the blessings and greetings began all over again. We immediately noticed that Abu Nasser looked exactly like a smaller, rounder version of his son.

I noticed a young man slip out the front door and soon return with bags of fresh produce. They hurried to prepare some hospitality offerings of *bizer*, roasted seeds, a beautiful tray of fresh fruits and, of course, glasses of hot sweet tea. It seemed like too short a time before we heard the knock on the gate which signaled that our faithful taxi driver had returned. We then had to make our apologies, once more exchange kisses, hugs, and blessings, and depart. I feel blessed that we were able to make that oh-so-short visit to the family of Ibrahim's good friend.

When we climbed back into our taxi, the driver made an astounding offer. He told Ibrahim that it would be a crime for him not to let our family tour at least two of the most famous sites in Damascus. He assured us that we could easily visit the Umayyad Mosque and the Mosque of Sitni Zaynab while still arriving in Al Husn that same night. Since Ibrahim was a captive of the driver's kindness, he couldn't very well argue with the wishes from the back seat. Consequently, my non-tourist husband was forced to agree, and we drove to see the largest and oldest mosque in the world.

The Umayyad Mosque, holy to both Sunni and Shia, is truly spectacular both in size and beauty. I marveled at its huge rectangular courtyard, tall minarets, and lovely mosaics. Our driver told us that the site was first a Christian basilica and that many believe it will be the site where Jesus will return at the End of Days. Devout followers also believe it is the burial place for John the Baptist's head. Ibrahim, a student of early Middle-Eastern history who admired Saladin for his fair-minded treatment, was pleased to visit the north wall, which contains the tomb of Saladin.

We needed to hurry on if we were also to see the Mosque of Sitni Zaynab. Ibrahim knew of Zaynab's importance, since she was the granddaughter of Muhammad. The guide explained that this shrine was the burial place of Lady Zaynab and greatly revered by Shia Muslims. My breath was caught by the beauty of its golden dome with its marvelous mosaics constructed from mirrors. I was so entranced that I nearly committed a grievous mistake when I handed our little Brownie camera to Tammy and asked her to photograph the glistening interior.

Immediately, guards came up and threatened to confiscate the camera or even arrest my young daughter. Photographs of their holy site were strictly forbidden, and foolish Americani tourists like me were very offensive indeed. I have carried my guilt all these years, feeling so chastened and embarrassed, but Tammy doesn't even remember the incident.

The drive back to Jordan was uneventful, except that we began to feel deep hunger as we drove on into the night. It dawned on me that the many cups of tea and servings of fruit were our sole nourishment during the long day. Once again, our splendid driver came to the rescue by stopping near the border at a tiny, pleasant restaurant called Naim Ali. Its owner served us a delicious meal, all the while apologizing for the smallness of his establishment. He told Ibrahim that his construction efforts were brought to a sudden halt because he ran out of steel. I hope he eventually did finish his building project and that his business thrived. When our trip was finally ended, our driver was handsomely rewarded by Ibrahim as we arrived at the family gate.

After returning from Syria, there were just a few quiet days left before we found ourselves in the throes of packing. As I struggled to fit everything back into our suitcases, I silently cursed myself for allowing each of us to bring so much. We never wore all those shoes. The girls and I had no need for the dressy clothing, and my knitting project with its many expensive skeins of wool was barely touched. In fact, I stopped knitting when my sisters-in-law repeatedly tried to take it out of my hands to knit it for me. It was obvious that they were much more skilled, but I could also see that they didn't relish working with wool in such hot weather. When someone explained to me that knitting was considered a winter activity, I gave up on my project and tucked it away in my bag.

Still, I was making some headway with my packing until the parting gifts began to accumulate. Homemade foods, lovely little religious icons, handcrafted linens, plus Subha's *hatta*, *shambar*, and *shursh*, a head-covering, long black dress, and head wrap. There was also a complete outfit of Toufiq's traditional clothing. They offered us the set of ancient coffee pots. Even shy Saad got into the act by slipping tiny trinkets like religious medals and prayer cards into the girl's hands.

I found it necessary to enlist Ibrahim's help in graciously resisting such determination to give away the entire collection of family treasures. He sat beside me and became the stern, determined husband, insisting in Arabic, "No room, no room!" He was able to convince them to keep the coffee pots, but then we received that coffee set by parcel post the following year. I confess that I was the one who melted when Miriam offered the *Mehbash*, the ancient coffee grinder. Ibrahim was adamant that we could not take it, and I found myself begging, "Come on, Abe, I'll carry it all the way home in my duffel bag." The argument continued while all of the family sat along the sidelines listening. It was my deepest wish to accept this wonderful gift. Finally, dear Miriam won Ibrahim over by calling out the only English words we ever heard her attempt, "Come on Abe, Come on Abe!" The roomful of family dissolved into laughter, and Ibrahim smilingly gave in to his mother's plea.

At last, the luggage was packed; we were dressed in our traveling clothes; the taxi was ordered; the relatives were assembled; and we sat in the shade of the courtyard. This became the hour I will remember forever. While we sat, sipping our final glasses of sweet tea, the family began the ritual of retelling all their favorite Joha stories. It was part of Ibrahim's previous visits home, but this time, I was experiencing it first-hand. As the tales were told in Arabic with much laughter, and then translated into English with repeated laughter, I came to appreciate this beautiful method of dealing with the impending sorrow of saying goodbye.

Finally, our transportation arrived. I stood to utter my poor Arabic farewell, *"Biddi atrukum;"* I would like to leave, now. Heartfelt wishes and blessings were heaped upon us, along with countless kisses, hugs, and tears. I shall always remember Miriam's last request to me, because it was never fulfilled. She made the motion of cradling a babe in her arms and said in Arabic for me to return soon with a baby son. I smiled but said nothing. No matter how much Miriam loved our girls, tradition dictated that Ibrahim should produce a male heir. I simply asked Ibrahim to translate my wish that she take good care of herself and that she must sit to wait for our next visit.

At long last, the four of us, along with our cumbersome luggage, were loaded into the taxi, and I was able to look back at our Jordanian family one last time before we turned the corner and headed towards Amman. I would not see Miriam or Toufiq again. Ibrahim was able to return for later visits, but they were both gone when we returned together in 2005.

Following that heart-wrenching farewell, I was amazed to learn that we were charged a head tax upon departure from Amman. It may be a usual expectation for more experienced travelers, but I was flabbergasted that I must pay a fee for the privilege of leaving the country! Yacoub's family departed Amman at the same time, and we visited with them a bit more while we spent six days in Cairo. Yacoub's sons, Khalid and Majid, enjoyed teasing our girls about their ritzy accommodations at the Cairo Hilton, while we stayed at the Semiramis, built at the end of the 19th century, with three lovely balconies all facing the Nile. It was clean with excellent service, and we enjoyed its gracious, old-fashioned décor and atmosphere.

It had a nightclub on the top floor, and Tammy was delighted to go on a date with Daddy one night to see the belly dancers. I helped put her hair up in a bun and get all dolled up with a skirt and gorgeous embroidered shawl. She remembered the outing as being one of the highlights of her time in Cairo. Laila stayed with me in the hotel room that night, but both of us did get to see the belly dancers on a different evening. Since Laila and her friend had taken belly dancing classes at the YWCA in Yakima, where she even sewed a dancing costume, she was excited to see real, live performers.

Ibrahim's relatives in Al Husn had primed him with firm instructions to provide a chance for us to enjoy some of the wonders of Egypt during our week's stay. Reluctantly, he was obliged to assume the role of tour director. Although he was experienced in negotiating travel independently during his many trips to the Middle East, I'm sure he must have felt under a greater burden to shepherd his family through the ins and outs of visiting the sites of Egypt. He was definitely not a normal tour guide! He had his mental list of all the places he was told that we must see, and he would have been most content if we could have accomplished it all in one day.

We visited the zoo, and then took a taxi out to see the Pyramids all in the same day! Nothing stands out in my memory about the zoo, although the girls seemed to enjoy it. What I do remember is our champion father defending us from pickpockets. As we strolled along the path, suddenly Ibrahim grabbed the girl's hands and pushed all of us in front of him. Then he turned to face two men who were following closely behind us. I don't understand much Arabic, but I do know cursing when I hear it, and Ibrahim let loose harsh, loud shouts. I could read the surprise on their faces. Quickly, they turned on their heels and melted back into the crowd of strollers. We surmised that the girls and I looked so obviously American that they planned their attack aloud in Arabic, not realizing that Ibrahim heard and understood every word they said. My journal entry that day states, "Abe very tired."

However exhausted we might have been, our drive to Giza was exciting as the Pyramids loomed into sight. They didn't really "loom" from a distance and appeared more like picture postcards. But when the driver approached Kofo, the largest, we were overwhelmed with its enormity. It is the oldest and largest and is one of the original Seven Wonders of the World. Each of the huge blocks in Kofo is the size of a railroad car and weighs two-and-a-half tons. Over two million of the stones were cut from another area in Egypt and transported by rolling them along on heavy logs. The guide told us that the thousands who built it were not necessarily slaves but were more likely native Egyptian agricultural laborers who worked when the Nile flooded the land nearby. I enjoyed the guide's description of them as "native volunteers."

Tourists are allowed to climb inside Kofo and stand directly in its burial chamber, so we got in line to make the climb. The dark, narrow, passage leading up to the tomb was musty smelling and cramped with no room to stand. Footholds were like a ladder slanted at an angle that forced us to employ both hands and feet, almost like crawling, while we worked our way up. We were warned that the close confines of the passage often cause distress. Laila later told me that she found it physically challenging. We were crouched in a passageway no more than four feet high, going a long way uphill, without fresh air, with people in front of us and behind. Laila also complained that whenever she craned her neck up to look ahead, all she could see was my butt. She actively forced herself to stay calm and was determined to make it to the top. We all felt pretty smug when the passage ended with a small opening into the perfectly square, stone burial chamber.

After we entered the chamber, we were able once more to stand straight. There was a beautiful echo, and I couldn't stop myself from softly singing a melody that the girls and I often sang as a round. I tried to get my daughters to join with me to sing in harmony, but they were embarrassed. I shall never forget the memory of that melody floating eerily inside the tomb. The other item of special interest was the tiny hole at the top of the small chamber. The guide explained that ancient Egyptians believed the soul of the dead needed this escape portal in order to travel in and out of the tomb.

After we emerged from Kofo, back into the sunshine, Ibrahim led us over to where drivers were standing beside their kneeling camels. I know that folk say camels can be mean-spirited, but I saw them as wonderful. Especially their long-lashed, beautiful, dark eyes. I noticed that their legs were hobbled and that large satchels of fodder were fastened back by their tails where it was impossible for them to reach until their driver deemed it to be feeding-time.

They were outfitted with fancy, colorful headgear made of tassels and bells. Even when kneeling, the back was as high as I am tall. I knew that it would be impossible for me to clamber up into the fancy leather saddle perched on top of the hump. But, a driver came over to me, literally grabbed hold of my legs and backside and lifted me into the saddle. After being put up there, Ibrahim came over speaking most impatiently, "What are you doing up on THAT camel? I just finished bargaining for this other one!" Too late! I was up there and not willing to go through the loading again. So, Ibrahim agreed that the girls could ride the one he had chosen.

On command from the driver, and with a loud, complaining bellow, the beast rose up on its front legs causing me to hang on for dear life as I was tipped way, way over backwards. Then the reverse; his back legs came up accompanied by another loud groan, and I was sure I was going to fall off right over his head. A camel does not walk like a horse. It moves both legs on one side at the same time and then both legs on the other side. This is why camels have been described as "ships of the desert," because they sway from side to side like a boat rising and falling in waves. I loved it!

I knew immediately that I would be able to make this glorious experience come alive for my kindergarten children when I was back in my Yakima classroom. And indeed I did! When it was time to study the letter "C," I read them a page from Dr. Seuss. "Big C, Little C. What begins with C? Camel on the ceiling, C, C, C." Then I got all my little kids up in a line, with loud groans and bellows and we rode our lurching, imaginary camels all around the classroom. An interesting footnote to this lesson happened many years later as Abe and I were standing in the check-out line of a big-box store. A woman behind Abe tapped him on the arm saying, "I'll bet you rode a camel too." Startled, Abe answered that he had, indeed, ridden many a camel. I was perplexed until she explained that she was one of my pupils who had gone on the camel ride that day so long ago in my kindergarten. One never knows when the past will come jumping out!

But, I didn't exert much effort at planning my future camel lesson as we rode up to the base of the Great Sphinx, a guardian statue carved of limestone with the head of a man and the body of a lion. Our ride was too short. Before we knew it, our camels were back at their resting place, and we went through the process of hanging on tightly while they knelt back down. I dearly hope those lovely animals were rewarded with some of their feed, but we didn't wait to see, because we were hot, tired, and thirsty, too.

Ibrahim ushered us over to a refreshment compound and bought us cool drinks and Egyptian ice cream. I am a lover of ice cream and was pleased to receive this treat, since cold things and dairy foods had been in short supply during our stay in the Middle East. But, I was leery about what was served at the refreshment booth, because it looked like it was full of dirt specks. We talked about it and agreed: We don't know if this is vanilla bean or dirt, but let's just enjoy it and hope for the best.

We took a taxi to a nearby restaurant for an excellent chicken dinner and then back to the Pyramids for the after-dark light show. We sat up in bleachers while music and lights played over the great structures in front of us. It was here that I learned from the announcer that the Sphinx was the largest statue in the ancient world, 240-feet long, and sixty-six feet high. We also learned that it came to be worshipped as the image of the god Horus.

The music, lights, and scenery were awe-inspiring. Yet, the announcer seemed to be trying to boost the drama even further, using the voice of a circus magic performer. We were annoyed by the way he tried to make his story even more mysterious and wondrous than the sights in front of us, as if that were possible.

The following day, Ibrahim got us up and off to tour Maniel Palace in central Cairo. This opulent structure was the home of King Farouk's uncle, Prince Mohamed Ali, who lived there until Gamal Abdul Nasser staged his military takeover in 1952, causing Farouk and Prince Mohamed Ali to flee. This palace was of interest to Ibrahim because Nasser's coup occurred while Ibrahim was politically active in Amman, and he was following Egyptian politics. I remember him emphasizing Egypt's unrest to our International Relations club in college, as we prepared to represent Egypt at the Model United Nations conference.

Tour brochures describe the palace as "One of Cairo's most eccentric tourist sites," because Prince Mohammed Ali apparently couldn't decide which architectural style he preferred, so he went for the lot: Ottoman, Moorish, Persian, and Rococo. I noticed that every ceiling and every window was decorated differently. One room was all in slate blue with furnishings that looked like lacy white filigree, while another long reception area had deep purple furnishings along each side and a brightly lit ceiling containing one huge decoration that looked like a series of long dark brown bars of some type of rare wood. Several ceilings and walls could have been Persian carpets if woven from wool rather than created with mosaic tiles. The state dining room was glistening golden from the window trimmings to the pillars along the walls, like gold lacework, down to the golden-colored parquet floor.

The beauty of these rooms was in stark contrast with the chamber containing King Farouk's horde of hunting trophies. Among many species of stuffed animals were more than 350 gazelles. My girls and I wanted to cry when we saw those beautiful animals killed and stuffed just to increase Farouk's collection. Although the furnishings and mosaics were beautiful, it was good to get away from there.

The following day we walked the short distance from our hotel to the Egyptian Museum in Tahrir Square. Approaching, I was entranced with a huge statue of what I assumed to be a lion. But, of course, upon closer inspection this impressive structure was a replica of the Sphinx. We were immediately approached by an onslaught of tour guides, and Ibrahim wisely hired one. This was a good decision, since we were totally bewildered with all that there was to see. The museum, designed in Neoclassical style with 107 halls, was filled with over 160,000 objects covering 5,000 years of Egypt's past.

Since our guide was somewhat limited in his English, I would have appreciated more labels and printed explanations. But I shall always be grateful for the chance to view the treasures of Tutankhamen, statuettes of divinities, and priceless displays of jewelry, and ancient items used in daily life. There was also an extensive collection of royal mummies. This created a hailstorm of questions from Tammy. When we approached a peacefully reposed mummy, Tammy tugged at my hand asking, "Mommy, is this how Grandma looks now that she is dead?"

I did my best to distract her attention to other displays, but she was insistent in her question as we came to each mummy. Finally, I stopped and faced her to explain earnestly, "Tammy, when you ask me this question, it hurts my feelings and makes me feel sad, because I miss Grandma so much." The kid finally got my meaning and left off with the questions, but as an adult, she still remembers being puzzled about it.

True to form, Ibrahim-the-tour-director was not satisfied with just visiting the museum. If he had to be tour guide, he was going to do a thorough job. His exhausting itinerary for the day crammed in our walking trip to the Suq.

The Americani stamp on our appearance also put a damper, on our visit to the Suq, the Khan al-Khalili Bazaar. It is one of the most fabulous and extensive markets in the Middle East, and Ibrahim had been instructed to take us to it. Because we stood out like sore thumbs as the tourists that we were, he laid down the rule that we could not walk beside him, but must stay half a block behind and just signal some way when we noticed what we wanted to purchase. Then, we were to wander on ahead while he negotiated a price. His reasoning was sound, because whenever I exhibited the slightest interest in an item, I was besieged with shopkeepers and hucksters pushing their wares in broken English.

The sights, sounds, and smells of the crowded Suq were overwhelming, yet exhilarating. Ibrahim had previously experienced Middle Eastern markets many times and had described his experiences of the market in Beirut, but this was a first for the rest of us. I was enthralled with the endless rows upon rows of gleaming gold stalls strung with necklaces and bracelets. I enjoyed studying the fragrant amber, green, yellow, and brown spices in an effort to identify those that Miriam had tucked into our suitcase. I recognized cumin, sage, cinnamon, nutmeg, allspice, pepper, and sumac. But there were many others that I could not name.

Tammy had her nose out for the strongly enticing stalls of falafel sellers and the slowly turning spits of roasting lamb kabob. Laila was entranced with the beautifully embroidered garments and the untold variety of fresh fruits and vegetables. Then, there were the cages of cackling live chickens and butcher-shops full of freshly plucked and gutted birds. They were strung up by their feet awaiting a housewife's evening stewpot. Bakers with clay ovens were producing mountains of fresh pocket bread, releasing wafts of fragrant yeast and causing us to salivate.

Every variation of delicate pastry and candy were arranged in colorful trays, begging our attention. We ended up purchasing some lovely alabaster figurines of Queen Nefertiti and a few small coffee table dishes made from the same stone. Ibrahim bargained for two leather hassocks which could fold flat in our suitcase and then be stuffed when we arrived home. Those hassocks graced our home for years. And above the bustle and calls of the hucksters, there floated the occasional, far-distant call to prayer from the muezzin in a mosque.

The next day, we hired a taxi to visit the Citadel. During the 12th century, Saladin built the Citadel on a hill above the city as a bastion of defense. The buildings were eventually torn down and replaced with a mosque built by Muhammad 'Ali in the 1800s. Nothing remains of the original fortress except a part of the walls and the well that supplied the water. My memory of the Mosque of Muhammad 'Ali is clouded due to the extreme heat of the day. I also remember feeling distressed that I was required to encase my relatively clean shoes with tourist-worn dusty foot coverings so as to not defile the mosque when I entered.

I was ashamed of my feelings, because I knew that I must show proper respect to the holy place. So, I followed directions correctly but could not dispel my inner irritations. It was a beautiful building, with two minarets and lovely architecture. But I found myself comparing it to the Dome of the Rock, and it didn't measure up. Another bout of guilty feelings hit me when I realized I was making such comparisons. Perhaps the crux of the matter was that our family's touristy days had stretched us to our limits. Obviously, it was time to pack it in and head for home. If everyone could see the wonders we saw and experience the hospitality we encountered, surely no one could have a single anti-Arab thought.

The driver who took us to the airport said, "Life requires that he who runs - - gets." It was 6:30 a.m. and we were his fare because the man who was hired to take us failed to show. I noted that it continued to be Friday, August 24th "forever and ever so long." The stopover in Rome again caused us to sit for hours in the plane due to technical difficulties. It was still Friday when we arrived in Chicago and went through customs and 3:00 a.m. on Saturday morning when we got to Seattle.

As we walked the corridors of SeaTac, it seemed strange to hear loudspeaker announcements being given only in English, rather than a mixture of Arabic, French, and German. Also, I now understood better the phrase "sea legs," which is usually attributed to ocean voyages. We were recovering from "air legs," due to the slightly lilting motion of an airplane's aisles, and it felt a bit weird to be walking on solid floors. I remember the marvelous taste and texture of the large vanilla ice cream cone Abe bought for each of us to celebrate our homecoming. Even though we had just eaten the motel's continental breakfast, that cold, familiar treat refreshed us.

It was a relief to board the commuter flight and head out for the last forty-five minutes of our journey. A group of friends met us at the airport and escorted us to our quiet, comfortable house on 18th Avenue. They'd mown the lawn and stocked the fridge. After a much-needed sleep in our own beds, it was easy enough to unpack our clothing, treasures, and laundry. I didn't even mind the task of tucking all those shoes back into their closets.

CHAPTER 17

———◆◇◆———

Our Farming Lives

NOT LONG AFTER OUR return, the bustle of preparation for school began for the girls and me. Abe had another month before his term began and used the time to work on the yard, visit with his coffee buddies, and travel on union business.

For Laila, the coming school year was significant since it would be her senior year at Davis High, and Tammy, as a sixth-grader, would begin the last year of elementary school. The annual tradition of preparing "first day of school" outfits loomed. Since we rarely splurged on store-bought," we called on our sewing skills. Laila, designed her own clothes, and I decided to wear things I'd taken to Jordan, so my only sewing task was a new outfit for Tammy. She was always pleased to use Laila's patterns, so the project was simplified.

That was a good thing, since school meetings, classroom preparations, and home visits were time-consuming. My class load was large, because I taught morning and afternoon half-day sessions for twenty-eight children each, and I called on all fifty-six incoming students.

In the Yakima School system, my home visits were unusual. But, I'd previously attended a workshop taught by a splendid instructor who believed strongly in the rewards that can be reaped from early-in-the-year home visits. He noted the most troubled kids sometimes had only one day of good behavior in their psyche, and after that one good day, he knocked at the family's door to report, "I just stopped by to let you know that your child had a very good day at school." The startled parent probably had never received positive feedback before, and the encouragement engendered by that visit made it possible for the troubled kid to feel success, carrying over for more good days of school.

The system worked well for me. During the two weeks before classes began, I mailed a letter in which I informed families that I would be coming by for a door-stop visit. Most parents made an effort to be home, and I was often invited inside. I found it to be one of my most successful tools in getting classes off to a good start. The school district learned of what I was doing and began encouraging other teachers to follow the practice. It came to be a way to fulfill the required early term parent contact.

At least one family remembers how important that home visit was, and my former student remembers serving cookies to the lady who was going to be his new teacher. Because sandwiching so many home visits into my schedule was time-consuming, I felt rushed almost beyond endurance during those two weeks. Laila remembers how stressed I was, and was vaguely proud, she says now, of my dedication and effort.

However, I could always count on significant assistance from Tammy. She loved to spend an afternoon in my empty classroom setting up the playhouse while I studied student records and wrote lesson plans. Each spring, all the dress-up clothes, doll clothes, and toy dishes were carried to our house for scrubbing. After I helped Tammy lug the big sack of paraphernalia back in the fall, she took over. She arranged the furniture, set out the dishes, dressed the dolls, and fixed their hairdos. We had one African-American doll (Baby Nancy) with long, black, curling tresses. Tammy relished taking great pains to style her hair. She did this even though, after the first day, none of the dolls were ever properly combed and dressed again until the following fall. Tammy was proud of her ability to arrange the playhouse beautifully, but she understood that its charm was fleeting. I felt grateful that Tammy chose to help me every fall. It became a special tradition that we both enjoyed, and we cherish the memory.

Over the years, she and I have both remarked about one item in the doll house. We were always amazed at how the little boy doll's fragile leather sandals were never lost or broken. We were in awe that such tiny things as those delicate sandals always turned up. It would have been easy for them to be destroyed by little hands or carried off in a child's pocket. But each fall, there they were, and the boy doll would once again be fully clothed.

While the girls and I rushed about during those two weeks before school began, Abe sought ways to make himself absent as much as possible. That suited me fine—no need to worry about proper meals. I was quite agreeable when he informed me of his plan to take off for a union meeting in Seattle. I was even more gratified to receive a Friday night dinner invitation and looked forward to a relaxed, yummy meal with friends.

Just as the girls and I headed out the kitchen door, there was a knock on the front door. Hardly anybody ever used that door, and I wondered who it might be as I hurried to answer. Much to my surprise, a handsome young Arab man stood there. It took me a minute to recognize him as Hana's younger brother, Subhi Ayyoub. Since Hana was now off to WSU in Pullman, her room had been offered to her young brother, who was prepared to begin his studies at YVC.

But, no notice of his arrival had been given. He just arrived! And, we were ready to leave for a thirty-minute drive up to the mountains for supper. I was surprised that he'd found his way all alone to our house but very grateful that he arrived before we were gone. It would be devastating, after his long trip, to arrive at nightfall to an empty house.

Later, Subhi explained that he had our address written on a piece of paper, which he gave to a taxi driver. He told me that he remembered knocking on the front door, being warmly welcomed by his Aunt Doris, and only then did he feel he was in safe hands. Considering that I didn't immediately change our plans and offer our young traveler a soft place to rest, I'm surprised that he felt safe in my hands. But, our friends had already prepared our meal, and we couldn't cancel at that late moment.

I knew the graciousness of our hosts, so I quickly phoned them requesting an extra place be set at their table. I felt comfortable bringing Subhi along. However, I now think about how strange the whole evening was for him. He must have been exhausted, wanting nothing more than a warm bed. Instead, he was whisked up into the mountains, without his Uncle Ibrahim along, to meet strangers and eat unfamiliar foods. I distinctly remember the entrée was Reuben Casserole, a delicious German dish of corned beef mixed with sauerkraut and topped with a buttery, crunchy bread-crumb crust. Our friends were excellent hosts and our nephew's English was sufficient for interesting conversation. He was resilient and able to hide his fatigue until we could drive him back to town.

Tammy, an eager sixth grader, was excited to have her cousin from Jerusalem come to live with us. Because he was new to our household, in her eyes he was instantly exotic. That first morning after he arrived, she could not leave him alone and let him sleep. She raced down to the basement where he was sleeping, paced around outside his door, peeked inside several times to see if he was up, until he came out to the family room and watched cartoons with her. She remembers his incredibly sweet smile and kind eyes. They didn't speak much that first morning, but she remembers his nice, quiet participation in her little cartoon ritual.

Before the weekend was over, Abe was home and took his young nephew to begin registration. As foreign student advisor, he knew exactly how to guide Subhi and help him adjust to new routines. He was an excellent student, and we enjoyed his addition to our household. Soon, Subhi was a busy student at YVC; Abe was back to teaching math classes; Laila was involved with senior-year activities and dance classes; Tammy was a sixth-grader, enjoying the role of lording it over the lower grades at her elementary school; and, I was embroiled in reigning over the activities of all my kindergarteners.

Those activities involved a field trip to the Yakima apple orchards to gather windfalls. We brought the boxes of apples back to the classroom where we made apple sauce and apple pies. One of the required learnings for my students was to count to 100, so I told them that they would each have a chance to make an individual apple pie as soon as we collected enough little pie pans. In the weekly home letter, I asked parents to save the Swanson's meat-pie pans. As the pans arrived, we counted them each day to see if we had enough. I remember one parent complaining, "When can we quit eating all those frozen meat pies?"

When we reached the golden number of sixty, I requested help from mothers to come to class and assist with the pie-baking activity. In advance, the school cooks mixed up a large batch of child-proof crust, wonderfully tender no matter how long the dough was worked. Parents always requested the recipe, and I'm sure that it is still being used in many Yakima homes.

We set up a cooking center, and six children at a time cut apples into small pieces using a regular table knife. It was okay to leave the peel on, but if they could get it off, they were allowed to eat their peelings. The children rolled out their dough on a piece of saran-wrap, using large plastic water glasses for rolling pins. Into the pan went dough, apples, sugar, and cinnamon. Little fingers patted and fussed till the pie met with the child's satisfaction.

Parents were able to rotate the entire class through the process in one session, while I directed the rest of the class in the other activities. Sometimes, the school cooks baked for me and in other years, I packed all those little pies home. The following day, each child was allowed to choose whether to eat the pie during snack-time or take it home to share. Often, they found it hard to choose and would eat part while saving a few crumbs to take home.

One year, the school provided ingredients, so early that morning, I grabbed the bowl of sugar from the supply shelf and we used it for the pies. When I tasted my sample pie at home that night, I discovered, to my horror, that I had grabbed a bowl of salt left over from some other teacher's salt and flour clay project. Needless to say, being my mother's daughter, I pulled a "Jo Rigney" behavior out of my hat and went around the room with a bowl of sugar and a large spoon to each child sitting at the snack table. I explained, "I think you will want a little more sugar on your pie," and heaped a big spoon of sugar on top of the crusts. Not a single child discovered my terrible mistake, but the rest of the teaching staff knew, since I thought it was too funny not to share.

Pie-baking day was not the only time that parents came to help at school. There was always an open invitation for moms and dads to come, and I had directions written out on boxes of activities that were best taught individually. When a parent walked through the door, I handed over a list of all the children's names and a box containing an individual learning game. Children soon learned to go quietly to get the next child on the list saying, "It's your turn to work with the helper." Parents were instructed to check off the child's name as each one finished and indicate whether the effort was successful or if it needed to be repeated.

I often had as many as three parents sitting around the room busily working with children while I taught the group lessons or directed activity times. One parent stoked her infant with cereal so she would sleep during class and brought her in a stroller. Another parent wanted so badly to help but was tied down with two toddlers. I told her to bring them with her as long as she took time before she left to put away the things they had pulled out for play. It bothered my class to see a little one pulling out blocks and making a mess while they were required to sit still for a lesson. I simply told them babies and toddlers are too little to know better, while they were big grown-up kindergartners.

In no time, my classes developed empathy for the "too little" ones, which then carried over to appreciation for special needs children. The school district quickly discovered that I was usually able and willing to take on the education of children who didn't fit the so-called normal pattern. Parents often requested that their special needs child be placed with me. I was agreeable with the arrangement, because I could see how much it helped a child of regular abilities to empathize with others who required extra help in order to learn.

I almost decided that I had taken on too great a challenge the year that a little boy with extreme behavioral problems was assigned to me. I discovered that he could not be trusted to roam freely in the classroom at any time. He tried to stick metal objects into the electrical outlets, tore up work posted on the walls, and dumped games or puzzles out into jumbled piles. That year, I taught with one hand, while my other one was taken up with holding his hand. However, even that paid dividends for the rest of the class. One little child came up to me one day when I really needed both hands to accomplish a task and said, "Mrs. Ayyoub, I'll hold his hand for you while you do that." And it worked! The disturbed child remained calm all the time his hand was being held by his classmate.

I loved working with the five-year-olds, particularly the active, inquisitive little boys who came my way. We had a required list of learning that must be accomplished for the year, but my years of kindergarten teaching occurred prior to the big push that academics have since made. Often school districts now test all kindergarten children on reading skills before they even enter first grade. Using the whole language method of listening to and learning to love literature, many of my students did accomplish good reading abilities during the year. But in my mind, it was not a "Make or Break" requirement. Research still attests to the fact that many youngsters are not going to mature into the skills needed for reading until age eight. This is particularly true for little boys who seem to require more large muscle development before they can sit to accomplish the tasks needed in reading. Consequently, I provided time every day for activities that kept the little guys on the go while at the same time they were develop-ing the listening, motor, and visual skills they needed.

One great kinesthetic activity I designed to challenge my active little boys cen-tered on a big hunk of tree stump set up in the corner. Children could choose ham-mering during what we called Choice Time. We had a can of nails and two sturdy hammers. Little boys flocked to that activity and spent their built up energies pound-ing nails into that stump. Little girls loved to get over there and pound away, too. By the end of a school year, one would be hard-pressed to locate a spot with room to pound another nail.

Our class planted a garden, played on balance beams, rode triangle scooters, co-operatively built large constructions with blocks, kept a pet rabbit, had an aquarium full of fish, and learned about each animal's special needs. I was honest with teaching students about life, and on the day our guinea pig had her baby, I answered their questions about birth. I almost snapped the year we had a pet boa constrictor in the classroom. Boas need to eat a live mouse, and I allowed the class to watch while it happened.

The next time the snake's owner brought the little mouse in its box for mealtime, the box and mouse mysteriously disappeared. My principal called me over to the office to report a strange call from a parent. Her little boy had taken home a live mouse in a little box saying that Mrs. Ayyoub had given it to him. It turned out the child was sad to learn that the little mouse was slated for snake dinner, so he stole it and lied about it. My principal suggested that perhaps my teaching was too graphic and that I should tone it down a bit. Needless to say, the boa went home before the next feeding time.

The area I called the cooking table was really just a large 8 x 10 sheet of one inch plywood placed over two permanently fixed saw horses. I sanded the top and gave it a couple of coats of varnish. The board could be removed and leaned against the wall when we made carpentry projects. We had large c-clamps to hold boards in place so that little children could use both hands to saw their wood into boats or toy cars. It was a delight to watch a child saw away on a project. Most children were still too short to operate the tools properly unless they were standing on one of our sturdy building blocks.

I could usually coerce some dads to volunteer when we took up carpentry, and there were always fifth grade students who loved to come over as student helpers. The fifth grade teachers liked to team up their classes with my students so that each kid had a permanent buddy for the whole year. The older kids prepared stories to read and we planned a buddy story time, once every week or so.

When the plywood top was in place on its saw horses, the large table served as an area for many art projects. This was the place where children, buttoned backwards into a man's shirt as protection against paint spills, were given a chance to finger paint on large sheets of butcher paper using a puddle of liquid laundry starch and powdered tempera paint. I had a strong cord stretched close by where their paintings were hung with clothes pins to dry.

As Christmas season approached, each child finger painted a large sheet with red, green, or yellow. When the paintings were dry, a parent helper supervised the children while they traced around a Christmas stocking pattern on their paintings folded in half. After the child cut out the stocking, the parent marked the edges with carefully-placed pencil marks and the child was allowed to use a hole-puncher to make holes around the edge. Then, a big blunt needle threaded with yarn laced up the stocking. We hung them all so that Santa could fill them with a surprise.

This prompted a great problem-solving lesson during circle discussion as I posed the question, "How can Santa get into the room to fill your stockings since the door is locked at night and the room has no chimney?" Their thinking was always clever and delightful. One year, I taught the son of a reporter from our local paper. The dad asked to sit in on the lesson and brought a photographer with him. The episode resulted in a great op-ed article in the paper.

Christmas was always an exciting time for my kindergarteners. They practiced and practiced so that they could sing, "We wish you a Merry Christmas" at the school program. We learned all the verses and even made Figgie Pudding in class as Christmas gifts for their parents. Since the Christmas program involved the entire school, my students got to come to school at night early in December to sing their song in front of a crowd of parents. Then, it was up to me to keep their bubbles of excitement under control with lots of art projects and activities until school dismissed for Christmas break three weeks later.

I remember feeling smug as I trundled home about 5:30 in the afternoon on December 23, 1973. I had stayed late that day to prepare all the necessary art materials for the last week of school. My kids had stolen the show earlier in the week with their darling performance at the program, and I was exuberantly singing, "We wish you a Merry Christmas" as I climbed out of the car and headed up the driveway towards the kitchen door. But surprisingly, Abe was standing outside and stopped me in mid-sentence of "We wish—." Taking me in his arms, he gave me a gentle hug and kiss. Highly unusual behavior from my dignified professor! Then, he held my shoulders at arm's length, looked me in the eyes, and told me that Dad had been found, sitting in his chair, dead from a heart attack. That moment destroyed my Merry Christmas.

Shock must have set in immediately, since I did not burst into a flood of tears. We walked into the house and sat to make plans as a family. Once again, I proposed that the girls stay in Yakima to finish their last week of school. But, I was met with strong resistance from both of them. They'd felt left out when Grandma died. Both girls stated firmly that they were not about to stay home this time. So, I informed their schools and headed back to my classroom to write detailed lesson plans for a substitute.

Since Abe's classes finished earlier in December than the public schools, the four of us were soon free to begin the long drive toward Nyssa. The miles to my parents' home were the same distance as always, but the winter road conditions and the heaviness we felt in our hearts made the trip seem interminable. We arrived late in the afternoon to a house already dark and exceedingly empty. Good neighbors stoked the coal furnace so it was warm enough, but I felt as though I might never become warm again. We went to bed with the hope that the morrow would find us a little refreshed.

The next morning, Dad's neighbors walked through the kitchen door with two dozen eggs and a huge package of bacon. They remembered that Grandpa always took pains to have bacon on hand when the grandkids arrived. While we sat around Mom's beloved oak table with coffee and food, they described how they had stopped by for a visit and walked in with their usual cheery hellos. They found him sitting in his recliner, and assumed he had just fallen asleep there as he often did.

But this time, he didn't respond to their greetings and was already cold to the touch. The cigarette he'd been smoking had fallen from his fingers and burned a hole in the chair. They told us that after the funeral home picked him up, they discovered his nitroglycerin pills in his pocket. Abe and I wondered if he no longer wished to live his lonely existence without Mom and chose to forego his medication when he felt the attack begin. The pillowslip on his bed attested to his long-endured grief and loneliness, because it was stained and yellowed with tears.

We were immediately faced with the practical necessities of notifying the relatives, writing the obituary, and planning the funeral. For some unknown reason, the pastor of the Nyssa Christian Church refused to officiate at Dad's service, so I made a quick drive to the Ontario Christian Church. Who knows what had transpired in the Nyssa church after Mom's death? The pastor was unknown to me, but perhaps he locked horns with Dad's temper.

Long-time friends in the church pitched in with their usual kindness toward a bereaved church family and prepared a potluck in the basement social hall after the service. I requested that the usual flood of casseroles, cakes, and pies should not be offered at the house, since we had just a few short days before we needed to head back to Yakima.

The actual service is just a blur in my memory. Once again, I opted not to view the remains of my parent. I wanted to remember him as I had last seen him, sitting in his chair, following our summer trip to the Oregon coast. However, some of my aunts and uncles told me that Dad looked very peaceful.

During the service, our family sat in a screened, darkened area of the funeral home behind the speaker's platform. After the sermon, Dad's Masonic friends assumed the role of pallbearers, and everyone drove to the bleak, wintery Owyhee cemetery where he was interred next to Mom. I've been back to the graveyard only once, many years later, when my girls wanted to see where their grandparents were buried. In my mind, they are not in those graves. They live in a better place in my memory.

Dad had used his time sitting alone in his chair to make careful plans and write directions for what I was to do after he died. He didn't write a will, but he'd informed me many months before that when the time came, I was to read the letter tucked into the drawer of his smoking stand. In it, he spelled out his detailed financial plans. He said that I should pay all the bills and then close out the bank account which was listed jointly in his name and mine. The account contained several thousand dollars, and I decided to keep a record of how the money was used so that Jim could receive his share after everything was settled.

Dad directed me to take his Datsun station wagon, which had my name on the registration, and he asked me to prepare the house for sale. He wanted Abe and me to recover the cost of the payments we'd made on the mortgage and to deduct from Jim's share the amounts Dad had loaned him over the years. Then, the balance was to be divided between the two of us. These tallies were all neatly recorded.

Jim was not there for Dad's funeral. He'd moved with his new wife and child to Spain. It was difficult to communicate so far away with Jim, but I finally connected by telephone and asked if there was anything special of Dad's that he wanted. He said that he would like to have Dad's watch and Masonic ring. Though I mailed them immediately, I'm sorry to say that the package never arrived.

I'll be forever grateful to the kindness of our Nyssa friends who continuously dropped in during the week we were there. Friends adopted Mitzie dog and Puss cat. Boise folk stayed around an extra day to help us take care of the miniscule but important details of putting an empty house to sleep for the rest of the winter. I made sure that utility accounts were transferred to our Yakima address. Finally, everything was done, and we could start our trek back home.

Abe was worried about the wintry drive ahead of us. Our car was outfitted with snow tires, but I would be driving Dad's Datsun, and we knew that its tires were going to slip and slide on ice. Also, we'd promised the Jubran's to stop in La Grande to pick up their niece, Kamly, a student at Eastern Oregon College, to bring her to Yakima for Christmas break. We agreed to caravan closely in case I ran into any difficulties.

This worked fine over the snowy roads between Nyssa and La Grande. We drove up to Kamly's residence, and she climbed in with Abe so they could converse in Arabic. The girls rode with me in Grandpa's new car. As I headed out of town, all of a sudden I lost sight of Abe. I stopped and waited a good long while, but he never appeared. Unbeknownst to me, Kamly discovered she had forgotten some things she planned on taking with her. This being an age long before instant communication by cell phone, Abe had no way of letting me know that he'd turned back.

Thus, the second leg of our trip became our trip through Hell! I learned later that Abe was frantic in his efforts to catch up with me, while I was furious with him for taking off and leaving me to find my way alone over the Blue Mountain Pass between La Grande and Pendleton. In 1973, that highway was still the old twisting, curving US 30. The dangerous stretches were not smoothed out until completion of I-84 in 1980. It was called Deadman's Pass with a 6% grade and several hairpin curves. Even now, Deadman's Pass has been the site of numerous truck and car crashes resulting from unpredictable and harsh weather.

I can attest that I experienced all those conditions as I inched my way over slippery ice with drifting snow changing to pouring sleet which kept my windshield wipers clicking and swishing while the inside windows fogged up. My vision was not helped by tears of frustration and fear flowing from eyes that had experienced too much grief over the last long week. Under it all dwelt my slow-burning rage because

Abe had failed to caravan as promised. Thank goodness for astute children who knew better than to attempt any conversation. They surely sensed that Mom had her dander up, and all of us remained very quiet.

It was way past dark when I finally pulled into our driveway. Abe was not there. The house was dark, and his car was missing. Still angry, I drove over to Jubran's, and it did not salve my spirits to find Abe's car parked in their driveway. I shall never forget the sensation of walking into Kitty and Aziz's living room! Of course, I felt relief to find Abe safe, and we quickly explained how the adventure played out for both of us. He had been sitting there with deep concern over our safety. Kamly was full of explanations and apologies for being the cause of the trouble. Kitty was trying to make everyone feel more relaxed with offers of Christmas treats and hot spiced punch. And, Aziz had already plied Abe with soothing liquid refreshment of a different kind.

But what struck me between the eyes and deep down into my heart was the beauty of Kitty's home decorated for Christmas. Lights glowed from their tree shining down on gifts piled high beneath it, all prettily wrapped. Poinsettias held places of honor, and soft music flowed over our heads. In my exhausted, stressed-out state, it seemed just too much for me to bear. I remember making quick excuses and getting my family out and on our way home to a house bereft of all Christmas cheer, no gifts, no tree, and none likely to appear without effort that I had no energy to exert.

When I got inside, I quietly told Abe that he would have to tend to the immediate needs of unpacking the cars and providing food for the girls. I walked into the bedroom, shut the door, and gave in to my need for tears of exhaustion and grief. I became a hermit in that room for the next two or three days while I sat at my desk, writing letters of thanks, and tending to the usual details after a family death. Abe, bless his heart, pitched in with uncomplaining kindness and understanding throughout my whole meltdown. Actually, I have no idea how we pulled off Christmas that year. Surely I must have done some "Ho, Ho, Ho" traditional stuff for the sake of the girls, but I come up blank when pressed for details.

Eventually, my grief settled down, and once more demands of daily life began to command my attention. One family ritual that year was plagued with disaster. The girls had come to expect that on the morning of their birthdays, they would discover a beautiful hand-made cake lovingly crafted by Mom during the night while they slept. But the night before Laila's birthday on February 2nd, I was exhausted. I started baking too late, and I failed to allow enough time for cooling before I attempted to assemble. As I lifted the tender layers from the pans, both of them crumbled into irreparable hunks and crumbs. After I failed miserably to glue the mess together with some frosting, I gave up in tears and flushed Laila's birthday cake down the toilet! In the morning, after offering an apology, I prepared pancakes for breakfast saying she would have to be satisfied with that. Either Abe or I produced a pretty store-bought cake for dessert that evening.

Our family was drawn into a myriad of activities involved with Laila's senior year of high school. I learned about an upcoming student exchange program with a school in Japan. A group of select students would travel from Japan to spend two weeks as guests in homes of Yakima high-school families and attend school with their host students. Then, during the summer, Davis High students would travel to spend two weeks in Japan with the same kids.

When I asked Laila why she hadn't told us about it, she answered that she was sure we would say no to the idea, because of the $200-$300 expense plus airfare, so she hadn't even considered it as an option. I decided to broach the subject with Abe, and as Laila predicted, his immediate response was a firm, "No!" But I disagreed and demanded that he explain why she couldn't go. Finally, he answered, "I've never been to Japan." At that point, he and I both began to laugh at his ridiculous rationale, which caused him to relent, and she received permission to go. In later years Laila told me I was her hero in that story. The experience of going to Japan enriched her world more than she ever thought possible, and she said it changed her life.

But before considering summer plans, we had to get the kid graduated. Her course work was under control because she was the type of student who always got good grades. And, she had plenty of energy left over to pursue her interest in dance and debate. The debate training also kept her involved with long hours of research, practice, and tournaments. Because of her debate experience, Laila developed an interest in pursuing a law career, and she began lobbying to attend Lewis & Clark College, a private institution located in Portland, Oregon. It was noted for its fine undergraduate College of Arts and Sciences and its pre-law program.

I knew that if she attended Lewis & Clark it would put a real strain on our finances. We had just blown our savings for the trip to Jordan. It did no good for Laila to apply for student financial-aid programs. She didn't qualify for assistance because both of her parents were employed with adequate incomes. I held out the hope that she might receive a scholarship, but Lewis & Clark was a prestigious college with top-notch students and competition for grants was highly competitive.

However, the main road-block came from her father. Following the family chain of command, she shared her wishes and dreams with me. In turn, I became her champion and took her arguments to Abe. He received the news in silence, his usual reaction to matters of consequence. Whether it was a wish to go out on a date with a boy or to attend an exorbitantly expensive college, we would be left dangling for days awaiting his reply, while he mulled over the situation.

Finally, on a Friday afternoon in mid-February, he made an unusual offer to take me out to dinner at the Thunderbird Restaurant, leaving the girls home to fend for themselves. I was pleased to accept, since dates alone with my husband were rare. Not only was it a lovely place to eat, but the Thunderbird Restaurant was well-known to Abe. He and his coffee-buddies were regular customers, and the waitresses greeted him as we entered. They were probably as surprised as I that he brought his wife to dine there in the early evening, with no others tagging along to join us.

I remember the salad and entrée were served before Abe finally broached what was on his mind. Just as I took my first bite, he looked directly at me and declared, "I don't want Laila to go to Lewis & Clark." He went on to explain his distrust of private colleges who charge too much. He believed that since Laila was a year younger than the rest of her classmates, she would be well-served to attend Yakima Valley Community College so that she could live at home, and we'd be able to afford her expenses.

The more I listened and argued unsuccessfully for Laila's cause, the more distress I felt. I finally realized that Laila was not going to get her wish, and I began to cry, with tears dripping down into food I couldn't eat. On top of it all, I was plagued with a runny nose, for which I had no hanky. I couldn't even use my napkin because it was cloth, not paper. Embarrassed over my behavior, I just knew that Abe's waitresses were probably watching and wondering what kind of woman Abe had for a wife. So I asked if we could leave, and Abe was more than willing to get out of there. His carefully-planned, reasonable discussion had gone completely awry.

I was grateful for the dark so that my puffy, tear-stained face was less visible. I sank miserably into the passenger seat of our Rambler as he started up the engine. Abe was obviously trying to think of some way to boost my spirits, because he remarked, "I think we need to take a drive out into the country. I have something I'd like to show to you." By that time, I was resigned to pretty much anything he had to offer.

We drove for ten miles, traveling the Old Naches Highway, out past the pear orchard and beyond the Lower Naches School where Laila had attended fourth grade. Soon after passing the school, Abe turned off to the right to ascend a short but steep, curving grade that evened out at the top into a bumpy graveled road, past a farm house on the left and a tumble-down barn on the right. When he came to the next driveway on the left, he drove on past for a few feet. Then he stopped, shut off the car's engine, and urged me to look carefully at the house situated slightly below us. He explained, "This spread is available, and the owners need to sell. If I bargain well, I think we have enough money for a down payment using the rest of the funds from Grandpa's savings account. What do you think?"

In the glow from the moonlight, I could make out a modern, split-level, cinder-block house. I could see what appeared to be new landscaping along a dirt bank ending in a flight of steps leading down to a big, grassy yard on the lower, front level. There was a spinney of weeping birch trees by the steps, and I could just barely make out four little evergreens and a baby dogwood. The back door opened out onto a sidewalk leading past a pump house and curving around an above-ground swimming pool to a large two-car garage with an adjacent car-port. Beyond the garage, I spotted what was obviously a chicken house with a fenced run for the hens. The moonlight didn't help me see the rest of the land, but Abe said there were almost three acres of pasture.

I sat there, soaking it all in. This explained his concern about having funds to pay for an expensive, private, college education for Laila. My tearful demeanor melted away and I turned to Abe with a wobbly smile to ask, "Can we buy it?"

On the way back into town, we had a much less emotional discussion, and we agreed to tell Laila not to dream of Lewis & Clark anymore. Abe decided to pursue the purchase of the farm and I began to map out a moving strategy if his negotiations were successful. All this before I had even seen the interior of the house!

We did purchase that farm. We made an appointment to have the realtor show us the house, and I fell in love with it. Entering from the back door, we could go straight down carpeted stairs to a completely finished lower level. I immediately knew that the laundry area would become my favorite hang-out because its abundant cupboards promised to hold all my sewing and crafting materials. We learned that this area had been a kitchen for the builder's family. They'd lived in the lower level for years while he worked on the main floor.

There were three finished bedrooms downstairs, a room for each of our girls and one for Subhi. The bathroom was nicely arranged, and there was a huge activity room with a Franklin stove. An outside entrance opened onto a patio and the large front yard. I decided that the other very small, dark room on the east side could hold shelving to house our large collection of books. We would actually have a library!

Upstairs, a family area adjoined a well-apportioned kitchen divided by a counter. At the same time that I was admiring, I began to plan that later, the kitchen counter tops would be changed and redesigned to provide a sit-down eating area. I really liked the red-brick design of the linoleum because it blended so well with the used-brick corner with another Franklin stove.

From the kitchen, a door led into a carpeted dining room with the living room off to its right. Again, the room arrangements were great, but I hated the green shag carpet, the wild green and gold wallpaper, and the gauzy green draperies. I made a mental note to learn about applying wallpaper and then practice my skills on the dining room, bedrooms, hallways, and bathrooms. All of these schemes eventually happened.

Standing in the living room, we looked through a large picture window with a view of the newly-landscaped area spreading out below. The front door opened onto a deck and cement stairs going down to the front lawn. To the right of the living room we entered a hallway leading to a master bath and a master bedroom. I couldn't believe the abundance of cupboards and closets in the small area. It seemed obvious that we would never be able to fill all of them, but twenty-seven years of living in that home proved me wrong!

What was there not to love? The asking price was $35,000. After the tour and a few days spent in discussion and financial figuring, Abe made an offer to pay an adequate down payment and assume the present mortgage. He made it contingent upon a satisfactory inspection report. We asked a trusted friend, skilled in construction, to inspect, and he determined that the main floor foundation was extremely well designed with support beams much stronger than usual. In fact, his exact words were, "This is fantastic! Buy it!"

Happily, the owners accepted our offer quickly. Almost before I had time to reconsider, we were committed to purchasing an acreage which came with a flock of chickens about whose care I knew nothing! In addition, we were still making monthly payments for the house in town, and we'd need to find renters until we could locate a buyer.

During this process, Abe and I took time to explain his wishes to Laila concerning her college plans. Laila reluctantly agreed to attend a year at YVC. Although there were other roads to law school, which she chose not to pursue, she has sometimes regretted that original decision. She believed that her characteristic passivity could be traced back to her acceptance of "the unreasonable hard stop" that her Dad's value system placed upon her.

On the other hand, I don't recall passivity being too obvious during the rest of Laila's senior year. We promised to provide rides to all and every activity for both girls while they finished their school year. I can attest to the fact that Laila aggressively held me to that bargain. I was constantly in the car transporting her to and from functions in town.

I knew that the scheduled possession date of our new home was going to create pressure. We needed to finish three months of school, which meant we'd be packing and moving before school let out. A large flock of chickens would be clucking at me for grain, and in the back of my mind dwelt the knowledge that Dad's empty house in Nyssa awaited my attention during that summer. Oh, and by the way, two Japanese students would be coming to live with us after our April spring vacation. No need to worry; pressure was something our family could handle.

During this time, we drove a dependable second-hand Rambler, which had seen years of constant use before it became ours. Then, Abe bought a second-hand trailer from another college buddy. He affixed a hitch to the Rambler, and we were set to move. My memory says that I did the lion's share of the work! During the weeks leading up to Easter, I came home to pack, after a full day of herding fifty-six kindergartners through their paces! Each night, Abe carefully loaded everything "the right way" into the Rambler while I prepared our evening meal. Then I began assembling the next items to be packed before getting to bed late at night.

The girls and Abe fended for themselves the next morning, because I awakened early to drive the ten-mile jaunt to our new house. I tried to be there at least two hours before school started so that I could wash drawers and cupboards, unload the car, feed and water the chickens, take a shower, dress for school, and get to work by 8:15. Strong doubts ran through my head on the first morning as I entered that cold, empty house, did my chores, and headed to the shower.

Eventually, it became home, but not without struggle. The first of those struggles was to make our home livable before our Japanese exchange students arrived. We bought a king-size bed for the master bedroom and put our "good old "54," from Corvallis days in the guest room downstairs. Tammy and Laila had to share a room with twin beds. When I drove Laila to Davis High School to meet our students, she was dismayed and very shy to discover that they were boys. They must have been just as dismayed to learn that their host family lived ten miles out in the country, away from all the excitement and action their friends had access to in town. Thank heavens for Subhi! He filled in as the guy who could relate and make them feel at ease.

We were far from settled in our new home when the students arrived. I managed to hang all the pictures, get the beds made, put towels in the bathrooms, and get the furniture in place, but that first-night supper for our guests was a long, long, time coming, because my cookware was still in a box in the basement. And what does one feed hungry Japanese teenagers? Of course, it never entered my head to ask them what they would like!

My decisions were based on many years of feeding Arab students, but my repertoire of American/Arab cuisine didn't seem too popular. I finally asked for help from the other host families who advised me to provide hamburgers, pizza, and ice cream. Cold cereal for breakfast was just fine, normal teen-guy food. I mentioned that I was at a loss to know what to offer to drink. Should it be lemonade, hot tea, soda? One mother looked at me rather strangely and replied, "My students like milk." I was embarrassed that I had made assumptions about them due to my experience with our many Arab students who generally shunned cold milk.

As it turned out, we overcame our discomforts and enjoyed the exchange-student experience so much that I encouraged Laila to invite all the Davis High School host families and their students to a final pot-luck picnic on our huge front lawn. The place was bursting with the music of sweet kids and their fun-loving chatter. They ate and played badminton and lawn darts and thoroughly enjoyed themselves.

So, we settled into our new digs. The first thing that struck us was the change in Abe's outlook on life. No more coming home to flop down silently on his mattress in front of the TV. Perhaps town living had caused him to sink into a sort of depression, but now he seemed to come alive. After all, he had grown up in a rural community, and this new setting was more like his early life. He spent his free time outside with various chores, such as chopping wood for winter, buying a calf to fatten on the tall pasture grass, and setting the irrigation pipes to keep everything growing green. He purchased a power mower and took on the lawn care as well. When he came inside, he would be full of plans for improvements. He designed a huge addition to the east side by tearing down the existing wooden deck and building a roof extending over a new cement patio. All of Abe's dreams came to fruition.

As the school year flew by, we proudly watched our first-born graduate from high school and excitedly begin preparations for her trip to Japan. Abe would hold down the fort at our new house while she was gone so that Tammy and I could travel to Nyssa and clear out my parents' home. Tammy remembered the trip with pleasure. We stopped at all the usual haunts along the way: the favorite picnic spot and the mandatory ice cream treat at the "48-Flavors" in La Grande. But, in the recesses of my mind dwelt the dismay I felt about parking in the weedy driveway and walking into that empty house.

It was just as bad as I expected. Friends had stocked the refrigerator for us. I still had girlfriends living in the area, and the long-time neighbors kindly greeted me. Also, Jim's first wife, Janey, lived in Nyssa with her new husband, but the house was empty of all life, although filled with memories! My parents' lives echoed to me from every nook and cranny. I prepared a simple meal for Tammy and me and sat her in front of the TV because we'd kept the electric utility paid up, knowing that we would be living there until the place was ready for sale. Then, I went into Mom's bedroom and sank down upon her bed.

As I sat there, the emptiness struck me with full force. Here I was in her musty, closed-up room that still held faint whiffs of her pancake makeup and perfume. Dad had moved nothing; shoes, clothing, jewelry, and cosmetics were all still in place. Though far from empty, filled with her years of collected clutter, the absence of her energetic personality caused a void to open up in the pit of my stomach. I knew I must sort through every drawer and every shoebox stuffed with bills, receipts, letters, and mementos. This room held the story of my mother's private life, and I felt that I had no right to invade it. But, I had to.

I knew Dad's room would be just as bad. The thought of going through all my parents' accumulated belongings, making decisions about distribution and disposal, emptying and cleaning, just swamped me. I'd never experienced such devastation before in all my thirty-nine years of life.

On the other hand, Tammy remembered it as a fun trip with Mom. I took her to Dad's favorite A&W drive-in and used the phone booth outside to call Aunt Dorothy and Uncle Walt. They'd invited Tammy to come visit for a week so that I could slog it out in the house undisturbed. When I hung up, the coin slot opened up and emptied its coin box into our hands and onto the floor. Tammy was sure we'd hit upon a magic phone booth. After that she walked daily to the A&W to check it out for more riches. Alas, it was just a one-shot-deal!

During the next week, Tammy and I drove to Boise, enjoyed one of Aunt Geneva's delicious fried chicken dinners, and stayed overnight with Aunt Dorothy and Uncle Walt. After leaving Tammy for her visit, I headed back to Nyssa and began the work in earnest. It was slow going, but I was brutal in my decision-making. Friends stopped by and marveled at the growing pile of discards in the front driveway. They offered to buy this or that item, but Abe had said his culture doesn't sell the belongings of the beloved dead. I happily offered things to people who wanted them.

Favorite pieces of furniture were distributed among friends and relatives. Janey took the oak table and chairs to be saved for Tony. Clothing was donated except for one frilly dress apron and a favorite green dress of Mom's with its matching green glass pin still attached. Those items are now in my cedar chest. All of Mom's shoebox receipts were piled into one big carton to be sorted later in Yakima. I kept some special items of furniture which had meaning for me: my grandmother's knick-knack shelf, the ancient Singer treadle sewing machine, a lovely antique mirrored dresser that Mom bought from my favorite pastor. Believe it or not, I kept my Dad's cloth handkerchiefs, and I still dig them out when a doozey of a cold needs major assistance.

I also kept the couch and chair that had been in our family all the time I was growing up. At one time, the couch became so worn that it was relegated to the basement as a home for mice, until Mom had it re-upholstered in the greens and golds of the 1960's. I also kept Dad's mustard-colored recliner. It sat in front of the Franklin stove at our new house and became my spot while I read or corrected schoolwork.

I learned that Mom had attended a class on furniture refinishing and the instructor delivered to me all the pieces of a table that Mom worked on. Considering her general lack of interest and ability for such a task, I was impressed with the fair-to-middling job she'd done in stripping down and sanding all its parts. I carried the pieces back to Yakima where we stored them in the basement for many years. Finally, in 1988, We finished it in time to hold Laila's wedding cake. My mother's rescued woodworking project became a wedding present for Laila.

Sorting my mother's kitchen was a more daunting task. A few of the things I wanted to keep were stored on the scuzzy, greasy top shelves: her graniteware platter, the ancient waffle iron and the antique flour sifter with its green-knobbed handle. I saved her red plastic pitcher and matching glasses in memory of the many company dinner tables they had graced. But the spices and foodstuffs were trashed, because everything was full of weevils. I thought I'd never get all those cupboards and shelves washed and acceptable for inspection by potential buyers. My mom didn't enjoy housekeeping, and her cupboards showed it.

There was a brass-wire divider in the living room where Mom displayed keepsakes. I packed up her tea-cup collection, the blue glass candy bowl with matching candle holders, the silver bud vases that had belonged to her mother, and a pink china teapot with its broken lid that my dad had glued back together. It was his present to her on their wedding day.

Then, there was the basement! It was still crammed with orange-crate shelving, dirty canning jars, piles of rags, and piles of just plain dirt. I kept a few of Dad's workbench tools, such as his clamp-on vise, but gave a lot away. I ruined my Kirby vacuum on the basement cement floor. Water seepage from outside irrigation had caused the corner wall to lime up, and after I brushed the walls, I vacuumed up the dust. Not good for motors, I learned!

I stayed for over a month, and as the days wore on, I became more tired and beat-up, feeling the task would never end. The outside of the house required major sprucing. Irrigation sprinklers had constantly beat against the aluminum siding, and Nyssa's water, with its high nitrate, sulphur and other mineral content left sediment on the walls. On one side, the aqua-colored siding was stained a dark orange-brown. I consulted experts at the local hardware store who instructed me to wear protective goggles and heavy rubber gloves while applying a potent acid with a small rag. After it was allowed to set for a while, I washed off the stain with detergent. Many a hot hour in the muggy Nyssa summer heat was spent cleaning that side of the house. But when I finished, it looked presentable.

As the work neared completion, I phoned Abe, who agreed to borrow a pickup and come with Subhi and another friend to load everything I'd set aside. By then, Tammy was back from Boise, and we were both so happy to see them. Their arrival meant the promise of an end to this loathsome labor. Before heading back to Yakima, we signed an agreement with a local real estate company. Within the year, we received a payout, which I distributed as directed by Dad's letter. Jim received his share, and my ties with Nyssa came to an end.

It was so good to get back to Yakima. We had much to learn about our new home and very little time to do it, because we heard that Naim and Siham would arrive to visit in July. It was exciting to think of showing it off to them, and I wanted our relatives to appreciate our choice of country living. This meant we must plunge into preparations for their arrival. Quite a few complications hindered our early efforts.

I asked Laila and Tammy to continue sharing their twin-bed arrangement, so the spare room was free. That worked out fairly well except that Tammy, whose bed was next to the outside wall, discovered that she must check her sheets every night because yellow-jackets crawled through the electric conduits and snuggled into her bed. She received more than one brutal sting as a result. Abe knew he'd be able to plug the holes when he changed the outside patio, but those repairs were on hold because of the expense.

A more immediate concern was care for the chickens. In my effort to teach responsibility, while also freeing me from the chore, I quickly assigned the task to Tammy. She hated feeding, watering, and gathering, because the ferocious old rooster always attacked. Many times she came tearfully limping back to the house with huge red welts on her legs. He also attacked Laila with blood in his eyes.

That bird became the first on the list to be butchered. I literally forced Laila's assistance because I hoped to promote my latest philosophy on feeding our family. I had just finished reading *Diet for a Small Planet*, which convinced me that what we eat should be produced by our own hands. Buying a package of chicken in the supermarket was totally removed from the actual process of raising and harvesting our own.

I knew how to butcher a chicken from watching my elders over the years. I caught our rooster with the wire leg-catcher, and wrestled his squawking body under control.

Laila was horrified to see me tuck his head between two nails pounded into a stump and whack it off with our short-handled axe. She was appalled to see his headless body flopping all over the driveway! After he finished bleeding, I showed her how to dip him into boiling water, strip away his stinky feathers, gut, and wash him. By the time he was cut up, neither of us had appetite for cooking him, so he was relegated to the freezer. When we finally did cook him into a stew, the meat was unchewable. And, Laila decided to become a vegetarian!

Somehow, Tammy managed to escape the butchering lesson, but I saw to it that she was saddled with maintaining the swimming pool. She was expected to vacuum, skim leaves and dead grasshoppers, and add the chemicals. I don't believe that Abe got into the pool even once. He complained about the cost of chemicals, and, I didn't appreciate its small size. It was not large enough to do laps, and invariably the winds came up, making it too chilly to enjoy. But Tammy and her friend loved it! Their favorite game involved standing at opposite sides of the pool, then running as fast as possible towards each other, making a whirlpool, then floating around and around for as long it would carry them. That game, plus practicing back flips in the water, occupied hours of pool time.

Because they loved the pool so intensely, I could foresee eventual trouble brewing over keeping it. And sure enough, the following summer, after experiencing the complicated process of wintering it over, I traded the pool and all its equipment in return for a monster-load of soil. We took advantage of Tammy's being gone to 4-H camp during the Great Pool Removal. When she returned, she found her beloved pool turned into a deep hole and a pile of dirt. She never quite got over it.

About that same time, I'd read another gardener's book that stated a gardener should work outside every day until she lost her enthusiasm. Consequently, I spent long, dusty hours with shovel and wheelbarrow filling in the hole so I could have my garden. I'd shovel, haul, and dump in the pesky wind until my face was coated with grit and all that showed was my pink mouth and tired dark eyes surrounded by wind-blown graying hair. I'd look at Abe and state, "I guess I've lost my enthusiasm." Abe laughed with me about it but never offered to help.

Over the years, that garden became precious to me. I loved a naturalized look with my flowers and planted varieties of perennials. I was always on the look-out for a new plant to tuck in somewhere. But, I often found life too full to be out in the garden every day tending it properly. Abe would occasionally stroll into the house and remark, "Doris, you need to get out and do some work in your garden. It is becoming way too 'naturalized'!"

However, he took over the lawn and pasture, and he quickly mastered the irrigation pipes. About three days of changing pipes were required in order to water the whole pasture. He nursed the plugged-sprinkler heads free from debris, repaired stubborn or broken ones, and then set about teaching the rest of us the "right way" of doing it.

I was so inept. I remember our young neighbor's disdain when I had no idea what she meant by, "You've blown a head." I had to be led out to see the huge shooting arc of water spiking from the broken sprinkler head. After she pointed out the main turn-off valve at the end of the pasture, I was soaked as I waded through the thigh-high pasture grass to crank the valve shut. Eventually, many years and several thousand dollars later, we were able to change the whole system to underground piping. But not soon enough to please me!

However, a neighbor's disdain was no preparation for the painful disillusionment that came next. To my face, everyone was very polite when I enrolled our daughter for fall term at the local junior high school. I initially felt quite comfortable with our choice for Tammy's school. But sadly, thanks to a gossipy member of the teaching staff, who knew us, I learned another side to the situation. At an in-service training session, the principal announced that they would need to quit talking about "those thieving A-rabs" because they were going to have one attending seventh grade that fall. I couldn't believe what I was hearing!

After I reported the incident to Abe, he became silent for a long time. Finally, we decided to chalk it up to a general dissatisfaction shown by many Americans over the recent Arab oil boycott. We opted not to tell the girls, because we felt that it would cloud Tammy's attitude about her new school. She was always so proud of her daddy's heritage.

In truth, we reacted just the way that many others have. We sucked it up and carried on as if nothing had happened. Perhaps we handled it well enough. After all, we learned of the incident through gossip. But since then, I've developed a greater admiration for people who stand up for their rights more overtly.

Thankfully, we were not yet aware of this incident when Naim and Siham arrived. We were still in our honeymoon period of living on our acreage. They loved the place as much as we did. Of course, we spent time with Siham in town as she purchased the many items on her "buy in America" list. Our happiest times were spent in quiet hours of rural living. One full day was spent on the chickens. Siham and Naim were experts at chicken processing, and with their good help, we made quick work of culling the flock to a more reasonable size and storing nice packages in the freezer. Also, Tammy had great fun sitting on my mother's White Mountain freezer while Naim cranked out homemade ice cream.

The most memorable happening for Tammy took place while she was not even home. Major changes in Tammy's life were usually decided when she was gone, it seems. While she attended her first week of 4-H camp, Naim and I discussed the problem of the overgrown pasture grass. He assured Abe and me that a goat would be just the ticket. I located a farmer with animals for sale. Then Naim, Laila, and I went out to look over the herd, and we selected a young Toggenberg doe. The farmer said she was a scrub goat, meaning she had no papers, but Naim said she was healthy, and Laila thought she was pretty. Besides, the price was right, only twenty dollars. When

Tammy arrived home, she found herself the owner of a beautiful goat with correct Toggenberg markings of brown velvet with white stockings.

Although our pasture was adequately fenced to contain Abe's Holstein steer, we quickly learned it was no match for a goat. We often heard the trip, trip, trip of hooves running back and forth on our deck, or witnessed this nimble, mischievous animal jump up on our car roof. At first, we tried staking her with a long chain. But she just pulled the stake up. We then attached her chain to a heavy cement block. Even with that, she grew powerful enough to drag that block wherever she chose to go. I sought advice from goat experts who explained that she was a herd animal and lonesome; she needed companions. Obviously, we acquired a second goat! Abe decided to construct a proper fence. His friends brought a block and tackle for stretching wire and soon built an excellent fence all around the pasture. We never heard the end of Abe's complaint that the twenty dollar bargain goat ended up costing him over two thousand dollars to keep her fenced in.

Then winter arrived, so we needed a barn. Once again, Abe came through and constructed a beautiful pole-barn with dirt floor, manger, tack room, and hay loft. That structure was finished in the cold dark evenings of November with me serving as assistant. "Hold the flashlight a little higher." "Hand me another large nail." "Wait 'til I measure with the level." He built a perfect barn, but I was literally frozen with impatience before it was finished.

November also was breeding time for goats. We sought out a registered Toggenberg buck, because Tammy learned that with careful breeding she could upgrade the kids to earn papers. When her doe began bleating and rapidly flagging her tail, we knew she was in heat. I laughingly told my friends that we were dressing in our oldest, raggedy clothes to attend a goat wedding.

There is nothing to compare with the odor of a buck in rut! It is much ranker than the perfume of a skunk. By the time a doe is bred, everyone involved is just as smelly. Because of this, we chose not to attempt breeding at our place and always took our goats out to a goat farm. That first year, we had to hitch up the trailer to our Rambler while Tammy rode in the trailer with her goat to ensure that she stayed lying down. In later years, we had a pick-up, but Tammy still rode in back with the goat.

All of this effort was so rewarding. Tammy just blossomed!

She was elected to office in her 4-H club; she assumed excellent responsibility for her animals; and we were in absolute awe when the kids were born. Some of the happiest times I've ever had with my daughter were spent snuggling under the

Tammy and Kids

warmth of a heat lamp at four in the morning while we struggled to teach those babies to nurse from a bottle. We had to capture their little wiggling heads between our knees and force them to take the nipple. Later, they always came running up to butt against our knees. Due to their first feeding experiences, they had learned that food comes from knees.

The experts told us not to allow the kids to nurse their mother because weaning was so difficult. So Tammy would rise early, clamber barefooted into farm boots, shrug on a coat over her nightgown, and head out into the frosty air to milk before hurrying to catch her school bus. I've always cherished her young girl comment, "I'm lucky. I get to go milk a warm goat."

That warm goat was a good milker and produced well over a gallon of milk every morning and night. Tammy carefully strained it, filled the baby bottles, and washed her equipment. We worked out a bargain to buy the milk, which gave her spending money and experience in financial record-keeping. All of the family, except Tammy, enjoyed drinking it, and I learned to make yogurt and several varieties of good cheese. At one time, Tammy had a customer who bought all the extra milk to feed her herd of baby goats. Some of Tammy's earnings were even stashed away for future college expenses.

Abe, as a good dad, willingly took over the task of milking if Tammy was going to be away on school activities. However, when Tammy came home, he would say to her, "Walk with me." Then she knew she was in for yet another lesson on the exact "right way" to do the whole process. "Now with the feed, best if you pour it out like this." And "Best if you wash her udder like this." He was gentle in his teaching, but it didn't seem to register with him that she had been doing the task successfully for months. Because he was so sure that he knew the best way of doing things, she listened politely to all his advice every time it was offered.

I took over caring for the baby goats during the day. I put the kids in the back seat of the Rambler and they went to kindergarten with me. We built a pen with plastic covering the floor and straw over that. The kindergartners were ecstatic, taking turns with bottle feeding and running with kids on leashes during recess. I remarked on how much fun it was to witness the kids chasing the kids.

In later years, a friend asked me if taking a carload of goats to school would be acceptable in the present-day Yakima school district. I answered, "Love me, love my goats! If I still had the stamina to herd kindergartners, the school would need to accept those darling baby animals in my classroom every spring."

Tammy stayed active with her 4-H goat projects throughout high school. She spent many days attending fairs to show her animals, and she relished every moment. I didn't relish the extra strain of hauling feed, tack, straw, animals, tent, and food back and forth while still fulfilling my teaching duties and keeping our home together. But the rewards of having this close experience with her made up for all the effort.

She received trophies and awards. Dressed all in dairy whites for her first fair, she was the only student to enter a goat. The judge asked her, "What makes a good goat?" Tammy described all her goat's best qualities with such assurance, and he awarded the Grand Champion Trophy! However, they didn't have a goat trophy prepared and had to order one to be delivered later. Even then, Tammy couldn't have been more proud.

Another of her awards is prominent in my memory because I managed to make a fool of myself during the occasion. Tammy was honored at a Yakima valley-wide banquet for her 4-H service and I, being the proud Mama, was invited to introduce myself. I felt flustered, but I stood and loudly announced, "I am Doris Valley from Upper Ayyoub." I wanted to disappear, but Tammy thought it was hilarious.

I was also an embarrassment during 4-H meetings. What was so satisfying about the 4-H organization was the expectation that parents should stay for the meetings and offer support to the members. This suited me fine, and I was pleased to transport Tammy to member's homes or serve as hostess at ours. Eager to learn, I asked more than my share of questions during the meetings. Abe noticed how I was dominating the conversation, and he quietly corrected me later. He said that when he heard me talking too much, he was going to say, "Doris, don't you think it's time for a nice cup of tea?" That became a signal, which lasted through many years of marriage, for me to put a lid on it!

Even though Abe was able to influence my actions by suggesting tea, my propensity to order other family members around wasn't inhibited until the population of the house began to change. My influence over Laila diminished when she headed off to the University of Washington for her sophomore year of college. And, Subhi bid us goodbye to finish his schooling in London. His room didn't stay vacant for long since Abe's niece Hanan, Nasser's daughter, soon arrived to begin her two years at YVC.

This meant that the basement domain was taken over by girls once more. Hanan was a sweetheart who willingly took on her share of household duties, and I never felt compelled to nag her as I regularly did with my daughter. Tammy, poor girl, received the brunt of my motherly expectations. Her piano practice is only one example.

By the time Tammy was in high school, she'd been taking piano lessons for many years and was beginning to develop some skill. But like most kids, she resisted the demands of daily practice sessions. For one thing, the piano was located in the basement recreation room which was quite cold in winter. In Tammy's opinion, other family members were all upstairs carrying on more interesting activities, like cooking, reading, or watching television, while she was banished to the freezing isolation down below. She hated my constant nagging about paying for lessons when she wasn't practicing.

On one of these occasions during her junior year, I decided to apply some leverage by reminding her that these lessons were expensive and that if she wasn't going to invest the effort in preparing for them, we would no longer invest in paying for them. She said, "Fine. I'll stop!" "Oh no, you won't!" I shouted back. "We expect you to continue with lessons until you graduate from high school, and you WILL practice."

Tammy was expected to practice either while I prepared supper or right after we ate so that we could listen and applaud. On occasion, I would walk over to the head of the stairs to clap, but more often than not, she would hear her father and me applauding from our comfy chairs in front of the wood stove or from the living room. We rarely sat downstairs in the cold and actually watched her play.

At some point, still smarting from the unfairness of it all, she devised a plan. She hooked up our portable tape recorder, stole one of Hanan's cassettes, and recorded an entire practice session. Then, several nights a week, she would sit on the piano bench in the cold basement, reading while the tape was playing. She said that she couldn't risk us coming to the top of the stairs to applaud her and find her nowhere near the piano, so she sat there, in constant fear that she would be caught in this massive deception.

While she came to realize that the thirty-minute practice seemed to take twice as long when she was just sitting at the piano as opposed to actually playing, she continued with her scheme because she just really needed to get away with something. We never noticed that she made the same errors each time she practiced. We never knew she did this until she was an adult and was commiserating with one of her nephews about sneaky things they had done.

This was just one of the instances where I assumed the role of lead parent when dealing with daily family concerns for Tammy, her goats, and all the 4-H activities. Abe took over in other areas to make our life comfortable while we lived on the acreage. One of his concerns dealt with keeping that huge house warm in winter and cool in summer. When we moved in, there was a not-so-efficient oil furnace in the basement. We soon removed that and installed an electric heat pump. But, Abe knew the electric bills would eat us up unless he supplemented with wood fires. He traded away the Franklin Stoves and installed an excellent, efficient American Home Heater upstairs and an Earth Stove downstairs. Then he developed a meticulous system for hauling, chopping, and stacking wood. He acquired wedges, mauls, and axes, and truly enjoyed his role as family woodsman.

Of course, there was a correct way to build a fire. Even before beginning to lay the fire, he had a ritual of carefully cleaning the stove's glass door with steel wool and a cotton-ball dipped in rubbing alcohol. The cotton ball then served as the fire-starter. Abe asked me to record the fire-building rules in detail so that they could be inserted into the manual that we prepared for our renters in the Corvallis house.

To Build a Fire

Unlike Jack London, you will be highly successful in having a warm place to live if you follow these rules:

1. Allow flame to rise when starting by building a stacked structure with wood.

2. Place kindling and starter at the bottom.

3. Starter can be a cotton ball soaked in rubbing alcohol.

4. Burn only dry, cured wood. No garbage, cardboard, or Christmas wrappings.

5. Burn clean with a hot fire and dry wood to help burn the carbon from chimney.

6. A continuous, slow-burning fire causes accumulated carbon build-up inside chimney.

7. Store wood covered outside.

8. Please be considerate of our newly refinished fir floor.

9. Keep your wood in a cardboard box in the entry room and off living room floor.

Each member of the family was subjected to serving as pupil while he taught us the right way to build a fire. Of course, we never actually had to build one, because he would hover and then take over. We were relegated to being his gofers. Once he asked me to go out to the wood pile to bring in one more piece of wood. When I came back with it, he said, "No, that's not the right piece," and he took it back outside to find the correct one.

We watched in fascination when he began the fire-building process by sifting every bit of cold ash through his fingers, rescuing any specks of charcoal that might still be somewhat combustible, and carefully piling them over in the corner of the firebox. After he was satisfied, he used his metal dustpan to scoop out all the finer cold ash to be stored in a cardboard box or a paper grocery bag. The little burnable charcoal bits were then stacked in the middle of the firebox and he began to build his new wood structure over it.

He always carried out this routine in the warmer part of the day, got everything just so, and then would leave it until the cold of the evening signaled him to touch it with a match. He loved to get things really going hot. I often felt a need to escape the room for several hours until the fire settled down a bit. But for Tammy, while the upstairs family rooms were blistering with too much heat, the basement where she slept, showered, and "practiced" piano, was frequently about 45°F. It was not Abe's usual custom to build a fire down there.

I was often able to use the stove top to simmer a pot of stew or chili overnight for the next day, which pleased Abe immensely. It brought back his

The right way to build a fire

memory of cooking beets on his little heater when he lived in Amman. The trick allowed me to work late after school knowing that the family would come home to an already prepared meal.

Besides being the chief fire-builder for the family, Abe was our snow-removal superintendent. He obviously garnered a great deal of satisfaction from shoveling our walks clean. Often, he'd head outside in the middle of the night to scrape away. If the snowfall was light, we teased him to hurry with his shoveling before the snow melted.

But, when the snowfall was heavy, it had its scary aspects.

And it snowed!

The turn-off for our road from the Old Naches Highway involved a curving hill. If a driver hesitated at the top of the curve, rounding the turn, it was possible for a vehicle to slip off and tumble down a steep embankment. This was doubly difficult for me, because I usually drove the pickup to work, and it was too light with nothing in the back to maintain good traction. During snowy weather, Abe loaded it up with heavy chunks of wood or several bales of hay under a tarp. We had chains for the truck, but Abe refused to allow me to drive with them installed all winter because they destroyed tires when driving on cleared roads. He knew how to install the chains as needed, and I thought I did, too.

But, one freaky, snowy Valentine's day, I headed out to the garage at around seven in the morning and realized I was in trouble. Abe had parked his car overnight at the foot of the hill by the main highway, so he and Tammy walked down the slippery road and drove off, while I was still busy preparing Valentine treats for two kindergarten class parties.

With the snow so deep, I knew better than to try going down that slick curve without chains. So, I laid the chains out on the garage floor just as I had observed Abe do, and backed the pickup on to them just as he did. But in the freezing cold, I discovered that my fingers did not have the strength to buckle them up. I was finally forced to give up, go back into the house, and call my principal to get a substitute teacher. Consequently, I sat at home in tears while someone else oversaw the excitement of my fifty-six kids opening Valentines and gobbling treats.

I was embarrassed. Two-thirds of our family made it to their schools that day. Deservedly or not, I blamed myself for not planning ahead a little better. After all, I could have parked at the bottom of the hill the night before; a plan that never even occurred to me! But yes, I would have hated the treacherous trudge down the snowy hill in the frosty, cold morning while trying to carry the tray of treats.

That was not the only occasion when that pickup and I got into trouble. Since I was always the last one to leave the house, I suffered alone. This time, it was a cooking day at school and I was running late, as usual. The children and I were going to bake a complicated concoction as gifts for parents, and I needed to gather all the ingredients from my home and take them to school. My head buzzed with details of what I must remember to bring: flour, eggs, shortening, sugar, spices, implements, recipe, etc. I finally had it all loaded into the pickup and I remarked out loud to myself. "There, I've remembered everything." So I climbed into the truck, feeling smug that I would be able to make it to school before the bell rang. I revved the engine and proceeded to back out of the garage. Ker slam! Bam! Kerklunk! I looked up and realized the one important item I'd overlooked. I hadn't opened the garage door!

I hopped out to survey the damage and realized that bumps and dents were going to show, but the truck still worked and the garage door still opened, although a bit crookedly. It struck me as hilarious, and I giggled all the way to school. My teaching associates and I enjoyed several good laughs that day over my foolishness. When I drove home that night, I prepared to enjoy the joke on me with Abe. Abe took one look at the damage to truck and garage door and didn't think it was at all funny! He just adopted his usual silence for the rest of the evening.

About the same time, the county sent out a notice that our road was to receive a name and we would be assigned a house number. Until then, our postal address was simply "Route 4." The county provided all residents with an opportunity to suggest a road name. I sent in our suggestion of "Ahsanshee Road" since we had chosen the name of "Ahsanshee Acres" for our place. After all, it was where we raised our very best daughters along with the very best goats. It was a distinct disappointment when the county didn't appreciate my suggestion and bestowed the address of 200 Barnes Road upon us. We were stuck with a mundane name, no offence to whoever Barnes was, and I resented it.

Possibly, my resentment had something to do with my forthcoming crime caper. I'm not really a vindictive woman, and I suspect that the theft of plants from the county had to do with my actually wanting that particular variety of rose, but still, I thought the county owed me something. For quite some time, I had been admiring the wild roses that grew along the roadside. I even learned their name, Rugosa Rose. They bloomed profusely in early summer and then produced large brightly-colored rose hips and deep red foliage in the fall. I knew that it was unlawful to dig public plants, but I also knew that roses could be started from cuttings which would not damage the mature plant.

So, one lovely fall morning, I stuck clippers and plastic bags in the car. On the way home that evening, I parked by the side of the road and urged Tammy to assist me in cutting canes from the bushes. We had good luck. No one apprehended us while we stole from the county, and no car rear-ended our illegally-parked vehicle. When I arrived home, I used root-tone on the cuttings and planted them along our lower bank under glass quart jars to winter over.

In the spring, I removed the jars to discover that the cuttings had indeed taken root and were sending up new little shoots. I was so proud of the accomplishment that when the Scholarship Board met at my home, I proceeded to brag about my illicit rose caper to two of the board members who also enjoyed gardening. I insisted they clamber down the steps to "ooh and ahh." To my utter dismay, I discovered that every little plant had been pulled up and lay dried and dead. I couldn't understand the mystery until I confronted Abe. It seems that he had decided to weed the area, something he never did, and he thought they were weeds! Why on earth did he finally decide to "help" me with my gardening?!

My, how the ladies did laugh at me and took great delight in reminding me of the fact that "Crime Does Not Pay!" I finally did get Rugosa Roses started after I searched local nurseries and purchased them. They flourished and the birds loved to feed on the rose hips each winter. I dried some hips and produced a lovely red lemony-flavored tea. But true to form, Abe never did like their wild rambling over the hillside and often complained because they were covered with thorns. Probably, he classified them in the same category as the wild blackberries which he fought on the Corvallis property.

Though Abe didn't exert much effort in caring for my "naturalized" flower gardens, the tomato-cucumber patch was a different matter. Between the garage and the barn was some land that initially must have been the dumping area for gravel and stones used during construction of the house. It was a total mess when we moved in.

Our Troy-Bilt tiller was way too expensive, yet necessary. I ordered it, only to discover it required Abe's strength to manipulate. Over the years, Abe's patient hours of removing rock, and adding mulch and manure resulted in a fine little patch where we planted vegetables and a nice peach tree. Early in the summer, I purchased Early Girl, Big Boy, or Celebrity tomato plants for the two of us to set. Abe quickly assumed the lead on the planting and nurturing ritual. Watering had to be done just so.

He carefully sculpted a circular dike to form a well around each little plant so that only the immediate area near the roots received water. Consequently, weeds between the plants received no encouragement from irrigation. In the cool of summer evenings, we could always find Abe in his customary squatting position, watering, pruning, staking, and creating windbreaks for his precious crop. Was he ever pleased with his harvest!

After two years of struggle on Ahsanshee Acres, I began to feel satisfied with my metamorphosis from city kid to farm woman. My mother's early training in canning and food preservation was being put to good use. I had learned the fundamentals of goat-rearing; I could change irrigation pipes in the pasture; and I was nurturing a flock of chickens that produced more eggs than our family could eat.

Abe and I both felt that our rich pasture grass also should be used to provide meat for us. Since his mainstay meals while growing up came from lamb, we chose to add a few sheep to our ever-growing herd of goats, but our sheep seemed to be more fragile and labor intensive than goats. The sheep collected cheat-grass seeds in their nostrils and around their eyes which often caused infection. They needed an annual drenching with smelly sheep-dip to control the insects in their wool, and they frightened easily and would stampede over nothing. Adverse weather conditions, such as a period of extra hot days, would lay them low.

I was inclined to believe the joke that our 4-H leader told about their fragility. He said never to tell a sheep that it is looking a bit poorly. It will immediately oblige by keeling over dead. However, one good characteristic showed up when Tammy went out to the pasture and called, "Goats!" Everybody came running, including the sheep, who must have thought they were goats. This meant that we didn't require the services of a sheep dog.

Somehow, we successfully managed to winter our flock and were able to help with lambing in the spring. I even thought I could learn to do my own shearing. That first spring, after two hours of torturously nicking the hide of one ewe, I released the poor blood-speckled animal back into the flock. She was obviously embarrassed, and her baby didn't even recognize her. I went inside and called a professional to shear the rest of the flock. Butchering was also relegated to the professionals. Both Tammy and Laila made themselves scarce on that dreadful day. And Laila became even more secure in the belief that she wanted to be a vegetarian.

But on a scale of needing professional help, our cow, Bonny, was the cause of my silliest farming fiasco. Abe wanted to have her bred in order to raise our own meat. That was all fine and good, except Bonny came in heat on a day when Abe was gone. The guy we contracted to do the artificial insemination was on his way to our house with the expectation that our animal would be tethered and ready, but Bonny was far out at the edge of the pasture. Although she was tame for Abe, she didn't trust me one iota. How to get her into the barn and tied up? I remembered that Abe tamed her by putting grain into a bucket and shaking it so she would be attracted to the rattle. Every few steps backward he'd pour a bit into a flat cardboard box-top and allow her to eat it. With the breeder due any minute, I said to myself, "I can do that, and I'd better be quick about it."

Picture a timid Doris, stumbling backwards through the uneven tufts of pasture grass, shaking a pail of grain, and offering soft words to encourage a skittish cow who is constantly bellowing out her distrustful stress. With a few relapses, when she backed off as if to bolt, I finally coaxed her up to the gate of the barn. I didn't dare turn around to watch where I was going for fear of losing her attention. Finally at the threshold of the barn, almost home free, I took one last backward step and BAM! With a loud whoop of surprise, down I went, landing directly on my butt!

The grain bucket went flying and I sat there ungraciously sprawled in front of Bonny. I'd forgotten that the threshold was actually a wide board. I was sure that all was lost because Bonny would take off in fright! But, I looked up at her, and exclaimed, "Excuse me!" Believe it or not, she kindly accepted my apology and stood there watching me with her big brown eyes while patiently waiting for more grain.

There wasn't much left in the bucket, but I held it out to her and enticed her inside to finish munching the rest of it in the jury-rigged manger that Abe built. As soon as her head was inside the stanchion, I tied her halter to its cross-bar and my job was finished. Thankfully, the breeder, who had just driven up, arrived too late to witness my prat fall. Only the cow and I knew about my lack of grace. And, as was my habit from younger days, I didn't confess.

Breeding took place in mid-August. This meant that we welcomed her darling baby calf the first week of May. Since Bonny was a good mother, Abe decided to allow the calf to nurse. We didn't need any cow's milk because we had more goat milk than we could use, but Abe insisted on bringing a container of her "first milk" into the kitchen with careful instructions on how I should heat it, add a bit of sugar, and produce a special custard. It brought back memories from his childhood of how his mother relished that treat. The rest of the family was allowed a small taste, but that particular "superior comestible" belonged to Abe.

The entire experience of raising the calf was an absolute delight for Abe. He spent precious time every day out in the pasture feeding grain to Bonny, while lovingly petting and brushing her little offspring. When Mount St. Helens erupted on May 18th, I am quite certain that Abe felt every bit as alarmed for the wellbeing of Bonny and her calf as he did for the safety of his wife and daughter!

Indeed, he should have been anxious because we were in danger. While he was home alone trying unsuccessfully to coax cow and calf into the barn, Tammy and I were hauling a trailer-load of goats home from a Sunday 4-H show. The volcano blew at 8:30 a.m., and a cloud of ash began to travel towards the northeastern section of Washington. By 9:45, it hit Yakima and turned the sunny day into the darkest of nights. Visibility was reduced to less than ten feet.

When I saw the dark cloud approaching while we were still at the goat show, I urged Tammy to help me quickly load up our tack and animals, and we headed out on an unfamiliar road to travel the thirty miles home. In no time, we were lost in a swirling, choking mist of ash that no amount of windshield wipers or headlights could overcome. I found myself heading towards the ditch again and again. It was terrifying to be confronted suddenly with the headlights of an approaching car and needing to swerve out of the way.

It didn't help that Tammy sat beside me dissolved in a puddle of frantic tears because our radio suggested that chemical contents of the ash were probably highly toxic, and all animals should be sheltered inside. Of course, her beloved goats were being dragged along behind us in an open trailer! The tension was almost unbearable, but after three desperately-long hours of creeping down the road, we finally reached the safety of our home to be greeted by a much-relieved Abe.

His story of trying to rescue Bonny and the calf bordered on the ridiculous. He couldn't entice Bonny to come to the barn, so he picked up the calf and trudged through the ever-thickening blanket of ash and deposited him in the barn. Bonny followed her calf, but immediately fled back out to the far corner of the pasture. Abe said he carried that calf into the barn three times before finally giving up.

As it turned out, the ash was not chemically toxic. I brazenly proved that for myself. One speculation broadcast on the radio said that it might be transformed to sulfuric acid when mixed with water. But, our stock tank was choked with ash and our animals needed to drink. I stood there by the tub, debating how to reach the plug so that it could be drained and cleaned. Finally, I decided just to find out if we had a tank of acid and plunged my arm to the bottom to pull the plug. Luckily, the radio conjecture was wrong.

School was closed for an entire week, while we spent every waking moment fighting the ash which carpeted everything six inches deep. The world was grey and the ash didn't melt or blow away. Abe shoveled the sidewalk only to realize we would also need to hire someone to shovel the roof, which once more piled the sidewalks high. Every inch of pasture had to be sprinkled to wash off the grass so that the animals could graze. While we trudged to set the pipes, the wet ash formed into heavy cement-like globs on our boots.

After fighting our own personal battle with the unremitting and ever-present ash, we were forced to make up the entire week of missed school days. I headed back for a wearisome lengthened school year, with antsy students, where all classroom surfaces were covered with a dusting of ash that filtered through every crack. The custodians tried to keep it cleaned up but children continually tracked it back in. We all felt cranky from breathing the dust-filled air, and it was necessary to rinse out our nostrils as often as possible. This uncomfortable condition didn't improve much during the remainder of the school term which stretched interminably into the first weeks of June.

In the midst of it all, Tammy was experiencing exhilarating years of high school. With encouragement from her family, she chose to transfer into Yakima's Davis High School following her sophomore year at Naches. There, she became very involved in the music program and student government during her last two years of school. She studied German, which allowed her to participate in a foreign-exchange program with a high school in West Germany, as it was then.

We hosted a German student for two weeks, which then qualified Tammy to travel to Germany during the summer after her junior year. Abe was more willing this second go-around to encourage his daughter to travel. And it paid off big time! By piquing her interest in travel, she decided to pursue a college minor in German, which helped her land her first job with Boise Cascade. They hired her in their Internal Audit department, which required 75% travel, primarily within North America, but occasionally to Germany and Austria.

Tammy achieved good grades in high school, while also finding time for music and stage craft. She sang in a the large high school chorus, called the Aeolians, as well as in a smaller select jazz ensemble known as Die Meister Singers. In addition, she took on important production and costuming roles for two of the school musicals. But as graduation approached, it became her turn to go through family negotiations on her plans for college. Tammy enlisted the help of her choir director for some counseling on how to prepare for the difficult discussions with her father about where to go for college. In so doing, she realized that her primary objective was not to live at home and not to attend YVC. Abe rather quickly agreed that Central Washington University, only thirty miles from Yakima, would be just fine.

Tammy applied and was accepted for fall term 1980. Our incomes were sufficient that she did not qualify for financial aid, so we were facing years of counting pennies with two girls in college. But we knew it was doable and we proudly celebrated her graduation during the spring.

CHAPTER 18

—⟡—

Our Fulfilled lives

AFTER SURVIVING THE TRIALS of Mount St. Helens, our life settled back into managing the acreage, harvesting our produce, and supporting both girls in college. Although we were not extravagant, there was never money left over at month's end. We usually found it necessary to take a loan from the Teacher's Credit Union at the beginning of each fall.

Laila graduated from the University of Washington, majoring in Psychology with a minor in Dance and headed off to Loyola Marymount in Los Angeles for graduate work in movement therapy. Tammy attended Central Washington University major-ing in Accounting with a minor in German. Abe continued shepherding freshmen and sophomore students through their struggles with math at Yakima Valley College and serving as Department of Math Chair.

I was faced with my previously announced decision to change schools. I knew that I planned to retire after ten more years, and I wanted to prove to myself that I was capable of successfully teaching students in an economically-depressed area. Up until that time, my experience was with children from middle-class, upwardly mobile families. So, I requested a transfer and was assigned to a third grade position.

Consequently, I was faced with packing up my classroom and saying good-bye to the kindergartners. On the last day of the year, as I carried my boxes into the new, ash-coated school room, I remember being depressed and fearful. What unimagined challenges had I bitten off, and would I ever feel secure with my decision?

I began my ten-year effort to adjust to the new challenge of working with young kids living in an area of Yakima with low household incomes where most of the pupils qualified for the free-lunch program.

That first fall was a huge adjustment for me. I discovered that my bag of disci-plinary tricks was totally ineffective with third-graders. They didn't respond to my singing directions that worked great with five-year-olds. These kids looked at me with a "what's up with this teach?" expression on their faces. I usually managed to get them settled into productive work each morning until recess. But all hell broke loose while they were out on the playground, and I was met with a line of angry, pushing, petulant children when I met them at the door. "He called me a mother!" "She's talking nasty to me!" "I won't stand in line next to him!" Until then, my vocabulary was so innocent that I didn't even know what they meant when they called each other a "mother."

I quickly adopted a more commanding tone of voice and I struggled to discover what would work so that I could accomplish more than just putting out fires. I learned to implement immediate feedback. Each student was required to keep each day's work in a folded-over sheet of newsprint and they were not dismissed to go home until I walked by each desk to check that assignments were in the folder. Then, I carried all those folders home, fed the family, cleaned up, prepared the next day's meal, and fell asleep in front of the fire.

I'd wake up about 3:00 a.m. and begin to check folders, keeping track of what each student needed to fix. When I arrived at school, I posted every kid's name with the work that must be done before going out for morning recess. Consequently, I had no break while monitoring their corrections. It was a grueling process as the students and I worked to become a cohesive classroom. I remember my positive self-talk as I drove to school each morning. "They are just children, Doris. They are just children."

Other teachers and I took advantage of every in-service that was offered on dealing with classroom behavior. With the help of a good principal, things began to turn around. I finally hit upon the plan of appointing a new classroom "president" each day. It was that child's responsibility to bring in a signed note from the playground supervisor that everyone in class had been trouble-free for the entire recess. Such a note gave the class a success mark on our chart working toward the goal of some special treat. When the class met the goal, I offered a new challenge. One of those rewards was a chance to cook something special during class time. Another was an ice cream party.

If the note came with a negative report, I removed a success mark from the chart accompanied by disgruntled moans from the kids. Rightly so, since it may have been only one child who misbehaved, but I was trying to emphasize that they could learn to be buddies out there and cooperate to achieve success.

The final challenge for the year was a swimming party at the YMCA. Meeting that goal was a real struggle, but we all felt full of pride when we loaded into a school bus and headed to the "Y." We had a ball. But even there, one particularly troubled kid caused a near disaster. The lifeguard lined the class up and set limits on how far a non-swimmer could go towards the deep end. This boy, the tallest and most aggressive in the class, immediately walked down towards the edge of the deepest section, jumped in, and was rescued by the guard. Another day, the same student became so unruly on the playground that the principal suspended him, and he missed the last week of school. I've worried over the years about whatever happened to him as he grew into adulthood. I admit that I wasn't entirely successful with all my kids that first year.

Most of the third-graders eventually came around. In fact, there was one small boy with whom I'd been particularly strict because he was noted for violent outbursts and temper tantrums. Yet, by the end of the year, he turned into my secret admirer. One morning, he stopped by the office to show our principal the special present he had for me. When the school bell rang, he rushed into our schoolroom to place the box proudly on my desk. I opened it in front of his excited eyes to discover a lavish, multi-layered French crystal necklace, circa 1950. Although it is possible that he might have snitched it from his mother's jewelry, knowing his temperament, I chose not to investigate. My principal concurred with that decision. I proudly wore that necklace every day until the school year finished.

I continued working in that same building until my retirement in 1990. However, during the last few years, I left third grade and moved back to my comfort level with younger children. The district was experimenting with the concept of "readiness-first" grades. My pupils were children who had already attended kindergarten yet didn't have the skills or maturity for success with regular first grade curriculum. Parents were advised that it meant adding an extra year to their child's elementary education.

Even though we emphasized it all year during parent-teacher conferences, many families were still surprised when their youngsters were not assigned to second grade the following year. I loved teaching them, but I soon noticed that many of my pupils were actually assigned to me due to behavior problems rather than academic shortcomings. It caused me to run a tight ship, and we still made good progress.

It was never a good day, if I had to be absent while a substitute teacher filled in. For that matter, I didn't find it wise even to step out of the room. Poor Abe discovered that! One day, he came by during lunch time to pick up a document. The kids were all seated at their separate desks eating, while one youngster sat on the teacher's tall stool to give his "show and tell" presentation. I told Abe that I knew exactly where the paper was in my car and asked him to stay with my class while I scooted out to retrieve it. I was gone less than five minutes, but I returned to find a white-faced husband and chaos among my students. It seems that one child thought the kid sitting on the stool had overstayed his turn. So, he got up from his desk and knocked the kid off the stool, causing tears, shouts, and name-calling. Because Abe was so startled by the incident, he grabbed the document and fled, never to return while school was in session.

After that, our friends often heard Abe bemoan the trials and tribulations of elementary teachers. I suspect he thought that *Blackboard Jungle* was alive and flourishing in American schools. I also know that discipline was never something he worried about during his years of teaching junior college. Once, I was free from school on a day when Abe was in the classroom. I went to the college to meet him for lunch and enjoyed the opportunity to peek through the small window of his classroom door where I could see him holding forth in front of a polite, deeply engrossed roomful of students. He had a sweet smile on his face and was obviously sharing a joke with them, because they erupted into laughter.

Abe enjoyed not only his classes, but also his co-workers. During this period, he decided to stop smoking, and it was a tremendously difficult challenge. The nurse in the health services center provided him with excellent support, and his department buddies did too. They'd pass by his office and josh him when they noticed him holding a carrot stick between his fingers as if it were a cigarette.

Throughout our marriage, Abe struggled with smoking. It is understandable given that he first began to light up at the tender age of ten. He knew it was detrimental to his health and while he was a student, it also interfered with his religious affiliations. I swear that I didn't nag when he was openly smoking, but I confess to being overly enthusiastic when he was going through a period of abstinence.

What dismayed me was his sneakiness when he pretended not to smoke while secretly indulging whenever I wasn't around. Ostensibly, he had refrained from smoking for over two years, but he placed himself in an untenable situation by secretly grabbing a puff when he could get away with it.

The funniest incident occurred during a night when Tammy and I joined Abe and his poker buddy for dinner at a nearby casino. We enjoyed a lovely salmon dinner, and Abe thought Tammy and I had gone home, while he planned on staying for a few more hours of poker. Unknown to him, I'd stopped off to use the restroom. As Tammy waited for me across the room, she looked up to see her father lighting up a cigarette just outside the entrance to the lavatories. She felt like she was moving in slow motion as she tried to warn her dad just as I emerged. She will never forget the look on my face as I exclaimed, "Brahim, you are smoking!" But, what cracked her up was his response, as he blew the smoke from his nostrils to reply, "No, I'm not!"

Our marriage survived, of course, but for a while, the trust level was in jeopardy. We worked it out as soon as he openly admitted what he was doing. I could accept that. In later years, when heart difficulties and early emphysema developed, he truly did quit for good.

Abe's weekly lesson plans never had to be written out in detail ready for inspection by his supervisor, as I was required to do. He woke up early, studied his textbook over coffee, jotted a few equations on a note card, stuck it in his shirt pocket, and headed off to teach. After class one day, his best student stopped him to ask what secret message he kept on the tip end of his chalk. It seems that when a student asked him a question, he had a habit of intently studying his piece of chalk before beginning to write out the answer in full detail on the board. She believed there must be some magic on the tip of that chalk. I agree there was magic involved in the way Abe could make the difficult concepts of mathematics come alive in his classes. Over the years, scores of students came back to thank him for his patient and gentle assistance as they strived to master the concepts.

With the help of great co-workers, I began to feel comfortable with my teaching assignment and was able to devote more time to family concerns. Even though our kids were living away from home, we were still deeply invested in support of their doings. Tammy became part of the Accounting leadership team at one Boise Cascade facility, a century-old paper mill in northern Vermont.

Laila finished her Master's degree in Social Work and began as a foster care worker in Los Angeles. She brought her boyfriend home to meet us during Christmas 1986, and we suspected that a wedding might be coming up in a couple of years. But first, they needed to work out some details, as he was previously married with three children. Our perception proved to be correct when Laila called home in the early spring of 1988 saying that the date was set and requesting an August wedding in our family garden. I glanced out the window as I took the call, gazing upon my "naturalized" weed patch and was compelled to exclaim, "What garden?"

We rose to the challenge. I hired a gardener who accomplished an excellent makeover of the lawn, where he planted a rose bed. He also helped me groom the weed patch by the back door. Laila sent swatches of her favorite shades of gold, mauve, and pink. Then, we selected plants that promised to bloom in those colors in August.

Laila wanted a tiered carrot cake decorated with white chocolate curls. She even sent me a photograph from a bridal book showing how she hoped it would look. Bravely, I decided to bake it myself. Having never produced a wedding cake, I signed up for a class in cake decorating at a local baking supply store. When I eagerly arrived for my first lesson, I was shocked with disappointment to learn that no one else had signed up and the class was cancelled.

But, the owner could see how important this was to me and offered to give private lessons. The lessons ran for six weeks, and my assignment was to produce a practice layer cake every week. I baked it, my instructor critiqued it, and then I carried it to the school staff room where eager colleagues commented on my efforts before devouring it. "Your frosting is too thick!" "Aren't you ever going to make a chocolate one?" "Hey, you're getting better every week!" "Keep bringing these in!"

Kitty and Aziz worked tirelessly to help us prepare for Laila's shindig. One night, as we sat around the dinner table making plans, Kitty jumped up and asked for soap and a dishpan. She couldn't stand the dirty chandelier for one more minute. This began our joke of having to wash every light bulb, which produced a classic photo to commemorate the effort.

Invitations went out, and wonder of wonders, everybody accepted. We were going to have a big party! It would be a major blending of cultures, all staying under one roof. Abe's oldest sister Subha and her husband, Rajah, decided to come from Jordan. This impressed us, since until that time Rajah had always refused to fly. I knew that the customs of an American wedding would be new to Abe's family

Is the light in the right spot?

because our simplified home celebration would be much different from the huge hotel weddings produced in Amman.

My beloved Aunt Dorothy and Aunt Geneva planned to fly from Boise. Although we arranged hotel accommodations for them the day before the wedding, they wished to stay with us for a few more days after the wedding, which meant we must arrange extra beds. We ended up buying a brand new sleeper sofa for the living room so that our bed could be given to my aunts.

Tammy was flying from her job in Vermont, and Laila would be coming with Richard, along with his sister, brother, and sister-in law from Los Angeles. Richard's three children, Lorraine, Ruth, and Rollie would soon become our new grandchildren and stay with us for a week after the wedding while the newlyweds took a honeymoon. I'd just barely met the children, and we hadn't yet met any of Richard's family. I began to feel uneasy about the comfort of all these new personalities who'd share our home during this oh-so-important family celebration.

I needn't have worried. When Subha arrived, she immediately agreed to prepare mounds of glorious broth-flavored rice for the wedding supper. This was no small undertaking, for we planned to feed over one hundred people. The rest of the menu was a work in progress for weeks ahead. I marinated chicken thighs, pre-roasted and froze them. We were able to secure the loan of three gas barbeques to broil the chicken to perfection right when needed. I found a lovely lady who agreed to come in as a caterer-assistant to allow me to enjoy the guests. This same caterer also baked up a huge supply of special cookies selected by Laila, who wanted every guest to have one as they signed the guest book. She believed that folks should have something delicious for munching as soon as they arrived. Laila formed that opinion when she was a little girl and required to wait too long to sample wedding goodies.

Laila was just as determined as I to do things herself. She decided to sew her own wedding dress, using a complicated pattern of piecing multitudinous pieces of lace into a mosaic design. I was sure that she was overly ambitious, and I had nightmares that she walked down the aisle in a see-through dress with no under slip. But, her lovely gown was finished on time, and I could have saved all that fretting. She also purchased gold rings for each child and involved them in the wedding ceremony as a promise of commitment to their care and happiness.

Then, came the actual day of the wedding festivities. Tammy remembers a chaotic moment with the children's rings that were fastened securely to a little cushion which Rollie was supposed to carry. While they waited at the top of the garden stairs for their cue to begin the procession, Ruthie decided to see if her finger would fit into Rollie's tiny gold band. Of course she could slip it on, but no way was it coming back off. Tammy, who was shepherding the children, could see that Ruthie was frantically close to tears. So Tammy looked directly into her eyes and commanded, "Ruthie, this ring is coming off right now!" Then she grabbed her little finger and painfully twisted off the ring. Ruthie's little face was a bit tear-stained from panic, but she was thrilled to be free of that ring.

Of the three children, the solemnity of the ceremony probably affected Lorraine the most. She realized that this wedding meant big changes in their family structure, and it was a scary prospect for an eleven-year-old. But little Rollie, full of nervous wriggles, was hard-pressed even to stand still in front of the altar. Only his Uncle Al's firm grip kept him in place until it was over. When finally released, he exploded into cartwheels all over the lawn, causing him to split out the crotch of the little maroon suit that Laila had sewn for him.

Laila waited nervously upstairs in our bedroom while the wedding-singer finished. This soloist was unknown to us but came recommended by one of our friends. Too late, we learned that she was less than adept. However, the processional music, a classical selection performed on a recorder was exquisite. The golden notes floated out into the sun-flecked evening air as the little group came down the stairs and up the aisle of white folding-chairs filled with guests. Abe in his newly-purchased wedding suit proudly escorted Laila on his arm.

Laila remembers being so flustered about getting into her costume and waiting for "that God-awful singing to stop" that she forgot her bouquet. Her girlfriend spotted the problem, ran inside to fetch it, and handed it to her as she arrived at the front of the gathering.

Throughout the wedding day, I was punch drunk from lack of sleep because the night before, after the entire household was in bed, I began final assembly of the wedding cake. I knew that I would nervously dissolve into disaster if I had children and relatives looking over my shoulder. The layers were baked weeks earlier and carefully frozen until I thawed them that day. It was meticulous work for an amateur, and I didn't finish applying the frosting and decorations until dawn, but it turned out beautifully.

I fell into bed for two hours while others decorated tables. Tammy managed much of it, and guests from Los Angeles arranged the flowers. Aziz took control of chilling the champagne. By the time we turned on the flood lights and the men started broiling the chicken, I realized that we had pulled off the whole affair with very few glitches. Subha's delicious rice was the "feast de résistance." Everyone raved about it long after other details of the meal were forgotten.

Cutting the cake

Subha was responsible for beginning the ululations, and we all delightedly joined in as Laila and Richard slipped off late in the evening to a little mountain cabin that we'd reserved for them. Many guests lingered on into the late night, and I felt much like a zombie before I finally found a chance to lie down.

The burden of aftermath responsibilities hit hard the following morning. Tammy collected rented materials in time for the pick-up crew to arrive. I felt like a bitchy taskmaster as I bossed everyone around. I was grateful that Subha didn't understand my words until I discovered that Rajah knew more English than I suspected and was translating everything to her. Then I was really embarrassed. However, we later learned that Subha and Rajah flew home to describe the American wedding in glorious detail. Members of their family called to say they'd been talking about it for several nights already and were still not finished.

We gathered up all the wedding flowers and donated them to a nursing home, while a mountain of leftover food was delivered to the Mission. Then, it was time to begin my role as Grandma. I worried that the kids might feel a bit lost and lonesome during that long week, but they tried to be agreeable with their new relatives, and I did the best I could. I got out the Slip 'N Slide for the front lawn and offered some craft projects that they all could do. The two younger children spent much of the week looking to Lorraine for comfort, and she was a good older sister to them. It helped that they all loved to watch TV. Though I didn't feel too successful, the three of them, as adults, have spoken of happy times spent with Grandma Doris and Grandpa Abe. So we must have done something right.

After Laila and her family returned to California, Abe and I were able to spend a few more days with Subha and Rajah before they returned home. Since we wanted them to experience the beauty of our mountains, we planned a leisurely drive over Chinook Pass the day before their flight, and Subha prepared a *Warak Dawali* picnic, grape leaves stuffed with rice and meat. It was a lovely, sunshiny day, and we all relaxed in a peaceful, forested spot. It served as respite after the hectic days of wedding celebration. Rajah enjoyed watching a little chipmunk brazenly scamper up onto the picnic table to snatch a morsel of food. It was a treasured day in our Washington woods. Though I had no way of knowing at the time, this trip marked the last time I would see them. Abe managed a trip to Michigan several years later when Subha flew there to visit her sons, but I didn't accompany him.

With everyone safely back to their homes, we were able to catch our breath during the last few weeks of that stressful summer before the push of another school year was upon us. Abe and I spent some time considering my desire to retire in June, 1990. He pulled out his calculator to run the numbers, knowing that by then I would be fifty-five and qualified to claim full retirement benefits. Also, since Abe was seven years older than I, he agreed that it would be possible for him to "pack it in" the same year. We wanted to have some time together to enjoy life without the daily school bell ringing in our brains. We began the countdown towards finishing our teaching careers.

I was perfectly willing for the staff at school to know my plans when the 1989–1990 school year rolled around. I even made a big to-do about sharing Jenny Joseph's poem: "When I am an old woman I shall wear purple / With a red hat that doesn't go, and doesn't suit me." I particularly loved the section in the poem which grants the liberty to sit down on the pavement when tired, press alarm bells, run a stick along the public railings, and generally do things that were frowned upon in my youth. In particular, I wanted to ring our old school bell vigorously. The bell was modeled after the US Liberty Bell in Philadelphia and was prominently displayed in the library, tempting passing school children. Rules about never ringing it were strictly enforced, but I proclaimed that I planned to ring it when I'd earned my liberty from teaching.

On the first day of my final year, my teacher friends presented me with 180 purple jelly beans. With them came instructions for me to eat one piece of candy each school day. Thus, I'd have an accurate countdown to retirement. I followed their directions religiously and enjoyed the year as a time of collecting lasting memories as I cleaned out closets and gave away teaching materials after I'd finished teaching each unit.

Also, I continued the "purple" plan by announcing my intention to sew a new purple dress for the last day of school. I found some fluffy purple netting and wrapped it around my father's silver-painted pith helmet to complete the costume. The staff staged a retirement party where all the guests lined up and individually presented small purple joke gifts. I was required to sit in a retirement rocking chair to receive their well-wishes. And, my fellow teachers insisted that I must indeed ring the bell, which I gladly did, long and loud!

Ring the Liberty Bell

Both Tammy and Laila flew in for the party. Abe stood in the background enjoying the scene. It was entirely "too much halleluiah!" But I loved every moment of it, and all the mischief made the sadness of saying good-bye to my life's work much easier to bear. There were some more serious awards and celebrations also. The school district honored me with the Crystal Apple Award for excellence in teaching accompanied by a check for $1000. The staff in my building took up a collection to fund a Yakima Valley Human Rights Scholarship in my honor.

I must admit to a feeling of let-down when the school year wound to a halt. But Abe wisely chose to teach the fall term with his retirement date falling on December 31, 1990. This allowed me some alone time for adjusting to a retirement routine. We'd heard horror tales of couples who found themselves unprepared for days of constant togetherness, and our staggered schedule avoided that. We made another wise decision for my sake, which was to get out of town during the early days of the following

September when all my co-workers headed back to school. I was pretty sure that my heart-strings would be pulled towards the routines of previous years, so we took off for an extended trip through the Canyon Lands, with our good friend Mary Jean Lord serving as tour director.

However, one thing did upset me about that fall. I had been a loyal champion of teachers' union activities during all my years of teaching. But most teachers just rolled with the punches, going along with whatever the school district set as policy. Wouldn't you know it? The very first year that I was no longer a teacher, the Yakima Education Association walked out on grievances, while I went driving off on a vacation trip! I felt downright disloyal for not being there to help walk the picket line.

That feeling was fleeting because Mary Jean did her homework and mapped out a glorious itinerary. We began at a lovely ranch house in Moab, Utah. That was where Mary Jean and I went for a moonlight swim. It was just too cold for our warm-blooded Arab, who preferred to stretch out and snooze after supper. I can still see the starry night, smell the moist breeze rippling over our faces, and hear the quiet night sounds coming from the trees and bushes surrounding that tiny pool. The day had been hot and dusty, so a dip in the cool water was delightfully refreshing.

Our trip included the cliff-dwellings of the ancient Anasazi peoples at Mesa Verde National Park, and we also visited Arches National Park, Monument Valley, Bryce Canyon, Grand Canyon, Lake Powell, and Four Corners Monument in Navajo country where the four states of Arizona, New Mexico, Utah, and Colorado intersect. I actually sat on the ground straddling the corners with my hands and feet each touching a different state!

The drive was enjoyable, with Mary Jean urging us to stop and explore many side roads. Being quite well versed in wild flowers, she was able to give me the names of many. I loved her final pronouncement when I requested the name of one more small yellow bloom. She tossed off, "Oh that is an ADYF." Since her answer made no sense to me, I pressed for clarification. "You know, Another Damn Yellow Flower!"

Abe surprised himself by actually enjoying much of that trip. He loved the night-time walk he took out to the Bryce Canyon rim to view the incredible star-lit sky, and he was deeply impressed with the Grand Canyon. I now understand that the area must have reminded him of home. We drove through exactly the same type of terrain in Jordan on our way to Petra.

Abe was long-suffering and patient throughout our slow, rambling trip solely because he had been assured of a visit to Vegas along our return route. When he hit Route 66 and headed toward his "promised land," I thought we would become another statistic among the speeding fools who drive that stretch too fast. If we suggested a stop, he would remind us that he'd seen enough red rock to satisfy a lifetime.

When we finally landed in "Abe's town," he insisted that we drop him at Harrah's, his favorite casino, and we saw little else of him unless we chased him down to join us for a meal. I learned later, however, that Abe was disappointed in Las Vegas, because he had trouble finding a good poker game. The big casinos, he said, didn't even have poker because they couldn't make as much money. After all his anticipation, that must have been a terrible disappointment. In 1990, there were no casinos in the Yakima area, so Abe had been stashing bills away in his money belt all year long waiting for his chance to play poker in Vegas. I have no idea if he won or lost, and I didn't ask. It was all the fun of playing the game.

Mary Jean and I didn't find much of interest to do. I asked our hotel clerk what there was to do for fun. After I nixed his suggestions for gambling and shows, he suggested "some nice churches in the area." His face fell when I told him that we "didn't do churches either." So, we wandered the strip, went to a show, did some laundry, and basically waited out the three days allotted to Abe.

When we'd served our sentence in Vegas, we headed home. There was one last place where Abe knew he could quench his thirst for poker. It was the small, unincorporated town of Jackpot, Nevada, right on the edge of the Idaho border. He planned an overnight there, ensconced Mary Jean and me in a motel, and headed for Cactus Pete's Casino. The stop at Jackpot was ample compensation for his disappointment in Las Vegas, because he found a good game and played until breakfast. After we checked out, he crawled into the back seat to sleep for the remainder of the trip, leaving Mary Jean and me to take turns driving.

I did a slow boil over that antic, but I was consoled somewhat because I knew he must immediately head back to teach his final term at YVC while I'd be able to recover my composure at leisure. However, my leisure time was scarce, since our eighteen year-old nephew, Omar, arrived from Jerusalem to begin his schooling. Omar was the youngest son of Abe's brother Suleiman. This was his first big venture out into the world, and Suleiman entrusted him to Abe. Omar made his home with us for the next four years.

My other occupation involved setting up an office downstairs and acquiring a computer. I applied wallpaper and paint to make the cold basement room more cheerful, and Abe sprung for a carpet to keep my feet warm. I created a computer desk by painting an old door a soft pastel and purchasing a set of file cabinets to place it on. The door-knob hole worked fine to thread all the cords through. We shopped for an expensive office chair, and Aziz helped me choose and set up my first-ever computer.

I surrounded myself with all kinds of writing aids, thesaurus, dictionary, and how-to manuals. I even took a class at YVC. This was when I began to spend long nights struggling to teach myself the skills needed to join the electronic age. When I stumbled up the stairs in the wee hours of the morning, Abe would ask me, "Did you learn anything?" My standard answer was, "I learned a whole bunch of things *not* to do." At retirement time, when teachers asked me what I was going to do in retirement, I'd always reply, "Oh, I'm finally going to have time to write!"

Yet, I must admit that I was deep into procrastination about seriously beginning my writing project. I used the excuse of learning computer skills and Omar's arrival for the delay. But, I cannot justify my procrastination by blaming Omar. He soon developed friendships and spent long hours with homework. Nor can I blame it on the needs of the farm. We gave away the goats and cut back on gardening. Truthfully, it was just not yet time for me to begin writing, because my thoughts and activities were occupied elsewhere.

In some ways, my excuses were legitimate. In the beginning, Omar didn't drive and was therefore dependent on Abe or me to provide transportation until he could get his license and take possession of the pickup. And, I struggled for a while to learn what our hungry kid liked to eat. He came from a home of fabulous cooks, and I catered to his likes and dislikes as best I could. He informed us that he was not fond of cooked onions or any yellow cooked vegetables. That placed a big hole in many of my menus. Sneakily, I began to sauté onions for a recipe and blend them up in the Cuisinart before adding them to a dish, so we had our customary flavors without the cooked onion texture. I eliminated cooked squash until pumpkin pie season.

Interestingly, his attitude changed when I blended cooked squash and made it into pumpkin pie. All of the leftover dessert had disappeared by the next morning. I enjoyed teasing Omar that he had learned to eat yellow vegetables! And he became completely won over when I made Enchiladas. The first time I served them, he astounded both Abe and me by rising from the supper table and exclaiming, "Damn Good Enchiladas, Aunt!" It has been our name for that dish ever since.

But I didn't spend all my time cooking. I also had a chance to do some traveling during that fall while Abe agreed to keep the homestead together. I took off with a friend for a flight to Quebec and New England, and to visit Tammy at her home in St. Albans, Vermont. Highlights of the trip included a visit to the Montréal Museum of Art where I sat for what seemed like hours in front of Renoir's *Mademoiselle Irene*. Prints are fine, but nothing can be compared with seeing the original! Later, with Tammy, we drove the coast of Maine and I ate my first whole lobster.

After we arrived home, it became a time of celebration for Abe, because of his birthday and his retirement. The college staff gave him a retirement dinner in December, and his co-workers took the opportunity to speak about his years at YVC. He was praised for his listening skills during Union negotiations and teased for mowing down a co-worker's saplings while helping to mow his lawn. One story was told of Abe's generosity as a professor. During an exam, a capable student was busily writing out the solution to a problem. Abe walked by, looked down, and softly murmured, "No, no, no." The student quickly spotted and corrected the error.

Even though Abe found speech-making extremely difficult, he did stand up to respond, saying he felt like Mark Twain had described, "as smug as a Christian with four aces." He said that his co-workers words had given him such full-satisfaction that it was just the same as if he were holding four aces in a poker game and feeling able to "whip the ass of anybody around the table." He thanked them for the chance to associate for thirty years with the best men and women anyone could hope to meet.

He was presented with a scrapbook of well-wishes from all the members of the faculty. In addition to the college dinner, he was fêted at several dinners in the homes of our friends. During all of these occasions, Abe's grin truly did exhibit his smug satisfaction in completing a job well done.

We assumed that the celebrations for Abe's retirement were complete at the end of December, and we began to enjoy our time together with several more trips. During the early spring, we flew to visit friends in Georgia. While there, we visited President Jimmy Carter's home town and saw his boyhood farm. We toured the Andersonville National Cemetery and the site of the historic Civil War prison at Camp Sumter. It caused me to focus sharply on the carnage caused by that war.

A much more restful outing was spent touring the Day Butterfly Center in the Calloway Gardens. We were ushered into a huge glass structure filled with fountains and plantings of all varieties with countless hundreds of butterflies fluttering over our heads and even settling for fleeting moments on our heads or shoulders. I could have spent hours there. We also visited President Franklin D. Roosevelt's Summer White House in Warm Springs, Georgia. I was impressed with the simplicity of its furnishings.

Before heading back to Yakima, our hosts drove us to Savannah after St. Patrick's Day. The long streamers of moss sweeping down from the glorious old oaks were entrancing. I was also quite taken with my evening meal of fried catfish, greens, and hushpuppies—delicate, crisply fried cornmeal fritters. The flavors reminded me of my father's Oklahoma heritage and my grandmother's kitchen.

During the flight home, Abe mentioned that he'd really like to try poker in Vegas again. So, when we reached the farm and were reassured that Omar was doing an excellent job of holding down the fort, we booked tickets and off we flew. This time, it was just the two of us. I spent all my waking hours in the swimming pool, while Abe spent his dollars at the poker table.

Eventually, all this traveling required a breather. I wanted time at home in front of my computer, and I also hoped to get the spring garden cleared of weeds. One morning in June, I dressed in grubbies and headed out to work. Soon, out came Abe all slicked up in his best sports coat and tie. The college staff had asked him to take part in commencement exercises, so he planned to don that mortar-board, collar, and robe one more time. When I offered to get cleaned up and go with him, he waved me off saying it was no big deal and urged me to keep on with what I was doing.

To this day, I am furious with myself for not insisting that I accompany him. When he arrived home in late afternoon, I learned that while I was home on my hands and knees in the dirt, he had indeed been the star of a very big deal. He told me that he lined up as usual with the rest of his department colleagues, but the president of the college came and pulled him out of line, insisting that he lead the procession into the hall. Once inside, he was ushered up to the stage and directed to take a seat with the presiding dignitaries. Strange as that seemed to him, it soon became even more surprising.

Selected students and staff began making their way, one at a time, to the podium where each gave a speech in praise of Abe Ayyoub's contributions to the college. The ceremony culminated with his being presented the President's Recognition Award for Dedicated Service to Students. I was overwhelmed with regret for failing to attend, but Abe never felt that I was remiss in not being there.

Abe and I continued to work the farm, take short trips, share holidays with our children, and entertain family members when they visited from overseas. On the surface, we seemed to be enjoying the rich rewards of retirement. But, we had become aware that we must do some watchful waiting about a potential health problem for Abe.

That spring, Abe went for his regular physical and learned that he had a noticeable heart murmur. At first he didn't feel too concerned, but our doctor urged that he should be referred to a specialist in Seattle. There, we learned that Abe's aortic heart valve was slowly failing. At that time, we were advised to postpone surgery until symptoms occurred. We were cautioned to watch for shortness of breath, dizzy spells, and fatigue. We took this advice seriously, but as time passed, we continued with our plans to drive to San Francisco and then on to Los Angeles during the fall of 1992. We wanted to arrive at Laila's home in time to welcome the birth of her second baby.

Our drive down I-5 included several important stops. Just out of Portland, Abe drove into a dealership where he traded his Mercedes diesel for a new Camry V-6. He'd wanted to make that change for a long time because his little Mercedes, although pretty and economical, had no power on hills. Our friend described it as a "gutless wonder." We were pleased to drive away from the dealer in our brand new car to check on the Corvallis property and then on to San Francisco for a week with Abe's sister, Naimeh.

After saying good-bye to Abe's family, we drove off again with the hope of reaching Los Angeles in one day. However, when we grew tired, we checked into a motel about sixty miles from our destination. I called Laila to let her know our plans and discovered that she was upset. She felt birth was imminent and she was home alone with three-year-old Jordan because Richard was away at the time. In distress, she said we were so near and she really needed us. She had been just holding on until we could arrive, take over the care of Jordan, and be available if she needed transport to the hospital. So we packed up our stuff and wearily headed on to Los Angeles.

Of course, it took more than an hour to arrive, since we were in unfamiliar Los Angeles traffic, but I'll always remember the clinging hug I received from little Jordan when we finally reached their home. He was up into my arms and draped around my body like a little guy who could feel the upset in the household. I'm quite sure that he was aware of his Mama's stress. Jordan knew that there was a new baby inside of Mama and would pat Laila's tummy, saying "Ing Ong."

And wouldn't you know? Baby didn't arrive until the doctor induced labor several days later. What an experience to be a part of the delivery of my daughter's child! Abe stayed with Jordan, and I followed Richard in our car when he drove her to the hospital. There were agonizing hours of waiting out the labor process and we were all tense. Jordan had been delivered by Caesarian, but Laila was determined to give natural birth to this baby. She was very concerned that her doctor might decide to operate.

Richard, on edge and without sleep, drove away to meet his commitments at work, believing that delivery was still a good way off. But he'd barely reached his place of work when the nurse advised me to call him back. He did make it back in time, and we were both allowed to stay beside Laila as her second little baby boy slipped into the world. What a wonder! I remember having difficulty containing my impatience to hold this tiny wee little one until Daddy had an opportunity to give first cuddles to his new baby son.

After Laila rested and baby was cleaned up to meet the family, Richard drove Abe, Jordan, Lorraine, Rollie and Ruthie to the hospital for a greeting. Laila had prepared some little gifts for Jordan, explaining that they were presents that his new little brother wanted him to have. She named the baby Abram Bell because she had figured out that Jordan was trying to say "Ding Dong" when he was patting Mama's tummy.

We stayed for another busy week enjoying our growing family. Since Tammy flew in from Vermont, we decided to have early Thanksgiving dinner while we were all together. There was much to be thankful for. But soon, it was time for us to head back to Yakima, ready to launch into the holiday season with dinner invitations.

One of those dinners was overshadowed with worry about Abe. We barely sat down to eat when he touched my arm to say the room was spinning around a ball of white light! All of us jumped up to escort him safely into the bedroom so that he could lie down. The dizzy spell cleared up, and Abe refused to be rushed to hospital as we urged. At first, our friends suggested that he might have over indulged in pre-dinner Scotch, but I knew he had nursed only his one usual drink. I also remembered that we had been warned to watch for these signs, but when the dizziness did not reoccur, we delayed going to the doctor until the next day.

Thus began phase two of watchful waiting. Our family doctor referred Abe to Dr. Vielbig, who ran all sorts of tests. He advised us that it was time to arrange for an aortic valve replacement. We asked him where would be the best venue for the surgery. He explained that he didn't do this surgery himself and that Yakima's operating staff often had many surgeries in a day. We felt that if Abe were the last patient for the day, the surgeon was bound to be more tired.

So, Abe sought some other options. He had an older swimming buddy at the YMCA who'd researched possibilities before selecting Dr. Rittenhouse at Providence Hospital in Seattle. Since Abe could see that his friend had successfully come through the procedure and was back to swimming, he determined to explore the same route.

Our next step would be an interview with Dr. Rittenhouse. I knew enough to request that medical records be sent in advance, but I had no idea what we should ask when we got there. We were grateful for the long-distance input from our daughters. They both planned on being in Seattle for the actual surgery, but we had to tough out this initial interview on our own.

My head was full of concerns. How many days would Abe be in hospital? Where does the family stay during the ordeal? How do I get him safely home after he has just had his chest cut open? The girls assured me that these kinds of concerns would all have workable solutions. They wanted to be confident that Dr. Rittenhouse was the best qualified surgeon available, and they gave me suggestions on how to ask the right questions.

I remember sitting in the office while we waited for the doctor to come in. His wall was covered with plaques describing his training and honors. Abe was immediately impressed that Dr. Rittenhouse had been honored for his extensive work in open-heart surgery on newborns. Abe observed, "I think if Dr. Rittenhouse could repair those tiny baby hearts, he can surely fix up mine."

When the doctor came in and shook hands, Abe was, as usual, able to rapidly judge the character of this great surgeon. He quickly felt confident about his ability, while I was determined to ask my one burning question. "How many of these surgeries like Abe's have you done? He smiled kindly and said, "I cannot recall the total number, but there have been over sixty during the last three months." I buttoned my lip then. It was obvious that the only amateur in the room was me!

His answer instilled us with confidence and relief that we were in good hands. Also, I realized that I shouldn't have felt foolish for asking. Everyone but the surgeon is an amateur when it comes to open heart surgeries. After that, we were carefully led through an explanation of the whole procedure and assured that Abe was an excellent candidate. We left the appointment with a sheaf of papers outlining what needed to be done in preparation.

During the next few weeks, all the logistics buzzed around in my head, while Abe appeared to go about life pretty much as usual. I couldn't understand how he remained on such an even keel, knowing that he would soon be undergoing a major, life-threatening operation. We discovered that his aortic valve might have been abnormal at birth, or it possibly became diseased over time. Abe was sixty-five years old, so it could have been either. However, we later learned that his brother, Naim, needed the same operation, which indicates heredity.

We also learned that Abe needed to make a choice between a biological valve made from pig tissue, which at that time had a five-year life, or a mechanical valve that was more durable and designed to last as long as ten years with less chance of early failure. But, the choice of a mechanical valve replacement meant that he would need to take a blood-thinner medication for the rest of his life.

Abe studied all the information with his usual attention to detail and chose the mechanical valve. I was pleased to learn that he fully expected to live many more years and wanted the longer-lasting valve. He had great fun warning us that another use for blood-thinners was rat poison. Although Abe maintained his stoicism about the whole adventure, it was frightening to me that he would have his sternum sawed open and his ribcage pried back to expose his heart. For an extended period of the operation, he would be attached to a bypass machine taking over the function of his heart and lungs.

Again and yet again, I silently wondered how Abe could remain so calm, because the more we studied what was going to take place, the more alarmed I felt. Consequently, I experienced a full-blown arthritis flare in both of my knees. As we packed up our personal needs for the extended stay in Seattle, it became painfully difficult for me even to carry things out to the car.

Laila planned to bring the children and meet us in Seattle while Tammy was able to take family leave and fly from Vermont to Yakima. It was a great relief to have her help with decisions and loading. During our last evening at home, Abe finally shared the reason for his serenity. He gathered us around the table for a "pre-celebration" dinner. This was his usual time and place to engage in conversation.

He started by saying that he had something important to discuss. He took hold of my hand to say, "You know, I've had a good life. And I've given it some careful thought during these last few days. I have decided that if I wake up after surgery, well and good. And if I don't, there's no better way to go." I couldn't hold back my tears, but it did explain why he remained so calm while I was going ballistic.

His comment about having a good life really struck a chord. I've always been aware of the constant adjustments he made in order to fit into our American way of life. Once, he was asked how long it had taken for him to feel comfortable in America. He thought about his answer for a while and then quietly replied, "I really never have felt comfortable."

That saddened me, but I was not surprised. Throughout our married life, I noticed a unique light of joy flood over his face whenever he was in the company of his Jordanian relatives, whether we were in Al Husn or his family was visiting here. I am reminded of a cartoon we once had showing a lonely, dejected young girl sitting atop her suitcase beside a deserted street with the caption, "I am a stranger here." So when Abe assured us that his life had been good, it meant the world to me. It gave me the courage to get up from the table and finish preparations for our trip.

For our benefit, Abe continued to maintain his outwardly light-hearted mood. I remember driving past a street sign in Seattle while we were searching for where we were to stay. The sign read SU, to indicate Seattle University, but when Abe saw it, he launched into a poem about a lovely, young Arab woman named Su Su. The poet was crazy in love with Su Su! I wish I could have recorded his rendition because it was a really sweet expression of love.

We eventually located the large family dormitory which was provided for a nominal rent by Providence Medical Center. It was connected to the hospital and made it possible for our whole family to stay together. This arrangement helped me, because I was leaning on family strength to get us through the ordeal.

The day of Abe's operation remains a blur. After we kissed him, and watched him trundled off on his gurney, we were ushered into a comfortable waiting room. Laila kept busy with the needs of her little ones, and Tammy decided to involve me with sorting and assembling the mass of jigsaw puzzles which were scattered over a large table. The pieces were all jumbled up, and she took on the challenge of working every puzzle in the room. Because of her zeal, I mistakenly concluded that she loved working jigsaws, and I sent her a gift of some complicated ones in later years. She eventually explained that she really had no interest, but had chosen to use the puzzles as a stress-reliever while we waited out the surgery.

I do remember a nurse coming to us after what seemed to be eons. She announced that Abe was now on the by-pass machine. The knowledge that my husband's heart was no longer beating, while he depended on a machine to maintain life, flooded me with a numbing, cold dread. Never mind the statistic that the overall risk of death during aortic valve surgery is less than 1%. My best love was under the knife and I could hardly breathe! That pressure was somewhat relieved when the nurse came back with the update that Abe was off the bypass machine and his heart was beating normally. We got up and danced a jig in celebration!

And then it was over. Dr. Rittenhouse gave us the news that Abe had come through the surgery well, and that we could see him as soon as he was out of recovery. Those next few hours were filled with relief as I sat beside my wan, sleeping husband, holding his warm hand. When he finally opened his eyes and smiled at me, the room lit up with sunshine.

Recovery had its scary concerns. We were informed that his sternum was held together with staples and that he must not, under any circumstances, twist his body or attempt to get out of bed until a nurse came to assist him. Through the long night, I dozed by his bed and, of course, had visions of the staples popping loose. He was on powerful pain medication which enabled him, the next morning, with the assistance of his skilled nurse, to sit, stand, and even walk a short distance in the hall. It seemed to me that nurses and aids were hovering with solicitous attention all the time, and I truly appreciated the excellent care he was receiving.

Soon we were able to move Abe to the annex. Laila and the boys stayed with us for the rest of the week, but Tammy's leave time was up, and she reluctantly flew back to Vermont. Before we knew it, Abe was released to ride in our car with the seat reclined while I drove to Yakima. We were greeted with many well-wishes from friends, and we began to pick up the pieces of our life.

Abe was serious about following doctor's orders and began a walking regime in our long driveway. He counted out the distance and calculated how many trips up and down it took to make a mile. He'd then come inside and record it in his record book. We figured he accumulated enough miles to make it all the way to Denver, before he finally slowed down to take up his more favored program of swimming.

His careful effort to maintain good health afforded us another nineteen years of happy life together. We traveled to France and went on our second trip to Jordan. After we sold the farm and moved to a condo in town, he opted to undergo corneal transplants. This allowed him to experience the joy of truly seeing colors again and to enjoy reading his beloved poetry.

Throughout those last years of sharing our morning coffee time, puzzling over the state of national affairs, and always finding something to laugh about together, I was often led to remember what Abe said to me when he first came alert after his surgery. Although he later said it was just the anesthesia speaking, I know better. He opened his eyes, squeezed my hand, and whispered, "Doris, if I could choose to do it all over again, marrying you and having the girls, I'd do it!" To that I must reply, "Ahsanshee! The Very Best!"

Afterword

———◆———

THROUGHOUT MOST OF MY adult life, I knew I had a story to tell that needed to be written down. But it was not until I retired from teaching that I seriously began to consider the project. An internet search led me to Susan Wittig Albert's Story Circle Network. I signed up for courses in writing Family History taught by Dr. A. Mary Murphy. Mary became my mentor and led me through the process of learning to write.

Mary, your skill, patience, humor, and insistence on my very best efforts have made this book possible. I also owe a heap of praise to my husband, Ibrahim, and my daughters, Laila and Tammy. They read, re-read and critiqued my efforts to the very end.

Rigney relatives, Ayyoub relatives, and Yakima friends all contributed their stories which made the book rich in detail. I owe special thanks to my nephew, Muhannad Ghanma, who offered technical assistance with the Arabic language. Many thanks go to Becky Scholl who spent hours with her red pen, as she read and critiqued the entire manuscript. And finally, A. Mary Murphy provided professional copyediting skill before publication.

So to you all, let me employ my limited Arabic to express my thanks. *Shukran* and *Teslam Edeykum*. Thank you and bless the hands of those who have helped me.

Glossary of Arabic Terms

Arabic Term	Meaning
Abu	father of
Ahlan wa sahlan	you are welcome
Ahsan	better
Al Diwan Al-malaki (The Royal Diwan)	building in king's courtyard for holding audiences with citizens
Al-hamdu lil-lah	praise God
Al-Ka's	the cup - a fountain at al Aqsa Mosque in Jerusalem
Al-Marjeh	a square in Damascus
Ala ta'rifu anna hadik el-akleh shatwiyeh?	don't you know that this is a winter meal?
Ana bahibbak	I love you
Ana thahiba ila al- maktaba	I am going to the library
Arabayeh	one-horse open carriage
Araq	a traditional alcoholic beverage in the Middle East, anise-flavored distilled alcoholic drink,
Baba ghannouge	eggplant dip
Bahar	cooking spice mix of cinnamon, allspice, nutmeg and black pepper
Baksheesh	gratuity

Arabic Term	Meaning
Baklava	rich sweet pastry made of layers of filo and chopped nuts, sweetened and held together with honey or syrup
Barhoumy	my Ibrahim (term of endearment)
Barjack	a decorative serving pot for coffee
Biddak shai?	would you like some tea?
Biddi atrukum	I would like to leave
Birkeh	a small pool of water
Bissa	cat
Bissat Tamam	Tammy's cat
Bizer	roasted seeds (usually pumpkin, water melon or sunflower seeds)
Dishdasheh	long, usually white gown worn by men and boys
Falafel	a deep-fried ball or patty made from ground chickpeas
Farika	green cracked wheat harvested and roasted
Fasoulia	green bean stew with meat and tomato.
Ghirbaal	sieve for sifting wheat
Gombaz	men's long sleeve gown, buttoned at the neck and has a wide shiny sash at the waist, open at the front.
Hadith	telling of a tale, a conversation
Hail wa dalleh	cardamom and a coffee pot
Haji	a pilgrim, commonly used to refer to an older man
Halawa or halva	sweet made from crushed sesame seeds and sugar
Haleeb	milk
Hatta	decorated headband worn by women
Hayat	life
Hummus	garbanzo bean dip
Ibnil Kalb, or Ibin Kalb	curse meaning "son of a dog"

Arabic Term	Meaning
Ilfaitteh	wild plant with a juicy stem and leaves similar to radish, usually boiled then sautéed with onions and olive oil
Ishbini	my godfather
Ithnain	two
Jameed	sun-dried salted fat free yogurt
Jelly	Jell-O
Joha	an Arab jokester
Jubne	cheese
Kabab	middle eastern dish of lamb usually flame roasted or grilled on a skewer
Ka'ek	special form of bread, shaped like a large thick donut
Kaif Halick?	how are you?
Kallouseh	a hat worn by a priest
Kam shubback fi darkum?	how many windows are in your house?
Kefta	a dish of ground lamb, onions, parsley and spices
Khiar	baby cucumbers
Khoury	a priest
Khubiz	bread
Kibbeh	meat dish of lamb, onions, bulgur wheat and spices, baked or deep fried
Kousa	zucchini
Kufiya with Agal	traditional middle eastern men's headdress
Kwaiseh	good, fine, a term used to express approval (feminine)
La	No
Lam bataal	not a bad idea, not too shabby
Labneh	yogurt strained through a cloth to remove whey

Arabic Term	Meaning
Mabsoota	I am fine
Majnoon	crazy
Malfouf	cabbage rolls
Mankal	clay brazier used in roasting coffee beans
Marhaba	hello
Mehbash	ancient wooden coffee grinder (a large mortar and pestle)
Mehmaseh	steel pan with a long handle used for roasting coffee beans
Mensaf	the Jordanian feast meal of lamb, rice and mlehiyeh (jameed sauce). traditionally eaten by hand
Meznuck	same as gombaz
Min Aina Laka Hatha	name of a newspaper meaning "Where did you get all this wealth from?"
Misbaha	worry beads
Mlehiyeh	sauce made from reconstituted Jameed
Moghrabia	pasta made from wheat flour and fine bulgur similar to couscous
Margat Adas	lentil soup (could also contain meat)
Na'am	yes,
Nimleh	an ant
Oud	a pear-shaped string instrument commonly used in Arabic music, similar to a lute
Rab El-eyoon	a doctor called the "God of Eyes."
Salaam Alekum	peace be upon you.
Samneh	clarified butter
Sesan mhammara	roasted chicken with spices (usually young male chickens used)
Shamandar	beets

Arabic Term	Meaning
Shambar	a black silk fabric worn under a woman's head dress, covers head neck
Shaneeneh	a yogurt beverage (skimmed or low fat)
Shukran	thank you
Shursh	women's long black dress
Snobar	pine nuts
Sphiha	pastry topped with seasoned ground meat
Sumac	reddish-purple spice used as garnish or to add a lemony taste to salads or meat
Suq	public market
Ta'alooli	come to me
Taboon	dome-shaped clay oven
Tabouleh	a salad (made with parsley, tomato, cucumber, onions, lemon, bulgur olive oil)
Tafadalou	come to eat (more in general: please come in, please come to eat or to drink)
Teslam edeykum	bless your hands
Tosbeir	a card game
Trouh wa tiji bissalameh	a blessing meaning "go and come back safely"
Ululations	a high-pitched call sung by women during times of celebration
Um	mother of
Wadi Musa	a city in southern Jordan near Petra, (valley of Moses)
Wahad be wahad	one by one
Warak Dawali	grape leaves stuffed with meat and rice
Za'ter	spice mixture of thyme, sumac and sesame seeds
Zeit zeitoon	olive oil
Zubdeh	butter